THE OFFICIAL

PRICE GUIDE
2ND EDITION

FIGURINES
&PLATES

HEIDI ANN VON RECKLINGHAUSEN

Published by

Krause Publications, a division of F + W Media, Inc.
700 East State Street • Iola, WI 54990-0001
715-445-2214 • 888-457-2873
www.krausebooks.com

To order books or other products call toll-free 1-800-258-0929
or visit us online at www.krausebooks.com or www.krausebooks.com

Hummel® and M. I. Hummel® are used under license from
Manufaktur Rödental GMBH/Germany
©ARS AG, Baar/Switzerland

Parts of the illustrations of the M.I. Hummel art in this collector guide
are printed under license of ARS AG, Baar/Switzerland.
ARS AG is not responsible for any information concerning the products
contained in this guide, in particular quotations of prices or descriptions
of products.

ISBN-13: 978-1-4402-3713-3
ISBN-10: 1-4402-3713-1

On Our Cover: Hum 196: Telling Her Secret; Hum 2: Little Fiddler;
Hum 153: Auf Wiedersehen; Hum 47: Goose Girl; and
Hum 280: Stormy Weather anniversary plate.
Back Cover: Hum 730: Just Resting 1985 anniversary bell sample;
Hum 415: Thoughtful; and Hum 498: All Smiles.
Spine: Hum 618: A Basket of Gifts.

Edited by Mary Sieber
Cover Design by Nicole MacMartin
Designed by Nicole MacMartin

Printed in China

10 9 8 7 6 5

Contents

Introduction

The 100-year anniversary celebration of Sister Maria Innocentia Hummel's birth— May 21, 1909—brought forth new interest in Sister Hummel's life, her drawings, her paintings, and the beloved M.I. Hummel figurines, which this book is about. Who would have thought that these cherished figurines that depict Sister Hummel's love of children, animals, nature, and her deep devotion to her Catholic faith, which were introduced by Franz W. Goebel at the Leipzig Trade Fair in March of 1935, would bring such incredible interest around the world shortly after World War II that it continues today?

This book is a reference for the collector, dealer, anyone owning just a few figurines, inheriting a collection, or contemplating starting a collection. New information has been found about existing figurines, rare figurines, as well as the new figurines developed from Sister Maria Innocentia Hummel's two-dimensional drawings, and the 2000 Series, which are sculpted by German master sculptors and produced in Germany.

This is a collector's guide—and nothing more. It should be used in conjunction with every other piece of information you may be able to obtain from other sources such as websites, books, and any seminars you may attend.

The information in this book was obtained from many of the same sources available to collectors, dealers, and other writers. It is a wealth of information obtained from historians, old company and dealer pamphlets, brochures, publications, dealers, collectors, conventions, conferences, and writers. It is the hope that it will prove to be helpful to all that purchase this book.

Included in this book is a brief history of Sister M.I. Hummel, explanation of the trademark system, photographs of each piece when possible, detailed descriptions of color and mold variations, glossary of terminology, description of production techniques, current production status and market value range, detecting restored pieces, remarks of interest, a comprehensive listing of all the pieces themselves, and more.

Chapter One

History & Preservation

The charm and innocence of rosy-cheeked children, captured in Sister M.I. Hummel's heartwarming artwork, have inspired one of the world's most beloved collectibles of all time.

T he story of the Hummel figurines is unique. It is practically required reading for those with an interest in the artist, her work, and the resulting three-dimensional fine earthenware renditions—the famous Hummel figurines.

These charming but simple figurines of boys and girls easily capture hearts. In them we see, perhaps, our son or daughter, sister or brother, or even ourselves when we were racing along the paths of happy childhood. When you see the School Boy or School Girl, you may be taken back to your own school days. Seeing the figurine Culprits could bring back the time when you purloined your first apple from a neighbor's tree and were promptly chased away by his dog. You will delight in the beauty of the Flower Madonna or Shepherd's Boy. You will love them all with their little round faces and big questioning eyes. These figurines will collect you, and if you have the collecting tendency, you will undoubtedly want to collect them.

You may ask yourself what artist is behind these beguiling figurines. Who is the person with the talent to portray beauty and innocence with such simplicity? The answer is Berta Hummel, a Franciscan sister called Maria Innocentia.

Berta Hummel was born on May 21, 1909, in Massing in lower Bavaria, which was located about 40 miles northeast of Munich, Germany. She grew up in a family of two brothers and three sisters in a home where music and art were part of everyday life. In this environment, her talent for art was encouraged and nourished by her parents.

Berta attended primary school between 1915 and 1921. During these early years, she demonstrated the great imagination so necessary for an artist. She created delightful little cards and printed verses for family celebrations, birthdays, anniversaries, and Christmas. Her subjects

Hum 81: School Girl.

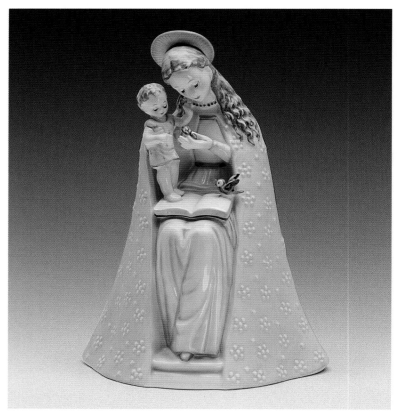

Hum 10: Flower Madonna.

were almost always the simple objects with which she was familiar: flowers, birds, animals, and her friends. In her simple child's world, she saw only the beautiful things around her.

When she finished primary school, Berta was enrolled in the Girls Finishing School in Simbach in 1921, in order to nurture and train her talent further and to give her a wider scope of education and experience. Here again, her artistic talent was recognized and upon finishing, it was decided that she should go to a place where she could further cultivate that talent and realize her desire to pursue art as a vocation. In 1927, Berta moved to Munich, where she entered the Academy of Fine and Applied Arts. There she lived the life of an artist, made friends, and painted to her heart's content. At the academy, she acquired full mastery of art history, theory, and technique. It was here also that she met two Franciscan sisters who, like herself, attended the academy.

There is an old adage that art and religion go together. Berta Hummel's life was no exception. She became friends with the two sisters and began to think that this might be the best way to serve. Over time, she decided to join the sisters in their pilgrimage for art and God, in spite of the fact that she had been offered a position at the academy.

For a time, Hummel divided her days between her talent for art and her love for humanity and hours of devotion and worship. Then she took the first step into a new life of sacrifice and love. After completing her term as a novice, the 25-year-old took the first vows in the Convent of Siessen on Aug. 30, 1934.

Hum 82: School Boy.

Although Berta Hummel (now Sister Maria Innocentia) gave her life over to an idea she thought greater than any worldly aspiration, the world became the recipient of her wonderful works. Within the walls and the beautiful surroundings of the centuries-old convent, she created the paintings and drawings that were to make her famous. Within these sacred confines, her artistic desires enjoyed unbounded impetus.

Little did her superiors dream that this modest blue-eyed artist who had joined their community would someday win worldwide renown. Much less did they realize what financial assistance Maria Innocentia's beloved convent would derive from her work as an artist.

During World War II, in 1945, after the French had occupied the region, the noble-minded artist's state of health was broken. On Nov. 6, 1946, at age 37, despite the best care, Sister Maria Innocentia died, leaving all her fellow sisters in deep mourning.

The M.I. Hummel figurines, modeled according to Sister Maria Innocentia's work, are known all over the world. They are her messengers, bringing pleasure to many, many people.

Facsimile of the well-known M.I. Hummel signature.

Hum 64: Shepherd's Boy.

W. Goebel Porzellanfabrik

In an area very near Coburg in northern Bavaria, Franz Detleff Goebel and his son, William Goebel, founded the company in 1871. Once known as Oeslau, the village is now known as Rödental.

Initially, the company manufactured slates, pencils, and marbles, and after 1879, it was well into the production of porcelain dinnerware and beer steins.

By the mid-1910s, a third generation, Max Louis Goebel, had taken the helm of the company and it began manufacturing fine earthenware products. His son, Franz Goebel, became active in the company, and the two of them developed a line of porcelain figurines that was well accepted on the international market.

Upon Max Louis' death in 1929, Franz took over the running of the company along with his brother-in-law Dr. Eugen Stocke, a trained economist, who was the financial manager of the operation.

By the early 1930s, Goebel had gained considerable experience and expertise in fashioning products of porcelain and fine earthenware.

Sister Maria Innocentia's art came to the attention of Franz in December 1933 in the form of religious note cards for the Christmas and New Year seasons. These cards were brand-new publications of her art by Ars Sacra Josef Muller Verlag. (This company has since evolved into ArsEdition, well known to collectors of prints and postcards of Hummel art.)

Remarkably, it was in March of the same year that the Siessen Convent had made an unsolicited inquiry of the Josef Muller firm regarding the possibility of reproducing their Sister Maria Innocentia's art.

Once Franz Goebel saw the cards in Munich, he conceived the idea of translating them into three-dimensional figurines. He sought and gained permission from the convent and Sister Maria Innocentia Hummel. The letter granting Goebel permission stated plainly that all proposed designs must be preapproved before the product could be manufactured. This is true to this day: The convent still has the final say as to whether a proposed design stays within the high standards insisted upon by M.I. Hummel.

After Franz Goebel gained permission for the company to produce the figurines, it took about a year to model the first examples, make the first molds, experiment with media, and make the first models of fine earthenware. The company presented the first figurines, Hum numbers 1 through 10 with the exception of Hum number 8, at the Leipzig Fair in 1935. They were a great success, and by the end of 1935, there were 46 models in the new line of Hummel figurines.

Production of Hummel figurines dwindled during the years of World War II, and toward the end of the war, production ceased completely. During the American Occupation, the United States Military Occupation Government allowed Goebel to resume operation. This included the production of Hummel figurines. During this period, the figurines became quite popular among U.S. servicemen in the occupation forces, and upon their return to the United States, many brought them home as gifts. This activity engendered a new popularity for Hummel figurines. Goebel Porzellanmanufaktur and its master sculptors and master painters continued to produce existing Hummels as well as new Hummels until Sept. 30, 2008, when the company closed its factory in Rödental due to financial strain. Goebel continued producing accessories in the gift and home area.

Manufaktur Rödental GmbH

In February 2009, Manufaktur Rödental GmbH took, under the direction of investor and managing director Jörg Köster, began manufacturing Hummel figurines at the original location in Rödental. Original M.I. Hummel artists are producing the M.I. Hummel figurines with the same quality and workmanship as before, while maintaining the relationship with Convent Siessen and the Hummel family. "Time for Hummel" is the theme for Manufaktur Rödental, crafting new figurines with new vision and enthusiasm. Trademark 9 was created to mark the new era of Hummel figurines. (See "Understanding Trademarks").

The Manufaktur Rödental Information Center

The new, recently remodeled location of the Manufaktur Rödental Information Center welcomes visitors from throughout the world. The center is still located at the factory, but is easier to get to now.

The display rooms show the history of M.I. Hummel figurines, with pieces from the archives as well as the newest introductions. The well-known, small museum with pieces from many German porcelain manufacturers and from Troy is also open for viewing.

The Information Center is open Monday through Friday from 9 a.m. to 5 p.m. and Saturday from 9 a.m. to 12 p.m. It is closed Sundays and on German holidays. Factory tours are available on Tuesdays at 10 a.m. and 2 p.m. Advance registration is required. Please call +49 - 95 63 - 75 293 - 33 to make reservations and for admission cost. Group tours (15 or more persons) are also available Monday through Friday from 9 a.m. to 2 p.m. Advance coordination is required (+49 - 95 63 - 75 293 - 33).

To request information or coordinate a visit, contact:

Manufaktur Rödental
Hummel Figurines
Information Center
Coburger Strasse 7
96472 Rödental, Germany
www.mihummel.de
Email: club@mihummel.de

M.I Hummel Club

The M.I. Hummel Club worldwide continues its service to current and new members alike. Throughout 2009, the club celebrated the 100th anniversary of Sister Maria Innocentia's birth on May 19, 1909. A chapter was written for each *INSIGHTS* magazine to commemorate her life. A seminar was given by Joan Ostroff, club ambassador, at the North American 2009 M.I. Hummel Convention held in Buffalo, New York. Ostroff commemorated Sister Maria Innocentia's life by drawing those who attended right into the life of Sister Maria Innocentia. Together with the sisters of Convent Siessen; Jörg Köster, Manufaktur Rödental; Hummel artists; the M.I. Hummel Club; and the convention attendees, a new chapter of M.I. Hummel figurines began.

For more information and/or membership in the M.I. Hummel Club in the United States and Canada, please visit www.mihummelclub.com.

A view of the entry to the Berta-Hummel-Museum in Massing, Germany.

Museums and Institutions

Das Berta-Hummel-Museum im Hummelhaus

This museum was opened in July 1994. It is located in the Hummel home in Massing, Bavaria, and was the birthplace of Berta Hummel and her home before she took her vows to become a nun.

The interior of the home was redesigned to accommodate the museum. Directed by Berta Hummel's nephew, Alfred Hummel, the museum houses the largest exhibit of Hummel figurines in Europe. More important is the large collection of paintings and drawings the artist accomplished before entering the convent.

Guided 30-45 minute tours are available by appointment only. Visit the museum's website at www.hummelmuseum.de for information on exhibitions, hours, news, the museum, Berta Hummel, gift shop, and various links. The site is written in both German and English.

Contact the museum at: Das Berta-Hummel-Museum im Hummelhaus Marktplatz 32, D - 84323 Massing; telephone: 08724/9602-50; fax: 08724/9602-99; e-mail: info@hummelmuseum.de.

The hours of operation are: Monday through Saturday, 9 a.m. to 5 p.m., and Sunday, 10 a.m. to 5 p.m. Admission is 5 euros for adults; 4 euros per person for groups of 15 persons or more; and 3 euros for children,

An interior view showing some of Berta Hummel's artwork.

college students, and handicapped individuals. Guided tours are 30 euros per person.

The Convent Siessen-Hummelsaal (Hall of Hummels)

Convent Siessen is a beautiful and peaceful place to visit. Here you will be able to visit the Baroque Church St. Mark's; convent gardens; The Chapel where "The Way of the Cross" paintings from Sister Maria Innocentia are located. In Hummelsaal, the convent maintains an exhibit of many of her original drawings and paintings. A selection of Hummel postcards, small prints, and books is offered for sale. There is also the opportunity to see her final resting place in the convent cemetery. The convent is a regular stop on annual club-sponsored tours.

An interior view showing childhood and family photos of Berta Hummel.

The convent is located just three kilometers out of Saulgau in southern Germany. The address is Kloster Siessen, D-88343 Saulgau, Germany. The hours of operation are: Tuesday through Saturday, 10 a.m. to noon and 2 p.m. to 4 p.m.; Sunday, 2 p.m. to 4:30 p.m.; it is closed on Mondays and on the first Sunday of every month. The convent is typically closed to the public from Dec. 28 through Jan. 31. It is best to phone ahead in case of religious celebrations or other unscheduled closings.

Visit the website at www.Klostersiessen.de; click on Kunst und Kultur, then click on Künstlerinnen, then M. Innocentia Hummel. This part of the site is written in both English and German. There is also a link to Hummelsaal. This area of the website is not written in English. The email address is: hummalsaal@klostersiessen.de. The telephone number is: (0 75 81) 80 124.

The Donald E. Stephens Museum of Hummels

The Donald E. Stephens Museum of Hummels was opened in 1986 in the Rosemont Exposition Center. Stephens, longtime mayor of Rosemont, Illinois, donated his magnificent Hummel collection to the village in 1984 for the purpose of establishing a museum.

The museum is probably the largest public display in the world of both current-production M.I. Hummel items and old, rare pieces. The collection does not stop there; it is constantly expanding. With guidance from the board of directors and with Stephens' expert consulting, the museum continues to seek out and acquire rare pieces.

The museum accommodates the Stephens Collection, a display of all current M.I. Hummel products, a facsimile factory that demonstrates the fashioning of the figurines, a display of other Goebel products, a display of ANRI figurines, special exhibits and shows, a retail store (known as The Village Gift Shop), and an auditorium.

The Donald E. Stephens Museum of Hummels is located on 9511 West Higgins Rd., Rosemont, IL 60018-4905. Hours are: Monday through Friday, 10 a.m. to 4 p.m., and Saturday from 9 a.m. to 3 p.m. For group tours and to confirm visiting hours, please call (847) 692-4000. Check the website for more information: www.stephenshummelmuseum.com. E-mail: stephansmuseum@rosemont.com.

Chapter Two

Collectors' Guide

Buying and selling M.I. Hummel collectibles, fakes and forgeries, trademarks, mold numbers and size designators.

Buying and Selling

The single, most important factor in any collecting discipline is knowledge. Before you spend your hard-earned funds to start or expand a collection, it is incumbent upon you to arm yourself with knowledge. If you've bought this book, you have made a good start. Now you must study it, learn from it, and refer to it often when you're on your hunt.

But don't stop there.

In today's market, there are many sources, some quite productive and some not so productive, as is true of any collectibles field. Supply and demand is a very important factor in the world of Hummel collecting. We have been through some extraordinary times. Nearly four decades ago, retailers had a very difficult time obtaining Hummel figurines and plates in any quantity, never had a choice of pieces, and often went for weeks with none in stock. They often had to order an assortment, and there were three monetary levels of assortments. In addition, it was often two to three months between ordering them and taking delivery. This was true for almost every Hummel retailer in the country. In those years of limited supply, even small dealers would see their shipments gone in a matter of days. There was a time in the late-1970s and early 1980s that dealers not only couldn't meet collectors' demands, but kept lists of collectors and what each collector was looking for. The result was most of their stock was presold, and what was left would sometimes literally be fought over.

The shows and conventions that featured Hummel saw great crowds in those early years of the surge in Hummel popularity. Frequently, the dealers would literally be cleaned out before half the show was over, leaving booths empty of all but tables and display fixtures.

Our economic times have changed all that, but the good news is that collectors now have many sources from which to choose. This is particularly true if you are not specializing in the older trademark pieces. These can be readily found in gift shops, jewelry stores, galleries, and shops specializing in collectibles. Even the popular television shopping programs feature Hummel figurine sales from time to time. They are also available by mail-order from various dealers around the country, many of whom also deal in the old trademark pieces.

A great way to find Hummels is by looking in various antiques and collectible publications. Many of them have classified advertising sections where dealers and collectors alike offer Hummel figurines and related pieces such as plates.

Productive sources, if you can get to them, are the large annual gatherings of dealers and collectors held around the country. Especially if you're trying to find the older-marked pieces, these shows can be a goldmine. But even if you're a collector of the newer pieces, attending the shows is fun and a good learning experience. They usually offer lectures and seminars by experts and dealers, all of whom are subject to much "brain-picking" by crowds of collectors. You also have the opportunity to meet other collectors and learn from them. Just be sure to pick the ones with this book under their arm: They are obviously the smartest!

The Internet has provided collectors of all sorts of Hummel-related pieces with a place not only to shop, but also to interact in chat rooms or online discussion panels with other collectors. Online appraisal services with trained appraisers can give you a value to your collection for a fee.

Using the Internet, the possibilities for expanding or selling a collection are endless. Take, for example, the number of Hummel-related collectibles on auction Web sites; on eBay.com, a search under the word "Hummel" will bring forth an average of more than 4,000 choices every day. The one caution about using the Internet for buying, however, is to beware of potential fraud. Without the opportunity to actually pick up and inspect a piece, it is sometimes difficult to legitimize authenticity. See "More About E-Buying" for a bit more detail on Internet buying.

You can sometimes find old trademark pieces in shops that sell both new and old pieces. There are a few around the country. With the increased awareness of the value of the older-marked pieces, it is very unlikely—but still possible—that some smaller, uninformed shops could have a few pieces bearing older trademarks, bought some years ago for sale at whatever the current retail price is for the newer ones.

Bargains? Yes, there are bargains to be found. Estate auctions and sales and country auctions are your best bet. Flea markets (especially in Europe), junk shops, attics, basements, relatives, friends, acquaintances, and neighbors are by far the best sources for bargains. In short, anywhere one might find curious old gifts, castaways, etc.

More About E-Buying

People flock to online Internet sites to shop for a wide array of collectibles. As more opportunities develop for making the best deal, collectors need to educate themselves on the proper methods of buying online, and by doing so, reduce the risk of possible abuse by an unscrupulous merchant.

E-Buying Tips

- Check out the seller. For company information, contact the state or local consumer protection agency and Better Business Bureau.

- Beware of out of focus pictures.

- Know when to buy – early morning or "night owl" shopping on an auction site may be beneficial.

- Be especially careful if the seller is a private individual.

- Get the seller's name, street address, and telephone number to check him/her out or follow up if there is a problem.

- Ask about returns, warranties, and service.

- Be wary of claims about collectibles.

- Use common sense and ask yourself: Is this the best way to buy this item? What is the most I am willing to bid?

- Get free insurance through the auction sites whenever possible.

- For assistance, check out these websites: www.fraud.com, www.ftc.gov, and www.bbbonline.com.

- Protect your financial information by using Pay-Pal.

- Don't be afraid to contact the website you bought the item from (i.e., eBay.com) if you are having a problem with a seller on the site.

The Price to Pay

The province of this book is primarily Hummel figurines and related articles. The majority of these collectibles was made by W. Goebel Porzellanfabrik (hereinafter called Goebel) and most recently by Manufaktur Rödental.

There are several factors that influence the actual selling price of the old and the new. The suggested retail price list addresses those pieces bearing the current production trademark. Each time the list is released, it reflects changes in the retail price. These changes are due primarily to the basic principle of supply and demand, economic influences of the world money market, ever-increasing material and production costs, the American market demand, and last, but certainly not least, an expanding interest in Germany and the rest of the European market.

The list does not necessarily reflect the actual price you may have to pay. Highly popular pieces in limited supply can go higher and some of the less popular pieces can go for less. This has been the case more in the recent past than now, but the phenomenon still occurs.

The value of Hummel figurines, plates, and other collectibles bearing trademarks other than the one currently being used in production is influenced by some of the same factors discussed earlier, to a greater or lesser extent. The law of supply and demand comes into even more prominent light with regard to pieces bearing the older trademarks, for they are no longer being made and the number of them on the market is finite. More simply, there are more collectors desiring them than there are available pieces. Generally speaking, the older the trademark, the more valuable or desirable the piece may be to a collector. One must realize, however, that this is not a hard and fast rule. In many instances there are larger numbers available of pieces bearing an older mark than there are of pieces bearing later trademarks. If the latter is a more desirable figure and is in much shorter supply, it is perfectly reasonable for it to be more valuable.

Another factor must be considered. The initial find of the rare International Figurines saw values shoot up as high as $20,000 each. At first, the figurines were thought to exist in just eight designs and in only one or two prototypes of each. Over the years, several more designs and multiples of the figurines have surfaced. Although they are still quite rare, most bring less than half of the original inflated value. So you see, values can fall as the result of an increase in supply of a rare or uncommon piece. This situation can be brought about artificially as well. If someone secretly buys up and hoards a large quantity of a popular piece for a period of time, the short supply will drive the value up. If that supply is suddenly dumped on the market, demand goes down. This has happened more than once in the past, but not so much today.

Yet another circumstance that may influence a fall in pricing is the reissue of a piece previously thought by collectors to be permanently out of production. This has happened because of collectors' past confusion over company terminology with regard to whether a piece was permanently or temporarily withdrawn from production. Many collectors wish to possess a particular item simply because they like it and have no interest in an older trademark version. These collectors will buy the newer piece simply because they can purchase it for less, although recent years have seen the last of the older trademarked pieces go for about the same. It follows naturally that demand for an even older trademark version will lessen under those circumstances.

You may find it surprising that many of the values in the old trademark listing are less than the values reflected in the current suggested retail price list. You have to realize that serious collectors of old mark Hummel collectibles have very little interest in the price of or the collecting of those pieces currently being produced, except where the list has an influence on the pricing structure of the secondary market. As we have seen, demand softens for some of the later old trademark pieces. That is not to say that those and the current production pieces are not valuable—quite the contrary. They will be collectible on the secondary market eventually. Make no bones about it, with the changing of trademarks and the passing of time will come the logical step into the secondary market. The principal market for the last two trademarks is found in the general public, not the seasoned collector. The heaviest trading in the collector market in the past couple of years has been in the Crown and Full Bee trademark pieces. The Stylized Bee and Three Line trademark pieces are currently remaining stable and the Last Bee trademark pieces are experiencing a stagnant market.

Selling M.I. Hummel Items

There is an old saying in the antique and collectibles world that goes like this: "You buy at retail and sell at wholesale." Although this is true in some cases, it is most assuredly (and thankfully) not the rule. The axiom can be true if you must sell and the only ready buyer is a dealer whose percent discount equals or exceeds the amount your item has appreciated in value. This can also be true if you have consigned your piece to an auction, although auctions usually allow you to set a reserve. A reserve is the lowest price you will sell at. If bidding doesn't reach your reserve, you still owe the auctioneer his fee, but you get your item back. This is the case whether you are dealing with a traditional auctioneer or an online auction site.

There are several other methods of selling, each of which has its own set of advantages and disadvantages. Bottom line – educate yourself about the piece(s) you are selling. This will help know what you have and its approximate worth.

Selling to a Dealer

The have-to-sell scenario is an obvious disadvantage, but selling to a dealer will, in most cases, be a painless experience. If you have been fortunate in your acquisitions and the collection has appreciated considerably, it may also be a profitable encounter. If you are not near the dealer and have to ship, then you run the risk of damage or loss.

Running Newspaper Ads

Selling to another collector in your local area is probably one of the easiest and most profitable ways to dispose of your piece(s). There is the advantage of personal examination and no shipping risks.

Running Collector Publication Ads

This is another fine way to get the best price, as long as the sale is to another collector. The same shipping risks exist here also, and you do have to consider the cost of the ad.

Answering Wanted Ads in Collector Publications

The only risk beyond the usual shipping risks is the possibility of the buyer being disappointed and wishing to return the pieces for a refund.

Selling Through a Local Dealer

If you are fortunate enough to have a dealer near you, he/she may take consignments for a percentage.

Selling on the Internet

Although shipping risks and those related to dissatisfied buyers also apply to Internet sales, one advantage over traditional advertisements is not having to pay to publicize your piece (if you have your own website). Websites also offer an opportunity to showcase not only the basic description of a piece, but also a photograph of it.

If you are not so technologically advanced that you can run your own website, selling via auction sites is relatively inexpensive as well. Such sites also offer a wide range of services, most notably for billing, which helps the seller lessen his/her risks of a fraudulent sale (buyers using bad checks, stolen credit cards, etc.).

Another advantage to selling on the Internet involves the web's far-reaching capabilities. The Internet provides worldwide exposure.

Utilize Collector Club Services

The M.I. Hummel Club has an online "members forum" in the members-only section of the website. A member can ask a question of other members, look for a particular Hummel, or sell a Hummel. There is also a collector's market form on the website that you may use. There is no charge for this service beyond membership dues. You must be a member, so you can enroll at www.mihummelclub.com or call membership services at 1-800-666-CLUB (2582). The address is: M.I. Hummel Club, M.I. Hummel Co., LLC, 3705 Quakerbridge Rd., STE 105, Mercerville, NJ 08619-9919. If you interested in joining a local chapter of the club, contact membership services, which will be able to put you in contact with the nearest local chapter in your area.

Possible Pitfalls

The determination of the authenticity of the piece in question is fairly easy in the greatest majority of instances. If you have no reason to suspect the piece of being a fake or forgery and it somewhere bears the incised M.I. Hummel signature, it is probably genuine. In a few instances, the pieces were simply too small for the incised signature to be placed on them without defacing them. Under these circumstances, the company usually places a paper or foil sticker where it is least obtrusive. Often these are lost from the piece over the years, but these small items are few in number and usually readily identifiable by the use of the incised mold number and trademark.

By carefully studying the section on how Manufaktur Rödental (Goebel) utilized mold numbers on the M.I. Hummel pieces, you will gain much more insight into correct identification.

Be ever-alert to the trademarks found on pieces and how to interpret them (see "Understanding Trademarks" later in this chapter). It is a complicated and sometimes confusing system, and you must know how marks are used and what they mean in order to know what you are buying.

Variations are rampant (see individual listings) in both size, coloration, and mold, and you may think you are buying one thing when you're actually getting something quite different.

When it comes to determining the value of broken but expertly restored pieces, they are generally worth significantly less than the current value of the unbroken "mint" pieces. This value is entirely dependent upon the availability of unbroken mint pieces bearing the same mold number, size designator, and trademark. In the case of a rare piece, however, it is often worth almost as much as the mint piece if expertly restored, due simply to its scarcity.

Detecting Restored Pieces

It is sometimes difficult—or impossible—for the average collector to detect an expert restoration of a Hummel figurine or article. The two most reliable methods are: 1) examination by long-wave ultraviolet light, and 2) examination by X-ray. Until very recently, one could rely almost 100 percent on ultraviolet light examination, but some restorative techniques have been developed in the past few years that are undetectable except by X-ray examination.

Examination by X-ray

Access to X-ray equipment might prove difficult. If you have a good friend who is a doctor or dentist with his/her own equipment, you might be able to get your X-ray by reimbursing expenses. A crack otherwise invisible to the naked eye may appear where the piece has been restored. If the piece does exhibit such a feature, it is safe to assume it is a restored piece. There are some restoration marks, however, that may not show up, so the X-ray examination is not foolproof. The latter represents state-of-the-art restoration.

Examination by Ultraviolet Light

When an undamaged piece is exposed to long-wave ultraviolet light, it will appear uniformly light purple in color; the value of the purple will vary with color on the piece. A crack or fracture with glue in it will appear a lighter color (usually orange or pink), patches

This 3" imitation Hummel appears to be a combination of Easter Time (Hum 384) and Playmates (Hum 58). No markings.

Plastic imitation of Hum 201, Retreat to Safety. It appears the mold for this piece was taken directly from a genuine Hummel figurine.

Plastic imitation of Hum 197, Be Patient.

will appear almost white, and most new paint will appear a much, much darker purple.

Fakes, Forgeries, Imitations, and Copies

Fakes and Forgeries

Though not widespread in number, there have been a few rather obvious alterations to the trademarks and to the figurines themselves, making them appear older or different from the norm and therefore more valuable. There have been additions or deletions of small parts (i.e. birds, flowers, etc.) to figures. Worse, one or two unscrupulous individuals have been reglazing colored figurines and other articles with a white overglaze to make them appear to be the relatively uncommon to rare all-white pieces. The serious collector can sometimes detect these imposters, but it is best left to the experts. Should you purchase a piece that is ultimately proven to be one of these fakes, any reputable dealer would replace your figurine if possible.

Imitations, Copies, and Reproductions of Original Hummels

Anyone interested in copies should consult the excellent book *Hummel Copycats* by Lawrence L. Wonsch (Wallace-Homestead, 1987). Wonsch shows that the collecting of copycat M.I. Hummels can be fascinating and fun.

There are many reproductions and imitations of the original Hummel pieces, some better than others, but so far, all are easily detectable upon the most casual examination if one is reasonably knowledgeable about what constitutes an original.

The most common of these imitations are those produced in Japan. They are similar in design motif but obviously not original when one applies the simplest of rules. See "Understanding Trademarks" later in this chapter.

Take note of the photo here of Retreat to Safety (Hum 201). To look at the photo is disconcerting because the figure appears to be genuine. When you hold this particular copy in your hand, however, it feels very light and is obviously inferior. Beneath the base is the phrase "Made in Hong Kong." Carl Luckey purchased this plastic copy in a truck stop gift shop in a Midwestern state in 1979 for $3.95. It was probably worth about 50 cents at the time. Over the years, many others have surfaced. In fact, there is a whole series of these plastic copies.

Many other figurines and articles make obvious attempts at copying the exact design of the genuine article. In every single instance, the falseness becomes immediately detectable as being made of materials and paints severely inferior to the quality exhibited by the real thing. Most are manufactured from a material similar to the plaster or plaster-like substance used in the manufacture of the various prizes one wins at a carnival game booth. Some of these actually bear a sticker proclaiming that they are genuine, authentic, or original Hummel pieces.

The Dubler Figures

During World War II, the Nazi government did not allow the Goebel company to carry on production of Hummel figurines. At that time, a New York firm known as Ars Sacra (a subsidiary of today's Ars Edition in Munich) produced a small collection of figurines very much like the original designs and others in the Hummel style, but not copying any particular design. Those that were Hummel copies usually bore a 5/8" x 1" foil sticker, as reproduced here. They often also had "B. Hummel" and either "ARS SACRA" or "Herbert Dubler, Inc." associated with the signature. Either version was usually incised into the top or side of the base of the figurine. Frequently a copyright date also appears in the same area. In Wonsch's guide, *Hummel Copycats*, more than 20 of these Dubler figures are pictured. His research indicates the possibility that 61 of these figures were designed and perhaps made.

Most Dubler pieces were made of a chalk-like or plaster of Paris-type substance, but a few were rendered in bronze, and some have even been found cast in silver. The Crestwick Co. of New York ostensibly distributed them in the United States. Crestwick later became Hummelwerk, an old U.S. distributing company owned by Goebel. It eventually evolved to Goebel operations in the United States.

Another name associated with Dubler was "Decorative Figurines, Inc." These figurines, also made of plaster of Paris, were almost exact copies.

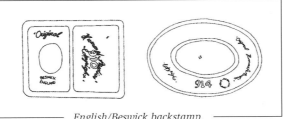

Reproduction of ARS SACRA sticker.

The English or Beswick Pieces

These interesting pieces are intriguing in that some mystery surrounds their origin. Collectors usually know them together as "The English Pieces." There has been speculation in the past that they have some claim to legitimacy, but there has never been any hard evidence found to support that notion. The backstamp "BESWICK-ENGLAND" indicates they were made by an old and respected English porcelain manufacturer that was later bought out by Royal Doulton. Royal Doulton finds no reference to the pieces in the records of Beswick that were obtained when Royal Doulton bought the company.

There have been 12 different designs identified with or without the Beswick backstamp, M.I. Hummel incised signature, and other markings. The mold numbers are 903 through 914. The number 907 model has never been found. The list follows:

903 *Trumpet Boy*	909 *Puppy Love*
904 *Book Worm*	910 *Meditation*
905 *Goose Girl*	911 *Max and Moritz*
906 *Strolling Along*	912 *Farm Boy*
907 *(No known name)*	913 *Globe Trotter*
908 *Stormy Weather*	914 *Shepherd's Boy*

The figurines are shiny and brightly colored in the faience tradition. Most of them bear the inscription "Original Hummel Studios Copyright" in script letters (see drawings) and some version of the Beswick backstamp. Most, but not all, also bear an incised M.I. Hummel signature along with the base inscriptions described above, and there have been some found with no markings at all. All are sought eagerly by many serious collectors.

English/Beswick Farm Boy (912).

English/Beswick backstamp.

English/Beswick Strolling Along (906).

Understanding Trademarks

Since 1935, there have been several changes in the trademarks on M.I. Hummel items. In later years of production, each new trademark design merely replaced the old one, but in the earlier years, frequently the new design trademark would be placed on a figurine that already bore the older style trademark. In some cases, a change from an incised trademark to a surface stamped version of the same mark would result in both appearing on the figure. The former represents a transition period from older to newer, and the latter resulted in what are called "Double Crown." This section is meant to give you an illustrated guide to the major trademarks and their evolution to the trademark presently used on M.I. Hummel items.

Many subtle differences will not be covered because they serve no significant purpose in identifying the era in which an item was produced. There are, however, a few that do help to date a piece. These will be discussed and illustrated. The dates of the early trademark changes are approximate in some cases, but probably accurate to within five years or so. Please bear in mind that the dates, although mostly derived from company records, are not necessarily as definite as they appear. There are documented examples where pieces vary from the stated years, both earlier and later. A number of words and phrases associated with various trademarks can, in some cases, help to date a piece.

Note: It is imperative that you understand that the various trademarks illustrated and discussed here were used by Goebel on all of its products, not just Hummel items, until about mid-1991, when a new mark was developed exclusively for use on M.I. Hummel items.

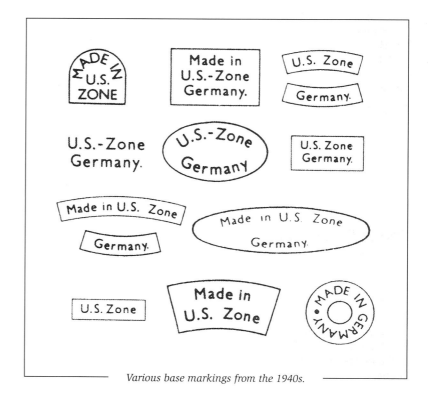

Various base markings from the 1940s.

The Crown Mark (TMK-1):1934-1950

The Crown Mark (TMK-1 or CM), sometimes referred to as the "Crown-WG," was used by Goebel on all of its products in 1935, when M.I. Hummel figurines were first made commercially available. Subtle variations have been noted, but the illustration here is all you need to identify the trademark. Those subtle differences are of no important significance to the collector. The letters WG below the crown in the mark are the initials of William Goebel, one of the founders of the company. The crown signifies his loyalty to the imperial family of Germany at the time of the mark's design, around 1900. The mark is sometimes found in an incised circle.

Another Crown-type mark is sometimes confusing to collectors; some refer to it as the "Narrow Crown" and others the "Wide Ducal Crown." This mark was introduced by Goebel in 1937 and used on many of its products. Goebel calls it the Wide Ducal Crown mark, so we shall adopt this name as well to alleviate confusion. To date, most dealers and collectors have thought this mark was never found on an M.I. Hummel piece. Goebel, however, in its newsletter *INSIGHTS* (Vol. 14, No. 3, pg. 8) stated that the mark was used "...rarely on figurines," so we will defer to the company and assume there might be some out there somewhere.

Often, as stated earlier, the Crown Mark will appear twice on the same piece, more often one mark incised and the other stamped. This is, as we know, the "Double Crown." When World War II ended and the United States Occupation Forces allowed Goebel to begin exporting, the pieces were marked as having been made in the occupied zone. The various forms and phrases to be found in this regard are illustrated below.

These marks were applied to the bases of the figurines, along with the other markings, from 1946 through 1948. They were sometimes applied under the glaze and often over the glaze. The latter were easily lost over the years through wear and cleaning if the owner was not careful. Between 1948 and 1949, the U.S. Zone mark requirement was dropped, and the word "Germany" took its place. With the partitioning of Germany into East and West, "W. Germany," "West Germany," or "Western Germany" began to appear most of the time instead.

Until the early 1950s the company occasionally used a WG or a WG to the right of the incised M.I. Hummel signature. When found, the signature is usually placed on the edge of, or the vertical edge of, the base. Some have been known to confuse this with the Crown Mark (TMK-1) when in fact it is not.

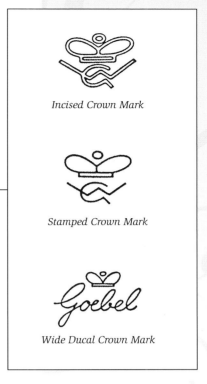

Incised Crown Mark

Stamped Crown Mark

Wide Ducal Crown Mark

The Hummel signature as a base rim marking.

The Full Bee Mark (TMK-2):1940-1959

In 1950, Goebel made a major change in its trademark. The company incorporated a bee in a V. It is thought that the bumblebee part of the mark was derived from a childhood nickname of Sister Maria Innocentia Hummel, meaning bumblebee. The bee flies within a V, which is the first letter of the German word for distributing company, Verkaufsgesellschaft. The mark was to honor M.I. Hummel, who died in 1946.

There are actually 12 variations of the Bee marks to be found on Goebel-produced M.I. Hummel items, but some are grouped together,

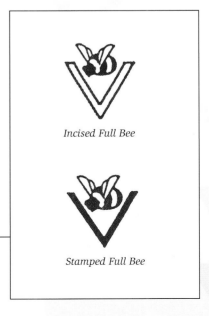

Incised Full Bee

Stamped Full Bee

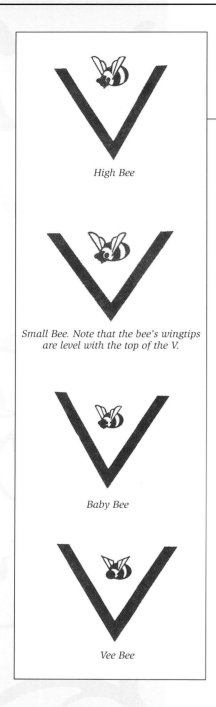

High Bee

Small Bee. Note that the bee's wingtips are level with the top of the V.

Baby Bee

Vee Bee

as the differences between them are not considered particularly significant. They will be detailed as a matter of interest.

The Full Bee mark, also referred to as TMK-2 or abbreviated FB, is the first of the Bee marks to appear. The mark evolved over nearly 20 years until the company began to modernize it. It is sometimes found in an incised circle. The history of the transition and illustrations of each major change follows. Each of them is still considered to be the Full Bee (TMK-2).

The very large bee flying in the V remained until around 1956, when the bee was reduced in size and lowered into the V. It can be found incised, stamped in black, or stamped in blue, in that order, through its evolution.

The Stylized Bee (TMK-3): 1958-1972

A major change in the way the bee is rendered in the trademark made its appearance in 1960. The Stylized Bee (TMK-3), sometimes abbreviated as Sty-Bee when written, as the major component of the trademark appeared in three basic forms through 1972. The first two are both classified as the Stylized Bee (TMK-3), but the third is considered a fourth step in the evolution, the Three Line Mark (TMK-4). It might interest you to know that Goebel reused the Crown-WG backstamp from 1969 until 1972. It is not always there, but when it shows, it is a small blue decal application. This was done to protect Goebel's copyright of the mark. It otherwise would have run out.

The Large Stylized Bee: This trademark was used primarily from 1960 through 1963. Notice in the illustration that the "W. Germany" is placed to the right of the bottom of the V. The color of the mark will be black or blue. It is sometimes found inside an incised circle. When you find the Large Stylized Bee mark, you will normally find a stamped "West" or "Western Germany" in black elsewhere on the base, but not always.

Large Stylized Bee

Small Stylized Bee

The Small Stylized Bee: This mark is also considered to be TMK-3. It was used concurrently with the Large Stylized Bee from about 1960 and continued in this use until about 1972. Note in the illustration that the "W. Germany" appears centered beneath the V and bee. The mark is usually rendered in blue, and it too is often accompanied by a stamped black "West" or "Western Germany." Collectors and dealers sometimes refer to the mark as the One Line Mark.

The Three Line Mark (TMK-4): 1964-1972

This trademark is sometimes abbreviated 3-line or 3LM in print. The trademark used the same stylized V and bee as the others, but also included three lines of wording beside it, as you can see. This major change appeared in blue.

Three Line Mark

The Last Bee Mark (TMK-5): 1972-1979

Actually developed and occasionally used as early as 1970, this major change was known by some collectors as the Last Bee Mark because the next change in the trademark no longer incorporated any form of the V and the bee. However, with the reinstatement of a bee in TMK-8 with the turn of the century, TMK-5 is not technically the "Last Bee" any longer. The mark was used until about mid-1979, when Goebel began to phase it out, completing the transition to the new trademark in 1980. There are three minor variations in the mark shown in the illustration. Generally, the mark was placed under the glaze from 1972 through 1976 and is found placed over the glaze from 1976 through 1979.

Last Bee Mark

The Missing Bee Mark (TMK 6): 1979-1991

The transition to this trademark began in 1979 and was complete by mid-1980. As you can see, Goebel removed the V and bee from the mark altogether. Many dealers and collectors lamented the passing of the traditional stylized V and bee, and for a while called the mark the Missing Bee. In conjunction with this change, the company instituted the practice of adding to the traditional artist's mark the date the artist finished painting the piece. Because the white overglaze pieces are not usually painted, it would be reasonable to assume that the date is omitted on them.

Missing Bee Mark

The Hummel Mark (TMK-7): 1991-1999

In 1991, Goebel made a move of historical importance. The company changed the trademark once again. This time, the change was not only symbolic of the reunification of the two Germanys by removal of the "West" from the mark, but very significant in another way. Until then, Goebel used the same trademark on virtually all of its products. The mark illustrated here was for exclusive use on Goebel products made from the paintings and drawings of M.I. Hummel.

Hummel Mark

The Millennium Bee (TMK-8): 2000-2008

Goebel decided to celebrate the beginning of a new century with a revival in a bee-adorned trademark. Seeking once again to honor the memory of Sister Maria Innocentia Hummel, a bumblebee, this time flying solo without the V, was reinstated into the mark in 2000 and ended in 2008. Goebel stopped production of the M.I. Hummel figurines on Sept. 30, 2008.

Millennium Bee Mark

The Manufaktur Rödental Mark (TKM-9): 2009-Present

Manufaktur Rödental purchased the rights to produce M.I. Hummel figurines from Goebel in 2009. This trademark signifies a new era for Hummel figurines while maintaining the same quality and workmanship from the master sculptors and master painters at the Rödental factory. This trademark has a full bee using yellow and black for the bumblebee, which circles around the words "Original M.I. Hummel Germany" with the registraton symbol next to M.I. Hummel. Manufaktur Rödental is underneath the circle with a copyright sign.

Manufaktur Rödental Mark

Other Base Marks

There are marks in addition to the U.S. Zone marks already covered that can be found on the bases and backs of Goebel Hummel items.

First of all, there are several colors of marks that you may encounter. The colors found to date are black, purple, red, brown, green, and blue.

The color blue has been used exclusively since 1972. There also have been several combinations of colors found.

The following list contains various words and marks found associated with the trademarks. There are probably more to be discovered, but these are representative.

    W. Germany – by W. Goebel (in script)
    W. Germany – W. Goebel (in script)
    GERMANY – Copr. W. Goebel
    Germany – by W. Goebel, Oeslau 1957
    WEST GERMANY – *II Gbl. 1948
    West Germany – OCCUPIED GERMANY
    WESTERN GERMANY – Western Germany

First Issue, Final Issue, and 125th Anniversary Backstamps

Starting in 1990, Goebel began stamping any newly issued piece with the words "First Issue," during the first year of production only. In 1991, the company began doing the same thing during the last year before retiring a piece, by marking each with the words "Final Issue." The words are also accompanied by the appropriate year date. The stamps are illustrated for you here. The first piece to bear the Final Issue backstamp was Hum 203, Signs of Spring, in both sizes. The Final Issue pieces will also be sold with a commemorative retirement medallion hung around them.

Goebel's 125th anniversary was in 1996, and all figures produced in that year bear the special backstamp.

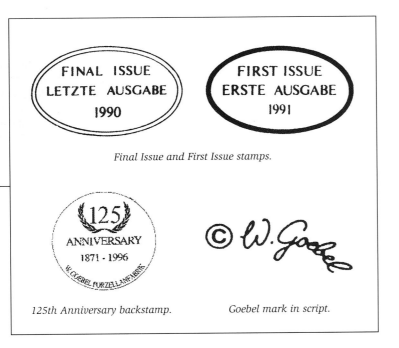

Final Issue and First Issue stamps.

125th Anniversary backstamp.   *Goebel mark in script.*

Mold Numbers and Size Designators

Mold Numbers

All Goebel-made Hummel items were made by the use of molds and each unique mold was assigned a number. The number is part of the mold and it, along with the size designator, becomes a part of the finished piece. It is generally incised on the underside of the base, but for practical reasons may appear elsewhere on the item.

Until the mid-1980s, it was thought by most collectors that the highest mold number normally used in production was in the mid-400s. Time and extensive research by writers, dealers, and serious collectors revealed, among other things, that the number in the Goebel design pool most likely exceeds 1,000 by a great deal. A large number of these have not yet been put into production, and those planned are designated Possible Future Editions (PFE). A few of these (presumably in sample form) have somehow found their way into the collector market, but the occurrence is exceedingly rare. When a PFE becomes a production piece, the earlier PFE example almost always bears an earlier trademark than the mark found on the production piece. It, therefore, retains its unique status. Of the remaining designs, some may be PFEs and some may never make it into the collection. The highest mold number used to date is 2358 for a regular figurine, but there are many gaps in numerical sequence and not every number between 1 and 2314 is currently designated for a figurine now or in the future. Additionally, there are several ball ornaments not produced by Goebel that have Hum numbers ranging from 3012 on up to 3021.

Note: Before we get into the explanation of the mold number system, let's eliminate the source of one area of confusion. Some price lists show an odd letter or number preceded by a slash mark associated with some Hummel mold numbers. Example: Flower Madonna, 10/l/W. The "W" and the slash are price list indications that this piece is finished in all white. The actual mold number found incised on the piece is "10/1" only. The "/W," meaning white overglaze finish, and the "/11" or "/6," meaning the normal color finish, are the decor indicators found in price lists. Remember that they are not part of the mold number itself.

The Size Designator Portion of the Mold Number

While the mold number as discussed earlier in this section was treated as separate from the size designator system, in reality, the two comprise what is sometimes called the Hummel number (Hum number), but more commonly, the mold number. It seems complicated, but isn't really if you factor out Goebel's occasional departure from the rules. The system has changed little over the years, but has been modified once or twice.

Beginning with the first commercial piece in 1935 and continuing to about 1952, the first size of a particular piece produced was considered by the factory to be the "standard" size. If plans were to produce a smaller or larger version, the factory would place a "0" (zero) or a decimal point after the model or mold number. Frequently, but not always, the "0" would be separated from the mold number by placing a slash mark (/) between them. There are many cases where the "0" or the decimal point did not appear. Apparently, this signified that at the time, there were no plans to produce other sizes of the same piece.

In the case of Hum 1, Puppy Love, there exists only one "standard" size and no size designator has ever been found on the figure. It is reasonable to assume, however, that subsequent changes in production plans would result in other sizes being produced. Therefore, the absence of the "0" or decimal point is not a reliable indicator that there exists only one standard size of the particular piece. In fact, there are some instances where later versions of a piece have been found bearing the "/0," decimal point, and even a "/I," which are smaller than the "standard" for that piece. In some cases, the decimal point appears along with the slash mark. The figurine Village Boy (Hum 51), for example, has been seen marked as: "51./0." It could be that when Goebel changed to the slash designator, it just didn't remove the decimal from the mold, but how do you explain the decimal point following the "0"?

The factory used Roman numerals or Arabic numbers in conjunction with the mold numbers to indicate larger or smaller sizes than the standard.

The best way for the collector to understand the system is by example. The figure Village Boy (Hum 51) has been produced in four different sizes. Example 51/0: The number 51 tells us that this is the figurine Village Boy and the "/0" indicates that it is the first size produced, therefore the standard size. In this case, the size of the piece is roughly 6 inches. The presence of the "/0" (or of a decimal point) is also an indication that the figurine was produced sometime prior to 1952.

As discussed earlier, not all the figures produced before 1952 were designated with the "/0" or decimal point, but if present, it is a great help in beginning to date a figure. The one exception currently known is the discontinuance of the use of the "/0" designator on Hum 353, Spring Dance. It was produced with the 353/0 mold and size designator about 1963, taken out of current production later, and recently reinstated once more.

By checking the reference for Hum 51, you will note that three more sizes exist: Hum 51/I/0, Hum 51/3/0, and Hum 51/ 1. Roman numerals are normally used to denote sizes larger than the standard and Arabic numbers indicate sizes smaller than the standard. When utilized in the normal manner, the Arabic number is always found to the left of the "0" designator. There are two exceptions to this norm: one specific, the other general. The specific known exception is Heavenly Angel, Hum 21/0/1/2. This is one of only two known instances of the use of a fractional size designator. The last two numbers are incised and read as one-half (1/2). The general exception is the occasional use of an Arabic number in the same manner as the Roman numeral. The Roman numeral size indicator is never used with the "0" designator present, and the Arabic number is never normally used without the "0" designator. Therefore, if you were to find a mold number 51/2, you would know to read it 51/II, and that it represents a piece larger than the standard.

Note: After the mold for Hum 218 (Birthday Serenade), the use of the "/0" size designator was eliminated. The mold number (51/II) does not exist. It is used here for illustrative purposes only.

Example 51/1

As before, the number 51 identifies the piece for us. The addition of the "/1" tells us that this is a larger figure than the standard. In this case, it is about 1 inch larger.

Example 51/2/0 and 51/3/0

Once again, we know the identity of the piece is Hum 51, Village Boy. In both cases, there is an Arabic number, the mold number, and the "/0," therefore we can assume both are smaller than the standard. The 51/2/0 is smaller than 5" and the 51/3/0 is even smaller still.

The "0" and decimal point size designators are no longer in use. Keeping in mind the cited exceptions, we can usually assume that a figure with the mold number and no accompanying Arabic or Roman numerals is the standard size for that model. If the mold number is accompanied by Roman numerals the figure is a larger size, ascending to larger sizes the higher the numeral.

There seems to be no set standard size or set increase in size for each of the Arabic or Roman numeral size designators used in the collection. The designators are individually specific to each model and bear no relation to the designators on other models.

Additional Designators

There are a number of pieces in the collection—table lamps, candy boxes, bookends, ashtrays, fonts, plaques, music boxes, candleholders, plates, and sets of figures—that may have additional or different designators. A list follows, with explanations of how each is marked.

Table lamps are numbered in the traditional manner. Some later price lists show the number preceded by an "M." Example: M/285.

Candy boxes (candy bowls) are covered cylindrical deep bowls, the cover being topped with one of the Hummel figures. They are numbered with the appropriate mold number for the figure and preceded with the Roman numeral "III." Example: "III/57" is a candy box topped with Hum 57, Chick Girl.

Bookends are both large figures with provisions for weighting with sand and smaller figures placed on wooden bookend bases. The only sand-weighted bookends are the Book Worms. The designation for a bookend is accomplished by placing an "A" and "III" after the assigned Hummel mold number for the bookends. Example: Hum 61/A and Hum 61/B are a set of bookends utilizing Hum 58 and Hum 47, Playmates and Chick Girl. These are the current designations. In some cases if the figurines are removed from the bookend bases they are indistinguishable from a regular figurine.

Ashtrays are numbered in the traditional manner.

Fonts are numbered in the traditional manner. Exception: There is a font, Hum 91 (Angel at Prayer), in two versions. One faces left; the other right. They are numbered 91/A and 91/B, respectively.

Plaques are numbered in the traditional manner.

Music boxes are round wooden containers in which there is a music box movement, topped with a traditional Hummel model that rotates as the music plays. The catalog and price list number for the music box is the Hummel number for the piece on the box followed by the letter "M." If the figure is removed from the top it will not have the "M" but will be marked in the traditional manner.

Candleholders are numbered in the traditional manner. They sometimes have Roman numerals to the left of the model designator in price lists. These indicate candle size: I = 0.6 cm, II = 1 cm.

Plates are numbered in the traditional manner. To date, none have been produced with the size designator, only the mold number.

Sets of figures are numbered with one model number sequence and followed by the designation /A, /B, /C ... /Z, to indicate each figure is part of one set. Example: The Nativity Set 214 contains 15 Hummel figures, numbers 214/A, 214/B, 214/C, and so on. In the case of nativity sets there are some letters that are not used. The letters "I" and "O" are not utilized because of the possibility of confusing them with the Roman numeral "I" or Arabic "1" and "0."

Additional Notes on Special Markings Sets

Any time there have been two or more pieces in the collection that were meant to be matched as a pair or set, the alphabetical listings A through Z are respectively applied to the Hummel mold numbers in some way. Exception: three figures, Hum 389, Hum 390, and Hum 391, sometimes called the Little Band. They do not bear the A, B, or C designating them as a set. The piece actually titled Little Band is Hum 392, an incorporation of these three figures on one base together.

Copyright Dates

The year date incised on the base of many M.I. Hummel pieces is the source of much confusion to some collectors. The year date is the copyright date, which is the date the original mold for that particular piece was made and not the date the piece was made. It bears no relationship whatsoever with the date of making the item, only the mold. As a matter of fact, there are many molds that are years old and still being used to make figures today. The copyright date doesn't always appear on the older pieces, but all those currently being made will have it.

Chapter Three

Delightful Art
Inspires
Beloved Figurines

Berta Hummel, born in 1909 in Massing, Bavaria, Germany, loved to paint already during her childhood. After her study at the Academy of Fine and Applied Arts in Munich, Germany, Berta Hummel entered the Franciscan Convent at Siessen, Germany. From 1931 to 1946, Sister Maria Innocentia Hummel created more than 600 paintings.

In 1934, W. Goebel Porzellanfabrik created the first Hummel figurines based on the original drawings of M. I. Hummel. Nearly 30 beautiful examples of her artwork, and the beloved figurines they inspired, are displayed in the following pages of this special section of the book for your enjoyment.

More information on M. I. Hummel can be found in the biography launched in 2009, *I Want to Give Joy! A Fateful Woman's Career,* www.arsedition.de.

Playmates figurine, Hum 58.

Playmates.

The Little Fiddler.

Little Fiddler figurine, Hum 2.

The Lucust Hunter.

Sensitive Hunter figurine, Hum 6.

Merry Wanderer figurine, Hum 11.

The Merry Wanderer.

Begging His Share figurine, Hum 9.

Begging His Share.

Child With Letter.

Meditation figurine, Hum 13.

Town Crier.

Hear Ye, Hear Ye figurine, Hum 15.

*Congratulations
figurine, Hum 17.*

Angel and Birds.

*Little Hiker
figurine,
Hum 16.*

Happy John.

Prayer Before Battle.

Prayer Before Battle figurine, Hum 20.

Chick Girl.

Chick Girl figurine, Hum 57.

*Wayside Harmony
figurine, Hum 111.*

Wayside Harmony.

*Just Resting
figurine,
Hum 112.*

Just Resting.

Mother's Helper.

Mother's
Helper
figurine,
Hum 133.

Bye-Bye!

Auf Wiedersehen
figurine, Hum 153.

*Doll Mother
figurine,
Hum 67.*

Doll Mother.

*Chimney
Sweep figurine,
Hum 12.*

Chimney Sweep.

The Botanist figurine, Hum 351.

Blue Belle.

The Run-a-way figurine, Hum 327.

The Runaway.

Goose Girl figurine, Hum 47.

Goose Girl.

Stormy Weather figurine, Hum 71.

Sunny Weather.

Have the Sun in Your Heart.

Umbrella Boy figurine,
Hum 152/A.

March Winds.

March Winds
figurine,
Hum 43.

Apple Tree Boy figurine, Hum 142.

Apple Tree Boy.

Apple Tree Girl figurine, Hum 141.

Apple Tree Girl.

Umbrella Girl.

*Umbrella Girl
figurine,
Hum 152/B.*

Max and Moritz.

*Max and Moritz
figurine, Hum 123.*

Chapter Four

Hummel Listings

The following list of Hummel pieces is arranged by Hummel mold number in ascending order. To fully understand all of the notations, you must read and study the first two chapters of this book carefully.

You will find the price listings almost complete, but it is impossible to conscientiously assign a value to each and every model that exists today. There are more than 1,500 pieces identified in this chapter; this number does not take into consideration variations due to mold size variation, color variation, and model design differences. When it was impossible to obtain pricing information on a particular figure size or variation, the appropriate space is left blank or the listing is omitted altogether. In the latter case, it was not possible to ascertain and document all existing models. From time to time it is possible to establish the existence of a piece but without sure information as to size or trademark. In these cases, the corresponding space is left blank.

As stated earlier, the sizes are approximate but as accurate as possible. Almost all lists are contradictory, but in most cases within reasonable agreement. The sizes listed are those most frequently encountered in those listings and notated as the "Basic Size/Basic Size." Most of the time, this is the smallest size for each figure. Frequently, however, there would be one smaller size listed, but the preponderance of other listings would indicate a 1/4" or 1/2" larger size. In these cases, the larger size was assumed the more representative.

For purposes of simplification, the various trademarks have been abbreviated in the list. Should you encounter any trouble interpreting the abbreviations, refer to the list below or to the glossary.

Trademark	Abbreviations	Dates
Crown	TMK-1	1934-1950
Full Bee	TMK-2	1940-1959
Stylized Bee	TMK-3	1958-1972
Three Line Mark	TMK-4	1964-1972
Last Bee	TMK-5	1972-1979
Missing Bee	TMK-6	1979-1991
Hummel Mark	TMK-7	1991-1999
Millennium Bee/Goebel Bee	TMK-8	2000-2008
Manufaktur Rödental Mark	TMK-9	2009-present

Hum 1: Puppy Love

Part of the original 46 pieces offered in 1935, Puppy Love was first known as the Little Violinist. It was first modeled by master sculptor Arthur Moeller in 1935 and can be found in Crown Mark (TMK-1) through TMK-6. It was retired in 1988, never to be produced again.

Many of the original group of 46 figurines have been found rendered in terra-cotta, and Puppy Love is no exception, although so far only one is known to exist in any private collection. It has an incised Crown Mark and incised number "T-1." It is valued at whatever a collector will pay.

Hum No.	Basic Size	Trademark	Current Value
1	5″	TMK-1	$2,900 Version 1
1	5″	TMK-1	$400 Version 3
1	5″	TMK-2	$500 Version 2
1	5″	TMK-2	$300 Version 3
1	5″	TMK-3	$375 Version 2
1	5″	TMK-3	$325 Version 3
1	5″	TMK-4	$275
1	5″	TMK-5	$225
1	5″	TMK-6	$200

Version 1: The most significant variation occurs in a Crown. In this variation, the head is tilted to the right instead of the typical left, he wears a black hat, and there is no necktie.

Version 2: Is found in TMK-2 and TMK-3. The boy's head has very little tilt towards his left shoulder.

Version 3: This is the current standard production model. The boy's head is tilted to his left shoulder and is, or close to, touching the violin. This version is found in all trademarks.

In the initial process of planning and modeling the figurines, there was no formal designation of the mold number, and Puppy Love has been found with the mold number FF 15. If found, this early sample with the original number is worth whatever a collector will pay for such a rare piece.

The last year of production in TMK-6 will have a "1988 FINAL ISSUE" stamp on the bottom.

A third early sample was produced in 1935 by Arthur Moeller, with an attached pot. If found, this piece would be worth the value of a rare piece. Puppy Love was also sold as a special edition that included a commemorative wooden base with a light pole and engraved plaque.

Hum 1: Puppy Love.

Hum 2: Little Fiddler

Originally known as the Violinist and then The Wandering Fiddler, this little fellow is almost always wearing a brown derby with an orange hatband. Modeled by master sculptor Arthur Moeller in 1935, the figure has been made in five sizes since its initial introduction as part of the original 46.

The two largest sizes were temporarily withdrawn from production in 1989. The smallest, Hum 2/4/0, was introduced into the line in 1984 and was temporarily withdrawn from the North American market on Dec. 31, 1997.

A few Little Fiddlers with the Crown Mark (TMK-1) have been found in doll face or faience finish. These are valued more than the regular Crown pieces. So few have come to market that the price should be determined between seller and buyer.

A mold number variation has been found with the mold number FF 16. In the days before the figurines were given the official "Hum" designation, the "FF" was used on Hum 1, 2, and 3. The value for this variation should be determined between seller and buyer.

Goebel produced a limited edition of 50 Hum 2/I pieces in 1985 for a company-sponsored contest in Europe to celebrate 50 years of M.I. Hummel figurines. The limited edition had a gold painted base and special backstamp that read, "50 Jahre M.I. Hummel-Figuren 1935-1985." A 12-1/4" version of Little Fiddler was introduced as part of the "Millennium Love " series, which also included Sweet Music (Hum 186/III), Serenade (Hum 85/III), Band Leader (Hum 129/III), and Soloist (Hum 135/III). These oversized pieces (Hum 85/III) were in limited supply and had to be special-ordered through an authorized M.I. Hummel retailer.

Hum No.	Basic Size	Trademark	Current Value
2/4/0	3-1/2"	TMK-6	$200
2/4/0 TW	3-1/2"	TMK-7	$175
2/0	6"	TMK-1	$550
2/0	6"	TMK-2	$400
2/0	6"	TMK-3	$325
2/0	6"	TMK-4	$325
2/0	6"	TMK-5	$175
2/0	6"	TMK-6	$175
2/0	6"	TMK-7	$175
2/0	6"	TMK-8	$260
2/I	7-1/2"	TMK-1	$550
2/I	7-1/2"	TMK-2	$500
2/I	7-1/2"	TMK-3	$400
2/I	7-1/2"	TMK-4	$450
2/I	7-1/2"	TMK-5	$300
2/I	7-1/2"	TMK-6	$1,200 LE 50 with gold-painted base
2/I	7-1/2"	TMK-6	$300
2/I TW	7-1/2"	TMK-7	$200 White Expressions of Youth
2/I TW	7-1/2"	TMK-7	$300 LE 200 for guild of specialist china and glass
2/I TW	7-1/2"	TMK-7	$300
2/II	11"	TMK-1	$1,300
2/II	11"	TMK-2	$925
2/II	11"	TMK-3	$850
2/II	11"	TMK-4	$825
2/II	11"	TMK-5	$725
2/II TW	11"	TMK-6	$700
2/III	12-1/4"	TMK-1	$2,000
2/III	12-1/4"	TMK-2	$1,850
2/III	12-1/4"	TMK-3	$1,600
2/III	12-1/4"	TMK-4	$1,400
2/III	12-1/4"	TMK-5	$1,100
2/III	12-1/4"	TMK-6	$1,100
2/III	12-1/4"	TMK-8	$1,550 retail

Left: Hum 2: Little Fiddler.
Right: The limited edition gold gilt base Little Fiddler, Hum 2/I.

The underside of the base of the gold-gilt base of Hum 2/I Little Fiddler, showing the trademark and the German language Golden Jubilee backstamp. It reads: "50 JAHRE M.I. HUMMEL-FIGUREN 1935-1985."

Hum 3: Book Worm

One of the original 46 released in 1935, this figure of a girl reading a book appears more than once in the collection and was originally called Little Book Worm. It is also found in a smaller size as Hum 8 and in the Hum 14/A and 14/B bookends, titled Book Worms, with a companion figure of a boy reading.

The larger Hum 3/II and Hum 3/III pieces have been out of current production for some time.

The Hum 3/III rarely comes to market in the older trademarks and is avidly sought by collectors.

The numbers 3/II and 3/III are occasionally found with the Arabic number size designator (3/2 and 3/3, respectively).

The two larger sizes (8" and 9-1/2") have been temporarily withdrawn from current production.

There is a mold number variation. Before the figurines were given "Hum" mold numbers, this figure was given the incised mold number FF 17. This mold number is very rare and no market price can be assessed

A few faience pieces have been found and would command a high price should one come to market.

Hum No.	Basic Size	Trademark	Current Value
3/I	5-1/2"	TMK-1	$675
3/I	5-1/2"	TMK-2	$550
3/I	5-1/2"	TMK-3	$400
3/I	5-1/2"	TMK-4	$325
3/I	5-1/2"	TMK-5	$250
3/I	5-1/2"	TMK-6	$250
3/I	5-1/2"	TMK-7	$250
3/I TW	5-1/2"	TMK-8	$200
3/II	8"	TMK-1	$1,500
3/II	8"	TMK-2	$1,175
3/II	8"	TMK-3	$700
3/II	8"	TMK-4	$650
3/II	8"	TMK-5	$525
3/II TW	8"	TMK-6	$475
3/III	9-1/2"	TMK-1	$2,500
3/III	9-1/2"	TMK-2	$2,200
3/III	9-1/2"	TMK-3	$1,200
3/III	9-1/2"	TMK-4	$900
3/III	9-1/2"	TMK-5	$800
3/III TW	9-1/2"	TMK-6	$800

Hum 3: Book Worm.

Hum 4: Little Fiddler

This is the same design as Hum 2, Little Fiddler. The difference is that this is a smaller size than Hum 2. It, too, was modeled by master sculptor Arthur Moeller in 1935 and originally named Violinist or The Wandering Fiddler. One wonders why the company used two different mold numbers for the same basic piece in the original 46 figurines released in 1935.

Another difference is that Hum 4 wears a black hat with an orange band, while Hum 2's hat is brown. The boy's vest, umbrella handle, and satchel handle sometimes can be found in yellow in TMK-1.

A few pieces have been found with the doll face and the faience style. Goebel documents indicated that this figurine in TMK-1 was made with an attached pot. If found it would be considered very very rare.

The 4-3/4 size designation is an average of the sizes found.

Hum No.	Basic Size	Trademark	Current Value
4	4-3/4"	TMK-1	$1,500 tilted head style
4	4-3/4"	TMK-1	$400
4	4-3/4"	TMK-2	$325
4	4-3/4"	TMK-3	$275
4	4-3/4"	TMK-4	$250
4	4-3/4"	TMK-5	$200
4	4-3/4"	TMK-6	$200
4	4-3/4"	TMK-7	$200
4	4-3/4"	TMK-8 CE	$200

Hum 4: Little Fiddler. The left piece is the doll face. Note the very pale face and hands, the completely different head position, and the lack of a neckerchief. Each has the decimal point mold number designation (4.), the Crown Mark, and measures 5-1/8".

Hum 5: Strolling Along

One of the first 46 figures released in 1935, Hum 5 appears in only one basic size, 4-3/4". This figure was modeled by Arthur Moeller in 1935.

Gerhard Skrobek restyled the figurine in 1962 and changed the position of the eyes. The TMK-6 figurines have the boy looking straight ahead, while the older ones have him looking to the side. There is also evidence that a sample was produced with an attached pot, which would be very rare and with a value to be determined between seller and buyer. Strolling Along was removed from production at the end of 1989, never to be made again.

Hum No.	Basic Size	Trademark	Current Value
5	4-3/4"	TMK-1	$425
5	4-3/4"	TMK-2	$300
5	4-3/4"	TMK-3	$225
5	4-3/4"	TMK-4	$200
5	4-3/4"	TMK-5	$150
5	4-3/4"	TMK-6 CE	$150

Hum 5: Strolling Along.

Hum 6: Sensitive Hunter

Called The Timid Hunter when first released among the original 46 figurines, it was modeled by Arthur Moeller in 1935.

The most notable variation is the shape of the suspenders on the boy's back. The suspenders form an "X" or "H." The "H" variation is found on all of the Crown Mark (TMK-1) figurines in the size 6 and 6/0. In the size 6/0, both styles of suspenders can be found in the TMK-3. The TMK-3 and up has the "X" style suspenders. Not enough of the 6/II in TMK-1 or TMK-2 have been found to know what the strap configuration may be. The color of the rabbit was usually orange, until 1981 when the company changed it to brown for all newly produced pieces.

In TMK-1 and TMK-2 there are variations in the size of the hat feather. The socks also can be found in different colors.

The smallest of the sizes listed here, Hum 6/2/0, was added in 1985 as the second in a series of new smaller figurines matching mini-plates of the same design.

On Dec. 31, 1984, Goebel announced the 7-1/2" size (Hum 6/II) was temporarily withdrawn from production status. In January 1999, the smallest size (6/2/0) was temporarily withdrawn. As of June 15, 2002, the 4-3/4" size (6/0) also was temporarily withdrawn.

Hum 6: Sensitive Hunter.

Hum No.	Basic Size	Trademark	Current Value
6/2/0	4"	TMK-6	$125
6/2/0 TW	4"	TMK-7	$125
6 CE	4-3/4"	TMK-1	$600 in "H" style
6/0	4-3/4"	TMK-1	$600
6/0	4-3/4"	TMK-2	$400 seldom seen in "X" style
6/0	4-3/4"	TMK-3	$325 either style
6/0	4-3/4"	TMK-4	$300
6/0	4-3/4"	TMK-5	$200
6/0	4-3/4"	TMK-6	$200
6/0	4-3/4"	TMK-7	$175
6/0 TW	4-3/4"	TMK-8	$150
6/I	5-1/2"	TMK-1	$700
6/I	5-1/2"	TMK-2	$550
6/I	5-1/2"	TMK-3	$325
6/I	5-1/2"	TMK-4	$300
6/I	5-1/2"	TMK-5	$200
6/I TW	5-1/2"	TMK-6	$200
6/II	7-1/2"	TMK-1	$1,500 seen only in "X" style
6/II	7-1/2"	TMK-2	$875
6/II	7-1/2"	TMK-3	$500
6/II	7-1/2"	TMK-4	$475
6/II	7-1/2"	TMK-5	$400
6/II TW	7-1/2"	TMK-6	$300

Hum 7: Merry Wanderer

Another of the 46 figurines released in 1935, the same design also appears as Hum 11 but in a smaller size. Originally modeled by master sculptor Arthur Moeller, the Merry Wanderer is probably found in more sizes and variations than any other single figure in the collection. There is even a huge six-foot replica of the figure on the factory grounds in Germany. An eight-foot-high Merry Wanderer was displayed on the grounds of the former location of the M.I. Hummel Club in Tarrytown, New York, and is now located at the U.S. company location in New Jersey. The Merry Wanderer is also the company's motif and is used on all correspondence.

The hardest size to find on the secondary market is Hum 7/III, which was temporarily withdrawn from production in 1991 (TMK-6). Trademarks 1, 2, and 3 have a base different from other sizes. Collectors refer to it variously as the "double step base," "stepped-up base," or the "stair step base." It is found on the Hum 7/I size of all the Crown Mark (TMK-1) and Full Bee (TMK-2) 7/I pieces. TMK-3 can be found in either style of base. The 7/I size has been found in the faience finish.

The 2009 Hummel Suggested Retail Price List places a $25,000 value on the 32" "Jumbo" Merry Wanderer. The early 7/X size were used as promotional figures in showrooms and shops. The later trademarks were made available to collectors and sold at retail. The 7/0 in a crown, however, has been spotted with four buttons and is difficult to find.

Hum No.	Basic Size	Trademark	Current Value
7/0	6-1/4"	TMK-1	$300
7/0	6-1/4"	TMK-2	$250
7/0	6-1/4"	TMK-3	$225
7/0	6-1/4"	TMK-4	$225
7/0	6-1/4"	TMK-5	$200
7/0	6-1/4"	TMK-6	$200
7/0	6-1/4"	TMK-7	$200
7/0 CE	6-1/4"	TMK-7	$200 made for Little Switzerland
7/0 CE	6-1/4"	TMK-8	$200
7/I	7"	TMK-1	$700 step base
7/I	7"	TMK-2	$650 step base
7/I	7"	TMK-3	$600 step base
7/I	7"	TMK-3	$500 standard base
7/I	7"	TMK-4	$450
7/I	7"	TMK-5	$375
7/I	7"	TMK-6	$275
7/I TW	7"	TMK-7	$200
7/I CE	7"	TMK-7	$200 Expressions of Youth
7/II	9-1/2"	TMK-1	$1,200
7/II	9-1/2"	TMK-2	$800
7/II	9-1/2"	TMK-3	$700
7/II	9-1/2"	TMK-4	$700
7/II	9-1/2"	TMK-5	$600
7/II	9-1/2"	TMK-6	$600
7/II TW	9-1/2"	TMK-7	$600
7/III	11-1/4"	TMK-1	$3,000
7/III	11-1/4"	TMK-2	$2,250
7/III	11-1/4"	TMK-3	$1,500
7/III	11-1/4"	TMK-4	$1,200
7/III	11-1/4"	TMK-5	$1,000
7/III TW	11-1/4"	TMK-6	$1,000
7/X	32"	TMK-5$	$12,000
7/X	32"	TMK-6$	$10,000
7/X	32"	TMK-7	$9,000
7/X	32"	TMK-8	$25,000 retail

Hum 7: Merry Wanderer.

Hum 8: Book Worm

This figure is the same as Hum 3/I, except smaller. First modeled by master sculptor Reinhold Unger in 1935, it was originally named Little Book Worm. It is one of the original 46 figurines to be offered at the Leipzig Fair that same year. At least one terra-cotta Book Worm is known to be in collectors' hands, and the value would be determined between the seller and buyer.

Hum No.	Basic Size	Trademark	Current Value
8	4"	TMK-1	$475
8	4"	TMK-2	$325
8	4"	TMK-3	$225
8	4"	TMK-4	$225
8	4"	TMK-5	$200
8	4"	TMK-6	$200
8	4"	TMK-7	$200
8	4"	TMK-8 TW	$200

Hum 8: Book Worm: a comparison between the normal skin coloration (left) and the pale coloration on the doll face piece. Both measure 4-1/4". The left bears a Stylized Bee Mark (TMK-3). The one on the right is a doll face piece with a Double Crown Mark (TMK-1).

Hum 9: Begging His Share

Begging His Share was originally designed by master sculptor Arthur Moeller in 1935 to be a candleholder. It was originally called Congratulatory Visit. The cake occasionally can be found without a hole for the candle, but in TMK-3 it was changed to a solid cake. It can be found with and without the candle-holding hole in the cake in TMK-3. In 1964, the hole was eliminated when the figurine was remodeled.

Hum No.	Basic Size	Trademark	Current Value
9	5-1/2"	TMK-1	$550
9	5-1/2"	TMK-2	$450
9	5-1/2"	TMK-3	$400 with hole in cake
9	5-1/2"	TMK-3	$300 without hole
9	5-1/2"	TMK-4	$225
9	5-1/2"	TMK-5	$175
9	5-1/2"	TMK-6	$150
9	5-1/2"	TMK-7 TW	$150
9/II	7-3/4"	TMK-9	$1,000 retail 75th Anniversary Edition

Although not a major variation in terms of value, the fact that the earliest of the TMK-1 pieces have brightly colored striped socks is worth mentioning.

This figurine has been found without a base. This no-base, large-shoes figure may have been intended to be utilized as a bookend piece, or it may have been simply an experiment. Whatever the case, if found it would command a premium price.

The 5-1/2" piece was temporarily withdrawn in January 1999. To pay tribute to Sister Innocentia Hummel 75 years later on 2010, the designers at Manufaktur Rödental, led by Master Sculptor Tamara Fuchs, redesigned Begging His Share to more closely match Sister Hummel's original drawing. This figurine is limited to 75 pieces worldwide. It has a commorative "75th Anniversary" backstamp, comes with a ceramic plaque with a copy of the original drawing, and a wooden easel for display. A ceramic oval white and gold plaque bearing the words "Special Edition 75 Years M.I. Hummel" written in both English and German, with an outline of the Merry Wanderer, is also included. Begging His Share was also part of QVC 100th Birthday-themed figurines. This figurine is 7-3/4" tall and has "Happy Birthday" painted on the base.

Hum 9/II: Begging His Share 75th Anniversary Edition.

Hum 9: Begging His Share.

Hum 10: Flower Madonna

Created in 1935 by master sculptor Reinhold Unger, this piece was listed in early catalogs as Virgin With Flowers and Sitting Madonna with Child. Theo A. Menzenbach restyled the figurine and made it approximately two inches shorter in TMK-3.

Several color and mold variations are known for this figure. In the 10/I and 10/III sizes, it appears in color and in white overglaze. The color cloak figurines, other than the powder blue (which is found in all trademarks), are found only in trademarks 1 and 2. Some of the cloak colors found are: tan, beige, ivory, brown, yellow, orange, and royal blue. In these colors the figurine will command at least $500 more than the prices below. Very few have been found in terra-cotta in 10/III (13") and in 10/I size (9-1/2") with the Crown Mark (TMK-1).

An open-style or "doughnut" type halo is found in the Crowns and TMK-2s. The figure was remodeled in the mid-1950s, eliminating the hole in the halo (closed halo).

The powder blue Madonnas are more popular but fetch only a slightly higher price. Because this figurine is so large, it is very susceptable to crazing, so those figurines without crazing are more desirable.

In 1996, the 50th anniversary of Sister M.I. Hummel's death, Goebel issued a special white edition of this piece in the 8-1/4" size for $225. The figure was on a hardwood base with a brass plaque.

Hum No.	Basic Size	Trademark	Current Value
10/I	8 1/2 to 9-1/2"	TMK-1	$600 open halo
10/I	9-1/2"	TMK-2	$450 open halo
10/I	8"	TMK-3	$375 remaining closed halos
10/I	8"	TMK-4	$375
10/I	8"	TMK-5	$275
10/I	8"	TMK-6	$200
10/I	8"	TMK-7 TW	$200
10/I	8"	TMK-7 TW	$225 50th Anniversary in white only
10/III	12 3/4"	TMK-1	$800 open halo
10/III	12 3/4"	TMK-2	$725 open halo
10/III	11-1/4"	TMK-3	$600 remaining closed halos
10/III	11-1/4"	TMK-4	$575
10/III	11-1/4"	TMK-5	$475
10/III	11-1/4"	TMK-6 TW	$375

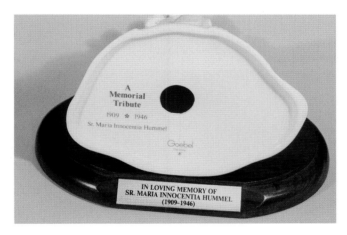

Base of a special edition white overglaze Flower Madonna and wood display stand.

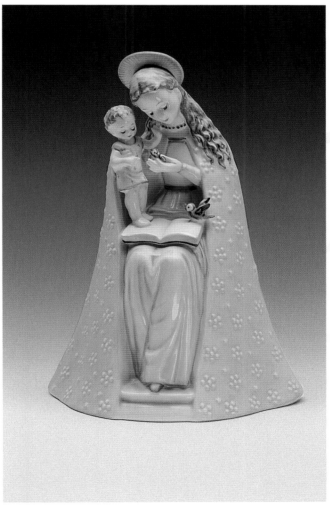

Hum 10: Flower Madonna.

Hum 11: Merry Wanderer

Hum 11 was first modeled by master sculptor Arthur Moeller in 1935. It is the same style as Hum 7.

Although most of these figures have a five-button vest, zero-, four-, six-, and seven-button versions have been found.

The Hum 11 model of the Merry Wanderer has been found with a faience finish, fetching a much higher price as other figurines in the faience style. The button variations are found in the 11, 11/0, and 11 2/0 variations, but only in trademarks 1, 2, and 3. Any of the pieces (other than those having five buttons) would have a higher value, but probably only to the person who collects such variations.

In 1993, as part of a special Disneyland and Disney World promotion, an unknown number of the small Merry Wanderers were given a special decal transfer mark beneath the base to commemorate the occasion. The piece was supposed to be sold along with a similar-sized limited edition Mickey Mouse. The Mickey Mouse has an incised mold number of 17322, a limited edition indicator, and TMK-7. The Merry Wanderer is a regular production 11/2/0. The problem was that the Merry Wanderers did not make it to the theme parks in time for the promotion.

The edition for the pair on a wooden base was 1,500. The first sales of them on the secondary market apparently took place at the site of the M.I. Hummel Club convention in Milwaukee, Wisconsin, in May 1993. Some private individuals were selling the figures out of their hotel rooms for a premium price per set.

The year 2011 marked the celebration of Sister Hummel's 75th anniversary of the beginning of her legacy. Manufaktur Rödental selected 50 figurines to bear the "75th Anniversary" backstamp. Merry Wanderer was one of those figurines. Only 75 of this figurine were available in North America with this backstamp.

Hum No.	Basic Size	Trademark	Current Value
11	4-3/4"	TMK-1	$625
11/2/0	4-1/4"	TMK-1	$475
11/2/0	4-1/4"	TMK-2	$275
11/2/0	4-1/4"	TMK-3	$250
11/2/0	4-1/4"	TMK-4	unknown if exists
11/2/0	4-1/4"	TMK-5	$100
11/2/0	4-1/4"	TMK-6	$125
11/2/0	4-1/4"	TMK-7	$100
11/2/0	4-1/4"	TMK-8	$100
11/2/0	4-1/4"	TMK-8	$150 Goebel 1871-2001 commemorative with Hummelscape
11/2/0	4-1/4"	TMK-8	$189 retail 75th Anniversary Backstamp
11/0	4-3/4"	TMK-1	$550
11/0	4-3/4"	TMK-2	$400
11/0	4-3/4"	TMK-3	$325
11/0	4-3/4"	TMK-4	unknown if exists
11/0	4-3/4"	TMK-5	$225
11/0	4-3/4"	TMK-6	$200
11/0	4-3/4"	TMK-7	$175
11/0	4-3/4"	TMK-7	$200 Special with red satchel, produced for Little Switzerland
11/0	4 3/4	TMK-8+1	$339 retail 70th Hummel Anniversary with tag LE 1935

Hum 11, Merry Wanderer. This piece bears the decimal mold number designator 11., a Double Crown Mark, and a split (quartered) base. It is not likely to be a demonstration piece, due to its age.

Hum 11: Merry Wanderer.

Hum 12: Chimney Sweep

When first introduced in 1935 as part of the original group displayed at the Leipzig Fair, this figure was called Smoky. It was first designed by master sculptor Arthur Moeller in 1935 with several minor restylings through the years.

The small 4" size was not added to the line until well into the 1950s, and consequently, no Crown Mark (TMK-1) pieces are found in that size. There are many variations in size, but none are significant. Examples found in sales lists are 4", 5-1/2", 6-1/4", and 6-3/8".

There was a surprise in store for those who bought the 1992 Sampler (a Hummel introductory kit). In it were the usual club membership discount and that year's figurine, Chimney Sweep. Along with the figure came a special display base of a rooftop and chimney.

In 1995, Goebel produced for German retail promotion a special edition of the Chimney Sweep with a gilded base. The edition was limited to 500 pieces.

Hum 12: Chimney Sweep.

Hum No.	Basic Size	Trademark	Current Value
12/4/0	3"	TMK-8	$99 retail
12/2/0	4"	TMK-2	$200
12/2/0	4"	TMK-3	$175
12/2/0	4"	TMK-4	$150
12/2/0	4"	TMK-5	$100
12/2/0	4"	TMK-6	$100
12/2/0	4"	TMK-7	$100
12/2/0	4"	TMK-8	$159 retail
12	6"	TMK-1	$550
12	6"	TMK-2	$375
12/I	5-1/2"	TMK-1	$450
12/I	5-1/2"	TMK-2	$375
12/I	5-1/2"	TMK-3	$275
12/I	5-1/2"	TMK-4	$275
12/I	5-1/2"	TMK-5	$200
12/I	5-1/2"	TMK-6	$200
12/I	5-1/2"	TMK-7	$200
12/I	5-1/2"	TMK-8+1	$379 retail 70th Hummel Anniversary with tag

Hum 13: Meditation

The Hum 13/0 and the Hum 13/II sizes were the first to be released in 1935 and were first modeled by Reinhold Unger. The piece was also called Little Messenger. The 13/II was restyled by Gerhard Skrobek in TMK-5; 13/2/0 was also modeled by Skrobeck; 13V was modeled by Theo A. Menzenback.

The most significant variations are with regard to the flowers in the baskets. When first released, 13/II had flowers in the basket. Flowers are found in TMK-1, 2, and 3. The piece was restyled by master sculptor Gerhard Skrobek to reflect no flowers in the basket in TMK-5.

Normally, the girl will have circles on her sleeves, but sometimes they are missing. Variations in Hum 13/0 are with regard to the pigtails. Some Crowns and Full Bee models of the figurine sported short pigtails with a painted red ribbon. Others had a red ribbon in a bow, while others had the pigtail on her left side flat against her face. Later the pigtails became prominent by sticking out from her face.

The larger Hum 13/V has a basket filled with flowers. It is scarce in the older trademarks and hardly ever found for sale. It was temporarily withdrawn from production on Dec. 31, 1989. Also temporarily withdrawn were 13/2/0 and 13/0 pieces in January 1999.

There is a very unusual and probably unique Meditation that has a bowl attached to its side. There have been three different figurines found with bowls attached. The other two are Goose Girl and Congratulations.

Meditation was re-released in the Christmas season of 2012 in a smaller size of 3-1/4". It is a TMK-9 figurine.

Hum No.	Basic Size	Trademark	Current Value
13/4/0	3-1/4"	TMK-8	$99 retail
13/2/0	4-1/4"	TMK-2	$200
13/2/0	4-1/4"	TMK-3	$200
13/2/0	4-1/4"	TMK-4	$175
13/2/0	4-1/4"	TMK-5	$150
13/2/0	4-1/4"	TMK-6 TW	$150
13/0	5	TMK-1	$475
13/0	5"	TMK-2	$400
13/0	5	TMK-3	$375
13/0	5"	TMK-4	$375
13/0	5"	TMK-5	$225
13/0	5"	TMK-6	$225
13/0	5"	TMK-7 TW	$225
13	7"	TMK-1	unknown value
13/I	5 1/4	TMK-1	unknown value
13/II	7"	TMK-1	$2,500 with flowers
13/II	7"	TMK-2	$1,850 with flowers
13/II	7"	TMK-3	$1,325 with flowers
13/II	7"	TMK-5	$275
13/II	7"	TMK-6 TW	$250
13/II	7"	TMK-8	$350 Revival Collection LE 2,000
13/V	13-3/4"	TMK-1	$2,750
13/V	13-3/4"	TMK-2	$2,250
13/V	13-3/4"	TMK-3	$1,000
13/V	13-3/4"	TMK-4	$850
13/V	13-3/4"	TMK-5	$675
13/V	13-3/4"	TMK-6	$700
13/V	13-3/4"	TMK-7	$700
13/V	13-3/4"	TMK-8	$1,500 retail
13/4/0	3-1/4"	TMK-9	$199 retail

Hum 13: Meditation.

Hum 13/4/0: Meditation.

14/A and Hum 14/B: Book Worm Bookends

The figurines were modeled by Reinhard Unger in 1935. There are two figures, a boy and a girl, which make a pair of bookends. The girl is the same as Hum 3 and 8, except the pictures in the book are in black and white instead of in color. Early marketed boy pieces were titled Learned Man. Typically the bookends were sold as a pair, but sometimes the boy was sold separately.

These bookends do not have wooden bases, unlike other bookends in the collection that typically have wooden bases. There are holes on the bottom where the figures are weighted with sand, etc., and are usually sealed with cork, a plastic plug, or a factory sticker, gold in color.

These bookends were temporarily withdrawn on Dec. 31, 1989, but in 1993, they could be purchased by mail-order from Danbury Mint, thus the existence of the TMK-7 pieces.

Hum No.	Basic Size	Trademark	Current Value
14 (Boy)	5-1/2"	TMK-1	$600-$800
14/A&B	5-1/2"	TMK-1	$800
14/A&B	5-1/2"	TMK-2	$475
14/A&B	5-1/2"	TMK-3	$400
14/A&B	5-1/2"	TMK-4	$400
14/A&B	5-1/2"	TMK-5	$400
14/A&B TW	5-1/2"	TMK-6	$350
14/A&B TW	5-1/2"	TMK-7	$350 Danbury Mint
14A	5-1/2	TMK-8+1	$389 retail 70th Anniversary with tag LE of 1935
14B	5-1/2	TMK-8+1	$389 retail 70th Anniversary with tag LE of 1935

70th Anniversary pieces come with wooden stand.

Hum 14/A and Hum 14/B: Book Worm bookends.

70th Anniversary Collection limited edition Book Worm bookends.

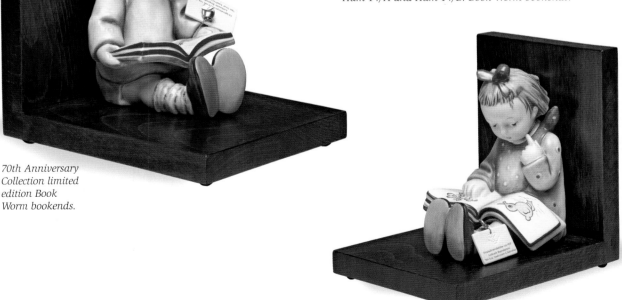

Hum 15: Hear Ye, Hear Ye

Among the first 46 to be released by Goebel at the Leipzig Fair, this figure was first called Night Watchman and remained so until around 1950. It was first modeled by master sculptor Arthur Moeller in 1935.

Hear Ye, Hear Ye can be found in the faience style, and its value would be determined by the seller and buyer.

Two variations have been found for Hear Ye, Hear Ye. The time on the watch hanging from his coat shows various times. Gloves with fingers can be found on older figurines, or as mittens with no fingers depicted. Figurines with gloves with fingers is more elusive.

In January 2002, QVC offered a special 1,000-piece limited edition Hear Ye! Hear Ye! Progression Set (Hum 15/0). The set consisted of three figurines—one in whiteware, one partially painted, and one completed—along with a wooden display stand with commemorative porcelain plaque and authentic Goebel painter's brush.

Both the 15/I and 15/II sizes have been temporarily withdrawn, while the 15/0 variation remains in production today.

Hum 15: Hear Ye, Hear Ye.

Hum No.	Basic Size	Trademark	Current Value
15/2/0	4"	TMK-6	$125
15/2/0	4"	TMK-7	$125
15/2/0	4"	TMK-8 CE	$199 retail
15/0	5"	TMK-1	$350
15/0	5"	TMK-2	$250
15/0	5"	TMK-3	$200
15/0	5"	TMK-4	$200
15/0	5"	TMK-5	$175
15/0	5"	TMK-6	$175
15/0	5"	TMK-7	$150
15/0	5"	TMK-8 CE	$225 Progression Set
15/0	5"	TMK-8	$300 70th Anniversary with tag LE 1935
15/I	6"	TMK-1	$500
15/I	6"	TMK-2	$450
15/I	6"	TMK-3	$350
15/I	6"	TMK-4	$350
15/I	6"	TMK-5	$250
15/I	6"	TMK-6	$250
15/I	6"	TMK-7 CE	$150
15/II	7-1/2"	TMK-1	$650
15/II	7-1/2"	TMK-2	$575
15/II	7-1/2"	TMK-3	$475
15/II	7-1/2"	TMK-4	$300
15/II	7-1/2"	TMK-5	$250
15/II	7-1/2"	TMK-6	$275
15/II	7-1/2"	TMK-7 CE	$150
15/II	7-1/2"	TMK-7 CE	$300 German employees Christmas figurine
15/II CE	7-1/2"	TMK-7	$250 Expressions of Youth

Hum 16: Little Hiker

Modeled by master sculptor Arthur Moeller, Little Hiker is one of the original 46 released in the 16/I and 16/2/0 sizes and was originally referred to as Happy-Go-Lucky.

Early painting samples have been found with a green jacket and blue hat. These are worth $750-$1,000.

The 16/I size has been temporarily withdrawn from production, and the 16/2/0 variation was permanently retired on Dec. 31, 2002. Those made in 2002 bear a "Final Issue 2002" backstamp and came with a "Final Issue" medallion.

Hum 16: Little Hiker.

Hum No.	Basic Size	Trademark	Current Value
16/2/0	4-1/4″	TMK-1	$350
16/2/0	4-1/4″	TMK-2	$200
16/2/0	4-1/4″	TMK-3	$175
16/2/0	4-1/4″	TMK-4	$160
16/2/0	4-1/4″	TMK-5	$150-$160
16/2/0	4-1/4″	TMK-6	$150
16/2/0	4-1/4″	TMK-7	$140
16/2/0	4-1/4″	TMK-8 CE	$145 Final Issue backstamp
16	5-1/2	TMK-1	$475
16	5-1/2	TMK-2	$400
16/I	5-1/2″	TMK-1	$475
16/I	5-1/2″	TMK-2	$400-$500
16/I	5-1/2″	TMK-3	$300
16/I	5-1/2″	TMK-4	$275
16/I	5-1/2″	TMK-5	$200
16/I	5-1/2″	TMK-6	$200
16/I	5-1/2″	TMK-7 TW	$175

Hum 17: Congratulations

One of the original 1935 releases, Congratulations was first modeled by master sculptor Reinhold Unger. The figurine was restyled by Gerhard Skrobeck in 1971. He added socks, new hair, and a textured finish. The flowers in the pot are larger, and the girl wears socks.

There is a very unusual, perhaps unique, version of this piece where a bowl is attached to the figurine's right rear. The figurine in this version does not have the normal base.

When first modeled, the girl had no socks. Later versions (after 1970) have a new hairstyle that appears to be a little longer. This change was made during the TMK-4 and TMK-5 eras, so you can find either version with these marks. Obviously, the no-socks piece would be the more desirable one.

A variation where the horn held by the girl has the handle of the horn pointing to the back instead of to the front has been found.

Once again, an early product book shows a sample with an attached pot. If found, that piece is worth whatever the seller and buyer agree on.

The final issue of this figurine was produced in 1999.

Hum No.	Basic Size	Trademark	Current Value
17/0	6″	TMK-1	$500 no socks
17/0	6″	TMK-2	$350 no socks
17/0	6″	TMK-3	$300 no socks
17/0	6″	TMK-4	$275 no socks
17/0	6″	TMK-5	$250 socks
17/0	6″	TMK-6	$225
17/0	6″	TMK-7 CE	$175 Final Issue backstamp
17/2	8-1/4″	TMK-1	$2,000

Hum 17: Congratulations.

Hum No.	Basic Size	Trademark	Current Value
17/2	8-1/4″	TMK-2	$1,750
17/2	8-1/4″	TMK-3	$1,500

Hum 18: Christ Child

Originally called Christmas Night, this figure is very similar to the Christ Child figure used in the Nativity Sets, Hum 214 and 260.

First modeled by master sculptor Reinhold Unger in 1935, it has been produced in a solid white overglaze and sold in Belgium. This white overglaze piece is rare and will fetch prices higher than the colored figurines. How many trademarks were made for Belguim has not yet been determined.

Christ Child was temporarily withdrawn from production at the end of 1990, was reinstated in 1997, and again temporarily withdrawn in January 1999.

Hum No.	Basic Size	Trademark	Current Value
18	3-3/4" x 6-1/2"	TMK-1	$250
18	3-3/4" x 6-1/2"	TMK-2	$225
18	3-3/4" x 6-1/2"	TMK-3	$175
18	3-1/4" x 6"	TMK-4	$200
18	3-1/4" x 6"	TMK-5	$150
18	3-1/4" x 6"	TMK-6	$125
18	3-1/4" x 6"	TMK-7 TW	$125

Hum 18: Christ Child.

Hum 19: Prayer Before Battle
Ashtray, Closed Number

Until 1986, when one of these surfaced in the United States, it was thought this was a closed number and the piece was never produced.

Even though one was found (temporarily), it may well be the only one ever made. The reason the term "temporarily" is used is as follows: It seems that a lady brought the piece to the Goebel Collectors' Club in Tarrytown, New York, for identification. The paint finish was badly damaged as a result of her having put it in a dishwasher to clean it. Goebel master sculptor Gerhard Skrobek, who was in Tarrytown, speculated that the reason the paint was damaged was because it was probably a sample piece, painted but never fired so that the paint had not bonded to the figurine.

Subsequent investigation of Goebel records revealed that the design was rejected by the Siessen Convent, and therefore never placed in production. Furthermore, there is no example in the company archives. How it got out of the factory and to the United States remains a mystery. It seems the woman left, taking her piece with her, and no one present could remember her name or where she was from.

The most recent footnote to this story: A noted and very serious collector pursued the search until he finally did find the ashtray and its owner. His attempt to purchase it, however, was rebuffed due to a sentimental attachment to the piece.

Hum No.	Basic Size	Trademark	Current Value
19	5-1/2"	TMK-1	$5,000-$10,000

Hum 20: Prayer Before Battle

First made by master sculptor Arthur Moeller in 1935, this piece has been listed at 4" and 4-1/2" in the price lists over the years.

The colors of the flag typically have white on top and blue on the bottom. Occasionally these can be found reversed. In the first three trademarks, the horn can be found in several variations. Some will have a deep hole in the end of the horn; on others it will be painted to look like a hole. The handle of the horn can be found pointing up or down. Pointing down is the norm. The horn can also be found missing entirely, including the strap the horn hangs from. These variations will command a higher price.

There has been one most unusual figure uncovered, which exhibits peculiar color variations. The horse is gray, black, and white instead of the normal tan, the wagon is a dark green with red wheels, the socks are the same green color, the clothes are dark green and brown, and the horn is a shiny gold. This may be a one-of-a-kind experimental piece that somehow made it out of the factory, but who knows? It is from the late Ed Wunner's collection.

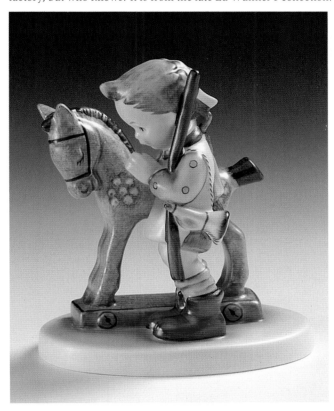

Hum 20: Prayer Before Battle.

Hum No.	Basic Size	Trademark	Current Value
20	4-1/4"	Arbeitmuster White	$450 with tag
20	4-1/4"	TMK-1	$450
20	4-1/4"	TMK-2	$375
20	4-1/4"	TMK-3	$300-$350
20	4-1/4"	TMK-4	$250
20	-1/4"	TMK-5	$200
20	4-1/4"	TMK-6	$200
20	4-1/4"	TMK-7	$200
20	4-1/4"	TMK-8	$219 retail
20	4-1/4"	TMK-8	$259 retail 70th Anniversary with tag LE 1935

Prayer Before Battle with peculiar color variations.

Another view of the Prayer Before Battle with unusual paint colors.

Hum 21: Heavenly Angel

First known as the Little Guardian or Celestial, this figure was among the 46 original releases in 1935 and was first modeled by master sculptor Reinhold Unger.

This is the same motif used on the famous 1971 annual plate, Hum 264, by Goebel and the Schmid company—the first-ever annual Hummel plate. The motif was also used for the tree topper, Hum 755.

The 21/0 size was the first to be introduced. It was followed by the larger sizes soon after.

The only variation of any significance in terms of value is the white overglaze model. It has not been found, but factory records indicate that it was produced. It is one of only two pieces in the Goebel collection where this "1/2" (one-half) designator is used. The other is Hum 78: Blessed Child.

Heavenly Angel is part of the "Expressions of Youth" series, which is written on the base of the figurine. The white figurines have only the facial features of eyes, eyebrows, and lips in color.

Both the 21/I and 21/II sizes have been temporarily withdrawn.

Hum 21: Heavenly Angel.

Hum No.	Basic Size	Trademark	Current Value
21/0	4-1/4"	TMK-1	$300
21/I	4-1/4"	TMK-2	$225
21/0	4-1/4"	TMK-3	$175
21/0	4-1/4"	TMK-4	$170
21/0	4-1/4"	TMK-5	$125
21/0	4-1/4"	TMK-6	$100
21/0	4-1/4"	TMK-7	$159 retail
21/0/1/2*	6"	TMK-1	$450
21/0/1/2*	6"	TMK-2	$425
21/0/1/2*	6"	TMK-3	$350
21/0/1/2*	6"	TMK-4	$300
21/0/1/2*	6"	TMK-5	$275
21/0/1/2*	6"	TMK-6	$275
21/0/1/2*	6"	TMK-7	$250
21/0/1/2*	6"	TMK-8	$299 retail
21/I	6-3/4"	TMK-1	$475
21/I	6-3/4"	TMK-2	$450
21/I	6-3/4"	TMK-3	$375
21/I	6-3/4"	TMK-4	$350
21/I	6-3/4"	TMK-5	$275
21/I	6-3/4"	TMK-6	$225
21/I	6-3/4"	TMK-7 TW	$200
21/II	8-3/4"	TMK-1	$800
21/II	8-3/4"	TMK-2	$700
21/II	8-3/4"	TMK-3	$600
21/II	8-3/4"	TMK-4	$500
21/II	8-3/4"	TMK-5	$375
21/II	8-3/4"	TMK-6	$350
21/II	8-3/4"	TMK-7 TW	$300
21/II	8-3/4"	TMK-7 TW	$225 Expressions of Youth

Hum 22: Angel With Bird
Holy Water Font

A figure sometimes known as Seated Angel With Bird or Sitting Angel, this piece was modeled by master sculptor Reinhold Unger. This font has two variations in bowl design.

As with most holy water fonts, it will have, or be without, a lip on the back of the bowl. The larger size can be found also with eyes open or closed. There are several color variations on the tree, flowers, and bird.

Hum No.	Basic Size	Trademark	Current Value
22	3-1/8" x 4-1/2"	TMK-1	$300
22/0	2-3/4" x 3-1/2"	TMK-1	$225
22/0	2-3/4" x 3-1/2"	TMK-2	$150
22/0	2-3/4" x 3-1/2"	TMK-3	$75
22/0	2-3/4" x 3-1/2"	TMK-4	$75
22/0	2-3/4" x 3-1/2"	TMK-5	$50
22/0	2-3/4" x 3-1/2"	TMK-6	$50
22/0	2-3/4" x 3-1/2"	TMK-7	$50
22/0	2-3/4" x 3-1/2"	TMK-8	$50
22/I	3-1/4" x 4-7/8"	TMK-1	$275
22/I	3-1/4" x 4-7/8"	TMK-2	$225
22/I	3-1/4" x 4-7/8"	TMK-3 CE	$175

Hum 22: Angel With Bird holy water font.

Hum 23: Adoration

Known in the early years as Ave Maria and At the Shrine, one of the 1935 group was first modeled by master sculptor Reinhold Unger and originally released in the smaller size. Soon after came the 23/III variation.

Early trademarks have rounded corners on the base while the newer ones are more square. The TMK-1 in size 23/I frequently does not have flowers on the base.

Both sizes have been produced in white overglaze, but they are quite scarce. The white overglaze was sold in Belguim. The number or trademarks have not been determined at this time. If found, they would demand a higher price than the colored pieces.

The 23/III size was temporarily withdrawn from production in January 1999.

Hum 23: Adoration.

Hum No.	Basic Size	Trademark	Current Value
23/I	6-1/4"	TMK-1	$700
23/I	6-1/4"	TMK-2	$550
23/I	6-1/4"	TMK-3	$475
23/I	6-1/4"	TMK-4	$400
23/I	6-1/4"	TMK-5	$350
23/I	6-1/4"	TMK-6	$325
23/I	6-1/4"	TMK-7	$250
23/I	6-1/4"	TMK-8	$250
23	9"	TMK-1	$900
23/III	9"	TMK-1	$900
23/III	9"	TMK-2	$850
23/III	9"	TMK-3	$825
23/III	9"	TMK-4	$700
23/III	9"	TMK-5	$625
23/III	9"	TMK-6	$600
23/III	9"	TMK-7	$575

Hum 24: Lullaby
Candleholder

This piece, which was modeled by both master sculptors Arthur Moeller and Reinhold Unger, is quite similar to Hum 262, except that this one is a candleholder. Its old name was Cradle Song. Variations can be found in the size and construction of the hole for the candle.

Hum 24: Lullaby candleholder.

Hum 24/I was listed as temporarily withdrawn at the end of 1989. By 1997, it was back on the suggested retail price list, only to be temporarily withdrawn again in January 1999. The larger 24/III was listed as temporarily withdrawn in 1982.

Both sizes are known to have been made in white in the Full Bee (TMK-2) and sold in Belguim. These would demand a higher price than the colored figurines.

Hum No.	Basic Size	Trademark	Current Value
24/I	3-1/4″ x 5″	TMK-1	$400
24/I	3-1/4″ x 5″	TMK-2	$350
24/I	3-1/4″ x 5″	TMK-3	$250
24/I	3-1/4″ x 5″	TMK-4	$250
24/I	3-1/4″ x 5″	TMK-5	$175
24/I	3-1/4″ x 5″	TMK-6	$150
24/I	3-1/4″ x 5″	TMK-7 TW	$150
24/I	3-1/4″ x 5″	TMK-7	$279 retail 70th Anniversary with tag LE 1935
24/III	6″ x 8-3/4″	TMK-1	$900
24/III	6″ x 8-3/4″	TMK-2	$875
24/III	6″ x 8-3/4″	TMK-3	$550
24/III	6″ x 8-3/4″	TMK-4	$500
24/III	6″ x 8-3/4″	TMK-5	$450
24/III	6″ x 8-3/4″	TMK-6 TW	$425

Hum 25: Angelic Sleep
Candleholder

This candleholder is one of the original 46 figures displayed at the Leipzig Fair in 1935 and was called Angel's Joy in some early company literature. The design is credited to both master sculptors Arthur Moeller and Reinhold Unger.

It was made in white overglaze for a short period for the Belguim market. The white overglaze production total is unknown, but the piece is very hard to find.

It was temporarily withdrawnon on Dec. 31, 1989.

Hum No.	Basic Size	Trademark	Current Value
25	3-1/2″ x 5″	TMK-1	$450
25	3-1/2″ x 5″	TMK-2	$375
25	3-1/2″ x 5″	TMK-3	$250
25	3-1/2″ x 5″	TMK-4	$200
25	3-1/2″ x 5″	TMK-5	$175
25	3-1/2″ x 5″	TMK-6 TW	$150

Hum 25: Angelic Sleep candleholder.

Hum 26: Child Jesus
Holy Water Font

This is one of the original 1935 releases and was first modeled by master sculptor Reinhold Unger.

The color of the robe is normally a deep orange-red. A very significant variation has appeared in the Stylized Bee (TMK-3) 26/0 size, in which the robe has also been found as either light blue or green.

The bowl on this font is fluted on the top edge. The Crown trademark can be found with and without a lip on the back edge of the bowl. Later trademarks have the lip.

The 26/0 size was temporarily withdrawn from production in January 1999.

Hum No.	Basic Size	Trademark	Current Value
26/0	2-3/4" x 5"	TMK-1	$250
26/0	2-3/4" x 5"	TMK-2	$125
26/0	2-3/4" x 5"	TMK-3	$75
26/0	2-3/4" x 5"	TMK-4	$50
26/0	2-3/4" x 5"	TMK-5	$40
26/0	2-3/4" x 5"	TMK-6	$40
26/0	2-3/4" x 5"	TMK-7	$40
26	3" x 5-3/4"	TMK-1	$450
26/I	3-1/4" x 6"	TMK-1	$300
26/I	3-1/4" x 6"	TMK-2	$275
26/I	3-1/4" x 6"	TMK-3	$250

Hum 26: Child Jesus holy water font.

Hum 27: Joyous News
Candleholder and Figurine

First modeled by master sculptor Reinhold Unger in 1935, this piece is considered to be hard to find in good condition in trademarks 1 and 2 in the 27/III size. The horn is found broken on many of these pieces.

The smaller size (27/I) was made as a candleholder and is very difficult to find.

Hum No.	Basic Size	Trademark	Current Value
27/I	2-3/4"	TMK-1	$575
27/I	2-3/4"	TMK-2	$500
27/III	4-1/4" x 4-3/4"	TMK-1	$750
27/III	4-1/4" x 4-3/4"	TMK-2	$700
27/III	4-1/4" x 4-3/4"	TMK-3	$675
27/III	4-1/4" x 4-3/4"	TMK-5	$275
27/III	4-1/4" x 4-3/4"	TMK-6	$250
27/III	4-1/4" x 4-3/4"	TMK-7	$225

Hum 27: Joyous News.

Hum 28: Wayside Devotion

This figurine is also one of the initial 1935 designs displayed at the Leipzig Fair and has been called The Little Shepherd and Evensong over the years. It was first modeled by master sculptor Reinhold Unger. (Hum 99: Eventide is the same figurine but is smaller and without the shrine.)

This figurine was also made for the Belguim market and is in the white overglaze. The white overglaze version is extremely difficult to locate.

The 70th Anniversary Edition of this figurine has a commorative tag.

The 28/III size was temporarily withdrawn from production on June 15, 2002.

Hum No.	Basic Size	Trademark	Current Value
28/II	7"	TMK-1	$900
28/II	7"	TMK-2	$750
28/II	7"	TMK-3	$600
28/II	7"	TMK-4	$500
28/II	7"	TMK-5	$350
28/II	7"	TMK-6	$300
28/II	7"	TMK-7	$275
28/II	7"	TMK-8	$350
28	8-3/4"	TMK-1	$1,100
28/III	8-3/4"	TMK-1	$1,000
28/III	8-3/4"	TMK-2	$850
28/III	8-3/4"	TMK-3	$800
28/III	8-3/4"	TMK-4	$700
28/III	8-3/4"	TMK-5	$550
28/III	8-3/4"	TMK-6	$500
28/III	8-3/4"	TMK-7 TW	$400 70th Anniversary Edition

Hum 28: Wayside Devotion.

Hum 29: Guardian Angel
Holy Water Font

This figure was first modeled in two sizes by master sculptor Reinhold Unger in 1935. A similar piece, Hum 248, is considered to be a redesign of Hum 29. The wings are frequently found to have been broken on this figurine.

Hum No.	Basic Size	Trademark	Current Value
29 CE	2-3/4" x 6"	TMK-1	$1,225
29/0	2-1/2" x 5-5/8"	TMK-1	$1,100
29/0	2-1/2" x 5-5/8"	TMK-2	$900
29/0 CE	2-1/2" x 5-5/8"	TMK-3	$800
29/I	3" x 6-3/8"	TMK-1	$1,400
29/I CE	3" x 6-3/8"	TMK-2	$1,200

Hum 29: Guardian Angel holy water font.

Hum 30/A and Hum 30/B: Ba-Bee Rings
Wall Plaques

Part of the original collection released in 1935, these wall plaques were first called Hummel Rings and were modeled by master sculptor Reinhold Unger. The rings were sold as a set and are priced as such.

Figures with the rings painted red in the Crown (TMK- 1) era are found in both sizes. The red ring figures are very difficult to find and have a blue hair ribbon instead of orange.

Hum No.	Basic Size	Trademark	Current Value
30/0 A&B	4-3/4" x 5"	TMK-1	$400
30/0 A&B	4-3/4" x 5"	TMK-1	$3,500 red rings
30/0 A&B	4-3/4" x 5"	TMK-2	$350
30/0 A&B	4-3/4" x 5"	TMK-3	$275
30/0 A&B	4-3/4" x 5"	TMK-4	$275
30/0 A&B	4-3/4" x 5"	TMK-5	$225
30/0 A&B	4-3/4" x 5"	TMK-6	$225
30/0 A&B	4-3/4" x 5"	TMK-7	$220
30/0 A&B	4-3/4" x 5"	TMK-8	$200
30/I A&B	5-1/4" x 6"	TMK-1	$1400
30/1 A&B	5-1/4" x 6"	TMK-1	$3,700 red rings

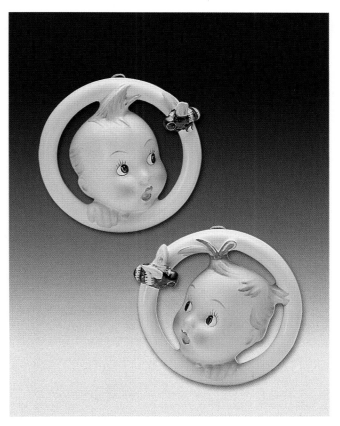

Hum 30/A and Hum 30/B: Ba-Bee Rings wall plaques.

Hum 31: Advent Group
Candleholder

This candleholder, which was first modeled by master sculptor Arthur Moeller in 1935, was often called Advent Group or Silent Night With White Child or Silent Night With Black Child. It is very similar to Hum 54: Silent Night. Hum 31 was produced first in 1935 with the other original 45 figurines.

Both versions have been found in the Crown Mark (TMK-1) only. (See also Hum 54, Hum 113, and Hum 754.) These two versions of Hum 31 are considered to be very rare. The number produced has never been determined.

Hum No.	Basic Size	Trademark	Current Value
31	3-1/2" x 5"	TMK-1	$12,000 black child
31	3-1/2" x 5"	TMK-1	$12,000 white child

Hum 31: Advent Group candleholder.

Hum 32: Little Gabriel

When first released in 1935, this figure was called Joyous News. Master sculptor Reinhold Unger is responsible for the first design.

The size designator for the 32/0 version was dropped in TMK-5 and had only the 32 thereafter. The first two trademarks of the larger 6" also had the 32 designator.

Little Gabriel was redesigned in 1982. The older pieces have the arms that are attached to each other up to the hands. The newer design has the arms separated. The wings were also made longer. Many of the pieces can be found with both the horn and wings broken. Perfect samples are difficult to find.

Hum 32: Little Gabriel.

Hum No.	Basic Size	Trademark	Current Value
32/0	5"	TMK-1	$600
32/0	5"	TMK-2	$450
32/0	5"	TMK-3	$275
32/0	5"	TMK-4	$250
32/0	5"	TMK-6	$175
32	5"	TMK-5	$175
32	5"	TMK-6	$150
32	5"	TMK-7 TW	$150
32	6"	TMK-1	$1,300
32	6"	TMK-2	$1,100
32/I	6"	TMK-1	$1,200
32/I	6"	TMK-2	$1,000
32/I	6"	TMK-3	$900

Hum 33: Joyful
Ashtray

Hum 33: Joyful ashtray.

This is an ashtray, first modeled by master sculptor Reinhold Unger in 1935, that utilizes a figure very similar to Hum 53: Joyful, with the addition of a small bird on the edge of the tray next to the figurine. This piece was temporarily removed from production on Dec. 31, 1984.

This figurine is another Hummel that was produced in the faience finish, but only a very few were produced.

Typically the figure wears a blue dress and orange shoes, but

Hum No.	Basic Size	Trademark	Current Value
33	3-1/2" x 6"	TMK-1	$350
33	3-1/2" x 6"	TMK-2	$300
33	3-1/2" x 6"	TMK-3	$225
33	3-1/2" x 6"	TMK-4	$200
33	3-1/2" x 6"	TMK-5	$125
33	3-1/2" x 6"	TMK-6	$125

a variation with the colors switched—orange dress and blue shoes—has been found (trademark unknown), much like the color changes in Hum 53: Joyful.

Since many of these Hummel were actually used as ashtrays, damage is not uncommon.

Hum 34: Singing Lesson
Ashtray

Master sculptor Arthur Moeller is credited with the design of this ashtray, which utilizes a figure very similar to Hum 64, with the addition of a small bird perched on the edge of the. Since many of these Hummels were actually used as ashtrays, damage is not uncommon.

This ashtray was listed as temporarily withdrawn from production at the end of 1989.

Hum No.	Basic Size	Trademark	Current Value
33	3-1/2" x 6"	TMK-1	$350
33	3-1/2" x 6"	TMK-2	$300
33	3-1/2" x 6"	TMK-3	$225
33	3-1/2" x 6"	TMK-4	$200
33	3-1/2" x 6"	TMK-5	$125
33	3-1/2" x 6"	TMK-6 TW	$125

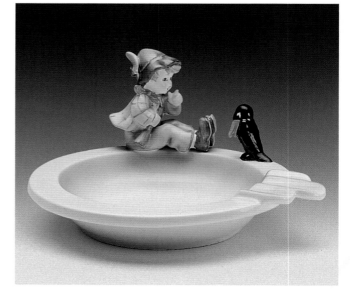

Hum 34: Singing Lesson ashtray.

Hum 35: Good Shepherd
Holy Water Font

Part of the original collection released in 1935, this figurine was designed by master sculptor Reinhold Unger. Hum 35 in the Crown trademark can be found with yellow lambs and green grass. This font also has a flared bowl. A lip is found on TMK-2 and up.

Hum 35: Good Shepherd holy water font.

Hum No.	Basic Size	Trademark	Current Value
35/0	2-1/4" x 4-3/4"	TMK-1	$200
35/0	2-1/4" x 4-3/4"	TMK-2	$150
35/0	2-1/4" x 4-3/4"	TMK-3	$75
35/0	2-1/4" x 4-3/4"	TMK-4	$70
35/0	2-1/4" x 4-3/4"	TMK-5	$50
35/0	2-1/4" x 4-3/4"	TMK-6	$50
35/0	2-1/2" x 4-3/4"	TMK-7	$50
35/0	2-1/2" x 4-3/4"	TMK-8	$50
35	2-1/4" x 4-3/4"	TMK-1 TW	$350 yellow lambs and green grass
35	2-1/4" x 4-3/4"	TMK-1 TW	$300
35/I	2-3/4" x 5-3/4"	TMK-1	$300
35/I	2-3/4" x 5-3/4"	TMK-2	$225
35/I	2-3/4" x 5-3/4"	TMK-3 TW	$175

Hum 36: Child With Flowers
Holy Water Font

Designed by master sculptor Reinhold Unger, this font is one of the original 46 figurines released in 1935. It also has been called Flower Angel and Angel With Flowers.

There have been only minor variations in the colors of the font. TMK-2 and up are found with a lip on the back of the bowl.

Hum 36: Child With Flowers holy water font.

Hum No.	Basic Size	Trademark	Current Value
36/0	3 1/2" x 4-1/2"	TMK-1	$150
36/0	3 1/2" x 4-1/2"	TMK-2	$100
36/0	3 1/2" x 4-1/2"	TMK-3	$75
36/0	3 1/2" x 4-1/2"	TMK-4	$75
36/0	3 1/2" x 4-1/2"	TMK-5	$50
36/0	3 1/2" x 4-1/2"	TMK-6	$50
36/0	3-1/2" x 4-1/2"	TMK-7	$50
36/0	3-1/2" x 4-1/2"	TMK-8	$50
36.	3-1/2" x 4-1/2"	TMK-1 CE	$200
36/I	3-1/2" x 4-1/2"	TMK-1	$200
36/I	3-1/2" x 4-1/2"	TMK-2	$175
36/I	3-1/2" x 4-1/2"	TMK-3 CE	$150

Hum 37: Herald Angels
Candleholder

This piece, which was designed by master sculptor Reinhold Unger, is a group of figures very similar to Hum 38, 39, and 40, placed together on a common round base with a candle receptacle in the center. There are two versions: low and high candleholder.

Hum No.	Basic Size	Trademark	Current Value
37	2-1/2" x 4"	TMK-1	$425
37	2-1/2" x 4"	TMK-2	$350
37	2-1/2" x 4"	TMK-3	$250
37	2-1/2" x 4"	TMK-4	$225
37	2-1/2" x 4"	TMK-5	$175
37	2-1/2" x 4"	TMK-6	$150

The higher holder is found on the older pieces. TMK-3 can be found in the low or high candleholder.

This figurine was also made in the faience style. The shoe color on the older pieces is a light purple while the shoes on the newer ones are brown. The older pieces also have a wider base.

This candleholder was temporarily withdrawn from production in 1989.

Hum 37: Herald Angels candleholder.

Hum 38, Hum 39, and Hum 40: Angel Trio
Candleholders

These three figures—Joyous News Angel With Lute, Joyous News Angel With Accordion, and Joyous News Angel With Trumpet—are presented as a set of three and are usually sold as a set. First modeled by master sculptor Reinhold Unger in 1935, these pieces have been called Little Heavenly Angels and Angel Trio in old company literature.

They each come in three versions according to size and candle size. The I/38/0, I/39/0, and I/40/0 versions are 2" tall and have a 0.6-cm candle diameter. The III/38/0, III/39/0, and III/40/0 versions are 2" tall and have a 1.0-cm candle diameter. The III/38/I, III/39/I, and III/40/I versions are 2-3/4" tall and have a 1.0-cm candle diameter. Early pieces do not carry a size designator and because the pieces are so small, the signature on the back or leg of the angel may simply read "Hum." Another variation is that size /0 has been found with green, brown, purple, and tan shoes.

Hum No.	Basic Size	Trademark	Current Value
I/38/0	2" x 2-1/2"	TMK-1	$150-$200
I/38/0	2" x 2-1/2"	TMK-2	$100-$125
I/38/0	2" x 2-1/2"	TMK-3	$95-$100
I/38/0	2" x 2-1/2"	TMK-4	$85-$95
I/38/0	2" x 2-1/2"	TMK-5	$80-$85
I/38/0	2" x 2-1/2"	TMK-6	$75-$80
I/38/0	2" x 2-1/2"	TMK-7	$70-$75
I/38/0	2" x 2-1/2"	TMK-8 TW	$70
III/38/0	2" x 2-1/2"	TMK-1	$150-$200
III/38/0	2" x 2-1/2"	TMK-2	$100-$125
III/38/0	2" x 2-1/2"	TMK-3	$90-$100
III/38/0	2" x 2-1/2"	TMK-4	$80-$90
III/38/0	2" x 2-1/2"	TMK-5	$70-$80
III/38/0	2" x 2-1/2"	TMK-6 TW	$60-$70
III/38/1	2-1/2" x 2-3/4"	TMK-1	$300-$350

Hum No.	Basic Size	Trademark	Current Value
III/38/1	2-1/2" x 2-3/4"	TMK-2	$250-$300
III/38/1	2-1/2" x 2-3/4"	TMK-3	$200-$250
I/39/0	2" x 2-1/2"	TMK-1	$150-$200
I/39/0	2" x 2-1/2"	TMK-2	$105-$125
I/39/0	2" x 2-1/2"	TMK-3	$95-$105
I/39/0	2" x 2-1/2"	TMK-4	$85-$95
I/39/0	2" x 2-1/2"	TMK-5	$80-$85
I/39/0	2" x 2-1/2"	TMK-6	$75-$80
I/39/0	2" x 2-1/2"	TMK-7	$70-$75
I/39/0	2" x 2-1/2"	TMK-8 TW	$70
III/39/0	2" x 2-1/2"	TMK-1	$150-$200
III/39/0	2" x 2-1/2"	TMK-2	$100-$125
III/39/0	2" x 2-1/2"	TMK-3	$90-$100
III/39/0	2" x 2-1/2"	TMK-4	$80-$90
III/39/0	2" x 2-1/2"	TMK-5	$70-$80
III/39/0	2" x 2-1/2"	TMK-6	$60-$70
III/39/1	2-1/2" x 2-3/4"	TMK-1	$300-$350
III/39/1	2-1/2" x 2-3/4"	TMK-2	$250-$300
III/39/1	2-1/2" x 2-3/4"	TMK-3 TW	$200-$250
I/40/0	2" x 2-1/2"	TMK-1	$150-$200
I/40/0	2" x 2-1/2"	TMK-2	$105-$125
I/40/0	2" x 2-1/2"	TMK-3	$95-$105
I/40/0	2" x 2-1/2"	TMK-4	$85-$95
I/40/0	2" x 2-1/2"	TMK-5	$80-$85
I/40/0	2" x 2-1/2"	TMK-6	$75-$80
I/40/0	2" x 2-1/2"	TMK-7	$70-$75
I/40/0	2" x 2-1/2"	TMK-8 TW	$70
III/40/0	2" x 2-1/2"	TMK-1	$150-$200
III/40/0	2" x 2-1/2"	TMK-2	$100-$125
III/40/0	2" x 2-1/2"	TMK-3	$90-$100
III/40/0	2" x 2-1/2"	TMK-4	$80-$90
III/40/0	2" x 2-1/2"	TMK-5	$70-$80
III/40/0	2" x 2-1/2"	TMK-6	$60-$70
III/40/1	2-1/2" x 2-3/4"	TMK-1	$300-$350
III/40/1	2-1/2" x 2-3/4"	TMK-2	$250-$300
III/40/1	2-1/2" x 2-3/4"	TMK-3	$200-$250

Hum 38, Hum 39, and Hum 40: Angel Trio candleholders.

Hum 41: Singing Lesson
Closed Number

This figure had been listed as a closed number, but the existence of the piece is now substantiated. Details are not known, but the piece is said to be similar to Singing Lesson (Hum 63) without the base. There are no known examples, but samples in this category have turned up from time to time. Collector value is $3,000-$7,000.

Hum 42: Good Shepherd

Master sculptor Reinhold Unger is credited with the design of this figurine in 1935.

The 42 mold number has been found with the decimal point designator. There are two very rare variations: a blue gown rather than the normal brownish-red color and a white gown with blue stars. This is found on the 42/0 size in the Crown (TMK-1) and Full Bee (TMK-2) figures.

It is no longer produced in the 7-1/2" size, and the 6-1/4" size was temporarily withdrawn in January 1999.

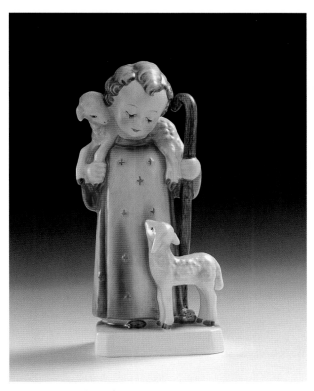
Hum 42: Good Shepherd.

Hum No.	Basic Size	Trademark	Current Value
42/0	6-1/4"	TMK-1	$450-$600
42/0	6-1/4"	TMK-2	$280-$430
42/0	6-1/4"	TMK-3	$225-$430
42/0	6-1/4"	TMK-4	$275-$325
42/0	6-1/4"	TMK-5	$275-$300

Hum No.	Basic Size	Trademark	Current Value
42/0	6-1/4"	TMK-6	$195-$225
42/0	6-1/4"	TMK-7	$195-$225
42/I	7-1/4" x 8"	TMK-3	$2,600-$4,000
42/I	7-1/2"	TMK-1	$4,200-$5,500
42/I	7-1/2"	TMK-2	$3,600-$4,500

Hum 43: March Winds

Hum 43: March Winds.

Designed by master sculptor Reinhold Unger, this figurine is one of the original 46 released in 1935 and has been called "Urchin" in old company catalogs.

There appear to be two slightly different designs. In the earlier pieces, the boy looks more toward the rear than in the newer ones, but there are no significant variations to be found.

A smaller size was added during the TMK-7 period, and that piece remains in production today. March Winds was also produced as a Progression Set and 70th Anniversary figurine.

Hum No.	Basic Size	Trademark	Current Value
43/5/0	2-3/4"	TMK-7	$55
43	5"	TMK-1	$250-$400
43	5"	TMK-2	$165-$225
43	5"	TMK-3	$160-$200
43	5"	TMK-4	$160-$175
43	5"	TMK-5	$125-$190
43	5"	TMK-6	$125-$190
43	4-3/4" x 5-1/2"	TMK-7	$115-$150
43	4-3/4" x 5-1/2"	TMK-8	$199 retail
43	4-3/4"	TMK-8	$250 Progression Set

Hum 44/A: Culprits and Hum 44/ B: Out of Danger

Table Lamps

Both of these lamps, designed my master sculptor Arthur Moeller, were part of the original 46 designs released in 1935. Both are about 8-1/2" tall and were temporarily withdrawn from production at the end of 1989.

There are no significant variations that would affect the collector value of either one; only minor changes such as the location of the switch.

Hum No.	Basic Size	Trademark	Current Value
44	8-1/2" to 9-1/2"	TMK-1	$390-$450
44/A	8-1/2" to 9-1/2"	TMK-1	$300-$390
44/A	8-1/2" to 9-1/2"	TMK-2	$260-$288
44/A	8-1/2" to 9-1/2"	TMK-3	$240-$288
44/A	8-1/2"	TMK-4	$225-$240
44/A	8-1/2"	TMK-5	$195-$230
44/A	8-1/2"	TMK-6	$200-$250
44/B	8-1/2" to 9-1/2"	TMK-1	$300-$390
44/B	8-1/2" to 9-1/2	TMK-2	$260-$300
44/B	8-1/2" to 9-1/2	TMK-3	$240-$260
44/B	8-1/2"	TMK-4	$225-$260
44/B	8-1/2"	TMK-5	$210-$250
44/B	8-1/2"	TMK-6	$195-$230

Hum 44/A: Culprits and Hum 44/B: Out of Danger table lamps.

Hum 45: Madonna With Halo and Hum 46: Madonna Without Halo

These Madonnas, designed by master sculptor Reinhold Unger, were part of the original 46 figures that were released in 1935 at the Leipzig Fair. They are often confusing to collectors because of their similarity.

Apparently, they are also occasionally confused with each other at the factory. Sometimes, the mold number appears on the wrong piece, possibly explained in some cases by the fact that the two pieces are identical without the halo, which is an add-on piece during assembly. The fact that they are sometimes found with both mold numbers incised on one piece lends evidence to the theory that the body is from the same mold and the mold number is impressed after assembly, but before firing.

At least nine legitimate variations have been found. The chief differences are in size, color, and glaze treatment. They are found in color and white overglaze. The known color variations are beige, rose, light blue, royal blue, and ivory. They have also been found in terra-cotta.

In 1982, both the 45/III and the 46/III were temporarily withdrawn from production, and in 1984, the 45/0 and 46/0 were also withdrawn temporarily. The 46/I was temporarily withdrawn in 1989, apparently leaving only the 45/I, Madonna With Halo, available to collectors.

While variations are rampant, only the appearance in terra-cotta, which is valued at $2,000-$3,000, and one other has any significant effect on value. There is a variation where there are red-painted stars on the underside of the halo. This variation can as much as triple the value for its counterpart without the stars.

Hum No.	Basic Siz e	Trademark	Value (White)	Value (Color)
45/0	10-1/2"	TMK-1	$75 -$120	$120-$165
45/0	10-1/2"	TMK-2	$55-$100	$60-$110
45/0	10-1/2"	TMK-3	$45-$85	$45-$85
45/0	10-1/2"	TMK-4	$30-$50	$45-$60
45/0	10-1/2"	TMK-5	$25-$45	$45-$50
45/0	10-1/2"	TMK-6	$20-$45	$45-$50
45/I	11-1/2" to 13-1/4"	TMK-1	$90-$120	$180-$240
45/I	11-1/2" to 13-1/4"	TMK-2	$60-$90	$105-$180
45/I	11-1/2" to 13-1/4"	TMK-3	$55-$60	$99-$105
45/I	11-1/2" to 13-1/4"	TMK-4	$55-$60	$95-$105
45/I	11-1/2" to 13-1/4"	TMK-5	$50-$60	$90-$105
45/I	11-1/2" to 13-1/4"	TMK-6	$45-$60	$90-$105
45/I	11-1/2" to 13-1/4"	TMK-7	$45-$60	$70-$105
45/I	11-1/2" to 13-1/4"	TMK-8	$45-$60	$60-$105
45/III	16-1/4"	TMK-1	$150-$210	$240-$360
45/III	16-1/4"	TMK-2	$105-$180	$200-$240
45/III	16-1/4"	TMK-3	$105-$140	$135-$200
45/III	16-1/4"	TMK-4	$70-$85	$150-$200
45/III	16-1/4"	TMK-5	$65-$70	$150-$200
45/III	16-1/4"	TMK-6	$40-$70	$150-$200
46/0	10-1/4"	TMK-2	$55-$85	$120-$165
46/0	10-1/4"	TMK-3	$35-$40	$100-$125
46/0	10-1/4"	TMK-4	$40-$70	$100-$125
46/0	10-1/4"	TMK-5	$40-$65	$100-$125
46/0	10-1/4"	TMK-6	$45-$65	$100-$125
46/I	11-1/4"	TMK-1	$180-$240	$180-$240
46/I	11-1/4"	TMK-2	$105-135	$105-$135
46/I	11-1/4"	TMK-3	$95-105	$125-$140
46/I	11-1/4"	TMK-4	$90-100	$125-$140
46/I	11-1/4"	TMK-5	$85-$95	$125-$140
46/I	11-1/4"	TMK-6	$80-$95	$125-$140
46/III	16"	TMK-1	$150-$210	$240-$360
46/III	16"	TMK-2	$105-185	$165-$225
46/III	16"	TMK-3	$85-140	$105-$130
46/III	16"	TMK-4	$70-$85	$95-$120
46/III	16"	TMK-5	$70-$85	$95-$110
46/III	16"	TMK-6	$70-$80	$90-$115
46/III	16"	TMK-8		$300 70th Anniversary

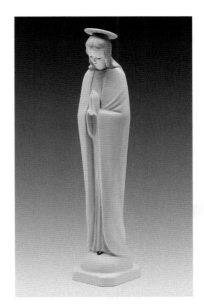

Hum 45: Madonna With Halo

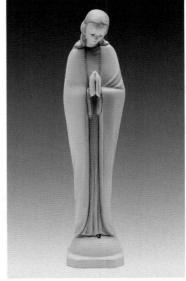

Hum 46: Madonna Without Halo.

Hum 47: Goose Girl

A very popular piece first modeled by master sculptor Arthur Moeller in 1936, this figurine is probably the most famous among collectors and non-collectors alike. Interestingly, for a model that dates back practically to day one and in three sizes, there are no variations significant enough to have an effect on collector value. The occurrence of the decimal designator might have a slight influence with some collectors, but not a great degree of significance.

There is, of course, the Goose Girl with a bowl attached. This piece is thought to be unique—a sample that somehow found its way into the collector market. There are two similar pieces with bowls attached: Congratulations (Hum 17) and Meditation (Hum 13).

The Goose Girl set is comprised of a 4" figurine and a bisque porcelain vase with a bas-relief image of Goose Girl. The vase was a first for Goebel. It has the TMK-7 trademark with 1989 copyright date decal on the bottom.

Hum No.	Basic Size	Trademark	Current Value
47/3/0	4"	TMK-1	$300-$390
47/3/0	4"	TMK-2	$180-$240
47/3/0	4"	TMK-3	$150-$180
47/3/0	4"	TMK-4	$135-$150
47/3/0	4"	TMK-5	$130-$140
47/3/0	4"	TMK-6	$125-$140
47/3/0	4" to 4-1/4"	TMK-7	$120-$130
47/3/0	4" to 4-1/4"	TMK-8	$200 retail
47	4"	TMK-7	$175-$225 figurine/vase set
47	5"	TMK-1	$480-$540
47/0	4-3/4"	TMK-1	$390-$480
47/0	4-3/4"	TMK-2	$240-$390
47/0	4-3/4"	TMK-3	$210-$240
47/0	4-3/4"	TMK-4	$180-$210
47/0	4-3/4"	TMK-5	$170-$180
47/0	4-3/4"	TMK-6	$160-$170
47/0	4-3/4"	TMK-7	$165-$170
47/0	4-3/4"	TMK-8	$275 retail
47/II	7-1/2"	TMK-1	$600-$780
47/II	7-1/2"	TMK-2	$420-$540
47/II	7-1/2"	TMK-3	$360-$420
47/II	7-1/2"	TMK-4	$300-$360
47/II	7-1/2"	TMK-5	$250-$265
47/II	7-1/2"	TMK-6	$250-$265
47/II	7" to 7-1/2"	TMK-7	$240-$250

Hum 47: Goose Girl.

Goose Girl bowl. This rare piece was found in Germany in 1989. It measures 4-7/8" and has an incised Crown Mark. Upon examining it closely, it appears that the bowl was attached to the figurine before firing, lending legitimacy to the speculation that it was fashioned by Goebel. The bowl is a Double Crown Mark piece and has an incised mold number "1". Two other bowl pieces have shown up with a different style of bowl: Meditation (Hum 13) and Congratulations (Hum 17).

Hum 48: Madonna
Wall Plaque

Master sculptor Reinhold Unger is credited with the design of this bas-relief plaque in 1936. It has been known to appear in a white overglaze in the 48/0 and the 48/II sizes in a bisque finish. The white overglaze pieces appear in the Crown Mark (TMK-1) and are very rare.

The 48/II can sometimes be found as 48/2. There are two variations of the 48/II in the Crown Mark (TMK-1).

The 48/II size was temporarily withdrawn on Dec. 31, 1984, and the 48/0 size was temporarily withdrawn at the end of 1989.

Hum No.	Basic Size	Trademark	Current Value
48/0	3" x 4"	TMK-1	$195-$225
48/0	3" x 4"	TMK-2	$135-$165
48/0	3" x 4"	TMK-3	$70-$80
48/0	3" x 4"	TMK-4	$60-$70
48/0	3" x 4"	TMK-5	$55-$60
48/0	3" x 4"	TMK-6	$55-$60
48	4-3/4" x 6"	TMK-1	$390-$510
48/II	4-3/4" x 6"	TMK-1	$330-$480
48/II	4-3/4" x 6"	TMK-2	$225-$315
48/II	4-3/4" x 6"	TMK-3	$115-150
48/II	4-3/4" x 5-3/4"	TMK-4	$99-115
48/II	4-3/4" x 6"	TMK-5	$80-$90

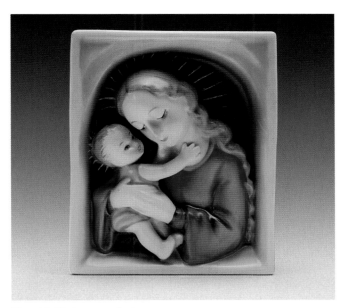

Hum 48: Madonna wall plaque.

Hum No.	Basic Size	Trademark	Current Value
48/II	4-3/4" x 6"	TMK-6	$80-$85
48/V	8-1/4" x 10-1/2"	TMK-1	$900-$1,200
48/V	8-1/4" x 10-1/2"	TMK-2	$750-$900
48/V	8-1/4" x 10-1/2"	TMK-3	$600-$750
48/II (white)	4-3/4" x 5-3/4"	TMK-3	$300-$360

Hum 49: To Market

Master sculptor Arthur Moeller first designed this piece in 1936, when it was then called "Brother and Sister."

The 49/I size was out of current production for at least 20 years and then was reinstated in the early 1980s. Goebel placed it on a temporarily withdrawn from production status on Dec. 31, 1984, and it remains so today. Also temporarily withdrawn, effective January 1999, was the 49/0 size. The smallest size at 4" (49/3/0) is the only one still in production today.

The 49 mold number has occasionally been found with the decimal point size designator. Some 49/0 versions have surfaced with no bottle in the basket. The 49/3/0 size is routinely produced with no bottle in the basket.

Hum 49: To Market.

Hum No.	Basic Size	Trademark	Current Value
49/3/0	4"	TMK-1	$300-$390
49/3/0	4"	TMK-2	$180-$225
49/3/0	4"	TMK-3	$150-$180
49/3/0	4"	TMK-4	$125-$140
49/3/0	4"	TMK-5	$120-$125
49/3/0	4"	TMK-6	$115-$120
40/3/0	4"	TMK-7	$110-$115
49/3/0	4"	TMK-8	$185 retail
49/0	5-1/2"	TMK-1	$450-$600
49/0	5-1/2"	TMK-2	$270-$375
49/0	5-1/4"	TMK-3	$255-$270
49/0	5-1/2"	TMK-4	$225-$255
49/0	5-1/2"	TMK-5	$210-$225
49/0	5-1/2"	TMK-6	$195-$210
49/0	5-1/2"	TMK-7	$195-$200
49	6-1/4"	TMK-1	$840-$1,020
49	6-1/4"	TMK-2	$720-$840
49	6-1/4"	TMK-5	$360-$420
49/I	6-1/4"	TMK-1	$840-$1,020
49/I	6-1/4"	TMK-2	$720-$840
49/I	6-1/4"	TMK-3	$330-$420
49/I	6-1/4"	TMK-4	$300-$330
49/I	6-1/4"	TMK-5	$270-$285
49	6-1/4"	TMK-6	$255-$270

Hum 50: Volunteers

Once called Playing Soldiers, this figurine was designed by master sculptor Reinhold Unger in 1936.

The 50/0 and 50/I sizes were out of production for some years and are difficult to find with the older trademarks. Both were reinstated in 1979. The 50/I was again withdrawn in December 1984 and the 50/0 version was temporarily withdrawn on June 15, 2002. The only variation still in production today, therefore, is 50/2/0.

The small Hum 50/2/0, Volunteers, was released with a special backstamp commemorating the allied victory in Operation Desert Storm. Limited to 10,000 pieces worldwide, it was to be sold only through military post and base exchanges at a retail price of $150-$175. This particular variation has dropped in value on the collector market.

In the wake of the terrorist attacks on the World Trade Center and Pentagon on Sept. 11, 2001, and the resulting American military effort, Goebel alerted its M.I. Hummel Club chapters that it would make a commitment to donate appropriately themed figurines to local chapters to be used as raffle prizes. Any proceeds from such fund-raising events would then go to benefit the families of the victims. Seven figurines, including this one, were selected as appropriate due to their patriotic or firefighter/police/medical personnel themes.

In 2002, a special edition of Volunteers was introduced in recognition of the figurine's 50th year in production. It carried a unique diamond-shaped "50th Anniversary" backstamp and came with a certificate of authenticity and a diamond-shaped anniversary medallion with "50" on it. Volunteers was also sold with the American flag in the rifle barrel.

Hum 50: Volunteers.

Hum No.	Basic Size	Trademark	Current Value
50/2/0	5"	TMK-1	$250-$305
50/2/0	5"	TMK-2	$255-$315
50/2/0	5"	TMK-3	$210-$240
50/2/0	5"	TMK-4	$195-$210
50/2/0	5"	TMK-5	$165-$180
50/2/0	5"	TMK-6	$140-$165
50/2/0	4-3/4" to 5"	TMK-7	$150-$160
50/2/0	4-3/4" to 5"	TMK-8	$235 retail
50/2/0	5"	TMK-8	$265 retail 50th Anniversary
50/0	5-1/2"	TMK-1	$515-$675
50/0	5-1/2"	TMK-2	$305-$395
50/0	5-1/2"	TMK-3	$270-$280
50/0	5-1/2" to 6"	TMK-$4	$240-$270
50/0	5-1/2"	TMK-5	$220-$240
50/0	5-1/2"	TMK-6	$210-$250
50/0	5-1/2" to 6"	TMK-7	$210-$250
50/0	4-3/4" to 6"	TMK-8	$350 retail
50	6-1/2"	TMK-1	$720-$900
50/I	6-1/2"	TMK-1	$450-$570
50/I	6-1/2"	TMK-2	$360-$450
50/I	6-1/2"	TMK-3	$330-$360
50/I	6-1/2" to 7"	TMK-4	$208-$305
50/I	6-1/2"	TMK-5	$275-$290
50/I	6-1/2"	TMK-6	$275-$290

Hum 51: Village Boy

Placed in production in the early years, master sculptor Arthur Moeller first designed this figurine in 1936.

The 51/I was taken out of production sometime in the 1960s, and the early figures are considered rare. Out of production for some 20 years, the 51/I was placed back in production for a short time and was once again placed on temporarily withdrawn status, effective Dec. 31, 1984. The 5" version (51/2/0) also was temporarily withdrawn from production, effective June 15, 2002.

In the mid-1990s, Goebel introduced a new, smaller size (51/5/0) as part of the six-piece "Pen Pals" series of personalized name card table decorations. However, that piece, too, has since been temporarily withdrawn from production.

There were many minor variations over the years, but the one most important to collectors occurs in the Crown Mark (TMK-1) 51/3/0 size. The boy wears a blue jacket and a yellow kerchief instead of the normal green jacket and red kerchief. This variation has dropped in value.

Hum 51: Village Boy.

Hum No.	Basic Size	Trademark	Current Value
51/5/0	2-3/4"	TMK-7	$55 retail
51/3/0	4"	TMK-1	$210-$270
51/3/0	4"	TMK-2	$135-$180
51/3/0	4"	TMK-3	$105-$120
51/3/0	4"	TMK-4	$95-$105
51/3/0	4"	TMK-5	$90-$95
51/3/0	4"	TMK-6	$90-$95
51/3/0	4"	TMK-7	$85-$90
51/3/0	4"	TMK-8	$140 retail
51/2/0	5"	TMK-1	$240-$315
51/2/0	5"	TMK-2	$150-$210
51/2/0	5"	TMK-3	$135-$150
51/2/0	5"	TMK-4	$120-$135
51/2/0	5"	TMK-5	$110-$120
51/2/0	5"	TMK-6	$105-$110
51/2/0	5"	TMK-7	$105-$110
51/2/0	5"	TMK-8	$175 retail
51/0	6"	TMK-1	$420-$540
51/0	6"	TMK-2	$270-$330
51/0	6"	TMK-3	$225-$240
51/0	6"	TMK-4	$195-$225
51/0	6"	TMK-6	$180-$195
51/0	6"	TMK-7	$175-$180
51/I	7-1/4"	TMK-1	$540-$690
51/I	7-1/4"	TMK-2	$480-$665
51/I	7-1/4"	TMK-3	$300-$360
51/I	7-1/4"	TMK-4	$240-$285
51/I	7-1/4"	TMK-5	$210-$240
51/I	7-1/4"	TMK-6	$195-$210
51	8"	TMK-1	$270-$335

Hum 52: Going to Grandma's

A very early figurine in the line, this figurine was designed by master sculptor Reinhold Unger in 1936 and called "Little Mothers of the Family" in early literature.

All of the older pieces in both sizes are found in the square base. A redesign and a new oval base were part of the transition to the Last Bee (TMK-5) era. You can, therefore, find TMK-5 pieces with either base, but the older, square base is the most desirable.

The figure has been found with the decimal designator in the Crown Mark (TMK-1).

The 52/I size was temporarily withdrawn on Dec. 31, 1984.

Hum 52: Going to Grandma's.

Hum No.	Basic Size	Trademark	Current Value
52/0	4-3/4"	TMK-1	$450-$600
52/0	4-3/4"	TMK-2	$270-$360
52/0	4-3/4"	TMK-3	$240-$270
52/0	4-3/4"	TMK-4	$195-$225
52/0	4-3/4"	TMK-5	$180-$195 square base
52/0	4-3/4"	TMK-5	$150-$165 oval base
52/0	4-3/4"	TMK-6	$175-$180
52/0	4-1/2" to 5"	TMK-7	$170-$175
52/0	4-1/2" to 5"	TMK-8	$285 retail
52	6"	TMK-1	$780-$960
52	6-1/4"	TMK-2	$510-$600
52/I	6"	TMK-1	$750-$900
52/I	6" to 6-1/2"	TMK-5	$255-$315 new oval
52/I	6"	TMK-2	$480-$540
52/I	6"	TMK-3	$390-$480
52/I	6"	TMK-5	$300-$480 old rectangle
52/I	6"	TMK-6	$240-$260

Hum 53: Joyful

This figurine, designed by master sculptor Reinhold Unger in 1936, was once known as Banjo Betty.

There are major size variations. As the figure emerged from the Crown Mark (TMK-1) era and transitioned into the Full Bee (TMK-2) period, it began to grow larger. Both the normal sizes and the larger variations appeared during the Full Bee period, and by the time the transition to the Stylized Bee (TMK-3) was finished, it was back to the normal 4" basic size. The oversize pieces consistently bring a higher price than the normal size pieces. They are valued at about 20%-25% more than the normal size.

A much rarer variation is the orange dress (instead of the normal blue) found on some very early Crown Mark (TMK-1) pieces. Collector value: $1,800-$2,100.

Similar to some of the other pieces, this piece was also produced in a sample with an attached bowl/pot, but was rejected by the Siessen Convent and never placed into production. If found, it is worth $3,000-$6,000.

This piece was temporarily withdrawn from production in January 1999.

Hum 53: Joyful.

Hum No.	Basic Size	Trademark	Current Value
53	4"	TMK-1	$210-$270
53	4"	TMK-2	$150-$185
53	4"	TMK-3	$115-$135
53	4"	TMK-4	$90-$105
53	4"	TMK-6	$90-$105
53	3-1/2"	TMK-7	$85-$100

Hum III/53: Joyful
Candy Box or Covered Box

There are two styles of candy boxes: bowl-like and jar-like. The transition from the old bowls to the new jars took place in the Stylized Bee (TMK-3) period. There are, therefore, old and new styles to be found with the Stylized Bee trademark. The older style would, of course, be the more desirable to collectors.

A newer version of the candy box (renamed "covered box") features a music staff with butterflies painted around the circumference.

This piece was temporarily withdrawn on Dec. 31, 1989; however, in 1996, a music box variation of the piece became available in Europe only. The music boxes are numbered IV/53, bear TMK-7, and have a brown banjo.

Hum III/53: Joyful candy box.

Hum No.	Basic Size	Trademark	Current Value
III/53	6-1/4"	TMK-1	$450-$510
III/53	6-1/4"	TMK-2	$345-$390
III/53	6-1/4"	TMK-3	$285-$330 old style
III/53	6-1/4"	TMK-3	$180-$210 new style
III/53	6-1/4"	TMK-4	$150-$195

Hum No.	Basic Size	Trademark	Current Value
III/53	6-1/4"	TMK-5	$135-$160
III/53	6-1/4"	TMK-6	$120-$145
IV/53	5-3/4"	TMK-7	$130-$150
IV/53	5-3/4"	TMK-9	$120

Hum 54: Silent Night
Candleholder

This piece, which was designed by master sculptor Reinhold Unger in 1936, is almost identical to the Hum 31: Advent Group candleholder, except that most of the Hum 31 figures have a black child on the left, and most of the Hum 54 figures have a white child on the left.

There have been at least three distinctly different molds.

The significant variation to be found, and the most valuable, is that of the black child. These can be found in the Crown Mark (TMK-1) and the Full Bee (TMK-2) trademarks only. They are valued at $4,500-$7,200. There is also an even more valuable piece with two black children in a Full Bee (TMK-2), which is worth $6,000-$9,000.

This piece was temporarily withdrawn in January 1999.

Hum No.	Basic Size	Trademark	Current Value
54	3-1/2" x 4-3/4"	TMK-1	$510-$665
54	3-1/2" x 4-3/4"	TMK-2	$330-$420
54	3-1/2" x 4-3/4"	TMK-3	$285-$300
54	3-1/2" x 4-3/4"	TMK-4	$255-$285
54	3-1/2" x 4-3/4"	TMK-5	$240-$255
54	3-1/2" x 4-3/4"	TMK-6	$225-$240
54	3-1/2" x 4-3/4"	TMK-1	$6,000-$7,200 with black child
54	3-1/2" x 4-3/4"	TMK-2	$4,500-$6,000 with black child
54	3-1/2" x 4-3/4"	TMK-2	$6,000-$9,000 two black children
54	3-1/2" x 4-3/4"	TMK-7	$220-$225

Hum 54: Silent Night candleholder.

Hum 55: Saint George

This figure, which was designed by master sculptor Reinhold Unger in 1936, is substantially different in style from most others in the collection and is difficult to locate most of the time.

The following sizes have been encountered in various lists: 6-1/4", 6-5/8", and 6-3/4". Some of the early TMK-1 pieces will have a bright red painted saddle. This is the rarest variation and brings $1,500-$1,800. There are reports of the existence of a white overglaze version as well.

This piece was temporarily withdrawn from production in January 1999.

Hum No.	Basic Size	Trademark	Current Value
55	6-3/4"	TMK-1	$1,500-$1,800 red saddle
55	6-3/4"	TMK-1	$600-$780
55	6-3/4"	TMK-2	$360-$450
55	6-3/4"	TMK-3	$270-$315
55	6-3/4"	TMK-4	$240-$270
55	6-3/4"	TMK-5	$225-$240
55	6-3/4"	TMK-6	$220-$240
55	6-3/4"	TMK-7	$210-$240

Hum 55: Saint George.

Hum 56/A: Culprits and Hum 56/B: Out of Danger

First modeled by master sculptor Arthur Moeller in 1936, Culprits was released in the mid-1930s. Out of Danger, which was also designed by Moeller, was not introduced until the early 1950s though. There have been minor changes over the years, including the fact that both the boy and girl had open eyes on older pieces and now have eyes cast down toward the dogs, but none of the changes have had any influence on normal collector values.

Hum 56/A: Culprits and Hum 56/B: Out of Danger.

Hum No.	Basic Size	Trademark	Current Value
56	6-1/4"	TMK-1	$515-$665
56	6-1/4"	TMK-2	$305-$400
56/A	6-1/4"	TMK-2	$305-$400
56/A	6-1/4"	TMK-3	$270-$300
56/A	6-1/4"	TMK-4	$260-$270
56/A	6-1/4"	TMK-5	$220-$250
56/A	6-1/4"	TMK-6	$210-$225
56/A	6-1/4"	TMK-7	$210-$225
56/A	6-1/4"	TMK-8	$210-$225
56/B	6-1/4"	TMK-2	$315-$360
56/B	6-1/4"	TMK-3	$270-$300
56/B	6-1/4"	TMK-4	$230-$285

Hum No.	Basic Size	Trademark	Current Value
56/B	6-1/4"	TMK-5	$220-$225
56/B	6-1/4"	TMK-6	$210-$215
56/B	6-1/4" to 6-3/4"	TMK-7	$210-$215
56/B	6-1/4" to 6-3/4"	TMK-8	$210-$215

Hum 57: Chick Girl

There are many mold types and sizes of this figurine, which was first designed by master sculptor Reinhold Unger in 1936 and then redesigned in 1964 by master sculptor Gerhard Skrobek. In the past, it has been called both Little Chicken Mother and The Little Chick Girl.

Like some of the other pieces, a sample of Chick Girl with a bowl/pot was produced in 1936, but never placed into production. If found, this piece would be worth $5,000-$7,000.

The chief mold variation shows different numbers of chicks on the base. For instance, the 57/0 has two chicks, and the larger, 57/I, has three. It also has been found with mold number and no size designator in the 4-1/4" size, "57."

Hum 57: Chick Girl.

Hum No.	Basic Size	Trademark	Current Value
57/2/0	3"	TMK-5	$130-$135
57/2/0	3"	TMK-6	$115-$120
57/2/0	3"	TMK-7	$110-$115
57/2/0	3"	TMK-8	$110-$115
57/0	3-1/2"	TMK-1	$305-$390
57/0	3-1/2"	TMK-2	$185-$225
57/0	3-1/2"	TMK-3	$150-$175
57/0	3-1/2"	TMK-4	$140-$155
57/0	3-1/2"	TMK-5	$125-$130
57/0	3-1/2"	TMK-6	$125-$130
57/0	3-1/2"	TMK-7	$115-$120
57/0	3-1/2"	TMK-8	$215 retail
57	4-1/4"	TMK-1	$485-$630
57/I	4-1/4"	TMK-1	$450-$600
57	4-1/4"	TMK-2	$305-$395
57/I	4-1/4"	TMK-2	$270-$360
57/I	4-1/4"	TMK-3	$250-$275
57/I	4-1/4"	TMK-4	$215-$240
57/I	4-1/4"	TMK-5	$210-$215
57/I	4-1/4"	TMK-6	$180-$210
57/I	4-1/4"	TMK-7	$190-$195

Hum III/57: Chick Girl
Candy Box

There are two styles of candy boxes: bowl-like and jar-like. The transition from the old bowls to the new jars took place in the Stylized Bee period, so both can be found with TMK-3. Naturally, the old style is the more desirable.

This piece was temporarily withdrawn on Dec. 31, 1989; however, in 1996, a music box variation of the piece became available in Europe only (just as occurred with Hum III/53: Joyful). The music boxes are numbered IV/ 57, bear TMK-7, and measure 6".

Hum III/57: Chick Girl candy box.

Hum No.	Basic Size	Trademark	Current Value
III/57	5-1/4"	TMK-1	$460-$510
III/57	5-1/4"	TMK-2	$350-$390
III/57 (old)	5-1/4"	TMK-3	$285-$330
III/57 (new)	5-1/4"	TMK-3	$185-$210
III/57	5-1/4"	TMK-4	$160-$175
III/57	5-1/4"	TMK-5	$140-$160
III/57	5-1/4"	TMK-6	$125-$140
IV/57	6"	TMK-7	$105 Europe only

Hum 58: Playmates

Originally known as Just Friends, this piece was designed by master sculptor Reinhold Unger in 1936. There are no variations in any trademark era that have any significant effect on value. A similar figure was used on bookend Hum 61/A and candy box Hum III/58.

Hum 58: Playmates.

Hum No.	Basic Size	Trademark	Current Value
58/2/0	3-1/2"	TMK-5	$120-$125
58/2/0	3-1/2"	TMK-6	$125-$130
58/2/0	3-1/2"	TMK-7	$120-$125
58/2/0	3-1/2"	TMK-8	$120-$125
58/0	4"	TMK-1	$350-$425
58/0	4"	TMK-2	$180-$225
58/0	4"	TMK-3	$160-$180
58/0	4"	TMK-4	$140-$165
58/0	4"	TMK-5	$125-$135
58/0	4"	TMK-6	$125-$135
58/0	4"	TMK-7	$115-$120
58/0	4"	TMK-8	$185-$195 closed edition
58	4-1/2"	TMK-1	$485-$595
58/I	4-1/2"	TMK-1	$450-$600
58	4-1/2"	TMK-2	$300-$360
58/I	4-1/2"	TMK-2	$275-$365
58/I	4-1/2"	TMK-3	$240-$270
58/I	4-1/2"	TMK-4	$210-$240
58/I	4-1/2"	TMK-5	$205-$210
58/I	4-1/2"	TMK-6	$190-$205
58/I	4-1/4"	TMK-7	$185-$195

Hum III/58: Playmates
Candy Box or Covered Box

Hum III/58: Playmates candy box.

There are two styles of candy boxes: bowl-like and jar-like. The transition from the old bowls to the new jars took place during the Stylized Bee (TMK-3) period, therefore each may be found with that trademark. The older style is, of course, more desirable to collectors.

This piece was temporarily withdrawn on Dec. 31, 1989; however, in 1996, Danbury Mint issued a new "M.I. Hummel" collector box that was sold by mail order only. It bears TMK-7.

Hum No.	Basic Size	Trademark	Current Value
III/58	5-1/4″	TMK-1	$460-$510
III/58	5-1/4″	TMK-2	$350-$395
III/58 (old)	5-1/4″	TMK-3	$285-$330
III/58 (new)	5-1/4″	TMK-3	$195-$210
III/58	5-1/4″	TMK-4	$160-$185
III/58	5-1/4″	TMK-5	$140-$160
III/58	5-1/4″	TMK-6	$125-$160
III/58	5-1/2″	TMK-7	$125-$145
IV/58	6-1/2″	TMK-7	$105 Europe only
IV/58	6-1/2″	TMK-9	$159 retail

Also in 1996, a music box variation of the piece became available in Europe only (just as occurred with Joyful, Hum III/53, and Chick Girl, Hum III/57). The music boxes are numbered IV/58, bear TMK-7, and have color graphics along the lower edge.

In the spring of 2010, Manufaktur Rödental reintroduced Playmates as a covered box featuring a rabbit eating grass.

Hum 59: Skier

Master sculptor Reinhold Unger created this figurine in 1936.

Newer models have metal ski poles and older models have wooden poles. For a short time, this piece was made with plastic poles. The poles are replaceable and are not considered significant in the valuation of the piece in the case of wooden and metal poles. There is, however, some difficulty with the plastic ski poles found on most of the Stylized Bee (TMK-3) pieces. The small round discs at the bottom of the poles are

Hum 59/4/0: Skier.

molded integral with the pole. Some collectors and dealers feel that the intact plastic ski poles on the Stylized Bee pieces are a bit more valuable than those with wooden or metal replacements.

Skier was re-released in a smaller size of 3-1/4″. A TMK-9, it is a mixed media figurine with wooden ski poles.

Hum No.	Basic Size	Trademark	Current Value
59.	5-1/4″	TMK-1	$425-$515
59	5-1/4″	TMK-1	$425-$515
59	5-1/4″	TMK-2	$255-$315
59	5-1/4″	TMK-3	$190-$210
59	5-1/4″	TMK-4	$170-$180
59	5-1/4″	TMK-5	$150-$170
59	5-1/4″	TMK-6	$150-$170
59	5″ to 6″	TMK-7	$140-$160
59	5″ to 6″	TMK-8	$235 retail
59/4/0	3-1/4″	TMK-9	$119 retail

Hum 59: Skier.

Hum 60/A and Hum 60/B: Farm Boy and Goose Girl
Bookends

The overall height of the bookends is 6", while the figurines themselves measure 4-3/4". Notice the lack of bases on the figurines. Most often the trademark is found stamped on the wooden base and not on the figurines. Noted collector Robert Miller has confirmed, by removing the boy from a 60/A bookend, that some of the earliest production pieces are occasionally found with the mold number incised on the bottom of the feet. The mold number has also been observed on the back of the slippers on other early pieces.

There are no significant variations affecting value.

These bookends were temporarily withdrawn from production status in Dec. 31, 1984.

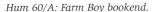

Hum 60/A: Farm Boy bookend.

Hum No.	Basic Size	Trademark	Current Value
60/A&B	6"	TMK-1	$575-$760
60/A&B	6"	TMK-2	$395-$575
60/A&B	6"	TMK-3	$255-$300
60/A&B	4-3/4"	TMK-4	$250-$260
60/A&B	6"	TMK-5	$250-$260
60/A&B	6"	TMK-6	$250-$260

Hum 61/A and Hum 61/B: Playmates and Chick Girl
Bookends

Overall height of each bookend is 6", while the figures are 4". Note that the figures used do not have the usual base. The trademark is usually marked on the wood portion. The trademark and mold number may or may not appear on the bottom of the figures if removed from the base. Some bookend pieces are marked so, especially the earliest.

The bookends were temporarily withdrawn on Dec. 31, 1984.

Hum 61/A: Playmates bookend.

Hum No.	Basic Size	Trademark	Current Value
61/A&B	6"	TMK-1	$575-$760
61/A&B	6"	TMK-2	$395-$575
61/A&B	6"	TMK-3	$255-$300
61/A&B	4"	TMK-4	$255-$300
61/A&B	6"	TMK-5	$250-$260
61/A&B	6"	TMK-6	$250-$260

Hum 62: Happy Pastime
Ashtray

Master sculptor Arthur Moeller first designed this piece in 1936 and there have been no significant variations affecting value since. This piece, as all ashtrays, has been temporarily withdrawn from production with no published reinstatement date.

The figure used is similar to Hum 69, except that the bird is positioned on the edge of the tray rather than on the girl's leg as on the Hum 69.

Hum No.	Basic Size	Trademark	Current Value
62	3-1/2" x 6-1/4"	TMK-1	$270-$390
62	3-1/2" x 6-1/4"	TMK-2	$180-$215
62	3-1/2" x 6-1/4"	TMK-3	$140-$150
62	3-1/2" x 6-1/4"	TMK-4	$120-$135
62	3-1/2" x 6-1/4"	TMK-5	$110-$120
62	3-1/2" x 6-1/4"	TMK-6	$95-$115

The Happy Pastime ashtray figure turned up in 1993 without its ashtray. This is an anomaly and has no significant value. It is interesting but is likely to be a unique accident. It apparently got packed and shipped out of the factory unnoticed.

Hum 62: Happy Pastime ashtray.

Hum 63: Singing Lesson

First designed by master sculptor Arthur Moeller in 1937 and called both Duet and Critic, Singing Lesson has changed a little over the years but has no significant variations. Occasionally it has been found with the decimal designator (63.) on the Crown Mark (TMK-1). This is an indication that it is an early Crown piece, but it does not have a significant impact on value.

Hum No.	Basic Size	Trademark	Current Value
63	2-3/4"	TMK-1	$270-$300
63	2-3/4"	TMK-2	$160-$220
63	2-3/4"	TMK-3	$115-$120
63	2-3/4"	TMK-4	$99-$110
63	2-3/4"	TMK-5	$95-$99
63	2-3/4"	TMK-6	$95-$99
63	2-3/4"	TMK-7	$90-$99
63	2-3/4"	TMK-8	$150 retail

Hum 63: Singing Lesson.

Hum III/63: Singing Lesson
Candy Box

There are two styles of bowls. The transition from the old to the new took place in the Stylized Bee (TMK-3) period, therefore both are found with the Stylized Bee trademark. The old style with this mark is, of course, more desirable to collectors.

In 1996, a music box variation of the piece became available in Europe only (just as occurred with Hum III/53: Joyful, Hum III/57: Chick Girl, and Hum III/58: Playmates). The music boxes are numbered IV/63, bear TMK-7, and have color graphics around the box.

Hum No.	Basic Size	Trademark	Current Value
III-63	5-1/4"	TMK-1	$450-$510
III-63	5-1/4"	TMK-2	$355-$390
III-63 (old)	5-1/4"	TMK-3	$290-$330
III-63 (new)	5-1/4"	TMK-3	$185-$220
III-63	5-1/4"	TMK-4	$150-$165
III-63	5-1/4"	TMK-5	$125-$145
III-63	5-1/4"	TMK-6	$125-$145
IV/63	4-3/4"	TMK-7	$105 Europe only

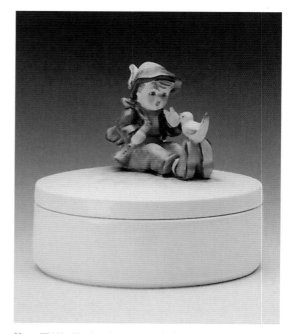

Hum III/63: Singing Lesson candy box.

Hum 64: Shepherd's Boy

Master sculptor Arthur Moeller first designed this figurine in 1937 and Gerhard Skrobek restyled it in the late-1970s with a new textured finish. It was originally called The Good Shepherd, and although there seem to be a number of size variations to be found, there are no significant variations that could affect the normal pricing of the various trademarked figurines.

Hum No.	Basic Size	Trademark	Current Value
64	5-1/2"	TMK-1	$420-$510
64	5-1/2"	TMK-2	$250-$275
64	5-1/2"	TMK-3	$215-$240
64	5-1/2"	TMK-4	$185-$215
64	5-1/2"	TMK-5	$175-$180
64	5-1/2"	TMK-6	$170-$180
64	5-1/2"	TMK-7	$170-$175
64	5-1/2"	TMK-8	$239 retail
64 III	13"	TMK-8 limited edition	$1,200 retail

Hum 64: Shepherd's Boy.

Hum 65: Farewell

Master sculptor Arthur Moeller designed this piece in 1937 and Gerhard Skrobek restyled it in 1964. Early company literature called this figurine So Long or Good Bye.

The first models of this figurine, the 65/0 size, in a small 4" basic size, are very rare and highly sought by serious collectors. Apparently a very limited number were made. They are found in the Crown Mark (TMK-1) and the Full Bee (TMK-2) only.

The 4-3/4" basic size carried the 65/I mold number for a while, but in the late-1970s it became 65 only. This size is also sometimes found with the decimal designator on the early Crown Mark and Full Bee mark pieces.

An interesting variation occurred in TMK-6 era. It seems that a few of the baskets were attached wrong, resulting in a gap between the arm and the basket on the inside. The pieces with this variation are valued a bit above normal by some collectors. Mistakes such as this are not common, but do happen on occasion. For instance, sometimes a bottle is inadvertently left out of a basket during assembly. Most of the time, it is only an interesting oddity, but enough of the incorrect-basket Farewell models were made that it is an attractive figure to some collectors.

Farewell is a retired figurine. The mold was scheduled to be broken on Dec. 31, 1993. All the items that were produced during 1993 bear a special "Final Issue" backstamp and were accompanied by a small medallion proclaiming it as a "Final Issue."

Hum 65: Farewell.

Hum No.	Basic Size	Trademark	Current Value
65/0	4"	TMK-2	$3,600-$4,800
65/0	4"	TMK-3	$3,000-$3,600
65.	4-3/4"	TMK-1	$460-$600
65/I	4-3/4"	TMK-1	$460-$600

Hum No.	Basic Size	Trademark	Current Value
65.	4-3/4"	TMK-2	$275-$345
65/I	4-3/4"	TMK-2	$270-$345
65/I	4-3/4"	TMK-3	$250-$275
65/I	4-3/4"	TMK-4	$210-$255
65/I	4-1/2" to 4-7/8"	TMK-5	$195-$220
65	4-3/4"	TMK-5	$195-$220
65	4-3/4"	TMK-6	$185-$200
65	4-3/4"	TMK-7	$170-$185

Hum 66: Farm Boy

A figure similar to that used in bookend Hum 60/A, this piece was modeled by master sculptor Arthur Moeller in 1937 and has been called Three Pals and Happy-Go-Lucky Fellow in the past. Older versions have larger shoes. In fact, in the older version, the whole piece appears fatter overall. It is occasionally found with the decimal point size designator.

Hum No.	Basic Size	Trademark	Current Value
66	5-1/4"	TMK-1	$450-$540
66	5-1/4"	TMK-2	$275-$345
66	5-1/4"	TMK-3	$210-$255
66	5-1/4"	TMK-4	$190-$220
66	5-1/4"	TMK-5	$175-$200 all are closed editions
66	5-1/4"	TMK-6	$175-$200
66	5" to 5-3/4"	TMK-7	$170-$185
66	5" to 5-3/4"	TMK-8	$180-$190

Hum 66: Farm Boy.

Hum 67: Doll Mother

Released in 1937 at the Leipzig Trade Fair, Doll Mother was designed by master sculptor Arthur Moeller and first known as Little Doll Mother and Little Mother of Dolls.

A color variation has surfaced whereby the blanket is white with red cross stripes rather than the typical pink blanket with red stripes. This unique piece bears TMK-1 and is worth $750-$1,000.

In 1997, a special 60th Anniversary Doll Mother figurine was issued with special backstamp and round gold medallion reading: "HUM 67 Doll Mother 1937-1997" and "60th."

Hum No.	Basic Size	Trademark	Current Value
67.	4-3/4"	TMK-1	$390-$510
67	4-3/4"	TMK-1	$390-$510
67	4-3/4"	TMK-2	$250-$305
67	4-3/4"	TMK-3	$200-$210
67	4-3/4"	TMK-4	$170-$195
67	4-3/4"	TMK-5	$150-$170
67	4-3/4"	TMK-6	$150-$155
67	4-1/4" to 4-3/4"	TMK-7	$150-$160
67	4-1/4" to 4-3/4"	TMK-8	$279 retail

Hum 67: Doll Mother.

Hum 68: Lost Sheep

Master sculptor Arthur Moeller modeled this piece in 1937, but it has been restyled by several modelers over the years.

Sizes found referenced in lists are as follows: 4-1/4", 4-1/2", 5-1/2", and 6-1/2". This figure is found most commonly with green pants. A reference to a figure with orange pants (6-1/2") was found, but the color variation considered rarest is the one with brown pants. The collector value for the brown pants variation is about 25% higher than the value for the normal green pants piece.

There are four or five different color variations involving the coat, pants, and shirt of the figure. Oversize pieces bring premium prices.

The decimal point designator has been found on some early Crown Mark (TMK-1) figures.

The 68/0 and 68/2/0 sizes were retired at the end of 1992. Each of them made in 1992 bear the special "Final Issue" backstamp and came with a special "Final Issue" medallion.

Hum 68: Lost Sheep.

Hum No.	Basic Size	Trademark	Current Value
68/2/0	4-1/2"	TMK-2	$150-$210
68/2/0	4-1/2"	TMK-3	$135-$150
68/2/0	4-1/2"	TMK-4	$115-$140
68/2/0	4-1/2"	TMK-5	$110-$115
68/2/0	4-1/2"	TMK-6	$105-$110
68/2/0	4-1/4" to 4-1/2"	TMK-7	$99-$105
68	5-1/2"	TMK-1	$360-$460
68	5-1/2"	TMK-2	$240-$300
68/0	5-1/2"	TMK-2	$210-$270
68	5-1/2"	TMK-3	$210-$240
68/0	5-1/2"	TMK-3	$210-$220
68/0	5-1/2"	TMK-4	$170-$185

Hum No.	Basic Size	Trademark	Current Value
68/0	5-1/2"	TMK-5	$150-$165
68/0	5-1/2"	TMK-6	$140-$150
68/0	5-1/2"	TMK-7	$120-$150

Hum 69: Happy Pastime

This figurine, which was modeled by master sculptor Arthur Moeller, was in a group of pieces that was issued a short time after the initial 46 were released. It was called Knitter in early company literature.

There have been changes over the years, but nothing significant enough to influence the normal pricing in any trademark era.

Happy Pastime was retired on Dec. 31, 1996. All figures produced in 1996 bear the "Final Issue" backstamp and came with a special gold commemorative tag.

Hum No.	Basic Size	Trademark	Current Value
69	3-1/4"	TMK-1	$300-$390
69	3-1/4"	TMK-2	$185-$250
69	3-1/4"	TMK-3	$150-$170
69	3-1/4"	TMK-4	$135-$150 all closed editions
69	3-1/4"	TMK-5	$120-$135
69	3-1/4"	TMK-6	$120-$130
69	3-1/4" to 3-1/2"	TMK-7	$115-$125

Hum 69: Happy Pastime.

Hum III/69: Happy Pastime
Candy Box

There are two styles of candy boxes: bowl-like and jar-like. The transition from the old bowls to the new jars took place during the Stylized Bee (TMK-3) period, so both the old and new can be found bearing that trademark.

This candy box was temporarily withdrawn in December 1989.

Hum III/69: Happy Pastime candy box.

Hum No.	Basic Size	Trademark	Current Value
III/69	6"	TMK-1	$450-$510
III/69	6"	TMK-2	$350-$395
III/69 (old)	6"	TMK-3	$290-$330
III/69 (new)	6"	TMK-3	$180-$210

Hum No.	Basic Size	Trademark	Current Value
III/69	6"	TMK-4	$155-$170
III/69	6"	TMK-5	$135-$150
III/69	6"	TMK-6	$120-$135

Hum 70: Holy Child

The collective effort of several modelers, this piece was released in 1937 and has also been called Child Jesus.

The piece has been known to exist in the rare white overglaze finish, which was sold only in Belgium, and in much sought-after oversize pieces, generally valued at about 20% above the normal value listed.

There was a general restyling of the whole collection over the years, to the more textured finish of the clothing of today's figures.

Hum 70: Holy Child.

Hum No.	Basic Size	Trademark	Current Value
70	6-3/4"	TMK-1	$450-$510
70	6-3/4"	TMK-2	$230-$300
70	6-3/4"	TMK-3	$210-$230
70	6-3/4"	TMK-4	$195-$210
70	6-3/4"	TMK-5	$180-$195
70	6-3/4"	TMK-6	$180-$190
70	6-3/4"	TMK-7	$170-$180

This figurine was temporarily withdrawn from production in 1999.

Hum 71: Stormy Weather

This figure, which was designed by master sculptor Reinhold Unger in 1937, has been known as Under One Roof.

Some earlier models were produced with a split base underneath. The split base model with the Full Bee (TMK-2) mark shows that the split is laterally oriented. The new models also have the split base, but it is oriented longitudinally.

A Crown Mark (TMK-1) Stormy Weather has been found that differs from the norm. Among other things, the boy figure in the piece has no kerchief. It is most likely a prototype, inasmuch as it is not signed.

Hum 71: Stormy Weather.

Other than the oddity described above, there were no significant variations over the years until the small 71/2/0 (5") was introduced. After a period of time, it became obvious that the method of painting the underside of the umbrella had changed. The first models exhibit the brush strokes of hand painting, while the later ones are airbrushed. Serious collectors seek out this variation. It is valued at about $500-$600.

Hum No.	Basic Size	Trademark	Current Value
71/2/0	5"	TMK-6	$225-$245
71/2/0	4-1/2" to 5"	TMK-7	$210-$220
71/2/0	4-1/2" to 5"	TMK-8	$279 retail
71	6-1/4"	TMK-1	$660-$785
71	6-1/4"	TMK-2	$480-$575
71	6-1/4"	TMK-3	$390-$405
71	6-1/4"	TMK-4	$360-$390
71	6-1/4"	TMK-5	$330-$360
71	6-1/4"	TMK-6	$315-$330
71/I	6-1/4"	TMK-6	$315-$345
71/I	6" to 6-1/4"	TMK-7	$305-$315
71/I	6" to 6-1/4"	TMK-8	$559 retail

The 71 mold number was changed to 71/I during TMK-6 period. The mold number can be found rendered either way on those pieces.

In 1997, a special variation of 71/2/0 was produced for QVC television and sold by mail order at $279.50 plus shipping and handling. This variation featured a yellow umbrella with tan-colored highlights, a decal signature on the back of the umbrella, and a special "60th Anniversary" backstamp.

Hum 72: Spring Cheer

Designed by master sculptor Reinhold Unger in 1937 and released soon after the initial issue of 46, this figurine was originally called Spring Flowers. It is modeled from the Hummel art called Just for You, H 271. Another piece modeled from the same artwork—Hum 793: Forever Yours—became the renewal premium for M.I. Hummel Club members who renew for their 20th year of membership.

There have been some significant variations in Spring Cheer over its years of production. It was initially released in a yellow dress and with no flowers in the right hand. These can be found in the Crown Mark (TMK-1), the Full Bee (TMK-2), and the Stylized Bee (TMK-3). During the Stylized Bee (TMK-3), the figure was produced with a green dress and flowers in the right hand. Current pieces are configured in the latter way. However, some of the old (no flowers in right hand) models were left over, and these were painted with a green dress to match the new model. This is the rarest of the two green dress models and is worth $1,200-$1,500.

The company lists the figurine as temporarily withdrawn from production as of Dec. 31, 1984.

Hum 72: Spring Cheer.

Hum No.	Basic Size	Trademark	Current Value
72	5"	TMK-1	$300-$390
72	5"	TMK-2	$195-$240
72	5"	TMK-3	$180-$195
72	5"	TMK-4	$150-$180
72	5"	TMK-5	$135-$150
72	5"	TMK-6	$120-$135

Hum 73: Little Helper

Master sculptor Reinhold Unger created this figurine in 1937 and it had been called Diligent Betsy and The Little Sister in early company literature.

There are no significant variations from any of the trademark eras affecting the normal values for this figurine. The TMK-8 piece, however, has been paired with the present-day rendition of Hum 554: Cheeky Fellow to create the Treehouse Treats collector's set.

Hum 73: Little Helper.

Hum No.	Basic Size	Trademark	Current Value
73	4-1/4"	TMK-1	$270-$300
73	4-1/4"	TMK-2	$150-$195
73	4-1/4"	TMK-3	$115-$120
73	4-1/4"	TMK-4	$95-$115
73	4-1/4"	TMK-5	$90-$100
73	4-1/4"	TMK-6	$90-$100
73	4-1/4" to 4-1/2"	TMK-7	$85-$95
73	4-1/4" to 4-1/2"	TMK-8	$85-$95

Hum 74: Little Gardener

This figure, which was modeled by master sculptor Reinhold Unger in 1937, was found in several lists with the following sizes: 4", 4-1/4", and 4-1/2". Earlier versions are found on an oval base, and more recent or current pieces are on the round base.

The major variation encountered is a dark green dress rather than the present lighter-colored dress. Some of the earliest models have a very light green or yellowish dress.

Some other variations make it easy to spot the older pieces. On the Crown

Hum 74: Little Gardener.

Mark (TMK-1) and Full Bee (TMK-2) figures, the flower at the base is tall and almost egg-shaped. On the Stylized Bee (TMK-3) figures, the flower is about one-half the height of the earlier flowers, and from the Last Bee (TMK-5) on, they are rather flattened in comparison. These variations, however, have no effect on the normal value of the piece for their respective

Hum No.	Basic Size	Trademark	Current Value
74	4-1/4"	TMK-1	$270-$300
74	4-1/4"	TMK-2	$150-$180
74	4-1/4"	TMK-3	$120-$135
74	4-1/4"	TMK-4	$300-$450
74	4-1/4"	TMK-5	$95-$105
74	4-1/4"	TMK-6	$90-$95
74	4" to 4-1/2"	TMK-7	$90-$95
74	4" to 4-1/2"	TMK-8	$90-$95

trademarks. They represent normal changes through the years.

There is one variation that bears watching. In the spring of 1992, Goebel took this figurine out of normal production for two years, resuming normal production in 1994. From the spring of 1992 until the end of the year, Little Gardener was used as a district managers' special promotional piece and each piece bears a special promotion backstamp. The only place they were available was at authorized M.I. Hummel dealers conducting district manager special promotions and in Canada at artists' promotions. Each of these pieces bears the appropriate backstamp identifying it as such. The figurines were available on a first-come, first-served basis.

Hum 75: White Angel
Holy Water Font

Although this piece, which was created in 1937 by master sculptor Reinhold Unger, was also known as Angelic Prayer or White Angel Font, it is not white, but painted with color. Terra-cotta variations have also surfaced over the years and those are worth $1,000-$1,500.

This piece was temporarily withdrawn from production in January 1999.

Hum No.	Basic Size	Trademark	Current Value
75	1-3/4" x 3-1/2"	TMK-1	$135-$165
75	1-3/4" x 3-1/2"	TMK-2	$80-$90
75	1-3/4" x 3-1/2"	TMK-3	$45-$60
75	1-3/4" x 3-1/2"	TMK-4	$40-$50
75	1-3/4" x 3-1/2"	TMK-5	$30-$40
75	1-3/4" x 3-1/2"	TMK-6	$30-$40
75	3-1/4" to 4-1/2"	TMK-7	$30-$40

Hum 75: White Angel holy water font.

Hum 76/A and Hum 76/B: Doll Mother and Prayer Before Battle
Bookends

Originally modeled by master sculptor Arthur Moeller, these bookends are unique. It is possible, but not likely, that they might be found in a collector's possession. There are no known examples in private hands, only those in factory archives.

Hum No.	Basic Size	Trademark	Current Value
76 A&B	–	TMK-1	$6,000-$9,000

Hum 76/A: Doll Mother bookend.

Hum 77: Cross With Doves
Holy Water Font

In past editions of this book, it was reported that there was only one example of this piece and it was in the factory archives. Created by master sculptor Reinhold Unger in 1937, it was thought that the piece never went into production as it was listed as a closed edition in October 1937. However, at least 10 now reside in private collections. The one in the accompanying photos is an incised Crown Mark (TMK-1) piece with the M.I. Hummel signature on the back. It has been reported in white. If sold, this font would likely bring $3,000-$6,000, in color or white.

Hum No.	Basic Size	Trademark	Current Value
77	1-3/4" x 6-1/4"	TMK-1	$3,000-$6,000

Hum 77: Cross With Doves holy water font

Backside of the Hum 77 font showing the Crown Mark and the M.I. Hummel incised signature.

Hum 78: Blessed Child

Known in the past as In the Crib and Infant of Krumbad, this piece was first designed by master sculptor Erich Lautensack in 1937. It was then redesigned in 1965 by master sculptor Gerhard Skrobek.

This figurine can be found in seven different sizes and three finishes. All sizes, except one, have been either retired or temporarily withdrawn from production, with no stated reintroduction date.

The normal finish is a sepia-tone bisque. The figures were available painted in full color for a time, then withdrawn, reissued, and finally discontinued. There was also a white overglaze finish reportedly produced for the European market only. The color pieces are valued at two times the normal price listed for the size, and the white overglaze figures are valued at about two to three times the normal price, also depending on the size.

There are two pieces still available. One is the small 78/ 0, 2-1/4" size, which is difficult to get because this size was discontinued in the Stylized Bee (TMK-3) period. It has been redesigned and issued in the sepia-tone finish without the 78/0 incised mold number. It bears only TMK- 6 or TMK-7 and is sold in the Siessen Convent only. It is unavailable elsewhere. The other one is also available only at the convent. It is the 4-1/2" Hum 78/II/1/2.

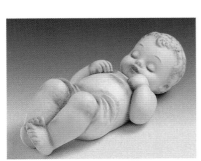

Hum 78: Blessed Child.

Hum No.	Basic Size	Trademark	Current Value
78/0	1-3/4"	TMK-2	$120-$180
78/0	1-3/4"	TMK-3	$90-$120
78/0	1-3/4"	TMK-6	$70-$80
78/I	2-1/2"	TMK-3	$30-$40
78/I	2-1/2"	TMK-4	$30-$40

Hum No.	Basic Size	Trademark	Current Value
78/I	2-1/2"	TMK-5	$30-$40
78/I	2-1/2"	TMK-6	$30-$40
78/II	3-1/2"	TMK-3	$30-$40
78/II	3-1/2"	TMK-4	$30-$40
78/II	3-1/2"	TMK-5	$30-$40
78/II	3-1/2"	TMK-6	$25-$40
78/III	5-1/4"	TMK-1	$210-$240
78/III	5-1/4"	TMK-2	$150-$210
78/III	5-1/4"	TMK-3	$40-$45
78/III	5-1/4"	TMK-4	$30-$40
78/III	5-1/4"	TMK-5	$30-$40
78/III	5-1/4"	TMK-6	$25-$40
78/V	7-3/4"	TMK-3	$80-$90
78/V	7-3/4"	TMK-4	$60-$75
78/V	7-3/4"	TMK-5	$90-$100
78/V	7-3/4"	TMK-6	$55-$90
78/VI	10"	TMK-1	$360-$510
78/VI	10"	TMK-2	$255-$325
78/VI	10"	TMK-3	$120-$150
78/VI	10"	TMK-4	$120-$250
78/VI	10"	TMK-5	$95-$105
78/VI	10"	TMK-6	$95-$105
78/VIII	13-1/2"	TMK-1	$450-$600
78/VIII	13-1/2"	TMK-2	$300-$450
78/VIII	13-1/2"	TMK-3	$210-$240
78/VIII	13-1/2"	TMK-4	$210-$240
78/VIII	13-1/2"	TMK-5	$180-$195
78/VIII	13-1/2"	TMK-6	$180-$195
78/II/1/2*	4"	TMK-6	$60-$90
78/II/1/2*	4-1/2"	TMK-7	$45-$60
78/II/1/2*	4-1/2"	TMK-8	$45-$60

*One of only two pieces in the collection to use this one-half designator. The other is Hum 21: Heavenly Angel.

Hum 79: Globe Trotter

One of the pre-World War II releases, this figurine was originally designed by master sculptor Arthur Moeller in 1937. There are no significant variations that directly affect the value of the pieces under the various trademarks, but there are some interesting variations that can help you spot the earlier figures without examining the marks. The Crown Mark (TMK-1) and Full Bee (TMK-2) exhibit a double weave in the baskets (see accompanying photos). With a redesign in 1955, the weaving changed from double weave to single weave during the Stylized Bee (TMK-3) era, so you may find them in either configuration in that trademark. A few of the older marked figures will also sport a dark green hat instead of the normal reddish brown color.

Globe Trotter was retired in 1991, but was redesigned and brought back to commemorate the M.I. Hummel Club Year 35 in 2011. Master sculptor Marion Huschka used a special molding process to achieve as much of the detail from Sister Maria Innocentia Hummel's original drawing. This 35th anniversary piece is almost 6" tall and painted with 24 colors, seven more than the original figurine. A porcelain postcard with a copy of the original artwork along with a wooden easel is included with the figurine. This is an exclusive to M.I. Hummel Club members who reach their 35th anniversary membership milestone. It is a TMK-9 figurine and has the TMK-9 backstamp and "35th Anniversary" backstamp.

Hum No.	Basic Size	Trademark	Current Value
79	5"	TMK-1	$360-$450
79	5"	TMK-2	$225-$300
79 (old style)	5"	TMK-3	$185-$220
79	5"	TMK-4	$170-$190
79	5"	TMK-5	$135-$165
79	5"	TMK-6	$135-$150
79	5" to 5-1/4"	TMK-7	$120-$135
79/I	6"	TMK-9	$499 retail M.I. Hummel Club Exclusive

Left: Hum 79: Globe Trotter. Rear view shows the different basket weave patterns discussed in text. The older figure is on the left.

Right: Hum 79/I: Globe Trotter 35th Anniversary club exclusive.

Hum 80: Little Scholar

Master sculptor Arthur Moeller designed this piece in 1937 and there have been no figures produced with variations that would affect their normal value. There is one variation, however, that may help you pick out the older pieces without examining the bases. The Crown Mark (TMK-1) and the Full Bee mark (TMK-2) pieces will have dark brown shoes instead of the lighter color of those produced later.

In 2002, a smaller 4-1/4" version of this figurine was introduced with model number Hum 80/2/0. It originally retailed for $175.

Hum No.	Basic Size	Trademark	Current Value
80	5-1/2"	TMK-1	$390-$480
80	5-1/2"	TMK-2	$230-$300
80	5-1/2"	TMK-3	$195-$210
80	5-1/2"	TMK-4	$170-$195
80	5-1/2"	TMK-5	$165-$170
80	5-1/2"	TMK-6	$135-$165
80	5-1/4" to 5-3/4"	TMK-7	$150-$165
80	5-1/4" to 5-3/4"	TMK-8	$279 retail
80/2/0	4-1/4"	TMK-8	$179 retail

Hum 80: Little Scholar.

Hum 81: School Girl

At one time called Primer Girl and Little Scholar, this figurine was designed by master sculptor Arthur Moeller in 1937.

There are no variations affecting the value of any of the models of this piece. There are, however, some worth noting. The smallest of the figures, the 81/2/0, has flowers in the basket. All other sizes are devoid of flowers. The older figures have a black book bag and a pink blouse.

The figure has been found with the decimal point designator on the Crown Mark (TMK-1) larger 5-1/4" basic size.

Goebel issued a special edition of this figurine in the Hum 81/2/0 size in 1996 in commemoration of the 125th anniversary of the company. Each figure bears a special "125th Anniversary" backstamp. In addition, the inscription "International Collectible Exposition" is placed around the base.

The larger 81/0 variation was temporarily withdrawn from production in 1999.

The year 2011 marked the celebration of Sister Hummel's 75th anniversary of the beginning of her legacy. Manufaktur Rödental selected 50 figurines to bear the "75th Anniversary" backstamp. School Girl was one of those figurines. Only 75 of them were available in North America with this backstamp. Each figurine was hand-numbered with a golden backstamp and a map of North America backstamp. A special porcelain plaque was included, and a notable emblem on the packaging hinted at the contents. Each figurine included a "75 Years of M.I. Hummel" certificate.

Hum No.	Basic Size	Trademark	Current Value
81/2/0	4-1/4"	TMK-1	$270-$360
81/2/0	4-1/4"	TMK-2	$150-$210
81/2/0	4-1/4"	TMK-3	$135-$160
81/2/0	4-1/4"	TMK-4	$120-$130
81/2/0	4-1/4"	TMK-5	$110-$120
81/2/0	4-1/4"	TMK-6	$105-$110
81/2/0	4-1/4" to 4-3/4"	TMK-7	$105-$110
81/2/0	4-1/4" to 4/3/4"	TMK-8	$175 retail
81.	5-1/4"	TMK-1	$360-$420
81/0	5-1/4"	TMK-1	$330-$420
81	5-1/4"	TMK-2	$210-$285
81/0	5-1/4"	TMK-2	$195-$270
81/0	5-1/4"	TMK-3	$180-$195
81/0	5-1/4"	TMK-4	$165-$180
81/0	5-1/4"	TMK-5	$150-$165
81/0	5-1/4"	TMK-6	$140-$150
81/0	4-3/4" to 5-1/4"	TMK-7	$135-$150 60th Anniversary Decal 1998

Hum 81: School Girl.

Hum 82: School Boy

Listed as Little Scholar, School Days, and Primer Boy in company literature throughout the years, this piece was originally crafted by master sculptor Arthur Moeller in 1938. Sizes found in various lists are 4", 4-3/4", 5-1/2", and 7-1/2". It is occasionally found having the decimal point size designator in the Crown Mark (TMK-1) pieces. There are no other significant variations.

The larger 82/II size was temporarily withdrawn from production in 1999.

The year 2011 marked the celebration of Sister Hummel's 75th anniversary of the beginning of her legacy. Manufaktur Rödental selected 50 figurines to bear the "75th Anniversary" backstamp. School Boy was one of those figurines. Only 75 of them were available in North America with this backstamp. Each figurine was hand-numbered with a golden backstamp and a map of North America backstamp. A special porcelain plaque was included, and a notable emblem on the packaging hinted at the contents. Each figurine included a "75 Years of M.I. Hummel" certificate.

Hum No.	Basic Size	Trademark	Current Value
82/2/0	4"	TMK-1	$270-$360
82/2/0	4"	TMK-2	$150-$210
82/2/0	4"	TMK-3	$135-$160
82/2/0	4"	TMK-4	$120-$130
82/2/0	4"	TMK-5	$110-$120
82/2/0	4"	TMK-6	$105-$115
82/2/0	4" to 4-1/2"	TMK-7	$105-$115
82/2/0	4" to 4-1/2"	TMK-8	$180 retail
82.	5-1/2"	TMK-1	$375-$465
82/0	4-3/4" to 6"	TMK-$1	$360-$450
82/0	5-1/2"	TMK-2	$210-$300
82/0	5-1/2"	TMK-3	$195-$220
82/0	5-1/2"	TMK-4	$165-$195
82/0	5-1/2"	TMK-5	$150-$165
82/0	5-1/2"	TMK-6	$145-$165
82/0	4-3/4" to 6"	TMK-7	$145-$160
82/0	4-3/4" to 6"	TMK-8	$150-$180
82/II	7-1/2"	TMK-1	$720-$960
82/II	7-1/2"	TMK-2	$540-$660
82/II	7-1/2"	TMK-3	$360-$420
82/II	7-1/2"	TMK-5	$330-$375
82/II	7-1/2"	TMK-6	$315-$330
82/II	7-1/2"	TMK-7	$300-$320

Hum 82: School Boy.

Hum 83: Angel Serenade With Lamb

Another piece in the collection with a similar name (Angel Serenade) is part of the Nativity Set. They do not look alike, but the name may confuse you.

Originally called Psalmist, this piece was designed by master sculptor Reinhold Unger in 1938.

There are no significant variations, only minor changes over the years. Until recently, these figures were apparently made in limited quantities (from the TMK-3 period to TMK-6 period), but now they seem to be readily available again.

Hum No.	Basic Size	Trademark	Current Value
83	5"	TMK-1	$390-$450
83	5"	TMK-2	$330-$345
83	5"	TMK-3	$240-$300
83	5"	TMK-4	$180-$240
83	5"	TMK-5	$165-$180
83	5"	TMK-6	$165-$180
83	5-1/2" to 5-3/4"	TMK-7	$165-$175 60th Anniversary Decal 1998

Hum 83: Angel Serenade With Lamb.

Hum 84: Worship

In 1938, master sculptor Reinhold Unger originally crafted this piece, which was previously called At the Wayside and Devotion. Sizes reported in various lists are 5", 6-3/4", and 14-1/2". The figure has been found with the decimal point size designator.

The 84/V size was temporarily withdrawn from production at the end of 1989 with no reinstatement date revealed.

Hum No.	Basic Size	Trademark	Current Value
84 white	5-1/4"	TMK-1	$720-$900
84	5-1/4"	TMK-1	$315-$375
84/0	5"	TMK-1	$300-$375
84/0	5"	TMK-2	$180-$225
84/0	5"	TMK-3	$135-$175
84/0	5"	TMK-4	$135-$165
84/0	5"	TMK-5	$120-$125
84/0	5"	TMK-6	$120-$125
84/0	5"	TMK-7	$115-$145 60th Anniversary Decal 1998
84/0	5"	TMK-8	$219 retail
84/V	13"	TMK-1	$1,200-$1,800
84/V	13"	TMK-2	$1,020-$1200
84/V	13"	TMK-3	$990-$1,050
84/V	13"	TMK-4	$970-$1,050
84/V	13"	TMK-5	$960-$1,020
84/V	13"	TMK-6	$950-$1,020

Hum 84: Worship.

Hum No.	Basic Size	Trademark	Current Value
84/V	13"	TMK-7	$930-$990
84/V	13"	TMK-8	$930-$990

Hum 85: Serenade

Introduced in the late-1930s and originally modeled by master sculptor Arthur Moeller, this figurine has undergone normal changes of style, colors, and finishes over the years, but none have had a significant impact on the collector value. It has been called The Flutist in some early company literature.

An interesting variation concerns the boy's fingers on the flute. You can find figures with some fingers extended while other versions have all fingers down. It seems, however, that there is no association with any particular mark or marks one way or the other.

The decimal designator can be found with the mold number on the older Crown Mark (TMK-1) pieces in both sizes.

There is a beautiful blue Hum 85 in the 7-1/2" size. It has no apparent markings. So far, this is the only one in a blue suit to

be found. It seems peculiar that the normal Serenades were not rendered in blue, as that is the color M.I. Hummel used in the original artwork (H 342) on which the piece is modeled. There has also been a Serenade found with the incised mold number 85/0. This one is painted with an airbrush rather than the usual brush. Both of these are most likely samples that did not obtain the approval of the convent.

Recently, a 12-1/2" version of Serenade was introduced as part of the "Millennium Love" series, which

Hum 85: Serenade.

Hum No.	Basic Size	Trademark	Current Value
85/4/0	3-1/2"	TMK-5	$80-$85
85/4/0	3-1/2"	TMK-6	$70-$80
85/4/0	3-1/2"	TMK-7	$70-$80
85/0	4-3/4"	TMK-1	$240-$300
85/0	4-3/4"	TMK-2	$135-$180
85/0	4-3/4"	TMK-3	$120-$135
85/0	4-3/4"	TMK-4	$110-$120
85/0	4-3/4"	TMK-5	$105-$110
85/0	4-3/4"	TMK-6	$99-$105
85/0	4-3/4" to 5-1/4"	TMK-7	$99-$105
85/0	4-3/4" to 5-1/4"	TMK-8	$179 retail
85.	7-1/2"	TMK-1	$750-$925
85/II	7-1/2"	TMK-1	$720-$900
85/II	7-1/2"	TMK-2	$450-$570
85	7-1/2"	TMK-2	$465-$585
85/II	7-1/2"	TMK-3	$390-$420
85/II	7-1/2"	TMK-4	$360-$390
85/II	7-1/2"	TMK-5	$330-$360
85/II	7-1/2"	TMK-6	$315-$330
85/II	7" to 7-1/2"	TMK-7	$300-$325
85/III	12-1/2"	TMK-8	$1,550 retail

also included Sweet Music (Hum 186/III), Little Fiddler (Hum 2/III), Band Leader (Hum 129/III), and Soloist (Hum 135/ III). These oversized pieces (Hum 85/III) were in limited supply and had to be special-ordered through an authorized M.I. Hummel retailer.

The 85/4/0 and 85/II size variations have been temporarily withdrawn from production.

Hum 86: Happiness

Another late-1930s entry into the collection, this piece was first crafted by master sculptor Reinhold Unger in 1938. Although its name has changed from the original Wandersong and Traveler's Song, there have been no other changes or variations significant enough to affect value. Sizes reported in various lists are 4-1/2", 4-1/4", 5", and 5-1/2".

Hum No.	Basic Size	Trademark	Current Value
86	4-3/4"	TMK-1	$240-$300
86	4-3/4"	TMK-2	$160-$215
86	4-3/4"	TMK-3	$120-$140
86	4-3/4"	TMK-4	$105-$120
86	4-3/4"	TMK-5	$105-$110
86	4-3/4"	TMK-6	$99-$105
86	4-1/2" to 5"	TMK-7	$95-$125 60th Anniversary Decal 1998
86	4-1/2" to 5"	TMK-8	$95

Hum 86: Happiness.

Hum 87: For Father

For Father is yet another late-1930s release, formerly called Father's Joy and originally designed by master sculptor Arthur Moeller in 1938.

The significant variations have to do with the beer stein and the color of the radishes. A few early Crown Mark (TMK-1) pieces have been found with the initials "HB" painted on the stein. The radishes on these figures have a definite greenish cast. These pieces are rare and can be priced as high as $2,000.

The other important variation is found on Full Bee (TMK-2) and Stylized Bee (TMK-3) trademark figures, where the radishes are colored orange to more closely resemble carrots than radishes. The collector value for this variation is $1,500-$2,400.

In 1996, Goebel announced the "Personal Touch" figurines, one of which was For Father. Goebel will inscribe onto the figure a personalization of your choice. The other three original figures used for personalization in the "Personal Touch" line were Bird Duet (Hum 69), Latest News (Hum 184), and The Guardian (Hum 455).

In the summer of 2002, a smaller 4-1/4" variation of For Father was announced. Sculpted by master

Hum 87: For Father.

Hum No.	Basic Size	Trademark	Current Value
87	5-1/2"	TMK-1	$420-$480
87	5-1/2"	TMK-2	$240-$330
87	5-1/2"	TMK-3	$195-$225
87	5-1/2"	TMK-4	$165-$200
87	5-1/2"	TMK-5	$165-$185
87	5-1/2"	TMK-6	$160-$175
87	5-1/2"	TMK-7	$165-$185 60th Anniversary Decal 1998
87	5-1/2"	TMK-8	$165-$175
87/2/0	4-1/4"	TMK-8	$165-$175 75th Anniversary Backstamp

sculptor Helmut Fischer, the smaller piece carries model number 87/2/0, a "First Issue 2002" backstamp, and TMK-8.

The year 2011 marked the celebration of Sister Hummel's 75th anniversary of the beginning of her legacy. Manufaktur Rödental selected 50 figurines to bear the "75th Anniversary" backstamp. For Father was one of those figurines. Only 75 of them were available in North America with this backstamp. Each figurine was hand-numbered with a golden backstamp and a map of North America backstamp. A special porcelain plaque was included, and a notable emblem on the packaging hinted at the contents. Each figurine included a "75 Years of M.I. Hummel" certificate.

Hum 88: Heavenly Protection

This figure, which was originally crafted by master sculptor Reinhold Unger, was first introduced in the late-1930s in the 9-1/4" size with a decimal designator 88. (with decimal) or 88 (without the decimal) in the Crown Mark (TMK-1), the Full Bee (TMK-2), and the Stylized Bee (TMK-3) trademarks.

The transition from the 88 to the 88/II mold number took quite some time. It began in the Full Bee era and was completed in the Stylized Bee era, so you can find the mold number rendered either way with either of those two trademarks.

The large size has been found in white overglaze in the Crown and Full Bee marks.

There is a similar piece in the Goebel line that some theorize may have either inspired Heavenly Protection or was inspired by it. It is mold number HS 1. Also see Hum 108.

Hum 88: Heavenly Protection.

Hum No.	Basic Size	Trademark	Current Value
88/I	6-3/4"	TMK-3	$390-$450
88/I	6-3/4"	TMK-4	$345-$395
88/I	6-3/4"	TMK-5	$330-$345
88/I	6-3/4"	TMK-6	$315-$325
88/I	6-1/4" to 6-3/4"	TMK-7	$315-$340 60th Anniversary Decal 1998
88/I	6-1/4" to 6-3/4"	TMK-8	$529 retail
88. or 88	9-1/4"	TMK-1	$1,080-$1,440
88. or 88	9-1/4"	TMK-2	$780-$960
88. or 88	9-1/4"	TMK-3	$660-$720
88/II	9-1/4"	TMK-2	$600-$780
88/II	9-1/4"	TMK-3	$600-$660
88/II	9-1/4"	TMK-4	$540-$600
88/II	9-1/4"	TMK-5	$510-$570
88/II	9-1/4"	TMK-6	$315-$510
88/II	8-3/4" to 9"	TMK-7	$480-$510

The larger 88/II size was temporarily withdrawn in 1994, reinstated for a short time, and once again withdrawn from production in 1999.

Hum 89: Little Cellist

Master sculptor Arthur Moeller originally designed this figurine in 1938 under the name Musician. Other than the name change, there have been no major variations over the years that would have an impact on the collector value of this figurine.

There are some differences worth noting, however. The newer models have a base that has flattened corners. The older models have squared-off corners. Also in the older models, the boy's  head is up and his eyes are wide open, whereas on the new models his head is down and his eyes are cast down as if concentrating on his steps. The transition from old to new style was during the Stylized Bee (TMK-3) era, so the old and the new can be found with this mark, the older obviously being the more desirable to collectors.

The larger 89/II size was temporarily withdrawn from production in 1993.

Hum 89: Little Cellist.

Hum No.	Basic Size	Trademark	Current Value
89/I	6"	TMK-1	$450-$510
89/I	6"	TMK-2	$270-$320
89/I	6"	TMK-3	$195-$200
89/I	6"	TMK-4	$170-$195
89/I	6"	TMK-5	$165-$175
89/I	6"	TMK-6	$160-$170
89/I	5-1/4" to 6-1/4"	TMK-7	$155-$190 60th Anniversary Decal 1998
89/I	5-1/4" to 6-1/4"	TMK-8	$279 retail
89.	8"	TMK-1	$840-$1,025
89	8"	TMK-1	$750-$960
89/II	7-1/2" to 7-3/4"	TMK-1	$720-$900
89/II	7-1/2" to 7-3/4"	TMK-2	$480-$600
89/II	7-1/2" to 7-3/4"	TMK-3	$390-$450
89/II	7-1/2" to 7-3/4"	TMK-4	$360-$390
89/II	7-1/2" to 7-3/4"	TMK-5	$300-$330
89/II	7-1/2" to 7-3/4"	TMK-6	$285-$300
89/II	7-1/2" to 7-3/4"	TMK-7	$270-$285

Hum 90/A and Hum 90/B: Eventide and Adoration
Bookends

Up until late 1984 it was thought that these pieces were never produced except in sample form and never were released on the market. The Adoration half of the set has been found, however. It is not likely that these bookends were ever put into production, but more than one was obviously made as at least two of the Adoration halves have made it into private collections.

Hum 90/A and Hum 90/B: Eventide and Adoration bookends.

Hum No.	Basic Size	Trademark	Current Value
90/A&B	–	–	$6,000-$9,000
90/B	4"	–	$3,000-$4,500

Hum 91/A and 91/B: Angel at Prayer
Holy Water Font

The angel facing left likely was made first since it exists in TMK-1 by itself and without an "A" designator. Thereafter, however, the fonts were released as a set with one facing left (91/A) and the other right (91/B).

The only notable variation in these figures is that the older ones have no halo and the newer models do. The transition from no halo to halo took place in the Stylized Bee (TMK-3) era, and both types of figures may be found in that trademark.

Hum 91/A and 91/B: Angel at Prayer holy water font.

Hum No.	Basic Size	Trademark	Current Value
91	3-1/4" x 4-1/2"	TMK-1	$240-$300
91/A&B	2" x 4-3/4"	TMK-1	$240-$300
91/A&B	2" x 4-3/4"	TMK-2	$120-$165
91/A&B	2" x 4-3/4"	TMK-3	$80-$95
91/A&B	2" x 4-3/4"	TMK-3	$80-$95
91/A&B	2" x 4-3/4"	TMK-4	$70-$80
91/A&B	2" x 4-3/4"	TMK-5	$70-$75
91/A&B	2" x 4-3/4"	TMK-6	$65-$70
91/A&B	3-3/8" x 5"	TMK-7	$65-$70
91/A&B	3-3/8" x 5"	TMK-8	$139 retail

Hum 92: Merry Wanderer
Wall Plaque

Hum No.	Basic Size	Trademark	Current Value
92	4-3/4" x 5-1/8"	TMK-1	$270-$345
92	4-3/4" x 5-1/8"	TMK-2	$170-$210
92	4-3/4" x 5-1/8"	TMK-3	$165-$185
92	4-3/4" x 5-1/8"	TMK-4	$110-$135
92	4-3/4" x 5-1/8"	TMK-5	$99-$105
92	4-3/4" x 5-1/8"	TMK-6	$90-$100

Master sculptor Arthur Moeller originally designed this piece in 1938, and it has gone through several redesigns since.

There are two distinct sizes to be found in the Crown (TMK-1) and Full Bee (TMK-2) trademark pieces. The newer ones are all in the smaller size. There are also some differences with regard to the placement of the incised M.I. Hummel signature, but there are no variations having a significant impact on the collector value. Some of the older Crown Mark pieces have been found with the decimal designator.

The piece was temporarily withdrawn from production in 1989.

Hum 92: Merry Wanderer wall plaque.

Hum 93: Little Fiddler
Wall Plaque

Hum No.	Basic Size	Trademark	Current Value
93	4-3/4" x 5-1/8"	TMK-1	$270-$345
93	4-3/4" x 5-1/8"	TMK-2	$165-$220
93	4-3/4" x 5-1/8"	TMK-3	$135-$165
93	4-3/4" x 5-1/8"	TMK-4	$105-$140
93	4-3/4" x 5-1/8"	TMK-5	$99-$105
93	4-3/4" x 5-1/8"	TMK-6	$90-$95
93 rare old style	–	TMK-1	$1,800-$2,400

Originally crafted by master sculptor Arthur Moeller in 1938, this plaque bears the Little Fiddler motif, which appears many times in the collection. The older models show less background detail. The older one is quite rare and is valued at $1,800-$2,400.

Some pieces display a 1938 copyright date, while others do not. Additionally, some bear the "M.I. Hummel" signature on both front and back, while other have it on either just the front or just the back.

This plaque was temporarily withdrawn from production on Dec. 31, 1989.

Hum 93: Little Fiddler wall plaque.

Hum 94: Surprise

Hum No.	Basic Size	Trademark	Current Value
94/3/0	4-1/4"	TMK-1	$270-$330
94/3/0	4-1/4"	TMK-2	$165-$230
94/3/0	4-1/4"	TMK-3	$135-$150
94/3/0	4-1/4"	TMK-4	$120-$135
94/3/0	4-1/4"	TMK-5	$120-$135
94/3/0	4-1/4"	TMK-6	$110-$120
94/3/0	4" to 4-1/4"	TMK-7	$105-$115
94/3/0	4" to 4-1/4"	TMK-8	$219 retail
94	5-1/2"	TMK-1	$480-$600
94	5-1/2"	TMK-2	$330-$420
94/I	5-1/2"	TMK-1	$450-$570
94/I	5-1/2"	TMK-2	$300-$390
94/I	5-1/2"	TMK-3	$255-$285
94/I	5-1/2"	TMK-4	$240-$255
94/I	5-1/2"	TMK-5	$210-$240
94/I	5-1/2"	TMK-6	$210-$225
94/I	5-1/4" to 5-1/2"	TMK-7	$195-$210

Designed by a group of sculptors and first placed in the line in the late-1930s in two basic sizes, this figurine continues in production in only the smaller of those sizes today. It has been called The Duet and Hansel and Gretel in past company literature, as well as What's Up?

The 94/I size has been found erroneously marked 94/II. The error was apparently caught early, for only a very few have shown up.

Older examples of the 94/I size have been found without the "/I".

The smaller 94/3/0 size is less detailed than the larger 94/I size, which was temporarily withdrawn from production in 1999.

Hum 94: Surprise.

Hum 95: Brother

Previously known as Our Hero and Hero of the Village and designed collectively by a group of sculptors, this figurine can be found in many size and color variations. For example, the older mold style comes with a blue coat.

The earliest Crown Mark (TMK-1) pieces can be found with the decimal point designator, but there are no other variations of any great significance. It is the same boy used in Surprise (Hum 94).

The 1998 piece bears a special "60th Anniversary" decal and metal tag.

Hum No.	Basic Size	Trademark	Current Value
95	5-1/2"	TMK-1	$450-$480
95	5-1/2"	TMK-2	$210-$300
95	5-1/2"	TMK-3	$185-$195
95	5-1/2"	TMK-4	$170-$180
95	5-1/2"	TMK-5	$150-$165
95	5-1/2"	TMK-6	$150-$165
95	5-1/4" to 5-3/4"	TMK-7	$145-$165 60th Anniversary Decal 1998
95	5-1/4" to 5-3/4"	TMK-8	$165-$175

Hum 95: Brother.

Hum 96: Little Shopper

Introduced in the late-1930s and formerly known as "Errand Girl," "Gretel," and "Meg," this figurine has changed little over the years. Like some of the other pieces crafted in 1938, it was the collective work of a group of sculptors. It is the same girl used in Hum 94: Surprise.

Hum No.	Basic Size	Trademark	Current Value
96	4-3/4"	TMK-1	$260-$330
96	4-3/4"	TMK-2	$165-$210
96	4-3/4"	TMK-3	$130-$150
96	4-3/4"	TMK-4	$115-$130
96	4-3/4"	TMK-5	$110-$125
96	4-3/4"	TMK-6	$105-$125
96	4-1/2" to 5"	TMK-7	$105-$115
96	4-1/2" to 5"	TMK-8	$105-$115

Hum 96: Little Shopper.

Hum 97: Trumpet Boy

Originally called The Little Musician, this piece was designed by master sculptor Arthur Moeller in 1938.

In addition to many size variations, there is an especially notable color variation. The boy's coat is normally green, but some of the older models, particularly those produced during the post-war U.S. Occupation era, have a blue painted coat.

Trumpet Boy in the Crown Mark (TMK-1) is fairly rare, but most assuredly exists. The Crown Mark era piece will have "Design Patent No. 116, 464" inscribed beneath (see accompanying photo).

A query with a photograph to Goebel regarding this anomaly brought the following response: "The Trumpet Boy shown in the photo seems to be a very old figurine dating back to pre-war years. The bottom of the piece allows the assumption that production date may go back as far as the late-1930s (possibly cast from the first model). The stamp Design Patent No. 116.464 indicates that the piece was originally shipped to England. All merchandise shipped at that time to that country was liable to be marked with the respective design patent number...." The collector value for a Trumpet Boy so marked is $1,000-$1,500.

Hum No.	Basic Size	Trademark	Current Value
97	4-3/4"	TMK-1	$240-$315
97	4-3/4"	TMK-2	$150-$180
97	4-3/4"	TMK-3	$120-$140
97	4-3/4"	TMK-4	$110-$135
97	4-3/4"	TMK-5	$105-$110
97	4-3/4"	TMK-6	$99-$105
97	4-3/4"	TMK-7	$90-$105

Hum 97: Trumpet Boy.

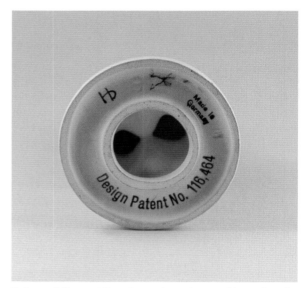

Bottom of Trumpet Boy shows the unique mold number discussed in the accompanying text.

Hum 98: Sister

This figure, which was crafted by master sculptor Arthur Moeller in 1938, was introduced in the late-1930s in the 5-3/4" basic size with the incised number 98, and a smaller size was introduced during the Stylized Bee (TMK-3) trademark period with the incised 98/2/0. The piece was originally known as The Shopper and The First Shopping in early company literature, and this is the same girl used in Hum 49: To Market.

Some of the larger size pieces from the Crown Mark (TMK-1) era through the Stylized Bee (TMK-3) era are found with the 98 mold number with and without the decimal designator (see Hum 788/B).

A special "60th Anniversary" decal appeared on the 1998 piece created in the smaller 98/2/0 size.

Hum 98: Sister.

Hum No.	Basic Size	Trademark	Current Value
98/5/0	2-3/4"	TMK-7	$55
98/2/0	4-3/4"	TMK-3	$140-$150
98/2/0	4-3/4"	TMK-4	$115-$135
98/2/0	4-3/4"	TMK-5	$110-$120
98/2/0	4-3/4"	TMK-6	$105-$120
98/0	4-12" to 4-3/4"	TMK-7	$105-$125 60th Anniversary decal 1998
98/0	4-1/2" to 4-3/4"	TMK-8	$105-$110
98.	5-1/4"	TMK-1	$330-$420
98.	5-3/4"	TMK-2	$210-$270
98.	5-3/4"	TMK-3	$195-$210
98/0	5-3/4"	TMK-3	$180-$195
98/0	5-3/4"	TMK-4	$165-$180
98/0	5-3/4"	TMK-5	$150-$165
98/0	5-3/4"	TMK-6	$150-$165
98/0	5-1/4" to 5-1/2"	TMK-7	$140-$160

The larger 98/0 size was temporarily withdrawn from production in 1999.

Hum 99: Eventide

Crafted by the collective efforts of a group of sculptors, this piece is almost identical to Hum 28: Wayside Devotion but without the shrine.

There are three versions of this figurine to be found. Apparently when first released in the late-1930s, the lambs were placed toward the left side of the base. For whatever reason, they were moved to the right side soon after and there they remained through the most recent production of the piece (TMK-7). This piece has also been found without the sheep. The collector value range for both the left-side sheep and the no sheep versions is $1,800-$2,100. There is also a rare white overglazed version valued at about the same amount.

This figurine was temporarily withdrawn from production in 1999. Eventide was reintroduced by Manufaktur Rödental under TMK-9 with the 100 years backstamp. The 100 years backstamp is only available for figurines produced in 2009.

Hum 99: Eventide.

Hum No.	Basic Size	Trademark	Current Value
99	4-3/4"	TMK-1	$570-$760
99	4-3/4"	TMK-2	$360-$450
99	4-3/4"	TMK-3	$300-$330
99	4-3/4"	TMK-4	$260-$300
99	4-3/4"	TMK-5	$240-$260
99	4-3/4"	TMK-6	$225-$240

Hum No.	Basic Size	Trademark	Current Value
99	4-1/4" x 5"	TMK-7	$220-$225
99 (rare version)	–	TMK-1	$1,800-$2,100
99	4-1/4" x 4-3/4"	TMK-9	$389 retail

Hum 100: Shrine
Table Lamp

In 1938, sculptor Erich Lautensack designed this extremely rare 7-1/2" table lamp containing a figure similar to Hum 23: Adoration. As far as can be determined, only three or four currently exist in collectors' hands. The lamps found so far bear the Crown (TMK-1) or the Full Bee (TMK-2) trademarks. There are two versions of the lamppost. The most common is the tree trunk post. The rarest is the fluted post.

Hum No.	Basic Size	Trademark	Current Value
100	7-1/2"	TMK-1	$4,800-$6,000
100	7-1/2"	TMK-2	$4,800-$6,000

Hum 101: To Market
Table Lamp

Hum 101: To Market table lamp.

This piece, which was designed by master sculptor Arthur Moeller in 1937, was quickly listed as a closed edition the same year. However, after a redesign by Moeller in 1952, a limited number were produced again in the early 1950s. This lamp is an adaptation of Hum 49: To Market.

There are two versions of this lamp with regard to the lamp stem or post. Of the few

Hum No.	Basic Size	Trademark	Current Value
101 (plain)	6-1/2"	TMK-1	$4,800-$6,000
101 (plain)	6-1/2"	TMK-2	$3,600-$4,800
101	7-1/2"	TMK-1	$900-$1,200 tree trunk
101	7-1/2"	TMK-2	$450-$600
101	7-1/2"	TMK-3	$300-$450

that have been found, most exhibit the "tree trunk" base, which was part of the 1950s redesign. Rarer are the less elaborate fluted stem and plain stem examples. The "plain" description refers only to the paint finish; the CM fluted stem is painted white, whereas the plain version is painted light beige. The plain version is found in both the Crown and the Full Bee trademarks.

Hum 102: Volunteers
Table Lamp

Another Erich Lautensack design from 1937, there are only a few examples of this piece known to exist in private collections. It was listed as a closed edition in April 1937 and the few found so far all bear the Crown Mark (TMK-1) and have a plain white post.

Hum 102: Volunteers table lamp.

Hum No.	Basic Size	Trademark	Current Value
102	7-1/2"	TMK-1	$4,800-$6,000

Hum 103: Farewell
Table Lamp

Master sculptor Erich Lautensack designed this extremely rare piece in 1937 and it was listed as a closed edition the very same year. Very few are known to exist.

Hum 103: Farewell table lamp.

Hum No.	Basic Size	Trademark	Current Value
103	7-1/2"	TMK-1	$4,800-$6,000

Hum 104: Eventide
Table Lamp

Very few examples of this table lamp, which was crafted by master sculptor Reinhold Unger in 1938, are known to be in collectors' hands at present. It is similar to the figurine of the same name, Hum 99, except for the positioning of the lambs, which are centered in front of the children on the lamp base rather than off to the right as in the figurine.

Hum No.	Basic Size	Trademark	Current Value
104	7-1/2"	TMK-1	$4,800-$6,000

Hum 105: Adoration With Bird

First discovered about 1977, this piece was not previously thought to exist. It bears the mold number 105. This number was a "closed number," a number supposedly never used and never intended for use on an original Hummel piece. There have been at least 10 to 15 pieces found since the initial discovery. Because of its similarity to Hum 23: Adoration, it was probably designed by master sculptor Reinhold Unger, although there are no records to verify that assumption. The major variation in the figures that have been found is in the girl's pigtail, in which some are very detailed and others are not.

Hum No.	Basic Size	Trademark	Current Value
105	4-3/4"	TMK-1	$4,200-$4,800

Hum 105: Adoration With Bird.

Hum 106: Merry Wanderer
Wall Plaque

Hum 106: Merry Wanderer wall plaque.

Limited examples have been found of this extremely rare plaque, which was designed by master sculptor Arthur Moeller in 1938 and apparently only made for a short time. Perhaps this is because the plaque is basically the same as Hum 92: Merry Wanderer plaque, except for the wooden frame. Of those that have been found, all have the Crown Mark (TMK-1).

Hum No.	Basic Size	Trademark	Current Value
106	6" x 6"	TMK-1	$1,800-$2,400

Hum 107: Little Fiddler
Wall Plaque

Hum 107: Little Fiddler wall plaque.

Limited examples of this extremely rare plaque have been found, even though it is listed as a closed edition. Crafted by master sculptor Arthur Moeller in 1938, it was apparently only made for a short time. Perhaps this is because the plaque is basically the same as Hum 93: Little Fiddler plaque, except for the wooden frame. Those that have been found all have the Crown Mark (TMK-1).

Hum No.	Basic Size	Trademark	Current Value
107	6" x 6"	TMK-1	$1,800-$2,400

Hum 108: Angel With Two Children at Feet
Wall Plaque in Relief, Closed Number

It is unlikely that any of these will ever find their way into collectors' hands since it is a closed number with only one reference in factory records in 1938. Master sculptor Reinhold Unger apparently designed it the same year, and it is thought that it was not approved by Siessen Convent for regular production.

A 1950s Goebel catalog lists the plaque as described, but it is not listed as a Hummel design. The deduction is made because of the description similar to the name and the mold number designation of 108 listed in factory records.

Hum No.	Basic Size	Trademark	Current Value
108	-	TMK-1	$6,000-$9,000
Goebel HS01	10-1/4"	TMK-1	$1,800-$3,000
Goebel HS01	10-1/4"	TMK-1 & 2	$1,500-$2,700

Hum 108: Angel With Two Children at Feet wall plaque in relief (closed number).

Hum 109: Happy Traveler

This figurine, which was designed by master sculptor Arthur Moeller in 1938, was placed in production in the late-1930s in a 5" basic size. An 8" basic size was added in the Full Bee (TMK-2) era and then retired in 1982.

There has been a curious variation to surface in the 109/0 size. The normal colors for the figurine are brown for the hat and green for the jacket. The variation has a green hat and a blue jacket. It has no trademark and is the only one known. It may be unique.

The 109/0 size was temporarily withdrawn from production on June 15, 2002.

Hum No.	w Size	Trademark	Current Value
109/0	4-3/4" to 5"	TMK-2	$165-$225
109/0 or 109	4-3/4" to 5"	TMK-3	$135-$150
109/0 or 109	4-3/4" to 5"	TMK-4	$120-$135
109/0 or 109	4-3/4" to 5"	TMK-5	$110-$120
109/0	4-3/4" to 5"	TMK-6	$110-$120
109/0	4-3/4" to 5"	TMK-7	$105-$110
109/0	4-3/4" to 5"	TMK-8	$175 retail
109/II	8"	TMK-1	$720-$900
109/II	8"	TMK-2	$480-$540
109/II	8"	TMK-3	$300-$330
109/II	8"	TMK-4	$270-$300
109/II	8"	TMK-5	$240-$255
109/II	8"	TMK-6	$230-$240

Hum 109: Happy Traveler.

Hum 110: Let's Sing

Master sculptor Reinhold Unger designed this piece, which was one of the group of new designs introduced in the late-1930s. Although there are many size variations, there have been no variations significant enough to have any impact on the normal pricing structure for the various pieces.

Hum 110: Let's Sing.

Hum No.	Basic Size	Trademark	Current Value
110	3-1/2"	TMK-1	$285-$360
110	3-1/2"	TMK-2	$200-$240
110/0	3-1/4"	TMK-1	$210-$300
110/0	3-1/4"	TMK-2	$135-$180
110/0	3-1/4"	TMK-3	$120-$135
110/0	3-1/4"	TMK-4	$115-$125
110/0	3-1/4"	TMK-5	$110-$120
110/0	3-1/4"	TMK-6	$110-$120
110/0	3" to 3-1/4"	TMK-7	$110-$120
110/0	3" to 3-1/4"	TMK-8	$179
110/I	3-7/8"	TMK-1	$125-$240
110/I	3-7/8"	TMK-2	$180-$240
110/I	3-7/8"	TMK-3	$150-$180
110/I	3-7/8"	TMK-4	$140-$150
110/I	3-7/8"	TMK-5	$125-$145
110/I	3-7/8"	TMK-6	$120-$130
110/I	3-1/4" to 4"	TMK-7	$120-$130
110/I	3-1/4" to 4"	TMK-8	$120-$130

Hum III/110: Let's Sing
Candy Box

There are two styles of candy boxes: bowl-like and jar-like. The transition from the old bowls to the new jars took place during the Stylized Bee (TMK-3) period. Therefore both the old and the new can be found in the Stylized Bee mark.

This piece was temporarily removed from production in 1989.

Hum III/110: Let's Sing candy box.

Hum No.	Basic Size	Trademark	Current Value
III/110	6"	TMK-1	$450-$510
III/110	6"	TMK-2	$345-$400
III/110 (old)	6"	TMK-3	$180-$225
III/110 (new)	6"	TMK-3	$100-$200
III/110	6"	TMK-4	$100-$150
III/110	6"	TMK-5	$100-$150
III/110	6"	TMK-6	$120-$150

Hum 111: Wayside Harmony

This figure, which was crafted in 1938 by master sculptor Reinhold Unger, was introduced in the late-1930s. It was previously called Just Sittin-Boy.

It has changed a bit over the years, but there are no variations that have any significant impact on the collector value. However, there does exist a curious variation where the bird is missing. This is an aberration wherein the bird was probably inadvertently left off during assembly. This sometimes happens to small parts and is not considered a rare variation.

This piece has been known to appear with Roman numeral size designators instead of the Arabic number indicated.

The Hum 111/I size was temporarily withdrawn from production on June 15, 2002.

Hum 111: Wayside Harmony.

Hum No.	Basic Size	Trademark	Current Value
111/3/0	3-3/4"	TMK-1	$270-$330
111/3/0	3-3/4"	TMK-2	$180-$240
111/3/0	3-3/4"	TMK-3	$140-$160
111/3/0	3-3/4"	TMK-4	$120-$145
111/3/0	3-3/4"	TMK-5	$110-$120
111/3/0	3-3/4"	TMK-6	$110-$115
111/3/0	3-3/4" to 4"	TMK-7	$110-$115
111/3/0	3-3/4" to 4"	TMK-8	$185 retail
111.	5"	TMK-1	$420-$510
111/I	5"	TMK-1	$390-$480
111/I	5"	TMK-2	$270-$330

Hum No.	Basic Size	Trademark	Current Value
111/I	5"	TMK-3	$240-$270
111/I	5"	TMK-4	$210-$240
111/I	5"	TMK-5	$150-$220
111/I	5"	TMK-6	$150-$200
111/I	5" to 5-1/2"	TMK-7	$195-$200

Hum II/111: Wayside Harmony
Table Lamp

Hum No.	Basic Size	Trademark	Current Value
II/111	7-1/2"	TMK-1	$480-$525
II/111	7-1/2"	TMK-2	$300-$500
II/111	7-1/2"	TMK-3	$230-$315

This lamp, which is the same design as the figurine of the same name (Hum 111), was made for a short period of time in the 1950s. Perhaps to avoid confusion and/or to conform with the mold numbering system, the lamp was slightly redesigned and assigned a new number, Hum 224/I. Whatever the reason, there are a few of these II/111 Wayside Harmony lamps around. They occur in the Crown (TMK-1), Full Bee (TMK-2), and Stylized Bee (TMK-3). The figures are quite scarce, but for some reason are not worth as much as some of the other equally as rare pieces.

Hum 112: Just Resting

Master sculptor Reinhold Unger designed this piece in 1938, when it was then called Just Sittin-Girl.

There have been no variations significant enough to influence the normal pricing structure of this piece. However, one example has been found of a curious variation on the 112/I size; there is no basket present on the base. This was probably the result of an inadvertent omission while it was being assembled, slipping by the quality control inspectors. This happens occasionally with small pieces such as bottles in baskets and birds. It is not usually considered important but merely a curiosity.

The larger 112/I size was temporarily withdrawn from production in 1999.

Hum No.	Basic Size	Trademark	Current Value
112/3/0	3-3/4"	TMK-1	$240-$330
112/3/0	3-3/4"`	TMK-2	$165-$210
112/3/0	3-3/4"	TMK-3	$145-$165
112/3/0	3-3/4"	TMK-4	$120-$140
112/3/0	3-3/4"	TMK-5	$110-$130
112/3/0	3-3/4"	TMK-6	$110-$120
112/3/0	3-3/4" to 4"	TMK-7	$105-$110
112/3/0	3-3/4" to 4"	TMK-8	$179 retail
112	5"	TMK-1	$420-$510
112/I	5"	TMK-1	$390-$480
112/I	5"	TMK-2	$270-$360
112/I	5"	TMK-3	$240-$300
112/I	5"	TMK-4	$210-$240

Hum 112: Just Resting.

Hum No.	Basic Size	Trademark	Current Value
112/I	5"	TMK-5	$150-$220
112/I	5"	TMK-6	$150-$220
112/I	4-3/4" to 5-1/2"	TMK-7	$195-$210

Hum II/112: Just Resting
Table Lamp

Hum No.	Basic Size	Trademark	Current Value
II/112	7-1/2"	TMK-1	$480-$525
II/112	7-1/2"	TMK-2	$300-$500
II/112	7-1/2"	TMK-3	$225-$315
112	7"	TMK-1 & 2	$3,000-$3,600

This lamp, which is the same design as the figurine of the same name (Hum 112), was made for a short period of time in the 1950s. Perhaps to avoid confusion and/or confirm the mold numbering system, the number was changed to 225/I with a concurrent slight redesign. Whatever the reason, there are a few of these II/112 Just Resting lamps around. They occur in the Crown (TMK-1), Full Bee (TMK-2), and Stylized Bee (TMK3). Although quite rare, for some reason these lamps, like the Wayside Harmony lamps (Hum II/111), are not worth as much as some of the equally hard to find pieces.

Hum 113: Heavenly Song
Candleholder

This four-figure piece, which was crafted in 1938 by master sculptor Arthur Moeller, is a candleholder. It is quite similar to Hum 54: Silent Night and was produced in extremely small numbers. Only a few are known to exist in private collections. The actual number is not known, but less than 50 would be a reasonable estimate. They do pop up from time to time and have been found in the Crown (TMK-1), Full Bee (TMK-2), Stylized Bee (TMK-3), and Last Bee (TMK-5), but it is extremely rare in any trademark. It has also been found in the faience style, but is extremely rare in that finish as well and would be worth $3,000-$5,000.

Goebel announced in 1981 that it was removing Heavenly Song from production permanently.

Hum No.	Basic Size	Trademark	Current Value
113	3-1/2" x 4-3/4"	TMK-1	$3,600-$6,000
113	3-1/2" x 4-3/4"	TMK-2	$2,700-$3,000
113	3-1/2" x 4-3/4"	TMK-3	$2,100-$2,700
113	3-1/2" x 4-3/4"	TMK-5	$1,800-$2,100

Hum 113: Heavenly Song candleholder. This is a rare porcelain-like figurine that may fall into the faience category. It has an incised Crown (TMK-1), but the incised M.I. Hummel signature is either too light to discern or is absent.

Hum 114: Let's Sing
Ashtray

This piece, which was crafted by master sculptor Reinhold Unger in 1938, is an ashtray with a figure very like Hum 110 at the edge of the dish. It is found with the figure on either the right or left side of the tray. Viewed from the front, the older ones have the figure on the right side. There are very few of this variation known. It was changed during the Full Bee (TMK-2), so it can be found with either the Crown or Full Bee trademark.

As is the case with all the ashtrays in the line, this piece is listed as temporarily withdrawn from production with no reinstatement date given.

Hum No.	Basic Size	Trademark	Current Value
114 (on right)	3-1/2" x 6-3/4"	TMK-1	$510-$600
114 (on right)	3-1/2" x 6-3/4"	TMK-2	$360-$510
114	3-1/2" x 6-3/4"	TMK-2	$305-$210
114	3-1/2" x 6-3/4"	TMK-3	$140-$155
114	3-1/2" x 6-3/4"	TMK-4	$105-$140
114	3-1/2" x 6-3/4"	TMK-5	$99-$105
114	3-1/2" x 6-3/4"	TMK-6	$90-$100

Hum 114: Let's Sing ashtray.

Hum 115: Girl With Nosegay, Hum 116: Girl With Fir Tree, & Hum 117: Boy With Horse

Advent Group Candleholders

This group of three figurines has a Christmas theme, and each of the figures is provided with a candle receptacle. Master sculptor Reinhold Unger is credited with the design in 1938.

The original models were made with the "Mel" prefix followed by 1, 2, and 3 for 115, 116, and 117, respectively. These were prototypes, but many apparently got into the market. These pieces tend to sell for $300-$350 apiece.

All three pieces in the 3-1/2" size were temporarily withdrawn from production on June 15, 2002.

Hum 115: Girl With Nosegay, Hum 116: Girl With Fir Tree, and Hum 117: Boy With Horse advent group candleholders.

Hum No.	Basic Size	Trademark	Current Value
115	3-1/2"	TMK-1	$120-$135
115	3-1/2"	TMK-2	$70-$80
115	3-1/2"	TMK-3	$55-$60
115	3-1/2"	TMK-4	$55-$60
115	3-1/2"	TMK-5	$45-$50
115	3-1/2"	TMK-6	$40-$45
115	3-1/2"	TMK-7	$40-$45
115	3-1/2"	TMK-8	$40-$45
116	3-1/2"	TMK-1	$120-$150
116	3-1/2"	TMK-2	$75-$85
116	3-1/2"	TMK-3	$55-$60
116	3-1/2"	TMK-4	$50-$60
116	3-1/2"	TMK-5	$45-$55
116	3-1/2"	TMK-6	$40-$45
116	3-1/2"	TMK-7	$40-$45
116	3-1/2"	TMK-8	$40-$50
117	3-1/2"	TMK-1	$120-$150
117	3-1/2"	TMK-2	$70-$85
117	3-1/2"	TMK-3	$55-$60
117	3-1/2"	TMK-4	$55-$60
117	3-1/2"	TMK-5	$45-$50
117	3-1/2"	TMK-6	$40-$50
117	3-1/2"	TMK-7	$40-$50
117	3-1/2"	TMK-8	$40-$50

Hum 118: Little Thrifty

This figurine, originally designed by master sculptor Arthur Moeller in 1939 and introduced in the late-1930s, is also a coin bank. It is usually found with a key and lockable metal plug beneath the base, but these are sometimes lost over the years.

Although not terribly significant in terms of value, there is a difference in design between the older and the newer pieces. The most obvious is a less thick base on the new design. This design change took place during the Stylized Bee (TMK-3) trademark period after a redesign by master sculptor Rudolf Wittman in 1963, so the old and the new designs can be found with that mark, but there is no bearing on value.

Little Thrifty was reintroduced by Manufaktur Rödental under TMK-9 with the 100 years backstamp. The 100 years backstamp is only available for figurines produced in 2009.

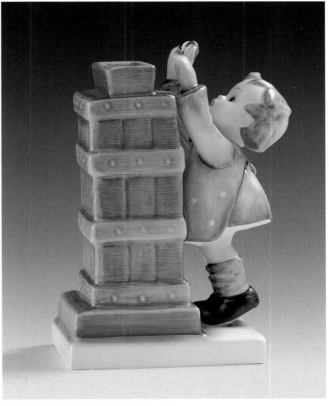

Hum 118: Little Thrifty.

Hum No.	Basic Size	Trademark	Current Value
118	5″	TMK-1	$330-$450
118	5″	TMK-2	$240-$270
118	5″	TMK-3	$135-$170
118	5″	TMK-4	$120-$125
118	5″	TMK-5	$120-$125
118	5″	TMK-6	$115-$120
118	5″	TMK-7	$110-$115
118	5″	TMK-8	$110-$115
118	5″	TMK-9	$199 retail

Hum 119: Postman

Master sculptor Arthur Moeller crafted this piece in 1939, and it was introduced about 1940.

This figure has been released in several different sizes and distinct mold variations, but only one size was listed until 1989, when a smaller version (119/2/0) was released. With the release of the 119/2/0, the larger 119 became 119/0 beginning with TMK-6 pieces.

There are no variations significant enough to influence normal values for the Postman.

Hum 119: Postman.

Hum No.	Basic Size	Trademark	Current Value
119/2/0	4-1/2″	TMK-6	$105-$115
119/2/0	4-1/2″	TMK-7	$105-$115
119/2/0	4-1/2″	TMK-8	$199 retail
119	5-1/4″	TMK-1	$360-$450
119	5-1/4″	TMK-2	$210-$270
119	4-3/4″	TMK-3	$180-$200
119	5-1/4″	TMK-4	$165-$180
119	5-1/4″	TMK-5	$150-$165
119	5-1/4″	TMK-6	$150-$165
119/0	5-1/4″	TMK-6	$150-$165
119/0	5-1/2″	TMK-7	$145-$160
119/0	5-1/2″	TMK-8	$150-$165
119/4/0	3-1/2″	TMK-8	$99 retail

Hum 120: Joyful and Let's Sing
Bookends

There are no examples known of these double figure bookends on wooden bases in private collections. Known from factory records only. It has been listed as a closed edition since 1939.

Hum No.	Basic Size	Trademark	Current Value
120	-	TMK-1	$6,000-$12,000

Hum 121: Wayside Harmony and Just Resting
Bookends

Only half of this two-piece bookend duo on wooden base is known to be in a private collection. It has been listed as a closed edition since 1939. The figures on the wooden base are very similar to the Hum 111 and Hum 112, but have different incised mold numbers.

Hum No.	Basic Size	Trademark	Current Value
121/A	-	TMK-1	$3,000-$6,000
121/B	-	TMK-1	$3,000-$6,000

Hum 121: Wayside Harmony bookend.

Hum 122: Puppy Love and Serenade With Dog
Bookends

No examples of this bookend ensemble on wooden bases are known to be in private collections. Listed as a closed edition in 1939, it exists in factory archives only.

Hum No.	Basic Size	Trademark	Current Value
122	-	TMK-1	$6,000-$12,000

Hum 122: Puppy Love bookend.

Hum 123: Max and Moritz

Released about 1940 and first designed by master sculptor Arthur Moeller, this figurine was once known as Good Friends.

An important variation has been found in a few Crown Mark (TMK-1) examples, where the figure has black hair rather than the lighter, blonde hair. In fact, these figures appear to be painted in darker colors overall. When found, these pieces are valued at about $1,500.

The same characters that make up this piece have been made into two new ones: Scamp (Hum 553) and Cheeky Fellow (Hum 554).

Hum No.	Basic Size	Trademark	Current Value
123	5-1/4″	TMK-1	$390-$480
123	5-1/4″	TMK-2	$240-$300
123	5-1/4″	TMK-3	$195-$225
123	5-1/4″	TMK-4	$180-$195
123	5-1/4″	TMK-5	$165-$180
123	5-1/4″	TMK-6	$165-$175
123	5″ to 5-1/2″	TMK-7	$155-$170
123	5″ to 5-1/2″	TMK-8	$279 retail

Hum 123: Max and Moritz.

Hum 124: Hello

First designed by master sculptor Arthur Moeller in 1939 and introduced around 1940, this figurine was once known as The Boss and Der Chef. This figurine is the same one used in the perpetual calendar bearing the same name, Hum 788/A.

When first released, it had gray pants and coat and a pink vest. This changed to green pants, brown coat, and pink vest, and then finally to the brown coat and pants with white vest used on the pieces from sometime in the Stylized Bee (TMK-3) period to the present. The variation in shortest supply is the green pants version.

The figure has been found with the decimal designator in the Crown (TMK-1) and Full Bee (TMK-2).

The larger 124/I size has been temporarily removed from production.

Hum No.	Basic Size	Trademark	Current Value
124	6-1/2″	TMK-1	$480-$600
124	6-1/2″	TMK-2	$270-$360
124/0	5-3/4″ to 6-1/4″	TMK-2	$240-$270
124/0	5-3/4″ to 6-1/4″	TMK-3	$210-$280
124/0	5-3/4″ to 6-1/4″	TMK-4	$180-$210
124/0	5-3/4″ to 6-1/4″	TMK-5	$165-$180
124/0	5-3/4″ to 6-1/4″	TMK-6	$130-$180
124/0	5-3/4″ to 6-1/4″	TMK-7	$130-$180
124/0	5-3/4″ to 6-1/4″	TMK-8	$130-$180
124/I	7″	TMK-1	$480-$600
124/I	7″	TMK-2	$270-$360
124/I	7″	TMK-3	$240-$270
124/I	7″	TMK-4	$210-$240
124/I	7″	TMK-5	$180-$210
124/I	7″	TMK-6	$195-$200

Hum 124: Hello.

Hum 125: Vacation Time
Wall Plaque

Originally called Happy Holidays and On Holiday, this piece was the original design of master sculptor Arthur Moeller. It was redesigned in 1960, however, leaving two distinctly different designs. The transition from the old to the new took place in the Stylized Bee (TMK-3) period, so you can find the old and the new styles in that trademark. The newest style has now lost one fence picket for a count of five. The old has six.

This piece was temporarily withdrawn from production in 1989, released again in 1998 as part of the Vacation Time Hummelscape package (TMK-7), and not produced again since.

Hum No.	Basic Size	Trademark	Current Value
125	4-3/8" x 5-1/4"	TMK-1	$360-$450
125	4-3/8" x 5-1/4"	TMK-2	$270-$330
125 (old)	4" x 4-3/4"	TMK-3	$225-$270
125 (new)	4" x 4-3/4"	TMK-3	$165-$210
125	4" x 4-3/4"	TMK-4	$165-$175
125	4" x 4-1/4"	TMK-5	$150-$165

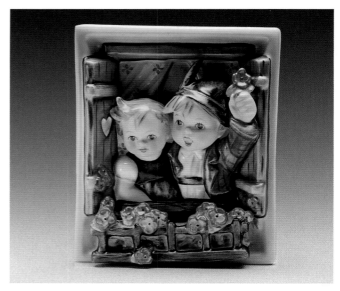

Hum 125: Vacation Time wall plaque.

Hum No.	Basic Size	Trademark	Current Value
125	4" x 4-1/4"	TMK-6	$150-$160
125	4" x 4-3/4"	TMK-7	$135-$150

Hum 126: Retreat to Safety
Wall Plaque

This plaque, which was first created by master sculptor Arthur Moeller in 1939, was in continuous production until 1989, when it was temporarily withdrawn from production. Although the colors differ, it is the same design as the

Hum 126: Retreat to Safety wall plaque.

Hum No.	Basic Size	Trademark	Current Value
126	4-3/4" x 4-3/4"	TMK-1	$330-$420
126	4-3/4" x 4-3/4"	TMK-2	$280-$300
126	4-3/4" x 4-3/4"	TMK-3	$165-$210
126	4-3/4" x 4-3/4"	TMK-4	$135-$170
126	4-3/4" x 4-3/4"	TMK-5	$120-$130
126	4-3/4" x 4-3/4"	TMK-6	$110-$120

figurine of the same name, Hum 201. There are no significant variations to affect collector values.

Hum 127: Doctor

Doctor, which was the original work of master sculptor Arthur Moeller, joined the line about 1940. It was formerly known as The Doll Doctor.

The sizes in various lists range from 4-3/4" to 5-1/4". The larger sizes are generally the older pieces.

On the Crown Mark (TMK-1) and Full Bee (TMK-2) figures, the doll's feet extend slightly beyond the edge of the base. They must have proven vulnerable to breakage because the feet were restyled so they no longer extended over the base. At presstime,

Hum 127: Doctor.

Hum No.	Basic Size	Trademark	Current Value
127	4-3/4"	TMK-1	$270-$390
127	4-3/4"	TMK-2	$180-$210
127	4-3/4"	TMK-3	$150-$170
127	4-3/4"	TMK-4	$120-$150
127	4-3/4"	TMK-5	$120-$130
127	4-3/4"	TMK-6	$110-$115
127	4-3/4" to 5-1/4"	TMK-7	$110-$115
127	4-3/4" to 5"	TMK-8	$219 retail
127/4/0	3-1/4"	TMK-9	N/A

Manufaktur Rödental planned to re-release this figurine in a smaller size of 3-1/4" in 2013. A new description was not available, but it will be a TMK-9 figurine with the TMK-9 backstamp.

Hum 128: Baker

Although this figure, which was first created by master sculptor Arthur Moeller in 1939, underwent changes over the years, none are important enough to influence the normal values of the pieces. Slight color variations do occur, and the older pieces (TMK-1) have open eyes.

Hum 128: Baker.

Hum No.	Basic Size	Trademark	Current Value
128	4-3/4″	TMK-1	$390-$450
128	4-3/4″	TMK-2	$210-$260
128	4-3/4″	TMK-3	$180-$195
128	4-3/4″	TMK-4	$180-$210
128	4-3/4″	TMK-5	$150-$170
128	4-3/4″	TMK-6	$165-$170
128	4-3/4″ to 5″	TMK-7	$140-$150
128	4-3/4″ to 5″	TMK-8	$259 retail

Hum 129: Band Leader

This piece, which was first referred to as Leader, was originally designed by master sculptor Arthur Moeller in 1939. There have been no significant mold variations.

Band Leader, like several other figurines, makes up the Hummel orchestra.

A new, smaller size (Hum 129/4/0) without the music stand was introduced in 1987 as the fourth in a four-part series of small figurines intended to match four mini-plates in the same motifs.

In the summer of 2002, a 13-1/2″ version of Band Leader was introduced as the fifth and final edition of the "Millennium Love" series, which also included Sweet Music (Hum 186/III), Soloist (Hum 135/III), Little Fiddler (Hum 2/III), and Serenade (Hum 85/III). These oversized pieces (Hum 129/III) were in limited supply and had to be special-ordered through an authorized M.I. Hummel retailer.

The smaller 129/4/0 size was temporarily withdrawn in 1997 and then listed as a closed edition in 1999.

Hum No.	Basic Size	Trademark	Current Value
129/4/0	3-1/2″	TMK-6	$80-$90
129/4/0	3-1/4″	TMK-7 CE	$75-$90
129	5-1/4″	TMK-1	$360-$450
129	5-1/4″	TMK-2	$210-$270
129	5-1/4″	TMK-3	$180-$210
129	5-1/4″	TMK-4	$165-$175
129	5-1/4″	TMK-5	$150-$170
129/0	5-1/4″	TMK-6	$150-$170
129/0	5″ to 5-1/4″	TMK-7	$140-$165
129/0	5″ to 5-1/4″	TMK-8	$140-$165
129/II (Special Edition)	–	TMK-7	$145 (Hong Kong only)
129/III	13-1/2″	TMK-8	$1,500 retail

Hum 129: Band Leader.

Hum 130: Duet

First crafted by master sculptor Arthur Moeller in 1939 and originally called The Songsters, this piece occurs in many size variations from 5" to 5-1/2".

Some older figures with the Crown Mark (TMK-1) have a very small lip on the front of the base, sort of a mini-version of the stepped or double base variation found on the Merry Wanderer. These lip base Duets also have incised musical notes on the sheet music and are more valuable than the regular pieces.

Another variation is the absence of the kerchief on the figure wearing the top hat. This is found on some Full Bee (TMK-2) and Stylized Bee (TMK-3) pieces. They have dropped in value.

This piece is another of the figurines that make up the Hummel orchestra. It is similar to the combined designs of Street Singer (Hum 131) and Soloist (Hum 135).

Duet was permanently retired in 1995, with the mold destroyed.

Hum No.	Basic Size	Trademark	Current Value
130	5-1/4"	TMK-1	$480-$600
130	5-1/4"	TMK-2	$330-$390
130	5-1/4"	TMK-3	$240-$270
130	5-1/4"	TMK-4	$195-$240
130	5-1/4"	TMK-5	$180-$205
130	5-1/4"	TMK-6	$190-$200
130	5" to 5-1/2"	TMK-7	$180-$195 retired
130	(without ties)	TMK-2 or 3	$1,200-$2,100
130	(with "lip" base)	TMK-1	$600-$900

Hum 130: Duet

Hum 131: Street Singer

This figure, which was designed by master sculptor Arthur Moeller in 1939 and formerly known as Soloist, is another of the Hummel orchestra pieces.

Although there have been size and minor color variations over the years, there are no significant mold variations to be found.

Hum No.	Basic Size	Trademark	Current Value
131	5" to 5-1/2"	TMK-1	$330-$420
131	5" to 5-1/2"	TMK-2	$225-$270
131	5" to 5-1/2"	TMK-3	$180-$210
131	5" to 5-1/2"	TMK-4	$165-$180
131	5" to 5-1/2"	TMK-5	$150-$165
131	5" to 5-1/2"	TMK-6	$150-$165
131	5" to 5-1/2"	TMK-7	$140-$155
131	5" to 5-1/2"	TMK-8	$70-$150 retired

Hum 131: Street Singer.

Hum 132: Star Gazer

Master sculptor Arthur Moeller originally crafted this piece in 1939, and it underwent a slight redesign in 1980 in with the textured finish was added and corners of the base were rounded.

A few of the older Crown Mark (TMK-1) pieces have a darker blue shirt, but the normal color on later pieces is a lighter blue or purple.

The straps on the boy's lederhosen are normally crossed in the back. If there are no straps, the value is increased, valued at about 20% above the normal value.

A special edition was released in 1996 for sale to the U.S. military troops stationed in Bosnia. The inscription read: "Looking for a Peaceful World." It is worth $500-$800.

This figurine was temporarily withdrawn from production on June 15, 2002.

Hum No.	Basic Size	Trademark	Current Value
132	4-3/4"	TMK-1	$360-$480
132	4-3/4"	TMK-2	$240-$300
132	4-3/4"	TMK-3	$200-$225
132	4-3/4"	TMK-4	$165-$195
132	4-3/4"	TMK-5	$165-$175
132	4-3/4"	TMK-6	$150-$170
132	4-3/4"	TMK-7	$150-$170
132	4-3/4" to 5"	TMK-8 TW	$165-$170

Hum 132: Star Gazer.

Hum 133: Mother's Helper

Created by master sculptor Arthur Moeller in 1939, this figurine has but one major variation to look for. Several Crown-era (TMK-1) pieces have surfaced with the stool reversed and only one leg of the stool showing when viewed from the rear. The norm has two legs visible from the rear. This unique variation is worth $750-$1,000.

This piece, with the presence of the cat, is similar to Hum 325: Helping Mother, which is a possible future edition.

Hum No.	Basic Size	Trademark	Current Value
133	5"	TMK-1	$330-$420
133	5"	TMK-2	$225-$270
133	5"	TMK-3	$180-$195
133	5"	TMK-4	$165-$180
133	5"	TMK-5	$150-$165
133	5"	TMK-6	$145-$150
133	4-3/4" to 5"	TMK-7	$145-$150
133	4-3/4" to 5"	TMK-8	$135-$150

Hum 133: Mother's Helper.

Hum 134: Quartet
Wall Plaque

Another of the circa 1940 releases, this plaque was designed by master sculptor Arthur Moeller in 1939.

The older pieces have the "M.I. Hummel" signature on the back, while the newer plaques have an incised front signature. Also of note on the older pieces is the existence of two holes for the cord to hang on the wall. The newer versions have a single, centered hole on the back. Despite these differences, there are no significant mold variations influencing the normal pricing structure.

This plaque was temporarily removed from production as of 1990.

Hum No.	Basic Size	Trademark	Current Value
134	5-1/2" x 6-1/4"	TMK-1	$480-$600
134	5-1/2" x 6-1/4"	TMK-2	$315-$375
134	5-1/2" x 6-1/4"	TMK-3	$230-$255
134	5-1/2" x 6-1/4"	TMK-4	$200-$225
134	5-1/2" x 6-1/4"	TMK-5	$160-$165
134	5-1/2" x 6-1/4"	TMK-6	$150-$165

Hum 134: Quartet wall plaque.

Hum 135: Soloist

Created by master sculptor Arthur Moeller in 1940 and released in the early 1940s as High Tenor, this piece has remained in continuous production since. It has no significant mold variations influencing price.

In 1986, a new smaller version, 135/4/0, was released as the third in a series of four small figurines and matching mini-plates. Because of the new size designator in the smaller model, the larger model is now incised with the mold number 135/0. This change occurred in TMK-6 era, only to be followed shortly thereafter by the temporary withdrawal of the smaller version (135/4/0) in 1997.

In 1996, an even smaller variation (135/5/0) was produced as part of the "Pen Pals" series of personalized name card table decorations. That size occurs in TMK-7 only and has not been produced since.

Recently, a 13" version of Soloist was introduced as part of the "Millennium Love" series, which also included Sweet Music (Hum 186/III), Little Fiddler (Hum 2/III), Band Leader (Hum 129/III), and Serenade (Hum 85/III). These oversized pieces (Hum 85/III) were in limited supply and had to be special-ordered through an authorized M.I. Hummel retailer.

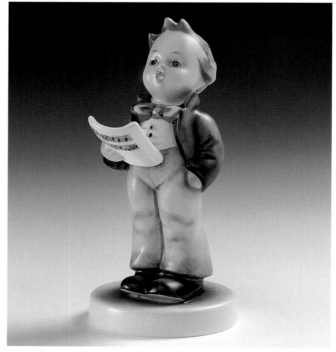

Hum 135: Soloist.

Hum No.	Basic Size	Trademark	Current Value
135/5/0	2-3/4"	TMK-7	$30-$50
135/4/0	3-1/2"	TMK-6	$75-$90
135/4/0	3"	TMK-7	$70-$75
135	4-3/4"	TMK-1	$240-$300
135	4-3/4"	TMK-2	$180-$210
135	4-3/4"	TMK-3	$120-$140
135	4-3/4"	TMK-4	$110-$120
135	4-3/4"	TMK-5	$105-$110

Hum No.	Basic Size	Trademark	Current Value
135	4-3/4"	TMK-6	$105-$110
135/0	4-3/4"	TMK-6	$99-$105
135/0	4-3/4"	TMK-7	$99-$105
135/0	4-3/4"	TMK-8	$179 retail
135/III	13"	TMK-8	$1,550 retail

Hum 136: Friends

Crafted by master sculptor Reinhold Unger in 1940 and released about the same time in two sizes, this figurine was formerly known as Good Friends and Friendship. Sizes found in various lists are 5", 10-3/4", and 11-1/2".

There have been at least two examples of this piece found that are made of terra-cotta. These are in the 10" size with incised Crown Mark (TMK-1). Another unique finish exists in dark chocolate brown in a 9-3/4" size. These are extremely rare pieces.

Also found in white overglaze in the Crown Mark (TMK-1), this very rare variation is valued at $4,000-$5,000.

The larger 136/V size was temporarily withdrawn from production in 1999.

The year 2011 marked the celebration of Sister Hummel's 75th anniversary of the beginning of her legacy. Manufaktur Rödental selected 50 figurines to bear the "75th Anniversary" backstamp. Friends was one of those figurines. Only 75 of them were available in North America with this backstamp. Each figurine was hand-numbered

Hum 136: Friends.

with a golden backstamp and a map of North America backstamp. A special porcelain plaque was included, and a notable emblem on the packaging hinted at the contents. Each figurine included a "75 Years of M.I. Hummel" certificate.

Hum No.	Basic Size	Trademark	Current Value
136/I	5" to 5-3/8"	TMK-1	$480-$570
136/I	5" to 5-3/8"	TMK-2	$240-$300
136/I	5" to 5-3/8"	TMK-3	$195-$225
136/I	5" to 5-3/8"	TMK-4	$165-$200
136/I	5" to 5-3/8"	TMK-5	$150-$165
136/I	5" to 5-3/8"	TMK-6	$245-$255
136/I	5" to 5-3/8"	TMK-7	$150-$165
136/I	5" to 5-3/8"	TMK-8	$150-$165
136	10-3/4"	TMK-1	$1,800-$2,400
136	10-3/4"	TMK-2	$1,200-$1,800
136 (terra-cotta)	10"	TMK-1	$6,000-$9,000
136 (dark brown)	9-3/4"	TMK-1	$6,000-$9,000
136/V	10-3/4" to 11"	TMK-1	$1,800-$2,400
136/V	10-3/4" to 11"	TMK-2	$1,050-$1,500
136/V	10-3/4" to 11"	TMK-3	$960-$1,050
136/V	10-3/4" to 11"	TMK-4	$900-$960
136/V	10-3/4" to 11"	TMK-5	$870-$900
136/V	10-3/4" to 11"	TMK-6	$840-$870
136/V	10-3/4" to 11"	TMK-7	$810-$870

Hum 137/A and Hum 137/B: Child in Bed
Wall Plaques

This set of plaques, which has been called Baby Ring With Ladybug and Ladybug Plaque in early company literature, was created by master sculptor Arthur Moeller in 1940. One child is looking to its right (137/A) and the other looking to its left (137/B). The mold number is found as 137/B until the Last Bee (TMK-5) era, when the B was dropped.

Until the mid-1980s, it was only speculated that there might have been a matching piece with the mold number 137/A. When one surfaced in Hungary and a few others followed, it was apparent that although they had indeed been produced, they are extremely rare.

A "Mel 14" variation has been found recently and although it has no "M.I. Hummel" signature, it does bear an incised "Mel 14" along with a Double Crown trademark.

Hum 137 was temporarily withdrawn from production in 1999.

Hum 137/B: Child in Bed wall plaque.

Hum No.	Basic Size	Trademark	Current Value
137/A	3" x 3"	TMK-1	$3,000-$4,200
137/B	3" x 3"	TMK-1	$210-$330
137/B	3" x 3"	TMK-2	$120-$135
137/B	3" x 3"	TMK-3	$70-$90
137/B	3" x 3"	TMK-4	$55-$70

Hum No.	Basic Size	Trademark	Current Value
137/B	3" x 3"	TMK-5	$50-$55
137	3" x 3"	TMK-5	$50-$55
137	3" x 3"	TMK-6	$40-$50
137	3" x 3"	TMK-7	$40-$45
MEL 14	3" x 3"	TMK-1	$1,200-$1,500

Hum 138: Tiny Baby in Crib
Wall Plaque

Although all factory records indicate that this piece was never released for sale to the consumer and only prototypes were produced, at least six are known to reside in private collections. Master sculptor Arthur Moeller created it in 1940.

These figures have also been found with the "Mel" designator as "Mel 15."

Hum No.	Basic Size	Trademark	Current Value
138	2-1/4" x 3"	TMK-1	$2,400-$3,000
138	2-1/4" x 3"	TMK-2	$1,800-$2,100
MEL 15	2-1/4" x 3"	TMK-1	$1,200-$1,500

Hum 138: Tiny Baby in Crib wall plaque.

Hum 139: Flitting Butterfly
Wall Plaque

Designed by master sculptor Arthur Moeller in 1940 and originally called Butterfly Plaque, this figure has not undergone any significant mold variation that would affect the normal value for the various trademarked pieces.

A few pieces bearing "Mel 16" do exist from 1940 and are worth substantially more than the regular variations.

This figure was out of production for some time, thus the absence of a Three

Hum No.	Basic Size	Trademark	Current Value
139	2-1/2" x 2-1/2"	TMK-1	$210-$330
139	2-1/2" x 2-1/2"	TMK-2	$120-$130
139	2-1/2" x 2-1/2"	TMK-3	$60-$90
139	2-1/2" x 2-1/2"	TMK-5	$45-$50
139	2-1/2" x 2-1/2"	TMK-6	$45-$50
139	2-1/2" x 2-1/2"	TMK-7	$45-$50
MEL 16	2-1/2" x 2-1/2"	TMK-1	$1,200-$1,500

Line (TMK-4) example. It was reissued in a new mold design with the same number during the Last Bee (TMK-5) period and continued in production until 1999 when it was temporarily withdrawn.

Hum 139: Flitting Butterfly wall plaque.

Hum 140: The Mail is Here
Wall Plaque

This plaque, also once known as Post Carriage and Mail Coach, predates the figurine by the same name and design (Hum 226). It was crafted by master sculptor Arthur Moeller in 1940 and introduced into the line the same year.

Although there are no significant mold variations, there is a finish variation of importance. Some of the early plaques were produced in white overglaze for the European market. These are found bearing the

Hum No.	Basic Size	Trademark	Current Value
140 (white overglaze)	4-1/2" x 6-3/4"	TMK-1	$600-$900
140	4-1/2" x 6-1/4"	TMK-1	$390-$570
140	4-1/2" x 6-1/4"	TMK-2	$270-$330
140	4-1/2" x 6-1/4"	TMK-3	$195-$210
140	4-1/2" x 6-1/4"	TMK-4	$180-$200
140	4-1/2" x 6-1/4"	TMK-5	$165-$180
140	4-1/2" x 6-1/4"	TMK-6	$150-$165

Crown Mark (TMK-1) and are valued at $600-$900.

There are minor variations noticeable in the doors and windows of the coach, as well as the handle of the horn, but none significantly affect values.

This plaque was temporarily withdrawn in 1989.

Hum 140: The Mail is Here wall plaque.

Hum 141: Apple Tree Girl

This figurine, which was designed by master sculptor Arthur Moeller in 1940, has also been known as Spring and Springtime. The following sizes are found in various lists: 4", 4-1/4", 6", 6-3/4", 10", 10-1/4", and 32".

In one list, references were made to a "rare old base" and a "brown base." These are apparently references to the "tree trunk base" variation. This variation will bring about 30% more than the value given in the chart below.

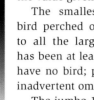

The smallest size (141/3/0) has no bird perched on the branch, in contrast to all the larger sizes. (Although there has been at least one, a 141/I, reported to have no bird; perhaps a factory worker's inadvertent omission.)

The jumbo 141/X size was temporarily withdrawn from production in 1990.

Hum 141: Apple Tree Girl.

Hum No.	Basic Size	Trademark	Current Value
141/3/0	4" to 4-1/4"	TMK-1	$270-$300
141/3/0	4" to 4-1/4"	TMK-2	$180-$210
141/3/0	4" to 4-1/4"	TMK-3	$135-$180
141/3/0	4" to 4-1/4"	TMK-4	$120-$180
141/3/0	4" to 4-1/4"	TMK-5	$110-$150

Hum No.	Basic Size	Trademark	Current Value
141/3/0	4" to 4-1/4"	TMK-6	$105-$150
141/3/0	4" to 4-1/4"	TMK-7	$105-$150
141/3/0	4" to 4-1/4"	TMK-8	$105-$150
141	6" to 6-3/4"	TMK-1	$480-$540
141	6" to 6-3/4"	TMK-2	$360-$420
141/I	6" to 6-3/4"	TMK-1	$420-$480
141/I	6" to 6-3/4"	TMK-2	$315-$375
141/I	6" to 6-3/4"	TMK-3	$255-$270
141/I	6" to 6-3/4"	TMK-4	$225-$255
141/I	6" to 6-3/4"	TMK-5	$210-$220
141/I	6" to 6-3/4"	TMK-6	$205-$210
141/I	6" to 6-3/4"	TMK-7	$200-$210
141/I	6" to 6-3/4"	TMK-8	$200-$210
141/V	10-1/4"	TMK-4	$900-$1,020
141/V	10-1/4"	TMK-5	$750-$900
141/V	10-1/4"	TMK-6	$860-$875
141/V	10-1/4"	TMK-7	$840-$860
141/V	10-1/4"	TMK-8	$900-$1,020
141/X*	32"	TMK-5	$9,000-$18,000
141/X*	32"	TMK-6	$9,000-$18,000
141/X*	32"	TMK-7	$9,000-$18,000
141/X	32"	TMK-8	$29,900 retail

*There are a few of these jumbo figures in collectors' hands. They are generally used as promotional figures in showrooms and shops. Rarely do they bring full retail price.

Hum 142: Apple Tree Boy

Apple Tree Girl's companion piece, this figure has also been known as Fall and Autumn. Just as with the girl, it too was crafted by master sculptor Arthur Moeller in 1940 and has been changed many times over the years. Sizes found in various lists are as follows: 3-3/4", 4", 4-1/2", 6", 6-7/8", 10", 10-1/4", 30", and 32".

In one list references were made to a "rare old base" and a "brown base." These are apparently references to the "tree trunk base" variation. This variation will bring about 30% more than the figure in the value chart here.

The smallest size (142/3/0) has no bird perched on the branch, in contrast to all the larger sizes.

Hum 142: Apple Tree Boy.

Hum No.	Basic Size	Trademark	Current Value
142/3/0	4" to 4-1/4"	TMK-1	$280-$300
142/3/0	4" to 4-1/4"	TMK-2	$180-$210
142/3/0	4" to 4-1/4"	TMK-3	$135-$180
142/3/0	4" to 4-1/4"	TMK-4	$120-$180
142/3/0	4" to 4-1/4"	TMK-5	$110-$160
142/3/0	4" to 4-1/4"	TMK-6	$105-$150
142/3/0	4" to 4-1/4"	TMK-7	$105-$150
142/3/0	4" to 4-1/4"	TMK-8	$105-$150

Hum No.	Basic Size	Trademark	Current Value
142	6" to 6-7/8"	TMK-1	$480-$540
142	6" to 6-7/8"	TMK-2	$360-$420
142/I	6" to 6-7/8"	TMK-1	$420-$480
142/I	6" to 6-7/8"	TMK-2	$315-$375
142/I	6" to 6-7/8"	TMK-3	$255-$270
142/I	6" to 6-7/8"	TMK-4	$220-$260
142/I	6" to 6-7/8"	TMK-5	$210-$220
142/I	6" to 6-7/8"	TMK-6	$205-$210
142/I	6" to 6-7/8"	TMK-7	$200-$210
142/I	6" to 6-7/8"	TMK-8	$200-$210
142/V	10-1/4"	TMK-3	$1,050-$1,200
142/V	10-1/4"	TMK-4	$900-$1,020
142/V	10-1/4"	TMK-5	$870-$900
142/V	10-1/4"	TMK-6	$870-$950
142/V	10-1/4"	TMK-7	$840-$870
142/V	10-1/4"	TMK-8	$900-$980
142/X*	30"	TMK-2	$15,600-$18,000
142/X*	30"	TMK-3	$10,200-$15,600
142/X*	30"	TMK-4	$9,600-$15,000
142/X*	30" to 32"	TMK-5	$9,000-$15,000
142/X*	30" to 32"	TMK-6	$9,000-$15,000
142/X*	30" to 32"	TMK-7	$9,000-$15,000
142/X*	30" to 32"	TMK-8	$29,900

*There are a few of these jumbo figures in collectors' hands. They are generally used as promotional figures in showrooms and shops. Rarely do they bring full retail price.

Hum 143: Boots

Hum 143: Boots.

Created by master sculptor Arthur Moeller in 1940 and originally called Shoemaker, this figure was first released around 1940 in the larger size and followed a short time later by the smaller size variation. Although many size variations have been found, none is significant in terms of affecting value.

Goebel retired both sizes of Boots in 1998, never to produce this figurine again.

Hum No.	Basic Size	Trademark	Current Value
143/0	5" to 5-1/2"	TMK-1	$330-$420
143/0	5" to 5-1/2"	TMK-2	$225-$270
143/0	5" to 5-1/2"	TMK-3	$180-$195
143/0	5" to 5-1/2"	TMK-4	$165-$180
143/0	5" to 5-1/2"	TMK-5	$150-$165
143/0	5" to 5-1/2"	TMK-6	$140-$150
143/0	5" to 5-1/2"	TMK-7	$225-$235
143/I	6-1/2" to 6-3/4"	TMK-1	$510-$600
143/I	6-1/2" to 6-3/4"	TMK-2	$360-$420
143/I	6-1/2" to 6-3/4"	TMK-3	$270-$315
143/I	6-1/2" to 6-3/4"	TMK-4	$255-$270
143/I	6-1/2" to 6-3/4"	TMK-5	$240-$255
143/I	6-1/2" to 6-3/4"	TMK-6	$225-$240
143/I	6-1/2" to 6-3/4"	TMK-7	$220-$225
143	6-3/4"	TMK-1	$540-$630
143	6-3/4"	TMK-2	$390-$450

Hum 144: Angelic Song

Formerly known as Angels and Holy Communion, this piece was created in 1941 by master sculptor Reinhold Unger. There are no significant variations of Angelic Song affecting the normal value of the pieces.

Hum No.	Basic Size	Trademark	Current Value
144	4"	TMK-1	$240-$315
144	4"	TMK-2	$165-$195
144	4"	TMK-3	$135-$150
144	4"	TMK-4	$120-$135
144	4"	TMK-5	$110-$125
144	4"	TMK-6	$110-$125
144	4"	TMK-7	$105-$125
144	4"	TMK-8	$105-$110

Hum 144: Angelic Song.

Hum 145: Little Guardian

Created by master sculptor Reinhold Unger in 1941, this piece is no longer in production. There are no variations significant enough to impact collector values, although the older pieces are just slightly bigger than the newer ones.

Hum No.	Basic Size	Trademark	Current Value
145	3-3/4" to 4"	TMK-1	$240-$300
145	3-3/4" to 4"	TMK-2	$165-$199
145	3-3/4" to 4"	TMK-3	$135-$150
145	3-3/4" to 4"	TMK-4	$120-$135
145	3-3/4" to 4"	TMK-5	$110-$120
145	3-3/4" to 4"	TMK-6	$110-$120
145	3-3/4" to 4"	TMK-7	$105-$115
145	3-3/4" to 4"	TMK-8	$105-$120

Hum 145: Little Guardian.

Hum 146: Angel Duet
Holy Water Font

Originally designed by master sculptor Reinhold Unger in 1941, this piece has undergone several redesigns throughout the years. There have been many variations with regard to the shapes and positions of the heads and wings of angels, but none significant.

This font was temporarily withdrawn from production in 1999.

Hum No.	Basic Size	Trademark	Current Value
146	3-1/2" x 4-3/4"	TMK-1	$105-$135
146	3-1/2" x 4-3/4"	TMK-2	$75-$90
146	3-1/2" x 4-3/4"	TMK-3	$50-$60
146	3-1/2" x 4-3/4"	TMK-4	$45-$50
146	3-1/2" x 4-3/4"	TMK-5	$45-$50
146	3-1/2" x 4-3/4"	TMK-6	$40-$50
146	3-1/2" x 4-3/4"	TMK-7	$35-$40

Hum 146: Angel Duet holy water font.

Hum 147: Angel Shrine
Holy Water Font

This figure, which was designed by master sculptor Reinhold Unger in 1941 and previously known as Angel Devotion, has been discontinued. There are no important mold or finish variations affecting its value, although some of the older pieces are slightly larger and the back of the font and water bowls have changed a bit over the years.

Hum No.	Basic Size	Trademark	Current Value
147	3-1/8" x 5-1/4"	TMK-1	$135-$165
147	3-1/8" x 5-1/4"	TMK-2	$75-$105
147	3" x 5"	TMK-3	$50-$60
147	3" x 5"	TMK-4	$45-$50
147	3" x 5"	TMK-5	$45-$50
147	3" x 5"	TMK-6	$40-$40
147	3" x 5"	TMK-7	$35-$40
147	3" x 5"	TMK-8	$35-$40

Hum 147: Angel Shrine holy water font.

Hum 148: Unknown
Closed Number

Listed as a closed number since 1941, records indicate that this piece could be a Farm Boy (Hum 66) with no base. No examples have ever been found. You can remove the figure from the bookend Hum 60/A and have the same figure, but the mold number will not be present.

Hum 149: Unknown
Closed Number

Records indicate that this piece, listed as a closed number since 1941, could be a Goose Girl (Hum 47) with no base. No known examples are in collectors' hands. You can remove the figure from the bookend Hum 60/B and have the same piece, but the mold number will not be present.

Hum 150: Happy Days

This piece, which was the collective effort of a group of sculptors and was once called Happy Little Troubadours, is referenced in numerous size variations throughout the years. It has been found with the decimal point designator. There are no mold or finish variations significant enough to influence values.

Both the 150/0 and 150/I sizes were temporarily withdrawn from production in 1999.

Hum No.	Basic Size	Trademark	Current Value
150/2/0	4-1/4″	TMK-2	$195-$240
150/2/0	4-1/4″	TMK-3	$150-$165
150/2/0	4-1/4″	TMK-4	$135-$150
150/2/0	4-1/4″	TMK-5	$130-$135
150/2/0	4-1/4″	TMK-6	$130-$135
150/2/0	4-1/4″	TMK-7	$120-$125
150/2/0	4-1/4″	TMK-8	$120-$125
150/0	5-1/4″	TMK-2	$315-$375
150/0	5-1/4″	TMK-3	$255-$285
150/0	5-1/4″	TMK-4	$240-$255
150/0	5-1/4″	TMK-5	$220-$235
150/0	5″ to 5-1/2″	TMK-6	$205-$220
150/0	5″ to 5-1/2″	TMK-7	$205-$210
150	6″	TMK-1	$780-$960

Hum 150: Happy Days

Hum No.	Basic Size	Trademark	Current Value
150	6″	TMK-2	$540-$600
150/I	6″	TMK-1	$750-$925
150/I	6″	TMK-2	$510-$570
150/I	6″	TMK-3	$425-$465
150/I	6″	TMK-5	$330-$360
150/I	6″	TMK-6	$315-$330
150/I	6-1/4″ to 6-1/2″	TMK-7	$330-$360

Hum 151: Madonna Holding Child

Sometimes called the Blue Cloak Madonna or Madonna with the Blue Cloak because of the most commonly found painted finish, this figure has appeared in other finishes. The rarest three finishes are those with the rich dark brown cloak, the dark blue cloak, and the ivory cloak. Always occurring in the Crown Mark (TMK-1), these are valued at $5,400-$7,200, depending on condition.

Sizes ranging from 12" to 14" have been referenced, and the figure has appeared with the Crown, Full Bee (TMK-2), and Stylized Bee (TMK-3) marks.

This figurine was temporarily withdrawn from production in 1989. It was back in production in a blue and white overglaze as per the 1993 Goebel price listing, but in 1995 was listed once again as temporarily withdrawn from production.

Hum No.	Basic Size	Color	TMK	Current Value
151	12-1/2″	blue	TMK-1	$1,200-$1,800
151	12-1/2″	blue	TMK-2	$1,200-$1,500
151	12-1/2″	blue	TMK-5	$555-$570
151	12-1/2″	blue	TMK-6	$540-$555
151	12-1/2″	white	TMK-1	$900-$1,500
151	12-1/2″	white	TMK-2	$600-$1,200
151	12-1/2″	white	TMK-5	$255-$270
151	12-1/2″	white	TMK-6	$240-$255

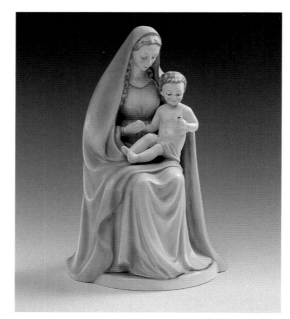

Hum 151: Madonna Holding Child.

Hum No.	Basic Size	Color	TMK	Current Value
151	12-1/2″	brown	TMK-1	$5,400-$7,200
151	12-1/2″	ivory	TMK-1	$5,400-$7,200
151	12-1/2″	dark blue	TMK-1	$5,400-$7,200

Hum 152/A: Umbrella Boy

Created by master sculptor Arthur Moeller in 1942 and introduced in one size in the early 1940s, the earliest Crown Mark (TMK-1) examples were produced with the incised mold number 152. Early literature calls the piece both In Safety and Boy Under Umbrella.

A second, smaller size was introduced in the Full Bee (TMK-2) period. There are no mold or finish variations that influence value.

The newest edition of this piece, Hum 152/A/2/0, was released in a "downsized edition" of 3-1/2" in 2002.

Hum No.	Basic Size	Trademark	Current Value
152/A/2/0	3-1/2"	TMK-8	$279 retail
152/0/A	5"	TMK-2	$660-$960
152/0/A	5"	TMK-3	$510-$600
152/0/A	5"	TMK-4	$450-$510
152/0/A	5"	TMK-5	$435-$450
152/0/A	5"	TMK-6	$420-$435
152/0/A	4-3/4"	TMK-7	$405-$420
152/0/A	4-3/4"	TMK-8	$405-$420
152	8"	TMK-1	$2,400-$4,200
152	8"	TMK-2	$1,440-$1,800
152/A	8"	TMK-2	$1,500-$1,800
152/A	8"	TMK-3	$1,140-$1,200
152/A	8"	TMK-4	$1,035-$1,080
152/II/A	8"	TMK-4	$1,025-$1,080
152/II/A	8"	TMK-5	$1,020-$1,035

Hum 152/A: Umbrella Boy.

Hum No.	Basic Size	Trademark	Current Value
152/II/A	8"	TMK-6	$1,035-$1,080
152/II/A	8"	TMK-7	$1,050-$1,075
152/II/A	8"	TMK-8	$980-$1,000

Hum 152/B: Umbrella Girl

Obviously created by master sculptor Arthur Moeller to match the Umbrella Boy, one wonders why this figure was introduced at the end of the 1940s, several years after Umbrella Boy.

In any case, it may be found in two sizes, the smaller appearing in the Full Bee (TMK-2) period. Also known early on as In Safety and Girl Under Umbrella. There are no significant variations influencing values.

The newest edition of this piece, Hum 152/B/2/0, was released in a "downsized edition" of 3-1/2" in 2002.

Hum No.	Basic Size	Trademark	Current Value
152/B/2/0	3-1/2"	TMK-8	$329 retail
152/0/B	4-3/4"	TMK-2	$720-$960
152/0/B	4-3/4"	TMK-3	$510-$600
152/0/B	4-3/4"	TMK-4	$450-$510
152/0/B	4-3/4"	TMK-5	$435-$450
152/0/B	4-3/4"	TMK-6	$420-$435
152/0/B	4-3/4"	TMK-7	$405-$420
152/0/B	4-3/4"	TMK-8	$405-$420
152/B	8"	TMK-1	$2,400-$4,200
152/B	8"	TMK-2	$1,320-$1,620
152/B	8"	TMK-3	$1,080-$1,200
152/B	8"	TMK-4	$1,050-$1,080

Hum 152/B: Umbrella Girl.

Hum No.	Basic Size	Trademark	Current Value
152/II/B	8"	TMK-4	$1,025-$1,080
152/II/B	8"	TMK-5	$1,020-$1,035
152/II/B	8"	TMK-6	$1,065-$1,080
152/II/B	8"	TMK-7	$1,050-$1,065
152/II/B	8"	TMK-8	$1,050-$1,065

Hum 153: Auf Wiedersehen

This figure, whose name means "goodbye" in English, was first released in the 1950s in the 7" basic size. It was designed by master sculptor Arthur Moeller in 1943 and was originally called Good Bye. A smaller size was introduced during the Full Bee (TMK-2) era. Both sizes have been restyled in recent years.

In a rare version of this double figure piece, the little boy wears a Tyrolean cap. This variation is found only in the 153/0 size. In most examples of these pieces, he wears no hat but is waving a handkerchief, as is the girl. The rare version is valued at about $1,800-$2,400. The 153/I size is listed as reinstated.

In 1993, Goebel issued a special edition of this figurine along with a replica of the Berlin Airlift Memorial at Templehof Airport in Berlin, Germany. This was to commemorate the Berlin Airlift at the end of World War II. Both pieces bear a special backstamp containing the flags of Germany, France, England, and the United States. The edition was limited to 25,000. The original issue was priced at $330 and is still valued at about the same.

Both sizes of this piece were permanently retired in December 2000 and will not be made again. Pieces made that year have "Final Issue 2000" backstamps and all gold "Final Issue" medallions in addition to TMK-8. The larger 153/I size was retired on QVC exclusively and came with a Hummelscape in a limited edition of 6,500 pieces.

Hum No.	Basic Size	Trademark	Current Value
153/0	5-1/2" to 6"	TMK-2	$255-$315
153/0	5-1/2" to 6"	TMK-3	$210-$240
153/0	5-1/2" to 6"	TMK-4	$190-$210
153/0	5-1/2" to 6"	TMK-5	$180-$190
153/0	5-1/2" to 6"	TMK-6	$170-$180
153/0	5-1/2" to 6"	TMK-7	$170-$180
153/0	5-1/2" to 6"	TMK-8	$170-$175
153/0 (hat)	5-1/4"	TMK-2	$1,800-$2,400
153	6-3/4" to 7"	TMK-1	$540-$720
153	6-3/4" to 7"	TMK-2	$390-$450
153/I	6-3/4" to 7"	TMK-1	$450-$640
153/I	6-3/4" to 7"	TMK-2	$360-$420
153/I	6-3/4" to 7"	TMK-3	$285-$315
153/I	6-3/4" to 7"	TMK-4	$255-$285
153/I	6-3/4" to 7"	TMK-5	$220-$235
153/I	6-3/4" to 7"	TMK-6	$200-$220
153/I	6-3/4" to 7"	TMK-7	$200-$205
153/I	6-3/4" to 7"	TMK-8	$200-$205

Special edition of Auf Wiedersehen on wood base with the porcelain Airlift Memorial replica piece. Both have a special backstamp and the edition is limited to 25,000. Wall: 7-1/2". Figurine: Hum 153/0, 5-1/2".

Hum 153: Auf Wiedersehen.

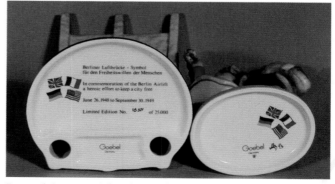

Bases of the memorial replica and Hum 153/0, respectively, showing the special markings.

Hum 154: Waiter

First crafted by master sculptor Arthur Moeller in 1943 and known as Chef of Service and Little Waiter, this figurine has appeared with several different labels on the wine bottle. All are

now produced with a "Rhine Wine" label. The variation in which the label on the bottle reads "Whiskey" is from the Full Bee (TMK-2) era and is valued at $960-$1,260.

Earlier versions of the piece have much darker pants than those in current production. The first figurines have a gray coat and gray striped trousers. In the 1950s, the coat became blue and the pants tan striped.

The larger 154/I size was temporarily withdrawn from production in 1999.

Hum 154: Waiter.

Hum No.	Basic Size	Trademark	Current Value
154/0	6" to 6-1/4"	TMK-1	$360-$480
154/0	6" to 6-1/4"	TMK-2	$225-$285
154/0	6" to 6-1/4"	TMK-3	$195-$210
154/0	6" to 6-1/4"	TMK-4	$180-$195
154/0	6" to 6-1/4"	TMK-5	$175-$185
154/0	6" to 6-1/4"	TMK-6	$165-$175
154/0	6" to 6-1/4"	TMK-7	$150-$165
154/0	6" to 6-1/4"	TMK-8	$150-$165
154/I	6-1/2" to 7"	TMK-1	$450-$600
154/I	6-1/2" to 7"	TMK-2	$300-$360
154/I	6-1/2" to 7"	TMK-3	$270-$300
154/I	6-1/2" to 7"	TMK-4	$375-$450
154/I	6-1/2" to 7"	TMK-5	$210-$225
154/I	6-1/2" to 7"	TMK-6	$205-$210
154/I	6-1/2" to 7"	TMK-7	$199-$335
154	6-1/2"	TMK-1	$510-$665
154	6-1/2"	TMK-2	$330-$420
154/0	6-1/4"	TMK-2	$960-$1,260 whiskey variation

Hum 155:
Madonna Holding Child
Closed Number

Records indicate this figure may be a Madonna holding child. Crafted by master sculptor Reinhold Unger, it has been a closed number since 1943. The photograph shown here is of the Madonna plaque. It is large, measuring 13" high. It has the incised "M.I. Hummel" signature and mold number, a Crown Mark (TMK-1) and "W. Goebel" on the back. Because it is unique and there is no trade data, no realistic collector value can be determined.

Hum 155: Madonna Holding Child.

Hum 156: Unknown
Closed Number

Records indicate this piece, which was created by master sculptor Arthur Moeller in 1943 and listed as a closed number ever since, may be a wall plaque of a mother and child. No known examples.

Hum 157 through Hum 162: Town Children
Closed Numbers

These are 1940s sample figurines where the children are dressed much more formally than in typical figurines. Master sculptor Arthur Moeller crafted the first three numbers in 1943, and master sculptor Reinhold Unger crafted the last three the same year. There are sample models of some of them in the Goebel archives and they are atypical of M.I. Hummel figurines. They do not wear the traditional costumes, but rather appear to be dressed in more modern clothes.

Sister Maria Innocentia is known to have asked on at least one occasion, "How shall I draw for the Americans?" One can speculate that these pieces, never approved by the convent, were an attempt to produce a few for the American market.

Until recently these numbers have been listed as unknown. Records indicate that the figurines were modeled and considered for production but never released. None are known outside the archives. The descriptions are as follows: standing boy with flower basket behind back (Hum 157); standing girl holding dog and with suitcase at her feet (Hum 158); standing girl cradling flowers in her arms (Hum 159); standing girl in tiered dress holding flower bouquet (Hum 160); standing girl with hands in pockets (Hum 161); and standing girl holding a handbag (Hum 162).

Hum 157 through Hum 162: "Town Children" (closed numbers).

Hum 163: Whitsuntide

This figure, which was originally named Christmas and is sometimes known as Happy New Year, was created by master sculptor Arthur Moeller in 1946. It is one of the early releases and was removed from production about 1960, then reinstated in 1977, and temporarily withdrawn in 1999. The older pieces are very scarce and highly sought by collectors.

In older versions, the angel appears holding a red or a yellow candle and is without the candle in newer models.

Hum 163: Whitsuntide.

Hum No.	Basic Size	Trademark	Current Value
163	7-1/4"	TMK-1	$600-$750
163	7-1/4"	TMK-2	$510-$600
163	7-1/4"	TMK-3	$390-$480
163	7-1/4"	TMK-5	$210-$235
163	7-1/4"	TMK-6	$200-$210
163	6-1/2" to 7"	TMK-7	$200-$205

Hum 164: Worship

Holy Water Font

Master sculptor Reinhold Unger crafted this font in 1946. From its introduction to the line in the mid-1940s to current production models, there have been no significant variations that have any impact on value.

Hum No.	Basic Size	Trademark	Current Value
164	3-1/4″ x 5″	TMK-1	$150-$180
164	3-1/4″ x 5″	TMK-2	$90-$120
164	3-1/4″ x 5″	TMK-3	$60-$95
164	3-1/4″ x 5″	TMK-4	$45-$55
164	3-1/4″ x 5″	TMK-6	$40-$45
164	3-1/4″ x 5″	TMK-7	$35-$40
164	3-1/4″ x 5″	TMK-8	$35-$40

Hum 164: Worship holy water font.

Hum 165: Swaying Lullaby

Wall Plaque

Created by master sculptor Arthur Moeller in 1946 and once called Child in a Hammock, this plaque was apparently made in limited quantities and then at some point was removed from production. It does occur in all trademarks, however, and was reinstated in 1978, only to be withdrawn from production again in 1989.

In 1999, it was reissued in TMK-7 along with a Sweet Dreams Hummelscape.

The translation of the inscription on the front of this piece is: "Dreaming of better times."

Hum No.	Basic Size	Trademark	Current Value
165	4-1/2″ x 5-1/4″	TMK-1	$480-$660
165	4-1/2″ x 5-1/4″	TMK-2	$330-$480
165	4-1/2″ x 5-1/4″	TMK-3	$225-$315
165	4-1/2″ x 5-1/4″	TMK-5	$135-$150
165	4-1/2″ x 5-1/4″	TMK-6	$100-$135

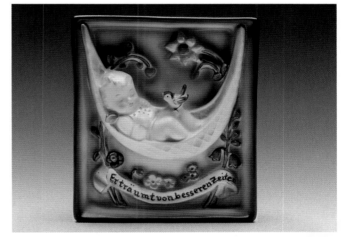

Hum 165: Swaying Lullaby wall plaque.

Hum No.	Basic Size	Trademark	Current Value
165	4-1/2″ x 5-1/4″	TMK-7	$120-$145 with Hummelscape

Hum 166: Boy With Bird

Ashtray

Originally designed by master sculptor Arthur Moeller in 1946 and introduced into the collection in the mid-1940s, this figure was in continuous production until 1989, when it was listed as temporarily withdrawn. There are no significant mold or finish variations.

Hum No.	Basic Size	Trademark	Current Value
166	3-1/4″ x 6-1/4″	TMK-1	$270-$390
166	3-1/4″ x 6-1/4″	TMK-2	$165-$195
166	3-1/4″ x 6-1/4″	TMK-3	$195-$210
166	3-1/4″ x 6-1/4″	TMK-4	$99-$120
166	3-1/4″ x 6-1/4″	TMK-5	$90-$95
166	3-1/4″ x 6-1/4″	TMK-6	$90-$95

Hum 166: Boy With Bird ashtray.

Hum 167: Angel With Bird

Holy Water Font

Sometimes called Angel Sitting or Angel-Bird, this font was crafted by master sculptor Reinhold Unger and first produced in the mid-1940s. There have been changes over the years but none that have any effect on the normal values.

Hum 167: Angel With Bird holy water font.

Hum No.	Basic Size	Trademark	Current Value
167	3-1/4" x 4-1/4"	TMK-1	$150-$180
167	3-1/4" x 4-1/4"	TMK-2	$90-$120
167	3-1/4" x 4-1/4"	TMK-3	$55-$80
167	3-1/4" x 4-1/4"	TMK-4	$45-$55
167	3-1/4" x 4-1/4"	TMK-5	$40-$45
167	3-1/4" x 4-1/4"	TMK-6	$40-$45
167	3-1/4" x 4-1/8"	TMK-7	$40-$45
167	3-1/4" x 4-1/8"	TMK-8	$40-$45

Hum 168: Standing Boy

Wall Plaque

Crafted by master sculptor Arthur Moeller in 1948, this piece must have been produced in limited numbers for the first 20 years because examples in the first three trademarks have never been available in any but small quantities.

It was taken out of production in the Stylized Bee (TMK-3) period, reinstated in 1978 and taken out of production yet again in 1989.

In 1979, this plaque served as the inspiration for a new figurine crafted in its likeness: Hum 399: Valentine Joy.

Hum No.	Basic Size	Trademark	Current Value
168	4-1/8" x 5-1/2"	TMK-1	$290-$395
168	4-1/8" x 5-1/2"	TMK-2	$180-$290
168	4-1/8" x 5-1/2"	TMK-3	$135-$150
168	4-1/8" x 5-1/2"	TMK-5	$135-$150
168	4-1/8" x 5-1/2"	TMK-6	$120-$135

Hum 168: Standing Boy wall plaque.

Hum 169: Bird Duet

There are many variations in this figure, which was designed by master sculptor Arthur Moeller in 1945, but none that have any impact on the normal values of the pieces. It was introduced in the 1940s and has been in continuous production since.

Goebel announced the production of "Personal Touch" figurines in 1996. At that time, four figurines in the line lent themselves well to this application of personalization: Bird Duet was

Hum 169: Bird Duet.

Hum No.	Basic Size	Trademark	Current Value
169	4"	TMK-1	$255-$330
169	4"	TMK-2	$150-$195
169	4"	TMK-3	$130-$140
169	4"	TMK-4	$120-$125
169	4"	TMK-5	$110-$120
169	4"	TMK-6	$105-$110
169	4"	TMK-7	$105-$110
169	4"	TMK-8	$105-$110

one of these. The other three were Latest News (Hum 184), The Guardian (Hum 455), and For Father (Hum 87).

This piece is also sold as a gift set with the Celestial Harmony Hummelscape.

Hum 170: School Boys

Originally crafted by master sculptor Reinhold Unger in 1943 and released in only one size in the 1940s, this figurine was introduced in a new smaller size in the Stylized Bee (TMK-3) period. The larger size, 170/III, was permanently retired by Goebel in 1982. It is now considered a closed edition.

Once called Difficult Problems, there are no variations important enough to affect values.

The middle boy was the inspiration for Hum 460: Authorized Retailer Plaque, which was released in 1986 in eight different languages.

Hum 170: School Boys.

Hum No.	Basic Size	Trademark	Current Value
170/I	7-1/2"	TMK-3	$990-$1,050
170/I	7-1/2"	TMK-4	$930-$960
170/I	7-1/2"	TMK-5	$900-$930
170/I	7-1/2"	TMK-6	$870-$900
170/I	7-1/2"	TMK-7	$840-$860
170/I	7-1/2"	TMK-8	$1,500 retail
170	10"	TMK-1	$2,400-$3,000
170	10"	TMK-2	$1,800-$2,400
170	10"	TMK-3	$1,320-$1,380
170/III	10"	TMK-3	$1,320-$1,380
170/III	10"	TMK-4	$1,260-$1,320

Hum No.	Basic Size	Trademark	Current Value
170/III	10"	TMK-5	$1,200-$1,260
170/III	10"	TMK-6	$1,140-$1,200

Hum 171: Little Sweeper

Little Sweeper was first designed by master sculptor Reinhold Unger in 1944 and released in the mid-1940s in one size, 171. A smaller size, 171/4/0, was introduced in 1988 as part of a four-piece series with matching mini-plates called the "Little Homemakers" series. As a result of this new mold number, the old 171 mold number was changed to 171/0. There are no variations significant enough to have an impact on collector values.

The smaller 171/4/0 size was temporarily withdrawn in 1997.

Hum No.	Basic Size	Trademark	Current Value
171/4/0	3"	TMK-6	$75-$85
171/4/0	3"	TMK-7	$70-$75
171	4-1/2"	TMK-1	$240-$300
171	4-1/2"	TMK-2	$150-$180
171	4-1/2"	TMK-3	$140-$145
171	4-1/2"	TMK-4	$120-$140
171	4-1/2"	TMK-5	$115-$120
171	4-1/2"	TMK-6	$110-$115
171/0	4-1/2"	TMK-6	$105-$110
171/0	4-1/2"	TMK-7	$105-$110
171/0	4-1/2"	TMK-8	$105-$110

Hum 171: Little Sweeper.

Hum 172: Festival Harmony
Angel With Mandolin

Master sculptor Reinhold Unger is responsible for this 1947 design in the larger size only with incised "172."

The major variations of this figure are found in the Crown (TMK-1) and Full Bee (TMK-2) marks. The earliest TMK-1 and some TMK-2 (very rare) have flowers extending from the base well up onto the gown, and the bird is perched on top of the flowers (rather than on the mandolin as in later models). This variation of the piece is valued at $1,500-$2,100, depending on condition and trademark.

The majority of the Full Bee pieces show the flowers just barely extending up over the bottom edge of the gown and the bird situated on the mandolin. The above variations invariably are found on pieces marked with the plain incised mold number 172.

There is one example in existence where the bird is perched on the arm, rather than on the mandolin. This was probably an error in assembly that somehow made it past the quality control inspection. There are several instances of this type of error among other figures with small pieces (such as bottles in baskets), and it usually does not influence value.

The 172/II size was temporarily withdrawn from production on Dec. 31, 1984, and the 172/0 and 172/4/0 sizes were withdrawn in 1999.

Hum 172: Festival Harmony (Angel With Mandolin).

Hum No.	Basic Size	Trademark	Current Value
172/4/0	3-1/8"	TMK-7	$70-$75
172/0	8"	TMK-3	$300-$390
172/0	8"	TMK-4	$240-$285
172/0	8"	TMK-5	$230-$240
172/0	8"	TMK-6	$220-$230
172/0	8"	TMK-7	$$-210-$220
172 (bird on flowers)	10-3/4"	TMK-1	$1,800-$2,100
172 (bird on flowers)	10-3/4"	TMK-2	$1,500-$1,800
172 (bird on mandolin)	10-3/4"	TMK-2	$750-$900
172 (bird on mandolin)	10-3/4"	TMK-3	$600-$740

Hum No.	Basic Size	Trademark	Current Value
172/II	10-3/4"	TMK-3	$390-$480
172/II	10-3/4"	TMK-4	$330-$360
172/II	10-3/4"	TMK-5	$285-$300
172/II	10-3/4"	TMK-6	$270-$285

Hum 173: Festival Harmony
Angel With Flute

Master sculptor Reinhold Unger is credited with this 1947 design in the larger size only with incised "173." It has been restyled several times throughout the years.

The major variations of this figure are to be found with the Crown (TMK-1) and Full Bee (TMK-2) marks. The Crown and some (very rare) Full Bee pieces have the flowers extending from the base well up onto the gown front. This variation of the piece is valued at $1,500-$2,100. Most of the Full Bee pieces have the flowers barely extending from the base up over the bottom edge of the gown. These variations are always found on the pieces marked with the plain incised 173 with no size designator.

The Hum 173 Crown and Full Bee trademarked figures seem to be in shorter supply than those same pieces in the 172 mold number. Probably they were not sold in the same quantities because of the flutes' vulnerability to breakage.

The 173/II size was temporarily withdrawn from production effective Dec. 31, 1984, and the other two sizes were withdrawn in 1999.

Hum 173: Festival Harmony (Angel With Flute).

Hum No.	Basic Size	Trademark	Current Value
173/4/0	3-1/8"	TMK-7	$70-$75
173/0	8"	TMK-3	$300-$390
173/0	8"	TMK-4	$290-$285
173/0	8"	TMK-5	$230-$240
173/0	8"	TMK-6	$220-$230
173/0	8"	TMK-7	$220-$235
173 (high flowers)	11"	TMK-1	$1,800-$2,100
173 (high flowers)	11"	TMK-2	$1,500-$1,800
173 (medium flowers)	11"	TMK-2	$750-$900
173 (low flowers)	11"	TMK-3	$360-$450
173/II	11"	TMK-3	$390-$480
173/II	11"	TMK-4	$330-$360
173/II	11"	TMK-5	$285-$300
173/II	11"	TMK-6	$270-$285

Hum 174: She Loves Me, She Loves Me Not

The work of master sculptor Arthur Moeller in 1945, this piece was released in the 1940s and has been in continuous production in one size since then.

The earliest models were produced with eyes open and a very small feather in the hat. A flower was added to the left fence post and the feather grew larger on the Full Bee (TMK-2) pieces, although some are found in the older style.

The third change was manifest by the time the Three Line Mark (TMK-4) was in use, where the fence post flower is missing and the boy's eyes are downcast. There are transition pieces for each of these changes, so you may encounter the changes associated with more than one trademark.

The current production pieces have the eyes cast downward.

Hum No.	Basic Size	Trademark	Current Value
174	4-1/4"	TMK-1	$330-$420
174	4-1/4"	TMK-2	$210-$270
174	4-1/4"	TMK-3	$175-$180
174	4-1/4"	TMK-4	$165-$175
174	4-1/4"	TMK-5	$150-$165
174	4-1/4"	TMK-6	$150-$165
174	4-1/4"	TMK-7	$145-$150
174	4-1/4"	TMK-8	$279 retail

Hum 174: She Loves Me, She Loves Me Not.

Hum 175: Mother's Darling

First known as Happy Harriet, this figurine was designed by master sculptor Arthur Moeller in 1945 with several revisions since.

The most significant variation of this figure is found in the color of the bags. The older versions have bags colored light pink and yellow-green. The newer ones are blue and red. These variations are insignificant except they allow the collector to spot older pieces without examining the bases. Differences in value are based on earlier trademarks, rather than color variation.

This figurine was permanently retired in 1997. During that year, all those produced carried the "Final Issue 1997" backstamp and came with small gold "Final Issue" medallion.

Hum 175: Mother's Darling.

Hum No.	Basic Size	Trademark	Current Value
175 (pink and green)	5-1/2"	TMK-1	$360-$480
175 (pink and green)	5-1/2"	TMK-2	$240-$315
175 (both ways)	5-1/2"	TMK-3	$195-$225
175	5-1/2"	TMK-4	$170-$195
175	5-1/2"	TMK-5	$165-$175

Hum No.	Basic Size	Trademark	Current Value
175	5-1/2"	TMK-6	$150-$165
175	5-1/2"	TMK-7	$145-$150

Hum 176: Happy Birthday

Created by master sculptor Arthur Moeller in only one size in 1945, the 176/0 has been written "176" (without using the "/0" designator) in the Crown (TMK-1) and Full Bee (TMK-2) marks. It utilizes the decimal point designator ("176.") in the Crown and Full Bee marks as well.

The smaller 176/0 size was introduced in the 1950s and the other piece was renumbered as 176/I.

There are no mold or finish variations that influence current value.

The larger 176/I size was temporarily withdrawn from production in 1999.

Hum 176: Happy Birthday.

Hum No.	Basic Size	Trademark	Current Value
176/0	5"	TMK-2	$240-$300
176/0	5"	TMK-3	$195-$225
176/0	5"	TMK-4	$180-$210
176/0	5"	TMK-5	$165-$170
176/0	5"	TMK-6	$165-$170
176/0	5"	TMK-7	$165-$170
176/0	5"	TMK-8	$279 retail
176	5-1/2"	TMK-1	$510-$690
176	5-1/2"	TMK-2	$360-$450
176/I	5-1/2"	TMK-1	$480-$600
176/I	5-1/2"	TMK-2	$330-$420
176/I	5-1/2"	TMK-3	$270-$315
176/I	5-1/2"	TMK-4	$235-$270
176/I	5-1/2"	TMK-5	$220-$240

Hum No.	Basic Size	Trademark	Current Value
176/I	5-1/2"	TMK-6	$345-$360
176/I	5-1/2"	TMK-7	$200-$205

Hum 177: School Girls

First designed by master sculptor Reinhold Unger in 1946 and produced in the 1940s, this figurine remains in the line today in a smaller size. It was originally known as Master Piece.

No mold or finish variations have an influence on value, outside the normal evolutionary changes on the various trademarked figures. There are similarities between this piece and Stitch in Time (Hum 255) and Knitting Lesson (Hum 256).

The smaller 177/I size was first issued in the 1960s with an incised 1961 copyright date.

The 177/III was permanently retired in 1982. It is now a closed edition, never to be produced again.

Hum 177: School Girls.

Hum No.	Basic Size	Trademark	Current Value
177/I	7-1/2"	TMK-3	$990-$1,050
177/I	7-1/2"	TMK-4	$945-$960
177/I	7-1/2"	TMK-5	$900-$945
177/I	7-1/2"	TMK-6	$870-$900
177/I	7-1/2"	TMK-7	$840-$870
177/I	7-1/2"	TMK-8	$1,500 retail
177	9-1/2"	TMK-1	$2,400-$3,000
177	9-1/2"	TMK-2	$1,800-$2,400
177	9-1/2"	TMK-3	$1,320-$1,380
177/III	9-1/2"	TMK-3	$1,320-$1,380
177/III	9-1/2"	TMK-4	$1,260-$1,320
177/III	9-1/2"	TMK-5	$1,200-$1,260
177/III	9-1/2"	TMK-6	$1,140-$1,200

Hum 178: The Photographer

This figure was created by master sculptor Reinhold Unger in 1948 in only one size and is still produced in the same size today. Color and mold variations do exist, but outside of the value differences due to trademark changes, the variations have no influence on the value of the pieces.

Hum No.	Basic Size	Trademark	Current Value
178	4-3/4"	TMK-1	$450-$660
178	4-3/4"	TMK-2	$300-$390
178	4-3/4"	TMK-3	$270-$300
178	4-3/4"	TMK-4	$220-$260
178	4-3/4"	TMK-5	$205-$225
178	4-3/4"	TMK-6	$205-$220
178	4-3/4"	TMK-7	$195-$345
178	4-3/4"	TMK-8	$369 retail

Hum 178: The Photographer.

Hum 179: Coquettes

The design of master sculptor Arthur Moeller in 1948, older versions of this figure have a blue dress and yellow flowers on  the back of the fence posts. The girls are a bit chubbier, and the hairstyle of the girl with the red kerchief is swept back.

First released around 1950, this figure was not produced with any mold or finish variations that significantly impact its price. It was temporarily withdrawn from production in 1999.

Hum 179: Coquettes.

Hum No.	Basic Size	Trademark	Current Value
179	5-1/4"	TMK-1	$480-$660
179	5-1/4"	TMK-2	$300-$390
179	5-1/4"	TMK-3	$270-$300
179	5-1/4"	TMK-4	$225-$270
179	5-1/4"	TMK-5	$210-$225
179	5-1/4"	TMK-6	$195-$210
179	5-1/4"	TMK-7	$195-$205

Hum 180: Tuneful Goodnight
Wall Plaque

Master sculptor Arthur Moeller designed this piece in 1946, when it was known as Happy Bugler plaque. This plaque is rare in the older marks. It was redesigned toward the end of the Last Bee (TMK-5) era. The newer design has the bugle in a more forward position, making it very vulnerable to breakage.

Hum 180: Tuneful Goodnight wall plaque.

Hum No.	Basic Size	Trademark	Current Value
180	4-1/2" x 4-1/4"	TMK-1	$540-$720 porcelain
180	5" x 4-3/4"	TMK-1	$360-$480
180	5" x 4-3/4"	TMK-2	$240-$330
180	5" x 4-3/4"	TMK-3	$210-$240
180	5" x 4-3/4"	TMK-4	$180-$210
180	5" x 4-3/4"	TMK-5	$135-$150
180	5" x 4-3/4"	TMK-6	$120-$135

Some of the early Crown (TMK-1) pieces are made of porcelain, rather than the usual ceramic material.

This piece was temporarily withdrawn in 1989.

Hum 181:
Old Man Reading Newspaper
Closed Number

Hum No.	Basic Size	Trademark	Current Value
181	6-3/4"	-	$9,000-$12,000

Sometimes referred to as Old People or The Mamas and the Papas, this figure and Hum 189 through Hum 191 and Hum 202 are the only known M.I. Hummel figurines to feature old people as the subjects. Designed by master sculptor Arthur Moeller in 1948, they are more like caricatures than realistic renderings.

An American collector discovered the first four in Europe. The fifth piece, a table lamp (Hum 202), turned up later. These discoveries filled in gaps in the mold number sequence previously designated closed numbers, the term Goebel applied to pieces never placed in production.

At least three complete sets of the five pieces are positively known to exist: one set in the company archives and two others in private collections. There have been other single pieces found, and there are reports of three or more sets in the United States. There is little doubt that some others do exist, either singly or in sets, but the number is likely to be extremely small. They were made in samples only and apparently rejected by the Siessen Convent as atypical of Hummel art.

Hum 181: Old Man Reading Newspaper (closed number).

Hum 182: Good Friends

Created by master sculptor Arthur Moeller in 1946 and released around the late-1940s, Good Friends remains in production today. It was first known as Friends.

Produced in one size only, there are no variations influencing the regular collector value for the various trademarked pieces.

Hum No.	Basic Size	Trademark	Current Value
182	4″	TMK-1	$330-$450
182	4″	TMK-2	$210-$285
182	4″	TMK-3	$180-$195
182	4″	TMK-4	$165-$180
182	4″	TMK-5	$150-$165
182	4″	TMK-6	$145-$150
182	4″	TMK-7	$140-$145
182	4″	TMK-8	$140-$165

Hum 182: Good Friends.

Hum 183: Forest Shrine

This figure, which was the work of master sculptor Reinhold Unger in 1946, was released some time around the late-1940s. Apparently the figures, once called Doe at Shrine, were produced in limited quantities because those with early trademarks are in short supply. They were removed from production some time around the end of the Stylized Bee (TMK-3) period, but put back in 1977. This is probably the reason they are not found bearing the Three Line Mark (TMK-4).

This piece was temporarily withdrawn from production in January 1999.

Hum No.	Basic Size	Trademark	Current Value
183	7″ x 9″	TMK-1	$900-$1,140
183	7″ x 9″	TMK-2	$600-$780
183	7″ x 9″	TMK-3	$420-$570
183	7″ x 9″	TMK-5	$390-$420
183	7″ x 9″	TMK-6	$375-$390
183	7″ x 9″	TMK-7	$240-$360

Hum 183: Forest Shrine.

Hum 184: Latest News

Hum 184: Latest News.

First produced by master sculptor Arthur Moeller in 1946, the older pieces have square bases and wide-open eyes. The figure was remodeled in the 1960s and given a round base and lowered eyes so the boy appears more like he is reading his paper.

Early Crown Mark (TMK-1) pieces can be found made of porcelain, rather than the typical ceramic material. These are rare and therefore worth more than the other Crown examples.

The figures are found with a variety of newspaper names. For a time the figures were produced with any name requested by merchants (i.e., their hometown newspapers). Later models bear the newspaper names: "Das Allerneuste," "Latest News," and "Munchener Presse." As of 1985, the only newspaper name used was "Latest News." These three titles are the most common. Some of the rarer titles can range in value from $750 to $1,500. Be careful in cleaning these items; if you rub too hard or use harsh cleaners, you may rub off the titles. The figures were also produced for a time with no titles.

In 1996, Goebel began producing a special limited edition of Latest News. This design used the U.S. Armed Forces newspaper masthead Stars and Stripes on the front page and a drawing of the famous Checkpoint Charlie of the Berlin Wall on the back page. The edition was limited to 20,000.

Another special edition produced in 1996 is titled The Chancellor's Visit. A special backstamp identifies it as such. This figure was accompanied by a wooden base with a brass plate reading: "In commemoration of Chancellor Dr. Helmut Kohl's historic meeting

Hum No.	Basic Size	Trademark	Current Value
184 (porcelain)	4-1/4" to 4-1/2"	TMK-1	$900-$1,200
184	5" to 5-1/4"	TMK-1	$480-$660
184	5" to 5-1/4"	TMK-2	$330-$420
184	5" to 5-1/4"	TMK-3	$255-$300
184	5" to 5-1/4"	TMK-4	$230-$255
184	5" to 5-1/4"	TMK-5	$220-$230
184	5"	TMK-6	$210-$225
184	5"	TMK-7	$205-$210
184	5"	TMK-8	$359 retail
184	5"	TMK-8 limited edition	$359 70th Anniversary

with President Bill Clinton, Milwaukee, Wisconsin, May 23, 1996." The newspaper is imprinted with the *Milwaukee Journal-Sentinel* masthead and the headline reads: "Clinton and Chancellor Helmut Kohl Meet in Milwaukee Today." An undisclosed number (probably very few) of these figures were produced in a limited edition for Mader's Tower Gallery.

There are two other special limited editions as well. The first, called A Celebration of Friendship Across the Seas, between Cobourg, Ontario, Canada and Coburg, Germany, 1798-1998, was produced in a limited edition of 1,998 figurines. Canadian and German flags accompany the figurine. The second is called Looney Tunes Spotlight Collection from Warner Brothers, produced in a limited edition of 7,958. The front of the newspaper on this version of the figurine reads, "Goebel Steps Into the Spotlight with Warner Brothers." A small book titled *Spotlight Collection* is included. Both of these figurines are TMK-7.

Goebel announced the production of "Personal Touch" figurines in 1996. At that time, four figurines in the line lent themselves well to this application: Latest News was one of these. The other three were: Bird Duet (Hum 169), The Guardian (Hum 455), and For Father (Hum 87).

Hum 185: Accordion Boy

Hum 185: Accordion Boy.

First styled by master sculptor Reinhold Unger in 1947, this piece remained in continuous production until 1994. Once called On the Alpine Pasture, there have been no significant variations in the mold or the finish that would affect value. Minor color variations do exist, however, in the accordion.

This piece is one of several figurines that comprise the Hummel orchestra.

Hum No.	Basic Size	Trademark	Current Value
185	5-1/4"	TMK-1	$330-$450
185	5-1/4"	TMK-2	$225-$270
185	5-1/4"	TMK-3	$180-$195
185	5-1/4"	TMK-4	$170-$180
185	5-1/4"	TMK-5	$145-$165
185	5-1/4"	TMK-6	$135-$150
185	5-1/4"	TMK-7	$120-$135

Goebel permanently retired Accordion Boy in 1994. It will never be produced again. Figures made in the final year of production bear the "Final Issue 1994" backstamp and came with the small gold "Final Issue" commemorative tag.

Hum 186: Sweet Music

This piece was the original work of master sculptor Reinhold Unger in 1947. It was once known as Playing to the Dance.

The most significant variation of Sweet Music is the striped slippers shown on the figure in the accompanying photo. It is found on the Crown Mark (TMK-1) figures and will bring $600-$900, depending upon condition. The plain painted slippers are also found on Crown Mark era figures.

It is one of several figurines that make up the Hummel orchestra.

Recently, a 12-1/2″ version of Sweet Music was introduced as part of the "Millennium Love" series, which also included Serenade (Hum 85/III), Little Fiddler (Hum 2/III), Band Leader (Hum 129/III), and Soloist (Hum 135/III). These oversized pieces (Hum 85/III) were in limited supply and had to be special-ordered through an authorized M.I. Hummel retailer

Hum 186: Sweet Music.

The most significant variation of Sweet Music is with striped slippers with the Crown Mark (TMK-1).

Hum No.	Basic Size	Trademark	Current Value
186 (striped slippers)	5″ to 5-1/2″	TMK-1	$600-$900
186	5-1/4″	TMK-1	$360-$450
186	5-1/4″	TMK-2	$240-$270
186	5-1/4″	TMK-3	$195-$210
186	5-1/4″	TMK-4	$180-$195

Hum No.	Basic Size	Trademark	Current Value
186	5-1/4″	TMK-5	$165-$170
186	5-1/4″	TMK-6	$165-$170
186	5″	TMK-7	$130-$150
186	5″	TMK-8	$130-$150
186/III	13-1/2″	TMK-8	$1,550 retail

Hum 187: Dealer Plaques and Display Plaques

Originally crafted by master sculptor Reinhold Unger in 1947, the 187 mold number was used on all dealer plaques until 1986, when it was taken out of production (see Hum 460).

The older pieces have the traditional bumblebee perched on top. The piece was redesigned in 1972 to have a raised round area known as the "moon top" in place of the traditional bumblebee and was imprinted with the Stylized Bee (TMK-3). The plaques in TMK-7 do not have this round medallion-like area. Some plaques have been found with the mold numbers 187/A and 187/C.

The accompanying picture is of a special edition of the display plaque made available for a short time to local chapter members of what was then the Goebel Collectors' Club. They were personalized with chapter and member name.

A number of the 187-mold plaques in existence in Europe were made specifically for individual stores and displayed the store name, in addition to the traditional wordings.

A suggested retail price list from a few years ago indicates the availability of a "Display Plaque Retailer" and a "Display Plaque Collector." The list suggested that each bore the 187 mold number. Neither is offered anymore.

A specially customized Hum 187 dealer plaque.

Hum 187: Display Plaque. A special edition commemorating 100 years of service by the Army and Air Force Exchange Service (AAFES).

Hum No.	Basic Size	Trademark	Current Value
187	5-1/2″ x 4″	TMK-1	$750-$960
187	5-1/2″ x 4″	TMK-2	$450-$540
187	5-1/2″ x 4″	TMK-3	$300-$360

Hum No.	Basic Size	Trademark	Current Value
187	5-1/2″ x 4″	TMK-4	$270-$300
187	5-1/2″ x 4″	TMK-5	$105-$135
187/A	5-1/2″ x 4″	TMK-5	$105-$135
187/A	5-1/2″ x 4″	TMK-6	$90-$105
187/A	5-1/2″ x 4″	TMK-6	$70-$85
187/A	5-1/2″ x 4″	TMK-7	$70-$85

Hum 188: Celestial Musician

Until 1983, this piece was made only in the 7" size, with a mold number of 188. Beginning in 1983, a smaller size was produced. The smaller size is 5-1/2" and bears the mold number 188/0. At the same time, the mold number of the 188 was changed to 188/I on the TMK-7 pieces to reflect the difference.

This figure, which was first designed by master sculptor Reinhold Unger in 1948, has reportedly surfaced in white overglaze. Other than that, there have been no significant variations that would influence normal values for the various trademarked pieces.

The 188/I size was temporarily withdrawn from production in 1999 and the 188/4/0 size was temporarily withdrawn on June 15, 2002.

Hum 188: Celestial Musician.

Hum No.	Basic Size	Trademark	Current Value
188/4/0	3-1/8"	TMK-7	$80-$85
188/4/0	3-1/8"	TMK-8	$80-$85
188/0	5"	TMK-6	$165-$175
188/0	5"	TMK-7	$135-$165
188/0	5"	TMK-8	$279 retail
188	7"	TMK-1	$900-$1,200
188	7"	TMK-2	$510-$660
188	7"	TMK-3	$255-$285
188	7"	TMK-4	$225-$255
188	7"	TMK-5	$200-$210
188	7"	TMK-6	$190-$195

Hum No.	Basic Size	Trademark	Current Value
188/I	7"	TMK-6	$185-$195
188/I	7"	TMK-7	$180-$185

Hum 189: Old Woman Knitting
Closed Number

(See description under Hum 181.)

Hum 189: Old Woman Knitting (closed number).

Hum No.	Basic Size	Current Value
189	6-3/4"	$9,000-$12,000

Hum 190: Old Woman Walking to Market
Closed Number

(See description under Hum 181.)

Hum 190: Old Woman Walking to Market (closed number).

Hum No.	Basic Size	Current Value
190	6-3/4"	$9,000-$12,000

Hum 191:
Old Man Walking to Market
Closed Number

(See description under Hum 181.)

Hum 191: Old Man Walking to Market (closed number).

Hum No.	Basic Size	Current Value
191	6-3/4"	$9,000-$12,000

Hum 193: Angel Duet
Candleholder

This candleholder, which was the original work of master sculptor Reinhold Unger in 1948, is essentially the same design as Hum 261 except that the 261 is not a candleholder.

This piece has been produced in two variations, noticeable in the rear view of the figure. One shows the angel not holding the songbook and with an arm around the waist of the other. In the other design, one angel has a hand on the shoulder of the other angel. Both versions are found in Crown Mark (TMK-1) and Full Bee (TMK-2). The transition to the new arm-around-waist figure took place during the Full Bee period.

This piece has been found in white overglaze. It is extremely rare and would be worth $3,000-$4,000 if found.

This candleholder was temporarily withdrawn from production in 1999.

Hum No.	Basic Size	Trademark	Current Value
193	5"	TMK-1	$785-$1,080
193	5"	TMK-2	$360-$420
193	5"	TMK-3	$195-$240
193	5"	TMK-4	$175-$195
193	5"	TMK-5	$165-$175
193	5"	TMK-6	$150-$165
193	5"	TMK-7	$150-$165

Hum 192: Candlelight
Candleholder

There are two distinct versions of this piece, which was first designed by master sculptor Reinhold Unger in 1948 and originally called Carrier of Light. The chief difference is found in the candle receptacle. This variation is found on the Crown Mark (TMK-1) and Full Bee (TMK-2) figurines. The transition from this older style to the newer one where the candle socket is held in the hand (no extension) took place in the Stylized Bee (TMK-3) era, so you may also find the old design so marked.

This candleholder was temporarily withdrawn from production in 1999.

Hum 192: Candlelight candleholder.

Hum No.	Basic Size	Trademark	Current Value
192	6-1/4"	TMK-1	$780-$1,080
192	6-3/4"	TMK-2	$480-$600
192 (long candle)	6-3/4"	TMK-3	$360-$420
192 (short candle)	6-3/4"	TMK-3	$210-$225
192	6-3/4"	TMK-4	$195-$210
192	6-3/4"	TMK-5	$175-$130
192	6-3/4"	TMK-6	$165-$175
192	6-3/4"	TMK-7	$165-$175

Hum 193: Angel Duet candleholder.

Hum 194: Watchful Angel

Once called Angelic Care and Guardian Angel, this figurine was designed by master sculptor Reinhold Unger in 1948 and entered the line shortly thereafter. There are no significant mold or finish variations reported. Most pieces have an incised 1948 copyright date.

Hum No.	Basic Size	Trademark	Current Value
194	6-1/2"	TMK-1	$960-$1,260
194	6-1/2"	TMK-2	$390-$480
194	6-1/2"	TMK-3	$285-$345
194	6-1/2"	TMK-4	$255-$300
194	6-1/2"	TMK-5	$250-$255
194	6-1/2"	TMK-6	$250-$255
194	6-1/2"	TMK-7	$240-$250
194	6-1/2"	TMK-8	$399 retail

Hum 194: Watchful Angel.

Hum 195: Barnyard Hero

Introduced into the line in 1948 and the work of master sculptor Reinhold Unger, this figure has undergone some major mold changes over the years, but most were associated with a trademark change or a change in the finish of the entire collection. None has had a significant influence on collector values.

The smaller 195/2/0 size was introduced in the 1950s and remains in production today. The larger 195/I size, however, was temporarily withdrawn from production in 1999.

Hum No.	Basic Size	Trademark	Current Value
195/2/0	3-3/4" to 4"	TMK-2	$240-$270
195/2/0	3-3/4" to 4"	TMK-3	$180-$195
195/2/0	3-3/4" to 4"	TMK-4	$150-$180
195/2/0	3-3/4" to 4"	TMK-5	$135-$140
195/2/0	3-3/4" to 4"	TMK-6	$130-$135
195/2/0	3-3/4" to 4"	TMK-7	$130-$135
195/2/0	3-3/4" to 4"	TMK-8	$219 retail
195	5-3/4" to 6"	TMK-1	$600-$720
195	5-3/4" to 6"	TMK-2	$390-$450
195/I	5-1/2"	TMK-2	$360-$450
195/I	5-1/2"	TMK-3	$285-$315
195/I	5-1/2"	TMK-4	$250-$285
195/I	5-1/2"	TMK-5	$225-$250
195/I	5-1/2"	TMK-6	$360-$375
195/I	5-1/2"	TMK-7	$210-$220

Hum 195: Barnyard Hero.

Hum 196: Telling Her Secret

This figurine, which was designed by master sculptor Reinhold Unger in 1948, was introduced shortly thereafter in a 6-3/4" basic size only. Its original name was The Secret, and the girl on the right is the same as that in Which Hand? (Hum 258).

During the Full Bee (TMK-2) period, a second, smaller size (196/0) was introduced. With this new size came a change of the mold number for the larger one, from 196 to 196/I. The Full Bee (TMK-2) can be found with either mold number.

The larger 196/I size and the smaller variation have been temporarily withdrawn.

Hum No.	Basic Size	Trademark	Current Value
196/0	5-1/4"	TMK-2	$390-$450
196/0	5-1/4"	TMK-3	$270-$300
196/0	5-1/4"	TMK-4	$240-$270
196/0	5-1/4"	TMK-5	$180-$230
196/0	5-1/4"	TMK-6	$210-$225
196/0	5-1/4"	TMK-7	$210-$225
196/0	5-1/4"	TMK-8	$399 retail
196	6-3/4"	TMK-1	$720-$900
196	6-3/4"	TMK-2	$480-$600
196/I	6-3/4"	TMK-2	$450-$570
196/I	6-3/4"	TMK-3	$300-$330
196/I	6-3/4"	TMK-4	$270-$300
196/I	6-3/4"	TMK-5	$255-$270
196/I	6-3/4"	TMK-6	$240-$255

Hum 196: Telling Her Secret.

Hum 197: Be Patient

There are no important mold or finish variations to be found on this late-1940s release, which was first crafted by master sculptor Reinhold Unger in 1948 and previously called Mother of Ducks. There is, however, a mold number variation that is significant. The figure was first produced in only one size with an incised mold number of 197. When a smaller size, 197/2/0, was produced in the Stylized Bee (TMK-3) period, the mold number on the larger one was changed to 197/I.

Attendees of the 1994 Disneyana Convention were given the opportunity to purchase a limited edition set of figurines on a wooden base. A regular-production Be Patient (Hum 197/2/0) bearing TMK-7 was paired with a Minnie Mouse figurine posed the same way. Minnie bears the incised mold number 17324, a limited edition indicator, and TMK-7.

Hum 197: Be Patient.

Hum No.	Basic Size	Trademark	Current Value
197/2/0	4-1/4"	TMK-2	$240-$300
197/2/0	4-1/4"	TMK-3	$180-$210
197/2/0	4-1/4"	TMK-4	$165-$180
197/2/0	4-1/4"	TMK-5	$145-$165
197/2/0	4-1/4"	TMK-6	$140-$145
197/2/0	4-1/4"	TMK-7	$140-$145
197/2/0	4-1/4"	TMK-8	$235
197	6-1/4"	TMK-1	$480-$600
197	6-1/4"	TMK-2	$330-$420
197/I	6-1/4"	TMK-2	$300-$390
197/I	6-1/4"	TMK-3	$255-$285
197/I	6-1/4"	TMK-4	$210-$255
197/I	6-1/4"	TMK-5	$210-$225
197/I	6-1/4"	TMK-6	$205-$225
197/I	6-1/4"	TMK-7	$200-$215

The issue price for the set was $395. It can now bring around $600-$750.

The larger 197/I size of Be Patient was temporarily withdrawn from production in 1999, but the smaller variation remains in production today.

Hum 198: Home From Market

There are no important mold or finish variations to be found on this late-1940s release, which was the design of master sculptor Arthur Moeller in 1948. There is, however, a mold number variation that is significant. The figure was first produced in only one size with the incised mold number 198. When a smaller size, 198/2/0, was issued in the Stylized Bee (TMK-3) period, the mold number of the larger figure changed to 198/I.

The larger 198//I size was temporarily withdrawn from production in 1999, but the smaller variation is still available today.

Hum 198: Home From Market.

Home From Market with a red line on the base. This indicates that this particular piece was a master model. Note the archive medallion wired and sealed around the legs.

Hum No.	Basic Size	Trademark	Current Value
198	4-1/2"	TMK-2	$225-$240
198/2/0	4-3/4"	TMK-2	$195-$225
198/2/0	4-3/4"	TMK-3	$150-$165
198/2/0	4-3/4"	TMK-4	$150-$165
198/2/0	4-3/4"	TMK-5	$130-$150
198/2/0	4-3/4"	TMK-6	$125-$130
198/2/0	4-3/4"	TMK-7	$120-$125
198/2/0	4-3/4"	TMK-8	$120-$125
198	5-3/4"	TMK-1	$390-$480
198	5-3/4"	TMK-2	$270-$330
198/I	5-3/4"	TMK-2	$280-$300

Hum No.	Basic Size	Trademark	Current Value
198/I	5-3/4"	TMK-3	$199-$225
198/I	5-3/4"	TMK-4	$165-$195
198/I	5-3/4"	TMK-5	$150-$165
198/I	5-3/4"	TMK-6	$135-$155
198/I	5-3/4"	TMK-7	$125-$150

Hum 199: Feeding Time

Crafted by master sculptor Arthur Moeller in 1948, there are no major mold or finish variations outside the normal evolution of this figurine. There is, however, a mold number variation that is important. This piece was first produced in the late-1940s in only one size with the incised mold number 199. It was also sometimes found as "199." with the decimal designator. When a new smaller size, 199/0, was introduced during the Stylized Bee (TMK-3) era, the number on the larger size was changed to 199/I.

The older pieces have blonde hair and the newer ones dark hair. The facial features are slightly different on the newer pieces as well.

The larger 199/I size was temporarily withdrawn from production in 1999 and retired in 2007.

In 2009 Manufaktur Rödental redesigned Feeding Time as a Masterpiece Collection figurine. This figurine was redesigned to mirror the original drawing of Sister Hummel. A ceramic postcard with a wooden easel displaying the original artwork was included. A worldwide limited edition of 1,250 figurines was made. A special Masterpiece backstamp, TMK-9 backstamp, and the numbered edition are found on the bottom of the figurine.

Hum 199: Feeding Time.

Hum 199/III: Feeding Time.

Hum No.	Basic Size	Trademark	Current Value
199/0	4-1/4"	TMK-2	$225-$300
199/0	4-1/4"	TMK-3	$195-$210
199/0	4-1/4"	TMK-4	$165-$180
199/0	4-1/4"	TMK-5	$150-$165
199/0	4-1/4"	TMK-6	$145-$150

Hum No.	Basic Size	Trademark	Current Value
199/0	4-1/4"	TMK-7	$135-$145
199/0	4-1/4"	TMK-8	$259 retail
199	5-3/4"	TMK-1	$480-$600
199	5-3/4"	TMK-2	$315-$375
199/I	5-3/4"	TMK-2	$285-$345
199/I	5-3/4"	TMK-3	$255-$285
199/I	5-3/4"	TMK-4	$235-$255
199/I	5-3/4"	TMK-5	$205-$225
199/I	5-3/4"	TMK-6	$195-$205
199/I	5-3/4"	TMK-7	$185-$195
199/III	13"	TMK-9	$1,500-$2,000

Hum 200: Little Goat Herder

There are no important mold or color variations outside those occurring during the normal evolution of the figurine, which was the original design of master sculptor Arthur Moeller in 1948. There is, however, a mold number variation that is significant. This figure was first produced in only one size, with the incised mold number 200. It also sometimes appeared as "200." with the decimal designator. When a new smaller basic size of 4-3/4" was introduced in the Stylized Bee (TMK-3) era, the mold number on the larger size was changed to 200/I.

Some of the Full Bee (TMK-2) pieces in the smaller size have been found with the "M.I." initials directly above the "Hummel," rather than next to it as is traditional.

In 2010 Little Goat Herder was redesigned and sculpted by master sculptor Marion Huschka to more closely reflect Sister Hummel's artwork. It was a Masterpiece Edition and limited to 1,250 figurines worldwide. It included a ceramic plaque of the original drawing and an easel for display.

Hum No.	Basic Size	Trademark	Current Value
200/0	4-3/4"	TMK-2	$240-$300
200/0	4-3/4"	TMK-3	$180-$195
200/0	4-3/4"	TMK-4	$170-$180
200/0	4-3/4"	TMK-5	$150-$170
200/0	4-3/4"	TMK-6	$145-$150
200/0	4-3/4"	TMK-7	$140-$145
200/0	4-3/4"	TMK-8	$259 retail
200	5-1/2"	TMK-1	$390-$510
200	5-1/2"	TMK-2	$300-$360
200/I	5-1/2"	TMK-2	$270-$330
200/I	5-1/2"	TMK-3	$210-$240
200/I	5-1/2"	TMK-4	$180-$210
200/I	5-1/2"	TMK-5	$170-$180
200/I	5-1/2"	TMK-6	$165-$170
200/I	5-1/2"	TMK-7	$160-$165
200/I	5-1/2"	TMK-8	$175-$180
200/III	13-1/4"	TMK-9 LE	$2,200

Hum 200: Little Goat Herder.

Hum 200/III: Little Goat Herder Masterpiece Edition.

Hum 201: Retreat to Safety

Designed by master sculptor Reinhold Unger in 1948 and once called Afraid, there are no important mold or finish variations outside those occurring during the normal evolution of this figure. There is, however, a significant mold number variation. The figure

was first produced in one size only with the incised mold number 201. It also sometimes appeared with the decimal point designator. When a new smaller size of 4" was introduced, the mold number on the 5-1/2" size was changed to 201/I.

The larger 201/I size was temporarily withdrawn from production in 1999.

Hum 201: Retreat to Safety.

Hum No.	Basic Size	Trademark	Current Value
201/2/0	4"	TMK-2	$240-$270
201/2/0	4"	TMK-3	$180-$195
201/2/0	4"	TMK-4	$150-$180
201/2/0	4"	TMK-5	$140-$145
201/2/0	4"	TMK-6	$135-$140
201/2/0	4"	TMK-7	$130-$135
201/2/0	4"	TMK-8	$219 retail
201	5-1/2"	TMK-1	$600-$720
201	5-1/2"	TMK-2	$390-$450
201/I	5-1/2"	TMK-2	$360-$420
201/I	5-1/2"	TMK-3	$285-$315
201/I	5-1/2"	TMK-4	$250-$285
201/I	5-1/2"	TMK-5	$225-$250
201/I	5-1/2"	TMK-6	$215-$225
201/I	5-1/2"	TMK-7	$210-$215

Hum 202: Old Man Reading Newspaper
Table Lamp, Closed Number

This is the same figure as Hum 181, except on a lamp. It was made as a sample only by master sculptor Arthur Moeller in 1948 after the Siessen Convent rejected it for production. It was listed as a closed number that same year. See further description under Hum 181.

Hum 202: Old Man Reading Newspaper table lamp (closed number).

Hum No.	Basic Size	Current Value
202	8-1/4"	$9,000-$12,000

Hum No.	Basic Size	Trademark	Current Value
203/2/0 (with two shoes)	4"	TMK-2	$720-$900
203/2/0	4"	TMK-2	$255-$300
203/2/0	4"	TMK-3	$210-$240
203/2/0	4"	TMK-4	$165-$210
203/2/0	4"	TMK-5	$150-$165
203/2/0	4"	TMK-6	$135-$165
203	5"	TMK-1	$450-$600
203	5"	TMK-2	$330-$390
203/I	5"	TMK-2	$300-$360
203/I	5"	TMK-3	$240-$270
203/I	5"	TMK-4	$210-$240

Hum 203: Signs of Spring
Closed Edition

Crafted by master sculptor Arthur Moeller and released about 1950, there is a significant mold variation in the 4" basic size, 203/2/0. This size, which was first called Scandal, was introduced in the Full Bee (TMK-2) period, when the figure had both feet on the ground and was wearing shoes. At some point during this period, it was remodeled so that her right foot was raised above the ground and the foot had no shoe. The first variation with the two shoes is scarcer.

Hum 203: Signs of Spring (closed edition).

Another mold variation is worthy of note. One version of this figure has four fence pickets instead of the usual three, and there are more flowers present.

There is also a variation in mold numbering. This figure was first released in the 201 mold number in only the 5" size. When the smaller 4" size, 203/2/0, was released in the Full Bee era, the mold number of the larger size was changed to 203/I. The earlier "203" is also occasionally found with the decimal designator.

Both sizes of Signs of Spring were permanently retired in 1990.

Hum No.	Basic Size	Trademark	Current Value
203/I	5"	TMK-5	$180-$195
203/I	5"	TMK-6	$165-$180

Hum 204: Weary Wanderer

This figurine, which was first known as Tired Little Traveler, was designed by master sculptor Reinhold Unger in 1949. Most pieces bear an incised 1949 copyright date.

There is a major variation associated with this figurine. The normal figurine has eyes painted with no color. The variation has blue eyes. There are only a handful of blue-eyed pieces presently known to be in collectors' hands. These are valued at about $2,000-$3,000 each.

Hum 204 was temporarily withdrawn from production in 1999 and was reintroduced in 2009 under TMK-9.

Hum 204: Weary Wanderer.

Hum No.	Basic Size	Trademark	Current Value
204	6″	TMK-1	$420-$540
204	6″	TMK-2	$300-$360
204	6″	TMK-3	$225-$255
204	6″	TMK-4	$195-$225
204	6″	TMK-5	$180-$195
204	6″	TMK-6	$175-$180
204	6″	TMK-7	$170-$175
204	6″	TMK-9	$299

Hum 205: German Language Dealer Plaque or Display Plaque

There are several merchant display plaques used by dealers. Master sculptor Reinhold Unger first designed each in 1949. The plaque has a large bumblebee perched atop the plaque and a Merry Wanderer figure attached to the right side. All are 5-1/2″ x 4-1/2″ in basic size. Although listed as a closed edition in 1949, some plaques do carry the Stylized Bee (TMK-3), which means they were produced after 1949. See other dealer plaques: Hum 187, 208, 209, 210, 211, and 213.

Hum 205: German language dealer plaque or display plaque.

Hum No.	Basic Size	Trademark	Current Value
205	5-1/2″ x 4-1/2″	TMK-1	$840-$1,020
205	5-1/2″ x 4-1/2″	TMK-2	$600-$720
205	5-1/2″ x 4-1/2″	TMK-3	$510-$600

Hum 206: Angel Cloud

Holy Water Font

Master sculptor Reinhold Unger is responsible for the design of this piece, which was released in the early 1950s and has been redesigned several times. The newer pieces carry an incised 1949 copyright date.

It has been in and out of production since the beginning but apparently in very limited quantities each time.

Hum 206: Angel Cloud holy water font.

Hum No.	Basic Size	Trademark	Current Value
206	2-1/4″ x 4-3/4″	TMK-1	210-$300
206	2-1/4″ x 4-3/4″	TMK-2	$150-$210
206	2-1/4″ x 4-3/4″	TMK-3	$120-$150
206	2-1/4″ x 4-3/4″	TMK-4	$40-$55
206	2-1/4″ x 4-3/4″	TMK-5	$40-$70
206	2-1/4″ x 4-3/4″	TMK-6	$35-$40
206	2-1/4″ x 4-3/4″	TMK-7	$35-$40

The older trademarks have always been in short supply.

This piece was once again temporarily withdrawn in 1999.

Hum 207: Heavenly Angel
Holy Water Font

Modeled by master sculptor Reinhold Unger in 1949 and first released in the early 1950s, this piece has the distinction of the highest mold number in the collection that can be found with the Crown Mark (TMK-1). There are a number of variations to be found, but none have any significant impact on collector value. This piece was the inspiration for the first Annual Plate (Hum 264), which was produced in 1971.

Hum 207: Heavenly Angel holy water font.

Hum No.	Basic Size	Trademark	Current Value
207	2" x 4-3/4"	TMK-1	$210-$300
207	2" x 4-3/4"	TMK-2	$90-$105
207	2" x 4-3/4"	TMK-3	$60-$75
207	2" x 4-3/4"	TMK-4	$45-$55
207	2" x 4-3/4"	TMK-5	$40-$45
207	2" x 4-3/4"	TMK-6	$40-$65
207	2" x 4-3/4"	TMK-7	$35-$40
207	2" x 4-3/4"	TMK-8	$60 retail

Hum 208: French Language Dealer Plaque

There are several merchant display plaques used by dealers. Each has a large bumblebee perched atop the plaque and a Merry Wanderer figure attached to the right side. All except the Spanish variation are 5-1/2" x 4-1/2" in basic size. See other dealer plaques: Hum 187, 205, 209, 210, 211, and 213.

Hum No.	Basic Size	Trademark	Current Value
208	5-1/2" x 4-1/2"	TMK-2	$2,400-$3,600
208	5-1/2" x 4-1/2"	TMK-3	$1,800-$2,400

Hum 209: Swedish Language Dealer Plaque

There are several merchant display plaques used by dealers. Each has a large bumblebee perched atop the plaque and a Merry Wanderer figure attached to the right side. All except the Spanish variation are 5-1/2" x 4-1/2" in basic size. Two distinctly different lettering designs have been found. See other dealer plaques: Hum 187, 205, 208, 210, 211, and 213.

Hum No.	Basic Size	Trademark	Current Value
209	5-1/2" x 4-1/2"	TMK-2	$2,400-$3,600

Hum 210: English Language Dealer Plaque

There are several merchant display plaques used by dealers. Each has a large bumblebee perched atop the plaque and a Merry Wanderer figure attached to the right side. All except the Spanish variation are 5-1/2" x 4-1/2" in basic size. Hum 210, the English language plaque, is a Schmid Brothers display plaque made specifically for this distributor. "Schmid Bros., Boston" is found molded in bas-relief on the suitcase. There are only four pieces known to exist. See other dealer plaques: Hum 187, 205, 208, 209, 211, and 213.

Hum No.	Basic Size	Trademark	Current Value
208	5-1/2" x 4-1/2"	TMK-2	$12,000-$15,000

Hum 211: English Language Dealer Plaque

There are several merchant display plaques used by dealers. Each has a large bumblebee perched atop the plaque and a Merry Wanderer figure attached to the right side. All except the Spanish variation are 5-1/2" x 4-1/2" in basic size. Hum 211, the English language plaque, is even rarer than the other English plaque, Hum 210. There are only two known examples of Hum 211 in collectors' hands. One is in white overglaze with no color and the other is in full color. The full-color example is the only dealer plaque to use the word "Oeslau" as the location of Goebel in Bavaria. The name has since been changed to Rödental, but this is not found on any plaques. See other dealer plaques: Hum 187, 205, 208, 209, 210, and 213.

Hum No.	Basic Size	Trademark	Current Value
211	5-1/2" x 4-1/2"	TMK-2	$12,000-$15,000

Hum 212: Orchestra
Closed Number

This was previously suspected to be another dealer plaque. Then it was thought that this number was intended to be utilized with the letters A through F as mold numbers for a set of musician pieces called "Orchestra." It is now known that this mold number was used for a short time merely as an inventory designation for the Hum 129: Band Leader and several of the musical figurines. The number was not incised on the figures.

Hum 214: Nativity Set.

Hum 214: Nativity Set

In the early Hum 214 sets, which were first designed by master sculptor Reinhold Unger in 1951, the Madonna and Infant Jesus were molded as one piece. The later figures are found as two separate pieces. The one-piece variations are closed editions.

Hum 366: Flying Angel is frequently used with this set. One old model camel and two more recently issued camels are also frequently used with the set, but these are not Hummel pieces.

Collectors may note the omission of 214/I in the listing below. It was assumed that the mold number was never used because of the possible confusion that might result from the

Hum 213: Spanish Language Dealer Plaque

There are several merchant display plaques used by dealers. Each has a large bumblebee perched atop the plaque and a Merry Wanderer figure attached to the right side. Hum 213, the Spanish language plaque, is slightly bigger than the other dealer plaques at 5-3/4" x 4-1/2". See other dealer plaques: Hum 187, 205, 208, 209, 210, and 211.

Hum No.	Basic Size	Trademark	Current Value
213	5-3/4" x 4-1/2"	TMK-2	$4,800-$6,000

similarity of the "I" and the "1" when incised as a mold number. The existence of a Hum 214/I has now been substantiated. The piece found is in white overglaze and is of two connected geese similar to the geese in the Goose Girl figure. It has the incised M.I. Hummel signature.

Because there are so many pieces under this listing, the following guide will first help you with the names matched to the Hum numbers for each figurine. The pricing list then follows that identifying list.

214/A and 214/A/I: Virgin Mary and Infant Jesus (one-piece variation)
214/A and 214/A/I: Virgin Mary
214/A (or 214 A/K) and 214/A/K/I: Infant Jesus
214/B and 214/B/I: Joseph
214/C and 214/C/I: Angel, standing (Good Night Angel)
214/D and 214/D/I: Angel, kneeling (Angel Serenade)
214/E and 214/E/I: We Congratulate
214/F and 214/F/I: Shepherd, standing with sheep
214/G and 214/G/I: Shepherd, kneeling
214/H and 214/H/I: Shepherd Boy, kneeling with flute (Little Tooter)
214/J and 214/J/I: Donkey
214/K and 214/K/I: Ox/cow
214/L and 214/L/I: Moorish king, standing
214/M and 214/M/I: King, kneeling on one knee
214/N and 214/N/I: King, kneeling with box
214/O and 214/O/I: Lamb
366 and 366/1: Flying Angel

There are also two wooden stables without Hum numbers to go with both the 12- to 16-piece sets and the three-piece sets.

Hum No.	Basic Size	Trademark	Current Value (Color)	Current Value (White)
214/A	6-1/2" one piece	TMK-2	$1,200-$1,500	$1,500-$1,800
214/A	6-1/4" to 6-1/2"	TMK-2	$180-$240	$240-$300
214/A	6-1/4" to 6-1/2"	TMK-3	$130-$175	$195-$240
214/A	6-1/4" to 6-1/2"	TMK-4	$135-$150	$150-$195
214/A	6-1/4" to 6-1/2"	TMK-5	$125-$135	$120-$135

Hum No.	Basic Size	Trademark	Current Value (Color)	Current Value (White)
214/A	6-1/4" to 6-1/2"	TMK-6	$120-$125	$120-$125
214/A/I	6-1/4" to 6-1/2"	TMK-7	$120-$125	N/A
214/A/M/I	6-1/4" to 6-1/2"	TMK-8	$130	N/A
214/A	1-1/2" x 3-1/2"	TMK-2	$70-$80	$130-$155
214/A	1-1/2" x 3-1/2"	TMK-3	$60-$65	$95-$130
214/A	1-1/2" x 3-1/2"	TMK-4	$60-$70	$55-$70
214/A	1-1/2" x 3-1/2"	TMK-5	$55-$65	$35-$45
214/A/K	1-1/2" x 3-1/2"	TMK-6	$50-$55	$35-$45
214/A/K/I	1-1/2" x 3-1/2"	TMK-7	$45-$50	N/A
214/A/K/I	1-1/2" x 3-1/2"	TMK-8	$45-450	N/A
214/B	7-1/2"	TMK-2	$180-$240	$210-$255
214/B	7-1/2"	TMK-3	$150-$170	$165-$210
214/B	7-1/2"	TMK-4	$135-$150	$135-$165
214/B	7-1/2"	TMK-5	$125-$135	$105-$120
214/B	7-1/2"	TMK-6	$125-$125	$90-$105
214/B/I	7-1/2"	TMK-7	$120-$125	N/A
214/B/I	7-1/2"	TMK-8	$120	N/A
214/C	3-1/2"	TMK-2	$95-$120	$225-$250
214/C	3-1/2"	TMK-3	$75-$90	$190-$225
214/C	3-1/2"	TMK-4	$70-$75	$165-$190
214/C	3-1/2"	TMK-5	$70-$75	N/A
214/C	3-1/2"	TMK-6	$65-$75	N/A
214/C/I	3-1/2"	TMK-7	$60-$65	N/A
214/C/I	3-1/2"	TMK-8	$60	N/A
214/C/I	3-1/2"	TMK-8	$70	N/A 50th Anniversary
214/D	3"	TMK-2	$95-$120	$145-$180
214/D	3"	TMK-3	$75-$85	$130-$145
214/D	3"	TMK-4	$70-$75	$105-$130
214/D	3"	TMK-5	$70-$75	N/A
214/D	3"	TMK-6	$65-$70	N/A
214/D/I	3"	TMK-7	$65-$70	N/A
214/D/I	3"	TMK-8	$60	N/A
214/D/I	3"	TMK-8	$70	N/A 50th Anniversary
214/E	3-3/4"	TMK-2	$195-$235	$240-$285
214/E	3-3/4"	TMK-3	$250-$285	$195-$240
214/E	3-3/4"	TMK-4	$130-$150	$165-$195
214/E	3-3/4"	TMK-5	$120-$125	N/A
214/E	3-3/4"	TMK-6	$115-$120	N/A
214/E/I	3-3/4"	TMK-7	$110-$115	N/A
214/E/I	3-3/4"	TMK-8	$110	N/A
214/E/I	3-1/2"	TMK-8	$120	N/A 50th Anniversary
214/F	7"	TMK-2	$205-$250	$375-$475
214/F	7"	TMK-3	$165-$175	$195-$240
214/F	7"	TMK-4	$140-$165	$140-$220
214/F	7"	TMK-5	$135-$140	N/A
214/F	7"	TMK-6	$135-$140	N/A
214/F/I	7"	TMK-7	$130-$135	N/A
214/F/I	7"	TMK-8	$219	N/A
214/G	5"	TMK-2	$160-$185	$165-$195
214/G	5"	TMK-3	$125-$165	$135-$165

Hum No.	Basic Size	Trademark	Current Value (Color)	Current Value (White)
214/G	5"	TMK-4	$105-$120	$105-$135
214/G	5"	TMK-5	$115-$120	N/A
214/G	5"	TMK-6	$110-$115	N/A
214/G/I	5"	TMK-7	$110-$115	N/A
214/G/I	5"	TMK-8	$179	N/A
214/H	3-3/4" to 4"	TMK-2	$140-$170	$165-$195
214/H	3-3/4" to 4"	TMK-3	$120-$140	$130-$165
214/H	3-3/4" to 4"	TMK-4	$120-$125	$105-$135
214/H	3-3/4" to 4"	TMK-5	$115-$120	N/A
214/H	3-3/4" to 4"	TMK-6	$110-$115	N/A
214/H/I	3-3/4" to 4"	TMK-7	$110-$115	N/A
214/H/I	3-3/4" to 4"	TMK-8	$179	N/A
214/J	5"	TMK-2	$85-$99	$110-$160
214/J	5"	TMK-3	$70-$75	$95-$110
214/J	5"	TMK-4	$70-$75	$80-$95
214/J	5"	TMK-5	$65-$70	N/A
214/J	5"	TMK-6	$60-$65	N/A
214/J/I	5"	TMK-7	$60-$65	N/A
214/J/I	5"	TMK-8	$99	N/A
214/K	3-1/2" to 6-1/4"	TMK-2	$80-$99	$110-$160
214/K	3-1/2" to 6-1/4"	TMK-3	$70-$75	$95-$110
214/K	3-1/2" to 6-1/4"	TMK-4	$70-$75	$80-$95
214/K	3-1/2" to 6-1/4"	TMK-5	$65-$70	N/A
214/K	3-1/2" to 6-1/4"	TMK-6	$60-$65	N/A
214/K/I	3-1/2" to 6-1/4"	TMK-7	$60-$65	N/A
214/K/I	3-1/2" to 6-1/4"	TMK-8	$55	N/A
214/L	8" to 8-1/4"	TMK-2	$210-$250	$230-$290
214/L	8" to 8-1/4"	TMK-3	$165-$195	$180-$230
214/L	8" to 8-1/4"	TMK-4	$140-$165	$135-$165
214/L	8" to 8-1/4"	TMK-5	$135-$140	N/A
214/L	8" to 8-1/4"	TMK-6	$135-$140	N/A
214/L/I	8" to 8-1/4"	TMK-7	$130-$135	N/A
214/L/I	8" to 8-1/4"	TMK-8	$219	N/A
214/M	5-1/2"	TMK-2	$190-$250	$230-$290
214/M	5-1/2"	TMK-3	$165-$185	$170-$230
214/M	5-1/2"	TMK-4	$140-$165	$135-$165
214/M	5-1/2"	TMK-5	$130-$135	N/A
214/M	5-1/2"	TMK-6	$125-$130	N/A
214/M/I	5-1/2"	TMK-7	$120-$125	N/A
214/M/I	5-1/2"	TMK-8	$219	N/A
214/N	5-1/2"	TMK-2	$190-$235	$230-$290
214/N	5-1/2"	TMK-3	$150-$170	$170-$230
214/N	5-1/2"	TMK-4	$130-$150	$135-$165
214/N	5-1/2"	TMK-5	$120-$125	N/A
214/N	5-1/2"	TMK-6	$110-$120	N/A
214/N/I	5-1/2"	TMK-7	$1115-$120	N/A
214/N/I	5-1/2"	TMK-8	$219	N/A
214/O	1-3/4" x 2-1/2"	TMK-2	$30-$35	$70-$80
214/O	1-3/4" x 2-1/2"	TMK-3	$30-$35	$55-$70
214/O	1-3/4" x 2-1/2"	TMK-4	$35-$40	$40-$45

Hum No.	Basic Size	Trademark	Current Value (Color)	Current Value (White)
214/O	1-3/4" x 2-1/2"	TMK-5	$32-$35	N/A
214/O	1-3/4" x 2-1/2"	TMK-6	$28-$32	N/A
214/O/I	1-3/4" x 2-1/2"	TMK-7	$25-$30	N/A
214/O/I	1-3/4" x 2-1/2"	TMK-8	$29	N/A
366	3-1/2"	TMK-4	$130-$165	$140-$170
366	3-1/2"	TMK-5	$99-$105	$95-$110
366	3-1/2"	TMK-6	$95-$99	$95-$110
366/I	3-1/2"	TMK-7	$95-$100	N/A
366/I	3-1/2"	TMK-8	$179	N/A

In 1988, Goebel introduced a smaller, third size of the Nativity Set. These are offered as three- or four-piece sets in the initial years of the offer and as separate pieces subsequently. Here is the pricing for those pieces:

Hum No.	Size	Figure	Trademark	Current Value
214/A/M/0	5-1/4"	Madonna	TMK-6	$95-$105
214/A/M/0	5-1/4"	Madonna	TMK-7	$95-$105
214/A/M/0	5-1/4"	Madonna	TMK-8	$165
214/A/K/0	2-7/8"	Infant Jesus	TMK-6	$35-$40
214/A/K/0	2-7/8"	Infant Jesus	TMK-7	$35-$40
214/A/K/0	2-7/8"	Infant Jesus	TMK-8	$55 Final Issue for all of these pieces
214/B/0	6-1/8"	Joseph	TMK-6	$105-$110
214/B/0	6-1/8"	Joseph	TMK-7	$95-$99
214/B/0	6-1/8"	Joseph	TMK-8	$165
214/D/0	2-7/8"	Angel Serenade	TMK-7/8	$95
214/J/0	3-7/8"	Donkey	TMK-6	$40-$45
214/J/0	3-7/8"	Donkey	TMK-7	$40-$45
214/J/0	3-7/8"	Donkey	TMK-8	$40-$45
214/K/0	2-3/4"	Ox	TMK-6	$40-$45
214/K/0	2-3/4"	Ox	TMK-7	$40-$45
214/K/0	2-3/4"	Ox	TMK-8	$65
214/O/0	1-1/2"	Lamb	TMK-6	$30-$35
214/O/0	1-1/2"	Lamb	TMK-7	$25-$30
214/O/0	1-1/2"	Lamb	TMK-8	$35
214/L/0	6-1/4"	King (standing)	TMK-6	$115-$120
214/L/0	6-1/4"	King (standing)	TMK-7	$110-$115
214/L/0	6-1/4"	King (standing)	TMK-8	$185
214/M/0	4-1/4"	King (on one knee)	TMK-6	$105-$110
214/M/0	4-1/4"	King (on one knee)	TMK-7	$105-$110
214/M/0	4-1/4"	King (on one knee)	TMK-8	$175
214/N/0	4-1/2"	King (on both knees)	TMK-6	$105-$110
214/N/0	4-1/2"	King (on both knees)	TMK-7	$105-$110
214/N/0	4-1/2"	King (on both knees)	TMK-8	$170
214/F/0	5-3/4"	Shepherd (standing)	TMK-6	$110-$120
214/F/0	5-3/4"	Shepherd (standing)	TMK-7	$110-$115
214/F/0	5-3/4"	Shepherd (standing)	TMK-8	$185
214/G/0	4"	Shepherd Boy	TMK-6	$95-$100

Hum No.	Size	Figure	Trademark	Current Value
214/G/0	4"	Shepherd Boy	TMK-7	$90-$95
214/G/0	4"	Shepherd Boy	TMK-8	$150
214/H/0	3-1/4"	Little Tooter	TMK-6	$75-$80
214/H/0	3-1/4"	Little Tooter	TMK-7	$75-$80
214/H/0	3-1/4"	Little Tooter	TMK-8	$123
366/0	2-3/4"	Flying Angel	TMK-6	$80-$85
366/0	2-3/4"	Flying Angel	TMK-7	$80-$85
366/0	2-3/4"	Flying Angel	TMK-8	$135

Manufaktur Rödental reissued the Nativity Set and individual pieces in three different sizes: small, large, and miniature. The small and large sets and individual pieces are listed below under Hum 214 numbering.

Small Nativity Set and Individual Figurines:

There are 16 individual figurines, Holy Family in white three-piece set, three-camel assortment, and a German wooden crèche, which is sold separately.

Small complete set of 16 figurines: $2,130 retail

Small Holy Family set of three figurines (white):

Hum 214: $225 retail

Camel assortment set of three figurines: $377

German wooden crèche (13-1/2"): $150

Large Nativity and Individual Pieces:

There are 16 individual figurines, Holy Family in white three-piece set, and three-camel set. Pricing is retail.

Large Nativity complete set: $3,200

Camel three-piece set: $497

Individual Large Nativity Figurines

Hum No.	Name	Size	Current Value
214/A/M/I	Virgin Mary	6-1/2"	$289
214/B/I	Joseph	7-1/2"	$289
214/A/K/I	Infant Jesus	1-1/2"	$129
214/H/I	Little Tooter	4"	$229
366/I	Flying Angel	3-1/2"	$269
214/M/I	King Kneeling	5-1/2"	$289
214/N/I	King Kneeling with Box	5-1/2"	$289
214/L/I	King Moorish	8-1/4"	$289
214/G/I	Shepherd Kneeling	4-1/4"	$229
214/F/I	Shepherd Standing	7"	$289
214/J/I	Donkey	4-3/4"	$129
214/O/I	Lamb	1-1/2"	$59
214/K/I	Ox	3-1/4"	$129
	Camel Kneeling	5"	$199
	Camel Laying	3-3/4"	$199
	Camel Standing	7-1/2"	$199

Individual Small Nativity Figurines

Hum No.	Name	Size	Current Value
214 A/M/O	Virgin Mary	5-1/4"	$199
214/B/O	Joseph	6"	$199
2230/C	Child Jesus	2-1/2"	$45
214/H/O	Little Tooter	3"	$145
366/0	Flying Angle	3"	$159
214/M/O	King Kneeling	4-1/4"	$199
214/N/O	King Kneeling with Box	4"	$199
214/L/O	King Moorish	6-1/4"	$219
214/G/O	Shepherd Kneeling	4"	$159
214/F/O	Shepherd Standing	5-1/2"	$219
214/J/O	Donkey	3-3/4"	$69
214/O/O	Lamb	1-1/4"	$39
214/K/O	Ox	2-3/4"	$69
	Camel Kneeling	4-1/4"	$159
	Camel Laying	3-1/4"	$159
	Camel Standing	6-1/2"	$159

Hum 215: Unknown
Closed Number

Not likely to be found. Records indicate it could possibly be a standing Jesus child holding a lamb in his arms.

Hum 216: Unknown
Closed Number

Not likely to be found. No known examples anywhere, if it exists. Records indicate it might be a Joyful (Hum 53) ashtray.

Hum 217: Boy With Toothache

This figurine, which was first crafted by master sculptor Arthur Moeller in 1951 and previously called At the Dentist and Toothache, was released in the 1950s. It has no significant mold or finish variations affecting the normal values.

Older models of the figure will have the "WG" after the M.I. Hummel incised signature. This mark is illustrated and discussed in the trademark section at the front of the book. Newer models carry the 1951 incised copyright date.

In 2002, a special edition of Boy With Toothache was introduced in

Hum No.	Basic Size	Trademark	Current Value
217	5-1/2"	TMK-2	$255-$315
217	5-1/2"	TMK-3	$195-$225
217	5-1/2"	TMK-4	$165-$190
217	5-1/2"	TMK-5	$160-$165
217	5-1/2"	TMK-6	$160-$165
217	5-1/2"	TMK-7	$145-$150
217	5-1/2"	TMK-8	$150-$155
217	5-1/2"	TMK-8	$150-$175 50th Anniversary

recognition of the figurine's 50th year in production. It carried a unique diamond-shaped 50th Anniversary backstamp and came with a certificate of authenticity and a diamond-shaped anniversary medallion with "50" on it.

Hum 217: Boy With Toothache.

Hum 218: Birthday Serenade

Master sculptor Reinhold Unger designed this piece in 1952. The most significant variation found of this figure is the "reverse mold variation." In the older versions of this double-figure piece, the girl plays the concertina and the boy plays the flute. In the newer models the instruments are the other way around.

The older Full Bee (TMK-2) pieces with the reverse mold were changed beginning in the next trademark period, the Stylized Bee (TMK-3), so you can find the old design in that mark as well. There must have been

many of the old design left in stock, for you can even find them bearing the Three Line Mark (TMK-4). Note that the boy lost his kerchief when he was given the concertina or accordion.

The larger 218/0 size was temporarily withdrawn from production in 1999.

Hum No.	Basic Size	Trademark	Current Value
218/2/0	4-1/4"	TMK-2	$390-$420
218/2/0 (old style)	4-1/4"	TMK-3	$360-$390
218/2/0 (new style)	4-1/4"	TMK-3	$165-$180
218/2/0 (old style)	4-1/4"	TMK-4	$285-$330
218/2/0 (new style)	4-1/4"	TMK-4	$150-$165
218/2/0	4-1/4"	TMK-5	$130-$140
218/2/0	4-1/4"	TMK-6	$125-$135
218/2/0	4-1/4"	TMK-7	$120-$125
218/2/0	4-1/4"	TMK-8	$120-$125
218/0	5-1/4"	TMK-2	$510-$590
218/0 (old style)	5-1/4"	TMK-3	$465-$525
218/0 (new style	5-1/4"	TMK-3	$270-$300
218/0 (old style)	5-1/4"	TMK-4	$440-$495
218/0 (new style)	5-1/4"	TMK-4	$227-$270
218/0	5-1/4"	TMK-5	$210-$225
218/0	5-1/4"	TMK-6	$200-$210
218	5-1/4"	TMK-2	$540-$600
218/I*	5-1/4"	TMK-2	$600-$900
218/I is a possible factory error.			

Hum 218: Birthday Serenade.

Hum 219/2/0: Little Velma

This figure, which has been known as Girl With Frog and was first crafted in 1952 by master sculptor Reinhold Unger, bears a number with the "closed number" designation, supposedly meaning a number that never has been and never will be used to designate a Hummel figurine. It is a girl sitting on a fence looking down at a frog on the ground. The factory never officially released it, although it has turned up due to a no longer practical policy of distributing pre-production samples. It was never placed in production due to its similarity to Hum 195 and Hum 201.

The owner of the first example of this figure to be uncovered has named it Little Velma. It was designed in 1952. At least 15 to 20 examples have been found to date, only in the Full Bee (TMK-2).

Hum 219/2/0: Little Velma.

Hum No.	Basic Size	Trademark	Current Value
219/2/0	4"	TMK-2	$2,400-$3,600

Hum 220: We Congratulate

We Congratulate is very similar to Hum 214/E (Nativity Set piece), except this figure is on a base and 214/E is not, and the girl has no wreath of flowers in her hair. A lederhosen strap was also added to the boy.

This piece, which was first designed by master sculptor Arthur Moeller in 1952, was introduced in the 1950s and has been produced with one variation of some significance. At first, the piece was produced with a 220/2/0 designator. It was soon dropped, leaving only the mold number 220 incised on the base.

Hum 220: We Congratulate.

Hum No.	Basic Size	Trademark	Current Value
220/2/0	4"	TMK-2	$285-$345
220	4"	TMK-2	$195-$240
220	4"	TMK-3	$150-$165
220	4"	TMK-4	$130-$150
220	4"	TMK-5	$120-$130
220	4"	TMK-6	$120-$130
220	4"	TMK-7	$110-$130
220	4"	TMK-8	$110-$130

Hum 221: Happy Pastime
Candy Box, Closed Number

Previously listed as unknown, it is now known that this is a pre-production sample made by master sculptor Arthur Moeller in 1952 and never released. It is essentially Hum 69: Happy Pastime affixed to the top of a round candy jar that is decorated with flowers. It is valued at $3,000-$6,000.

Hum 221: Happy Pastime candy box (closed number).

Hum 222: Madonna
Wall Plaque

An extremely rare piece, which was first designed by master sculptor Reinhold Unger in 1952, it has been out of current production for some time. Similar in design to Madonna Plaque (Hum 48), this plaque is unique in that a metal frame surrounds it. This piece has been found with several different designs of wire frame around it. Most were originally made with a felt backing. Each may be found with any design of the wire frame or no frame at all.

Madonna wall plaque has no apparent mark other than the mold number.

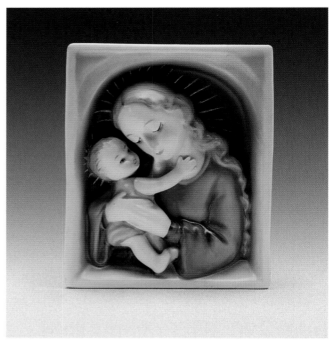

Hum 222: Madonna wall plaque.

Hum No.	Basic Size	Trademark	Current Value
222	4" x 5"	TMK-2	$450-$750
222	4" x 5"	TMK-3	$450-$600

Hum 223: To Market
Table Lamp

First crafted by master sculptor Arthur Moeller in 1937 as Hum 101 and later restyled and introduced in the 1950s, this lamp was temporarily withdrawn from production in 1989. There are no mold or finish variations significant enough to affect normal values. See Hum 101 entry for a description of a lamp of similar design.

Hum 223: To Market table lamp.

Hum No.	Basic Size	Trademark	Current Value
223	9-1/2"	TMK-2	$420-$510
223	9-1/2"	TMK-3	$390-$420
223	9-1/2"	TMK-4	$345-$390
223	9-1/2"	TMK-5	$325-$345
223	9-1/2"	TMK-6	$315-$330
223	9-1/2"	TMK-7	$300-$310
223	9-1/2"	TMK-8	$495

Hum 224: Wayside Harmony
Table Lamp

First introduced as a redesign of the Hum 111 lamp in the 1950s, this lamp, which was the work of master sculptor Reinhold Unger in 1952, was produced in two sizes. Both were temporarily withdrawn from production in 1989. There are no finish or mold variations that have an impact on normal values.

Hum 224: Wayside Harmony.

Hum No.	Basic Size	Trademark	Current Value
224/I	7-1/2"	TMK-2	$330-$360
224/I	7-1/2"	TMK-3	$270-$285
224/I	7-1/2"	TMK-4	$255-$270
224/I	7-1/2"	TMK-5	$240-$255
224/I	7-1/2"	TMK-6	$210-$240
224/I	7-1/2"	TMK-7	$210-$240
224/I	7-1/2"	TMK-8	$350
224	9-1/2"	TMK-2	$390-$480
224	9-1/2"	TMK-3	$305-$365
224/II	9-1/2"	TMK-2	$390-$480
224/II	9-1/2"	TMK-3	$300-$360
224/II	9-1/2"	TMK-4	$285-$300
224/II	9-1/2"	TMK-5	$270-$285
224/II	9-1/2"	TMK-6	$240-$270
224/II	9-1/2"	TMK-7	$240-$270
224/II	9-1/2"	TMK-8	$400

Hum 225: Just Resting
Table Lamp

First crafted by master sculptor Reinhold Unger in 1952 and released in the 1950s as a redesign of Hum 112, it was listed as temporarily withdrawn from production by Goebel in 1989.

Hum 225: Just Resting table lamp.

Hum No.	Basic Size	Trademark	Current Value
225/I	7-1/2"	TMK-2	$330-$390
225/I	7-1/2"	TMK-3	$270-$285

Hum No.	Basic Size	Trademark	Current Value
225/I	7-1/2"	TMK-4	$255-$270
225/I	7-1/2"	TMK-5	$240-$255
225/I	7-1/2"	TMK-6	$210-$240
225/I	7-1/2"	TMK-7	$210-$240
225/I	7-1/2"	TMK-8	$350
225	7-1/2"	TMK-2	$390-$480
225	7-1/2"	TMK-3	$300-$360
225/II	9-1/2"	TMK-2	$390-$480
225/II	9-1/2"	TMK-3	$300-$360
225/II	9-1/2"	TMK-4	$285-$300
225/II	9-1/2"	TMK-5	$270-$285
225/II	9-1/2"	TMK-6	$240-$270
225/II	9-1/2"	TMK-7	$240-$270
225/II	9-1/2"	TMK-8	$400

Hum 226: The Mail is Here

First crafted by master sculptor Arthur Moeller in 1952 and introduced into the line in the 1950s, it was known as Mail Coach. This name is still favored by many collectors. Incidentally, this figure was preceded by a wall plaque utilizing the same motif (Hum 140).

The piece generally carries an incised 1952 copyright date and some older pieces have a very light "M.I. Hummel" signature, while others have the signature painted on due to the light impression.

There are no major variations affecting normal values.

Hum No.	Basic Size	Trademark	Current Value
226	4-1/4" x 6-1/4"	TMK-2	$660-$840
226	4-1/4" x 6-1/4"	TMK-3	$510-$660
226	4-1/4" x 6-1/4"	TMK-4	$420-$480
226	4-1/4" x 6-1/4"	TMK-5	$390-$480
226	4-1/4" x 6-1/4"	TMK-6	$375-$450
226	4-1/4" x 6-1/4"	TMK-7	$365-$435
226	4-1/4" x 6-1/4"	TMK-8	$720 retail

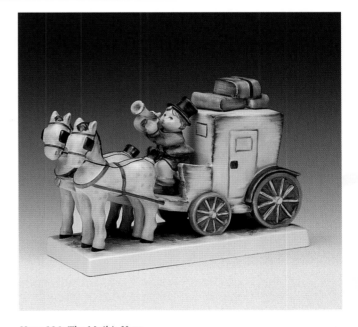

Hum 226: The Mail is Here.

Hum 227: She Loves Me, She Loves Me Not
Table Lamp

This piece, which was the work of master sculptor Arthur Moeller in 1953, is a 7-1/2" lamp base utilizing Hum 174 as part of the design. Older pieces depict the figure much larger and the boy's eyes open.

Goebel listed it as temporarily withdrawn from production in 1989.

Hum 227: She Loves Me, She Loves Me Not table lamp.

Hum No.	Basic Size	Trademark	Current Value
227	7-1/2"	TMK-2	$390-$510
227	7-1/2"	TMK-3	$285-$315
227	7-1/2"	TMK-4	$255-$285
227	7-1/2"	TMK-5	$240-$315
227	7-1/2"	TMK-6	$225-$240

Hum 228: Good Friends
Table Lamp

This piece, another crafted by master sculptor Arthur Moeller in 1953, is a 7-1/2" lamp base utilizing Hum 182 as part of the design. The older pieces have a much larger figure, even though the overall size remained 7-1/2".

Goebel listed it as temporarily withdrawn from production in 1989.

Hum 228: Good Friends table lamp.

Hum No.	Basic Size	Trademark	Current Value
228	7-1/2"	TMK-2	$390-$510
228	7-1/2"	TMK-3	$285-$315
228	7-1/2"	TMK-4	$255-$285
228	7-1/2"	TMK-5	$240-$315
228	7-1/2"	TMK-6	$225-$240

Hum 229: Apple Tree Girl
Table Lamp

This 7-1/2" table lamp, which was designed by master sculptor Arthur Moeller in 1953, utilized Hum 141 as part of the design. It was previously known as Spring and Springtime, and the older pieces have a much larger figure, even though the overall size remained 7-1/2".

It was listed as temporarily out of production in 1989.

Hum 229: Apple Tree Girl table lamp.

Hum No.	Basic Size	Trademark	Current Value
229	7-1/2"	TMK-2	$540-$600
229	7-1/2"	TMK-3	$285-$315
229	7-1/2"	TMK-4	$255-$285
229	7-1/2"	TMK-5	$240-$255
229	7-1/2"	TMK-6	$225-$240

Hum 230: Apple Tree Boy
Table Lamp

This 7-1/2" lamp base, which was designed by master sculptor Arthur Moeller in 1953, utilized Hum 142 as part of the design. It was previously known as both Autumn and Fall, and the older pieces have a much larger figure, even though the overall size remained 7-1/2".

This piece was listed as temporarily withdrawn from production in 1989.

Hum 230: Apple Tree Boy table lamp.

Hum No.	Basic Size	Trademark	Current Value
230	7-1/2"	TMK-2	$540-$600
230	7-1/2"	TMK-3	$285-$315
230	7-1/2"	TMK-4	$255-$285
230	7-1/2"	TMK-5	$240-$255
230	7-1/2"	TMK-6	$225-$240

Hum 231: Birthday Serenade
Table Lamp

This particular lamp, which was first designed by master sculptor Reinhold Unger, was out of production for many years. It utilizes Hum 218: Birthday Serenade as its design. The old model is found in the Full Bee (TMK-2) and reflects the same old mold design (girl with accordion and boy with flute). These old mold design lamps measure about 9-3/4" tall and are fairly scarce.

In 1976, Hum 231 was reissued after master sculptor Rudolf Wittman redesigned it with the instruments reversed. Now the girl plays the flute, and the boy plays the accordion. The newer pieces are found with the TMK-5 and TMK-6. (See Hum 234.)

Goebel listed this lamp as temporarily withdrawn from production as of Dec. 31, 1989.

Hum 231: Birthday Serenade table lamp.

Hum No.	Basic Size	Trademark	Current Value
231	9-3/4"	TMK-2	$1,200-$1,800
231	9-3/4"	TMK-5	$330-$360
231	9-3/4"	TMK-6	$300-$330

Hum 232: Happy Days
Table Lamp

The Happy Days table lamp was first designed by master sculptor Reinhold Unger in 1954 and placed into production in the 1950s. Essentially the same design as Hum 232 (only larger), it was apparently made in limited numbers in the early days because those with the Full Bee (TMK-2) trademark have always been in short supply.

After a redesign in 1976, the figures were available in TMK-5 and TMK-6, but the factory listed them as temporarily withdrawn from production in late-1989.

Hum No.	Basic Size	Trademark	Current Value
232	9-3/4″	TMK-2	$720-$1,020
232	9-3/4″	TMK-5	$300-$330
232	9-3/4″	TMK-6	$255-$315

Hum 232: Happy Days table lamp.

Hum 233: Unknown
Closed Number

This figure is unlikely to be found. There is evidence to suggest that this is a preliminary design for Bird Watcher (Hum 300). No known examples anywhere.

Hum 235: Happy Days
Table Lamp

Hum 235: Happy Days table lamp.

Hum 235 is a smaller size (7-3/4″) of the Hum 232 lamp. It too was first crafted by master sculptor Reinhold Unger in 1954 and placed in production in the 1950s, only to be removed shortly thereafter.

It was reissued in a new design in the late-1970s—as was the larger lamp—only to be withdrawn from production again in 1989. Unlike the larger lamp, however, this one can be found in all trademarks starting with TMK-2 through TMK-6.

Hum 234: Birthday Serenade
Table Lamp

This lamp, like the larger Hum 231 table lamp of the same name, was first designed by master sculptor Reinhold Unger and apparently also removed from production or limited in production for a time after its initial release. Unlike the Hum 231 lamp, however, it can be found in all trademarks through TMK-6 beginning with the Full Bee (TMK-2).

It was redesigned by master sculptor Rudolf Wittman in the late-1970s with the instruments reversed, just as the Hum 231 lamp was. It can be found in the old or new styles in the Full Bee.

It was temporarily withdrawn from production in 1989.

Hum No.	Basic Size	Trademark	Current Value
234	7-3/4″	TMK-2	$960-$1,260
234	7-3/4″	TMK-3	$660-$960
234	7-3/4″	TMK-4	$300-$660
234	7-3/4″	TMK-5	$270-$300
234	7-3/4″	TMK-6	$255-$270

Hum No.	Basic Size	Trademark	Current Value
235	7-3/4″	TMK-2	$540-$665
235	7-3/4″	TMK-3	$375-$510
235	7-3/4″	TMK-4	$300-$375
235	7-3/4″	TMK-5	$285-$300
235	7-3/4″	TMK-6	$270-$285

Hum 236/A and Hum 236/B: No Name
Closed Number

Only one example of each of these is known to exist at this time. They were first designed by master sculptor Arthur Moeller in 1954, but for whatever reason, not approved by the Siessen Convent for production.

The figures are two angels, one at the base of a tree and the other seated on a tree limb. Hum 236/A has one angel playing a harp at the base of a tree and the other seated on a tree limb above singing. The Hum 236/B has the tree angel blowing a horn and the seated angel playing a lute. No known examples exist outside the factory archives.

Hum No.	Basic Size	Trademark	Current Value
236/A	6-1/2"	TMK-2	$6,000-$9,000
236/B	6-1/2"	TMK-2	$6,000-$9,000

Hum 236/A and Hum 236/B: Angel on Tree (closed number).

Hum 237: Star Gazer
Wall Plaque, Closed Number

This piece is a plaque using the Star Gazer figurine in white overglaze as its design. It is a 1954 design that was again rejected by the Siessen Convent. Only one is known to exist in a private collection.

Hum No.	Basic Size	Trademark	Current Value
237	4-3/4" x 5"	TMK-2	$6,000-$9,000

Hum 238/A: Angel With Lute, Hum 238/B: Angel With Accordion, Hum 238/C: Angel With Trumpet
Angel Trio Set

These three pieces, which were designed by master sculptor Gerhard Skrobek in 1967, are usually sold as a set and referred to as the Angel Trio. In current production, they can be found in all trademarks since the Three Line Mark (TMK-4). On rare

occasions, they can also be found in TMK-3; those pieces are worth $100-$125.

Each is 2" to 2-1/2" high and carries an incised 1967 copyright date.

They are essentially the same set as the Angel Trio (Hum 38, 39, and 40), but the three Hum 238 pieces are not candleholders.

Hum No.	Basic Size	Trademark	Current Value
238/A	2" to 2-1/2"	TMK-4	$60-$75
238/A	2" to 2-1/2"	TMK-5	$55-$60
238/A	2" to 2-1/2"	TMK-6	$45-$55
238/A	2" to 2-1/2"	TMK-7	$40-$45
238/A	2" to 2-1/2"	TMK-8	$40-$45
238/B	2" to 2-1/2"	TMK-4	$60-$75
238/B	2" to 2-1/2"	TMK-5	$55-$60
238/B	2" to 2-1/2"	TMK-6	$45-$55
238/B	2" to 2-1/2"	TMK-7	$40-$45
238/B	2" to 2-1/2"	TMK-8	$40-$45
238/C	2" to 2-1/2"	TMK-4	$60-$75
238/C	2" to 2-1/2"	TMK-5	$55-$60
238/C	2" to 2-1/2"	TMK-6	$45-$55
238/C	2" to 2-1/2"	TMK-7	$40-$45
238/C	2" to 2-1/2"	TMK-8	$40-$45

Hum 238/A: Angel With Lute, Hum 238/B: Angel With Accordion, Hum 238/C: Angel With Trumpet (Angel Trio Set).

Hum 239/A: Girl With Nosegay, Hum 239/B: Girl With Doll, Hum 239/C: Boy With Horse, & Hum 239/D: Girl With Fir Tree

The first three figures (Hum 239/A, 239/B, and 239/C) have traditionally been sold as a set and were known as Children Trio ever since they were placed into production in the 1960s. They are essentially the same as the Hum 115, Hum 116, and Hum 117, except that the three Hum 239 pieces have no receptacle for holding a candle. In 1997, the trio was expanded with a fourth figure, Girl With Fir Tree (Hum 239/D).

Also in 1997, a set of four ornaments was introduced. The ornaments are the same as the Hum 239 figurines, except they have brass ring hangers on top instead of bases on the bottom. They are designated with a "/0" after the regular Hum number. A variation of the ornaments is sold in Europe, does not include the brass hanging ring or the base, and is differentiated by a "/X" after the regular Hum number rather than the "/0."

Girl With Fir Tree (Hum 239/D) was re-released in the Innocent Reflections Series. Innocent Reflections are white ceramic figurines on which a glaze is fired on the figurine to make it glisten. A coating of 21-karat gold is delicately painted on certain details on each figurine, then fired for 3-1/2 hours. On this figurine the tree is painted in gold. This figurine is TMK-9.

Hum 239/A: Girl With Nosegay, Hum 239/B: Girl With Doll, Hum 239/C: Boy With Horse, and Hum 239/D: Girl With Fir Tree.

Hum No.	Basic Size	Trademark	Current Value
239/A	3-1/2"	TMK-3	$90-$120
239/A	3-1/2"	TMK-4	$55-$70
239/A	3-1/2"	TMK-5	$50-$70
239/A	3-1/2"	TMK-6	$45-$70
239/A	3-1/2"	TMK-7	$40-$70
239/A	3-1/2"	TMK-8	$40-$70
239/A/0	3"	TMK-7 and 8	$40-$70
239/A/X	3"	TMK-7 and 8	$40-$70
239/B	3-1/2"	TMK-3	$90-$120
239/B	3-1/2"	TMK-4	$55-$70
239/B	3-1/2"	TMK-5	$50-$70
239/B	3-1/2"	TMK-6	$45-$70
239/B	3-1/2"	TMK-7	$40-$70
239/B	3-1/2"	TMK-8	$40-$70
239/B/0	3"	TMK-7 and 8	$40-$70
239/B/X	3"	TMK-7 and 8	$40-$70

Hum No.	Basic Size	Trademark	Current Value
239/C	3-1/2"	TMK-3	$90-$120
239/C	3-1/2"	TMK-4	$55-$70
239/C	3-1/2"	TMK-5	$50-$70
239/C	3-1/2"	TMK-6	$45-$70
239/C	3-1/2"	TMK-7	$40-$70
239/C	3-1/2"	TMK-8	$40-$70
239/C/0	3"	TMK-7 and 8	$40-$70
239/C/X	3"	TMK-7 and 8	$40-$70
239/D	3-1/2"	TMK-7	$40-$70
239/D	3-1/2"	TMK-8	$40-$70
239/D/0	3"	TMK-7 and 8	$40-$70
239/D/X	3"	TMK-7 and 8	$40-$70
239/D/0	3-1/2"	TMK-9	$79 retail

Hum 239/E: Little Flag Bearer

Little Flag Bearer depicts a young child holding a toy horse under his left arm and a U.S. flag in his right hand. It is marked with the "First Issue 2003" backstamp with an American flag on the bottom of the piece.

Hum No.	Basic Size	Trademark	Current Value
239/E	3-1/2"	TMK-8	$69.50 retail

Hum 240: Little Drummer

Placed into production in the 1950s, this figurine was the original work of master sculptor Reinhold Unger in 1955. It is usually found with an incised copyright date of 1955. There are no variations significant enough to affect normal values for this piece.

Attendees at the 1993 Disneyana Convention were given the opportunity to purchase a pair of figurines on a wooden base. The figurines were a normal production model of the Little Drummer (Hum 240), and a matching Donald Duck figurine in the same pose. The Donald Duck drummer is marked with an incised mold number of 17323, TMK-7, and a limited edition notation. The edition was limited to 1,500. They were originally sold for $300 and are now valued at $500-$750.

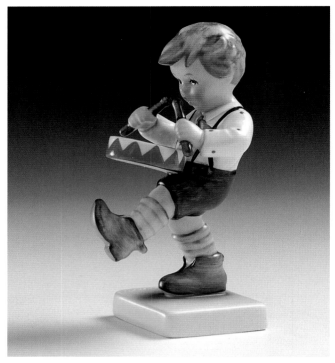

Hum No.	Basic Size	Trademark	Current Value
240	4-1/4"	TMK-2	$185-$225
240	4-1/4"	TMK-3	$145-$160
240	4-1/4"	TMK-4	$120-$150
240	4-1/4"	TMK-5	$115-$120
240	4-1/4"	TMK-6	$110-$120
240	4-1/4"	TMK-7	$110-$120
240	4-1/4"	TMK-8	$105-$120

Hum 240: Little Drummer.

Hum 241: Joyous News, Angel With Lute

Holy Water Font, Closed Number

The mold number 241 for this font, which was first designed by master sculptor Reinhold Unger in 1955, was used by mistake on the next piece listed (Angel Lights). This font design was produced only in sample form and never put into regular production. There is only a handful known to exist outside the factory archives, one of which is part of the Don Stephens Collection in Rosemont, Illinois.

Hum No.	Basic Size	Trademark	Current Value
241	3" x 4-1/2"	TMK-2	$900-$1,200

Hum 241: Angel Lights

Candleholder

The work of master sculptor Gerhard Skrobek in 1976, this piece was first released in 1978 as Angel Bridge. It is in the form of an arch placed on a plate. A figure sits attached to the top of the arch, with candle receptacles down each side of the arch. It is not attached to the plate base.

It has been suspended from production since Jan. 1, 1990.

Hum 241: Angel Lights candleholder.

Hum No.	Basic Size	Trademark	Current Value
241	10-1/3" x 8-1/3"	TMK-5	$240-$300
241	10-1/3" x 8-1/3"	TMK-6	$180-$210

Hum 242: Angel Joyous News With Trumpet
Holy Water Font, Closed Number

This font, which was the design of master sculptor Reinhold Unger in 1955, was produced as a sample only and never put into production. Although once predicted that this piece would not likely find its way into private collections, a handful of pieces have since made their way into the collections of several individuals.

Hum 242: Angel Joyous News With Trumpet holy water font (closed number).

Hum No.	Basic Size	Trademark	Current Value
242	3″ x 4-1/2″	TMK-2	$900-$1,200

Hum 243: Madonna and Child
Holy Water Font

Even though this piece, which was designed by master sculptor Reinhold Unger in 1955, was apparently not released until the 1960s, it can be found in all trademarks starting with the Full Bee (TMK-2). There are no significant variations affecting normal values for this figure.

Hum No.	Basic Size	Trademark	Current Value
243	3-1/4″ x 4″	TMK-2	$150-$180
243	3-1/4″ x 4″	TMK-3	$65-$85
243	3-1/4″ x 4″	TMK-4	$50-$65
243	3-1/4″ x 4″	TMK-5	$45-$50
243	3-1/4″ x 4″	TMK-6	$40-$45
243	3-1/4″ x 4″	TMK-7	$40-$45
243	3-1/4″ x 4″	TMK-8	$40-$45

Hum 243: Madonna and Child holy water font.

Hum 244-245: Open Numbers

Hum 246: Holy Family
Holy Water Font

This font, which was originally designed by master sculptor Theo Menzenbach in 1955, was released into the line in the mid-1950s. It is usually found with the incised copyright date of 1955. There are no significant mold or finish variations affecting normal values.

Hum 246: Holy Family holy water font.

Hum No.	Basic Size	Trademark	Current Value
246	3″ x 4″	TMK-2	$150-$180
246	3″ x 4″	TMK-3	$65-$85
246	3″ x 4″	TMK-4	$50-$65
246	3″ x 4″	TMK-5	$75-$80
246	3″ x 4″	TMK-6	$40-$45
246	3″ x 4″	TMK-7	$40-$40
246	3″ x 4″	TMK-8	$40-$45

Hum 247: Standing Madonna With Child
Closed Number

This beautiful piece was the work of master sculptor Reinhold Unger, designed in 1965 but apparently rejected by the Siessen Convent. It exists in sample form only in the factory archives.

Hum 247: Standing Madonna With Child (closed number).

Hum No.	Basic Size	Current Value
247	11-1/2"	$6,000-$9,000
247	13"	$6,000-$9,000

Hum 248: Guardian Angel
Holy Water Font

This piece is a redesigned version of Hum 29, which is no longer in production. When placed in the collection as designed by master sculptor Gerhard Skrobek in 1958, it measured 2-3/8" x 5-3/8" and carried mold number is 248/0. A larger 2-3/4" x 6-1/4" piece was also designed (248/I) but never put into regular production.

This font was temporarily withdrawn from production in 1999.

Hum 248: Guardian Angel holy water font.

Hum No.	Basic Size	Trademark	Current Value
248/I	2-3/4" x 6-1/4"	TMK-3	$600-$900
248/0	2-3/8" x 5-3/8"	TMK-3	$120-$165
248/0	2-3/8" x 5-3/8"	TMK-4	$50-$65
248/0	2-1/4" x 5-1/2"	TMK-5	$45-$50
248/0	2-1/4" x 5-1/2"	TMK-6	$40-$45
248/0	2-1/4" x 5-1/2"	TMK-7	$40-$45

Hum 249: Madonna and Child
Plaque in Relief, Closed Number

Molded as a sample only, this plaque was never put into the line. It is essentially the same design as Hum 48: Madonna Plaque with the background cut away. No known examples outside the Goebel archives.

Hum 249: Madonna and Child plaque in relief (closed number).

Hum No.	Basic Size	Current Value
249	6-3/4" x 8-3/4"	$6,000-$9,000

Hum 250/A: Little Goat Herder and Hum 250/B: Feeding Time
Bookends

These bookends were the collective efforts of several designers and were placed in the line in 1964. If the figurines are removed from the wooden bookend bases, they are indistinguishable from the regular pieces (Hum 199 and Hum 200).

These figures were temporarily withdrawn from production at the end of 1989.

Hum 250/A: Little Goat Herder and Hum 250/B: Feeding Time bookends.

Hum No.	Basic Size	Trademark	Current Value
250/A &B	5-1/2"	TMK-2	$330-$450
250/A &B	5-1/2"	TMK-3	$225-$225

Hum No.	Basic Size	Trademark	Current Value
250/A &B	5-1/2"	TMK-5	$195-$210
250/A &B	5-1/2"	TMK-6	$180-$195

Hum 251/A: Good Friends and Hum 251/B: She Loves Me, She Loves Me Not
Bookends

These bookends were the collective efforts of several designers and were placed into the line in 1964. If the figurines are removed from the wooden bookend bases, they are indistinguishable from the regular production figurines (Hum 174 and Hum 182).

Goebel listed these pieces as temporarily withdrawn from production in 1989.

They are priced here as a set.

Hum 251/A: Good Friends and Hum 251/B: She Loves Me, She Loves Me Not bookends.

Hum No.	Basic Size	Trademark	Current Value
251/A & B	5-1/2"	TMK-2	$330-$450
251/A & B	5-1/2"	TMK-3	$225-$255

Hum No.	Basic Size	Trademark	Current Value
251/A & B	5-1/2"	TMK-5	$195-$210
251/A & B	5-1/2"	TMK-6	$180-$195

Hum 252/A: Apple Tree Boy and Hum 252/B: Apple Tree Girl
Bookends

Another collective designing effort, these bookends were placed in the collection in 1964. If the figures are removed from the bookends they are indistinguishable from the regular figurines (Hum 141 and Hum 142).

The bookends were temporarily withdrawn from production at the end of 1989.

They are priced here as a set.

Hum 252/A: Apple Tree Boy and Hum 252/B: Apple Tree Girl bookends.

Hum No.	Basic Size	Trademark	Current Value
252/A & B	5-1/2"	TMK-3	$225-$255
252/A & B	5-1/2"	TMK-5	$195-$210
252/A & B	5-1/2"	TMK-6	$180-$195

Hum 253: Unknown
Closed Number

Goebel records indicate that this piece was a design much like the girl in Hum 52: Going to Grandma's. There is no evidence that it was ever produced, and there are no known examples in the archives or anywhere else.

Hum 254: Girl With Mandolin
Closed Number

This figurine depicts a girl playing the mandolin. It was modeled in 1962 and is similar to Hum 150: Happy Days. Factory archives have samples only. Hum 557 is a slightly smaller version of this figurine issued in 1995.

Hum No.	Basic Size	Trademark	Current Value
254	4-1/4"	CN	$3,000-$6,000

Hum 255: A Stitch in Time

First released in 1964 as a result of the combined efforts of several designers, this piece is similar to one of the girls depicted in Knitting Lesson (Hum 256) and School Girls (Hum 177). It has a 1963 incised copyright date. There are no significant variations that might affect normal values.

In 1990 a smaller size, 3", was added as part of a four-figurine series matching miniature plates in the same series. When this figure was introduced, the mold number for the larger size was changed to 255/I.

The 3" variation (255/4/0) was temporarily withdrawn in December 1997, followed by withdrawal of the larger size (255/I) in January 1999.

Hum 255: A Stitch in Time.

Hum No.	Basic Size	Trademark	Current Value
255/4/0	3"	TMK-6	$75-$85
255/4/0	3"	TMK-7	$70-$75
255	6-3/4"	TMK-3	$330-$480
255	6-3/4"	TMK-4	$225-$255

Hum No.	Basic Size	Trademark	Current Value
255	6-3/4"	TMK-5	$210-$225
255	6-3/4"	TMK-6	$200-$210
255/I	6-3/4"	TMK-7	$195-$200

Hum 256: Knitting Lesson

Introduced in 1964 with an incised 1963 copyright date, Knitting Lesson has no significant variations that might affect normal values. It is similar to the girls used in School Girls (Hum 177).

This figurine was temporarily withdrawn from production in 1999.

Hum No.	Basic Size	Trademark	Current Value
256	7-1/2"	TMK-3	$525-$665
256	7-1/2"	TMK-4	$375-$450
256	7-1/2"	TMK-5	$330-$345
256	7-1/2"	TMK-6	$325-$330
256	7-1/2"	TMK-7	$315-$325

Hum 256: Knitting Lesson.

Hum 257: For Mother

The collective work of several sculptors, this piece was introduced in the United States in 1964 and carries a 1963 incised copyright date. There are no significant mold or finish variations.

A new smaller-size figurine was released as a part of a four-piece series with matching mini-plates in 1985. When this was done the mold number for the larger size was changed to 257/0.

The 257/0 variation was temporarily withdrawn from production on June 15, 2002.

Hum No.	Basic Size	Trademark	Current Value
257/5/0	2-3/4"	TMK-7	$55
257/2/0	4"	TMK-6	$195-$95
257/2/0	4"	TMK-7	$90-$95
257/2/0	4"	TMK-8	$150 retail
257	5-1/4"	TMK-3	$375-$525
257	5-1/4"	TMK-4	$165-$180
257	5-1/4"	TMK-5	$160-$165
257/0	5-1/4"	TMK-6	$150-$155
257/0	5-1/4"	TMK-7	$145-$150
257/0	5-1/4"	TMK-8	$145-$150

Hum 257: For Mother.

Hum 258: Which Hand?

Designed by a team of sculptors and first released in the United States in 1964, this piece has an incised copyright date of 1963. The girl is similar in design to *Telling Her Secret* (Hum 196). There are no mold or finish variation that would affect normal values.

Hum No.	Basic Size	Trademark	Current Value
258	5-1/4"	TMK-3	$375-$495
258	5-1/4"	TMK-4	$165-$180
258	5-1/4"	TMK-5	$150-$165
258	5-1/4"	TMK-6	$145-$150
258	5-1/4"	TMK-7	$140-$150
258	5-1/4"	TMK-8	$140-$150
258	5-1/4"	TMK-8	$270 Progression Set LE of 1,000

Hum 258: Which Hand?

Hum 259: Girl With Accordion
Closed Number

This piece, which was the collective work of several designers in 1962, is almost exactly the same design as that of the girl with concertina or accordion in Hum 218 (Birthday Serenade). It was produced in sample form only and never placed into production. Only one is known to reside in a private collection.

Hum No.	Basic Size	Current Value
259	4"	$6,000-$9,000

Hum 260: Nativity Set
Large

The work of master sculptor Gerhard Skrobek in 1968, there was only sketchy information concerning complete nativity sets in this size and little more about the individual pieces in any of the many price lists studied. Below is a listing of each piece in the Hum 260 Nativity Set.

The set has been temporarily withdrawn from production since December 1989.

Hum 260: Large nativity set.

Hum No.	Basic Size	Figure	Trademark	Value
260	16-piece set	all 16 (including stable)	TMK-4	$3,450-$3,534
260	16-piece set	all 16 (including stable)	TMK-5	$3,534-$3,630
260	16-piece set	all 16 (including stable)	TMK-6	$2,524-$3,630
260/A	9-3/4"	Madonna	TMK-4	$375-$400
260/A	9-3/4"	Madonna	TMK-5	$360-$375
260/A	9-3/4"	Madonna	TMK-6	$345-$360
260/B	11-3/4"	Joseph	TMK-4	$375-$390
260/B	11-3/4"	Joseph	TMK-5	$360-$375
260/B	11-3/4"	Joseph	TMK-6	$345-$360
260/C	5-3/4"	Infant Jesus	TMK-4	$85-$90
260/C	5-3/4"	Infant Jesus	TMK-5	$80-$85
260/C	5-3/4"	Infant Jesus	TMK-6	$80-$85
260/D	5-1/4"	Goodnight (Angel Standing)	TMK-4	$105-$110
260/D	5-1/4"	Goodnight (Angel Standing)	TMK-5	$105-$110
260/D	5-1/4"	Goodnight (Angel Standing)	TMK-6	$99-$105
260/E	4-1/4"	Angel Serenade (Kneeling)	TMK-4	$105-$110
260/E	4-1/4"	Angel Serenade (Kneeling)	TMK-5	$99-$105
260/E	4-1/4"	Angel Serenade (Kneeling)	TMK-6	$95-$99
260/F	6-1/4"	We Congratulate	TMK-4	$265-$275
260/F	6-1/4"	We Congratulate	TMK-5	$260-$265
260/F	6-1/4"	We Congratulate	TMK-6	$250-$255
260/G	11-3/4"	Shepherd (Standing)	TMK-4	$375-$390
260/G	11-3/4"	Shepherd (Standing)	TMK-5	$360-$375
260/G	11-3/4"	Shepherd (Standing)	TMK-6	$360-$370
260/H	3-3/4"	Sheep and Lamb	TMK-4	$75-$80
260/H	3-3/4"	Sheep and Lamb	TMK-5	$70-$75
260/H	3-3/4"	Sheep and Lamb	TMK-6	$70-$75
260/J	7"	Shepherd Boy (Kneeling)	TMK-4	$210-$225
260/J	7"	Shepherd Boy (Kneeling)	TMK-5	$210-$220
260/J	7"	Shepherd Boy (Kneeling)	TMK-6	$205-$210
260/K	5-1/8"	Little Tooter	TMK-4	$125-$135
260/K	5-1/8"	Little Tooter	TMK-5	$120-$125
260/K	5-1/8"	Little Tooter	TMK-6	$120-$125

Hum No.	Basic Size	Figure	Trademark	Value
260/L	7-1/2"	Donkey	TMK-4	$105-$110
260/L	7-1/2"	Donkey	TMK-5	$99-$105
260/L	7-1/2"	Donkey	TMK-6	$95-$99
260/M	6" x 11"	Cow (Lying)	TMK-4	$110-$115
260/M	6" x 11"	Cow (Lying)	TMK-5	$105-$110
260/M	6" x 11"	Cow (Lying)	TMK-6	$105-$110
260/N	12-3/4"	Moor King (Standing)	TMK-4	$355-$365
260/N	12-3/4"	Moor King (Standing)	TMK-5	$360-$355
260/N	12-3/4"	Moor King (Standing)	TMK-6	$350-$355
260/O	12"	King (Standing)	TMK-4	$360-$370
260/O	12"	King (Standing)	TMK-5	$355-$360
260/O	12"	King (Standing)	TMK-6	$350-$355
260/P	9"	King (Kneeling)	TMK-4	$340-$345
260/P	9"	King (Kneeling)	TMK-5	$335-$345
260/P	9"	King (Kneeling)	TMK-6	$330-$335
260/R	3-1/4" x 4"	Sheep (Lying)	TMK-4	$50-$55
260/R	3-1/4" x 4"	Sheep (Lying)	TMK-5	$45-$50
260/R	3-1/4" x 4"	Sheep (Lying)	TMK-6	$40-$45
260/S		Stable	N/A	$450

Hum 261: Angel Duet

This figure, which was the design of master sculptor Gerhard Skrobek in 1968, is essentially the same design as Hum 193, the candleholder of the same name, but this piece does not have a provision for a candle. It was apparently produced in very limited quantities, for it is somewhat difficult to find bearing the older, Three-Line Mark (TMK-4).

There are no major variations affecting value. Each piece carries an incised 1968 copyright date and there is no reverse mold variation as in the Hum 193 candleholder.

Hum 261: Angel Duet.

Hum No.	Basic Size	Trademark	Current Value
261	5-1/2"	TMK-4	$390-$510
261	5-1/2"	TMK-5	$165-$180
261	5-1/2"	TMK-6	$165-$175
261	5-1/2"	TMK-7	$165-$170
261	5-1/2"	TMK-8	$165-$170

Hum 262: Heavenly Lullaby

First designed by master sculptor Gerhard Skrobek in 1968, this figure has undergone no significant mold variations. It bears an incised copyright date of 1968.

This figure is the same design as Hum 24/I (Lullaby) but does not have a provision for a candle. It was apparently produced in very limited quantities, for it is very difficult to locate in older trademarks.

This piece was temporarily withdrawn from production in 1999.

Hum 262: Heavenly Lullaby.

Hum No.	Basic Size	Trademark	Current Value
262	3-1/2" x 5"	TMK-4	$390-$515
262	3-1/2" x 5"	TMK-5	$140-$180
262	3-1/2" x 5"	TMK-6	$130-$170
262	3-1/2" x 5"	TMK-7	$120-$130

Hum 263: Merry Wanderer
Plaque in Relief

A very rare plaque of the familiar Merry Wanderer motif, this piece was created by master sculptor Gerhard Skrobek in 1968. There is only one known to be outside the factory collection and in a private collection. As far as can be determined there are no more on the collector market. It is known to bear the Three Line Mark (TMK-4).

It appears to have been made from a regular Merry Wanderer mold with the base cut off and the backside flattened.

Hum No.	Basic Size	Trademark	Current Value
263	4" x 5-3/8"	TMK-4	$6,000-$9,000

Hum 263: Merry Wanderer plaque in relief, shown from the front and back.

Hum 264-279, 283-291: Annual Plates

In 1971, the factory produced its first annual plate. This plate utilized the Heavenly Angel (Hum 21) design and was released to the Goebel factory workers to commemorate the 100th anniversary of the W. Goebel firm. The plate was subsequently produced for regular sales without the factory worker inscription. It was received so well in the United States, it was decided that a similar plate would be released annually from then on. The 1971 plate was not released to European dealers.

Since 1971, Goebel has released one new design per year through 1991, each bearing a traditional Hummel figurine motif. The 1991 plate, Come Back Soon (Hum 291), marked the final issue in the 25-year series. The plates and their current market value are listed on the following pages.

There are three versions of this plate. The first is the "normal version." The second differs from the first only in that it has no holes for hanging. It was exported to England where tariff laws in 1971 placed a higher duty on the plate if it had holes than if not. The law states that holes make it a decorative object, subject to a higher duty rate. The third variation is the special original edition produced only for the Goebel factory workers. There is an inscription on the backside of the lower rim. It reads in German as follows: "Gewidmet Aller Mitarbeitern Im Jubilaumsjahr. Wirdanken ihnen fur ihre mitarbeit." Roughly translated, this means "thanks to the workers for their fine service." This last plate is the least common of the three, hence the most sought-after.

There are three known versions of the 1972 Goebel annual plate. The first is the "normal" one with the regular backstamp and the current Goebel trademark. The second has the same backstamp but bears the Three-Line Mark instead of the current mark. The third is exactly the same as the second but does not bear the inscription "Hand Painted," and the "2nd" is omitted from the identification of the plate as an annual plate.

Hum 264: Heavenly Angel 1971 annual plate.

Hum 265: Hear ye, Hear Ye 1972 annual plate.

Hum 266: Globe-Trotter 1973 annual plate.

Hum 267: Goose Girl 1974 annual plate.

Hum 268: Ride Into Christmas 1975 annual plate.

Hum 265: Apple Tree Girl 1976 annual plate.

Hum	Size	Plate Design	Trademark	Year	Current Value
264	7-1/2"	Heavenly Angel	TMK-4	1971	$300-$450
264	7-1/2"	Heavenly Angel*	TMK-4	1971	$720-$900
265	7-1/2"	Hear Ye, Hear Ye	TMK-4	1972	$50-$75
265	7-1/2"	Hear Ye, Hear Ye**	TMK-5	1972	$50-$75
266	7-1/2"	Globe Trotter	TMK-5	1973	$50-$120
267	7-1/2"	Goose Girl	TMK-5	1974	$50-$75
268	7-1/2"	Ride Into Christmas***	TMK-5	1975	$50-$75
269	7-1/2"	Apple Tree Girl****	TMK-5	1976	$50-$75
270	7-1/2"	Apple Tree Boy*****	TMK-5	1977	$3,000
270	7-1/2"	Apple Tree Boy	TMK-5	1977	$50-$75
271	7-1/2"	Happy Pastime	TMK-5	1978	$50-$75
272	7-1/2"	Singing Lesson	TMK-5	1979	$40-$60
273	7-1/2"	School Girl	TMK-6	1980	$40-$60
274	7-1/2"	Umbrella Boy	TMK-6	1981	$50-$75
275	7-1/2"	Umbrella Girl	TMK-6	1982	$75-$90
276	7-1/2"	Postman	TMK-6	1983	$90-$120
277	7-1/2"	Little Helper	TMK-6	1984	$50-$75
278	7-1/2"	Chick Girl	TMK-6	1985	$50-$75
279	7-1/2"	Playmates	TMK-6	1986	$75-$120
283	7-1/2"	Feeding Time	TMK-6	1987	$120-$180
284	7-1/2"	Little Goat Herder	TMK-6	1988	$75-$90
285	7-1/2"	Farm Boy	TMK-6	1989	$60-$90
286	7-1/2"	Shepherd's Boy	TMK-6	1990	$90-$120
287	7-1/2"	Just Resting	TMK-6	1991	$90-$120
287	7-1/2"	Just Resting	TMK-7	1991	$90-$120
288	7-1/2"	Wayside Harmony	TMK-7	1992	$90-$120
289	7-1/2"	Doll Bath	TMK-7	1993	$90-$120
290	7-1/2"	Doctor	TMK-7	1994	$90-$120
291	7-1/2"	Come Back Soon	TMK-7	1995	$105-$120

In 1971, Goebel presented each of its employees a copy of the 1971 annual plate design, only with a special inscription on the back.

** Made at the same time as the Last Bee marked plate and represents a transition. Not appreciably more valuable.

*** Late in 1983 an annual plate was found in Germany. It was a 1975 Annual Plate but instead of the Ride Into Christmas motif it was a Little Fiddler. No doubt that this was a prototype plate considered for 1975, but obviously not selected. How it managed to find its way out of the factory is unknown. It may have been the only one.

**** Somehow a number of the 1976 Annual Plates were inadvertently given the incorrect backstamp "Wildlife Third Edition, Barn Owl" and they were released. How many got out is unknown. It has no value significance.

*****Early sample.

Hum 270: Apple Tree Boy 1977 annual plate.

Hum 271: Happy Pastime 1978 annual plate.

Hum 272: Singing Lesson 1979 annual plate.

Hum 273: School Girl 1980 annual plate.

Hum 274: Umbrella Boy 1981 annual plate.

Hum 275: Umbrella Girl 1982 annual plate.

Hum 276: Postman 1983 annual plate.

Hum 277: Little Helper 1984 annual plate.

Hum 278: Chick Girl 1985 annual plate.

Hum 279: Playmates 1986 annual plate.

Hum 283: Feeding Time 1987 annual plate.

Hum 284: Little Goat Herder 1988 annual plate.

Hum 285: Farm Boy 1989 annual plate.

Hum 286: Shepherd's Boy 1990 annual plate.

Hum 287: Just Resting 1991 annual plate.

Hum 288: Wayside Harmony 1992 annual plate.

Hum 289: Doll Bath 1993 annual plate.

Hum 290: Doctor 1994 annual plate.

Hum 291: Come Back Soon 1995 annual plate.

Hum 280, 281, 282: Anniversary Plates

These three anniversary plates are all larger (10") than the annual plates. Hum 280 utilizes the Stormy Weather (Hum 71) design. Hum 281 only uses one figure from the Spring Dance (Hum 353) figurine and the second girl from the Ring Around the Rosie figurine (Hum 348); it was incorrectly labeled Spring Dance on the back. Hum 282 uses the design from the figurine Auf Wiedersehen (Hum 153).

Hum	Size	Plate Design	Trademark	Year	Current Value
280	10"	Stormy Weather	TMK-5	1975	$60-$90
281	10"	Ring Around the Rosie	TMK-6	1980	$60-$90
282	10"	Auf Wiedersehen	TMK-6	1985	$60-$90

Hum 280: Stormy Weather anniversary plate.

Hum 281: Ring Around the Rosie anniversary plate.

Hum 282: Auf Wiedersehen anniversary plate.

Hum 292, 293, 294, 295: Friends Forever
Plate Series

This is a four-plate series designed by master sculptor Gerhard Skrobek in 1991 and introduced in 1992. At 7" diameter, the plates are smaller than the annual plates and have a decorative border.

Hum No.	Design	Trademark	Year	Current Value
292	Meditation	TMK-7	1992	$60-$90
293	For Father	TMK-7	1993	$60-$90
294	Sweet Greetings	TMK-7	1994	$60-$90
295	Surprise	TMK-7	1995	$60-$90

Friends Forever plate series, featuring Hum 292: Mediation, Hum 293: For Father, Hum 294: Sweet Gatherings, and Hum 295: Surprise.

Hum 296, 297, 298, 299: Four Seasons

Plate Series

This plate series, which is the work of master sculptor Helmut Fischer, began in 1996. The plates measure 7-1/2" in diameter and contrary to the norm, the plate design elements are three-dimensional: less than figural and more than bas-relief. The first in the series was issued at $195. It bears a 1996 copyright date and a "First Issue" backstamp.

Hum No.	Design	Trademark	Year	Current Value
296	Winter Melody	TMK-7	1996	$100-$120
297	Springtime Serenade	TMK-7	1997	$100-$120
298	Summertime Stroll	TMK-7	1998	$100-$120
299	Autumn Glory	TMK-7	1999	$100-$120

Four Seasons plate series, featuring Hum 296: Winter Melody, Hum 297: Springtime Serenade, Hum 298: Summertime Stroll, and Hum 299: Autumn Glory.

Hum 300: Bird Watcher

First known as Tenderness, this figure was released in 1979. It was originally modeled by master sculptor Gerhard Skrobek (the first piece he ever modeled) in the Full Bee (TMK-2) period. Samples in that trademark have an incised copyright date of 1954 and are more valuable than the others. Early samples were, however, also made in TMK-3 and TMK-4, so these are quite valuable as well.

Far more easy to locate are the regular production pieces bearing the 1956 copyright date. They start with the Last Bee (TMK-5) and have been in continuous production since.

Hum No.	Basic Size	Trademark	Current Value
300	5"	TMK-2	$2,400-$3,000
300	5"	TMK-3	$1,200-$1,500
300	5"	TMK-4	$900-$1,200
300	5"	TMK-5	$165-$170
300	5"	TMK-6	$150-$165
300	5"	TMK-7	$150-$165
300	5"	TMK-8	$150-$165

Hum 300: Bird Watcher.

Hum 301: Christmas Angel

A new release in 1989 and originally called Delivery Angel, this piece was originally designed by master sculptor Theo Menzenbach in 1957, during the Stylized Bee (TMK-3) period. It was made in prototype with that trademark and given an incised copyright date of 1957. These early samples are far more valuable than those made after the redesign.

With the redesign by master sculptor Gerhard Skrobek in the late-1980s, the figure was made slightly smaller than the sample and released with TMK-6 and the same 1957 copyright date. This piece remains in production today.

Hum No.	Basic Size	Trademark	Current Value
301	6-1/4"	TMK-3	$2,400-$3,000
301	6-1/4"	TMK-6	$180-$185
301	6-1/4"	TMK-7	$175-$180
301	6-1/4"	TMK-8	$319 retail

Hum 301: Christmas Angel.

Hum 302: Concentration
Possible Future Edition

This figure was first designed by master sculptor Arthur Moeller in 1955 and made in sample form in the Full Bee (TMK-2) era, but regular production has not yet begun. It was originally known as Knit One, Purl Two and the girl is similar to Stitch in Time (Hum 255). The example in the accompanying photograph has the Full Bee (TMK-2) and a 1956 copyright date.

Hum No.	Basic Size	Trademark	Current Value
302	5"	TMK-2	$2,400-$3,000

Base of Concentration showing the Full Bee (TMK-2) trademark in an incised circle.

Hum 302: Concentration, shown here in a rare sample.

Hum 303: Arithmetic Lesson
Possible Future Edition

First designed by master sculptor Arthur Moeller in 1955 and made in sample form in the Full Bee (TMK-2) era, this figure appears to be a combination of one boy and one girl from Hum 170 (School Boys) and Hum 177 (School Girls). The boy in this figure, which was originally known as School Lesson, is also much like the boy in the Dealer Plaque (Hum 460). Note the line around the base in the accompanying photograph: a red line like that indicates that this is a sample figurine.

Hum No.	Basic Size	Trademark	Current Value
303	5-1/4"	TMK-2	$2,400-$3,000

Hum 303: Arithmetic Lesson, another rare sample.

Hum 304: The Artist

This figurine, which was the original work of master sculptor Karl Wagner in 1955, was placed in regular production about 1970 after it was restyled by master sculptor Gerhard Skrobek. There is reason to believe it may have been made in extremely limited quantities in the Full Bee (TMK-2) era and somewhat limited in the Stylized Bee (TMK-3) era. The figure in the accompanying photograph bears that mark and a 1955 incised copyright date.

Base of The Artist, showing the inked-in incised mold number indicating that this is a figurine from the mother mold, a master model.

Hum No.	Basic Size	Trademark	Current Value
304	5-1/4"	TMK-2	$2,400-$3,000
304	5-1/4"	TMK-3	$1,200-$1,800
304	5-1/4"	TMK-4	$600-$720
304	5-1/4"	TMK-5	$180-$225
304	5-1/4"	TMK-6	$175-$185
304	5-1/4"	TMK-7	$175-$180
304	5-1/4"	TMK-8	$329 retail

Hum 304: The Artist.

Hum 305: The Builder

The first sample of this figure, which was created by master sculptor Gerhard Skrobek in 1955, was made in the Full Bee (TMK-2) period and bears that trademark. These early samples are substantially more valuable than the figures made since.

This figurine was originally introduced into the line in 1963, and there are no significant mold or finish variations affecting the normal values, but a Full Bee trademarked piece is rare.

It was temporarily withdrawn from production on June 15, 2002.

Hum No.	Basic Size	Trademark	Current Value
305	5-1/2"	TMK-2	$2,400-$3,000
305	5-1/2"	TMK-3	$600-$900
305	5-1/2"	TMK-4	$195-$225
305	5-1/2"	TMK-5	$180-$200
305	5-1/2"	TMK-6	$175-$180
305	5-1/2"	TMK-7	$175-$180
305	5-1/2"	TMK-8	$175-$180

Hum 305: The Builder.

Hum 306: Little Bookkeeper

The first example of this figure, which was created by master sculptor Arthur Moeller in 1955, was made in the Full Bee (TMK-2) era, and those prototypes bear that trademark. These early samples are substantially more valuable than the figures made since.

There are no significant mold or finish variations affecting normal values, but a Full Bee trademarked example is rare.

Temporarily withdrawn from production on June 15, 2002.

Hum No.	Basic Size	Trademark	Current Value
306	4-3/4"	TMK-2	$2,400-$3,000
306	4-3/4"	TMK-3	$600-$900
306	4-3/4"	TMK-4	$225-$270
306	4-3/4"	TMK-5	$210-$225
306	4-3/4"	TMK-6	$205-$210
306	4-3/4"	TMK-7	$200-$205
306	4-3/4"	TMK-8	$200-$205

Hum 306: Little Bookkeeper.

Hum 307: Good Hunting

This figure, which was the result of combined efforts by master sculptor Reinhold Unger and Helmut Wehlte in 1955, was first introduced in 1962, in the Full Bee (TMK-2) era. These early samples are substantially more valuable than the figures made since.

Figures with the Stylized Bee (TMK-3) trademark and later are the most common.

In older versions of this piece, the boy holds the binoculars significantly lower than they are held in the figure made today, but this and any other mold and finish variations have no effect on normal values. The variations merely reflect the normal changes in the evolution of the figurine.

Hum No.	Basic Size	Trademark	Current Value
307	5-1/4"	TMK-2	$2,400-$3,000
307	5-1/4"	TMK-3	$600-$900
307	5-1/4"	TMK-4	$225-$255
307	5-1/4"	TMK-5	$180-$195
307	5-1/4"	TMK-6	$175-$190
307	5-1/4"	TMK-7	$170-$185
307	5-1/4"	TMK-8	$170-$180

Hum 307: Good Hunting.

Hum 308: Little Tailor

This figure, which was first designed by master sculptor Horst Ashermann in 1955, was first produced in the Full Bee (TMK-2) era, but not placed in the line until 1972. There are a few of the Full Bee and Stylized Bee (TMK-3) pieces around, but they are rare.

There was a major mold redesign in the Last Bee (TMK-5) era, and the old and new figures may be found in that trademark, although the old style is difficult to find. Early pieces carry the incised 1955 copyright date, while the newer styles have a 1972 incised copyright date.

This figurine was temporarily withdrawn as a TMK-8 figurine. In 2009 Manufaktur Rödental reintroduced Little Tailor in a larger size as a TMK-9 figurine.

Hum 308: Little Tailor.

Hum No.	Basic Size	Trademark	Current Value
308	5-1/2″	TMK-2	$2,400-$3,000
308	5-1/2″	TMK-3	$1,200-$1,800
308	5-1/2″	TMK-4	$600-$900
308 (old style)	5-1/2″	TMK-5	$480-$540
308 (new style)	5-1/2″	TMK-5	$180-$205
308	5-1/2″	TMK-6	$175-$190
308	5-1/2″	TMK-7	$175-$185
308	5-1/2″	TMK-8	$175-$180
308	5-1/2″	TMK-9	$369 retail

Hum 309: With Loving Greetings

When first released in 1983, the suggested retail price for this piece was $80, but an early sample piece, which was the work of master sculptor Karl Wagner in 1955, was made during the Full Bee (TMK-2) era. These pieces are substantially more valuable than any made since.

This piece, more complex because of a paintbrush under the boy's arm, was judged too vulnerable to breakage and was removed from the production model. Samples can also be found in TMK-3, TMK-4, and TMK-5.

When first introduced into the line in 1983, the inkwell was colored blue, and the writing on the tablet was turquoise. In late-1987, the color of the inkwell was changed to brown and the color of the writing to blue. This change was made during the TMK-6 period and can be found with the old or the new color in that trademark.

Hum 309: With Loving Greetings.

Hum No.	Basic Size	Trademark	Current Value
309	3-1/2″	TMK-2	$2,400-$3,000
309	3-1/2″	TMK-3	$1,800-$2,400
309	3-1/2″	TMK-4	$1,200-$1,800
309	3-1/2″	TMK-5	$600-$1,200
309 (blue pot)	3-1/2″	TMK-6	$150-$180

Hum No.	Basic Size	Trademark	Current Value
309 (brown pot)	3-1/2″	TMK-6	$130-$145
309	3-1/2″	TMK-7	$125-$135
309	3-1/2″	TMK-8	$125-$130

Hum 310: Searching Angel
Wall Plaque

This piece, which has been called Angelic Concern, was first fashioned by master sculptor Gerhard Skrobek in 1955 during the Full Bee (TMK-2) period, but was not released for sale until 1979. This early sample is very rare, but it has been found. Other samples were also made during the Stylized Bee (TMK-

Hum 310: Searching Angel wall plaque.

Hum No.	Basic Size	Trademark	Current Value
310	4″ x 2-1/2″	TMK-2	$1,200-$1,800
310	4″ x 2-1/2″	TMK-3	$720-$1,020
310	4″ x 2-1/2″	TMK-4	$600-$900
310	4″ x 2-1/2″	TMK-5	$180-$300
310	4″ x 2-1/2″	TMK-6	$85-$90
310	4″ x 2-1/2″	TMK-7	$85-$90

3) and Three Line (TMK-4) periods. Pieces carry an incised 1955 copyright date.

This plaque was temporarily withdrawn from production in January 1999.

Hum 311: Kiss Me

Kiss Me was first designed by master sculptor Reinhold Unger in 1955 and made in the Full Bee (TMK-2) era, but it was not released for sale until 1961, during the Stylized Bee (TMK-3) period. A few of these Full Bee pieces have made their way into the collectors' market. They are very rare and, therefore, substantially more valuable than pieces made since.

The mold was reworked later so that the doll the girl is holding did not appear to be a child. The figures can, therefore, be found either way in both the Stylized Bee (TMK-3) and Three Line (TMK-4) periods.

Hum No.	Basic Size	Trademark	Current Value
311	6″	TMK-2	$2,400-$3,000
311 (old style)	6″	TMK-3	$480-$665
311 (new style)	6″	TMK-3	$270-$300
311 (old style)	6″	TMK-4	$390-$300
311 (new style)	6″	TMK-4	$225-$270
311	6″	TMK-5	$210-$225
311	6″	TMK-6	$205-$210
311	6″	TMK-7	$200-$210
311	6″	TMK-8	$359 retail

Hum 311: Kiss Me.

Hum 312: Honey Lover

This piece, which was created by master sculptor Helmut Wehlte in 1955, was first found illustrated as a possible future edition (PFE) in the Golden Anniversary Album when the book was released in 1984. At that point in time, a few had somehow already made their way into collectors' hands.

The figure is now officially on

Hum 312: Honey Lover.

Hum No.	Basic Size	Trademark	Current Value
312	3-3/4″	TMK-2	$2,400-$3,000
312/I	3-3/4″	TMK-6	$240-$300
312/I	3-3/4″	TMK-7	$140-$150
312/I	3-3/4″	TMK-8	$295

the market, having been released as a special M.I. Hummel Club exclusive in 1991. Released at $190, it is available to members after the 15th anniversary of their club membership.

Hum 313: Sunny Morning

This piece, which was designed by master sculptor Arthur Moeller in 1955 and originally called Slumber Serenade, was a new release for 2003 with mold number 313/0. Those issued in 2003 carried the "First Issue 2003" backstamp as well as TMK-8.

Early samples were made in the mid-1950s carrying the Full Bee (TMK-2). Somehow, at least three prototype pieces have made it into the collectors' market.

Hum No.	Basic Size	Trademark	Current Value
313	3-3/4"	TMK-2	$2,400-$3,000
313/0	4-1/4"	TMK-8	$319 retail

Hum 313: Sunny Morning.

Hum 314: Confidentially

Hum 314: Confidentially.

Even though this figure was first introduced into the line in 1972, the Last Bee (TMK-5) period, it can also be found as early samples in the Full Bee (TMK-2), Stylized Bee (TMK-3), and the Three Line (TMK-4) eras.

It was the original design of master sculptor Horst Ashermann in 1955, but master sculptor Gerhard Skrobek redesigned the figure shortly after releasing it. The new and old styles include changes in the stand, the addition of a tie on the boy, and a change in the finish texture. The old and new styles can be found with the Last Bee (TMK-5).

This piece was temporarily withdrawn from production in 1999.

Hum No.	Basic Size	Trademark	Current Value
314	5-1/2"	TMK-2	$2,400-$3,000
314	5-1/2"	TMK-3	$1,200-$1,800
314	5-1/2"	TMK-4	$600-$1,800
314 (old style)	5-1/2"	TMK-5	$480-$570
314 (new style)	5-1/2"	TMK-5	$210-$235
314	5-1/2"	TMK-6	$200-$210
314	5-1/2"	TMK-7	$195-$205

Hum 315: Mountaineer

Hum 315: Mountaineer.

Modeled by master sculptor Gerhard Skrobek in 1955 and released in 1964 (TMK-3 period) at the World's Fair in New York City, this figure is also found, albeit rarely, as an early sample with the Full Bee (TMK-2) trademark.

There are no mold or finish variations that would have any effect on the normal values, although older pieces are slightly smaller and have a green stick rather than the dark gray stick of the newer pieces.

The year 2011 marked the celebration of Sister Hummel's 75th anniversary of the beginning of her legacy. Manufaktur Rödental selected 50 figurines to bear the "75th Anniversary" backstamp. Mountaineer was one of those figurines. Only 75 of them were available in North America with this backstamp. Each figurine was hand-numbered with a golden backstamp and a map of North America backstamp. A special porcelain plaque was included and a notable emblem on the packaging hinted at the contents. Each figurine included a "75 Years of M.I. Hummel" certificate.

Hum No.	Basic Size	Trademark	Current Value
315	5-1/4"	TMK-2	$2,400-$3,000
315	5-1/4"	TMK-3	$450-$600
315	5-1/4"	TMK-4	$170-$240
315	5-1/4"	TMK-5	$165-$175
315	5-1/4"	TMK-6	$160-$165
315	5-1/4"	TMK-7	$150-$160
315	5-1/4"	TMK-8	$279

Hum 316: Relaxation

This piece, which was once called Nightly Ritual, was designed and produced in prototype by master sculptor Karl Wagner in 1955, in the Full Bee (TMK-2) period.

The piece was produced as a M.I. Hummel Club 25-year membership exclusive. The inscription on the bottom reads: "EXCLUSIVE EDITION Twenty-Five Year Membership M.I. HUMMEL CLUB" and carries the special club backstamp.

Hum No.	Basic Size	Trademark	Current Value
316	4"	TMK-2	$2,400-$3,000
316	4"	TMK-8	$390

Hum 316: Relaxation.

Hum 317: Not For You

Even though this figurine, which was created by master sculptor Arthur Moeller in 1955, was not released for sale until 1961 during the Stylized Bee (TMK-3) period, it is occasionally found as an early sample bearing the Full Bee (TMK-2) trademark.

There are no mold or finish variations that affect the normal values for the figures with the various trademarks.

Hum No.	Basic Size	Trademark	Current Value
317	5-1/2"	TMK-2	$2,400-$3,000
317	5-1/2"	TMK-3	$450-$600
317	5-1/2"	TMK-4	$185-$195
317	5-1/2"	TMK-5	$175-$195
317	5-1/2"	TMK-6	$170-$175
317	5-1/2"	TMK-7	$180-$190
317	5-1/2"	TMK-8	$180-$190

Hum 317: Not For You.

Hum 318: Art Critic

This figure was first designed by master sculptor Horst Ashermann in 1955 and produced in prototype during the Full Bee (TMK-2) era, but was not released until 1991. At least two of these figures, marked with the Full Bee trademark, have found their way into the collectors' market. These early prototypes are worth substantially more than anything released since.

These figurines carry a 1955 incised copyright date and "First Issue 1991" backstamp in the first year of production. There are no significant mold or finish variations affecting the normal values.

The piece was temporarily withdrawn from production in 1999.

Hum No.	Basic Size	Trademark	Current Value
318	5-3/4"	TMK-2	$2,400-$3,000
318	5-3/4"	TMK-6	$180-$205
318	5-3/4"	TMK-7	$190-$200

Art Critic TMK-7 demonstration piece with "First Issue" backstamp and incised 1955 copyright date.

Hum 318: Art Critic.

Hum 319: Doll Bath

This figure was first designed by master sculptor Gerhard Skrobek in 1956 and produced in early sample form during the Full Bee (TMK-2) period, but was not released until 1962, during the Stylized Bee (TMK-3) period. There are some pieces out there with the Full Bee trademark, and these early samples are worth substantially more than the later releases.

In the 1970s, the entire collection underwent a change from the old smooth surface finish to a textured finish. Unlike many of the other figures in the collection, this one made a clean break from the old style finish (found only in the TMK-4 pieces) to the new textured finish (found on the TMK-5 pieces and all thereafter).

Hum No.	Basic Size	Trademark	Current Value
319	5-1/4"	TMK-2	$2,400-$3,000
319	5-1/4"	TMK-3	$450-$600
319	5-1/4"	TMK-4	$225-$270
319	5-1/4"	TMK-5	$210-$225
319	5-1/4"	TMK-6	$200-$220
319	5-1/4"	TMK-7	$200-$205
319	5-1/4"	TMK-8	$359 retail

Both of these figures of Doll Bath bear the Three Line Mark (TMK-4). The one on the left has an incised 1956 copyright date and the other has a copyright date of 197? It is impossible to discern the fourth digit.

Hum 319: Doll Bath.

Hum 320: The Professor

First produced in prototype by master sculptor Gerhard Skrobek in 1955 during the Full Bee (TMK-2) era, this figure was not released until 1991.

The new pieces bear the mold number 320/0, but the Full Bee pieces have the mold number 320 with no size designator. These sample pieces are considerably larger than the production pieces and are worth considerably more than those released into production.

There are no significant variations affecting the normal collector values.

The 320/0 size was temporarily withdrawn from production on June 15, 2002.

Hum 320: The Professor.

The base of Hum 320 master model. Note the inked incised mold number. This is routinely done on pieces made from the mother or master mold.

Hum No.	Basic Size	Trademark	Current Value
320	5-3/4"	TMK-2	$2,400-$3,000
320/0	4-3/4"	TMK-7	$145-$160
320/0	4-3/4"	TMK-8	$160-165

Hum 321: Wash Day

In the first sample figurines, made in 1955 by master sculptor Reinhold Unger and Helmut Wehlte, the laundry being held up was much longer and attached to the rest of the laundry down in the basket. This was during the Full Bee (TMK-2) period. It is possible, though unlikely, that you will find this figure. These early samples are marked with the Full Bee (TMK-2) trademark and are significantly more valuable than the later variations.

In 1989, a new smaller version of this piece was issued as a part of a four-piece series with matching mini-plates. These versions do not have the laundry basket. They have an incised mold number of 321/4/0. When this mold was issued, Goebel changed the number on the larger piece to 321/I. You may find it either way on those figures with TMK-6 trademark.

The smaller 321/4/0 size was temporarily withdrawn from production in 1997.

Hum No.	Basic Size	Trademark	Current Value
321/4/0	3"	TMK-6	$75-$85
321/4/0	3"	TMK-7	$70-$75
321	5-3/4"	TMK-2	$2,400-$3,000
321	5-3/4"	TMK-3	$450-$600
321	5-3/4"	TMK-4	$240-$270
321	5-3/4"	TMK-5	$260-$280
321	5-3/4"	TMK-6	$215-$260
321/I	5-3/4"	TMK-6	$215-$250
321/I	5-3/4"	TMK-7	$210-$250
321/I	5-3/4"	TMK-8	$365 retail

Hum 321: Wash Day.

Hum 322: Little Pharmacist

This figurine was first designed by master sculptor Karl Wagner in 1955 and those early samples bear the Full Bee (TMK-2) trademark and are worth considerably more than regular production pieces.

There are several variations in the labeling of the medicine bottle at the figure's feet. The version written in German was temporarily withdrawn from production as of Dec. 31, 1984.

Hum 322: Little Pharmacist.

One of the most difficult pieces to find is the version with "Castor Oil" on the bottle in Spanish ("Castor bil"). When found, it is on the Three Line Mark (TMK-4) pieces and is worth considerably more than the other variations at $1,200-$1,800.

In 1988 Little Pharmacist was redesigned, and all subsequent production of the figure reflects the following changes. The

Hum No.	Basic Size	Trademark	Current Value
322	6"	TMK-2	$2,400-$3,000
322	6"	TMK-3	$450-$600
322	6"	TMK-4	$195-$240
322 (Spanish)	6"	TMK-4	$1,200-$1,800
322	6"	TMK-5	$180-$195
322	6"	TMK-6	$175-$200
322	6"	TMK-7	$170-$175
322	6"	TMK-8	$170-$175

base was made shallower with rounded corners, which made the figure shorter than its former 6" size (now 5-3/4"). The coat is now curved in front at the bottom line. A breast pocket was added, the strap (in back) was made wider and a second button was added. The figure's bow tie was straightened and the eyeglass stems made to disappear into his hair.

Somehow in 1990 an unknown (but probably very small) number of these figures were produced with the bottle label in German ("Rizinusol") and the prescription in English ("Recipe"). A TMK-6 Little Pharmacist with these words has a collector value of $600-$900.

Hum 323: Merry Christmas
Wall Plaque

Designed and made in sample form by master sculptor Gerhard Skrobek in 1955, during the Full Bee (TMK-2) period, this plaque was not offered for sale until 1979. The TMK-2 samples are worth significantly more than figures made since.

Samples were also made during the Stylized Bee (TMK-3) and Three Line (TMK-4) periods, and those too are worth more than the versions eventually released to the public during the Last Bee (TMK-5) era.

This plaque was temporarily withdrawn from production in January 1999.

Hum No.	Basic Size	Trademark	Current Value
323	4" x 5-1/4"	TMK-2	$1,200-$1,800
323	4" x 5-1/4"	TMK-2	$720-$1,020
323	4" x 5-1/4"	TMK-2	$600-$900
323	4" x 5-1/4"	TMK-5	$180-$300
323	4" x 5-1/4"	TMK-6	$90-$95
323	4" x 5-1/4"	TMK-7	$85-$90

Hum 323: Merry Christmas wall plaque.

Hum 324: At the Fence
Possible Future Edition

Base markings of At the Fence.

Hum 324: At the Fence rare sample.

This figure was designed by master sculptor Arthur Moeller in 1955 and produced in sample form in the 1950s, but has not yet been put into regular production and offered for sale. The one in the picture is marked with the Full Bee (TMK-2), as you can see. Somehow it managed to make it into the collectors' market. Notice the line painted around the base; this denotes a painter's sample, a model that the Goebel painters try to duplicate when producing the figurines.

Hum No.	Basic Size	Trademark	Current Value
324	4-3/4"	TMK-2	$2,400-$3,000

Hum 325: Helping Mother
Possible Future Edition

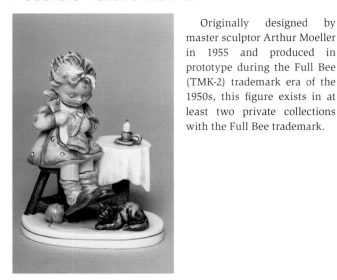

Hum 325: Helping Mother rare sample.

Originally designed by master sculptor Arthur Moeller in 1955 and produced in prototype during the Full Bee (TMK-2) trademark era of the 1950s, this figure exists in at least two private collections with the Full Bee trademark.

Hum No.	Basic Size	Trademark	Current Value
325	5"	TMK-2	$2,400-$3,000

Hum 326: Being Punished
Possible Future Edition

The original design and prototype figure by master sculptor Gerhard Skrobek was made in 1957. Those figures, which were originally called Naughty Boy, have an incised 1955 copyright date and bear the Full Bee (TMK-2) trademark.

Hum No.	Basic Size	Trademark	Current Value
326	4" x 5"	TMK-2	$2,400-$3,000

Although the piece has not yet been released, more than one has made its way into the collector market. There may also be early samples with the Stylized Bee (TMK-3) trademark, but those reports have not been substantiated.

Hum 327: The Run-a-way

Originally designed by master sculptor Helmut Wehlte in 1955, this figure was not released until 1972. Samples were produced with the Full Bee (TMK-2) and Stylized Bee (TMK-3) trademarks.

The early samples are worth substantially more than figures made since, with the Full Bee variations the most desirable.

There exist at least two variations of Hum 327, due to a redesign by master sculptor Gerhard Skrobek in 1972. They have both been found with the Last Bee (TMK-5) trademark, although each bears a different copyright date.

Hum 327: The Run-a-way.

Hum No.	Basic Size	Trademark	Current Value
327	5-1/4"	TMK-2	$2,400-$3,000
327	5-1/4"	TMK-3	$1,200-$1,800
327	5-1/4"	TMK-4	$660-$720
327 (old style)	5-1/4"	TMK-5	$540-$600
327 (new style)	5-1/4"	TMK-5	$180-$195
327	5-1/4"	TMK-6	$175-$180
327	5-1/4"	TMK-7	$180-$185
327	5-1/4"	TMK-8	$180-$185

The older design (1955 copyright date) has flowers in the basket, gray jacket, gray hair, and the crook on the cane is turned more sideways. The newer design (1972 copyright date) has no flowers, a green hat, blue jacket, and the cane is situated with the crook pointing up.

Hum 328: Carnival

The original design was the work of master sculptors Reinhold Unger and Helmut Wehlte in 1955, and samples of this figure were made in the mid-1950s. Those sample pieces have a copyright date of 1955 and bear the Full Bee (TMK-2).

When the piece was put into regular production and offered for sale in the 1960s, it had the Three Line Mark (TMK-4), but a few have been found bearing the Stylized Bee (TMK-3) as well.

There are no major mold or finish variations affecting the normal values, although older pieces are slightly larger and do depict the object under the boy's arm as a noisemaker or "slapstick."

This piece was temporarily withdrawn from production in 1999.

Hum No.	Basic Size	Trademark	Current Value
328	6"	TMK-2	$2,400-$3,000
328	6"	TMK-3	$450-$600
328	6"	TMK-4	$190-$210
328	6"	TMK-5	$165-$170
328	6"	TMK-6	$150-$165
328	6"	TMK-7	$145-$150

Hum 328: Carnival.

Hum 329: Off to School
Possible Future Edition

This figure, which was first known as Kindergarten Romance, was originally designed by master sculptor Arthur Moeller in 1955 and samples were made during the Full Bee (TMK-2) and Stylized Bee (TMK-3) periods. It consists of a boy and girl walking along. The girl has a book satchel in the crook of her left arm. The boy figure is substantially similar to Hum 82: School Boy.

Hum No.	Basic Size	Trademark	Current Value
329	5"	TMK-2	$2,400-$3,000
329	5"	TMK-3	$1,800-$2,400

Hum 330: Baking Day

This figure, once called Kneading Dough, was first made in sample form by master sculptor Gerhard Skrobek in 1955. These early examples bear the 1955 copyright date, as do the pieces made since. The figure was not released until 1985, during TMK-6 period, but samples were produced in every trademark leading up to the release. Such samples are worth substantially more than the figures released thereafter.

There are no significant mold or finish variations affecting normal values.

The piece was temporarily withdrawn from production in January 1999.

Hum No.	Basic Size	Trademark	Current Value
330	5-1/4"	TMK-2	$2,400-$3,000
330	5-1/4"	TMK-3	$1,500-$1,800
330	5-1/4"	TMK-4	$1,200-$1,500
330	5-1/4"	TMK-5	$900-$1,200
330	5-1/4"	TMK-6	$200-$220
330	5-1/4"	TMK-7	$180-$220

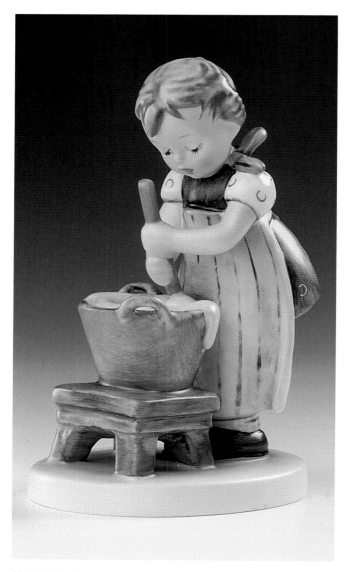

Hum 330: Baking Day.

Hum 331: Crossroads

Master sculptor Arthur Moeller first made Crossroads in 1955, with early samples bearing both the Full Bee (TMK-2) and Stylized Bee (TMK-3) trademarks.

It has been reported that there is a variation regarding the position of the trombone. The reported variation is that the horn is reversed so that it points down instead of up. It is the result of a mistake in the assembly of the parts of the factory and is likely to be the only one in existence.

In 1990, Goebel issued a special edition of Crossroads to commemorate the demise of the Berlin Wall. Limited to 20,000 worldwide, it is the same figure except the "HALT" sign on the post is placed at the base of the post as if it had fallen or been torn down. Production of this edition took place during the transition from TMK-6 to TMK-7. Interestingly, it has been reported that only about 3,500 of the 20,000 were given the TMK-7.

The third variation is another edition created for the U.S. military forces. As with the special "Desert Storm" edition of Hum 50 (Volunteers), this one was sold through military base exchange stores only. This

Hum 331: Crossroads.

Hum No.	Basic Size	Trademark	Current Value
331	6-3/4″	TMK-2	$2,400-$3,000
331	6-3/4″	TMK-3	$1,200-$1,800
331	6-3/4″	TMK-4	$450-$600
331	6-3/4″	TMK-5	$300-$330
331	6-3/4″	TMK-6	$290-$300 original
331	6-3/4″	TMK-6	$450-$540 commemorative
331	6-3/4″	TMK-7	$570-$1,200 commemorative
331	6-3/4″	TMK-7	$285-$290 original
331	6-3/4″	TMK-7	$360-$465 Desert Storm
331	6-3/4″	TMK-8	$510

Desert Storm edition was a three-piece set. The figure is the regular production model with the sign on the post, but it has an American and German flag beneath the glaze under the base. A second piece is a representation of a piece of the wall with "Berlin Wall" on it in bas-relief. It also has the flags underneath along with the inscription "With esteem and grateful appreciation to the United States Military Forces for the preservation of peace and freedom." That same inscription is found on a brass plate on the front of the third piece, a wooden display base. The Berlin Wall piece is limited to 20,000 worldwide and sequentially hand-numbered beneath the base in the traditional manner of marking limited editions. The initial release price in 1992 was $265 for the set. It is valued at about $700 today.

Hum 332: Soldier Boy

Hum 332: Soldier Boy.

Originally designed by master sculptor Gerhard Skrobek in 1955 and produced in prototype in the 1950s, this figure was not released for sale to the general public until 1963. The early samples, bearing the Full Bee (TMK-2) and a 1955 incised copyright date, are worth substantially more than the pieces released since.

Pieces later than TMK-2 have a 1957 incised copyright date.

There is a variation on the color of the cap medallion. It is painted red on older pieces and blue on the newer ones. The transition from red to blue took place in the Three Line Mark (TMK-4) period and can be found both ways bearing that trademark.

Goebel released a special limited edition in 1994 consisting of the figurine, a small porcelain replica of the shack at Checkpoint Charlie of Berlin Wall fame, and a wooden base with a sign and brass ID plate (see accompanying photograph). The edition was limited to 20,000 and the pieces each bear a special backstamp identifying them appropriately. The release price was $330 and is still valued at about the same today.

This figurine was temporarily withdrawn from production in 1999.

Hum No.	Basic Size	Trademark	Current Value
332	6″	TMK-2	$2,400-$3,000
332	6″	TMK-3	$600-$900
332 (red)	6″	TMK-4	$150-$210
332 (blue)	6″	TMK-4	$175-$185
332	6″	TMK-5	$165-$180
332	6″	TMK-6	$165-$175
332	6″	TMK-7	$165-$170
332	6″	TMK-9	$279 retail

Left: The special edition Checkpoint Charlie Soldier Boy display.

Right: The bases of the Soldier Boy and Checkpoint Charlie Shack showing the special markings.

Soldier Boy was introduced separately and exclusively by QVC in the fall of 2009. In spring of 2010, Manufaktur Rödental made the figurine available in honor of those serving in the military. It is a TMK-9 figurine with the TMK-9 backstamp.

Hum 333: Blessed Event

This figure was designed by master sculptor Arthur Moeller in 1955 and produced as samples in the 1950s, but not released until 1964 (TMK-4 era) at the World's Fair in New York City. The samples in both the Full Bee (TMK-2) and Stylized Bee (TMK-3) eras are worth substantially more than the pieces released since.

No significant variations have been reported, although pieces can be found with 1955, 1956, or 1957 incised copyright dates.

Hum No.	Basic Size	Trademark	Current Value
333	5-1/2"	TMK-2	$2,400-$3,000
333	5-1/2"	TMK-3	$450-$600
333	5-1/2"	TMK-4	$255-$360
333	5-1/2"	TMK-5	$240-$255
333	5-1/2"	TMK-6	$235-$240
333	5-1/2"	TMK-7	$230-$235
333	5-1/2"	TMK-8	$389 retail

Hum 333: Blessed Event.

Hum 334: Homeward Bound

Homeward Bound was first made in sample form in the mid-1950s by master sculptor Arthur Moeller, but it was not released until 1971. Samples are known to exist in both the Full Bee (TMK-2) and Stylized Bee (TMK-3) trademarks. The Full Bee samples are especially valuable.

Older models of this design have a support molded in beneath the goat. The newer versions do not have this support. Examples of both styles exist in both the Three Line (TMK-4) and Last Bee (TMK-5) periods.

The piece was temporarily withdrawn from production in January 1999.

Hum No.	Basic Size	Trademark	Current Value
334	5"	TMK-2	$2,400-$3,000
334	5"	TMK-3	$600-$900
334 (old style)	5"	TMK-4	$420-$510
334 (new style)	5"	TMK-4	$275-$300
334 (old style)	5"	TMK-5	$285-$300
334 (new style)	5"	TMK-5	$240-$260
334	5"	TMK-6	$235-$240
334	5"	TMK-7	$220-$225

Hum 334: Homeward Bound.

Hum 335: Lucky Boy

Designed in 1956 by master sculptor Arthur Moeller and produced in sample form (called Fair Prizes) in both the Full Bee (TMK-2) and Stylized Bee (TMK-3) periods, this figurine was released in 1995. One example has a red line painted around the base, used by the factory to denote a figure that is used as a sample model for the factory artists.

Lucky Boy was released in special limited edition in a 4-1/2" size (Hum 335/0). It was part of Goebel's 1995 celebration of 60 years of Hummel figurines; 250 U.S. dealers participated in Goebel's M.I. Hummel 60th Anniversary Open House. The figurine was limited to 25,000 worldwide with 15,000 of them bearing a special 60th anniversary backstamp. Collectors could only purchase figurines from participating dealers during the year. The other 10,000 pieces were made available in 1996 with the Goebel 125th anniversary backstamp. None will ever again be produced in this size. The release price was $190.

Base of Lucky Boy showing Stylized Bee (TMK-3) trademark.

Hum 335: Lucky Boy.

Hum No.	Basic Size	Trademark	Current Value
335	5"	TMK-2	$2,400-$3,000
335	5"	TMK-3	$1,800-$2,400
335/0	4-1/2"	TMK-7	$115-$150

Hum 336: Close Harmony

This figure was crafted by master sculptor Gerhard Skrobek in 1956 and first produced in sample form in the Full Bee (TMK-2) era, but not released until the early 1960s. The early samples are worth substantially more than the pieces released since.

Inexplicably, this piece can be found with any one of three copyright dates: 1955, 1956, or 1957. There is a 1962 copyright date that is explained by a redesign in that year. Even more peculiar is that those in production currently are yet another redesign, but they bear the 1955

Hum 336: Close Harmony.

Hum No.	Basic Size	Trademark	Current Value
336	5-1/2"	TMK-2	$2,400-$3,000
336	5-1/2"	TMK-3	$600-$900
336	5-1/2"	TMK-4	$235-$315
336	5-1/2"	TMK-5	$220-$240
336	5-1/2"	TMK-6	$215-$240
336	5-1/2"	TMK-7	$215-$235
336	5-1/2"	TMK-8	$215-$230

copyright date. This strange circumstance makes the pieces with the later copyright date of 1962 more valuable than those with the 1955 copyright date that are currently in production. This is the only figure in the collection that can be found with four different copyright dates.

This figure was temporarily withdrawn from production on June 15, 2002.

Hum 337: Cinderella

Produced first in the Full Bee (TMK-2) era as samples by master sculptor Arthur Moeller and with more samples produced during the Stylized Bee (TMK-3), Cinderella was not placed in the collection until 1972. The early samples will bring premium prices.

Early pieces have either a 1958 or 1960 copyright date. Restyled in 1972 by master sculptor Gerhard Skrobek, the redesigned version carries a 1972 copyright date.

In the first versions of this figure, the eyes are open. Newer figures have the eyes closed. These variations represent two entirely different molds. Both versions have appeared bearing the Last Bee trademark (TMK-5).

Hum 337: Cinderella.

Hum No.	Basic Size	Trademark	Current Value
337	5-1/2"	TMK-2	$2,400-$3,000
337	5-1/2"	TMK-3	$1,800-$2,400
337	5-1/2"	TMK-4	$900-$1,020
337 (old style)	5-1/2"	TMK-5	$720-$900
337 (new style)	5-1/2"	TMK-5	$210-$225
337	5-1/2"	TMK-6	$210-$225
337	5-1/2"	TMK-6	$200-$210
337	5-1/2"	TMK-6	$355

Hum 338: Birthday Cake
Candleholder

Birthday Cake, which was the work of master sculptor Gerhard Skrobek in 1956 and was originally called A Birthday Wish, was added to the line in 1989. It measures 3-3/4" and has a receptacle for a candle as you can see in the accompanying photo. It has an incised copyright date of 1956.

There are two versions to be found. The differences are with regard to the texture of the top of the cake surface. About the first 2,000 pieces were produced with a smooth texture. This was changed to a rough texture ostensibly to correspond to the style of today.

It does exist in the Full Bee (TMK-2) prototype and has also turned up in the Stylized Bee (TMK-3).

Birthday Cake became part of QVC's Sister Hummel's 100th birthday celebration. The figurines sold had "Alles Gute zum Geburtstag" painted on the base.

This piece was temporarily withdrawn from production in January 1999.

Hum 338: Birthday Cake candleholder.

Hum No.	Basic Size	Trademark	Current Value
338	3-3/4"	TMK-2	$2,400-$3,000
338	3-3/4"	TMK-3	$1,800-$2,400
338	3-3/4"	TMK-6	$105-$110
338	3-3/4"	TMK-7	$100-$105

Hum 339: Behave!

In 1956, master sculptor Helmut Wehlte created Behave!, which was first known as Walking Her Dog.

The figurine was released in 1996 as a M.I. Hummel Club exclusive for the club. It has a special club backstamp in commemoration of 20 years of membership; issued only by those eligible returning a redemption card. It measures 5-1/2". The release price was $350. Notice the considerable difference between the sample piece and the regular production figurine.

Hum No.	Basic Size	Trademark	Current Value
339	5-1/2"	TMK-2	$3,000-$6,000
339	5-1/2"	TMK-3	$2400-$3,000
339	5-1/2"	TMK-7	$270-$300
339	5-1/2"	TMK-8 EE	$360

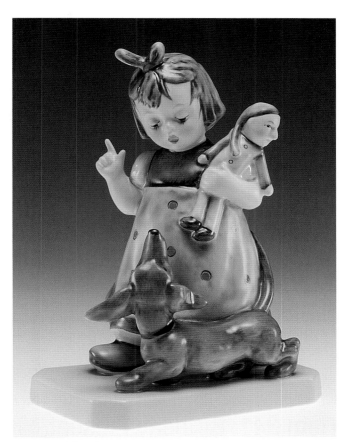

A TMK-7 version of Behave! showing base marks.

Hum 339: Behave!

Factory "sample" of Behave! showing base markings that include a 1956 copyright date and Stylized Bee (TMK-3).

Hum 340: Letter to Santa Claus

The first sample models of Letter to Santa Claus, which were designed by master sculptor Helmut Wehlte in 1956, were an inch smaller (6-1/4") and had a tree trunk instead of a milled lumber post for the mailbox. The lumber post was the final design approved for production. Early samples exist in the Full Bee (TMK-2) both with the tree trunk post as well as the lumber post. Samples can also be found with the Stylized Bee (TMK-3). As always, the samples are worth substantially more than the figures released since.

The piece was first released in 1971 at $30. It was restyled with a new textured finish. This was a general change throughout the collection in the TMK-5 period and can be found either way bearing that trademark. The old pieces sport gray-green pants and the newer ones have red-orange pants.

Hum No.	Basic Size	Trademark	Current Value
340 (tree trunk post-prototype)	6-1/4"	TMK-2	$9,000-$12,000
340 (lumber post)	7-1/4"	TMK-2	$2,400-$3,000
340	7-1/4"	TMK-3	$1,800-$2,400
340	7-1/4"	TMK-4	$450-$600
340	7-1/4"	TMK-5	$240-$260
340	7-1/4"	TMK-6	$235-$240
340	7-1/4"	TMK-7	$235-$240
340	7-1/4"	TMK-8	$400

Hum 340: Letter to Santa Claus.

Hum 341: Birthday Present

Birthday Present, in 5" sample form bearing the Full Bee (TMK-2), Stylized Bee (TMK-3), and Three Line (TMK-4) trademarks, was found on the collectors' market long before its release in 1994. These early sample models, which were designed by master sculptor Gerhard Skrobek in 1956, are worth substantially more than the figures released since.

The production figurine is smaller at 3-3/4" and bears the "First Issue" and "SPECIAL EVENT" backstamps, as it was part of a district manager promotion during 1994. It was available in this configuration during that year only. The release price was $140.

This piece continues in general production today.

Hum No.	Basic Size	Trademark	Current Value
341	5" to 5-1/3"	TMK-2	$2,400-$3,000
341	5" to 5-1/3"	TMK-3	$1,800-$2,400
341	5" to 5-1/3"	TMK-4	$1,200-$1,800
341/3/0	3-3/4"	TMK-7	$105-$120
341/3/0	3-3/4"	TMK-8	$105-$120

Hum 341: Birthday Present.

Hum 342: Mischief Maker

The work of master sculptor Arthur Moeller in 1956, Mischief Maker exists in sample form with either the Full Bee (TMK-2) or Stylized Bee (TMK-3) trademarks.

This figure was not released for sale until 1972 at $26.50. There are no significant variations affecting normal values.

It was temporarily withdrawn from production in January 1999.

Hum No.	Basic Size	Trademark	Current Value
342	5″	TMK-2	$2,400-$3,000
342	5″	TMK-3	$1,200-$1,800
342	5″	TMK-4	$450-$600
342	5″	TMK-5	$210-$220
342	5″	TMK-6	$200-$210
342	5″	TMK-7	$185-$195

Hum 342: Mischief Maker.

Hum 343: Christmas Song

Originally known as Singing Angel in early company records, Christmas Song was one of six new designs released by Goebel in 1981. The work of master sculptor Gerhard Skrobek in 1956, there are early samples bearing the Full Bee (TMK-2), Stylized Bee (TMK-3), and Three Line (TMK-4) trademarks. As always, these are worth substantially more than the figures released since.

A smaller 3-1/2" version (Hum 343/4/0) was released in 1996 as part of Goebel's 125th anniversary. Those pieces carry an incised 1991 copyright date, TMK-7, and a combination "First Issue 1996" and "125th Anniversary Goebel" backstamp.

Hum No.	Basic Size	Trademark	Current Value
343/4/0	3-1/2″	TMK-7	$95-$110
343/4/0	3-1/2″	TMK-8	$135
343	6-1/4″	TMK-2	$2,400-$5,000
343	6-1/4″	TMK-3	$1,200-$1,800
343	6-1/4″	TMK-4	$600-$1,200
343	6-1/4″	TMK-5	$450-$600
343	6-1/4″	TMK-6	$160-$165
343	6-1/4″	TMK-7	$150-$160
343/I	6-1/4″	TMK-8	$279

Hum 343: Christmas Song.

Hum 344: Feathered Friends

First designed by master sculptor Gerhard Skrobek and made in sample form in the mid-1950s, this piece was not released until 1972. Figurines have been found on the collectors' market, however, that bear earlier marks: Full Bee (TMK-2) and Stylized Bee (TMK-3). These are considered early samples and are worth substantially more than the figures released since.

There are no major mold or finish variations to be found that affect normal collector values.

The year 2011 marked the celebration of Sister Hummel's 75th anniversary of the beginning of her legacy. Manufaktur Rödental selected 50 figurines to bear the "75th Anniversary" backstamp. Feathered Friends was one of those figurines. Only 75 of them were available in North America with this backstamp. Each figurine was hand-numbered with a golden backstamp and a map of North America backstamp. A special porcelain plaque was included, and a notable emblem on the packaging hinted at the contents. Each figurine included a "75 Years of M.I. Hummel" certificate.

Hum 344: Feathered Friends.

Hum No.	Basic Size	Trademark	Current Value
344	4-3/4"	TMK-2	$2,400-$3,000
344	4-3/4"	TMK-3	$1,200-$1,800
344	4-3/4"	TMK-4	$450-$600
344	4-3/4"	TMK-5	$210-$220

Hum No.	Basic Size	Trademark	Current Value
344	4-3/4"	TMK-6	$200-$210
344	4-3/4"	TMK-7	$205-$210
344	4-3/4"	TMK-8	$359

Hum 345: A Fair Measure

A Fair Measure, the work of master sculptor Helmut Wehlte, was first made as samples in the mid-1950s, but it was not released until 1962. Early samples bear the Full Bee (TMK-2) and Stylized Bee (TMK-3) and are worth substantially more than the figures produced since.

At least two variations of this figure exist. The older design (1956 copyright date) shows the boy with his eyes wide open. In the newer design (1972 copyright date), the boy is looking down so that it appears that he is looking at his work. This transition from eyes up to eyes down took place during the Last Bee (TMK-5) and can be found both ways with that trademark.

This figurine was temporarily withdrawn from production in January 1999 as a TMK-7 figurine. In 2009 Manufaktur Rödental reintroduced A Fair Measure in a larger size as a TMK-9 figurine.

Hum No.	Basic Size	Trademark	Current Value
345	4-3/4"	TMK-2	$2,400-$3,000
345	4-3/4"	TMK-3	$1,200-$1,800
345	4-3/4"	TMK-4	$600-$720
345 (old style)	4-3/4"	TMK-5	$480-$600
345 (new style)	4-3/4"	TMK-5	$210-$280
345	4-3/4"	TMK-6	$200-$210
345	4-3/4"	TMK-7	$195-$205
345	5-1/2"	TMK-9	$359 retail

Hum 345: A Fair Measure.

Hum 346: Smart Little Sister

The creation of master sculptor Gerhard Skrobek in 1956, samples of Smart Little Sister were first made in the 1950s but not released for sale until 1962. It is nevertheless found with the earlier Full Bee (TMK-2) trademark, albeit rarely. The Stylized Bee (TMK-3) figures are not so rare; they seem to be available in a somewhat limited quantity.

There are no significant variations affecting normal values.

Hum 346: Smart Little Sister.

Hum No.	Basic Size	Trademark	Current Value
346	4-3/4"	TMK-2	$2,400-$3,000
346	4-3/4"	TMK-3	$600-$900
346	4-3/4"	TMK-4	$200-$215
346	4-3/4"	TMK-5	$180-$195
346	4-3/4"	TMK-6	$175-$180
346	4-3/4"	TMK-7	$170-$175
346	4-3/4"	TMK-8	$279

Hum 347: Adventure Bound

Also known as Seven Swabians, this large, complicated multi-figure piece was crafted by Theo R. Menzenbach and first made as a sample in the mid-1950s but was not released for sale until 1971. It carries a 1971 incised copyright date.

There are at least three Full Bee (TMK-2) trademarked pieces known to be in private collections. These early samples are worth substantially more than pieces made since.

No significant variations affect normal collector value.

Hum 347: Adventure Bound.

Hum No.	Basic Size	Trademark	Current Value
347	7-1/4" x 8"	TMK-2	$6,000-$9,000
347	7-1/4" x 8"	TMK-4	$2,700-$3,300
347	7-1/4" x 8"	TMK-5	$2,400-$2,760
347	7-1/4" x 8"	TMK-6	$2,400-$2,450
347	7-1/4" x 8"	TMK-7	$2,400-$2,450
347	7-1/4" x 8"	TMK-8	$1,200-$2,500

Hum 348: Ring Around the Rosie

This figure was first modeled in 1957 by master sculptor Gerhard Skrobek but was not released until 1960 for the 25th anniversary of M.I. Hummel figurines. Sizes found in various price lists range from 6-3/4" to 7". The older ones tend to be the larger ones. They all bear a 1957 copyright date.

There are no significant variations affecting normal values.

Hum 348: Ring Around the Rosie.

Hum No.	Basic Size	Trademark	Current Value
348	6-3/4" to 7"	TMK-2	$6,000-$9,000
348	6-3/4" to 7"	TMK-3	$2,400-$3,000
348	6-3/4"	TMK-4	$2,100-$2,400
348	6-3/4"	TMK-5	$2,100-$3,200
348	6-3/4"	TMK-6	$1,800-$1,950
348	6-3/4"	TMK-7	$1,725-$1,950
348	6-3/4"	TMK-8	$3,200

Hum 349: Florist

Florist, which was originally known as Flower Lover and crafted by master sculptor Gerhard Skrobek in 1957, was put into regular production as a new release for 2003. Those issued in 2003 carried the "First Issue 2003" backstamp as well as TMK-8. This figurine was the fourth edition in the matching plate and figurine series. The plate (Hum 924) has the same name and was the Annual Plate for 2003.

Early samples do exist in earlier trademarks, but only one example is known to be in a private collection.

Hum No.	Basic Size	Trademark	Current Value
349	6-3/4" to 7-1/2"	TMK-2	$2,400-$3,000
349	6-3/4" to 7-1/2"	TMK-3	$1,800-$2,400
349	6-3/4" to 7-1/2"	TMK-4	$1,200-$1,800
349/0	5-1/4"	TMK-8	$300

Hum 349: Florist.

Hum 350: On Holiday

First known as Holiday Shopper and made in the Stylized Bee (TMK-3) period, On Holiday was a new release in 1981. Apparently a few samples, which were the work of master sculptor Gerhard Skrobek in 1964, were made in the Stylized Bee (TMK-3) and the Three Line (TMK-4) trademarks, for there have been a few uncovered. The remainder are found in TMK-5 or later trademarks.

In 2002, On Holiday was added to Goebel's special "Work in Progress" series of collectors' sets. The series featured the figurine in

three stages: one whiteware, one partially painted, and one complete. The set includes an authentic brush used by a Goebel painter and wooden display base. This was a limited edition of 500 sequentially numbered pieces available through QVC only. Hear Ye! Hear Ye! (Hum 15/0) was offered in the same type of progression set earlier in the year.

No significant mold or finish variations affect normal collector values.

Hum 350: On Holiday.

Hum No.	Basic Size	Trademark	Current Value
350	5-1/2"	TMK-3	$2,400-$3,000
350	4-1/4"	TMK-4	$1,200-$1,800
350	4-1/4"	TMK-5	$900-$1,200
350	4-1/4"	TMK-6	$110-$120
350	4-1/4"	TMK-7	$110-$120
350	4-1/4"	TMK-8	$110-$120
350	4-1/4"	TMK-8 LE	$240-$300

Hum 351: The Botanist

First known as Remembering on early company literature, The Botanist was the 1965 design of master sculptor Gerhard Skrobek. It was not released, however, until 1982.

There is a very rare example of The Botanist known to exist with the Three Line Mark (TMK-4) and a 1965 copyright date. This is apparently an early sample. Another sample found with a 1965 copyright date has TMK-5 on it. All the newer pieces bear the 1972 copyright date.

Hum 351: The Botanist.

Hum No.	Basic Size	Trademark	Current Value
351	4"	TMK-4	$1,200-$1,800
351	4"	TMK-5	$900-$1,200
351	4"	TMK-6	$130-$135
351	4"	TMK-7	$125-$135
351	4"	TMK-8	$219
351 4/0	3"	TMK-8	$45

Hum 352: Sweet Greetings

Sweet Greetings was among six new designs to be released in 1981, but it was modeled much earlier—in 1964—by master sculptor Gerhard Skrobek. Its original name was Musical Morning.

Like a few other new releases of the time, it was apparently produced in limited numbers as samples in the Three Line Mark (TMK-4) era, for at least one figure is known to exist bearing that mark. Both the sample piece and the new release have a copyright date of 1965, although the sample is larger at 6-1/4".

The year 2011 marked the celebration of Sister Hummel's 75th anniversary of the beginning of her legacy. Manufaktur Rödental selected 50 figurines to bear the "75th Anniversary" backstamp. Sweet Greetings was one of those figurines. Only 75 of them were available in North America with this backstamp. Each figurine was hand-numbered with a golden backstamp and a map of North America backstamp. A special porcelain plaque was included, and a notable emblem on the packaging hinted at the contents. Each figurine included a "75 Years of M.I. Hummel" certificate.

Hum No.	Basic Size	Trademark	Current Value
352	6-1/4"	TMK-4	$2,400-$3,000
352	4-1/4"	TMK-5	$720-$1,200
352	4-1/4"	TMK-6	$130-$135
352	4-1/4"	TMK-7	$125-$135
352	4-1/4"	TMK-8	$219

Hum 352: Sweet Greetings.

Hum 353: Spring Dance

Spring Dance, the work of several sculptors combined, first appeared in 1964. Early samples with the Stylized Bee Mark (TMK-3) do exist in both the 4-3/4" and 6-1/2" sizes. These samples are rare and worth substantially more than the pieces released since.

The smaller size, 353/0, was released in 1978. The 353/0 with a Three Line Mark (TMK-4) is quite rare.

The larger size, 353/I, was temporarily withdrawn from production in 1982.

There are no significant variations that affect normal collector value.

During the winter of 2010, Manufaktur Rödental reintroduced Spring Dance in a slightly smaller size of 5-1/2". It is a TMK-9 figurine with the TMK-9 backstamp.

Hum No.	Basic Size	Trademark	Current Value
353/0	4-3/4"	TMK-3	$1,800-$3,000
353/0	4-3/4"	TMK-4	$1,200-$1,800
353/0	4-3/4"	TMK-5	$235-$250
353/0	4-3/4"	TMK-6	$230-$235
353/0	4-3/4"	TMK-7	$225-$250
353/0	4-3/4"	TMK-8	$399
353/I	6-1/2"	TMK-3	$600-$1,200
353/I	6-1/2"	TMK-4	$390-$450
353/I	6-1/2"	TMK-5	$345-$360

Hum 353: Spring Dance.

Hum No.	Basic Size	Trademark	Current Value
353/I	6-1/2"	TMK-6	$330-$345
353	6-1/2"	TMK-3	$1,800-$3,000
353/0	5-1/2"	TMK-9	$389

Hum 354/A: Angel With Lantern, Hum 354/B: Angel With Trumpet, and Hum 354/C: Angel With Bird

Holy Water Fonts, Closed Numbers

These fonts have closed number designations. Three fonts exist in the Goebel archives as factory samples only. Apparently they were never produced in quantity because Siessen Convent did not approve the designs.

Hum 354/A: Angel With Lantern, Hum 354/B: Angel With Trumpet, and Hum 354/C: Angel With Bird holy water fonts (closed numbers).

Hum 355: Autumn Harvest

Created by master sculptor Gerhard Skrobek in 1963 and first produced as a sample in the Stylized Bee (TMK-3) era, Autumn Harvest was not released for sale in any quantity until 1972. The earliest production pieces bear the Three Line Mark (TMK-4), but they are apparently in fairly short supply.

The figures have an incised copyright date of 1971.

There are no significant variations affecting normal collector values; however, the piece was permanently retired on Dec. 31, 2002. Those figurines made in 2002 bear a "Final Issue 2002" backstamp and came a with "Final Issue" medallion.

Hum No.	Basic Size	Trademark	Current Value
355	5″	TMK-3	$1,200-$1,800
355	5″	TMK-4	$600-$900
355	5″	TMK-5	$150-$170
355	5″	TMK-6	$145-$160
355	5″	TMK-7	$145-$160
355	5″	TMK-8	$145-$160

Hum 355: Autumn Harvest.

Hum 356: Gay Adventure

Gay Adventure, the design of master sculptor Gerhard Skrobek, was first produced as a sample in 1963 and was known as Joyful Adventure at the time. Early samples bear the Stylized Bee (TMK-3).

It was released for sale in 1972, bearing a 1971 incised copyright date.

There are no significant variations affecting normal collector values.

It was temporarily withdrawn from production on June 15, 2002.

Hum 356: Gay Adventure.

Hum No.	Basic Size	Trademark	Current Value
356	4-3/4″	TMK-3	$1,200-$1,800
356	4-3/4″	TMK-4	$600-$900
356	4-3/4″	TMK-5	$145-$160
356	4-3/4″	TMK-6	$140-$160
356	4-3/4″	TMK-7	$145-$160
356	4-3/4″	TMK-8	$145-$160

Hum 357: Guiding Angel, Hum 358: Shining Light, and Hum 359: Tuneful Angel

Originally crafted in 1958 by master sculptor Reinhold Unger with a 1960 copyright date, these angel pieces were not released until 1972. The issue price that year was $11 each.

They are sometimes sold as a set, although they are priced individually here.

There are no significant variations affecting normal values.

Hum No.	Basic Size	Trademark	Current Value
357	2-3/4"	TMK-4	$105-$135
357	2-3/4"	TMK-5	$70-$75
357	2-3/4"	TMK-6	$70-$75
357	2-3/4"	TMK-7	$65-$70
357	2-3/4"	TMK-8	$99
358	2-3/4"	TMK-4	$105-$135
358	2-3/4"	TMK-5	$70-$75
358	2-3/4"	TMK-6	$70-$75
358	2-3/4"	TMK-7	$70-$75
358	2-3/4"	TMK-8	$99
359	2-3/4"	TMK-4	$105-$135
359	2-3/4"	TMK-5	$70-$75
359	2-3/4"	TMK-6	$70-$75
359	2-3/4"	TMK-7	$70-$75
359	2-3/4"	TMK-8	$99

Hum 357: Guiding Angel, Hum 358: Shining Light, and Hum 359: Tuneful Angel.

Hum 360/A: Boy, Hum 360/B: Girl, and Hum 360/C: Boy and Girl
Wall Vases

Stylized Bee trademarked wall vases are considered rare. They were first produced in 1959, the work of master sculptor Gerhard Skrobek. For whatever reason, they were discontinued about 1960. All three pieces were then restyled and reissued in 1979 with TMK-5 and continued in production in TMK-6. They were temporarily withdrawn from production once again on Dec. 31, 1989.

Of the three, Boy and Girl (Hum 360/A) seems to be the most easily found. All three appear with the earliest and rarest Stylized Bee (TMK-3) trademark. Their basic size is 4-1/2" x 6".

Hum No.	Basic Size	Trademark	Current Value
360/A	4-1/2" x 6"	TMK-3	$315-$450
360/A	4-1/2" x 6"	TMK-5	$105-$135
360/A	4-1/2" x 6"	TMK-6	$99-$120
360/B	4-1/2" x 6"	TMK-3	$300-$450
360/B	4-1/2" x 6"	TMK-5	$90-$135
360/B	4-1/2" x 6"	TMK-6	$85-$120
360/C	4-1/2" x 6"	TMK-3	$300-$450
360/C	4-1/2" x 6"	TMK-5	$90-$135
360/C	4-1/2" x 6"	TMK-6	$85-$120

Hum 360/A: Boy, Hum 360/B: Girl, and Hum 360/C: Boy and Girl wall vases.

Hum 361: Favorite Pet

First made in prototype by master sculptor Theo R. Menzenbach in 1959, Favorite Pet was released for sale at the World's Fair in New York City in 1964. Early samples exist with the Full Bee Mark (TMK-2) and are worth significantly more than the figures released since. All pieces carry a 1960 incised copyright date.

There are no significant variations affecting normal collector values.

Hum No.	Basic Size	Trademark	Current Value
361	4-1/2"	TMK-2	$2,400-$3,000
361	4-1/2"	TMK-3	$720-$1,020
361	4-1/2"	TMK-4	$225-$270
361	4-1/2"	TMK-5	$210-$225
361	4-1/2"	TMK-6	$200-$210
361	4-1/2"	TMK-7	$195-$200
361	4-1/2"	TMK-8	$195-$200

Hum 361: Favorite Pet.

Hum 362: Forget Me Not

Made in sample form by master sculptor Theo R. Menzenbach in 1959 and originally listed as Thoughtful, this piece bears the Last Bee (TMK-5) trademark and a copyright date of 1959. Early samples exist in the factory archives in the Full Bee (TMK-2), Stylized Bee (TMK-3), and Three Line (TMK-4) trademarks. Formerly a PFE, it is now classified as the 30-year anniversary figurine. The flowers in the basket are removable and can be used as a decorative pin on your lapel. The pin was only available free for charter M.I. Hummel Club members. The figurine has "Exclusive Edition M.I. Hummel Club" 30-year membership in a half-moon decal on the bottom.

Hum No.	Basic Size	Trademark	Current Value
362	4-1/4"	TMK-2	$2,400-$3,000
362	4-1/4"	TMK-3	$1,800-$2,400
362	4-1/4"	TMK-4	$1,200-$1,800
362	4-1/4"	TMK-5	$600-$1,200
362	4-1/4"	TMK-8	$350

Hum 362: Forget Me Not early sample.

Base markings on Forget Me Not.

Hum 363: Big Housecleaning

The original sample models of Big Housecleaning, created by master sculptor Gerhard Skrobek in 1959, were made during the Full Bee (TMK-2) era. Released in 1972 at $28.50 apiece, these figurines bear an incised 1960 copyright date.

There are no significant variations affecting normal value for the figures.

It was temporarily withdrawn from production in January 1999 as a TMK-7 figurine. In 2009 Manufaktur Rödental reintroduced Big Housecleaning as a TMK-9 figurine.

Hum No.	Basic Size	Trademark	Current Value
363	4"	TMK-2	$2,400-$5,300
363	4"	TMK-3	$1,200-$1,800
363	4"	TMK-4	$600-$900
363	4"	TMK-5	$210-$225
363	4"	TMK-6	$200-$210
363	4"	TMK-7	$190-$200
363	4"	TMK-9	$299 retail

Hum 363: Big Housecleaning.

Hum 364: Supreme Protection

Supreme Protection, the fine craftsmanship of master sculptor Gerhard Skrobek in 1963, is a 9" full-color Madonna and child and is the first limited edition figurine ever offered to the general public by Goebel. Released in 1984, the piece had been scheduled to be produced during that year only, in commemoration and celebration of what would have been Sister M.I. Hummel's 75th birthday. The figure has a special backstamp written in gold lettering identifying it as such: "M.I. Hummel—IN CELEBRATION OF THE 75th ANNIVERSARY OF THE BIRTH OF SISTER M.I. HUMMEL."

As the first figures became available, it was discovered that some 3,000 to 3,500 of them were released with a mistake in the stamp. M.I. Hummel came out as "M.J. Hummel." The factory tried at first to correct the mistake by modifying the "J" in the decal to appear as an "I." However, they attempted to change it by cutting the decal and, unfortunately, the modification didn't come off too well; the result demonstrated their attempt quite obviously. As a consequence, there are three backstamp versions to be found: the correct backstamp, the poorly modified backstamp, and the "M.J. Hummel" incorrect backstamp. This particular backstamp variation is apparently in strong demand.

These Hum 364 figures have been found bearing the Three Line (TMK-4) and Last Bee (TMK-5) trademarks, but they are rare. They were probably sample pieces never meant to be sold.

Hum No.	Basic Size	Trademark	Current Value
364	9"	TMK-4	$1,800-$2,400
364	9"	TMK-5	$1,200-$1,800
364 (regular signature)	9"	TMK-6	$210-$240
364 (M.J. variation)	9"	TMK-6	$210-$360
364 (M.J. altered version)	9"	TMK-6	$360-$510

Hum 364: Supreme Protection.

Hum 365: Hummele

Hummele was produced as a special exclusive edition to M.I. Hummel Club members to commemorate Goebel's 90th anniversary in 1999. It was made for that year only and retired on May 31, 2000. It is the first club figurine to bear backstamp TMK-8.

This cute little cherub was first made in prototype by master sculptor Gerhard Skrobek in 1963 and has been listed in company records as both The Wee Angel and Littlest Angel. The Three Line (TMK-4) trademark sample has blue eyes.

Hum No.	Basic Size	Trademark	Current Value
365	2-3/4"	TMK-4	$1,200-$1,800
365	2-3/4"	TMK-8	$90-$110

Hum 365: Hummele.

Hum 366: Flying Angel

Flying Angel, which was created by master sculptor Gerhard Skrobek in 1963, is commonly used with the nativity sets and has been produced in painted versions as well as white overglaze. The white ones are rare and valued at $300-$350.

The larger variation was first released in the Three Line (TMK-4) period and has remained in production throughout the years. It was renumbered as 366/I in TMK-8. The new smaller version (366/0) was introduced in 1989.

There are no significant variations affecting normal values.

Hum No.	Basic Size	Trademark	Current Value
366/0	3"	TMK-6	$80-$85
366/0	3"	TMK-7	$75-$130
366/0	3"	TMK-8	$133
366	3-1/2"	TMK-4	$135-$165
366	3-1/2"	TMK-5	$99-$105
366	3-1/2"	TMK-6	$95-$99
366	3-1/2"	TMK-7	$95-$99
366/I	3-1/2"	TMK-8	$179

Hum 366: Flying Angel.

Hum 367: Busy Student

The combined efforts of several sculptors, Busy Student was released in 1964 and has been continuously available since then. It has an incised 1963 copyright date and is similar to the girl in Smart Little Sister (Hum 346).

There are no significant variations in color, size, or design that affect normal values.

Hum No.	Basic Size	Trademark	Current Value
367	4-1/4"	TMK-3	$510-$600
367	4-1/4"	TMK-4	$135-$165
367	4-1/4"	TMK-5	$120-$130
367	4-1/4"	TMK-6	$120-$125
367	4-1/4"	TMK-7	$120-$125
367	4-1/4"	TMK-8	$120-$125

Hum 367: Busy Student.

Hum 368: Lute Song
Possible Future Edition

Hum No.	Basic Size	Trademark	Current Value
368	5"	TMK-4	$1,200-$1,800

Lute Song, which was designed by master sculptor Gerhard Skrobek in 1964 and first known as Lute Player, is a standing girl playing the lute. This design is substantially similar to the girl in Close Harmony (Hum 336).

An early sample with the Three Line Mark (TMK-4) is known to exist.

Hum 369: Follow the Leader

Follow the Leader was first made in prototype by master sculptor Gerhard Skrobek in 1964, but was not released for sale until 1972 at $110. It carries a 1964 incised copyright date.

Early samples bearing the Stylized Bee (TMK-3) exist and are worth substantially more than figures released since.

There are no significant variations to affect the normal values.

Hum No.	Basic Size	Trademark	Current Value
369	7"	TMK-3	$2,400-$3,000
369	7"	TMK-4	$960-$1,325
369	7"	TMK-5	$840-$925
369	7"	TMK-6	$780-$840
369	7"	TMK-7	$780-$840
369	7"	TMK-8	$780-$840

Hum 369: Follow the Leader.

Hum 370: Companions
Possible Future Edition

Companions, the work of master sculptor Gerhard Skrobek in 1964, is much like To Market (Hum 49), except that the girl has been replaced with a boy that is remarkably like the boy of Hum 51 (Village Boy). It has been listed as Brotherly Love in old company literature.

Hum No.	Basic Size	Trademark	Current Value
370	5"	TMK-3	$2,400-$5,000
370	5"	TMK-4	$1,800-$2,400
370	5"	TMK-5	$1,200-$1,800

This piece has been found as samples in the Stylized Bee (TMK-3), Three Line (TMK-4), and Last Bee (TMK-5) eras, but has yet to be put into regular production.

Hum 371: Daddy's Girls

Daddy's Girls, which was crafted by master sculptor Gerhard Skrobek in 1964, was a new addition to the line in 1989 at $130. It has an incised copyright date of 1964 on the underside of the base. It was first known as Sisterly Love.

Because it was first made as a sample in the Three Line (TMK-4) and Last Bee (TMK-5) periods, early samples exist with those trademarks.

Hum No.	Basic Size	Trademark	Current Value
371	4-3/4"	TMK-4	$1,800-$2,400
371	4-3/4"	TMK-5	$1,200-$1,800
371	4-3/4"	TMK-6	$165-$170
371	4-3/4"	TMK-7	$165-$170
371	4-3/4"	TMK-8	$279

Hum 371: Daddy's Girls.

Hum 372: Blessed Mother
Possible Future Edition

Hum No.	Basic Size	Trademark	Current Value
372	10-1/4"	TMK-4	$1,800-$2,400

Blessed Mother, which is credited to master sculptor Gerhard Skrobek in 1964, is a standing Madonna and child. It was once known as Virgin Mother and Child.

An early sample is known to exist in the Three Line Mark (TMK-4), but the figure has yet to be placed into regular production.

Hum 373: Just Fishing

Just Fishing, which was designed in 1964 by master sculptor Gerhard Skrobek, was released in early 1985 at a suggested retail price of $85. Once called The Fisherman, it measures 4-1/4" x 4-1/2" and carries a 1965 incised copyright date.

Early Goebel promotional materials referred to this piece as an ashtray. This was in error, probably due to the tray-like base representing the pond.

Hum 373: Just Fishing.

Hum No.	Basic Size	Trademark	Current Value
373	4-1/4" x 4-1/2"	TMK-4	$1,800-$2,400
373	4-1/4" x 4-1/2"	TMK-5	$600-$900
373	4-1/4" x 4-1/2"	TMK-6	$165-$185
373	4-1/4" x 4-1/2"	TMK-7	$165-$170

Early samples exist with the Three Line Mark (TMK-4) and are worth substantially more than the figures released since.

Just Fishing was temporarily withdrawn from production in January 1999.

Hum 374: Lost Stocking

Made as a sample by master sculptor Gerhard Skrobek in 1965, Lost Stocking was not released for sale until 1972 in the Three Line (TMK-4) trademark period. The suggested retail price at release was $17.50.

Early samples bearing the Stylized Bee (TMK-3) do exist and are worth substantially more than the figures released since.

No significant variations affect normal values.

It was temporarily withdrawn from production on June 15, 2002.

Hum No.	Basic Size	Trademark	Current Value
374	4-1/2"	TMK-3	$1,800-$2,400
374	4-1/2"	TMK-4	$600-$900
374	4-1/2"	TMK-5	$115-$120
374	4-1/2"	TMK-6	$110-$115
374	4-1/2"	TMK-7	$110-$115
374	4-1/2"	TMK-8	$110-$115

Hum 374: Lost Stocking.

Hum 375: Morning Stroll

First produced in sample form by master sculptor Gerhard Skrobek in 1964 with the Three Line Mark (TMK-4), Morning Stroll was released in 1994. It measures 3-3/4" (a full inch smaller than the pre-production sample, which had been known as Walking the Baby). Those produced in 1994 bear a "First Issue" backstamp. The production piece is known as Hum 375/3/0.

Hum No.	Basic Size	Trademark	Current Value
375	4-3/4"	TMK-4	$1,800-$2,400
375/3/0	3-3/4"	TMK-7	$130-$135
375/3/0	3-3/4"	TMK-8	$130-$135

Hum 375: Morning Stroll.

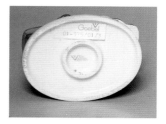

This is an early factory sample of Morning Stroll. The base shows the Three Line Mark (TMK-4).

Hum 376: Little Nurse

Little Nurse, which was the original design of master sculptor Gerhard Skrobek in 1965, was one of the two designs released in 1982.

Although most of them are found with TMK-6, it is known that at least one exists bearing TMK-5 with a 1965 copyright date. TMK-6 or later trademarked pieces have a 1972 copyright date.

Early samples, which were originally called First Aid, are also known to carry the Three Line Mark (TMK-4).

In the wake of the terrorist attacks on the World Trade Center and Pentagon on Sept. 11, 2001, and the resulting American military effort, Goebel alerted its M.I. Hummel Club chapters that it would donate appropriately themed figurines to local chapters to be used as raffle prizes. Proceeds from such fund-raising events would benefit the families of the victims. Seven figurines, including this one, were selected as appropriate due to their patriotic or firefighter/police/medical personnel themes.

Little Nurse was a closed edition, but in celebration of the figurine's 25th anniversary in 2009, a commemorative edition was released with a 25th Anniversary backstamp and hangtag.

Hum 376: Little Nurse.

Hum No.	Basic Size	Trademark	Current Value
376	4"	TMK-4	$1,800-$2,400
376	4"	TMK-5	$1,200-$1,800

Hum No.	Basic Size	Trademark	Current Value
376	4"	TMK-6	$175-$180
376	4"	TMK-7	$175-$180
376	4"	TMK-8 CE	$175-$180

Hum 377: Bashful

Bashful was first made in sample form by master sculptor Gerhard Skrobek in 1966 with the Three Line Mark (TMK-4) and can be found in samples bearing TMK-4 as well as production models with the same mark. Both the samples and the production models in that mark are fairly scarce. Later marks are more easily found.

There are no significant variations that affect normal values. The older pieces generally have a 1966 copyright date and sometimes a 1971 copyright date, but the new production figurines do not have an incised copyright date at all.

Hum No.	Basic Size	Trademark	Current Value
377 (sample)	4-3/4"	TMK-4	$1,800-$2,400
377	4-3/4"	TMK-4	$600-$900
377	4-3/4"	TMK-5	$150-$165
377	4-3/4"	TMK-6	$145-$150
377	4-3/4"	TMK-7	$140-$150
377	4-3/4"	TMK-8	$250

Hum 377: Bashful.

Hum 378: Easter Greetings

The early sample models of Easter Greetings were made by master sculptor Gerhard Skrobek in 1966 during the Three Line Mark (TMK-4) period of production and can be found in samples bearing TMK-4 as well as production models with the same mark. Both the early samples and the regular production figurines bearing this mark are scarce. They have an incised copyright date of 1966 or 1971.

There are no significant mold or finish variations affecting normal collector values.

The figure was temporarily withdrawn from production in January 1999.

Hum 378: Easter Greetings.

Hum No.	Basic Size	Trademark	Current Value
378 (sample)	5-1/2"	TMK-4	$1,800-$2,400
378	5-1/2"	TMK-4	$600-$900
378	5-1/2"	TMK-5	$150-$165
378	5-1/2"	TMK-6	$145-$150
378	5-1/2"	TMK-7	$140-$145

Hum 379: Don't Be Shy

Don't Be Shy was the design of master sculptor Gerhard Skrobek in 1966 as a possible future edition (PFE). It depicts a little girl with a kerchief on her head feeding a bird perched on a fencepost. Originally called One For Me, One For You, early samples exist in the Stylized Bee (TMK-3) and Three Line (TMK-4) periods.

Forty-seven years later—one of the longest waiting periods in M.I. Hummel history—Don't Be Shy was released as a M.I. Hummel Club Year 37 Exclusive with the TMK-9 backstamp.

Hum 379/I: Don't Be Shy.

Hum No.	Basic Size	Trademark	Current Value
379	4-1/4"	TMK-3	$2,400-$3,000
379	4-1/4"	TMK-4	$1,800-$2,400
379/I	6"	TMK-9	$419 retail

Hum 380: Daisies Don't Tell

Daisies Don't Tell was the Goebel Collectors' Club Special Edition figure offered exclusively to club members in 1981. As with all the others, it could be purchased by current members with redemption cards for $80 in the United States and $95 in Canada. As of May 31, 1985, it was no longer available, except on the secondary market.

The work of master sculptor Gerhard Skrobek in 1966, it was originally called Does He? The copyright date is 1972. There is at least one early sample known to exist bearing the Three Line Mark (TMK-4) and one with a copyright date of 1966. This latter piece is exceedingly rare.

Hum 380: Daisies Don't Tell.

Hum No.	Basic Size	Trademark	Current Value
380	5"	TMK-4	$1,800-$2,400
380	5"	TMK-5	$600-$1,200
380	5"	TMK-6	$165-$180

Hum 381: Flower Vendor

Master sculptor Gerhard Skrobek designed Flower Vendor in 1966, but it was not released until 1972 at the end of the Stylized Bee (TMK-3) and Three Line Mark (TMK-4) era. It can only be found in the latter (considered an early sample and are fairly scarce). It has a 1971 incised copyright date but has been found in rare occurrence with a 1967 copyright date.

There are no significant variations affecting values.

Hum No.	Basic Size	Trademark	Current Value
381	5-1/2″	TMK-4	$1,800-$2,400
381	5-1/2″	TMK-5	$190-$210
381	5-1/2″	TMK-6	$185-$205
381	5-1/2″	TMK-7	$180-$200
381	5-1/2″	TMK-8	$180-$200

Hum 381: Flower Vendor.

Hum 382: Visiting an Invalid

Visiting an Invalid, the creation of master sculptor Gerhard Skrobek in 1966, was released first in 1972 during the Three Line (TMK-4) era but is scarce and hard to find with that trademark.

There are no significant variations in color, size, or design.

It was temporarily withdrawn from production in January 1999.

The year 2011 marked the celebration of Sister Hummel's 75th anniversary of the beginning of her legacy. Manufaktur Rödental selected 50 figurines to bear the "75th Anniversary"

Hum No.	Basic Size	Trademark	Current Value
382	4-15/16″	TMK-4	$600-$900
382	4-15/16″	TMK-5	$150-$165
382	4-15/16″	TMK-6	$145-$150
382	4-15/16″	TMK-7	$135-$140

Hum 382: Visiting an Invalid.

backstamp. Visiting an Invalid was one of those figurines. Only 75 of them were available in North America with this backstamp. Each figurine was hand-numbered with a golden backstamp and a map of North America backstamp. A special porcelain plaque was included, and a notable emblem on the packaging hinted at the contents. Each figurine included a "75 Years of M.I. Hummel" certificate.

Hum 383: Going Home

Crafted by master sculptor Gerhard Skrobek in 1966, this new piece for 1985 was released at a suggested retail price of $125. The first examples, initially known as Fancy Free, were apparently made in the prototype phase in the Three Line Mark (TMK-4) period.

There are no significant variations that influence collector values, but the piece has been made into two separate figurines: Grandma's Girl (Hum 561) and Grandpa's Boy (Hum 562).

Hum No.	Basic Size	Trademark	Current Value
383	5″	TMK-4	$1,800-$2,400
383	5″	TMK-5	$1,200-$1,800
383	5″	TMK-6	$235-$255
383	5″	TMK-7	$230-$240
383	5″	TMK-8	$399

Hum 383: Going Home.

Hum 384: Easter Time

Occasionally called Easter Playmates, this figurine was first produced in sample form by master sculptor Gerhard Skrobek in 1967 during the Three Line Mark (TMK-4). It was first released for sale in 1972, at the very end of that period, so the figures are fairly scarce in that trademark. It bears an incised 1971 copyright date.

There are no significant variations that affect collector value.

The year 2011 marked the celebration of Sister Hummel's 75th anniversary of the beginning of her legacy. Manufaktur Rödental selected 50 figurines to bear the "75th Anniversary" backstamp. Easter Time was one of those figurines. Only 75 of this figurine were available in North America with this backstamp. Each figurine was hand-numbered with a golden backstamp and a map of North America backstamp. A special porcelain plaque was included, and a notable emblem on the packaging hinted at the contents. Each figurine included a "75 Years of M.I. Hummel" certificate.

Hum 384: Easter Time.

Hum No.	Basic Size	Trademark	Current Value
384	3-15/16"	TMK-4	$600-$900
384	3-15/16"	TMK-5	$180-$200
384	3-15/16"	TMK-6	$175-$185

Hum No.	Basic Size	Trademark	Current Value
384	3-15/16"	TMK-7	$175-$185
384	3-15/16"	TMK-8	$279

Hum 385: Chicken-Licken

Chicken-Licken, first designed by master sculptor Gerhard Skrobek in 1967, was one of the 24 pieces first released in 1972 with the Three Line Mark (TMK-4). It has a copyright date of 1971 and has been in production ever since. The original release price was $28.50.

In 1990, Goebel released a smaller size, 3-1/4", with the incised mold number 385/4/0. The recommended retail price at release time was $85. That variation was temporarily withdrawn from production in 1997 and has since been made a closed edition.

There are no significant variations affecting collector value.

Hum 385: Chicken-Licken.

Hum No.	Basic Size	Trademark	Current Value
385/4/0	3-1/4"	TMK-6	$75-$90
385/4/0	3-1/4"	TMK-7	$70-$80
385	4-3/4"	TMK-4	$600-$900
385	4-3/4"	TMK-5	$210-$225
385	4-3/4"	TMK-6	$200-$230
385	4-3/4"	TMK-7	$200-$210
385	4-3/4"	TMK-8	$200-$210

Hum 386: On Secret Path

The original design of master sculptor Gerhard Skrobek in 1967, On Secret Path is one of the 24 pieces first released in 1972 in the Three Line (TMK-4) trademark. It has a 1971 copyright and originally sold for $26.50.

There are no significant variations affecting the collector value.

It was temporarily withdrawn from production on June 15, 2002.

Hum 386: On Secret Path.

Hum No.	Basic Size	Trademark	Current Value
386	5-1/4"	TMK-4	$600-$900
386	5-1/4"	TMK-5	$180-$195
386	5-1/4"	TMK-6	$175-$185
386	5-1/4"	TMK-7	$175-$185
386	5-1/4"	TMK-8	$175-$180

Hum 387: Valentine Gift

This rather special figure, which was the original design of master sculptor Gerhard Skrobek in 1967, was the first special edition figurine available only to members of the Goebel Collectors Club (now the M.I. Hummel Club), an organization sponsored by, and a division of, the Goebel firm. The figure was originally released in 1977 at $45 with a redemption card obtained through membership in the club. The size is 5-3/4" and inscription on blue decal read: "EXCLUSIVE SPECIAL EDITION No. 1 FOR MEMBERS OF THE GOEBEL COLLECTORS' CLUB." The most commonly found piece bears TMK-5.

Older pieces (TMK-4) are significantly more valuable, especially those with a bird sitting on top of the heart, which is inscribed with "i hab di gern" (translation: "I love you very much"). A few TMK-4 pieces without the inscription have surfaced over the years and sell for the same as the TMK-4 pieces without the bird ($2,000-$3,000).

As of May 31, 1984, Hum 387 in the 5-3/4" size was no longer available except on the secondary market.

In 2012 Valentine Gift (HUM 387/III) was released as a Masterpiece Edition. At 13-1/4", Valentine Gift was redesigned by master sculptor Marion Huschka, reflecting Sister Hummel's original artwork more closely. The larger size allowed for the inclusion of flowers in the girl's arms and basket, a songbird at her feet, and the heart, which is still inscribed "i hab di gern." Valentine Gift, a TMK-9 figurine, was produced in a worldwide limited edition of 999 pieces.

Hum 387: Valentine Gift.

Hum 387/III: Valentine Gift Masterpiece Edition.

Hum No.	Basic Size	Trademark	Current Value
387 (with bird)	5-3/4"	TMK-4	$3,000-$4,500
387	5-3/4"	TMK-4	$1,200-$1,800
387	5-3/4"	TMK-5	$285-$360
387/III	13-1/4"	TMK-9 LE	$2,400

Hum 388: Little Band
Candleholder

The original design of master sculptor Gerhard Skrobek in 1967, Little Band is a three-figure piece utilizing Hum 389, 390, and 391 on one base. It contains a candle receptacle. It was released in the Three Line (TMK-4) period and bears a 1968 incised copyright date.

This piece was temporarily withdrawn from production on Dec. 31, 1990.

Hum 388: Little Band candleholder.

Hum No.	Basic Size	Trademark	Current Value
368	3" x 4-3/4"	TMK-4	$210-$270
368	3" x 4-3/4"	TMK-5	$180-$210
368	3" x 4-3/4"	TMK-6	$150-$180

Hum 388/M: Little Band
Candleholder and Music Box

This is the same piece as Hum 388, but it is mounted on a wooden base with a music box inside. When the music box plays, the Little Band figure rotates. No significant variations affect collector values, but there are variations known in the type of music box as well as the tune played.

Goebel placed this figure on a list of pieces taken out of production temporarily on Dec. 31, 1990.

Hum 388/M: Little Band candleholder and music box.

Hum No.	Basic Size	Trademark	Current Value
388/M	4-3/4" x 5"	TMK-4	$285-$300
388/M	4-3/4" x 5"	TMK-5	$270-$285
388/M	4-3/4" x 5"	TMK-6	$240-$255

Hum 389: Girl With Sheet Music, Hum 390: Boy With Accordion, and Hum 391: Girl With Trumpet

Little Band

These three pieces, which were designed by master sculptor Gerhard Skrobek in 1968, are the same figures used on Hum 388, 388/M, 392, and 392/M. They each carry an incised 1968 copyright date.

No significant variations affect collector values for the various trademarked pieces.

Hum 391: Girl With Trumpet was temporarily withdrawn from production on June 15, 2002.

Hum No.	Basic Size	Trademark	Current Value
389	2-1/2"	TMK-4	$135-$165
389	2-1/2"	TMK-5	$75-$80
389	2-1/2"	TMK-6	$70-$75
389	2-1/2"	TMK-7	$65-$70
389	2-1/2"	TMK-8	$99
IV/389 (music box)	4-3/4"	TMK-8 LE	$110
390	2-1/2"	TMK-4	$135-$165
390	2-1/2"	TMK-5	$70-$75
390	2-1/2"	TMK-6	$70-$75
390	2-1/2"	TMK-7	$65-$70
390	2-1/2"	TMK-8	$99
IV/390 (music box)	4-3/4"	TMK-8	$110
391	2-1/2"	TMK-4	$135-$165
391	2-1/2"	TMK-5	$70-$75
391	2-1/2"	TMK-6	$70-$75
391	2-1/2"	TMK-7	$65-$70
391	2-1/2"	TMK-8	$99

Hum 389: Girl With Sheet Music, Hum 390: Boy With Accordion, and Hum 391: Girl With Trumpet (Little Band).

Hum 392: Little Band

This piece, which was modeled by master sculptor Gerhard Skrobek in 1968, is the same as Hum 388 except that it has no provision for a candle. It has a 1968 incised copyright date. There are no significant variations affecting collector value.

Little Band is listed as temporarily withdrawn from current production status.

Hum No.	Basic Size	Trademark	Current Value
392	4-3/4" x 3"	TMK-4	$210-$270
392	4-3/4" x 3"	TMK-5	$180-$195
392	4-3/4" x 3"	TMK-6	$165-$180

Hum 392/M: Little Band
Music Box

This piece is the same piece as Hum 392, but it is placed atop a base with a music box inside. When the music plays the piece revolves.

There are no significant mold or finish variations affecting values; however, there are variations in the type of music box as well as the tunes played.

This music box was temporarily withdrawn from production in 1990.

Hum No.	Basic Size	Trademark	Current Value
392/M	4-1/4" x 5"	TMK-4	$285-$300
392/M	4-1/4" x 5"	TMK-5	$270-$285
392/M	4-1/4" x 5"	TMK-6	$240-$255

Hum 392/M: Little Band music box.

Hum 393: Dove
Holy Water Font, Possible Future Edition

Hum No.	Basic Size	Trademark	Current Value
393	2-3/4" x 4-1/4"	TMK-4	$1,200-$1,800

The design of this font, which was created by master sculptor Gerhard Skrobek in 1968, includes a flying dove and a banner with the inscription: "+KOMM+HEILIGER+GUEST+." This translates into English as: "Come Holy Spirit."

Only one known example exists outside Goebel archives. It is an early sample that bears the Three Line Mark (TMK-4).

Hum 394: Timid Little Sister

This two-figure piece, which was first designed by master sculptor Gerhard Skrobek in 1972, was a new design released with five others in 1981. When released, the price was $190.

An early sample has been found with the Last Bee trademark (TMK-5) and is worth considerably more than those made since. Both the older pieces and the commonly found, more recent pieces bear the 1972 copyright date.

There are no significant variations that affect collector value, although on occasion, the girl can be found with eyelashes.

Hum No.	Basic Size	Trademark	Current Value
394	7"	TMK-5	$1,800-$2,400
394	7"	TMK-6	$310-$315
394	7"	TMK-7	$300-$310
394	7"	TMK-8	$300-$310

Hum 394: Timid Little Sister.

Hum 395: Shepherd Boy

This 6-3/4" figurine was first made as a sample by master sculptor Gerhard Skrobek in 1971 and later released in 1996 in a smaller 4-7/8" size with mold number 395/0. The first year's figures will be marked with a combination "First Issue 1996" and "125th Anniversary Goebel" backstamp, TMK-7, and an incised 1972 copyright date.

An early sample, once called Young Shepherd, has been found bearing the Last Bee (TMK-5) with a 1989 copyright date. It is worth significantly more than those figures released since.

Shepherd Boy was temporarily withdrawn from production on June 15, 2002.

Hum No.	Basic Size	Trademark	Current Value
395	6-3/4"	TMK-5	$1,800-$2,400
395/0	4-7/8"	TMK-7	$180-$185
395/0	4-7/8"	TMK-8	$170-$180

Hum 395: Shepherd Boy.

Hum 396: Ride Into Christmas

Ride Into Christmas, which was first designed by master sculptor Gerhard Skrobek in 1970 and released in 1972, remains quite popular and is in great demand by collectors. In fact, in the summer 2002 edition of the M.I. Hummel Club's *INSIGHTS* newsletter, it is noted that Skrobek considered this piece his favorite design of the hundreds he modeled during his many years at Goebel.

Goebel released a smaller version in 1982. The release of the smaller piece necessitated a change in the mold number of the larger one from 396 to 396/I.

The larger size bears a copyright date of 1971 and the smaller has a 1981 copyright date. There are no significant production variations that affect collector values for these pieces, although it should be noted that the same design was used on the 1975 Annual Plate (Hum 268).

The year 2011 marked the celebration of Sister Hummel's 75th anniversary of the beginning of her legacy. Manufaktur Rödental selected 50 figurines to bear the "75th Anniversary" backstamp. Ride Into Christmas was one of those figurines. Only 75 of them were available in North America with this backstamp. Each figurine was hand-numbered with a golden backstamp and a map of North America backstamp. A special porcelain plaque was included, and a notable emblem on the packaging hinted at the contents. Each figurine included a "75 Years of M.I. Hummel" certificate.

Hum No.	Basic Size	Trademark	Current Value
396/2/0	4-1/4"	TMK-6	$165-$175
396/2/0	4-1/4"	TMK-7	$165-$170
396/2/0	4-1/4"	TMK-8	$279
396	5-3/4"	TMK-4	$1,200-$1,500
396	5-3/4"	TMK-5	$330-$345
396	5-3/4"	TMK-6	$315-$345
396/I	5-3/4"	TMK-6	$300-$315
396/I	5-3/4"	TMK-7	$295-$300
396/I	5-3/4"	TMK-8	$530
396/III	9"	TMK-8	$1,550 retail

This version of Ride Into Christmas is a demonstration piece with the TMK-6 and an incised 1971 copyright date.

Hum 396: Ride Into Christmas.

Hum 397: The Poet

The Poet, which master sculptor Gerhard Skrobek first crafted in 1973, was released in 1994 in a 6" size. Those produced in 1994 bear the "First Issue" backstamp, are marked Hum 397/I, and were temporarily withdrawn from production on June 15, 2002.

The figure was first made in sample form with the Three Line Mark (TMK-4), which is worth substantially more than any figures made since.

A smaller size (4") was issued in 1998 as a M.I. Hummel Club Exclusive (397/3/0). It was called Poet at the Podium and was crafted by master sculptor Helmut Fischer in 1988. Like other club figurines, it came with a redemption card. It was retired in May 2000.

Hum No.	Basic Size	Trademark	Current Value
397	6"	TMK-4	$1,800-$2,400
397/3/0	4"	TMK-7	$90-$105
397/I	6"	TMK-7	$170-$175
397/I	6"	TMK-8	$170-$175

Hum 397: The Poet.

Hum 398: Spring Bouquet
Possible Future Edition

Hum No.	Basic Size	Trademark	Current Value
398	6-1/4"	TMK-5	$1,800-$2,400

This figurine, which was designed by master sculptor Gerhard Skrobek in 1973, is a girl picking flowers. She holds a bouquet in her left arm. Early samples have been found with the Last Bee (TMK-5), but the figure has yet to be put into regular production.

Hum 399: Valentine Joy

This figurine, which was designed by master sculptor Gerhard Skrobek, is the fourth special edition offered exclusively to the members of the Goebel Collectors' Club (now the M.I. Hummel Club). Issued in 1980-'81, the figures bear a 1979 copyright date and were available for $95 with the club redemption card. Each carries a special inscription on a blue decal that read: "EXCLUSIVE SPECIAL EDITION No. 4 FOR MEMBERS OF THE GOEBEL COLLECTORS' CLUB."

The wording on the heart translates to "I like you."

Although there are existing early samples with TMK-5 that are somewhat larger, with a rounded base and bird at the boy's feet, the piece is normally found with TMK-6. The early samples carry a 1973 incised copyright date.

Hum No.	Basic Size	Trademark	Current Value
399	6-1/4"	TMK-5	$3,000-$4,500
399	5-3/4"	TMK-6	$150-$180

Hum 399: Valentine Joy.

Hum 400: Well Done!
Possible Future Edition

Well Done! is a figure of two standing boys originally crafted by master sculptor Gerhard Skrobek in 1973. The boy wearing shorts pats the shoulder of the other, who wears long pants.

Hum No.	Basic Size	Trademark	Current Value
400	6-1/4"	TMK-5	$1,800-$2,400

Early samples are known to exist with TMK-5, but the piece has yet to be put into regular production.

Hum 401: Forty Winks

Another Gerhard Skrobek design from 1973, Forty Winks features a girl seated next to a small boy, asleep with his head on her right shoulder. Early samples are known to exist with in TMK-5.

The year 2011 marked the celebration of Sister Hummel's 75th anniversary of the beginning of her legacy. Manufaktur Rödental selected 50 figurines to bear the "75th Anniversary" backstamp. Forty Winks was one of those figurines. Only 75 of them were available in North America with this backstamp. Each figurine was hand-numbered with a golden backstamp and a map of North America backstamp. A special porcelain plaque was included, and a notable emblem on the packaging hinted at the contents. Each figurine included a "75 Years of M.I. Hummel" certificate.

Hum 401: Forty Winks.

Hum No.	Basic Size	Trademark	Current Value
401 (early sample)	5-1/4"	TMK-5	$1,800-$2,400
401	5-1/4"	TMK-5	$319

Hum 402: True Friendship

Master sculptor Gerhard Skrobek originally designed True Friendship in 1973. It was first released in 2002, but early samples are known to exist with the Last Bee Mark (TMK-5).

Hum No.	Basic Size	Trademark	Current Value
402	4-3/4"	TMK-5	$1,800-$2,400
402	5-1/4"	TMK-8	$399

Hum 402: True Friendship.

Hum 403: An Apple a Day

An Apple a Day, which was designed by master sculptor Gerhard Skrobek in 1973, was released in 1989. It carries an incised 1974 copyright date. The price at the time of release was $195.

The fact that the design was copyrighted in the TMK-5 era makes it possible that the figure exists, at least as a sample, with that trademark. There are, however, no known examples of such sample pieces in private collections.

There are no significant variations that affect collector value.

Hum No.	Basic Size	Trademark	Current Value
403	6-1/2"	TMK-5	$1,800-$2,400
403	6-1/2"	TMK-6	$200-$210
403	6-1/2"	TMK-7	$210-$200
403	6-1/2"	TMK-8	$195-$200
403 4/0	3-1/2"	TMK-8	$99

Hum 403: An Apple a Day.

Hum 404: Sad Song

Sad Song, which is a 1973 design by master sculptor Gerhard Skrobek, features a standing boy singing. He looks as if he is about to cry and holds the sheet music behind his back with his right hand. Early samples are known to exist with TMK-5, but the piece has yet to be placed into regular production.

Hum 404: Sad Song.

Hum No.	Basic Size	Trademark	Current Value
404	6-1/4"	TMK-5	$1,800-$2,400
404	6-1/4"	TMK-8 EE	$295

Hum 405: Sing With Me

Sing With Me, which was designed by master sculptor Gerhard Skrobek in 1973, was first released in 1985, although an early sample is known to exist in TMK-6. A copyright date of either 1973 or 1974 is found incised on the underside of the base. There are no significant variations that affect collector value.

Sing With Me was temporarily withdrawn from production in January 1999.

Hum 405: Sing With Me.

Hum No.	Basic Size	Trademark	Current Value
405	5"	TMK-5	$1,800-$2,400
405	5"	TMK-6	$225-$330
405	5"	TMK-7	$210-$215
405	5"	TMK-8	$199-$210

Hum 406: Pleasant Journey

Released in 1987, Pleasant Journey, like the Chapel Time clock, is limited to those produced in 1987. The figure, which was crafted by master sculptor Gerhard Skrobek in 1974, is

considered a closed edition. The original release price was $500.

Early samples in the Goebel archives bear TMK-5. The production figure, however, is found only with TMK-6.

Hum 406: Pleasant Journey.

Hum No.	Basic Size	Trademark	Current Value
406	7-1/8" x 6-1/2"	TMK-5	$3,000-$3,600
406	7-1/8" x 6-1/2"	TMK-6	$1,650-$1,800

It was the second figurine in the "Century Collection" and carries a 1976 incised copyright date, the name "PLEASANT JOURNEY," and a blue decal with the following inscription: "M.I. HUMMEL CENTURY COLLECTION 1987 XX."

There are no variations affecting the figure's value.

Hum 407: Flute Song

In 1974 master sculptor Gerhard Skrobek, using Sister Hummel's original artwork, designed Flute Song, a shepherd playing a gentle tune to entertain his friend in the meadow. The boy is seated on what appears to be a stump. Early samples bear TMK-5.

For M.I. Hummel Club Year 34 in 2010, Flute Song was introduced as the exclusive club figurine. This new figurine

Hum 407: Flute Song.

Hum No.	Basic Size	Trademark	Current Value
407	6"	TMK-5	$1,800-$2,400
407	6"	TMK-9	$599 retail

was redesigned in 2009 by master sculptor Marion Huschka. There are differences in the color and size of the shepherd's bag, his pants are lighter brown, he sits on a rock, and the lamb is snow white with a red collar and a bell. It has a TMK-9 backstamp with M.I. Hummel Club 2010 incorporated on the backstamp. A ceramic plaque depicting the original drawing and a wooden easel are included.

Hum 408: Smiling Through

Smiling Through was a redemption piece available only to members of the former Goebel Collectors' Club, now the M.I. Hummel Club. It was released in 1985 at $125 to those with a redemption card. The mold number incised on the bottom of this figurine is actually 408/0. The reason for this is that a larger version was modeled by master sculptor Gerhard Skrobek in 1976 but was never released. It was made as a sample only. This larger version was 5-1/2", while the one released to club members was 4-3/4".

As of May 31, 1987, these figurines were available only on the secondary market and found only in TMK-6. They carry a 1983 incised copyright date and blue decal with special inscription: "EXCLUSIVE SPECIAL EDITION No. 9 FOR MEMBERS OF THE GOEBEL COLLECTORS' CLUB."

There are no significant variations that affect value.

Hum No.	Basic Size	Trademark	Current Value
408	5-1/2"	TMK-5	$2,400-$3,000
408/0	4-3/4"	TMK-6	$210-$225

Hum 408: Smiling Through.

Hum 409: Coffee Break

Coffee Break was a special edition piece that was introduced in 1984 and available exclusively to members of the former Goebel Collectors' Club, now the M.I. Hummel Club. It was available to members with a redemption card until May 31, 1986. The issue price for Coffee Break was $90.

It is now available only on the secondary market and only in TMK-6; however, early samples made by master sculptor Gerhard Skrobek from an original Sister M.I. Hummel drawing do exist with TMK-5. The regular production pieces carry an incised 1976 copyright date, along with blue decal with special inscription: "EXCLUSIVE SPECIAL EDITION No. 8 FOR MEMBERS OF THE GOEBEL COLLECTORS' CLUB."

Hum No.	Basic Size	Trademark	Current Value
409	4″	TMK-5	$1,800-$2,400
409	4″	TMK-6	$180-$195

Hum 409: Coffee Break.

Hum 410: Little Architect

New for 1993, Little Architect, which was crafted by master sculptor Gerhard Skrobek in 1978 and formerly known as Truant, bears the mold number 410/I. It carries an incised 1978 copyright date, and first-year pieces carry the "First Issue 1993" decal.

Early samples are known to exist with TMK-5, but the regular production pieces began with TMK-7. This piece remains in production today.

Hum No.	Basic Size	Trademark	Current Value
410	6″	TMK-5	$1,800-$2,400
410/I	6″	TMK-7	$205-$210
410/I	6″	TMK-8	$365

Hum 410: Little Architect.

Hum 411: Do I Dare?

Do I Dare?, which was crafted by master sculptor Gerhard Skrobek in 1978, features a standing girl holding a flower in her left hand and a basket in the crook of her right arm. Early samples exist with TMK-5, but the piece has yet to be placed into regular production.

Do I Dare? was a gift to attendees of the 2005 M.I. Hummel Convention held in Boston. "2005-M.I. Hummel Club Convention Boston, MA" is written on the side of the base. The regular issue was released in 2006 without the convention marking, but has a "First Issue 2006" backstamp, incised 1988 copyright date, and TMK-8. It was formerly a possible future edition.

Hum No.	Basic Size	Trademark	Current Value
411	6″	TMK-5	$1,800-$2,400
411	4″	TMK-8	$149

Hum 411: Do I Dare?

Hum 412: Bath Time

The design of master sculptor Gerhard Skrobek in 1978, Bath Time was released for sale in 1990 during the TMK-6 era, but early samples exist with TMK-5. It bears a 1978 incised copyright date and was $300 when issued. There are no significant variations that affect the collector value.

Bath Time was temporarily withdrawn from production on June 15, 2002.

Hum 412: Bath Time.

Hum No.	Basic Size	Trademark	Current Value
412	6-1/4"	TMK-5	$1,800-$2,400
412	6-1/4"	TMK-6	$320-$325
412	6-1/4"	TMK-7	$300-$325
412	6-1/4"	TMK-8	$300-$325

Hum 413: Whistler's Duet

Whistler's Duet, which master sculptor Gerhard Skrobek crafted in 1979, was released in late 1991. Early samples exist with TMK-5. It carries an incised 1979 copyright date and was $235 when released. No significant variations affect the collector value.

This piece was temporarily withdrawn from production on June 15, 2002.

Hum 413: Whistler's Duet.

Hum No.	Basic Size	Trademark	Current Value
413	4" to 4-1/2"	TMK-5	$1,800-$2,400
413	4" to 4-1/2"	TMK-6	$300-$600
413	4" to 4-1/2"	TMK-7	$190-$200

Hum 414: In Tune

One of six new designs released in 1981, In Tune was modeled by master sculptor Gerhard Skrobek in 1979. Early samples exist bearing TMK-5. Its basic size is 4", it carries a 1979 incised copyright date, and it is a matching figurine to the 1981 Annual Bell with the same name (Hum 703). Later, in 1997, the Springtime Serenade plate (Hum 297) also carried the same motif. There are no significant variations that affect the collector value.

The figure was temporarily withdrawn from production in January 1999.

Hum No.	Basic Size	Trademark	Current Value
414	4"	TMK-5	$1,800-$2,400
414	4"	TMK-6	$200-$210
414	4"	TMK-7	$195-$200
414	4"	TMK-8	$259

Hum 414: In Tune.

Hum 415: Thoughtful

Thoughtful, which was the original work of master sculptor Gerhard Skrobek in 1979, was another of the new designs released by Goebel in 1981. It is a matching piece to the 1980 Annual Bell with the same name (Hum 702). The figurine has a 1980 incised copyright date and was $105 the year it was issued.

In 1996, Goebel issued a special edition of 2,000 Thoughtful figurines in conjunction with the release of master sculptor Gerhard Skrobek's new book, *Hummels and Me, Life Stories*. The title page on the special edition figurine's book is the same as Skrobek's book. The figurines were signed by Skrobek, and they bear the 125th anniversary backstamp. Collectors who bought that particular figurine in that year received the book for no extra charge.

Hum 415: Thoughtful.

Hum No.	Basic Size	Trademark	Current Value
415 (early sample)	4-1/2"	TMK-5	$1,800-$2,400
415	4-1/2"	TMK-6	$165-$170
415 (special edition)	4-1/2"	TMK-7	$165-$195
415	4-1/2"	TMK-7	$170-$180
415	4-1/2"	TMK-8	$279

Hum 416: Jubilee

Beginning in January 1985, this very special figurine was made available to collectors. Production was limited to the number sold during 1985. The figure, which was crafted by master sculptor Gerhard Skrobek in 1979, has a special backstamp reading: "50 YEARS M.I. HUMMEL FIGURINES, 1935-1985." Right below the backstamp is the slogan, "The Love Lives On." This piece was made in celebration of the golden anniversary of Hummel figurines. The factory-recommended retail price was $200.

At least two of these figures are found with "75" instead of "50" on the golden anniversary figure. The speculation is that this piece was originally designed to celebrate the 75th anniversary of M.I. Hummel's birthday.

Another unusual variation is one where the circle around the "50" is a shiny gold gilt. This particular piece, one of only two known to be in private collections, bears TMK-5. Apparently Goebel had an idea for the golden anniversary, but the gilt didn't come out to the company's satisfaction after being fired, and the idea was scrapped. These figures are unique, and there is no way to realistically assign a value to them.

The normal Jubilees are found only with TMK-6 and an incised 1980 copyright date.

Hum 416: Jubilee.

A variation of Jubilee with the gold gilt 50.

Hum No.	Basic Size	Trademark	Current Value
416	6-1/4"	TMK-6	$300-$360

Hum 417: Where Did You Get That?
Possible Future Edition

Crafted by master sculptor Gerhard Skrobek in 1982, Where Did You Get That? is a figure of a standing boy and girl. The boy holds his hat in both hands. It has three apples in it. The girl dangles her doll in her left hand. It is 5-1/4", carries a 1982 incised copyright date, and although it has never been put into regular production, the two figurines that make up the piece exist separately as Gift From a Friend (Hum 485) and I Wonder (Hum 486).

Hum 418: What's New?

Added to the line in 1990, What's New? was first modeled in 1980 by master sculptor Gerhard Skrobek. It has an incised 1980 copyright date and had a suggested retail price of $200 when released.

The M.I. Hummel Club announced a new edition of What's New? to honor the club's 20th anniversary. It was an exclusive members-only edition for the club year 1996-1997. The newspaper the girl reads has the M.I. Hummel Club newsletter masthead (*INSIGHTS: North American Edition*) with an American or Canadian flag and the club dates. The inside also pictures the club's exclusive anniversary piece, Celebrate With Song, in full color. It was released to club members at $310.

Hum 418: What's New?

Hum No.	Basic Size	Trademark	Current Value
418	5-1/4"	TMK-6	$200-$235
418 (special edition)	5-1/4"	TMK-7	$200-$235

Hum No.	Basic Size	Trademark	Current Value
418	5-1/4"	TMK-7	$200-$225
418	5-1/4"	TMK-8	$210-$225

Hum 419: Good Luck
Possible Future Edition

In this 6-1/4" figure, a standing boy has his left hand in his pocket and holds an umbrella under his right arm. Crafted in 1981 by master sculptor Gerhard Skrobek, it is a possible future edition only at this time.

Hum 420: Is It Raining?

Is It Raining?, the design of master sculptor Gerhard Skrobek in 1981, was added to the line in 1989. It has a copyright date of 1981, and its retail price at release was $175. There are no significant variations to affect the collector value.

Hum No.	Basic Size	Trademark	Current Value
420	6"	TMK-6	$200-$230
420	6"	TMK-7	$195-$225
420	6"	TMK-8	$369

Hum 420: Is It Raining?

Hum 421: It's Cold

It's Cold was the sixth in a series of special offers made exclusively to members of the former Goebel Collectors' Club, now the M.I. Hummel Club. It was initially available only from the club, requiring a special redemption card issued to members.

This figurine, the work of master sculptor Gerhard Skrobek following an original drawing by Sister M.I. Hummel, bears a 1981 incised copyright date and

was sold with redemption card for $80. It is found only bearing TMK-6 and a blue decal with the special inscription: "EXCLUSIVE SPECIAL EDITION No. 6 FOR MEMBERS OF THE GOEBEL COLLECTORS' CLUB."

There are no significant variations that affect the collector value of this figurine.

Hum 421: It's Cold.

Hum No.	Basic Size	Trademark	Current Value
421	5" to 5-1/4"	TMK-6 EE	$210-$240
421 4/0	3-1/4"	TMK-8"OE	$99

Hum 422: What Now?

What Now?, designed by master sculptor Gerhard Skrobek following an original drawing by Sister M.I. Hummel, was the seventh special edition issued for members of the Goebel Collectors' Club, now the M.I. Hummel Club. A redemption card was required for purchase of this figurine at $90.

What Now? stands 5-1/4" high, and since May 31, 1985, has been

available only on the secondary market. It carries a 1981 incised copyright date and blue decal with this special inscription: "EXCLUSIVE SPECIAL EDITION No. 7 FOR MEMBERS OF THE GOEBEL COLLECTORS' CLUB."

There are no variations that affect this figure's value.

Hum 422: What Now?

Hum No.	Basic Size	Trademark	Current Value
422	5-1/4"	TMK-6	$210-$240

Hum 423: Horse Trainer

Horse Trainer, which was designed by master sculptor Gerhard Skrobek in 1980, was added to the line in 1990 at a suggested retail price of $155. It carries a 1981 incised copyright date. There are no variations that affect this value.

Hum No.	Basic Size	Trademark	Current Value
423	4-1/2"	TMK-6	$165-$170
423	4-1/2"	TMK-7	$160-$165
423	4-1/2"	TMK-8	$268

Hum 423: Horse Trainer.

Hum 424: Sleep Tight

A 1990 release, Sleep Tight was first crafted in 1980 by master sculptor Gerhard Skrobek. It bears an incised 1981 copyright date and has no significant variation affecting value.

Hum 424: Sleep Tight.

Hum No.	Basic Size	Trademark	Current Value
424	4-1/2"	TMK-6	$165-$170
424	4-1/2"	TMK-7	$160-$170
424	4-1/2"	TMK-8	$200-$250

Hum 425: Pleasant Moment

This 4-1/2" figure, the design of master sculptor Gerhard Skrobek in 1980, portrays two seated girls. One holds flowers in her left hand, while the other reaches down with her right hand toward a yellow butterfly. It carries a 1981 incised copyright date. Part of the 2008 Premier Collection, Pleasant Moment was released in fall 2007 and has TMK-8.

Pleasant Moment was also a signature piece at the 2011 M.I. Hummel National Convention held at Walt Disney World in Orlando, Florida. Those who attended the convention had the opportunity to purchase this figurine with Mickey Mouse ears painted on the white apron and inside the butterfly. The words "It's Magic" were painted on the front base of the figurine. Master painter Ulrich Tendara painted and signed the figurines sold at the convention.

Hum No.	Basic Size	Trademark	Current Value
425	4-1/2"	TMK-8	$429 retail

Hum 426: Pay Attention

When Pay Attention was placed in production, it was not in its original 5-3/4" size. A 4-1/4" size (Hum 426/3/0), crafted by master sculptor Helmut Fischer in 1997, was released in 1999.

First modeled by master sculptor Gerhard Skrobek in 1980, the figurine depicts a girl sitting on a fence while holding flowers and a basket. She is looking away from a crowing blackbird perched on the fencepost behind her. The original pieces carry an incised 1981 copyright date, while the newer, smaller pieces have a 1997 copyright date. The original 1999 issue price was $175. The 5-3/4" size, bearing TMK-6, is now considered an early sample.

The year 2011 marked the celebration of Sister Hummel's 75th anniversary of the beginning of her legacy. Manufaktur Rödental selected 50 figurines to bear the "75th Anniversary" backstamp. Pay Attention was one of those figurines. Only

75 of them were available in North America with this backstamp. Each figurine was hand-numbered with a golden backstamp and a map of North America backstamp. A special porcelain plaque was included, and a notable emblem on the packaging hinted at the contents. Each figurine included a "75 Years of M.I. Hummel" certificate.

Hum 426: Pay Attention.

Hum No.	Basic Size	Trademark	Current Value
426	5-3/4"	TMK-6	$900-$1,200
426/3/0	4-1/2"	TMK-7	$110-$120
426/3/0	4-1/2"	TMK-8	$190

Hum 427: Where Are You?

When Where Are You? was placed in production, it was not in its original 5-3/4" size. A 4-1/4" size (Hum 427/3/0), crafted by master sculptor Helmut Fischer in 1997, was released in 1999.

In this figurine, a boy sits on a fence and holds a bouquet of flowers while a bird is perched on a fencepost. It was originally designed in 1980 by master sculptor Gerhard Skrobek, and those larger pieces carry a 1981 incised copyright date. The 5-3/4"

size, bearing TMK-6, is now considered an early sample.

The newer, smaller pieces carry TMK-7 and a 1997 copyright date. The original 1999 issue price was $175.

Hum 427: Where Are You?

Hum No.	Basic Size	Trademark	Current Value
427	5-3/4"	TMK-6	$900-$1,200
427/3/0	4-1/2"	TMK-7	$110-$120
427/3/0	4-1/2"	TMK-8	$190

Hum 428: Summertime Surprise

Once listed as a possible future edition under the name I Won't Hurt You, this figurine has since been placed into production, but not in the original 5-3/4" size. A 3-1/2" size (Hum 428/3/0) was released in 1997. In it, a boy with a hiking staff in his left hand looks down at a ladybug in his right hand.

Master sculptor Gerhard Skrobek was responsible for the original design of this piece in 1980. The 5-3/4" size, bearing TMK-6 and a 1981 incised copyright date, is now considered an early sample.

The newer, smaller pieces, which were the redesign of master sculptor Helmut Fischer, carry an incised 1989 copyright date and TMK-7. The original 1997 price was $140.

Hum No.	Basic Size	Trademark	Current Value
428	5-3/4"	TMK-6	$1,200-$1,800
428/3/0	3-1/2"	TMK-7	$95-$100
428/3/0	3-1/2"	TMK-8	$139

Hum 428: Summertime Surprise.

Hum 429: Hello World

Hello World was released in 1989 as an exclusive edition available to members of the former Goebel Collectors' Club, now the M.I. Hummel Club, with a redemption card bearing the expiration date of May 31, 1990. It was designed in 1980 by master sculptor Gerhard Skrobek and carries an incised 1983 copyright date in addition to either TMK-6 or TMK-7. It further carries the special club

Hum 429: Hello World.

Hum No.	Basic Size	Trademark	Current Value
429	5-1/2"	TMK-6	$210-$240
429	5-1/2"	TMK-7	$180-$210

"EXCLUSIVE EDITION" inscription on a blue decal.

There are two variations to be found. In 1989, the club changed from the Goebel Collectors' Club to the M.I. Hummel Club. Apparently a few figures were released with the old special edition backstamp before the error was discovered. All those subsequently released bear the M.I. Hummel Club backstamp.

Hum 430: In D Major

This 1989 release, originally designed by master sculptor Gerhard Skrobek in 1980, carries a 1981 copyright date incised beneath the base and was released at $135. "K B" appears on the boundary stone the little boy is sitting on, and can be seen only by looking at the back of the figurine. This is a reference to "Koenigreich Bayern," which translated to English means "Kingdom of Bavaria."

There are no significant variations to affect the value, although the piece was temporarily withdrawn from production on June 15, 2002.

Hum No.	Basic Size	Trademark	Current Value
430	4-1/4"	TMK-6	$145-$160
430	4-1/4"	TMK-7	$145-$155
430	4-1/4"	TMK-8	$145-$150

Hum 430: In D Major.

Hum 431: The Surprise

The Surprise, introduced in 1988, was the 12th special edition for members of the former Goebel Collectors' Club, now the M.I. Hummel Club. The expiration date on the redemption card was May 31, 1990.

The Surprise bears the incised copyright date of 1981 as well as the same date in decal beneath TMK-7. This figure, which was first modeled by master sculptor Gerhard Skrobek in 1980, was the first to also bear the little bumblebee that was to appear on all special editions for club members. It further carries a blue decal with the inscription: "EXCLUSIVE SPECIAL EDITION No. 12 FOR MEMBERS OF THE GOEBEL COLLECTORS' CLUB."

It exists in TMK-6 as both an early sample and the exclusive member piece, but the sample is worth significantly more than the club piece. There is no club inscription on the sample piece.

Hum No.	Basic Size	Trademark	Current Value
431	4-1/4" to 5-1/2"	TMK-6	$1,200-$1,800
431	4-1/4" to 5-1/2"	TMK-6	$180-$210

Hum 431: The Surprise.

Hum 432: Knit One, Purl One

Knit One, Purl One, the design of master sculptor Gerhard Skrobek in 1982, was a new addition to the line in 1983. It was made to go with the 1982 annual bell named Knit One of the same motif (Hum 705). The figurine has an incised 1982 copyright date and no base. It was originally issued at $52.

There are no significant variations to affect collector values.

Hum 432: Knit One, Purl One.

Hum No.	Basic Size	Trademark	Current Value
432	3"	TMK-6	$90-$95
432	3"	TMK-7	$85-$90
432	3"	TMK-8	$179

Hum 433: Sing Along

Released in 1987 at $145, Sing Along bears an incised copyright date of 1982 and was made to go with the 1986 annual bell of the same name and motif (Hum 708). Master sculptor Gerhard Skrobek first modeled it in 1981.

There are no variations to affect the collector value. It was temporarily withdrawn from production in January 1999.

Hum 433: Sing Along.

Hum No.	Basic Size	Trademark	Current Value
433	4-1/2"	TMK-6	$200-$205
433	4-1/2"	TMK-7	$185-$195

Hum 434: Friend or Foe?

This 4" figure, released in 1991 at a $190 suggested retail price, bears an incised 1982 copyright date. Master sculptor Gerhard Skrobek first designed the piece in 1981.

There are no variations to affect the price of the normal production pieces. It was temporarily withdrawn from production on June 15, 2002.

Hum 434: Friend or Foe?

Friend or Foe? demonstration piece with TMK-7, incised 1982 copyright date, and measuring 3-7/8".

Hum No.	Basic Size	Trademark	Current Value
434	4"	TMK-6	$165-$170
434	4"	TMK-7	$160-$165
434	4"	TMK-8	$255

Hum 435: Delicious

Originally made by master sculptor Gerhard Skrobek in 6" samples bearing a TMK-6, Delicious was not released until 1996 in a 3-7/8" size (Hum 435/3/0). It has an incised 1988 copyright date and two special backstamps: "First Issue 1996" and "125th Anniversary Goebel." Both appear only on those pieces produced in 1996. The issue price was $155 in the year of release, but the early samples are now worth significantly more than those released since.

This piece (435/3/0) was temporarily withdrawn from production on June 15, 2002.

Hum No.	Basic Size	Trademark	Current Value
435	6"	TMK-6	$1,200-$1,800
435/3/0	3-7/8"	TMK-7	$105-$110
435/3/0	3-7/8"	TMK-8	$175

Hum 435: Delicious.

Hum 436: An Emergency

This 5-3/4" figurine, crafted by master sculptor Gerhard Skrobek in 1981, portrays a boy with a bandage on his head. He is about to push the button on the doctor's gate. The figurine was released in 2007.

Hum No.	Basic Size	Trademark	Current Value
436	5-3/4"	TMK-8	$319

Hum 436: An Emergency.

Hum 437: Tuba Player

Tuba Player, the 1982 design of master sculptor Gerhard Skrobek, was released in the winter of 1989 with a 1983 copyright date. Suggested retail price in 1989 was $160.

There are no variations to affect the value. It was temporarily withdrawn from production on June 15, 2002.

Hum No.	Basic Size	Trademark	Current Value
437	6-1/4″	TMK-6	$195-$205
437	6-1/4″	TMK-7	$190-$200
437	6-1/4″	TMK-8	$190-$200

Hum 437: Tuba Player.

Hum 438: Sounds of the Mandolin

This 3-3/4" figure was released in 1988 for $65 as one of three musical angel pieces. The other two were Hum 454: Song of Praise and Hum 453: The Accompanist. Sculpted by master sculptor Gerhard Skrobek in 1982, it carries an incised 1984 copyright date and was originally called Mandolin Serenade.

There are no variations to affect that value; however, it was temporarily withdrawn from production on June 15, 2002.

Hum No.	Basic Size	Trademark	Current Value
438	3-3/4″	TMK-6	$95-$100
438	3-3/4″	TMK-7	$95-$100
438	3-3/4″	TMK-8	$90-$100

Hum 438: Sounds of the Mandolin.

Hum 439: A Gentle Glow
Candleholder

Released in 1987 at $110, A Gentle Glow portrays a small standing child originally modeled by master sculptor Gerhard Skrobek in 1982. The candle receptacle appears to be resting on greenery that the child holds up with both hands. It carries a 1983 incised copyright date.

The figurine is found only in TMK-6 and TMK-7 as it was temporarily withdrawn from production in January 1999. There are no variations to affect the collector value.

Hum No.	Basic Size	Trademark	Current Value
439	5-1/4″ to 5-1/2″	TMK-6	$120-$150
439	5-1/4″ to 5-1/2″	TMK-7	$115-$150

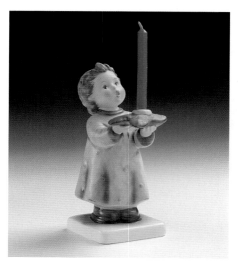

Hum 439: A Gentle Glow candleholder.

Hum 440: Birthday Candle
Candleholder

This 5-1/2" candleholder, which was designed by master sculptor Gerhard Skrobek following an original M.I. Hummel drawing, was the 10th exclusive edition available to members of the Goebel Collectors' Club, now known as the M.I. Hummel Club. It bears a

1983 copyright date and the following inscription on a blue decal: "EXCLUSIVE SPECIAL EDITION No. 10 FOR MEMBERS OF THE GOEBEL COLLECTORS' CLUB." It was released at $95, and the redemption card cut-off date was May 31, 1988. The figure was released in conjunction with the 10th anniversary celebration of the founding of the club. This piece is found in TMK-6 only. There are no variations affecting value.

Hum 440: Birthday Candle candleholder.

Hum No.	Basic Size	Trademark	Current Value
440	5-1/2"	TMK-6	$210-$240

Hum 441: Call to Worship
Clock

Introduced in 1988, Call to Worship was only the second clock ever made from a Hummel design. (The first was Chapel Time, Hum 442.) First crafted by master sculptor Gerhard Skrobek in 1982, it stands 13" tall and chimes every hour. You can choose from two tunes by moving a switch beneath the figure. The tunes are "Ave Maria" and "Westminster Chimes."

Call to Worship was the second offering in what Goebel called the Century Collection, a group of pieces produced in the 20th century with a one-year limited production. Figures in the collection bear the Roman numeral "XX" on their bases. The suggested retail price in 1988 was $600. These figures can be found in TMK-6 only with an incised 1983 copyright date. There are no variations that affect value.

Hum 441: Call to Worship clock.

Hum No.	Basic Size	Trademark	Current Value
441	13"	TMK-6	$840-$900

Hum 442: Chapel Time
Clock

Chapel Time was the first clock to be put into production and released by Goebel. It was limited to one year of production (1986) and could not be made again in the 20th century. Included with the artist's mark and date on the bottom is the Roman numeral "XX," indicating the 20th century. The base also bears TMK-6, incised 1983 copyright date, and a blue M.I. Hummel

signature with the inscription, "The Love Lives On."

The original design of master sculptor Gerhard Skrobek in 1982, Chapel Time exists in several variations, mostly regarding the windows. So far the most common version has all windows closed and painted except for the four in the belfry. The rarest version has all windows closed and painted.

Hum 442: Chapel Time clock.

According to Goebel, this rare version was a pre-production run numbering 800 to 1,000 pieces. Reportedly, a few of these have been found with the two small round windows in the gables open. A third version has open windows in the gables and belfry. There are other variations with regard to the base and size of the hole in the bottom (to replace the battery), but these are not presently considered significant.

The following is a breakdown of the values of the three variations:

Hum No.	Basic Size	Trademark	Current Value
442	11-1/2"	TMK-6	$1,050-$1,200 belfry and gable windows open
442	11-1/2"	TMK-6	$1,200-$1,500 painted windows variation
442	11-1/2"	TMK-6	$1,500-$1,800 belfry windows open, gable painted

Hum 443: Country Song
Clock, Possible Future Edition

This 8" figurine, modeled by master sculptor Gerhard Skrobek in 1982, features a boy blowing a horn. He is seated on a flower-covered mound. Blue flowers are used instead of numbers on the clock face. The piece bears a 1983 copyright date. At this time it is a possible future edition only.

Hum 444-445: Open Numbers

Hum 446: A Personal Message
Possible Future Edition

First designed by master sculptor Gerhard Skrobek in 1983, this 3-3/4" piece features a girl on her knees using a large pen to write on paper. There is an inkwell to her left. This piece looks somewhat like Hum 309: With Loving Greetings. At this time, it is a possible future edition only.

Hum 447: Morning Concert

Morning Concert, first sculpted by master sculptor Gerhard Skrobek from an original Sister Hummel drawing, was the 11th exclusive special edition piece made and offered exclusively for members of the former Goebel Collectors' Club, now the M.I. Hummel Club. It was available to members until the expiration date of May 31, 1989.

Morning Concert has a copyright date of 1984 incised beneath the base and the special edition club backstamp in decal underglaze. It carries the following inscription on a blue decal: "EXCLUSIVE SPECIAL EDITION No. 11 FOR MEMBERS OF THE GOEBEL COLLECTORS' CLUB." It was available to members for $98.

There are no significant variations.

Hum No.	Basic Size	Trademark	Current Value
447	5-1/4"	TMK-6	$150-$180

Hum 447: Morning Concert.

Hum 448: Children's Prayer
Possible Future Edition

Children's Prayer is an 8-1/4" figure of a boy and girl standing, looking up at a roadside shrine of Jesus on the cross. It was modeled by master sculptor Gerhard Skrobek in 1983 and has a 1984 incised copyright date. At this time it is a possible future edition only.

Hum 449: The Little Pair

In 1990, the M.I. Hummel Club began offering special figures to members who had passed certain milestones in their membership. The Little Pair was made available by redemption card to only those members who attained or surpassed their 10th year of membership. Each carried a special backstamp commemorating the occasion. This piece was retired in May 2000 and is now only available on the secondary market.

Hum No.	Basic Size	Trademark	Current Value
449	5" to 5-1/4"	TMK-6	$210-$240
449	5" to 5-1/4"	TMK-7	$130-$140
449	5" to 5-1/4"	TMK-8	$130-140

Hum 449: The Little Pair.

Hum 450: Will It Sting?

Will It Sting? was released as an exclusive special edition to M.I. Hummel Club members to mark the club's 24th year. Released in 2000, the exclusive figure (Hum 450/0) was designed by master sculptor Helmut Fischer at a smaller size than the earlier TMK-6 sample that was crafted by master sculptor Gerhard Skrobek in 1984, which was 5-3/4".

The figure, a girl looking at a bee perched on a plant at her feet, carries the inscription applied as a blue decal on the bottom: "EXCLUSIVE EDITION 2000/01 M.I. HUMMEL CLUB." Like other club exclusives, a redemption card was necessary for purchase for an issue price of $260 in 2000.

Hum No.	Basic Size	Trademark	Current Value
450	5-3/4"	TMK-6	$1,200-$1,800
450/0	5"	TMK-8	$160-$175

Hum 450: Will It Sting?

Hum 451: Just Dozing

Released in 1995, Just Dozing was first modeled by master sculptor Gerhard Skrobek in 1984 and has an incised 1984 copyright date. Those produced in 1995 bear the "First Issue 1995" backstamp. It was originally released at $220. Just Dozing is a companion to Hum 2122: Sweet Nap.

Hum No.	Basic Size	Trademark	Current Value
451	4-1/4"	TMK-7	$155-$175
451	4-1/4"	TMK-8	$279

Hum 451: Just Dozing.

Hum 452: Flying High

Flying High was the first in a series of hanging ornaments, however, it was not the first Hummel hanging ornament. The first was Flying Angel (Hum 366), commonly used with the nativity sets.

Flying High was modeled by master sculptor Gerhard Skrobek in 1984 and introduced as the 1988 (first edition) ornament at $75. It has a 1984 incised copyright date.

There are three variations with regard to additional marks. When first released, there were no additional markings; these undated pieces are the most sought-after. The second variation has the 1988 date as well as a decal reading "First Edition" beneath the skirt. The third variation has "1988" painted on the back of the gown but no "First Edition."

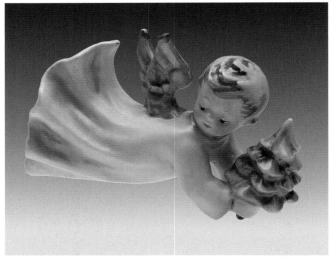

Hum 452: Flying High.

Hum No.	Basic Size	Trademark	Current Value
452	4-1/2" x 2-3/4"	TMK-6	$150-$180 no marks
452	4-1/2" x 2-3/4"	TMK-6	$105-$120 "First Edition"
452	4-1/2" x 2-3/4"	TMK-6	$105-$120 "1988"

Hum 453: The Accompanist

The Accompanist, along with Hum 454: Song of Praise and Hum 438: Sounds of the Mandolin, was introduced in 1988 as a trio of angel musicians. It was released at $39.

The figurine, which was designed by master sculptor Gerhard Skrobek in 1984, measures 3-1/4" high and has an incised copyright date of 1984. It is not found with any earlier trademark than TMK-6.

Hum 453: The Accompanist.

Hum No.	Basic Size	Trademark	Current Value
453	3-1/4"	TMK-6	$75-$80
453	3-1/4"	TMK-7	$70-$75
453	3-1/4"	TMK-8	$135

Hum 454: Song of Praise

Song of Praise was one of three angel musician figures introduced in 1988. The others were Hum 453: The Accompanist and Hum 438: Sounds of the Mandolin. It was released at $39.

Song of Praise, which was modeled by master sculptor Gerhard Skrobek in 1984, stands 3" high and has an incised copyright date of 1984. It is not found with any earlier trademark than TMK-6.

Hum 454: Song of Praise.

Hum No.	Basic Size	Trademark	Current Value
454	3"	TMK-6	$75-$80
454	3"	TMK-7	$70-$75
454	3"	TMK-8	$135

Hum 455: The Guardian

A 1991 release, The Guardian was first crafted by master sculptor Gerhard Skrobek in 1984. It bears an incised copyright date of 1984. Those made in 1991 bear the "First Issue 1991" backstamp dated 1991. These are not found in trademarks earlier than TMK-6. The suggested retail price at the time of release was $145.

In 1996, Goebel announced "Personal Touch" figurines. There were four figurines in the line at the time that lent themselves well to this application. The Guardian was one of these. The other three were Bird Duet (Hum 69), Latest News (Hum 184), and For Father (Hum 87). A permanent personalization of choice could be fired onto the piece. (The bird is removed for the inscription.)

Hum 455: The Guardian.

Hum No.	Basic Size	Trademark	Current Value
455	2-3/4" x 3-1/2"	TMK-6	$115-$120
455	2-3/4" x 3-1/2"	TMK-7	$110-$115
455	2-3/4" x 3-1/2"	TMK-8	$200

Hum 456: Sleep, Little One, Sleep
Possible Future Edition

This 4-1/4" figurine, which was the design of master sculptor Gerhard Skrobek in 1984, depicts an angel standing beside a baby in a cradle, apparently rocking the child to sleep. At this time it is a possible future edition only.

Hum 457: Sound the Trumpet

Sound the Trumpet, which was first modeled by master sculptor Gerhard Skrobek in 1984, was introduced in 1988 at a price of $45. It has an incised copyright date of 1984. The piece is not found in trademarks earlier than TMK-6. It was temporarily withdrawn from production on June 15, 2002.

Hum 457: Sound the Trumpet.

Hum No.	Basic Size	Trademark	Current Value
457	3"	TMK-6	$80-$85
457	3"	TMK-7	$75-$80
457	3"	TMK-8	$75-$80

Hum 458: Storybook Time

Storybook Time was introduced as new for 1992 in the fall 1991 issue of *INSIGHTS*, the M.I. Hummel Club newsletter, with the name Story Time. It was first crafted by master sculptor Gerhard Skrobek in 1984 and carries an incised 1985 copyright date. The release price was $330.

Hum 458: Storybook Time.

Hum No.	Basic Size	Trademark	Current Value
458	5-1/4"	TMK-7	$280-$350
458	5-1/4"	TMK-8	$270-$340

Hum 459: In the Meadow

In the Meadow, which was the original work of master sculptor Gerhard Skrobek in 1984, was released in 1987 as one of five 1987 releases. The release price was $110. It has an incised copyright date of 1985 beneath the base.

In the Meadow was temporarily withdrawn from production on June 15, 2002.

Hum No.	Basic Size	Trademark	Current Value
459	4"	TMK-6	$150-$160
459	4"	TMK-7	$150-$155
459	4"	TMK-8	$150-$160

Hum 459: In the Meadow.

Hum 460: Tally
Dealer Plaque

Tally dealer plaque was introduced in 1986. Many assumed it was to replace the Hum 187: Merry Wanderer dealer plaque that had been used since the 1940s, but in 1990, the Merry Wanderer style was reissued.

When Tally was first introduced, there was apparently a shortage, and dealers were limited to one figure each, but the shortage was soon alleviated. The boy on the plaque is very similar to the center figure in School Boys (Hum 170). The base of the plaque bears an incised copyright date of 1984.

There are no structural, size (all are 5" x 6"), or color variations presently known, but there are variations in the language used on the front of the plaque. German, Swedish, French, Italian, Spanish, Dutch, and Japanese are used on the plaques. The Japanese variation was issued in 1996. In addition, there is a version for British dealers and one for the American market, for a total of nine different

Hum No.	Variation	Trademark	Current Value
460	Dutch	TMK-6	$540-$900
460	Dutch	TMK-7	$180-$300
460	English/U.S.	TMK-6	$120-$135
460	English/Britain	TMK-6	$300-$450
460	English/Britain	TMK-7	$180-$300
460	French	TMK-6	$450-$600
460	French	TMK-7	$180-$300
460	German	TMK-6	$450-$600
460	German	TMK-7	$180-$300
460	Italian	TMK-6	$540-$900
460	Italian	TMK-7	$180-$300
460	Japanese	TMK-7	$300-$450
460	Spanish	TMK-6	$540-$900
460	Spanish	TMK-7	$180-$300
460	Swedish	TMK-6	$450-$600
460	Swedish	TMK-7	$180-$300

Hum 460: Tally dealer plaque.

versions. The plaque was released as $85 in the United States. The U.S. variation was closed in December 1989, and the others were temporarily withdrawn from production in January 1999.

Hum 461: In the Orchard
Possible Future Edition

This 5-1/2" figurine, which was first modeled by master sculptor Gerhard Skrobek in 1984, depicts a girl standing next to an apple tree sapling that is tied to a wooden post for support. The child has an apple in her left hand and a shovel in the other. At this time it is a possible future edition only.

Hum 462: Tit For Tat

This 3-3/4" figurine, designed by master sculptor Gerhard Skrobek in 1984, depicts a boy sitting next to a bird perched on a wooden post. The boy has a feather in his right hand and the bird is tugging at a lock of the boy's hair in retaliation. The piece was first released in 2004 with an incised 1985 copyright date and TMK-8. Limited editions of 600 have the Caribbean Collection backstamp, a band of flowers on the side of base, and "First Issue 2004" backstamp.

Hum No.	Basic Size	Trademark	Current Value
462	3-3/4"	TMK-8 OE	$279

Hum 462: Tit For Tat.

Hum 463/0: My Wish is Small

My Wish is Small was a M.I. Hummel Club exclusive offering for the 16th club year, available only in TMK-7, although early samples exist bearing TMK-6. Such samples, which have a square base instead of the round base of the regular production figurines, are worth significantly more than the pieces made since.

Hum 463: My Wish is Small.

Hum No.	Basic Size	Trademark	Current Value
463/0	5-1/2"	TMK-6	$1,200-$1,500
463/0	5-1/2"	TMK-7	$150-$180

The figure, which was modeled by master sculptor Gerhard Skrobek in 1985, was available exclusively to members with redemption cards for $170. It bears an incised 1985 copyright date, TMK-7, and special inscription on a blue decal: "EXCLUSIVE EDITION 1992/93 M.I. HUMMEL CLUB."

This piece was permanently retired on May 31, 1994, and the mold was destroyed.

Hum 464: Young Scholar
Possible Future Edition

According to Goebel factory records, master sculptor Gerhard Skrobek modeled this 5-1/8" figurine in 1985. It depicts a boy wearing a hat and jacket while sitting on a wooden bench reading a book. A basket rests beside him on the bench at his left. At this time it is listed as a possible future edition only.

Hum No.	Basic Size	Trademark	Current Value
465	4-1/4"	TMK-6 CE	$2,400-$3,000 early sample

Hum 465: Where Shall I Go?
Possible Future Edition

Sculpted by master sculptor Gerhard Skrobek in 1985, Where Shall I Go? is approximately 4-1/4" and depicts a boy kneeling while holding a toy train. There is no base. At this time it is a possible future edition only. Robert and Ruth Miller own the original drawing of Jochen Edinger, the inspiration for the figurine.

Hum 466: Do Re Mi
Possible Future Edition

This 5-1/2" figurine, modeled by master sculptor Gerhard Skrobek in 1985, depicts two girls standing beside one another in short dresses singing joyfully. At this time it is listed as a possible future edition only.

Hum 467: The Kindergartner

A new release at $100 in 1987, The Kindergartner was first crafted by master sculptor Gerhard Skrobek in 1985. It bears a copyright date of 1986 incised beneath the base. This figure is not found with trademarks earlier than TMK-6, and it remains in production today.

Hum No.	Basic Size	Trademark	Current Value
467	5-1/4"	TMK-6	$145-$150
467	5-1/4"	TMK-7	$140-$145
467	5-1/4"	TMK-8 TW	$145-$150
467	3-1/4"	TMK-8 OE	$70

Hum 467: The Kindergartner.

Hum 468: Come On
Possible Future Edition

This 5-1/4" figurine, modeled by master sculptor Gerhard Skrobek in 1986, depicts a little boy walking with a stick in his right hand and a lamb tugging at his jacket on his left. At this time it is listed as a possible future edition only.

Hum 469: Starting Young
Possible Future Edition

This 4-3/4" figurine, first designed by master sculptor Gerhard Skrobek in 1986, depicts two girls: one sewing and one knitting. At this time it is listed as a possible future edition only.

Hum 470: Time Out

This 4-1/4" figurine, first crafted by master sculptor Gerhard Skrobek in 1986, is of a boy taking a rest, sitting with one shoe off and his mandolin tucked under his left arm. Released in 2008, this figurine is a TMK-8 and has the TMK-8 backstamp along with the "75th Anniversary" backstamp.

The year 2011 marked the celebration of Sister Hummel's 75th anniversary of the beginning of her legacy. Manufaktur Rödental selected 50 figurines to bear the "75th Anniversary" backstamp. Time Out was one of those figurines. Only 75 of them were available in North America with this backstamp. Each figurine was hand-numbered with a golden backstamp and a map of North America backstamp. A special porcelain plaque was included, and a notable emblem on the packaging hinted at the contents. Each figurine included a "75 Years of M.I. Hummel" certificate.

Hum No.	Basic Size	Trademark	Current Value
470	4-1/4"	TMK-8	$279

Hum 470: Time Out.

Hum 471: Harmony in Four Parts

Harmony in Four Parts was the 1989 addition to the "Century Collection." These pieces were limited to one production year and were not produced again in the 20th century. They bear a special backstamp indicating such. The stamp on this figure is 1989 underlined with the Roman numeral "XX" beneath it in the center of a circle made up of the M.I. Hummel signature and the words "CENTURY COLLECTION." The copyright date is 1987, and it was released at $850.

Designed by master sculptor Gerhard Skrobek in 1986, the lamppost was originally made of the same fine earthenware used to render Hummel pieces, but it was soon noted that the post was very easily broken. To alleviate this problem, Goebel began using a metal post. Although there is presently no difference in the value of the figures, it is reasonable to assume that the earthenware post version may become uncommon and more desirable to serious collectors, and consequently become more valuable. Only time will tell.

Hum No.	Basic Size	Trademark	Current Value
471	9-3/4"	TMK-6	$1,200-$1,500

Hum 471: Harmony in Four Parts.

Hum 472: On Our Way

This unusual piece, which was first crafted by master sculptor Gerhard Skrobek in 1986, was introduced as new for 1992 in the fall 1991 issue of *INSIGHTS*, the M.I. Hummel Club newsletter. On Our Way was the "Century Collection" piece for 1992, which means its availability was limited by the number produced during the one year of production.

The figure bears a special identifying backstamp and is accompanied by a certificate of authenticity. In addition to an incised 1987 copyright date, the piece also carries a special inscription on a blue decal: "M.I. HUMMEL CENTURY COLLECTION 1992 XX." The release price was $950.

Early samples exist in TMK-6 and are worth more than the figures made since.

Hum No.	Basic Size	Trademark	Current Value
472	8" to 8-1/4"	TMK-6	$1,200-$1,800
472	8" to 8-1/4"	TMK-7	$720-$900

Hum 472: On Our Way.

Hum 473: Ruprecht
Knecht Ruprecht

Ruprecht was produced in 1987 as a limited edition of 20,000 sequentially numbered pieces. It was modeled by master sculptor Gerhard Skrobek in 1986 and carries a 1987 incised copyright date. Early samples, which were called Father Christmas, exist in TMK-6 and are worth significantly more than the figures made since.

This piece is considered a companion to Saint Nicholas Day (Hum 2012), which was released the same year with matching edition numbers. Both pieces were offered at a reduced M.I. Hummel Club price of $1,000 per set.

Hum No.	Basic Size	Trademark	Current Value
473	6"	TMK-6	$1,200-1,800
473	6"	TMK-7	$300-$360

Hum 473: Ruprecht (Knecht Ruprecht).

Hum 474: Gentle Care
Possible Future Edition

This 6" figurine was first modeled by master sculptor Gerhard Skrobek in 1986. It shows two girls wearing long dresses and handkerchiefs in their hair. One girl carries a lamb while the other holds a basketful of apples. At this time it is listed as a possible future edition only.

Hum 475: Make a Wish

This piece was a new release in 1989 and bears a 1987 incised copyright date. The original design of master sculptor Gerhard Skrobek in 1986, these figures cannot be found with trademarks earlier than TMK-6. The original issue price was $135.

Make a Wish was temporarily withdrawn from production in 1999.

Hum No.	Basic Size	Trademark	Current Value
475	4-1/2"	TMK-6	$145-$150
475	4-1/2"	TMK-7	$135-$140

Hum 475: Make a Wish.

Hum 476: A Winter Song

This figurine, which was modeled by master sculptor Gerhard Skrobek in 1987, was a 1988 release and was priced at $45 when introduced. It bears an incised copyright date of 1987 and appears with TMK-6 or later trademarks. There are no significant variations affecting collector value.

Hum No.	Basic Size	Trademark	Current Value
476	4″	TMK-6	$90-$95
476	4″	TMK-7	$90-$95
476	4″	TMK-8	$145

Hum 476: A Winter Song.

Hum 477: A Budding Maestro

The work of master sculptor Gerhard Skrobek in 1987, A Budding Maestro was released in 1988 at $45 and is found with TMK-6 or later trademarks. It carries an incised 1987 copyright date.

There are no significant variations. It was temporarily withdrawn from production in January 1999.

Hum No.	Basic Size	Trademark	Current Value
477	4″	TMK-6	$80-$85
477	4″	TMK-7	$70-$75

Hum 477: A Budding Maestro.

Hum 478: I'm Here

I'm Here was released in 1989 as a new addition to the line. First modeled by master sculptor Gerhard Skrobek in 1987, it carries a 1987 incised copyright date. The price at release was $50. This piece is not found with trademarks earlier than TMK-6.

There are no significant variations. The piece was temporarily withdrawn from production on June 15, 2002.

Hum No.	Basic Size	Trademark	Current Value
478	3″	TMK-6	$90-$95
478	3″	TMK-7	$85-$95
478	3″	TMK-8	$85-$95

Hum 478: I'm Here.

Hum 479: I Brought You a Gift

On June 1, 1989, the 4" bisque plaque with the Merry Wanderer motif, which had been given to every new member of the Goebel Collectors' Club, was officially retired. On the same date, the club became the M.I. Hummel Club, and a new membership premium, I Brought You a Gift, was introduced. At the time of transition, each renewing and new member was given the new premium.

Crafted by master sculptor Gerhard Skrobek in 1987, I Brought You a Gift has the incised copyright date of 1987 on the underside of the base. There are two variations with regard to the club special edition backstamp. If you will look at the accompanying photograph of the base, you will note the old club name underneath the bumblebee. This is found on the early examples. Newer ones have the M.I. Hummel Club name on them.

This figurine was permanently retired on May 31, 1996.

Hum 479: I Brought You a Gift.

I Bought You a Gift bearing TMK-6, incised 1987 copyright date, and the special club exclusive backstamp. Note the club name is the old "Goebel Collectors Club" name instead of the current M.I. Hummel Club moniker.

Hum No.	Basic Size	Trademark	Current Value
479	4"	TMK-6	$90-$110
479	4"	TMK-7	$75-$90

Hum 480: Hosanna

Released in 1989, this figurine was first modeled by master sculptor Gerhard Skrobek in 1987 and therefore carries a 1987 copyright date incised under the base. The suggested retail price at the time of the release was $68. Hum 480 is not found with trademarks earlier than TMK-6.

Hosanna was temporarily withdrawn from production on June 15, 2002.

Hum 480: Hosanna.

Hum No.	Basic Size	Trademark	Current Value
480	4"	TMK-6	$85-$90
480	4"	TMK-7	$80-$85
480	4"	TMK-8	$80-$85

Hum 481: Love From Above
1989 Christmas Ornament

This ornament is the second edition in the hanging ornament series that began with the 1988 Flying High (Hum 452). The design of master sculptor Gerhard Skrobek in 1987, it bears a 1987 incised copyright date and TMK-6. It was released at $75.

Hum No.	Basic Size	Trademark	Current Value
481	3-1/4″	TMK-6	$75-$90

Hum 481: Love From Above 1989 Christmas ornament.

Hum 482: One For You, One For Me

This piece was a new release in 1989. It was first crafted by master sculptor Gerhard Skrobek in 1987 and thereby carries a 1987 incised copyright date. It was originally priced at $50.

The 3″ figurine is not found with trademarks earlier than TMK-6. It was temporarily withdrawn from production on June 15, 2002.

A 2-3/4″ piece was introduced in 1996 as part of the "Pen Pals" figurines line, which is a series of personalized name card decorations. That piece was temporarily withdrawn in January 1999.

Hum No.	Basic Size	Trademark	Current Value
482/5/0	2-3/4″	TMK-7	$55
482	3″	TMK-6	$80-$85
482	3″	TMK-7	$80-$85
482	3″	TMK-8	$80-$85

Hum 482: One For You, One For Me.

Hum 483: I'll Protect Him

New in 1989, this figure was designed by master sculptor Gerhard Skrobek in 1987 and bears an incised copyright date of 1987 on the underside of the base. The release price was $55. It is not found with trademarks earlier than TMK-6. It was temporarily withdrawn from production on June 15, 2002.

Hum No.	Basic Size	Trademark	Current Value
483	3-3/4″	TMK-6	$70-$75
483	3-3/4″	TMK-7	$65-$70
483	3-3/4″	TMK-8	$65-$70

Hum 483: I'll Protect Him.

Hum 484: Peace on Earth
1990 Christmas Ornament

The third in an annual series of M.I. Hummel Christmas ornaments, this one was released in 1990 at a suggested retail price of $80. It was modeled by master sculptor Gerhard Skrobek in 1987 and carries a 1987 incised copyright date. It is found only in TMK-6.

Hum 484: Peace On Earth 1990 Christmas ornament.

Hum No.	Basic Size	Trademark	Current Value
484	3-1/4″	TMK-6	$75-$80

Hum 485: A Gift From a Friend

This little fellow, crafted by master sculptor Gerhard Skrobek in 1988, was offered exclusively to members of the M.I. Hummel club in the club year 1991-1992. Its availability to members at $160 with redemption card was subject to the cut-off date of May 31, 1993. It carries a 1988 incised copyright date and special decaled club inscription: "EXCLUSIVE EDITION 1991/92 M.I. HUMMEL CLUB." A large black bumblebee is located on the bottom.

This figurine is found in both TMK-6 and TMK-7, but the older mark is slightly more valuable than the new. There are no significant variations.

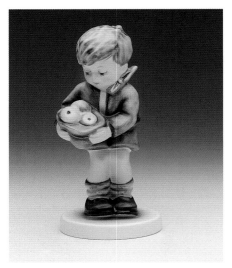

Hum 485: A Gift From a Friend.

Hum No.	Basic Size	Trademark	Current Value
485	5″	TMK-6	$170-$190
485	5″	TMK-7	$150-$180

Hum 486: I Wonder

I Wonder, which was first modeled by master sculptor Helmut Fischer in 1988, was a club exclusive offered only to members of the M.I. Hummel Club during the club year of June 1, 1990, to May 31, 1991. The figurines were offered by way of a redemption card at $140. Each piece bears the bumblebee club backstamp, as well as 1988 incised copyright date and special decaled club inscription: "EXCLUSIVE EDITION 1990/91 M.I. HUMMEL CLUB." It is found in both TMK-6 and TMK-7, but the older mark is slightly more valuable than the new.

Somehow, an estimated 300 of these escaped the factory with the erroneous year date "1991/92" on the backstamp, according to Goebel. Only time will tell if this variation becomes significant.

Hum 486: I Wonder.

I Wonder demonstration piece with TMK-7, M.I. Hummel Club special backstamp, and incised 1988 copyright date.

Hum No.	Basic Size	Trademark	Current Value
486	5-1/4″	TMK-6	$170-$190
486	5-1/4″	TMK-7	$150-$180

Hum 487: Let's Tell the World

First crafted by master sculptor Gerhard Skrobek in 1987 and released in 1990 as part of the "Century Collection", Let's Tell the World was limited to one year (1990) and the edition was listed as closed in the 1992 Goebel price list. The actual number of figures produced is not known.

Each piece bears a special backstamp commemorating the 55th anniversary of M.I. Hummel figurines and an incised 1988 copyright date. A blue decal was also applied with special inscription: "M.I. HUMMEL CENTURY COLLECTION 1990 XX" and "1935-1990 – 55 Years of M.I. Hummel Figurines." Released at $875, they are available only in TMK-6.

Hum No.	Basic Size	Trademark	Current Value
487	10-1/2" x 7"	TMK-6	$900-$1,080

Hum 487: Let's Tell the World.

Hum 488: What's That?

This figurine, modeled by master sculptor Helmut Fischer in 1988, was produced in 1997 as an exclusive preview edition for members of the M.I. Hummel Club. It carries an incised 1988 copyright date as well as TMK-7. A decal on the underside of the base reads, "EXCLUSIVE EDITION 1997/98 M.I. HUMMEL CLUB." It was originally issued to collectors at $150.

What's That? is a companion to One, Two, Three (Hum 555).

Hum No.	Basic Size	Trademark	Current Value
488	4"	TMK-7	$105-$115

Hum 488: What's That?

Hum 489: Pretty Please

This figurine, which was introduced in 1996, is part of an informal series of paired pieces called "Cozy Companions." The piece paired with this one is No Thank You (Hum 535).

Pretty Please, which was crafted by master sculptor Helmut Fischer in 1988, has an incised copyright date of 1988 and bears both the "First Issue 1996" and the "125th Anniversary" backstamps during the initial year of production. The issue price was $120.

It was temporarily withdrawn from production on June 15, 2002.

Hum No.	Basic Size	Trademark	Current Value
489	3-1/2"	TMK-7	$85-$90
489	3-1/2"	TMK-8	$135

Hum 489: Pretty Please.

Hum 490: Carefree

Another figurine in the informal annual series of paired pieces called "Cozy Companions," Carefree was paired with Free Spirit (Hum 564). First designed by master sculptor Helmut Fischer in 1988, Carefree bears an incised copyright date of 1988. Those released in the first year of production have the "First Issue 1997" backstamp. The release price was $120.

Hum No.	Basic Size	Trademark	Current Value
490	3-1/2"	TMK-7	$85-$90
490	3-1/2"	TMK-8	$135

Hum 490: Carefree.

Hum 491-492: Open Numbers

Hum 493: Two Hands, One Treat

This special 4" figurine, the design of master sculptor Helmut Fischer in 1988, was a M.I. Hummel Club exclusive. It was made available as a renewal premium, a gift, to those members renewing their membership in the club year 1991-1992. The club placed a $65 value on the piece at that time.

Two Hands, One Treat, which carries an incised 1988 copyright date, is found only with TMK-7. A special decaled club inscription reads: "M.I. HUMMEL CLUB." There is also a black flying bumblebee to signify a club piece.

Hum No.	Basic Size	Trademark	Current Value
493	4"	TMK-7	$75-$90

Hum 493: Two Hands, One Treat.

Hum 494: Open Number

Hum 495: Evening Prayer

Introduced in the fall 1991 at $95, Evening Prayer was first modeled by master sculptor Helmut Fischer in 1988. It has an incised 1988 mold induction. There are no significant variations to affect collector value, although it is noteworthy to mention that the girl is similar to Doll Mother (Hum 67).

Hum No.	Basic Size	Trademark	Current Value
495	3-3/4"	TMK-7	$80-$85
495	3-3/4"	TMK-8	$80-$85

Hum 495: Evening Prayer.

Hum 496-497: Open Numbers

Hum 498: All Smiles

This 4" figurine, modeled by master sculptor Helmut Fischer in 1988, was released in 1997 as a sequentially numbered limited edition of 25,000 pieces. The original retail price was $175. The piece carries a 1988 incised copyright date and is similar to the girl from Telling Her Secret (Hum 196), except with no pigtails and a longer dress.

Hum No.	Basic Size	Trademark	Current Value
498	4"	TMK-7	$120-$135

Hum 498: All Smiles.

Hum 499: Open Number

Hum 500: Flowers For Mother
Mother's Day Plate, Possible Future Edition

This plate was listed in the index of *M.I. Hummel: The Golden Anniversary Album*. It was not illustrated, however, and little else is known about why it has never been issued.

Hum 501-511: Doll Parts

These mold numbers were utilized to identify the heads, arms, and legs of the eight porcelain dolls released by Goebel, starting in 1984. There were eight different heads; the left and right hands were the same on each doll, which accounts for the 10 mold numbers used. Hum 501 through 508 were doll heads; Hum 509 and 511 were arms and legs; and Hum 510 was an actual doll (Carnival Doll).

Hum 512-524: Dolls

These are the mold numbers used to identify the dolls made by the Danbury Mint as well as two produced by Goebel. Since the early 1950s, Hummel dolls have been produced. These dolls were originally produced with rubber heads but changed to vinyl in 1964. Later, in 1983, the porcelain-style of doll was introduced.

Originally, the dolls were 16" tall and had the "M.I. Hummel" signature incised on the back of the neck. In 1961, however, the dolls were downsized to 10". Today they range in size from 10" to 16". Each Hummel doll is worth between $120 and $150.

Manufaktur Rödental continued the tradition of M. I. Hummel dolls in 2012 when Hum P/353: Rosi Doll was introduced in a worldwide limited edition of 99 dolls. Rosi Doll was inspired by the classic M.I. Hummel motif Ring Around the Rosie and is 14-1/2" tall. It features a ceramic head, modeled by master sculptor Marion Huschka, and a soft body made of muslin. The back of the head bears the Manufaktur Rödental trademark, model number, and edition number. The doll also comes with a certificate of authenticity.

Hum P/353: Rosi Doll.

Hum No.	Doll
Hum 512	Umbrella Girl Doll
Hum 513	Little Fiddler Doll
Hum 514	Friend or Foe? Doll
Hum 515	Kiss Me Doll
Hum 516	Merry Wanderer Doll
Hum 517	Goose Girl Doll
Hum 518	Umbrella Boy Doll
Hum 519	Ride Into Christmas Doll
Hum 520	Possible Future Edition
Hum 521	School Girl Doll (by Goebel Retailers)
Hum 522	Little Scholar Doll (by Goebel Retailers)
Hum 523	Possible Future Edition
Hum 524	Valentine Gift Doll
Hum 950	Apple Tree Girl Doll (by Goebel Retailers)
Hum 951	Apple Tree Boy Doll (by Goebel Retailers)
Hum 960	Ride Into Christmas Doll (by Goebel Retailers)
Hum P/353	Rosi Doll (Manufaktur Rödental) LE $1,599 retail

Hum 512: Umbrella Girl porcelain doll.

Hum 513: Little Fiddler porcelain doll.

Hum 514: Friend or Foe? porcelain doll.

Hum 516: Merry Wanderer porcelain doll.

Hum 517: Goose Girl porcelain doll.

Hum 518: Umbrella Boy porcelain doll.

Hum 519: Ride Into Christmas porcelain doll.

Hum 521: School Girl porcelain doll.

Hum 522: Little Scholar porcelain doll.

Hum 525-529: Open Numbers

Hum 530: Land in Sight

This large, complicated piece is very special. The design of master sculptor Gerhard Skrobek in 1988, Land in Sight is a sequentially numbered limited edition of 30,000 worldwide, released in the fall of 1991 to commemorate Columbus' discovery of America. It carries a 1988 incised copyright date and special inscription that reads: "1492 – The Quincentennial of America's Discovery." A medallion accompanies the figurine. These pieces, which were priced at $1,600 at time of release, are found only in TMK-7.

Hum No.	Basic Size	Trademark	Current Value
530	9" x 9-1/2"	TMK-7	$1,080-$1,350

Hum 530: Land in Sight.

Hum 531-532: Open Numbers

Hum 533: Ooh, My Tooth

This figurine was modeled by master sculptor Gerhard Skrobek in 1988 and first issued in 1995 with a "SPECIAL EVENT" backstamp, as it was available at district manager promotions and in-store events. It also carries an incised 1988 copyright date, and those pieces issued the first year carry the "First Issue 1995" backstamp. The original retail price was $110.

It was temporarily withdrawn from production on June 15, 2002.

Hum No.	Basic Size	Trademark	Current Value
533	3"	TMK-7	$90-$95
533	3"	TMK-8	$90-$95

Hum 533: Ooh, My Tooth.

Hum 534: A Nap

This piece was introduced as new for 1991 in the fall issue of the M.I. Hummel Club newsletter, *INSIGHTS*. It was modeled by master sculptor Gerhard Skrobek in 1988 and bears an incised 1988 copyright date. A Nap was originally released at $100.

Hum No.	Basic Size	Trademark	Current Value 5
34	2-1/4"	TMK-6	$90-$95
534	2-1/4"	TMK-7	$85-$90
534	2-1/4"	TMK-8	$150

Hum 534: A Nap.

Hum 535: No Thank You

This piece is part of an informal series of paired figurines called "Cozy Companions." Its companion piece is Pretty Please (Hum 489).

The 1996 release carried the "125th Anniversary" and "First Issue 1996" backstamps. Modeled by master sculptor Helmut Fischer in 1988, it therefore has an incised 1988 copyright date. The issue price was $120.

Hum No.	Basic Size	Trademark	Current Value
535	3-1/2"	TMK-7	$80-$85
535	3-1/2"	TMK-8	$80-$85

Hum 535: No Thank You.

Hum 536: Christmas Surprise

This figurine, modeled by master sculptor Helmut Fischer in 1988, was produced in a limited edition of 15,000 pieces and was sold exclusively by QVC in 1998. It bears a 1988 incised copyright date as well as TMK-7. Original issue price was $139.50. It came with the Hummelscape Musikfest display as a collector's set. The figurine was introduced, retired, and had its mold broken all on the same day.

An ornament variation also exists as 536/3/0/0 at 3-1/4" in TMK-8.

Hum No.	Basic Size	Trademark	Current Value
536/3/0	4"	TMK-7	$105-$120
536/3/0/0	3-1/4"	TMK-8	$50-$55

Hum 536: Christmas Surprise.

Hum 537: Open Number

Hum 538: School's Out

First crafted by master sculptor Helmut Fischer in 1988, this was a new piece for 1997. It measures 4" and has a 1988 incised copyright date. The first year of production has the "First Issue 1997" oval decal on the bottom. The original suggested retail price was $170. There are no significant variations to affect collector values.

Hum 538: School's Out.

Hum No.	Basic Size	Trademark	Current Value
538	4"	TMK-7	$115-$120
538	4"	TMK-8	$115-$120

Hum 539: Good News

This figurine, modeled by master sculptor Helmut Fischer in 1988 and thereby carrying a 1988 incised copyright date, was first released at the 1996 M.I. Hummel Club Convention in Coburg, Germany. It was issued to the U.S. market in 1997 at a retail price of $180.

Good News was a part of Goebel's Personalization Program, whereby two letters or two numbers were permanently applied by a Goebel authorized artisan.

Hum 539: Good News.

Hum No.	Basic Size	Trademark	Current Value
539	4-1/2"	TMK-7	$125-$135
539	4-1/2"	TMK-8	$125-$135

Hum 540: Best Wishes

Modeled by master sculptor Helmut Fischer in 1988 and carrying an incised 1988 copyright date, this figurine was first released at the 1996 M.I. Hummel Club Convention in Coburg, Germany, and later released in the United States in 1997. It originally retailed for $180.

As part of Goebel's "Personal Touch" program, Best Wishes could have two letters or two numbers applied by a Goebel authorized artisan. It was also a 1997 "SPECIAL EVENT" piece with a flying bumblebee decal applied to the flowers.

Hum 540: Best Wishes.

Hum No.	Basic Size	Trademark	Current Value
540	4-5/8"	TMK-7	$120-$130
540	4-5/8"	TMK-8	$200

Hum 541: Sweet As Can Be

Modeled by master sculptor Helmut Fischer in 1988, a special preview edition of this figure was offered only to members of the M.I. Hummel Club for the 17th club year. The figures were given the standard club exclusive backstamp for 1993 and were put into regular production with the regular trademark afterward.

Goebel placed a value of $125 on the figure in the spring of 1993. Each carried a 1988 incised copyright date, black club bumblebee, and special decaled inscription: "EXCLUSIVE EDITION 1993/94 M.I. HUMMEL CLUB."

The M.I. Hummel Birthday Sampler Set released in 1998 features Sweet As Can Be along with a Happy Birthday Hummelscape.

Hum 541: Sweet As Can Be.

Hum No.	Basic Size	Trademark	Current Value
541	4-1/8"	TMK-7	$105-$110
541	4-1/8"	TMK-8	$149

Hum 542: Open Number

Hum 544: Open Number

Hum 543: I'm Sorry
Possible Future Edition

I'm Sorry was modeled by master sculptor Gerhard Skrobek in 1988 and carries an incised copyright date of 1988. It depicts a little boy, eyes cast downward and arms behind his back, looking quite apologetic. At this time it is listed as a possible future edition only.

Hum 545: Come Back Soon

This figure, which was first designed by master sculptor Helmut Fischer in 1989, was first released in 1995. In the first year of production, each figure was given the special "First Issue 1995" oval decal on the bottom. These pieces have a 1989 copyright date and the TMK-7. The original issue price was $135.

For some inexplicable reason, the pieces produced after the first year are in a slightly different style from an obviously different mold. They bear a 1988 copyright date and the earlier TMK-6. It appears that Goebel produced many of the regular figurines in advance of the "First Issue" pieces released in 1995.

This figurine matches the 25th and final installation in the annual plate series.

Come Back Soon was temporarily withdrawn from production on June 15, 2002.

Hum 545: Come Back Soon.

Left: The regular production figure of Come Back Soon with TMK-6. Right: The 1995 "First Issue" version with TMK-7.

Bases of Come Back Soon showing trademarks and backstamps.

Hum No.	Basic Size	Trademark	Current Value
545	4-1/4"	TMK-6	$180-$300
545	4-1/4"	TMK-7	$110-$115
545	4-1/4"	TMK-8	$110-$115

Hum 546: Open Number

Hum 547: Bunny's Mother

Bunny's Mother was available in North America in January 2006 as part of the "Animal Friends" collection. It has an incised 2005 copyright date and TMK-8. It was also available in A Mother's Love Collector Set with a heart-shaped wooden base in spring 2006. Bunny's Mother made its initial appearance in 2005 in Europe, with a bunny backstamp.

Hum No.	Basic Size	Trademark	Current Value
547 4/0	2-3/4"	TMK-8 CE	$109

Hum 548: Flower Girl

In 1990, Flower Girl became available only to members of the M.I. Hummel Club and then only upon or after the fifth anniversary of their membership. It was modeled by master sculptor Helmut Fischer in 1989 and bears a special "EXCLUSIVE EDITION" backstamp to indicate its unique status. As with any of the club anniversary exclusives, members attained this piece by way of a redemption card. The original price was $105.

Flower Girl was retired on May 31, 2000.

Hum No.	Basic Size	Trademark	Current Value
548	4-1/2"	TMK-6	$105-$135
548	4-1/2"	TMK-7	$150-$175
548	4-1/2"	TMK-8	$150

Hum 548: Flower Girl.

Hum 549: A Sweet Offering

Modeled by master sculptor Helmut Fischer in 1992, A Sweet Offering was a M.I. Hummel Club exclusive for members only. Free to members renewing their membership for club year 1993-1994, it carries mold number 549/3/0 and has a basic size of 3-1/2". It has a 1992 copyright date and carries the inscription: "M.I. HUMMEL CLUB Membership Year 1993/94." Goebel valued the piece originally at $80.

Hum No.	Basic Size	Trademark	Current Value
549/3/0	3-1/2"	TMK-7	$90-$95

Hum 549: A Sweet Offering.

Hum 550, 551, 552: Open Numbers

Hum 553: Scamp

The design of master sculptor Helmut Fischer in 1989, Scamp was new in 1992. It has a basic size of 3-1/2" and an incised copyright date of 1989. The original suggested retail price was $95. It is considered a companion piece to Pixie (Hum 768) as part of the "Cozy Companions" series.

There are no known significant variations, but it is interesting to note the similarity to Max in Hum 123.

Hum No.	Basic Size	Trademark	Current Value
553	3-1/2"	TMK-7	$90-$135
553	3-1/2"	TMK-8	$90-$135

Hum 553: Scamp.

Hum 554: Cheeky Fellow

Cheeky Fellow, which was modeled by master sculptor Helmut Fischer in 1989 and similar to Moritz in Hum 123, was offered in a special preview edition exclusively to members of the M.I. Hummel Club for the 1992-1993 club year. Figures produced that year were given the standard club exclusive backstamp. Those produced later became regular production pieces and no longer had the special marking. Each carries a 1989 incised copyright date. Goebel placed a value of $120 on the figure when released.

Hum No.	Basic Size	Trademark	Current Value
554	4-1/8"	TMK-7	$90-$135
554	4-1/8"	TMK-8	$90-$135

Hum 554: Cheeky Fellow.

Hum 555: One, Two, Three

One, Two, Three, modeled by master sculptor Helmut Fischer in 1989, was released in 1996. It was an exclusive edition available to members of the M.I. Hummel Club only and therefore carries special club backstamp and the following inscription on a blue decal: "EXCLUSIVE EDITION 1996/97 M.I. HUMMEL CLUB." It has an incised copyright date of 1989. One, Two, Three was released at $145. The 1997 companion piece is What's That? (Hum 488).

Hum No.	Basic Size	Trademark	Current Value
555	3-7/8"	TMK-7	$90-$150

Hum 555: One, Two, Three.

Hum 556: One Plus One

One Plus One was first made available in a limited form. Although it was released in 1993, it was not made available through normal channels, but rather only at authorized dealer promotions that were billed as district manager promotions in the United States and Canadian artist promotions in Canada. The figures were made available for purchase by anyone interested on a first-come, first-served basis.

Hum No.	Basic Size	Trademark	Current Value
556	4″	TMK-7	$105-$120 special event
556	4″	TMK-7	$105-$115
556	4″	TMK-8	$105-$115

These pieces, first crafted by master sculptor Helmut Fischer in 1989, bear a "SPECIAL EVENT" backstamp, along with the regular markings (1989 incised copyright date), to indicate they were part of the promotion.

They sold for $115 at these events, were in regular production for a time, and are now temporarily withdrawn from production.

Hum 556: One Plus One.

Hum 557: Strum Along

Strum Along was first issued in 1995 to members of the M.I. Hummel Club. Modeled by master sculptor Helmut Fischer in 1989, this figurine has a 1989 incised copyright date. It carries the inscription: "EXCLUSIVE EDITION 1995/96 M.I. HUMMEL CLUB." The issue price in 1995 was $135.

Strum Along was later reintroduced as an open edition without "exclusive edition" wording on the backstamp.

Hum No.	Basic Size	Trademark	Current Value
557	3-7/8″	TMK-7	$105-$155
557	3-7/8″	TMK-8	$155
557/III	13″	TMK-9	$2,300-$3,100

In 2009 Manufaktur Rödental redesigned Strum Along as a set with Hum 558/III: Little Troubadour. A mixed media figurine in a new size of 13", it features a yellow ribbon with a red stripe down the center attached to the girl's mandolin. The set of both figurines together is a closer match to Sister Hummel's original artwork. A ceramic plaque with a wooden easel for display of the original artwork is included.

Hum 557: Strum Along.

Hum 558: Little Troubadour

Released in 1994, this figurine, modeled by master sculptor Helmut Fischer in 1989, has an incised 1989 copyright date. It was an exclusive edition reserved for members of the M.I. Hummel Club, and it bears the special club backstamp and special decaled inscription: "EXCLUSIVE EDITION 1994/95 M.I. HUMMEL CLUB." The original issue price was $130.

In 2009 Manufaktur Rödental redesigned Little Troubadour as a set with Hum 557/III: Strum Along. A mixed media figurine in a new size of 13", it features a yellow ribbon with a red stripe down the center attached to the boy's mandolin. The set of both figurines together is a closer match to Sister Hummel's original artwork. A ceramic plaque with a wooden easel for display of the original artwork is included.

Hum 558: Little Troubadour.

Hum No.	Basic Size	Trademark	Current Value
558	4-1/8″	TMK-7	$90-$145
558	4-1/8″	TMK-8	$90-$145
558/III	13″	TMK-9	$2,300-$3,100

Hum 557III and Hum 558/III: Strum Along and Little Troubadour set.

Hum 559: Heart and Soul

This figurine, which was first designed by master sculptor Helmut Fischer in 1988, is part of an informal annual series of paired figurines called "Cozy Companions." It is paired with From the Heart (Hum 761).

Released in 1996, Heart and Soul has an incised copyright date of 1989. Those produced in 1996 will bear both the "First Issue 1996" and the "125th Anniversary" back stamps. The suggested retail price at release was $120.

Hum No.	Basic Size	Trademark	Current Value
559	3-5/8"	TMK-7	$90-$135
559	3-5/8"	TMK-8	$90-$135

Hum 559: Heart and Soul.

Hum 560: Lucky Fellow

Modeled by master sculptor Helmut Fischer in 1989, this figure was given free to members who renewed their membership in the club year 1992-1993. Lucky Fellow carries a 1989 copyright date and the inscription: "M.I. HUMMEL CLUB." Goebel valued it at $75 when first released.

Hum No.	Basic Size	Trademark	Current Value
560	3-5/8"	TMK-7	$60-$90

Hum 560: Lucky Fellow.

Hum 561: Grandma's Girl

Modeled by master sculptor Helmut Fischer in 1989, Grandma's Girl was first released in 1990. It carries a 1989 incised copyright date and is essentially a smaller version of the same girl as the one on Going Home (Hum 383). The original price at time of release was $100.

In 1993, on the day after the first M.I. Hummel Club Convention, a special meeting was held for local chapter members from all over the United States and Canada. Each member of the 650 attending was given either Hum 561: Grandma's Girl or Hum 562: Grandpa's Boy. On the side of each base was the inscription: "1993 – M.I. Hummel Club Convention." Goebel master sculptor Gerhard Skrobek also signed each figurine.

The year 2011 marked the celebration of Sister Hummel's 75th anniversary of the beginning of her legacy. Manufaktur Rödental selected 50 figurines to bear the "75th Anniversary" backstamp. Grandma's Girl was one of those figurines. Only 75 of them were available in North America with this backstamp. Each figurine was hand-numbered with a golden backstamp and a map of North America backstamp. A special porcelain plaque was included, and a notable emblem on the packaging hinted at the contents. Each figurine included a "75 Years of M.I. Hummel" certificate.

Hum 561: Grandma's Girl.

Hum No.	Basic Size	Trademark	Current Value
561	4"	TMK-6	$110-$150
561	4"	TMK-7	$110-$150
561	4"	TMK-8	$180

Hum 562: Grandpa's Boy

Modeled by master sculptor Helmut Fischer in 1989, this piece was first released in 1990. It carries a 1989 incised copyright date and is essentially a smaller version of the same boy from Going Home (Hum 383). The original price at time of release was $100.

In 1993, on the day after the first M.I. Hummel Club Convention, a special meeting was held for local chapter members from all over the United States and Canada. Each member of the 650 attending was given either Hum 561: Grandma's Girl or Hum 562: Grandpa's Boy. On the side of each base was the inscription: "1993 – M.I. Hummel Club Convention." Goebel master sculptor Gerhard Skrobek also signed each figurine.

The year 2011 marked the celebration of Sister Hummel's 75th anniversary of the beginning of her legacy. Manufaktur Rödental selected 50 figurines to bear the "75th Anniversary" backstamp. Grandpa's Boy was one of those figurines. Only 75 of them were available in North America with this backstamp. Each figurine was hand-numbered with a golden backstamp and a map of North America backstamp. A special porcelain plaque was included, and a notable emblem on the packaging hinted at the contents. Each figurine included a "75 Years of M.I. Hummel" certificate.

Hum 562: Grandpa's Boy.

Hum No.	Basic Size	Trademark	Current Value
562	4-1/4"	TMK-6	$120-$150
562	4-1/4"	TMK-7	$110-$150
562	4-1/4"	TMK-8	$180

Hum 563: Little Visitor

Little Visitor, modeled by master sculptor Helmut Fischer in 1991, has the mold number 563/0, indicating that another size might be offered. This one measures 5-1/8" and has an incised 1991 copyright date.

Little Visitor was a M.I. Hummel Club exclusive available only to club members. It was released in 1994 and bears the special club backstamp, as well as the inscription: "EXCLUSIVE EDITION 1994/95 M.I. HUMMEL CLUB." The original price to members was $180.

Hum No.	Basic Size	Trademark	Current Value
563/0	5-1/8"	TMK-7	$120-$125

Hum 563: Little Visitor.

Hum 564: Free Spirit

Free Spirit was part of the "Cozy Companions" informal annual series of paired figurines. The pair for this piece is Carefree (Hum 490).

Free Spirit, modeled by master sculptor Helmut Fischer in 1988, has an incised copyright date of 1988 and a "First Issue 1997" backstamp. Both this figure and Carefree were released in the fall of 1996; Free Spirit was then priced at $120.

Hum No.	Basic Size	Trademark	Current Value
564	3-1/2"	TMK-7	$90-$135
564	3-1/2"	TMK-8	$135

Hum 564: Free Spirit.

Hum 565: Open Number

Hum 566: The Angler

Modeled by master sculptor Gerhard Skrobek in 1989, this figure was released in 1995 at $320. It measures nearly 6" and bears a 1989 incised copyright date. Each figure produced during 1995 bears the "First Issue 1995" backstamp.

Hum No.	Basic Size	Trademark	Current Value
566	5-7/8"	TMK-7	$240-$245
566	5-7/8"	TMK-8	$240-$245

Hum 566: The Angler.

Hum 567-568: Open Numbers

Hum 569: A Free Flight

A Free Flight was released in 1993 and carries a 1989 incised copyright date. Modeled by master sculptor Gerhard Skrobek in 1989, this piece was issued with a "First Edition 1993" oval decal on the underside. Retail price when issued was $185.

A special Canadian piece was produced with the words "O Canada" on the front of the base with a maple leaf on the front of the boy's paper. The retail price for this special edition was about $200.

A Free Flight was temporarily withdrawn from production on June 15, 2002.

Hum No.	Basic Size	Trademark	Current Value
569	4-3/4"	TMK-7	$125-$145
569	4-3/4"	TMK-8	$125-$145

Hum 569: A Free Flight.

Hum 570: Open Number

Hum 571: Angelic Guide
1991 Christmas Ornament

This ornament, modeled by master sculptor Gerhard Skrobek, was released in 1991 with an incised copyright date of 1989. It was the fourth in the annual series of M.I. Hummel figural ornaments. It has a metal ring atop the angel's head for hanging as an ornament. The issue price in 1991 was $95.

Hum No.	Basic Size	Trademark	Current Value
571	4″	TMK-6	$95-$120
571	4″	TMK-7	$85-$110

Hum 571: Angelic Guide 1991 Christmas ornament.

Hum 572: Country Devotion
Possible Future Edition

Modeled by Gerhard Skrobek in 1989, Country Devotion has an incised 1989 copyright date. It depicts a boy and girl standing at the foot of a country shrine. The girl has her head bowed and hands folded in prayer, and a basket of flowers hangs from her left arm. The boy, who is significantly smaller, holds his hat in his hands while he gazes upward. A small coniferous tree and wooden fence also adorn the base next to the shrine. At this time it is still listed as a possible future edition.

A rare model of Country Devotion, with TMK-6 and the copyright date of 1989, appeared on eBay in February 2013. The master painter sign was Neu7/89. The figurine sported a tag from Goebel noting "MODELL Falsch," meaning "model wrong," and also that it was a PFE. It measured 10-3/4". This rare model of Country Devotion was auctioned for $4,649.

Hum 573: Loving Wishes/Will You Be Mine?

This figurine goes by two names. Will You Be Mine was issued in 2004 in Europe with an incised 2002 copyright date and a "First Issue 2004" backstamp. Loving Wishes, a limited edition of 10,000, was available with the Loving Letters Hummelscape in North America. It features an incised 2002 copyright date and Special Edition and bouquet backstamps.

Hum 573: Will You Be Mine?

Hum No.	Basic Size	Trademark	Current Value
573 2/0	4-1/2″	TMK-8 OE	$219

Hum 574: Rock-A-Bye

Rock-A-Bye is the "Century Collection" piece for 1994, the ninth piece in the series. Production in the 20th century was limited to only that one year. The figure has a special Century Collection backstamp, incised 1991 copyright date, TMK-7, and special decaled inscription: "M.I. HUMMEL CENTURY COLLECTION 1994 XX." Modeled by master sculptor Helmut Fischer in 1991, the original 1994 issue price was $1,150.

Hum 574: Rock-A-Bye.

Hum No.	Basic Size	Trademark	Current Value
574	7-1/2″	TMK-7	$840-$960

Hum 575-582, 585, 586: Angels of Christmas
Ornament Series

This series of ornaments was modeled by master sculptor Helmut Fischer in 1988 and made by Goebel in 1990 for mail-order distribution by the Danbury Mint. The figures were made in full color for Danbury. Each carries an incised "M.I. Hummel" signature and TMK-6, but no incised model number.

In 1992, Goebel made these pieces available as the Christmas Angels, but the finish is different. These small ornaments appear to have been made from the same molds as the Danbury Mint pieces, but they are rendered in white overglaze with only their eyes and lips painted in color (in the same fashion as the "Expressions of Youth" series). The wing tips are flashed in 14-karat gold.

Hum No.	Name	Size	Current Value (Color)	Current Value (White)
Hum 575	Heavenly Angel	3"	$45-$50 (TMK-6)	$40 (TMK-7)
Hum 576	Festival Harmony With Mandolin	3"	$45-$50 (TMK-6)	$40 (TMK-7)
Hum 577	Festival Harmony With Flute	3"	$45-$50 (TMK-6)	$40 (TMK-7)
Hum 578	Celestial Musician	3"	$45-$50 (TMK-6)	$40 (TMK-7)
Hum 579	Song of Praise	2-1/2"	$45-$50 (TMK-6)	$40 (TMK-7)
Hum 580	Angel With Lute	2-1/2"	$45-$50 (TMK-6)	$40 (TMK-7)
Hum 581	Prayer of Thanks	3"	$45-$50 (TMK-6)	$40 (TMK-7)
Hum 582	Gentle Song	3"	$45-$50 (TMK-6)	$40 (TMK-7)
Hum 585	Angel in Cloud	2-1/2"	$45-$50 (TMK-6)	$40 (TMK-7)
Hum 586	Angel With Trumpet	2-1/2"	$45-$50 (TMK-6)	$40 (TMK-7)

Hum 575-582, 585, 586: Angels of Christmas ornament series.

Hum 583, 584, 587-595: Open Numbers

Hum 596: Thanksgiving Prayer
Christmas Ornament

Modeled by master sculptor Helmut Fischer in 1995, Thanksgiving Prayer was first released in 1997 without an incised copyright date. It does, however, have an incised model number of 596, as well as an oval "First Issue 1997" sticker on the lower part of the gown. The issue price in 1997 was $120.

Hum No.	Basic Size	Trademark	Current Value
596	3"	TMK-7	$80-$85

Hum 596: Thanksgiving Prayer ornament.

Hum 597: Echoes of Joy
Christmas Ornament

Master sculptor Helmut Fischer modeled Echoes of Joy in 1996. The ornament was first released in 1997 with a "First Issue 1998" sticker attached. An incised "M.I. Hummel" signature appeared on the backside. The issue price was $120 in 1997.

This ornament was temporarily withdrawn from production on June 15, 2002, as were the Echoes of Joy figurines (Hum 642/0 and 642/4/0).

Hum No.	Basic Size	Trademark	Current Value
597	2-3/4" to 3"	TMK-7	$80-$85

Hum 597: Echoes of Joy ornament.

Hum 598: Joyful Noise
Christmas Ornament

Master sculptor Helmut Fischer modeled Joyful Noise in 1995. The ornament was first released in 1998 with a "First Issue 1999" oval sticker. An incised "M.I. Hummel" signature appears on the backside. The issue price was $120 in 1998.

It was temporarily withdrawn from production on June 15, 2002.

Hum No.	Basic Size	Trademark	Current Value
598	2-3/4" to 3"	TMK-7	$80-$85

Hum 598: Joyful Noise ornament.

Hum 599: Light the Way
Christmas Ornament

Modeled by master sculptor Helmut Fischer in 1995, Light the Way was first released in 2000 with a "First Issue 2000" oval sticker. An incised "Hummel" signature appeared on the backside. The issue price was $120 in 1999.

This ornament was temporarily withdrawn from production on June 15, 2002, as were both sizes of the Light the Way figurine (Hum 715/4/0 and 715/0).

Hum No.	Basic Size	Trademark	Current Value
599	2-3/4" to 3"	TMK-7	$80-$85

Hum 599: Light the Way ornament.

Hum 600: We Wish You the Best

Modeled by master sculptor Helmut Fischer in 1989, We Wish You the Best was the sixth figurine in the "Century Collection," produced as a limited edition for one year. It has an incised 1989 copyright date and circular inscription on a blue decal reading: "M.I. HUMMEL CENTURY COLLECTION 1991 XX." The issue price in 1991 was $1,300.

Hum No.	Basic Size	Trademark	Current Value
600	8-1/4" x 9-1/2"	TMK-6	$1,140-$1,260
600	8-1/4" x 9-1/2"	TMK-7	$1,050-$1,140

Hum 600: We Wish You the Best.

Hum 601-607: Open Numbers

Hum 608: Blossom Time

A 1996 release, Blossom Time has the "125th Anniversary" and the "First Issue 1996" backstamps. Modeled by master sculptor Helmut Fischer in 1989, it measures 3-1/8" and has an incised copyright date of 1990. The original release price was $155.

Hum No.	Basic Size	Trademark	Current Value
608	3-1/8"	TMK-7	$105-$130
608	3-1/8"	TMK-8	$105-$130

Hum 608: Blossom Time.

Hum IV/608: Blossom Time
Music Box

Modeled by master sculptor Helmut Fischer, Blossom Time music box was issued in 1999 at $250. It carries a 1999 incised copyright date and was produced in a limited edition of only 500 pieces that were sold exclusively through the former Hummel Museum in New Braunfels, Texas. The box played "Edelweiss."

Hum No.	Basic Size	Trademark	Current Value
IV/608	5-1/2"	TMK-7	$180-$240

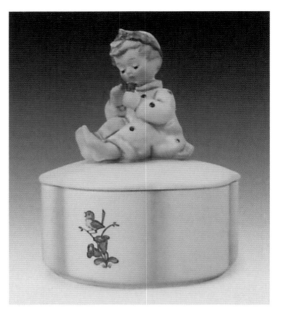

Hum IV/608: Blossom Time music box.

Hum 609: Open Number

Hum 610: April Showers

Master sculptor Helmut Fischer modeled April Showers in 1989 as a 9-3/8" figure. It carries a 1990 incised copyright date and depicts a boy and girl huddled beneath an umbrella while sitting on a wooden fence. It was first released in spring 2005 as an exclusive edition for the 2005/2006 club year for members of the M.I. Hummel Club. It features a "Special April Showers" backstamp in addition to the incised 1990 copyright date, TMK-8, and "Special Edition 2005 M.I Hummel Club" backstamp. It is a sequentially numbered figurine.

Hum No.	Basic Size	Trademark	Current Value
610	9-1/2"	TMK-8 EE	$450

Hum 610: April Showers.

Hum 611: Sunny Song
Possible Future Edition

Modeled by master sculptor Helmut Fischer in 1989 as a 5-1/8" figurine, Sunny Song portrays a girl singing and holding flowers while a boy sits next to her playing a horn. It bears a 1990 incised copyright date. At this time it is listed as a possible future edition only.

Hum 612: Lazybones

Modeled by master sculptor Helmut Fischer in 1989 as a 3-7/8" figurine with an incised 1990 copyright date, Lazybones is listed as a possible future edition. It features a boy lying on his stomach gazing at a bird perched on a plant.

Hum No.	Basic Size	Trademark	Current Value
612 2/0	3-1/4"	TMK-8 OE	$259

Hum 613: What's Up?
Possible Future Edition

Modeled by master sculptor Helmut Fischer in 1989 as a 5-1/2" figure, What's Up? depicts a boy sitting casually on a bench. The figurine has a 1990 incised copyright date. At this time it is listed as a possible future edition only.

Hum 614: Harmonica Player
Possible Future Edition

Harmonica Player, modeled by master sculptor Helmut Fischer in 1989, depicts a boy playing a harmonica. It measures 5-1/2" and has a 1990 incised copyright date. It is currently listed as a possible future edition only.

Hum 615: Private Conversation

Modeled by master sculptor Helmut Fischer in 1989, this figurine was put into production as an exclusive edition for members of the M.I. Hummel Club. This figurine has a 1990 incised copyright date and decal inscription: "EXCLUSIVE EDITION 1999/2000 M.I. HUMMEL CLUB." The issue price was $260 and was not available after May 2000.

Hum No.	Basic Size	Trademark	Current Value
615	4-1/2"	TMK-7	$160-$200

Hum 615: Private Conversation.

Hum 616: Parade of Lights

This 6" figurine, released in 1993, seems to be a cousin of Carnival (Hum 328). Designed by master sculptor Helmut Fischer, Parade of Lights has an incised copyright date of 1990 and "First Issue 1993" backstamp the first year it was released. The original issue price was $235.

Hum No.	Basic Size	Trademark	Current Value
616	6"	TMK-7	$210-$250
616	6"	TMK-8	$285

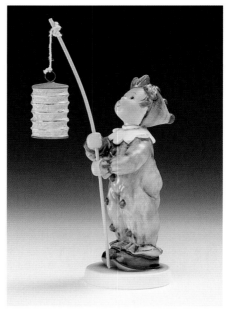

Hum 616: Parade of Lights.

Hum 617: Open Number

Hum 618: A Basket of Gifts

Master sculptor Helmut Fischer modeled A Basket of Gifts in 1990. Released in 2002, it carries a "First Issue 2002" backstamp, 1990 incised copyright date, and TMK-8.

Hum No.	Basic Size	Trademark	Current Value
618	5-1/4"	TMK-8	$375

Hum 618: A Basket of Gifts.

Hum 619: Garden Gift

Garden Gift, sculpted by master sculptor Helmut Fischer, was issued in fall 2003 and has a "First Issue 2004" backstamp, incised 2003 copyright date, and TMK-8.

A limited edition of 150 Arbeitsmuster Editions were available in October 2003 to members of the M.I. Hummel Club in North America. These editions have an incised 2003 copyright date, "First Issue 2004" backstamp, and TMK-8.

Hum No.	Basic Size	Trademark	Current Value
619	4-3/4"	TMK-8 OE	$279

Hum 619: Garden Gift.

Hum 620: A Story From Grandma

Goebel introduced this relatively large, complicated 8" figurine as an M.I. Hummel Club exclusive in 1995. It was a companion piece to At Grandpa's (Hum 621), which was introduced a year earlier. If you bought At Grandpa's, you were given the opportunity to reserve A Story from Grandma with the same sequential limited edition number as the first. Once these reserved pieces were sold, the figurine was released to the general membership of the club. A Story From Grandma was limited to 10,000 pieces worldwide. Modeled by the Goebel team of artists in 1993, it carries an incised copyright date of that year. It was released at $1,300.

Hum No.	Basic Size	Trademark	Current Value
620	8"	TMK-7	$900-$1,600

Hum 620: A Story From Grandma.

Hum 621: At Grandpa's

In 1994, Goebel announced production of the first M.I. Hummel figurine to feature an adult. Modeled by the Goebel team of artists in 1993, At Grandpa's was introduced in a limited edition of 10,000 sequentially numbered pieces for exclusive sale to members of the M.I. Hummel Club. The edition was limited in sale "from June 1, 1994 until May 31, 1995, or unless the edition is sold out." Each bears the club exclusive backstamp, incised 1993 copyright date, and was released at $1,300.

A companion piece, A Story From Grandma (Hum 620), was released the following year.

Hum No.	Basic Size	Trademark	Current Value
621	9"	TMK-7	$900-$1,600

Hum 621: At Grandpa's.

Hum 622: Light Up the Night
1992 Christmas Ornament

Light Up the Night was another in the annual series of ornaments. Modeled by master sculptor Gerhard Skrobek in 1990, it was released in 1w992 as the fifth edition to the series. It has an incised 1990 copyright date and was issued at $95.

Hum No.	Basic Size	Trademark	Current Value
622	3-1/4"	TMK-7	$90-$150

Hum 622: Light Up the Night 1992 Christmas ornament.

Hum 623: Herald on High
1993 Christmas Ornament

Herald on High was another in the annual series of ornaments. Modeled by master sculptor Gerhard Skrobek in 1990, the ornament was released in 1993 as the sixth and final issue in the series. The ornament has a "Final Issue" decal. The issue price in 1993 was $155.

Hum No.	Basic Size	Trademark	Current Value
623	2-3/4" x 4-1/2"	TMK-7	$90-$150

Hum 623: Herald on High 1993 Christmas ornament.

Hum 624: Fresh Blossoms

Fresh Blossoms is one of four figurines in the "Heart of Hummel" collection and features a heart backstamp and TMK-8. It was first issued in 2006 in a limited edition of 5,000. The other pieces in the collection are Hum 908: Gone-A-Wandering, Hum 2235: Lucky Friend, and Hum 2237: Sunday Stroll.

Hum No.	Basic Size	Trademark	Current Value
624	4-1/2"	TMK-8 LE	$199

Hum 624: Fresh Blossoms.

Hum 625: Goose Girl

Vase

Goose Girl vase was modeled by master sculptor Helmut Fischer and released in 1997 in combination with the small size 47/3/0 Goose Girl figurine.

This porcelain vase features a bas-relief design of the Goose Girl motif and has a 1989 copyright date. The issue price for the combination figurine and vase was $200.

Hum No.	Basic Size	Trademark	Current Value
625	4" x 3-1/2"	TMK-7	$50-$75

Hum 625: Goose Girl vase.

Hum 626: I Didn't Do It

I Didn't Do It, modeled by master sculptor Helmut Fischer in 1992 with a basic size of 5-1/2", was the M.I. Hummel Club exclusive offering for the club year 1993-1994. It was available for $175 to members with redemption cards. It has the special club exclusive backstamp, 1992 incised copyright date, and inscription on a decal under the base that reads: "EXCLUSIVE EDITION 1993/94 M.I. HUMMEL CLUB."

Hum No.	Basic Size	Trademark	Current Value
626	5-1/2"	TMK-7	$150-$225

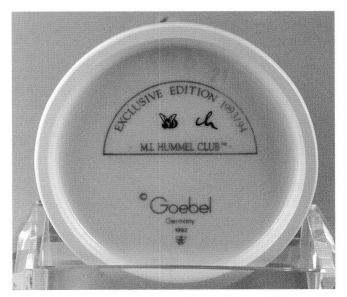

Base of I Didn't Do It showing the M.I. Hummel Club special backstamp.

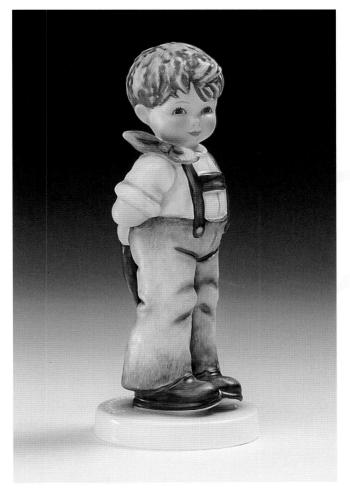

Hum 626: I Didn't Do It.

Hum 627: Open Number

Hum 628: Gentle Fellowship

Modeled by master sculptor Helmut Fischer in 1992, Gentle Fellowship was released in 1995 as the third and final figurine issued in the "UNICEF Commemorative Series." This piece bears the special UNICEF backstamp and has an incised 1992 copyright date. It is the only M.I. Hummel figurine to date that depicts two black African children. The design was taken from a drawing made during the 1930s when the Siessen Convent was beginning to develop missionary work in Africa.

The figurine was limited in production to 25,000 sequentially numbered pieces. The suggested retail price at release was $550.

As with the two previous figures in the series, for each one sold, a $25 donation was made to the United States Committee for UNICEF.

Hum 628: Gentle Fellowship.

Base of Gentle Fellowship showing the special backstamp.

Hum No.	Size	Trademark	Retail Value
628	5-3/4"	TMK-7	$360-$500

Hum 629: From Me to You

This figurine, which was modeled by master sculptor Helmut Fischer in 1992, was given to members of the M.I. Hummel Club who renewed their membership for the 1995-1996 club year. It measures 3-1/2" and has a 1992 incised copyright date. At the time of release, the club valued it at $85. It bears the special inscription, applied by decal, that reads: "M.I. HUMMEL CLUB Membership Year 1995/96."

Hum 629: From Me to You.

Hum No.	Size	Trademark	Current Value
629	3-1/2"	TMK-7	$80-$125

Hum 630: For Keeps

Modeled by master sculptor Helmut Fischer in 1992, For Keeps measures 3-1/2" and bears an incised copyright date of 1992. It was the renewal premium given free to members of the M.I. Hummel Club when they renewed their membership for the club year 1994-1995. It has the special inscription: "M.I. HUMMEL CLUB Membership Year 1994/95."

Hum 630: For Keeps.

Hum No.	Size	Trademark	Current Value
630	3-1/2"	TMK-7	$80-$125

Hum 631: Open Number

Hum 632: At Play

Modeled by master sculptor Helmut Fischer in 1990, At Play was released in 1998 exclusively for members of the M.I. Hummel Club. A special decal on the underside reads: "EXCLUSIVE EDITION 1998/99 M.I. HUMMEL CLUB." The issue price in 1998 was $260. It is now listed as a closed edition.

Hum No.	Size	Trademark	Current Value
632	3-1/2"	TMK-7	$170-$200

Hum 632: At Play.

Hum 633: I'm Carefree

Modeled by master sculptor Helmut Fischer in 1990 and released in 1994, I'm Carefree carries an incised copyright date of 1990.

When the piece was first released, the M.I. Hummel signature was located on the rear of the wagon. Later, the signature was moved to the backside of the piece, beneath the bird. It is thought that fewer than 1,000 of these were produced with the signature on the rear end of the wagon, and this "rear signature" variation brings a premium on the secondary market.

All the figurines produced in 1994 bear the "First Issue 1994" backstamp. The issue price was $365.

I'm Carefree was temporarily withdrawn from production on June 15, 2002.

Hum No.	Size	Trademark	Current Value
633	4-3/4" x 4-1/4"	TMK-7	$480-$600 rear signature
633	4-3/4" x 4-1/4"	TMK-7	$265-$300 side signature
633	4-3/4" x 4-1/4"	TMK-8	$265-$300

Hum 633: I'm Carefree.

Hum 634: Sunshower

Modeled by master sculptor Helmut Fischer in 1990, Sunshower was produced as a limited edition of 10,000 pieces to commemorate the 60th anniversary of Hum 71: Stormy Weather. It carries a 1990 incised copyright date. It was released as Hum 634/2/0 in 1997 at an issue price of $360.

Hum No.	Size	Trademark	Current Value
634/2/0	4-1/2"	TMK-7	$280-$359
634/2/0	4-1/2"	TMK-8	$359

Hum 634: Sunshower.

Hum 635: Welcome Spring

Welcome Spring is the 1993 "Century Collection" piece. It was modeled by master sculptor Helmut Fischer in 1990 and bears an incised 1990 copyright date. Production was limited to that one year during the 20th century. The figure is marked so on the base and comes with a certificate of authenticity. The decal inscription on the underside of the base reads: "M.I. HUMMEL CENTURY COLLECTION 1993 XX." The release price was $1,085.

Hum No.	Size	Trademark	Current Value
635	12-1/4"	TMK-7	$960-$1,100

Hum 635: Welcome Spring.

Hum 636-637: Open Numbers

Hum 638: The Botanist

Vase

Modeled by master sculptor Helmut Fischer, this porcelain vase has a bas-relief image of The Botanist (Hum 351). The vase was sold in combination with The Botanist figurine in 1998 for $210. The vase has a fired decal with a 1997 copyright date and incised "M.I. Hummel" signature.

Hum No.	Size	Trademark	Current Value
638	4" x 3-1/2"	TMK-7	$50-$75

Hum 638: The Botanist vase.

Hum 639-640: Open Numbers

Hum 641: Thanksgiving Prayer

Modeled by master sculptor Helmut Fischer in 1991 and 1995, Thanksgiving Prayer is a miniature-size figurine with the mold number 641/0. Several pieces are released each year, each with the same theme, to form a Christmas group consisting of a mini-figurine, Christmas tree ornament, bell, and plate. This mini-size figurine measures 5", has a 1991 copyright date, and if produced during the first year, bears the 1995 Limited Issue backstamp. (Compare to Hum 596.) A second, even smaller

Hum No.	Size	Trademark	Current Value
641/4/0	3-1/4"	TMK-7	$80-$130
641/4/0	3-1/4"	TMK-8	$80-$130
641/0	5"	TMK-7	$120-$180
641/0	5"	TMK-8	$120-$180

size was later introduced and numbered 641/4/0. Both sizes were first sold in the United States in 1997. Original issue prices were $180 for the large size (641/0) and $120 for the smaller size (641/4/0).

Both sizes were temporarily withdrawn from production on June 15, 2002.

Hum 641: Thanksgiving Prayer.

Hum 642: Echoes of Joy

Modeled by master sculptor Helmut Fischer in 1991 and 1995, two sizes of Echoes of Joy were introduced to the U.S. market in 1997 and have a "First Issue 1998" decal fired on the underside of the base. Original issue prices were $180 for the larger size (642/0) and $120 for the smaller size (642/4/0).

Both sizes were temporarily withdrawn from production on June 15, 2002, as was the Echoes of Joy ornament (Hum 597).

Hum No.	Size	Trademark	Current Value
642/4/0	3-1/8"	TMK-7	$80-$130
642/4/0	3-1/8"	TMK-8	$80-$130
642/0	5-1/8"	TMK-7	$120-$180
642/0	5-1/8"	TMK-8	$120-$180

Hum 642: Echoes of Joy.

Hum 643: Joyful Noise

Joyful Noise was produced in two sizes. Modeled by master sculptor Helmut Fischer in 1991 and 1996, both sizes were introduced in the U.S. market in 1999 and have a "First Issue 1999" decal fired on the underside of the base. Original issue prices were $180 for the larger size (643/0) and $120 for the smaller (643/4/0) size.

Both sizes were temporarily withdrawn from production on June 15, 2002, as was the Joyful Noise ornament (Hum 598).

Hum No.	Size	Trademark	Current Value
643/4/0	3"	TMK-7	$80-$130
643/4/0	3"	TMK-8	$80-$130
643/0	5"	TMK-7	$120-$180
643/0	5"	TMK-8	$120-$180

Hum 643: Joyful Noise.

Hum 644: Open Number

Hum 645: Christmas Song
Annual Ornament

Modeled by master sculptor Helmut Fischer in 1991, Christmas Song is part of the annual ornament series. It matches a miniature figurine and Christmas plate of the same design. It carries an incised "Hummel" signature on the rear side and "125th Anniversary Goebel" on the lower part of the angel's gown. The original issue price was $115 in 1996.

Hum 645: Christmas Song annual ornament.

Hum No.	Size	Trademark	Current Value
645	3-1/4"	TMK-7	$80-$120

Hum 646: Celestial Musician
Annual Ornament

Modeled by master sculptor Gerhard Skrobek in 1991, Celestial Musician is part of the annual ornament series. It matches a miniature figurine and Christmas plate of the same design. The original issue price was $90 in 1993. It carries an incised "Hummel" signature on rear side.

Hum 646: Celestial Musician 1993 annual ornament.

Hum No.	Size	Trademark	Current Value
646	2-7/8"	TMK-7	$80-$100

Hum 647: Festival Harmony With Mandolin
Annual Ornament

Modeled by master sculptor Helmut Fischer in 1991, Festival Harmony With Mandolin is part of the annual ornament series. It matches a miniature figurine and Christmas plate of the same design. It carries an incised "Hummel" signature on the rear side. The original issue price was $95 when first released in the United States in 1994.

Hum No.	Size	Trademark	Current Value
647	2-3/4"	TMK-7	$80-$100

Hum 647: Festival Harmony With Mandolin annual ornament.

Hum 648: Festival Harmony With Flute

Annual Ornament

Modeled by master sculptor Helmut Fischer in 1991, Festival Harmony With Flute is part of the annual ornament series. It matches a miniature figurine and Christmas plate in the same design. It carries an incised "Hummel" signature on the rear side. The original issue price was $100 when issued in 1995.

Hum No.	Size	Trademark	Current Value
648	2-3/4″	TMK-7	$80-$100

Hum 648: Festival Harmony With Flute annual ornament.

Hum 649: Fascination

Modeled by master sculptor Helmut Fischer in 1990, Fascination was produced as a limited edition of 25,000 sequentially numbered pieces to commemorate Goebel's 125th anniversary. It was released in a quantity of 15,000 pieces in the United States at a retail price of $190 in 1996.

Hum No.	Size	Trademark	Current Value
649/0	4-3/4″	TMK-7	$120-$190

Hum 649: Fascination.

Hum 650-657: Open Numbers

Hum 658: Playful Blessing

Modeled by master sculptor Helmut Fischer in 1992, Playful Blessing was produced as an exclusive edition for members of the M.I. Hummel Club. Introduced in 1997, Playful Blessing has an incised 1992 copyright date and this inscription: "EXCLUSIVE EDITION 1997/98 M.I. HUMMEL CLUB." The issue price in 1997 was $260.

Hum No.	Size	Trademark	Current Value
658	3-1/2″	TMK-7	$170-$260

Hum 658: Playful Blessing.

Hum 659: Open Number

Hum 660: Fond Goodbye

This was the 12th piece in the "Century Collection." Modeled by master sculptor Helmut Fischer in 1991, it was released in the United States in 1997. During the 20th century, the edition was limited to production in 1997. The figures are marked with the Century Collection backstamp and accompanied with a certificate of authenticity. The decal inscription on the underside of the base reads: "M.I. HUMMEL CENTURY COLLECTION 1997 XX." The suggested retail price at the time of release was $1,450.

Hum No.	Size	Trademark	Current Value
660	6-7/8" x 11"	TMK-7	$960-$1,450

Hum 660: Fond Goodbye.

Hum 661: My Little Lamb

As part of the "Animal Friends" collection, My Little Lamb was offered to collectors in North America in 2006. It featured an incised 2005 copyright date, standing lamb backstamp, and TMK-8.

The figurine was available in Europe in fall 2005 (with a standing lamb backstamp) representing spring in a "Four Seasons" collector series with Hum 2218: Springtime Friends, Hum 197/4/0: Be Patient, and Hum 2227: Morning Call.

Hum 661: My Little Lamb.

Hum No.	Size	Trademark	Current Value
661	3-1/4"	TMK-8	$119

Hum 662: Friends Together

Friends Together was released in the summer of 1993 in two basic sizes. The smaller of the two, Hum 662/0 at 4", is the regular production figure. It bears a special Commemorative Edition backstamp. The larger size, Hum 662/1 at 6", is a limited edition of 25,000 worldwide. This was the first of three cooperative fund-raising efforts between Goebel and the U.S. Committee for UNICEF. The art from which the figurine is taken was done by Sister M.I. Hummel in connection with Siessen Convent and its African missionary work during the 1930s.

The figurine was available exclusively to members of the M.I. Hummel Club on a first-come, first-served basis for roughly one month prior to its general release to the public on Sept. 3, 1993. These figures were not marked with the special club exclusive backstamp and are not considered club pieces. The suggested retail price for the 4" size at release was $260. The release price for the limited edition 6" size was $475, with $25 of that amount contributed to UNICEF.

Hum 662: Friends Together.

Hum No.	Size	Trademark	Current Value
662/0	4-1/4"	TMK-7	$210-$260
662/0	4-1/4"	TMK-8	$210-$260
662/1	6"	TMK-7	$360-$475

Hum 663-666: Open Numbers

Hum 667: Pretty as a Picture
Possible Future Edition

Modeled by master sculptor Gerhard Skrobek in 1992, Pretty as a Picture (7-1/8") has an incised 1992 copyright date. It depicts a boy and girl standing beside one another as the subject for an aspiring young boy photographer who kneels down to view the two through his camera, which is propped on a wooden tripod. It is listed as a possible future edition.

Hum 668: Strike Up the Band

Strike Up the Band, modeled by master sculptor Helmut Fischer in 1993 and released in 1995, is the 10th piece in the "Century Collection." All figures in the "Century Collection" are limited in number to those produced in one designated year of the 20th century. This piece has an incised copyright date of 1992 and special decal inscription on the base underside that reads: "M.I. HUMMEL CENTURY COLLECTION 1995 XX." The suggested retail price was $1,200 when released.

Hum No.	Size	Trademark	Current Value
668	7-3/8"	TMK-7	$840-$1,200

Hum 668: Strike Up the Band.

Hum 669-674: Kitchen Moulds

Modeled by master sculptor Helmut Fischer in 1989, six kitchen moulds were released in 1991 and distributed exclusively by the Danbury Mint in the United States. One mould was released every three months. Each bears an incised "M.I. Hummel" signature and either TMK-6 or TMK-7. The price at issue was $99 each.

Hum No.	Size	Design	Trademark	Current Value
669	7-1/2"	Baking Day	TMK-6 or 7	$99-$115
670	7-1/2"	A Fair Measure	TMK-6 or 7	$99-$115
671	7-1/2"	Sweet as Can Be	TMK-6 or 7	$99-$115
672	8"	For Father	TMK-6 or 7	$99-$115
673	8"	Supper's Coming	TMK-6 or 7	$99-$115
674	8"	Baker	TMK-6 or 7	$99-$115

Hum 669-674: kitchen moulds.

Hum 675: Open Number

Hum 676, 677: Apple Tree Girl and Apple Tree Boy
Candleholders

These candleholders were modeled by master sculptor Helmut Fischer in 1988 and distributed exclusively in the United States by the Danbury Mint in 1989. Each has a 1988 incised copyright date. The retail price at issue was $142.50 each.

Hum 676, 677: Apple Tree Girl and Apple Tree Boy candleholders.

Hum No.	Size	Trademark	Current Value
676	6-3/4"	TMK-6 or 7	$120-$150
677	6-3/4"	TMK-6 or 7	$120-$150

Hum 678, 679: She Loves Me, She Loves Me Not and Good Friends
Candleholders

Modeled by master sculptor Helmut Fischer in 1989, these candleholders were distributed exclusively in the United States by the Danbury Mint in 1990. Each has an incised 1989 copyright date. The retail price at issue was $142.50 each.

Hum 678, 679: She Loves Me Not and Good Friends candleholders.

Hum No.	Size	Trademark	Current Value
678	6-1/4"	TMK-6 or 7	$120-$150
679	6-1/4"	TMK-6 or 7	$120-$150

Hum 680-683: Open Numbers

Hum 684: Thoughtful
Trinket Box

Modeled by master sculptor Helmut Fischer in 2001 and released in 2002, this 3-1/2"-diameter round box bears the image of the figurine with the same name (Hum 415) on top of the lid, along with the "M.I. Hummel" signature. Small train images embellish the sides of the box.

Hum No.	Size	Trademark	Current Value
684	3-1/2"	TMK-8	$25-$40

Hum 684: Thoughtful trinket box.

Hum 685: Book Worm
Trinket Box

Released in 2002, this 3-1/2"-diameter round box is another design by master sculptor Helmut Fischer in 2001. It carries the image of the figurine with the same name (Hum 8) on top of the lid, along with the "M.I. Hummel" signature. Small duck images (like those in the figurine's book) embellish the sides of the box.

Hum No.	Size	Trademark	Current Value
685	3-1/2"	TMK-8	$25-$40

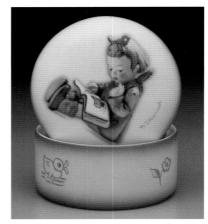

Hum 685: Book Worm trinket box.

Hum 686: Sweet Greetings
Trinket Box

Modeled by master sculptor Helmut Fischer in 2001and released in 2002, this 3-1/5" x 3-1/4" heart-shaped box bears the image of the figurine with the same name (Hum 352) on top of the lid, along with the "M.I. Hummel" signature. Small heart images embellish the sides of the box.

Hum 686: Sweet Greetings trinket box.

Hum No.	Size	Trademark	Current Value
686	3-1/2" x 3-1/4"	TMK-8	$25-$40

Hum 687: She Loves Me, She Loves Me Not
Trinket Box

Released in 2002, this 3-1/4" x 3-3/4" heart-shaped box bears the image of the figurine with the same name (Hum 174) on top of the lid, along with the "M.I. Hummel" signature. Small bird images embellish the sides of the box. It was modeled in 2001 by master sculptor Helmut Fischer.

Hum 687: She Loves Me, She Loves Me Not trinket box.

Hum No.	Size	Trademark	Current Value
687	3-1/4" x 3-3/4"	TMK-8	$25-$40

Hum 688: Umbrella Boy
Trinket Box

Modeled by master sculptor Helmut Fischer in 2001 and released in 2002, this 5"-diameter round box bears the instantly recognizable Umbrella Boy image on top of the lid, along with the "M.I. Hummel" signature. Small images of kites blowing in the wind embellish the sides of the box.

Hum No.	Size	Trademark	Current Value
688	5"	TMK-8	$25-$40

Hum 688: Umbrella Boy Trinket Box.

Hum 689: Umbrella Girl
Trinket Box

Released in 2002, this 5"-diameter round box is the same in size and shape as Hum 688 except that it has the Umbrella Girl image on top of the lid, along with the "M.I. Hummel" signature. Small images of kites blowing in the wind embellish the sides of the box. Like the other trinket boxes released that year, Umbrella Girl was designed by master sculptor Helmut Fischer in 2001.

Hum No.	Size	Trademark	Current Value
689	5"	TMK-8	$25-$40

Hum 689: Umbrella Girl trinket box.

Hum 690: Smiling Through
Wall Plaque

Hum No.	Size	Trademark	Current Value
690	5-3/4"	TMK-5	$25-$40

Modeled by master sculptor Gerhard Skrobek from an original Sister M.I. Hummel drawing, this is the second special edition produced in 1978 exclusively for members of the former Goebel Collectors' Club, now the M.I. Hummel Club. It was available only through membership in the club. Members received a redemption certificate upon receipt of their annual dues, and they could purchase the piece for $55 through dealers who were official representatives of the club.

The plaque bears TMK-5 and carries a decaled inscription that reads: 'EXCLUSIVE SPECIAL EDITION No. 2 HUM 690 FOR MEMBERS OF THE GOEBEL COLLECTORS' CLUB." As of May 31, 1984, it was no longer available as a redemption piece.

Hum 690: Smiling Through wall plaque.

Hum 691: Open Number

Hum 692: Christmas Song
1996 Annual Christmas Plate

Modeled by master sculptor Helmut Fischer in 1994, Christmas Song plate has a 1994 copyright date and an incised "M.I. Hummel" signature on the front. It was issued in 1996 as part of the annual Christmas plate series at $130.

Hum No.	Size	Trademark	Current Value
692	5-7/8"	TMK-7	$25-$40

Hum 692: Christmas Song grouping for 1996 comprising the mini-figurine, Hum 343/0, the plate, and the ornament, Hum 645.

Hum 693: Festival Harmony With Flute
1995 Annual Christmas Plate

Modeled by master sculptor Helmut Fischer in 1994, this plate was issued in 1995 as part of the annual Christmas plate series at $125. It has a 1994 copyright date and an incised "M.I. Hummel" signature on the front of the plate.

Hum No.	Size	Trademark	Current Value
693	5-7/8"	TMK-7	$25-$40

Hum 693: Festival Harmony With Flute grouping for 1995 comprising the mini-figurine, Hum 173/4/0, the plate, and the ornament, Hum 647.

Hum 694: Thanksgiving Prayer
1997 Annual Christmas Plate

Modeled by master sculptor Helmut Fischer in 1994, this plate was issued in 1997 as part of the annual Christmas plate series at $40. It has a 1995 copyright date and an incised "M.I. Hummel" signature on the front of the plate.

Hum 694: Thanksgiving Prayer 1997 annual Christmas plate.

Hum No.	Size	Trademark	Current Value
694	5-7/8"	TMK-7	$25-$40

Hum 695: Echoes of Joy
1998 Annual Christmas Plate

Modeled by master sculptor Helmut Fischer in 1996, this plate was issued in 1998 as part of the annual Christmas plate series at $145. It has a 1996 copyright date and an incised "M.I. Hummel" signature on the front of the plate.

Hum 695: Echoes of Joy 1998 annual Christmas plate.

Hum No.	Size	Trademark	Current Value
695	5-7/8"	TMK-7	$25-$60

Hum 696: Joyful Noise
1999 Annual Christmas Plate

Joyful Noise is part of the annual Christmas plate series. Modeled by master sculptor Helmut Fischer in 1995, it was issued in 1999 at $145. The plate has a 1996 copyright date and an incised "M.I. Hummel" signature on the front.

Hum 696: Joyful Noise 1999 annual Christmas plate.

Hum No.	Size	Trademark	Current Value
696	5-7/8"	TMK-7	$25-$60

Hum 697: Light the Way
2000 Annual Christmas Plate

Light the Way is part of the annual Christmas plate series. Modeled by master sculptor Helmut Fischer in 1995, it was issued at $145 in 2000. The plate has a 1996 copyright date and an incised "M.I. Hummel" signature on the front. The design is based on the figurine of the same name (Hum 715).

Hum 697: Light the Way 2000 annual Christmas plate.

Hum No.	Size	Trademark	Current Value
697	5-7/8"	TMK-7	$25-$60

Hum 698: Heart's Delight

Modeled by master sculptor Helmut Fischer in 1996, Heart's Delight was issued in 1998 for $220. It has an incised copyright date of 1996. The figurine sits on a small wooden chair.

This piece is considered part of the Kid's Club Collector's Set, which was first offered in 2002 and includes Practice Makes Perfect (Hum 771) and Love in Bloom (Hum 699). The set retailed for $650.

In February 2009, the "temporarily withdrawn" status was removed from Heart's Delight, and, to celebrate its 10th anniversary, it was featured exclusively on QVC. The figurines purchased on QVC have a 10th Anniversary backstamp.

Hum No.	Size	Trademark	Current Value
698	4"	TMK-7	$150-$220
698	4"	TMK-8 TW	$150-$220

Hum 698: Heart's Delight.

Hum 699: Love in Bloom

Modeled by master sculptor Helmut Fischer in 1996, Love in Bloom was issued in the United States in 1997 at a retail price of $220, including the wooden wagon. The figurine has an incised copyright date of 1996.

Hum No.	Size	Trademark	Current Value
699	4-1/4"	TMK-7	$150-$220
699	4-1/4"	TMK-8	$150-$220

Love in Bloom is considered a part of the Kid's Club Collector's Set, which was first offered in 2002 and includes Practice Makes Perfect (Hum 771) and Heart's Delight (Hum 698). The set retailed for $650.

Hum 699: Love In Bloom.

Hum 700-714: Annual Bells

Goebel issued annual bells from 1978 through 1992. Each bell measures 6" and has a bas-relief image on the front.

Hum No.	Design	Year	Trademark	Current Value
700	Let's Sing	1978	TMK-5	$20-$40
701	Farewell	1979	TMK-5	$20-$30
702	Thoughtful	1980	TMK-6	$20-$40
703	In Tune	1981	TMK-6	$20-$40
704	She Loves Me,	1982	TMK-6	$20-$40
705	Knit One, Purl One	1983	TMK-6	$20-$40
706	Mountaineer	1984	TMK-6	$20-$40
707	Girl With Sheet Music	1985	TMK-6	$20-$40
708	Sing Along	1986	TMK-6	$20-$40
709	With Loving Greetings	1987	TMK-6	$20-$40
710	Busy Student	1988	TMK-6	$20-$40
711	Latest News	1989	TMK-6	$20-$40
712	What's New?	1990	TMK-6	$20-$40
713	Favorite Pet	1991	TMK-6	$20-$40
714	Whistler's Duet	1992	TMK-6	$20-$40

Hum 700-714: Annual Bells.

Hum 715: Light the Way

Modeled by master sculptor Helmut Fischer in 1995, Light the Way was first released at a retail price of $120 in 1999 for the 715/4/0 size. The larger size, 715/0, was released at $180. Both carry the "First Issue 2000" backstamp, with the larger piece bearing a 1995 copyright date and the smaller an incised 1996 copyright date.

Both sizes were temporarily withdrawn from production on June 15, 2002, as was the Light the Way ornament (Hum 599).

Hum No.	Size	Trademark	Current Value
715/4/0	3"	TMK-8	$95-$130
715/0	5"	TMK-8	$110-$180

Hum 715: Light the Way.

Hum 716: Open Number

Hum 717: Valentine Gift
Display Plaque

This plaque was a M.I. Hummel Club exclusive to celebrate the 20th anniversary of the club. It is 5-1/4" high and utilizes the first club exclusive figurine design, Valentine Gift (Hum 387). It was available to any member from March 1996 through December of the same year for $250. For an extra $20, the purchaser could have it personalized.

The piece carries an incised 1995 copyright date and incised "M.I. Hummel" signature diagonally on the back.

Hum No.	Size	Trademark	Current Value
717	5-1/4" x 6-1/2"	TMK-7	$180-$250

Hum 717: Valentine Gift display plaque.

Hum 718: Heavenly Angels

Modeled by master sculptor Helmut Fischer in 1996, Heavenly Angels were released in the United States in 1999 at the retail price of $90 each. They were sold exclusively through the Danbury Mint, which added a hardwood display case at no additional charge.

Hum No.	Design	Trademark	Current Value
718/A	Let It Shine	TMK-7	$60-$90
718/B	Hush-A-Bye	TMK-7	$60-$90
718/C	Holy Offering	TMK-7	$60-$90
718/D	Join in Song	TMK-7	$60-$90
718/E	Peaceful Sounds	TMK-7	$60-$90
214/D/0	Angel Serenade	TMK-7	$60-$90

Hum 718: Heavenly Angels.

Hum 719: Open Number

Hum 720: On Parade

Modeled by master sculptor Helmut Fischer in 1994, On Parade was issued in the United States in 1998. It carries an incised 1995 copyright date and "First Issue 1998" decal backstamp in the first year of production. The retail price at time of issue was $165.

Hum No.	Size	Trademark	Current Value
720	4-3/4"	TMK-7	$165-$180
720	4-3/4"	TMK-8	$180

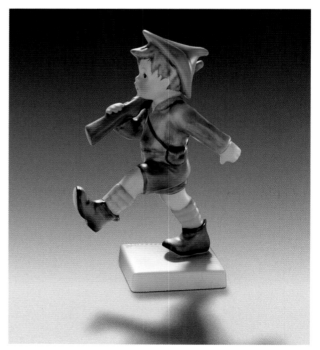

Hum 720: On Parade.

Hum 721: Trio of Wishes

Trio of Wishes is the second (1997) in a series of three called the "Trio Collection." Modeled by master sculptor Helmut Fischer in 1995, Trio of Wishes was released at $475. It has an incised 1995 copyright date and comes with a hardwood display base. Production was limited to 20,000 sequentially numbered pieces. The other two figurines in the series are Tuneful Trio (Hum 757) and Traveling Trio (Hum 787).

Hum No.	Size	Trademark	Current Value
721	4-1/2"	TMK-7	$360-$475

Hum 721: Trio of Wishes.

Hum 722: Little Visitor

Plaque

Modeled by master sculptor Helmut Fischer in 1995, Little Visitor plaque carries an incised 1995 copyright date. Produced for purchase at the visitors center at the Goebel factory in Rödental, Germany, it was available with personalization at a price of approximately $120.

Hum No.	Size	Trademark	Current Value
722	4-3/4" x 5"	TMK-7	$95-$120
722	4-3/4" x 5"	TMK-8	$120

Hum 722: Little Visitor plaque.

Hum 723: Silent Vigil

Possible Future Edition

Modeled by master sculptor Helmut Fischer in 1995, Silent Vigil bears an incised 1995 copyright date. The 6-3/4" figurine depicts a scene first used on a postcard drawing of Mary and Joseph watching over the Baby Jesus. Mary is seated on a wooden stool on one side of a cradle while Joseph stands on the other side. This piece is listed as a possible future edition.

Hum 724-725: Open Numbers

Hum 726: Soldier Boy

Plaque

Modeled by master sculptor Helmut Fischer in 1996, Soldier Boy plaque bears an incised 1996 copyright date. It was released in 1996 exclusively by the U.S. Military post exchanges as a limited edition of 7,500 pieces. The original issue price was $140.

Hum No.	Size	Trademark	Current Value
726	5-1/2" x 6-3/4"	TMK-7	$120-$140

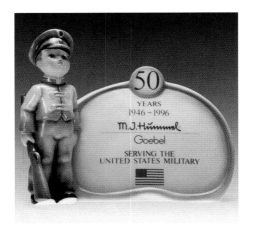

Hum 726: Soldier Boy plaque.

Hum 727: Garden Treasures

Modeled by master sculptor Helmut Fischer in 1996, Garden Treasures was released in the United States as the free gift for renewing membership in the M. I. Hummel Club for the 1998-1999 membership year. In addition to a black flying bumblebee on the bottom, the piece also has the inscription: "M.I. HUMMEL CLUB Membership year 1998/99."

Hum No.	Size	Trademark	Current Value
727	3-1/2"	TMK-7	$90-$100

Hum 727: Garden Treasures.

Hum 728: Open Number

Hum 729: Nature's Gift

Modeled by master sculptor Helmut Fischer in 1996, Nature's Gift was released in the United States as the free gift for renewing membership in the M. I. Hummel Club for the 1997-1998 membership year. It has a black flying bumblebee on the bottom as well as the inscription: "M.I. HUMMEL CLUB Membership Year 1997-1998."

Hum No.	Size	Trademark	Current Value
729	3-1/2"	TMK-7	$90-$100

Hum 729: Nature's Gift.

Hum 730: Just Resting
1985 Anniversary Bell

Although Just Resting anniversary bell was announced and listed in the index of the M.I. Hummel: Golden Anniversary Album, it has never been produced for release to the general public. The original intention was to release it as a companion piece for a plate in the anniversary plate series, but since the plate series was cancelled, apparently so was the bell. Modeled by master sculptor Gerhard Skrobek in 1978, what are likely samples are known to exist in several private collections.

Hum No.	Size	Trademark	Current Value
730	7-1/8" x 4"	TMK-6	$900-$1,200

Hum 730: Just Resting 1985 anniversary bell sample.

Hum 731: Best Friends

Modeled by master sculptor Helmut Fischer in 1992, this 5-1/2" figurine bears a 1992 incised copyright date. It depicts two girls walking arm in arm; one carries flowers and the other has a book/book strap slung over her shoulder. It was released in 2005, has a "First Issue 2006" backstamp, and TMK-8.

In celebration of Sister Hummel's 75th anniversary of the beginning of her legacy, Manufaktur Rödental selected 50 figurines to bear the "75th Anniversary" backstamp. Best Friends was one of those figurines. Only 75 of them were available in North America with this backstamp. Each figurine was hand-numbered with a golden backstamp and a map of North America backstamp. A special porcelain plaque was included, and a notable emblem on the packaging hinted at the contents. Each figurine included a "75 Years of M.I. Hummel" certificate.

Hum No.	Size	Trademark	Current Value
731	5-1/2"	TMK-8 OE	$399

Hum 731: Best Friends.

Hum 732: For My Sweetheart
Possible Future Edition

Modeled by master sculptor Helmut Fischer in 1992, this 5-3/4" figurine carries an incised 1993 copyright date. It depicts a boy wearing long pants and a hat with guitar slung over his shoulder while he looks at a flower in his hand. This figurine is listed as a possible future edition.

Hum 733-734: Open Numbers

Hum 735-738: Celebration Plate Series

A series of four 6-1/4" plates was made available exclusively to members of the former Goebel Collectors' Club, now the M.I. Hummel Club, to celebrate the club's 10th anniversary. One plate was released each year, starting in 1986. Modeled by master sculptor Gerhard Skrobek in 1985, each plate was originally sold only by redemption card to members of the M. I. Hummel Club. Each has an incised "M.I. Hummel" signature and special decal inscription on the back that reads: 'EXCLUSIVELY FOR MEMBERS OF THE GOEBEL COLLECTORS' CLUB."

Hum No.	Design	Year	Current Value
735	It's Cold	1989	$50-$60
736	Daisies Don't Tell	1988	$50-$60
737	Valentine Joy	1987	$50-$60
738	Valentine Gift	1986	$50-$60

Hum 735-738: Celebration plate series.

Hum 739/I: Call to Glory

Call to Glory was released in 1994, and all pieces produced that year bear the "First Issue 1994" backstamp. The figure has an incised copyright date of 1992, measures 5-3/4", and comes with three flags: German, European Common Market, and United States. The suggested retail price at time of release was $250. A special edition of this figurine was made for attendees of the M.I. Hummel Club Convention in Orlando, Florida.

In the wake of the terrorist attacks on the World Trade Center and Pentagon on Sept. 11, 2001, and the resulting American military effort, Goebel alerted its M.I. Hummel Club chapters that it would donate appropriately themed figurines to local chapters to be used as raffle prizes. Proceeds from such fundraising events benefited the families of the victims. Seven figurines, including this one, were selected as appropriate due to their patriotic or firefighter/police/medical personnel themes.

Hum No.	Size	Trademark	Current Value
739/I	5-3/4"	TMK-7	$250-$295
739/I	5-3/4"	TMK-8	$295

Hum 739/I: Call to Glory.

Hum 740: Open Number

Hum 741-744: Little Music Makers
Mini-Plate Series

This is a four-plate series of 4" diameter plates. At the time the plates were issued, small figurines in matching motifs were also issued. All were modeled by master sculptor Gerhard Skrobek in 1982. The plates were limited in number to the amount produced during each year of the release. They are all found with TMK-6. There is no explanation for the non-sequential mold number/year of release situation.

Hum No.	Design	Year	Current Value
741	Serenade	1985	$25-$30
742	Band Leader	1987	$25-$30
743	Soloist	1986	$25-$30
744	Little Fiddler	1984	$25-$30

Hum 741-744: Little Music Makers mini-plate series.

Hum 745-748: Little Homemakers
Mini-Plate Series

This four-piece mini-plate series began in 1988. The plates are 4" in diameter. A small matching figurine was issued with each plate. Master sculptor Gerhard Skrobek modeled all of them in 1986. Each plate was limited to the number produced in the year of issue. All but the last one in the series bear TMK-6. The last one, produced in 1991, is found with TMK-7.

Hum No.	Design	Year	Current Value
745	Little Sweeper	1988	$25-$30
746	Wash Day	1989	$25-$30
747	A Stitch in Time	1990	$25-$30
748	Chicken-Licken	1991	$25-$30

Hum 745-748: Little Homemakers mini-plate series.

Hum 749: Open Number

Hum 750: Goose Girl
Anniversary Clock

Goose Girl anniversary clock is one of the most unusual Hummel items ever produced. Modeled by master sculptor Helmut Fischer in 1993, it was first issued in the United States in 1995. The face of the clock, which carries an incised "M.I. Hummel" signature, is approximately 4" in diameter and features the Goose Girl rendered in bas-relief. The overall height, including the dome, is 12". The release price was $200.

Hum 750: Goose Girl anniversary clock.

Hum No.	Trademark	Current Value
750	TMK-7	$200-$250
750	TMK-8	$200-$225

Hum 751: Love's Bounty

Love's Bounty is the 11th piece in the "Century Collection." Production of this figure was limited to one year only in the 20th century. This particular piece is in commemoration of Goebel's 125th anniversary, and each figure is so marked with special "125th Anniversary" backstamp. In addition, each bears the "Century Collection" backstamp and special decal inscription: "M.I. HUMMEL CENTURY COLLECTION 1996 XX." It has an incised copyright date of 1993. Modeled by master sculptor Helmut Fischer in 1993, Love's Bounty was released in 1996 at a retail price of $1,200.

Hum 751: Love's Bounty.

Hum No.	Size	Trademark	Current Value
751	6-1/2" x 8-1/2"	TMK-7	$1,100-$1,200

Hum 752: Open Number

Hum 753: Togetherness

Modeled by master sculptor Helmut Fischer in 1993, Togetherness bears a 1994 copyright date. It depicts a boy and girl, each sitting on a wooden stool on either side of a tablecloth-draped table. The girl sews while the boy reads a book resting on the tabletop. A cat plays at their feet.

Togetherness was released in 2006 as an exclusive edition for the 2006-2007 club year of the M.I. Hummel Club. It is the third piece in the "Young Love" series and features TMK-8, "Special Togetherness" backstamp, and Special Edition 2006 M.I. Hummel Club backstamp.

Hum No.	Size	Trademark	Current Value
753	5-3/4" x 6"	TMK-8 EE	$745

Hum 753: Togetherness.

Hum 754: We Come in Peace

We Come in Peace, released in 1994, is a special commemorative UNICEF piece. Modeled by Helmut Fischer in 1993, it is quite similar to Hum 31 and Hum 113, but was redesigned especially for this release. It has a 1993 copyright date and a special backstamp identifying it as a UNICEF piece. The price at release was $350.

A $25 donation was made to the United States Committee for UNICEF for each figurine sold.

Hum No.	Size	Trademark	Current Value
754	3-1/2" x 5"	TMK-7	$240-$350

Hum 754: We Come in Peace.

Hum 755: Heavenly Angel
Tree Topper

Heavenly Angel tree topper is another very unusual M.I. Hummel item. The familiar Heavenly Angel (Hum 21) theme was rendered as a topmost ornament for a Christmas tree. It is open from the bottom so that it may be placed at the treetop, or it can be slipped over a wood base for display.

The figure, modeled by master sculptor Helmut Fischer in 1992, was released in 1994. Those produced during that first year have the "First Issue 1994" backstamp. It has a copyright date of 1992 and was issued at $450.

Goebel temporarily withdrew this piece from production in January 1999.

Hum No.	Size	Trademark	Current Value
755	7-3/4"	TMK-7	$450-$500

Hum 755: Heavenly Angel tree topper.

Hum 756: The Artist
Display Plaque

Three variations of The Artist display plaque, Hum 756, from left: piece to mark the 1993 opening of the M.I. Hummel Museum in New Braunfels, Texas, and two other pieces that were released in the German market only for events there in the 1990s.

In 1993, Goebel released The Artist (Hum 304) in display plaque form to commemorate the opening of the former M.I. Hummel Museum in New Braunfels, Texas. At the time, it sold for $260. It was available with the "Grand Opening" wording in 1993 only. Thereafter, it was made without that inscription. The museum used the plaque as its logo on letterhead and more until it closed its doors.

Modeled by master sculptor Helmut Fischer in 1993, there are two more The Artist display plaques, both produced for German consumption and in very limited quantities. Each has a 1993 copyright date.

Hum No.	Size	Trademark	Current Value
756	5" x 6-3/4"	TMK-7	$240-$300

Hum 757: Tuneful Trio

Tuneful Trio was the first edition in a series called the "Trio Collection." Issued on a hardwood base in 1996 in a limited edition of 20,000, each figure bears a "125th Anniversary" backstamp as well as an incised 1993 copyright date. The figurine, modeled by master sculptor Helmut Fischer in 1993, had a suggested retail price of $450 at release. The second in the series is A Trio of Wishes (Hum 721) and the third is Traveling Trio (Hum 787).

Hum No.	Size	Trademark	Current Value
757	4-7/8"	TMK-7	$450-$500

Hum 757: Tuneful Trio.

Hum 758: Nimble Fingers

Modeled by master sculptor Helmut Fischer in 1993, Nimble Fingers was the second figurine in the collection to be fashioned so it must be seated. It came with a separate wooden bench. Its companion piece is To Keep You Warm (Hum 759), which came out a year before with a 1993 copyright date. Those made in 1996, the year of release, bear the "First Issue 1996" backstamp. The release price was $225.

Hum No.	Size	Trademark	Current Value
758	4-1/2"	TMK-7	$225-$250
758	4-1/2"	TMK-8	$250

Hum 758: Nimble Fingers.

Hum 759: To Keep You Warm

Modeled by master sculptor Helmut Fischer in 1993 and released in 1995, To Keep You Warm was the first M.I. Hummel figurine to be fashioned so that it must be seated. As you can see from the photo, a wooden chair was provided with the figure. To Keep You Warm bears a 1993 copyright date and has both the "First Issue 1995" and the "125th Anniversary" backstamps if made during 1995. It was issued at a retail price of $195.

Nimble Fingers (Hum 758) was issued the following year and is considered a companion piece.

Hum No.	Size	Trademark	Current Value
759	5"	TMK-7	$195-$260
759	5"	TMK-8	$195-$260

Hum 759: To Keep You Warm.

Hum 760: Country Suitor

Country Suitor was released in 1995 as a M.I. Hummel Club exclusive. Modeled by master sculptor Helmut Fischer in 1993, it has an incised copyright date of 1993. It has the black club flying bumblebee as well as decal inscription: "EXCLUSIVE EDITION 1995/96 M.I. HUMMEL CLUB." The release price was $195.

Hum No.	Size	Trademark	Current Value
760	5-1/2"	TMK-7	$195-$225

Hum 760: Country Suitor.

Hum 761: From the Heart

From the Heart was part of an informal annual series of paired figurines called "Cozy Companions." The other figurine in this pair is Heart and Soul (Hum 559). Both were released in 1996.

From the Heart was modeled by master sculptor Helmut Fischer in 1993 and has an incised 1993 copyright date. Those produced in 1996 bear both the "First Issue 1996" and the "125th Anniversary" backstamps. It was released at a suggested retail price of $120.

Hum No.	Size	Trademark	Current Value
761	5-1/2"	TMK-7	$120-$135
761	5-1/2"	TMK-8	$120-$135

Hum 761: From the Heart.

Hum 762: Roses Are Red

Modeled by master sculptor Helmut Fischer in 1993, Roses Are Red carries a 1993 incised copyright date. It was first released in the United States in 1997 at the retail price of $120. There are no significant variations to affect collector values.

At presstime, Manufaktur Rödental planned to re-release this figurine at 3-1/2" tall in 2013. A new description was not available, but it will be a TMK-9 figurine with the TMK-9 backstamp.

Hum No.	Size	Trademark	Current Value
762	3-7/8"	TMK-7	$120-$135
762	3-7/8"	TMK-8	$135
762	3-1/2"	TMK-9	$199 retail

Hum 762: Roses Are Red.

Hum 763: Happy Returns
Possible Future Edition

Modeled by master sculptor Gerhard Skrobek in 1993, this 7-1/8" figurine has an incised copyright date of 1994. The piece shows a boy and girl standing side by side while a dog stands at their feet. The boy is holding a birthday cake, while the girl clutches a potted flower plant with bird perched atop. It is listed as a possible future edition.

Hum 764: Mission Madonna
Possible Future Edition

Modeled by master sculptor Helmut Fischer in 1993, this 10-1/2" piece depicts a Madonna holding a Caucasian child while two African-American children play at her feet: one standing with a flower and the other seated. It is listed as a possible future edition.

Hum 765: First Love

Modeled by master sculptor Helmut Fischer in 1993, First Love bears a 1994 incised copyright date. It features a boy similar to She Loves Me, She Loves Me Not (Hum 174) and a girl from the Hummel drawing "He Loves Me?" seated next to each other near a wooden fence. Each has a flower in his/her hand and two birds rest on the fence on either side of them.

First Love was released in 2004 as an exclusive edition to members of the M.I. Hummel Club for the 2004-2005 club year. It is the first issue in the "Young Love" series. It has "Special Edition 2004 M.I. Hummel Club" and "First Love" backstamps and TMK-8.

Hum 765: First Love.

Hum No.	Size	Trademark	Current Value
765	6-1/2" x 6-3/4"	TMK-8 EE	$945

Hum 766: Here's My Heart

Modeled by master sculptor Helmut Fischer in 1994, Here's My Heart was issued as the 1998 "Century Collection" release and was produced for only one year as a limited edition. It bears an incised 1994 copyright date as well as decal inscription: "M.I. HUMMEL CENTURY COLLECTION 1998 XX." The issue price was $1,375.

Hum No.	Size	Trademark	Current Value
766	10-3/4"	TMK-7	$960-$1,375

Hum 766: Here's My Heart.

Hum 767: Puppy Love
Display Plaque

Modeled by master sculptor Helmut Fischer in 1993, Puppy Love display plaque is a special edition created to celebrate the 60th anniversary of the making of Hummel figurines. It features Puppy Love, the first in the series of original figurines released in 1935. The plaque in the accompanying photograph has a 1993 copyright date and "Special Edition 1995" backstamp in German and English. Available only during 1995, the original issue price was $240.

Hum No.	Size	Trademark	Current Value
767	4-1/2" x 7-1/4"	TMK-7	$180-$240

Hum 767: Puppy Love 60-year anniversary display plaque.

Hum 768: Pixie

Pixie, modeled by master sculptor Helmut Fischer in 1994, was released in 1995. Each piece made that year had the "First Issue 1995" backstamp. It has an incised 1994 copyright date. The suggested retail price for Pixie in 1995 was $105. Pixie is part of an informal series of paired figurines called "Cozy Companions." Its companion piece is Scamp (Hum 553).

In the fall of 2009 Manufaktur Rödental introduced Pixie in a larger size of 5-1/2" tall. It is a TMK-9 figurine.

Hum No.	Size	Trademark	Current Value
768	3-1/2"	TMK-7	$105-$140
768	3-1/2"	TMK-8	$140
768/I	5-1/2"	TMK-9	$279 retail

Hum 768: Pixie.　　*Hum 768/I: Pixie.*

Hum 769-770: Open Numbers

Hum 771: Practice Makes Perfect

Modeled by master sculptor Helmut Fischer in 1994, Practice Makes Perfect is one of only a few figures in the collection that was fashioned to be seated on something. In this case, a rocking chair is supplied with the figurine. It has an incised 1994 copyright date and was released in the United States in 1997. The first year of production bears the "First Issue 1997" backstamp. The suggested retail price at time of issue was $250.

This piece is considered a part of the Kid's Club Collector's Set, which was first offered in 2002 and also included Love in Bloom (Hum 699) and Heart's Delight (Hum 698). The set retailed for $650.

Practice Makes Perfect was temporarily withdrawn from production on June 15, 2002.

Hum No.	Size	Trademark	Current Value
771	3-1/4"	TMK 8 OE	$139
771	4-3/4"	TMK-7	$250-$280
771	4-3/4"	TMK-8	$280

Hum 771: Practice Makes Perfect.

Hum 772-774: Open Numbers

Hum 775-786: Christmas Bell Series

Christmas bells were released in three four-year series: 1989-1992, 1993-1996, and 1997-2000. The bells have pinecone-shaped clappers and all measure 3-1/4" in height.

Master sculptor Helmut Fischer modeled all the bells between 1987 and 1996. Issue prices at the time of release were: $35 in 1989, $37.50 in 1990, $39.50 in 1991, $45 in 1992, $50 in 1993 and 1994, $55 in 1995, $65 in 1996, $68 in 1997, and $70 in 1998, 1999, and 2000. With the exception of Hum 775 and 776, which bears TMK-6, and Hum 786, which bears TMK-8, the rest of the bells bear TMK-7.

The only significant variation to be found is with regard to color. Some 250 to 300 of the 1990 bell were made in greenish-yellow color and given to company representatives as a Christmas present from Goebel.

Hum No.	Year	Design	Current Value
775	1989	Ride Into Christmas	$25-$30
776	1990	Letter to Santa Claus	$25-$30
777	1991	Hear Ye, Hear Ye	$25-$30
778	1992	Harmony in Four Parts	$25-$30
779	1993	Celestial Musician	$25-$30
780	1994	Festival Harmony With Mandolin	$25-$30
781	1995	Festival Harmony With Flute	$25-$30
782	1996	Christmas Song	$25-$35
783	1997	Thanksgiving Prayer	$25-$30
784	1998	Echoes of Joy	$25-$30
785	1999	Joyful Noise	$25-$30
786	2000	Light the Way	$25-$30

Hum 775: Ride Into Christmas 1989 Christmas bell.

Hum 776: Letter to Santa Claus 1990 Christmas bell.

Hum 777: Hear Ye, Hear Ye 1991 Christmas bell.

Hum 778: Harmony in Four Parts 1992 Christmas bell.

Hum 779: Celestial Musician 1993 Christmas bell.

Celestial Musician bell showing the location of the markings in the bells.

Hum 780: Festival Harmony (Mandolin) 1994 Christmas bell.

Hum 781: Festival Harmony (Flute) 1995 Christmas bell.

Hum 782: Christmas Song 1996 Christmas bell.

Hum 783: Thanksgiving Prayer 1997 Christmas bell.

Hum 784: Echoes of Joy 1998 Christmas bell.

Hum 785: A Joyful Noise 1999 Christmas bell.

Hum 786: Light the Way 2000 Christmas bell.

Hum 787: Traveling Trio

Traveling Trio was the third edition in a series called the "Trio Collection." Modeled by master sculptor Helmut Fischer in 1995 and issued in 1997 in a limited edition of 20,000 sequentially numbered figurines, Hum 787 bears a 1995 incised copyright date. The figurine measures 5-1/4". The suggested retail price at release was $490. First in the series was Tuneful Trio (Hum 757) and second in the series was A Trio of Wishes (Hum 721).

Hum No.	Size	Trademark	Current Value
787	5-1/4"	TMK-7	$490-$500

Hum 787: Traveling Trio.

Hum 788/A: Hello and Hum 788/B: Sister

Perpetual Calendars

Modeled by master sculptor Helmut Fischer in 1995 and released that summer, both of these pieces bear an incised 1995 copyright date. Each has wooden holder for calendar cards in which the month is written in both English and German. Both were released at a suggested retail price of $295 and both were temporarily withdrawn from production on June 15, 2002.

Hum 788/A: Hello perpetual calendar.

Hum 788/B: Sister perpetual calendar.

Hum No.	Size	Trademark	Current Value
788/A	7-1/2" x 6-1/8"	TMK-7	$100-$180
788/B	7-1/2" x 5-5/8"	TMK-7	$100-$180

Hum 789: Open Number

Hum 790: Celebrate With Song

This unusual figurine, modeled by master sculptor Helmut Fischer in 1994, was issued in 1996 as an exclusive M.I. Hummel Club piece. Sold only to those with redemption certificates from the club, it celebrates the 20th anniversary of the club. The valid redemption period ended May 31, 1998. It has an incised 1994 copyright date and the decal inscription: "EXCLUSIVE EDITION 1996/97 M.I. HUMMEL CLUB 1977 (20) 1997." It was priced at $295 at the time of release.

Hum No.	Size	Trademark	Current Value
790	5-7/8"	TMK-7	$180-$250

Hum 790: Celebrate With Song.

Hum 791: May Dance

Modeled by master sculptor Helmut Fischer in 1996, May Dance bears a "SPECIAL EVENT" decal since it was produced for sale only at "Mai Fest" celebrations during the year 2000. It also carries a 1996 incised copyright date. The original issue price was $199.

Hum No.	Size	Trademark	Current Value
791	7"	TMK-8	$130-$199

Hum 791: May Dance.

Hum 792: Open Number

Hum 793: Forever Yours

Forever Yours, modeled by master sculptor Helmut Fischer in 1994, bears a 1994 incised copyright date. It was the renewal gift for members of the M.I. Hummel Club who renewed their membership for the club year 1996-1997. The figure has the special club backstamp as well as the "First Issue 1996/97" backstamp and medallion. The inscription reads: "M.I. HUMMEL CLUB." The issue price was a $60 value as the gift with membership.

Hum 793: Forever Yours.

Hum No.	Size	Trademark	Current Value
793	4-1/8"	TMK-7	$55-$100

Hum 794/I: Best Buddies

Best Buddies was first sculpted by master sculptor Gerhard Skrobeck in 1955 as Being Punished wall plaque (Hum 326, PFE) and then as the 4-3/4" figurine by master sculptor Helmut Fischer in 1995. Based on an original drawing by Sister M.I. Hummel, the figurine depicts a boy who is taking a "time out" while his cat comes to snuggle and maybe share some soup. The figurine has an incised 1996 copyright date. Best Buddies was released in 2012, is a M.I. Hummel Club Year 36 exclusive, and is a TMK-9 figurine.

Hum 794/I: Best Buddies.

Hum No.	Size	Trademark	Current Value
794/I	4-3/4"	TMK-9	$419 retail

Hum 795: From My Garden

From My Garden, modeled by master sculptor Helmut Fischer in 1994, has a mold number of 795/0, which suggests that there may be another size in the offering. It has a copyright date of 1994 and bears the "First Issue 1997" backstamp. The original release price was $180.

Hum No.	Size	Trademark	Current Value
795/0	4-7/8"	TMK-7	$180-$220
795/0	4-7/8"	TMK-8	$200
795/1	5-1/2"	PFE	

Hum 795: From My Garden.

Hum 796: Brave Voyager

Modeled by master sculptor Helmut Fischer in 1994, this 3-7/8" figurine has an incised 1994 copyright date. It depicts a boy holding a horn and sitting in a little Viking ship, just like the postcard drawing of the same name.

Hum No.	Size	Trademark	Current Value
796	4"	TMK-8	$499

Hum 797: Rainy Day Bouquet
Possible Future Edition

Modeled by master sculptor Helmut Fischer in 1994, this 5-1/8" figurine is listed as a possible future edition. It has an incised 1995 copyright date and depicts a girl standing under an umbrella while holding a bouquet of flowers in her right hand.

Hum 798: Open Number

Hum 799: Vagabond

Originally modeled by master sculptor Helmut Fischer in 1994, this 5-7/8" figurine has an incised 1995 copyright date. It portrays a boy holding a walking stick in his right hand and mandolin strung to his back. A bird sits atop the end of the instrument. Master sculptor Marion Huschka redesigned Vagabond to mirror the original drawing by Sister M.I. Hummel. Vagabond was introduced in spring of 2011 as a M.I. Hummel Club Year 35 exclusive. This figurine is a little taller than the original possible future edition (PFE). It is a TMK-9 figurine with the TMK-9 backstamp and the 2011 M.I. Hummel Club backstamp.

Hum No.	Size	Trademark	Current Value
799	6"	TMK-9	$429 retail

Hum 799: Vagabond.

Hum 800: Proud Moments

Modeled by master sculptor Helmut Fischer in 1998, Proud Moments has an incised 1998 copyright date along with a "First Issue 2000 MILLENNIUM" oval decal and TMK-8. It was first released in the United States in the fall of 1999 at an original issue price of $300.

Hum No.	Size	Trademark	Current Value
800	3-5/8"	TMK-8	$279

Hum 800: Proud Moments.

Hum 801: Open Number

Hum 802: Brave Soldier

Brave Soldier was modeled by master sculptor Helmut Fischer in 1996 and has an incised 1997 copyright date. This 5-1/8" figurine depicts a boy holding a gun.

A larger version (8") sold exclusively through the AAFES catalog and at U.S. Military Post Exchanges in a limited edition of 3,000 with the inscription "Ambassadors of Freedom" and TMK-8.

Hum No.	Size	Trademark	Current Value
802	5-1/4"	PFE	
802/II	8"	TMK-8 LE	$228

Hum 802: Brave Soldier.

Hum 803: Little Fisherman

Little Fisherman was released in the fall of 2003 with a "First Issue 2004" backstamp. The mixed media piece features a boy holding a wooden fishing pole with a ceramic fish on the end. It has an incised 1997 copyright date and TMK-8.

Hum No.	Size	Trademark	Current Value
803	3-1/2"	TMK-8 OE	$69.95

Hum 803: Little Fisherman.

Hum 804: Love Petals

This piece of a girl holding a flower was issued in 2003 with a "First Issue 2003" backstamp. It was part of the "Create-A-Gift" collection when paired with a Sentiment Occasion base. It has an incised 1997 copyright date and TMK-8.

Hum No.	Size	Trademark	Current Value
804	3-1/2"	TMK-8 OE	$69.50

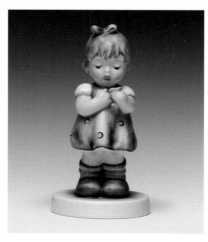

Hum 804: Love Petals.

Hum 805: Little Toddler
Possible Future Edition

Modeled by master sculptor Helmut Fischer in 1996, this 2-3/4" figurine features a toddler lying on his stomach while pushing up on his arms. It has an incised 1997 copyright date. It is a possible future edition.

Hum 806-813, 824, 825, 831-832, 834, 841-842, 851-854, 904, 913, 947 and 968: International Figurines

All international figurines were modeled by master sculptors Arthur Moeller or Reinhold Unger in 1940. Since 1976, several duplicates of some models and new variations of others have been found, usually selling in the $10,000 to $15,000 price range. They are as follows:

Hum No.	Description	Hum No.	Description	Hum No.	Description
806	Bulgarian Boy	824(B)	Swedish Boy	852(A)	Hungarian Girl
807	Bulgarian Girl	825(A)	Swedish Girl	852(B)	Hungarian Girl
808	Bulgarian Boy	825(B)	Swedish Girl	853(A)	Hungarian Boy
809	Bulgarian Girl	831	Slovak Boy	853(B)	Hungarian Boy
810(A)	Bulgarian Girl	832(B)	Slovak Girl	854	Hungarian Girl
810(B)	Bulgarian Girl	832	Slovak Boy	904	Serbian Boy
811	Bulgarian Boy	834	Slovak Boy	913	Serbian Girl (auctioned on eBay in February 2013 for $5,100)
812(A)	Serbian Girl	841	Czech Boy		
812(B)	Serbian Girl	842(A)	Czech Girl	947	Serbian Girl
813	Serbian Boy	842(B)	Czech Girl	968	Serbian Boy
824(A)	Swedish Boy	851	Hungarian Boy		

Hum 806: Bulgarian Boy   Hum 807: Bulgarian Girl   Hum 808: Bulgarian Girl   Hum 809: Bulgarian Girl   Hum 810: Bulgarian Girl   Hum 810: Bulgarian Girl

Hum 811: Bulgarian Boy   Hum 812: Serbian Girl   Hum 812: Serbian Girl   Hum 813: Serbian Boy   Hum 824: Swedish Boy   Hum 825: Swedish Girl

Hum 814: Peaceful Blessing

Modeled by master sculptor Helmut Fischer in 1997, this piece has an incised 1997 copyright date along with the "First Issue 1999" oval decal backstamp and TMK-7. It was first released in the United States in the fall of 1998 at an original issue price of $180.

Hum 814: Peaceful Blessing.

Hum No.	Size	Trademark	Current Value
814	4-1/2"	TMK-7	$180-$200
814	4-1/2"	TMK-8	$195

Hum 815: Heavenly Prayer

Modeled by master sculptor Helmut Fischer in 1997, this figurine was first released in the fall of 1998 for 1999. It has an incised 1997 copyright date, along with the TMK-7, and the "First Issue 1999" oval decal. The official issue price was $180 in 1999.

Hum 815: Heavenly Prayer.

Hum No.	Size	Trademark	Current Value
815	4-7/8"	TMK-7	$180-$200
815	4-7/8"	TMK-8	$195

Hum 816-819: Open Numbers

Hum 820: Adieu
Plaque

Modeled by master sculptor Helmut Fischer in 1997, Adieu has an incised 1997 copyright date. It was first released in Cayman Islands British West Indies in 1999 in a limited edition of approximately 300 pieces. It was sold exclusively (by Kirk Freeport Plaza, Ltd.) with 10 other models of M.I. Hummel figurines with a special floral backstamp and the words "Caribbean Collection." The issue price was $127 plus shipping/handling.

Hum No.	Size	Trademark	Current Value
820	3-3/4" x 6"	TMK-7	$95-$125

Hum 820: Adieu plaque.

Hum 821: Open Number

Hum 822: Hummelnest
Plaque

Modeled by master sculptor Helmut Fischer in 1997, Hummelnest was first released in the fall of 1997 as the new visitors' plaque that could be personalized for visiting the former Goebel factory in Rödental, Germany. The original issue price was DM195 (approximately $100 U.S.). It has an incised 1997 copyright date, along with the TMK-7. The plaque was released again in 2004 as a special edition for M.I. Hummel Club local chapter members.

Hum 822: Hummelnest plaque.

Hum No.	Size	Trademark	Current Value
822	5-1/4" x 4-3/8"	TMK-7 CE	$125
822	5-1/4" x 4-3/8"	TMK-8 OE	$125

Hum 823: Open Number

Hum 824-825: Swedish Figurines
See Hum 806: International Figurines.

Hum 826: Little Maestro

First issued in 2000, Little Maestro came as part of a limited edition gift set that was limited to 20,000 numbered pieces worldwide. The set included the 5-3/4" figurine and a 5-1/4" Steiff teddy bear. The bear had a consecutively numbered white ear tag and button-in-ear and wore a medallion at its neck that depicted the figurine image.

Hum No.	Size	Trademark	Current Value
826 (set)	5-3/4"	TMK-8	$320-$350

Hum 826: Little Maestro.

Hum 827: Daydreamer
Plaque

Modeled by master sculptor Helmut Fischer in 1998, Daydreamer has an incised 1998 copyright date along with the TMK-7 and the "First Issue 2000 MILLENNIUM" oval decal backstamp. It was first released in 1999 as the new visitor's plaque to those visiting the Goebel factory in Rödental, Germany. The official issue price was $140.

Hum No.	Size	Trademark	Current Value
827	3-1/2" x 4-3/8"	TMK-7	$140
827	3-1/2" x 4-3/8"	TMK-8	$140

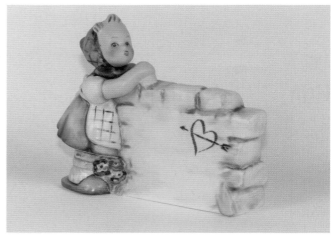
Hum 827: Daydreamer plaque.

Hum 828: Over the Horizon
Plaque

Released in the United States in 2000, Over the Horizon was originally only available during artist promotions. Modeled by master sculptor Helmut Fischer, it carries a 1998 copyright date. The original retail price was $140.

Hum No.	Size	Trademark	Current Value
828	3-1/4"	TMK-8	$140

Hum 828: Over the Horizon plaque.

Hum 829: Where to Go?

Modeled by master sculptor Helmut Fischer, this special limited edition figurine was part of a four-piece set that was released in 1999 through U.S. Military Post Exchanges in Europe to mark the 10-year anniversary of the fall of the Berlin Wall. Similar to Crossroads (Hum 331), Where to Go? carries an incised 1999 copyright date.

Hum 829: Where to Go?

Hum No.	Size	Trademark	Current Value
829 (Set)	6-1/2"	TMK-7	$358

The Enduring Glow of Freedom Set consists of two figurines: Where To Go? (Hum 829) and Happy Traveler (Hum 109). The set was limited to 5,000 sequentially numbered pieces worldwide. It came with a wooden base that had an engraved brass plaque on the front that read: "Commemorating the 10 Year Anniversary of the Fall of the Berlin Wall and the Sweet Glow of Freedom for all of Germany. 1989 – November – 1999." The colorful rainbow is made of plastic and fits firmly in a slot on the wooden base. The set originally sold for $358.

Hum 830: Open Number

Hum 831-834: Slovak Figurines

See Hum 806: International Figurines.

Hum 835: Garden Splendor

Released in 2000, Garden Splendor was first modeled by master sculptor Helmut Fischer and carries a 1998 incised copyright date as well as "First Issue 2000" special backstamp in the first year of production. This figurine also is the subject of a plate by the same name (Hum 921).

The year 2011 marked the celebration of Sister Hummel's 75th anniversary of the beginning of her legacy. Manufaktur Rödental selected 50 figurines to bear the "75th Anniversary" backstamp. Garden Splendor was one of those figurines. Only 75 of them were available in North America with this backstamp. Each figurine was hand-numbered with a golden backstamp and a map of North America backstamp. A special porcelain plaque was included, and a notable emblem on the packaging hinted at the contents. Each figurine included a "75 Years of M.I. Hummel" certificate.

Hum 835: Garden Splendor.

Hum No.	Size	Trademark	Current Value
835	3-1/4"	TMK-8	$219

Hum 836: Afternoon Nap

Released in 2001, this piece was first modeled by master sculptor Helmut Fischer in 1999 and carries a 1999 incised copyright date as well as "First Issue 2001" special backstamp in the first year of production. This figurine also is the subject of a plate by the same name (Hum 922).

The year 2011 marked the celebration of Sister Hummel's 75th anniversary of the beginning of her legacy. Manufaktur Rödental selected 50 figurines to bear the "75th Anniversary" backstamp. Afternoon Nap was one of those figurines. Only 75 of them were available in North America with this backstamp. Each figurine was hand-numbered with a golden backstamp and a map of North America backstamp. A special porcelain plaque was included, and a notable emblem on the packaging hinted at the contents. Each figurine included a "75 Years of M.I. Hummel" certificate.

Hum 836: Afternoon Nap.

Hum No.	Size	Trademark	Current Value
836	3-1/2"	TMK-8	$225

Hum 837: Bumblebee Friend

This figurine, released in 2002, was first modeled by master sculptor Helmut Fischer in 2000. It carries a 2000 incised copyright date as well as "First Issue 2002" backstamp in the first year of production. The same motif was used for the 2002 annual plate that carries the same name (Hum 923).

Hum No.	Size	Trademark	Current Value
837	5-1/4"	TMK-8	$279

Hum 837: Bumblebee Friend.

Hum 838: Christmas By Candlelight

This piece, released in 2001, was modeled by master sculptor Helmut Fischer in 2000. It measures 7-1/2" and carries TMK-8 and an incised 2000 copyright date, as well as a special "First Issue 2001" backstamp in the first year of production.

Hum No.	Size	Trademark	Current Value
838	7-1/2"	TMK-8	$215

Hum 838: Christmas By Candlelight.

Hum 839-844: Open Numbers

Hum 841-842: Czech Figurines

See Hum 806: International Figurines.

Hum 845: Too Shy to Sing

Too Shy to Sing was a free gift to members joining the M.I. Hummel Club for the 2003-2004 year. It has an incised 2002 copyright date, "Club Exclusive" backstamp, Exclusive Edition, EE, and TMK-8. Part of the first year of the "Kinder Choir," Too Shy to Sing was sculpted by master sculptor Helmut Fischer.

Hum No.	Size	Trademark	Current Value
845	4"	TMK-8 EE	$90

Hum 845: Too Shy to Sing.

Hum 846: Hitting the High Note

Hitting the High Note, released in 2004, was an exclusive edition available to members joining the M.I. Hummel Club for the 2004-2005 year. It has an incised 2002 copyright date, "Club Exclusive" backstamp, EE, exclusive edition backstamp, and TMK-8. Sculpted by Helmut Fischer, it was part of the second year of "Kinder Choir." It comes with a wood and ceramic lamppost.

Hum No.	Size	Trademark	Current Value
846	4"	TMK-8 EE	$110

Hum 846: Hitting the High Note.

Hum 847: Lamplight Caroler

Sculpted by Helmut Fischer, this figurine, part of the fourth year of "Kinder Choir," was issued in 2006. It was an exclusive edition for the M. I. Hummel Club for the 2006-2007 club year. It features an incised 2002 copyright date, TMK-8, "Club Exclusive" backstamp, and EE, exclusive edition backstamp.

Hum No.	Size	Trademark	Current Value
847	4"	TMK-8 EE	$110

Hum 847: Lamplight Caroler.

Hum 848: Steadfast Soprano

This figurine, which was released in 2005, was a free gift to members of the M.I. Hummel Club for 2005-2006. It is part of the third year of "Kinder Choir." It has an incised 2002 copyright date, "Club Exclusive" backstamp, Exclusive Edition, EE, 2005-2006 backstamp, and TMK-8.

Hum No.	Size	Trademark	Current Value
848	4"	TMK-8 EE	$100

Hum 848: Steadfast Soprano.

Hum 849: Double Delight

This piece, which was introduced in 2009, bears the special backstamp that commemorates the 100th anniversary of the birth of M.I. Hummel. It is one of the first TMK-9 figurines and has an incised copyright year, mold number on the bottom of the piece, and the 100th Anniversary backstamp.

Hum No.	Size	Trademark	Current Value
849	4-1/2"	TMK-9	$200-$269

Hum 849: Double Delight.

Hum 850: Open Number

Hum 851-854: Hungarian Figurines

See Hum 806: International Figurines.

Hum 855: Millennium Madonna

On Christmas Eve 1999, Pope John Paul II opened the holy doors at St. Peter's Basilica in Rome to mark the beginning of Jubilee 2000, the Holy Year. Jubilee 2000 ended on Epiphany 2001, when the Supreme Pontiff sealed the doors of St. Peter's, marking the closing of the Holy Year. But the spirit of Holy Year 2000 lives on with Millennium Madonna, which was released in 2000 to mark this event. It was a special limited edition of 7,500 numbered pieces worldwide. Modeled by master sculptor Helmut Fischer, it carries the "First Issue 2000" backstamp as well as TMK-8. It comes in a special, hinged, velvet-lined case. It is listed as a closed edition.

Hum 855: Millennium Madonna.

Hum No.	Size	Trademark	Current Value
855	10-1/4"	TMK-7	$495-$550

Hum 856: A Heartfelt Gift

Produced in a limited edition of 7,500, this figurine of a girl holding a Swarovski crystal heart was issued in 2003 and has an incised 2003 copyright date, limited edition backstamp, and TMK-8. It came in a heart-shaped presentation tin. It was the first piece in the "Swarovski" series of mixed media figurines.

Hum 856: A Heartfelt Gift.

Hum No.	Size	Trademark	Current Value
856	5-1/2"	TMK-8 LE	$275

Hum 857: Accordion Ballad

Part of the "Create-A-Gift" collection when paired with a Sentiment Occasion base, Accordion Ballad was issued in 2004, has an incised 2003 copyright date, and TMK-8.

Hum No.	Size	Trademark	Current Value
857	5-1/2"	TMK-8 OE	$70

Hum 858/A: A Favorite Pet

Easter Egg

This piece, which came with a wooden stand, was issued in 2001. It has an inscribed M.I. Hummel signature and a blue ink decal of "Special Edition 2001" on the back of the egg, and TMK-8 and 858/A under the base of the egg. It is temporarily withdrawn.

Hum No.	Size	Trademark	Current Value
858/A	5-1/2"	TMK-8 TW	$56

Hum 858/A: Favorite Pet Easter egg.

Hum 859: Open Number

Hum 860-874: Miniature Bells

Ten miniature bells were released in January 2000 and another five were released in 2001. Modeled by master sculptor Helmut Fischer in 1999, each miniature bell is a reproduction of the larger annual bells and originally retailed for DM 49 (about $24.50 apiece). Wooden display racks in two different finishes—"Countrystyle" and "Light Brown"—were also available for DM 95 (about $47.50). All measure 3-3/4", carry TMK-8, and are currently worth $25.

Hum No.	Design
860	Let's Sing
861	Farewell
862	Thoughtful
863	In Tune
864	She Loves Me, She Loves Me Not
865	Knit One, Purl One
866	Mountaineer
867	Girl With Sheet Music
868	Sing Along
869	With Loving Greetings
870	Busy Student
871	Latest News
872	What's New?
873	Favorite Pet
874	Whistler's Duet

Hum 860-874: miniature bells.

Hum 875: Open Number

Hum 876/A: Heavenly Angel
Ornament

This bell-shaped bas-relief Christmas ornament, measuring 3-1/4" with an incised "M.I. Hummel" signature on the front, was released in 1999 as part of what is now a series of nine decorative ornaments. In addition to this piece, the series, which was modeled by master sculptor Helmut Fischer in 1999, included the following: Hum 877/A, Hum 878/A, Hum 879/A, Hum 880/A, Hum 2099/A, Hum 2110/A, Hum 2111/A, and Hum 2129/A.

Hum 876/A: Heavenly Angel ornament.

Hum No.	Size	Trademark	Current Value
876/A	3-1/4"	TMK-7	$20

Hum 877/A: Ride Into Christmas
Ornament

Released in 1999, this decorative bas-relief Christmas ornament is in the shape of a Christmas tree and was the design of master sculptor Helmut Fischer in 1999. It measures 4-1/4" and has an incised "M.I. Hummel" signature on the front. It is another in the series of similar ornaments (see Hum 876/A).

Hum No.	Size	Trademark	Current Value
877/A	4-1/4"	TMK-7	$10

Hum 877/A: Ride Into Christmas ornament.

Hum 878/A: Sleep Tight
Ornament

This decorative bas-relief Christmas ornament in the shape of a ball ornament with bow was modeled by master sculptor Helmut Fischer in 1999. Measuring 3-1/2" with an incised "M.I. Hummel" signature on the front, it was released in 1999 as part of what is now a series of similar ornaments (see Hum 876/A).

Hum No.	Size	Trademark	Current Value
878/A	3-1/2"	TMK-7	$10

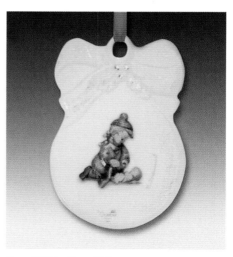

Hum 878/A: Sleep Tight ornament.

Hum 879/A: Christmas Song

Ornament

This bas-relief ornament is in the shape of a candlestick and was released new for 2002. Designed by master sculptor Helmut Fischer in 1999, it has an incised "M.I. Hummel" signature on the front. It is another in the series of similar decorative ornaments (see Hum 876/A).

Hum 879/A: Christmas Song ornament.

Hum No.	Size	Trademark	Current Value
879/A	3-1/2"	TMK-8	$10

Hum 880/A: Hear Ye, Hear Ye

Ornament

Released new for 2002, this bas-relief Christmas ornament is in the shape of a lantern. Master sculptor Helmut Fischer modeled it in 1999. It has an incised "M.I. Hummel" signature on the front. It is another in the series of similar decorative ornaments (see Hum 876/A).

Hum 880/A: Hear Ye, Hear Ye ornament.

Hum No.	Size	Trademark	Current Value
880/A	4-1/4"	TMK-8	$10

Hum 881-884: New Baby Gifts

Released new for 2003, the New Baby Gift Set features four pieces, all of which display The Guardian (Hum 445) motif. The pieces are: Baby's First Christmas ornament (Hum 881/A); an earthenware framed picture (Hum 882/A); earthenware birth certificate/storybook with pen (Hum 883/A); and The Guardian round trinket box (Hum 884).

Hum No.	Basic Size	Trademark	Current Value
881/A	3-1/2"	TMK-8	$22.50
882/A	5-1/2"	TMK-8	$75
883/A	5-1/2"	TMK-8	$50
884	4"	TMK-8	$50

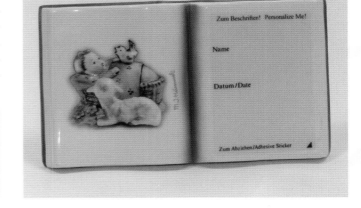

Hum 881/A, 882/A, 883/A, and 884: New Baby Gift Set.

Hum 885: Fishing Adventure

Part of the By the Sea Hummelscape, Fishing Adventure was issued in 2004 in a limited edition of 5,000. The mixed media figurine, which features a wooden fishing pole and ceramic fish, boasts sea sounds and light. The piece has an incised 2003 copyright date and TMK-8.

Hum No.	Size	Trademark	Current Value
885	5"	TMK-8 TW	$250

Hum 885: Fishing Adventure.

Hum 886-899: Century Collection Miniature Plates
Closed Edition

The "Century Collection" miniature plates feature each of the limited edition M.I. Hummel figurines on a single plate. Each plate measures 4" in diameter and is worth $30. A wall display in walnut was available for $100.

Hum No.	Design	Year
886	Chapel Time	1986
887	Pleasant Journey	1987
888	Call to Worship	1988
889	Harmony in Four Parts	1989
890	Let's Tell the World	1990
891	We Wish You the Best	1991
892	On Our Way	1992
893	Welcome Spring	1993
894	Rock-A-Bye	1994
895	Strike Up the Band	1995
896	Love's Bounty	1996
897	Fond Goodbye	1997
898	Here's My Heart	1998
899	Fanfare	1999

Hum 886-899: Century Collection mini plates.

Hum 900: Merry Wanderer
Plaque

Modeled in 1998 by master sculptor Helmut Fischer, the Merry Wanderer plaque was a M.I. Hummel Club exclusive. It has an incised 1998 copyright date, along with TMK-8 and "Original Goebel archival plaque ca. 1947" incised on the back of the collectors' club plaque only. It was first released in United States in the fall of 1999 for $195 with member's redemption card.

Hum No.	Size	Trademark	Current Value
900	4" x 5-3/4"	TMK-8	$120 retailer plaque
900	4" x 5-3/4"	TMK-8	$120 collector's plaque

Hum 900: Merry Wanderer plaque.

Hum 901: Open Number

Hum 902: Sunflowers, My Love?

This mixed media figurine depicts a boy holding a sunflower in which a Swarovski crystal sparkles in the center. Produced in a limited edition of 7,500, this figure was issued in 2004. It has an incised 2004 copyright date, "Limited Edition" backstamp, TMK-8, and came with a round presentation tin. It was the second piece in the "Swarovski" series of mixed media figurines.

Hum 902: Sunflowers, My Love?

Hum No.	Size	Trademark	Current Value
902	5-1/2"	TMK-8 LE	$275

Hum 903: Adoring Children

Introduced in 2006, Adoring Children is part of the Children's Nativity Set. It features TMK-8. The year 2011 marked the celebration of Sister Hummel's 75th anniversary of the beginning of her legacy. Manufaktur Rödental selected 50 figurines to bear the "75th Anniversary" backstamp. Adoring Children was one of those figurines. Only 75 of them were available in North America with this backstamp. Each figurine was hand-numbered with a golden backstamp and a map of North America backstamp. A special porcelain plaque was included and a notable emblem on the packaging hinted at the contents. Each figurine included a "75 Years of M.I. Hummel" certificate.

Hum 903: Adoring Children.

Hum No.	Size	Trademark	Current Value
903	4-1/2"	TMK-8 OE	$259

Hum 904: Serbian Boy

See Hum 806: International Figurines.

Hum 904: Serbian Boy.

Hum 905: Come With Me

Come With Me is made up of two pieces: a heart base and the Come With Me figurine. The heart base has the words: "A mother holds a child's hand for a short while...but holds their heart forever." The figurine features an incised 2006 copyright date, flower backstamp, and TMK-8. Manufaktur Rödental anticipates releasing this figurine sometime in 2013 and then re-introducing it as a TMK-9 figurine with the TMK-9 backstamp.

Hum No.	Size	Trademark	Current Value
905	3-1/2"; 3-3/4" with base	TMK-8	$99
905	3-1/4"	TMK-9	N/A

Hum 905: Come With Me.

Hum 906: I Will Follow You

I Will Follow You, introduced in 2007, is the companion to Come With Me (Hum 905). It features TMK-8. Manufaktur Rödental anticipates releasing this figurine sometime in 2013 and will re-introduce it in a slightly smaller size of 3-1/4" as a TMK-9 figurine bearing the TMK-9 backstamp.

Hum No.	Size	Trademark	Current Value
906	3-1/2"	TMK-8	$109
906	3-1/4"	TMK-9	N/A

Hum 906: I Will Follow You.

Hum 907: Big Fish

Big Fish, which features a boy holding a fishing pole with a fish on the line, is part of the "Little Companions" collection and has a fish picture backstamp. Big Fish was also available with a special Hummelscape produced in a limited edition.

Hum No.	Size	Trademark	Current Value
907	2-3/4"	TMK-8	$99

Hum 907: Big Fish.

Hum 908: Gone A-Wandering

Gone A-Wandering, produced in a limited edition of 5,000, is one of four "Heart of Hummel" collection pieces. Issued in 2006, it has a heart backstamp and TMK-8. The other three pieces in the collection are Hum 624: Fresh Blossoms, Hum 2235: Lucky Friend, and Hum 2237: Sunday Stroll.

Hum 908: Gone A-Wandering.

Hum No.	Size	Trademark	Current Value
908	4-1/2"	TMK-8 LE	$199

Hum 909: Gifts of Love

Gifts of Love is an Exclusive Edition for the 2006-2007 club year for members of the M.I. Hummel Club. Issued in 2006, it has an incised 2005 copyright date, "Club Exclusive" backstamp, and TMK-8.

Hum 909: Gifts of Love.

Hum No.	Size	Trademark	Current Value
909	5-1/4"	TMK-8 EE	$350

Hum 911: Harmony & Lyric

Harmony & Lyric was the club exclusive for club year 31. It comes with a ceramic plaque featuring the original artwork of Sister M.I. Hummel and a wooden easel for display. Harmony & Lyric is the second piece in a series that began with Hum 404: Sad Song.

Hum No.	Size	Trademark	Current Value
911	5-3/4"	TMK-8	$350

Hum 911: Harmony & Lyric

Hum 912/A through 912/D: Spring Time, Spring Waltz, Spring Love, and Spring Fancy

These four figurines are part of the Sounds of Spring collection. They are based on an earlier M.I. Hummel motif, Ring Around the Rosie, and perform on a dance floor that rotates and is topped by a May pole. Hum 912/B was the M.I. Hummel Club piece for 2007-2008.

Hum No.	Size	Trademark	Current Value
912/A	4″	TMK-8	$125
912/B	4″	TMK-8	$125
912/C	4″	TMK-8	$125
912/D	4″	TMK-8	$125

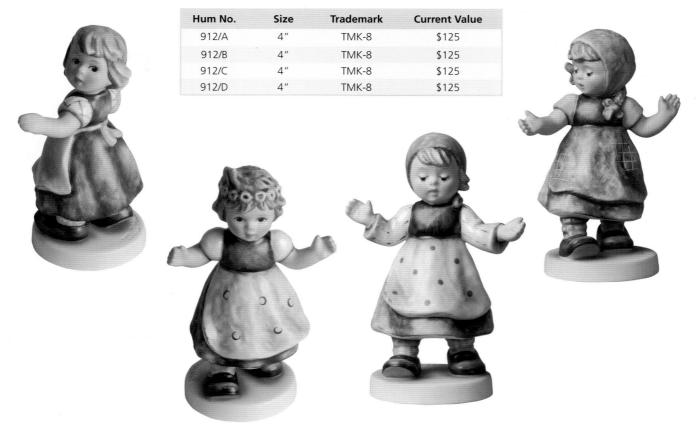

Hum 912/A, B, C, D: Spring Time, Spring Waltz, Spring Love, and Spring Fancy.

Hum 913: Serbian Girl

See Hum 806: International Figurines.

Hum 913: Serbian Girl.

Hum 914: Blumenkinder

This double figurine, whose name is translated to mean "flower children," was introduced in 2007 as part of the "Premier Collection." It is a TMK-8 figurine with the TMK-8 backstamp.

The year 2011 marked the celebration of Sister Hummel's 75th anniversary of the beginning of her legacy. Manufaktur Rödental selected 50 figurines to bear the "75th Anniversary" backstamp. Blumenkinder was one of those figurines. Only 75 of them were available in North America with this backstamp. Each figurine was hand-numbered, with a golden backstamp and a map of North America backstamp. A special porcelain plaque was included and a notable emblem on the packaging hinted at the contents. Each figurine included a "75 Years of M.I. Hummel" certificate.

Hum No.	Size	Trademark	Current Value
914	4-3/4"	TMK-8	$269

Hum 914: Blumenkinder.

Hum 915: Tuning Up

Tuning Up, released in 2008, was the M.I. Hummel Club exclusive for club year 32. It came with a ceramic postcard and wooden easel and features TMK-8. It is the third piece in a series with Hum 404: Sad Song and Hum 911: Harmony & Lyric.

Hum No.	Size	Trademark	Current Value
915	5-1/2"	TMK-8	$449

Hum 915: Tuning Up.

Hum 920: Star Gazer
Annual Plate

Modeled by master sculptor Helmut Fischer in 1990, this plate has an incised 1999 copyright date along with TMK-8. It is a part of the "Millennium" plate series, bears a special "60th Anniversary" backstamp honoring Hum 132: Star Gazer. The official issue price was $198 in 2000.

Hum No.	Size	Trademark	Current Value
920	7-1/2"	TMK-8	$125-$198

Hum 920: Star Gazer annual plate.

Hum 921: Garden Splendor
Annual Plate

With the design of the figurine of the same name (Hum 835), this plate was introduced new in 2000 as that year's edition in the annual plate series.

Hum No.	Size	Trademark	Current Value
921	7"	TMK-8	$125-$198

Hum 921: Garden Splendor annual plate.

Hum 922: Afternoon Nap
Annual Plate

The 2001 installment in the annual plate series, Afternoon Nap is adorned with the image of the figurine of the same name (Hum 836). Master sculptor Helmut Fischer modeled it in 1999.

Hum 922: Afternoon Nap annual plate.

Hum No.	Size	Trademark	Current Value
922	7"	TMK-8	$125-$198

Hum 923: Bumblebee Friend
Annual Plate

Carrying the image of the figurine with the same name (Hum 837), Bumblebee Friend was the 2002 edition in the annual plate series. It was modeled by master sculptor Helmut Fischer in 1999.

Hum 923: Bumblebee Friend annual plate.

Hum No.	Size	Trademark	Current Value
923	7"	TMK-8	$125-$198

Hum 924: The Florist
Annual Plate

In the annual plate series, The Florist was new for 2003. It is paired with the 5-1/4" figurine of the same name (Hum 349/0).

Hum No.	Size	Trademark	Current Value
924	7"	TMK-8	$125-$200

Hum 925: Garden Gift
Annual Plate

This plate, the fifth and final issue in the annual plate series, was issued in 2003. It has an incised M.I. Hummel signature, incised 2003 copyright date, and TMK-8.

Hum No.	Size	Trademark	Current Value
925	7"	TMK-8 CE	$125-$200

Hum 926-946: Open Numbers

Hum 947: Serbian Girl

See Hum 806: International Figurines.

Hum 947: Serbian Girl.

Hum 948-949: Open Numbers

Hum 950: Apple Tree Girl
Doll

Released in 1998, Apple Tree Girl doll was a companion to Apple Tree Boy doll, Hum 951, and was Goebel's continuation of the doll series begun by the Danbury Mint (see Hum 512-524). This doll was costumed by world-renowned doll designer Bette Ball and is seated in its own tree display stand, detailed with apples, apple blossoms, and a bird. Master sculptor Marion Huschka modeled it in 1996.

Hum No.	Size	Trademark	Current Value
950	13″	TMK-7	$100-$250

Hum 951: Apple Tree Boy
Doll

The companion to Hum 950: Apple Tree Girl doll, Apple Tree Boy doll was released in 1998 and was Goebel's continuation of the doll series begun by the Danbury Mint (see Hum 512-524). Apple Tree Boy doll was costumed by world-renowned doll designer Bette Ball and is seated in its own tree display stand, detailed with apples, apple blossoms, and a bird. Master sculptor Marion Huschka modeled it in 1996.

Hum No.	Size	Trademark	Current Value
951	13″	TMK-7	$100-$250

Hum 952-959: Open Numbers

Hum 960: Ride Into Christmas
Doll

Released in 1999, Ride Into Christmas is another addition to the doll series begun by Danbury Mint (see Hum 512-524). It was modeled by master sculptor Helmut Fischer in 1997 and measures 11".

Hum No.	Size	Trademark	Current Value
960	11"	TMK-7	$100-$200

Hum 961-967: Open Numbers

Hum 968: Serbian Boy

See Hum 806: International Figurines.

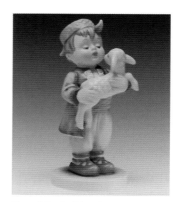

Hum 968: Serbian Boy.

Hum 969: Puppy Love
Clock

This item, which includes a wooden clock case, commemorated the 70th anniversary of Hummel figurines in 2005. The clock face, which is ceramic, features Hum 1: Puppy Love.

Hum No.	Size	Trademark	Current Value
969	10-1/4"	TMK-8 CE	$250

Hum 969: Puppy Love clock.

Hum 970: In Tune

Clock

This item, which includes a wooden clock case, was released in 2005. Its ceramic clock face depicts Hum 414: In Tune.

Hum No.	Size	Trademark	Current Value
970	11-1/2"	TMK-8 OE	$250

Hum 970: In Tune clock.

Hum 971-995: M.I. Hummel Miniature Plate Series

Each plate in this 25-piece series has a 1995 copyright date as part of the TMK-7 applied by blue decal on the back. Each measures 3-1/4" and is a reproduction of the larger annual plates with the same names.

They were produced in 1995 for the European market only, but then were available in the United States though the Danbury Mint. They retailed at $19.95 each. A custom wooden wall display was also available for $19.95.

Hum No.	Design	Year
971	Heavenly Angel	1997
972	Hear Ye, Hear Ye	1997
973	Happy Traveler	1997
974	Goose Girl	1997
975	Ride Into Christmas	1997
976	Apple Tree Girl	1997
977	Apple Tree Boy	1997
978	Happy Pastime	1997
979	Singing Lesson	1997
980	School Girl	1997
981	Umbrella Boy	1997
982	Umbrella Girl	1997
983	Postman	1998
984	Little Helper	1998
985	Chick Girl	1998
986	Playmates	1998
987	Feeding Time	1998
988	Little Goat Herder	1998
989	Farm Boy	1998
990	Shepherd's Boy	1998
991	Just Resting	1998
992	Wayside Harmony	1998
993	Doll Bath	1998
994	Doctor	1998
995	Come Back Soon	1998

Hum 971-995: M.I. Hummel miniature plate series.

Hum 996: Scamp
Trinket Box

Released in 2002, Scamp 4" x 3" oval box was modeled by master sculptor Helmut Fischer in 2001. It bears the image of the figurine with the same name (Hum 553) on top of the lid, along with the "M.I. Hummel" signature. Small cattail-like images embellish the sides of the box.

Hum No.	Size	Trademark	Current Value
996	4" x 3"	TMK-8	$20-$40

Hum 996: Scamp trinket box.

Hum 997: Pixie
Trinket Box

Modeled by master sculptor Helmut Fischer in 2001 and released in 2002, Pixie 4" x 3" oval box bears the image of the figurine with the same name (Hum 768) on top of the lid, along with the "M.I. Hummel" signature. Small rural homestead images embellish the sides of the box.

Hum No.	Size	Trademark	Current Value
997	4" x 3"	TMK-8	$20-$40

Hum 997: Pixie trinket box.

Hum 998-1998: Open Numbers

Hum 1999: Fanfare

The 14th and final figurine in the "Century Collection," Fanfare was released in 1999 and was produced for this one year only in the 20th century. This was attested by a certificate of authenticity and a special stamp on the bottom of the figurines. The inscription reads: "M.I. HUMMEL 1999 XX FINAL EDITION—CENTURY COLLECTION." Modeled by master sculptors Helmut Fischer and Marion Huschka in 1993, the piece bears an incised 1993 copyright date. An incised "M.I. Hummel" signature appears on the back. It came with a hardwood base with brass plaque that reads: "CENTURY COLLECTION 1999 LETZTE AUSGABE – FINAL EDITION."

Hum No.	Size	Trademark	Current Value
1999	11"	TMK-7	$1,200-$1,300

Hum 1999: Fanfare.

Hum 2000: Worldwide Wanderers

Worldwide Wanderers was modeled by master sculptors Helmut Fischer and Tamara Fuchs in 1998 and released in the United States in 1999. A worldwide limited and numbered edition of 2,000 pieces, it has a 1998 incised copyright date, special "Year 2000 Millennium" backstamp, and TMK-8. It comes with velvet-covered base and porcelain certificate of authenticity. The original issue price was $4,500. It is a closed edition.

Hum No.	Size	Trademark	Current Value
2000	8″	TMK-8	$4,500

Hum 2000: Worldwide Wanderers.

Hum 2001: Christmas is Coming

Christmas is Coming depicts a young lad holding a lantern and pulling a sleigh with a present and a small Christmas tree in a basket on it. A TMK-9 figurine, it has the TMK-9 backstamp.

Hum No.	Size	Trademark	Current Value
2001	5-1/2″	TMK-9	$459 retail

Hum 2001: Christmas is Coming.

Hum 2002: Making New Friends

Released in September 1996, Making New Friends was modeled by master sculptor Helmut Fischer and has a 1996 copyright date. Those produced in 1996 have the "First Issue 1996" and the "125th Anniversary" backstamps applied to the bottom on blue decal. The original issue price was $595.

Hum No.	Size	Trademark	Current Value
2002	6-1/2″	TMK-7	$595-$600
2002	6-1/2″	TMK-8	$625

Hum 2002: Making New Friends.

319

Hum 2003: Dearly Beloved

Modeled by master sculptor Helmut Fischer in 1997, Dearly Beloved was first released in 1998. It bears a 1997 incised copyright date, and those released in that first production year carry a "First Issue 1998" special backstamp. The piece came with a neutral brass plaque affixed to wooden base, which could be engraved by a specialist. The original issue price was $450.

Hum No.	Size	Trademark	Current Value
2003	6-5/8″	TMK-7	$250-$450
2003	6-5/8″	TMK-8	$450
203/2/0	4-1/4″	TMK-8	$219

Hum 2003: Dearly Beloved.

Hum 2004: Pretzel Girl

Pretzel Girl, modeled by master sculptor Helmut Fischer in 1996, was first released in the United States in 1999. Pieces produced that year carry a "First Issue 1999" backstamp. It has an incised 1996 copyright date and an original release price of $185. It is considered a companion piece to Pretzel Boy (Hum 2093).

Several Special Event Collector's Set pieces were issued, including two with "Germany" backstamps, one with "Two Flags, USA," and another with "M.I. Hummel Club Convention, Germany." This is listed as a closed edition in the United States.

Hum No.	Size	Trademark	Current Value
2004	4″	TMK-7	$185-$200

Hum 2004: Pretzel Girl.

Hum 2005-2006: Open Numbers

Hum 2007: Tender Love

Modeled by master sculptor Helmut Fischer in 1996, this 4-1/4" figurine was issued as a limited edition in 1998 for the Spring Open House event at participating U.S. retailers. Production consisted of a worldwide limited and numbered edition of 25,000 pieces. It has an incised copyright date of 1996, and its original retail price was $198. It is a closed edition.

Hum No.	Size	Trademark	Current Value
2007	4-1/4"	TMK-7	$198

Hum 2007: Tender Love.

Hum 2008: Frisky Friends

This 4-1/4" figurine, modeled by master sculptor Helmut Fischer in 1996, was issued as a limited edition in 1997 for the Fall Open House event at participating U.S. retailers. Production consisted of a worldwide limited and numbered edition of 25,000 pieces. It has an incised copyright date of 1996, and its original retail price was $198. It is a closed edition.

Hum No.	Size	Trademark	Current Value
2008	4-1/4"	TMK-7	$198

Hum 2008: Frisky Friends.

Hum 2009: Sleepy Doll

Sleep Doll depicts a young girl cradling her doll. This figurine is a TMK-9 with the TMK-9 backstamp.

Hum No.	Size	Trademark	Current Value
2009	4"	TMK-9	$199 retail

Hum 2009: Sleepy Doll.

2010: Open Number

Hum 2011: Little Landscaper

Sold first as part of the limited edition Little Landscaper Collector's Set on QVC in March 2002, this figurine was later available at authorized M.I. Hummel retailers for $200. The set features the 4-1/4" figurine, which was modeled by master sculptor Helmut Fischer in 1996, and the Bountiful Garden Hummelscape. It carries a "First Issue 2002" backstamp and TMK-8.

Hum No.	Size	Trademark	Current Value
2011	4-14"	TMK-8	$200-$259

Hum 2011: Little Landscaper.

Hum 2012: Saint Nicholas Day

Saint Nicholas Day was modeled by master sculptor Helmut Fischer in 1996 and released in the United States in 1997. This 6-3/4" figurine, with a copyright date of 1996 and TMK-7, was distributed worldwide in a limited and numbered edition of 20,000 pieces. It is considered a companion piece to Ruprecht (Hum 473, formerly called Father Christmas), and was sold as a matching-numbered set originally for $1,000. On its own, the piece was originally priced at $650. It is a closed edition.

Hum No.	Size	Trademark	Current Value
2012	6-3/4"	TMK-7	$250-$450

Hum 2012: Saint Nicholas Day.

Hum 2013: Surprise Visit

Surprise Visit became available for the first time in July 2002 as part of QVC's 14th year of hosting M.I. Hummel shows. The piece carries a "First Issue 2003" backstamp and TMK-8. It was sold as part of the Surprise Visit Collector's Set, which also included the musical Bee Happy display that plays "In the Good Old Summertime." The set was available on QVC only through Sept. 1, 2002, and then available separately at retailers beginning in December 2002.

Hum No.	Size	Trademark	Current Value
2013	4"	TMK-8	$219

Hum 2013: Surprise Visit.

Hum 2014: Christmas Delivery

First released in 1997 in a 5-3/4" size (Hum 2014/I), Christmas Delivery was also produced in a smaller 4-1/4" size (Hum 2014/2/0) beginning in 2000. In the first years of production, each figure carried the "First Issue" backstamp. Modeled by master sculptor Helmut Fischer, this design is a combination of Ride Into Christmas (Hum 396) and Sleep Tight (Hum 424).

The year 2011 marked the celebration of Sister Hummel's 75th anniversary of the beginning of her legacy. Manufaktur Rödental selected 50 figurines to bear the "75th Anniversary" backstamp. Christmas Delivery was one of those figurines. Only 75 of them were available in North America with this backstamp. Each figurine was hand-numbered, with a golden backstamp and a map of North America backstamp. A special porcelain plaque was included, and a notable emblem on the packaging hinted at the contents. Each figurine included a "75 Years of M.I. Hummel" certificate.

Hum 2014: Christmas Delivery.

Hum No.	Size	Trademark	Current Value
2014/I	5-3/4"	TMK-7	$495-$500
2014/I	5-3/4"	TMK-8	$530
2014/2/0	4-1/4"	TMK-8	$279
2014/III	8-1/2"	TMK-8	$1,550

Hum 2015: Wonder of Christmas

Modeled by master sculptor Helmut Fischer in 1997, this 7" figure was first released in 1998 in a worldwide limited and numbered edition of 20,000. It carries an incised 1997 copyright date and TMK-7.

Hum 2015 is also available in a Wonder of Christmas Collector's Set, which pairs the figurine with a Steiff teddy bear. The set's bear is a worldwide limited and numbered edition of 20,000. The backstamp contained a "First Issue" marking in the year it was released, 1998. The original price of the set was $575.

Hum 2015: Wonder of Christmas Collector's Set with Steiff bear.

Hum No.	Size	Trademark	Current Value
2015	7"	TMK-7	$400-$500
2015	7"	TMK-8	$400-$500

Hum 2016: Tasty Treats

This figurine of a boy and girl standing by a gingerbread house was issued in 2009. It features a special backstamp commemorating the 100th anniversary of the birth of Sister M.I. Hummel and TMK-9. The mold number and copyright year are incised on the bottom of the piece.

Hum No.	Size	Trademark	Current Value
2016	6-1/4"	TMK-9	$529 retail

Hum 2016: Tasty Treats.

Hum 2017: Open Number

Hum 2018: Toyland Express

Introduced in the summer of 2002, Toyland Express was made available only during special Toyland Events held from Sept. 1 through Dec. 31, 2002. The piece, which was modeled by master sculptor Helmut Fischer in 1998, carries a special "Little Town Train" backstamp and came with a free handmade Goebel beehive pin. It is considered a companion to the spring 2002 Toyland Event figurine, My Favorite Pony (Hum 2019).

Hum No.	Size	Trademark	Current Value
2018	4-1/4"	TMK-8	$219

Hum 2018: Toyland Express.

Hum 2019: My Favorite Pony

My Favorite Pony was made available only during special Toyland Events held in the spring of 2002, from March 1 through June 30. The piece, which was modeled by master sculptor Helmut Fischer in 1998, carried a "SPECIAL EVENT" backstamp and TMK-8 and came with a handmade Goebel basket of flowers porcelain pin. It is considered a companion to the fall 2002 Toyland Event figurine, Toyland Express (Hum 2018).

A variation of this piece was made available in March 2002 through QVC. Called Darling Duckling, the figurine was essentially the same as My Favorite Pony except that in place of a pony, a wooden duck was affixed. Since the girl figurine and the size is the same for both pieces, Darling Duckling carries the same model number—2019—as My Favorite Pony, along with an "EXCLUSIVE EDITION" backstamp. QVC sold the figurine as part of the Towne Square Collector's Set, which also included a musical Hummelscape. Despite the variation between duck and pony, Darling Duckling is priced the same as the regular variation of My Favorite Pony.

Hum No.	Size	Trademark	Current Value
2019	4-1/4"	TMK-8	$150-$219

Hum 2019: My Favorite Pony.

Hum 2020: Riding Lesson

Modeled by master sculptor Helmut Fischer, this 4-1/2" figurine was first released in the United States in 2001. It carries a "First Issue 2001" special backstamp in the first year of production, along with TMK-8. It is considered an unofficial companion piece to Cowboy Corral (Hum 2021).

Hum No.	Size	Trademark	Current Value
2020	4-1/2"	TMK-8	$150-$219

Hum 2020: Riding Lesson.

Hum 2021: Cowboy Corral

This 4-1/4" figurine, modeled by master sculptor Helmut Fischer, was first released in the United States in 2001. An unofficial companion piece to Riding Lesson (Hum 2020), it carries a "First Issue 2001" special backstamp in the first year of production, along with TMK-8. It is one of two M.I. Hummel figurines to win *Collector Editions* magazine's Award of Excellence for 2001; the other was Scooter Time (Hum 2070).

Hum No.	Size	Trademark	Current Value
2021	4-1/4"	TMK-8	$150-219

Hum 2021: Cowboy Corral.

Hum 2022-2024: Open Numbers

Hum 2025/A: Wishes Come True

Modeled by master sculptor Helmut Fischer in 1997, this 6-1/2" figurine was the exclusive annual edition for members of the M.I. Hummel Club in club year 2000-2001. It carries an incised 1997 copyright date as well as the club exclusive backstamp and TMK-8. As with any of the club exclusives, it was received by way of a redemption card. This original issue price was $695.

Hum No.	Size	Trademark	Current Value
2025/A	6-1/2"	TMK-8	$250-$695

Hum 2025/A: Wishes Come True.

Hum 2026: Good Tidings

This figurine, which was issued in 2003, is part of a collector set with the Tidings of Joy Hummelscape. Good Tidings has the Exclusive Edition, EE, and Christmas tree backstamps, an incised 2003 copyright date, and TMK-8. A mixed media piece, it features a wooden sled and packages.

Hum No.	Size	Trademark	Current Value
2026	4-1/4"	TMK-8 OE	$199

Hum 2026: Good Tidings.

Hum 2027: Easter's Coming

Modeled by master sculptor Helmut Fischer, this 4" figurine was first released in the United States in 2001. It carries a "First Issue" special backstamp in the first year of production, along with TMK-8. It was also sold as part of the Easter Basket collector's set.

Hum No.	Size	Trademark	Current Value
2027	4"	TMK-8	$179-$240

Hum 2027: Easter's Coming.

Hum 2028: Winter Adventure

This 4-1/4" figurine, modeled by master sculptor Helmut Fischer, was first released in the United States in 2001. It carries a "First Issue" special backstamp in the first year of production, along with TMK-8. It came as part of a collector's set, which included the figurine and the Slalom Slopes Hummelscape.

Hum No.	Size	Trademark	Current Value
2028	4-1/4"	TMK-8	$139-$230

Hum 2028: Winter Adventure.

Hum 2029: Open Number

Hum 2030: Firefighter

Modeled by master sculptor Helmut Fischer in 1997, this 4-1/4" figurine was first released in the United States in late

1999. It carries a "First Issue 2000 Millennium" special backstamp in the first year of production, along with TMK-8. It comes with a complimentary Hummelscape titled To the Rescue.

In the wake of the terrorist attacks on the World Trade Center and Pentagon on Sept. 11, 2001 and the resulting American military effort, Goebel alerted its M.I. Hummel Club chapters that it would donate appropriately

Hum 2030: Firefighter.

Hum No.	Size	Trademark	Current Value
2030	4-1/4"	TMK-8	$180-$250
2030	4-1/4"	TMK-9	$129 retail

themed figurines to local chapters to be used as raffle prizes. Any proceeds from such fund-raising events would then go to benefit the families of the victims. Seven figurines, including this one, were selected as appropriate due to their patriotic or firefighter/police/medical personnel themes.

Firefighter was re-released in the winter of 2013 in the "Innocent Reflections" series, a series of white ceramic figurines on which a glaze is fired to make it glisten. A coating of 21-karat gold is painted on certain details of each figurine, then fired for 3-1/2 hours. On this figurine, the firefighter hat, water nozzle, and bucket handle are painted in gold. This figurine is TMK-9.

Hum 2031: Catch of the Day

This 4-1/4" figurine, modeled by master sculptor Helmut Fischer, was first released in the United States in 2000. It carries a "First Issue" special backstamp in the first year of production, along with TMK-8. A complimentary Fisherman's Feast Hummelscape is included to form a collector's set.

Hum No.	Size	Trademark	Current Value
2031	4-1/4"	TMK-8	$175-$205

Hum 2031: Catch of the Day.

Hum 2032: Puppy Pause

This 4-1/4" figurine, modeled by master sculptor Marion Huschka in 1997, was first released in the United States in

2001. It carries a "First Issue 2001" special backstamp in the first year of production, along with TMK-8. It is to dog lovers what Kitty Kisses (Hum 2033), which was released at the same time, is to cat lovers.

The year 2011 marked the celebration of Sister Hummel's 75th anniversary of the beginning of her legacy. Manufaktur

Hum 2032: Puppy Pause.

Hum No.	Size	Trademark	Current Value
2032	4-1/4"	TMK-8	$150-$219

Rödental selected 50 figurines to bear the "75th Anniversary" backstamp. Puppy Pause was one of those figurines. Only 75 of them were available in North America with this backstamp. Each figurine was hand-numbered, with a golden backstamp and a map of North America backstamp. A special porcelain plaque was included, and a notable emblem on the packaging hinted at the contents. Each figurine included a "75 Years of M.I. Hummel" certificate.

Hum 2033: Kitty Kisses

First issued in 2001, Kitty Kisses was modeled by master sculptor Marion Huschka in 1997. It carries a "First Issue 2001" special backstamp in the first year of production, as well as TMK-8. It is to cat lovers what Puppy Pause (Hum 2032), which was released at the same time, is to dog lovers.

The year 2011 marked the celebration of Sister Hummel's 75th anniversary of the beginning of her legacy. Manufaktur Rödental selected 50 figurines to bear the "75th Anniversary" backstamp. Kitty Kisses was one of those figurines. Only 75 of them were available in North America with this backstamp. Each figurine was hand-numbered, with a golden backstamp and a map of North America backstamp. A special porcelain plaque was included, and a notable emblem on the packaging hinted at the contents. Each figurine included a "75 Years of M.I. Hummel" certificate.

Hum No.	Size	Trademark	Current Value
2033	4-1/4"	TMK-8	$150-219

Hum 2033: Kitty Kisses.

Hum 2034: Good Luck Charm

Good Luck Charm, which was first released in 2001, carries the special "First Issue 2001" backstamp in the first year of production. Modeled by master sculptor Marion Huschka in 1998, it is 4-1/2" and the original suggested retail price was $190.

Hum No.	Size	Trademark	Current Value
2034	4-1/2"	TMK-8	$110-$179

Hum 2034: Good Luck Charm.

Hum 2035: First Snow

Modeled by master sculptor Helmut Fischer in 1997, First Snow was first released with its companion piece Let It Snow (Hum 2036) in the United States in 1999. It carries a "First Issue" special backstamp

Hum No.	Size	Trademark	Current Value
2035	5-1/2"	TMK-7	$250-$370
2035	5-1/4"	TMK-8	$250-$360
2035/4/0	3-1/4"	TMK-8	$149

in the first year of production, along with TMK-7. The two figurines were part of the Frosty Friends collector's set, which also contained a white Steiff snowman-like bear. The set was released as a worldwide limited and sequentially numbered edition of 20,000.

The year 2011 marked the celebration of Sister Hummel's 75th anniversary of

the beginning of her legacy. Manufaktur Rödental selected 50 figurines to bear the "75th Anniversary" backstamp. First Snow was one of those figurines. Only 75 of them were available in North America with this backstamp. Each figurine was hand-numbered, with a golden backstamp and a map of North America backstamp. A special porcelain plaque was included, and a notable emblem on the packaging hinted at the contents. Each figurine included a "75 Years of M.I. Hummel" certificate.

Hum 2035: First Snow.

Hum 2036: Let It Snow

Modeled by master sculptor Helmut Fischer in 1997, Let It Snow, along with its companion piece First Snow (Hum 2035),

was first released in the United States in 1999. It carries a "First Issue" special backstamp in the first year of production, along with TMK-7. The two figurines were part of the Frosty Friends collector's set, which also contained a white Steiff snowman-like bear. The set was released as a worldwide limited and sequentially numbered edition of 20,000.

Hum 2036: Let It Snow.

Hum No.	Size	Trademark	Current Value
2036	5"	TMK-7	$250-$280
2036	5"	TMK-8	$258
2036/4/0	3.5"	TMK-8	$139

The year 2011 marked the celebration of Sister Hummel's 75th anniversary of the beginning of her legacy. Manufaktur Rödental selected 50 figurines to bear the "75th Anniversary" backstamp. Let It Snow was one of those figurines. Only 75 of them were available in North America with this backstamp. Each figurine was hand-numbered, with a golden backstamp and a map of North America backstamp. A special porcelain plaque was included, and a notable emblem on the packaging hinted at the contents. Each figurine included a "75 Years of M.I. Hummel" certificate.

Hum 2037: Star Light, Star Bright

This mixed media figurine of a child with a dog, with removable leash and metal dog tag, was issued in 2005. It has a "First Issue 2005" backstamp, incised 1998 copyright date, and TMK-8.

The year 2011 marked the celebration of Sister Hummel's 75th anniversary of the beginning of her legacy. Manufaktur Rödental selected 50 figurines to bear the "75th Anniversary" backstamp.

Hum 2037: Star Light, Star Bright.

Hum No.	Size	Trademark	Current Value
2037	5-1/4"	TMK-8 OE	$275-$305

Star Light, Star Bright was one of those figurines. Only 75 of them were available in North America with this backstamp. Each figurine was hand-numbered, with a golden backstamp and a map of North America backstamp. A special porcelain plaque was included, and a notable emblem on the packaging hinted at the contents. Each figurine included a "75 Years of M.I. Hummel" certificate.

Hum 2038: In the Kitchen

Released in late 1999, In the Kitchen was modeled by master sculptor Helmut Fischer in 1998 and carries a 1998 copyright date. Sold on QVC, it bears TMK-8 and the "First Issue 2000 MILLENNIUM" backstamp. Like Hum 2030, it came with a free Hummelscape, Painting Pals.

Hum No.	Size	Trademark	Current Value
2038	4-1/2"	TMK-8	$150-$200
2038	4-1/2"	TMK-7 CE	$150-$200

Hum 2038: In the Kitchen.

Hum 2039: Halt!

First designed by master sculptor Helmut Fischer in 1997, Halt! was released in 2000. It carries a 1998 copyright date as well as the "First Issue 2000" special backstamp in the first year of production. It is one of the figurines in the "Off to Work" series. As part of a collector's set, the figurine is sold with a complementary Duck Crossing Hummelscape. The issue price of this piece was $250.

In the wake of the terrorist attacks on the World Trade Center and Pentagon on Sept. 11, 2001 and the resulting American military effort, Goebel alerted its M.I. Hummel Club chapters that it would donate appropriately themed figurines to local chapters to be used as raffle prizes. Any proceeds from such fund-raising events would then go to benefit the families of the victims. Seven figurines, including this one, were selected as appropriate due to their patriotic or firefighter/police/medical personnel themes.

Hum No.	Size	Trademark	Current Value
2039	4-3/4"	TMK-8	$150-$200

Hum 2039: Halt!

Hum 2040: One Coat or Two?

First issued in 2000, this piece is the work of master sculptor Helmut Fischer, who modeled it in 1998. It carries a 1998 incised copyright date and the special "First Issue 2000" backstamp in the first year of production. The figurine was available as part of a collector's set with a Hummelscape. The original issue price was $250.

Hum No.	Size	Trademark	Current Value
2040	4-1/2"	TMK-8	$150-$200

Hum 2040: One Coat or Two?

Hum 2041: Open Number

Hum 2042: Hocus Pocus

Hocus Pocus is the first magic-themed M.I. Hummel Club Exclusive in a Preview Edition of 400 pieces. It depicts a young boy performing magic with a rabbit in a hat. It is a M.I. Hummel Club Exclusive Preview Edition of 400 pieces. It has the "M.I. Hummel Club Exclusive" backstamp along with the TMK-9 backstamp.

Hum 2042: Hocus Pocus.

Hum No.	Size	Trademark	Current Value
2042	4"	TMK-9 LE	$199

Hum 2043/A: Just Horsin' Around

Introduced in 2007, Just Horsin' Around depicts a girl riding a hobby horse. It features TMK-8 and is a companion to Hum 2043/B: Pony Express.

The year 2011 marked the celebration of Sister Hummel's 75th anniversary of the beginning of her legacy. Manufaktur Rödental selected 50 figurines to bear the "75th Anniversary" backstamp. Just Horsin' Around was one of those figurines. Only 75 of them were available in North America with this backstamp. Each figurine was hand-numbered, with a golden backstamp and a map of North America backstamp. A special porcelain plaque was included, and a notable emblem on the packaging hinted at the contents. Each figurine included a "75 Years of M.I. Hummel" certificate.

Hum 2043/A: Just Horsin' Around.

Hum No.	Size	Trademark	Current Value
2043/A	4"	TMK-8	$189

Hum 2043/B: Pony Express

Issued in 2007, Pony Express depicts a boy riding a hobbyhorse. It is part of the "Time to Play" series and has TMK-8. It is a companion to Hum 2043/A: Just Horsin' Around.

Hum 2043/B: Pony Express.

Hum No.	Size	Trademark	Current Value
2043/B	4-1/4"	TMK-8	$189

Hum 2044: All Aboard

Another piece in the "Off to Work" series, this figurine was modeled by master sculptor Helmut Fischer is 1996. It carries an incised 1997 copyright date. Those pieces made in the first year of production carry the special "First Issue" backstamp. The Homeward Bound Hummelscape is included as part of a collector's set. The original issue price was $250.

Hum 2044: All Aboard.

Hum No.	Size	Trademark	Current Value
2044	5"	TMK-8	$205-$210

Hum 2045: Trail Blazer

Introduced in the fall of 2006, Trail Blazer was an M.I. Hummel Club 30th anniversary edition. With a "First Issue 2007" backstamp and TMK-8, it was produced in a limited edition of 100. It is the companion to Gretl (Hum 2247).

The year 2009 was the 20th anniversary of master painter Ulrich Tendera's tour through North America. To mark this event, Manufaktur Rödental introduced a commemorative version of this figurine for QVC. The letter "U" for Ulrich and a bumblebee symbol appear on the boy's shirt, 2009 is marked on his shorts, and the inscription "20 Years on Tour" appears beneath his feet on the rocky ground. Each figurine has Tendera's signature and a hand-signed commemorative certificate. This figurine was only available in 2009.

The year 2011 marked the celebration of Sister Hummel's 75th anniversary of the beginning of her legacy. Manufaktur Rödental selected 50 figurines to bear the "75th Anniversary" backstamp. Trail Blazer was one of those figurines. Only 75 of them were available in North America with this backstamp. Each figurine is hand-numbered, with a golden backstamp and a map of North America backstamp. A special porcelain plaque was included, and a notable emblem on the packaging hinted at the contents. Each figurine included a "75 Years of M.I. Hummel" certificate.

Hum 2045: Trail Blazer.

Hum No.	Size	Trademark	Current Value
2045	4-1/4"	TMK-8	$180-$250
2045	4-1/2"	TMK-9	$180-$250

Hum 2046: Open Number

Hum 2047: Winter Sleigh Ride

Part of the Home for the Holidays Hummelscape, Winter Sleigh Ride was issued in 2002. It has an incised 1998 copyright date, Exclusive Edition, EE, backstamp, and TMK-8. It is a mixed media figurine featuring a wooden sled and twine rope.

Hum No.	Size	Trademark	Current Value
2047	4"	TMK-8	$225

Hum 2048: Little Patriot

Released in 2002 and issued for the U.S. military in a limited edition of 3,000, Little Patriot is second in the "Ambassadors of Freedom" series. It features TMK-8.

Hum 2048: Little Patriot.

Hum No.	Size	Trademark	Current Value
2048/II	8"	TMK-8 LE	$450-$550

Hum 2049/A: Cuddles

Modeled by master sculptor Helmut Fischer in 1997, Cuddles was first issued as a 3-1/2" figurine in 1998 at $80. Hum 2049/A carries the special "First Issue 1998" backstamp in the first year of production, along with incised 1997 copyright date and TMK-7. It is considered an unofficial

Hum No.	Size	Trademark	Current Value
2049/A	3-1/2"	TMK-7	$70-$75
2049/A/0	3"	TMK-8	$70-75
2049/A	3-1/2"	TMK-8	$70

companion to My Best Friend (Hum 2049/B).

A smaller 3-1/4" ornament variation of this piece was issued later with model number 2049/A/0 and TMK-8.

Hum 2049/A: Cuddles.

Hum 2049/B: My Best Friend

First issued as a 3-1/2" figurine in 1998 at $80, My Best Friend carries the special "First Issue 1998" backstamp in the first year of production, an incised 1997 copyright date, and TMK-7. Master sculptor Helmut Fischer first modeled this piece in 1997. It is considered an unofficial companion to Cuddles (Hum 2049/A), which was issued the same year.

A smaller 3-1/4" ornament variation of this piece was issued later with model number 2049/B/0 and TMK-8.

Hum No.	Size	Trademark	Current Value
2049/B	3-1/2"	TMK-7 CE	$70-$75
2049/B/0	3-1/4"	TMK-8 TW	$70-$75
2049/B	3-1/4"	TMK-8	$70

Hum 2049/B: My Best Friend.

Hum 2050/A: Messages of Love

First issued in 1999, Messages of Love was modeled by master sculptor Helmut Fischer in 1997. It carries an incised 1997 copyright date, a "First Issue 1999" special backstamp in the first year of production, and TMK-7. Newer pieces bear TMK-8. It is considered a companion piece to Be Mine (Hum 2050/B), which was issued the same year.

In 1999, some pieces also bore a special edition backstamp "Hummel, Bumble Bee" for an event held in the United States. These special editions were available for one year only and are now listed as closed editions.

Hum No.	Size	Trademark	Current Value
2050/A	3-1/4"	TMK-7	$70-$75
2050/A	3-1/4"	TMK-8	$70-$75

Hum 2050/A: Messages of Love.

Hum 2050/B: Be Mine

First issued in 1999, this 3-1/2" piece was modeled by master sculptor Helmut Fischer in 1997. It carries a "First Issue 1999" special backstamp in the first year of production, incised 1997 copyright date, and TMK-7. Newer pieces now carry TMK-8. It is considered a companion piece to Messages of Love (Hum 2050/A), which was issued the same year.

Hum 2050/B: Be Mine.

Hum No.	Size	Trademark	Current Value
2050/B	3-1/2"	TMK-7	$70-$75
2050/B	3-1/2"	TMK-8	$75

Hum 2051/A: Once Upon a Time

Once Upon a Time, the design of master sculptor Helmut Fischer in 1997, was first released in 1998, and any of those pieces issued in the first year of production will carry the special "First Issue 1998" backstamp, incised 1997 copyright date, and

TMK-7. Newer pieces will carry TMK-8. The original issue price was $80. Once Upon a Time is considered a companion piece to Let's Play (Hum 2051/B).

There are two editions of this figurine that carry special backstamps. One was issued in 1998 as a promotional piece for the "Miller's Expo" in the United States, and the other in 2000 for an event in Germany. Pieces carrying these special backstamps were issued only for one year and are now considered closed editions.

Hum 2051/A: Once Upon a Time.

Hum No.	Size	Trademark	Current Value
2051/A	3-1/2"	TMK-7	$70-$75
2051/A	3-1/2"	TMK-8	$75

Hum 2051/B: Let's Play

First issued in 1998, Let's Play was crafted by master sculptor Helmut Fischer in 1997 and carries a 1997 incised copyright date. Those pieces issued in the first year of production carry the "First Issue 1998" special backstamp and TMK-7. Newer pieces carry TMK-8. The original issue price was $80.

Hum 2051/B: Let's Play.

Hum No.	Size	Trademark	Current Value
2051/B	3-1/2"	TMK-7	$70-$75
2051/B	3-1/2"	TMK-8	$75

Hum 2052: Pigtails

Pigtails, which was modeled by master sculptor Helmut Fischer in 1998, was released in 1999 as the free exclusive renewal figurine for members of the M.I. Hummel Club in club year 1999-2000. It carries an incised copyright date of 1998, special club bumblebee marking, TMK-7, and decal inscription: "MI.I. HUMMEL CLUB Membership Year 1999/2000." It is a companion piece to Lucky Charmer (Hum 2071).

Hum 2052: Pigtails.

Hum No.	Size	Trademark	Current Value
2052	3-1/2"	TMK-7	$70-$80

Hum 2053: Playful Pals

Modeled by master sculptor Helmut Fischer in 1997, this figurine was issued in 1998 as a limited and numbered edition of 25,000 pieces worldwide. It has an incised 1997 copyright date and TMK-7, but does not carry a "First Issue" backstamp. It came with a free Autumn Frolic Hummelscape. It is now listed as a closed edition.

Hum No.	Size	Trademark	Current Value
2053	3-1/2"	TMK-7	$110-$150

Hum 2053: Playful Pals.

Hum 2054-2057: Open Numbers

Hum 2058/A: Skating Lesson

Modeled by master sculptor Helmut Fischer in 1998, this winter-themed figurine was first issued in 2000 along with its companion piece, Skate in Stride (Hum 2058/B). Those released in the first year of production carry the special "First Issue 2000" backstamp, incised 1998 copyright date, and TMK-8. The two figurines together make up the Icy Adventure Collector's Set, which retailed for $375 and included the Icy Adventure Hummelscape.

Hum No.	Size	Trademark	Current Value
2058/A	3-1/4"	TMK-8	$110-$150

Hum 2058/A: Skating Lesson.

Hum 2058/B: Skate in Stride

Modeled by master sculptor Helmut Fischer in 1998, this winter-themed figurine was first issued in 2000 along with its companion piece, Skating Lesson (Hum 2058/A). Those released in the first year of production carry the special "First Issue 2000" backstamp, incised 1998 copyright date, and TMK-8. The two figurines together make up the Icy Adventure Collector's Set, which retailed for $375 and included the Icy Adventure Hummelscape.

Hum No.	Size	Trademark	Current Value
2058/B	3"	TMK-8	$110-$155

Hum 2058/B: Skate In Stride.

Hum 2059: Merry Wandress

Merry Wandress, issued in 2004, was available in North America with an incised 2004 copyright date and "North American Limited Edition" and "First Issue 2005" backstamps. It was produced in an unknown limited edition and was a companion piece to Hum 11/2/0: Merry Wanderer.

The year 2011 marked the celebration of Sister Hummel's 75th anniversary of the beginning of her legacy. Manufaktur Rödental selected 50 figurines to bear the "75th Anniversary" backstamp. Merry Wandress was one of those figurines. Only 75 of them were available in North America with this backstamp. Each figurine was hand-numbered, with a golden backstamp and a map of North America backstamp. A special porcelain plaque was included, and a notable emblem on the packaging hinted at the contents. Each figurine included a "75 Years of M.I. Hummel" certificate.

Hum 2059: Merry Wandress.

Hum No.	Size	Trademark	Current Value
2059	4-1/4″	TMK-8	$125-$180

Hum 2060: European Wanderer

Hum 2060: European Wanderer.

Hum No.	Size	Trademark	Current Value
2060	3-1/2″	TMK-8	$100-$200

This 3-1/2" figurine came as part of a three-piece set released in 1999. The set, which included the figurine, a ceramic globe, and a black hardwood base, was modeled by master sculptors Helmut Fischer and Tamara Fuchs in 1998 and carries an incised 1998 copyright date and TMK-8. An oval decal backstamp reads: "First Issue 2000 MILLENNIUM." The original issue price was $250. This regular open edition was temporarily withdrawn from production on June 15, 2002.

Several editions of Hum 2060 were issued with special backstamps in 1999, including U.S. military pieces and figurines made available in Australia and the Caribbean. These special edition pieces are closed.

In total, there were five similar figurines issued in 1999, depicting the continents of Australia, Asia, Europe, America, and Africa (Hum 2060-2064). Together, these pieces were available in a "Millennium Collection" set that included a black pentagonal wooden base for display. The original issue price of the set was $1,250. It is considered a closed edition.

Hum 2061: American Wanderer

Hum 2061: American Wanderer.

Hum No.	Size	Trademark	Current Value
2061	4-1/4″	TMK-8	$100-$200

This 4-1/4" figurine came as part of a three-piece set released in 1999. The set, which included the figurine, a ceramic globe, and a black hardwood base, was modeled by master sculptors Helmut Fischer and Tamara Fuchs in 1998 and carries an incised 1998 copyright date and TMK-8. An oval decal backstamp reads: "First Issue 2000 MILLENNIUM." The original issue price was $250. This regular open edition was temporarily withdrawn from production on June 15, 2002.

Several editions of Hum 2061 were issued with special backstamps in 1999, including U.S. military pieces and figurines made available in Canada and Germany. These special edition pieces are closed.

In total, there were five similar figurines issued in 1999, depicting the continents of Australia, Asia, Europe, America, and Africa (Hum 2060-2064). Together, these pieces were available in a "Millennium Collection" set that included a black pentagonal wooden base for display. The original issue price of the set was $1,250. It is considered a closed edition.

Hum 2062: African Wanderer

This 3-1/2" figurine came as part of a three-piece set released in 1999. The set, which included the figurine, a ceramic globe, and a black hardwood base, was modeled by master sculptors Helmut Fischer and Tamara Fuchs in 1998 and carries an incised 1998 copyright date and TMK-8. An oval decal backstamp reads:  "First Issue 2000 MILLENNIUM." The original issue price was $250. This regular open edition was temporarily withdrawn from production on June 15, 2002.

Hum 2062: African Wanderer.

Hum No.	Size	Trademark	Current Value
2062	3-1/2"	TMK-8	$100-$200

A U.S. military edition of Hum 2062 was issued in 1999 with special backstamp. These special edition pieces are closed.

In total, there were five similar figurines issued in 1999, depicting the continents of Australia, Asia, Europe, America, and Africa (Hum 2060-2064). Together, these pieces were available in a "Millennium Collection" set that included a black pentagonal wooden base for display. The original issue price of the set was $1,250. It is considered a closed edition.

Hum 2063: Asian Wanderer

This 4" figurine came as part of a three-piece set released in 1999. The set, which included the figurine, a ceramic globe, and a black hardwood base, was modeled by master sculptors Helmut Fischer and Tamara Fuchs in 1998 and carries an incised 1998 copyright date and TMK-8. An  oval decal backstamp reads: "First Issue 2000 MILLENNIUM." The original issue price was $250. This regular open edition was temporarily withdrawn from production on June 15, 2002.

Hum 2063: Asian Wanderer.

Hum No.	Size	Trademark	Current Value
2063	4"	TMK-8	$100-$200

A U.S. military edition of Hum 2063 was issued in 1999 with special backstamp. These special edition pieces are closed.

In total, there were five similar figurines issued in 1999, depicting the continents of Australia, Asia, Europe, America, and Africa (Hum 2060-2064). Together, these pieces were available in a "Millennium Collection" set that included a black pentagonal wooden base for display. The original issue price of the set was $1,250. It is considered a closed edition.

Hum 2064: Australian Wanderer

This 3-1/2" figurine came as part of a three-piece set released in 1999. The set, which included the figurine, a ceramic globe, and a black hardwood base, was modeled by master sculptors Helmut Fischer and Tamara Fuchs in 1998 and carries an incised 1998 copyright date and TMK-8. An oval decal backstamp reads: "First Issue 2000 MILLENNIUM." The original issue price was $250. This regular open edition was temporarily withdrawn from production on June 15, 2002.

A U.S. military edition of Hum 2064 was issued in 1999 with special backstamp. These special edition pieces are closed.

In total, there were five similar figurines issued in 1999, depicting the continents of Australia, Asia, Europe, America, and Africa (Hum 2060-2064). Together, these pieces were available in a "Millennium Collection" set that included a black pentagonal wooden base for display. The original issue price of the set was $1,250. It is considered a closed edition.

Hum No.	Size	Trademark	Current Value
2064	3-1/2"	TMK-8	$100-$200

Hum 2064: Australian Wanderer.

Hum 2065: Open Number

Hum 2066: Peaceful Offering

Modeled by master sculptor Helmut Fischer in 1998, Peaceful Offering was released in 1999 as a limited and numbered edition of 25,000 pieces. It carries an incised 1998 copyright date and TMK-7, but does not have a "First Issue" backstamp. The figurine came as a collectors set with the free Friendship in Bloom Hummelscape. This piece is a closed edition.

Hum No.	Size	Trademark	Current Value
2066	4-1/4"	TMK-7	$100-$200

Hum 2066: Peaceful Offering.

Hum 2067/A: Sweet Treats

Modeled by master sculptor Helmut Fischer in 1998, the ornament variation (2067/A/0) of Sweet Treats was released in 1999 in the United States only as a limited and numbered edition of 25,000 pieces. It carries a stamped 1998 copyright date and TMK-7 on its feet and a small brass ring on the head for hanging as an ornament. It could either be purchased for $75 in 1999 or obtained as a free gift to members of the M.I. Hummel Club who had redemption cards and purchased $150 in Hummel products.

The figurine (Hum 2067/A) was issued in 2000 and carries an incised 1998 copyright date, TMK-8, and "First Issue 2000" special backstamp in the first year of production.

Sweet Treats was re-released in the "Innocent Reflections" series, a series of white ceramic figurines on which a glaze is fired to make it glisten. A coating of 21-karat gold is painted on certain details of each figurine, then fired for 3-1/2 hours. On this figurine, the "sweet treat" is painted in gold. This figurine is TMK-9.

Hum 2067/A: Sweet Treats.

Hum No.	Size	Trademark	Current Value
2067/A	3-1/4"	TMK-8	$70-$75
2067/A/0	3-1/4"	TMK-7	$70-$75
2067/A/0	3-1/4"	TMK-8	$70-$75
2067/A	3-1/4"	TMK-9	$79 retail

Hum 2067/B: For Me?

Like its companion piece (Hum 2067/A: Sweet Treats), For Me? exists in both ornament and figurine form.

Modeled by master sculptor Helmut Fischer in 1998, the ornament variation (2067/A/0) of this piece was released in 2000 in the United States only as a limited and numbered edition of 25,000 pieces. It carries a stamped 1998 copyright date and TMK-8 on its feet and a small brass ring on the head for hanging as an ornament.

The figurine (Hum 2067/A) was issued in 2000 and carries an incised 1998 copyright date, TMK-8, and "First Issue 2000" special backstamp in the first year of production.

Hum 2067/B: For Me?

Hum No.	Size	Trademark	Current Value
2067/B	3-1/2"	TMK-8	$70-$75
2067/B/0	3-1/4"	TMK-8	$70-$75

Hum 2068/A: Bumblebee Blossom

Bumblebee Blossom, issued in 2003, has an incised 1999 copyright date, "First Issue 2004" backstamp, and TMK-8. It was part of the "Create-A-Gift" collection when paired with a Sentiment Occasion base. It was also available in a limited edition of 500 with a "Caribbean Collection" backstamp, and in a limited edition of 600 with a "Swiss Collection" backstamp, each with a special base.

Hum No.	Size	Trademark	Current Value
2068/A	3-1/4"	TMK-8 OE	$70-$75

Hum 2068/A: Bumblebee Blossom.

Hum 2068/B: A Four-Leaf Clover/Pledge to America

Sculpted by Helmut Fischer, A Four-Leaf Clover was issued in 2003 with an incised 1999 copyright date, "First Issue 2003" backstamp, and TMK-8. It was part of the "Create-A-Gift" collection when paired with a Sentiment Occasion base. It was also available in a limited edition of 600 with a "Swiss Collection" backstamp and special base. As Pledge to America, released in 2004, the boy holds an American flag instead of a clover. This variation has an incised 1999 copyright date, "Special Edition" and U.S. flag backstamps, and TMK-8.

Hum No.	Size	Trademark	Current Value
2068/B	3-1/4"	TMK-8 OE	$70-$75

Hum 2068/B: A Four-Leaf Clover/Pledge to America.

Hum 2069/A: Monkey Business/ Freedom Day

Sculpted by Helmut Fischer, Monkey Business was issued in 2003 with an incised 1999 copyright date, "First Issue 2003" backstamp, and TMK-8. It was part of the "Create-A-Gift" collection when paired with a Sentiment Occasion base. It was also available as Freedom Day, in which the monkey was replaced with an American flag. This variation, issued in 2005, has an incised 1998 copyright date, "Special Edition" and U.S. flag backstamps, and TMK-8.

Hum No.	Size	Trademark	Current Value
2069/A	3-1/4"	TMK-8 OE	$70-$75

Hum 2069/A: Monkey Business/Freedom Day.

Hum 2070: Scooter Time

From the "Wonder of Childhood" collection, Scooter Time is the second edition in the series. It is a M.I. Hummel Club members' exclusive presented for club year 25, which means it was retired on May 31, 2002. Modeled by master sculptor Helmut Fischer, it comes with a wooden base bearing an engraved brass plaque and special club "EXCLUSIVE EDITION" backstamp. It was one of two M.I. Hummel figurines to win *Collector Editions* magazine's Award of Excellence for 2001; the other was Cowboy Corral (Hum 2021).

Hum No.	Size	Trademark	Current Value
2070	6-3/4"	TMK-8	$500-$695

Hum 2070: Scooter Time.

Hum 2071: Lucky Charmer

Modeled by master sculptor Helmut Fischer in 1999, Lucky Charmer was released in 1999 as an exclusive annual edition for members of the M.I. Hummel Club in club year 1999-2000. It has an incised 1999 copyright date as well as special club bumblebee symbol and decal inscription that reads: "M.I. HUMMEL CLUB Membership Year 1999/2000." The official issue price was $90 with redemption card in 1999. This figurine was retired May 31, 2000.

Hum 2071: Lucky Charmer.

Hum No.	Size	Trademark	Current Value
2071	3-1/2"	TMK-7	$70-$75

Hum 2072: Winter Days

Winter Days, issued in 2004, has a "First Issue 2004" backstamp, incised copyright date, and TMK-8. It was available with the "Winter Days" base with Fenton Art Glass evergreens.

Hum 2072: Winter Days

Hum No.	Size	Trademark	Current Value
2072	6-1/4"	TMK-8 OE	$359-$500

Hum 2073/A: Ring in the Season

Modeled in 1999 and carrying that year's incised copyright date, this 4" figurine was released in 2001. Pieces produced in 2001 bear the special "First Issue 2001" backstamp and TMK-8. This holiday piece is a companion to Christmas Carol (Hum 2073/B), which was issued the same year.

Hum 2073/A: Ring in the Season.

Hum No.	Size	Trademark	Current Value
2073/A	4"	TMK-8	$95-$139

Hum 2073/B: Christmas Carol

Modeled in 1999 and carrying that year's incised copyright date, this 4" figurine was released in 2001. Pieces produced in 2001 bear the special "First Issue 2001" backstamp and TMK-8. This holiday piece is a companion to Ring in the Season (Hum 2073/A).

Hum 2072: Winter Days

Hum No.	Size	Trademark	Current Value
2073/B	4"	TMK-8	$95-$139

Hum 2074/A: Christmas Gift

The design of master sculptor Helmut Fischer in 1998, Christmas Gift was released first as a 3-1/4" ornament (Hum 2074/A/0) in 1998 and then as a 3-1/2" figurine (Hum 2074/A) in 1999.

The ornament was available in the United States only as a free gift when $150 of Hummel merchandise was purchased from participating retailers.

The figurine was released with 1998 incised copyright date, TMK-7, and "First Issue 1998" backstamp the first year of production. Newer pieces bear TMK-8. The original issue price was $90.

Hum No.	Size	Trademark	Current Value
2074/A	3-1/2"	TMK-7	$90-$95
2074/A	3-1/2"	TMK-8	$90-$95
2074/A/0	3-1/4"	TMK-7	$80-$90

Hum 2073/B: Christmas Carol.

Hum 2075: Comfort and Care

Originally crafted in 1998, this piece was released in 2000 as part of the "Off to Work" series. The 4-1/4" figurine, which carried the special "First Issue 2000" backstamp in the first year of production and incised 1998 copyright date, came with the Healing Hands Hummelscape included.

In the wake of the terrorist attacks on the World Trade Center and Pentagon on Sept. 11, 2001 and the resulting American military effort, Goebel alerted its M.I. Hummel Club chapters that it would donate appropriately themed figurines to local chapters to be used as raffle prizes. Any proceeds from such fund-raising events would then go to benefit the families of the victims. Seven figurines, including this one, were selected as appropriate due to their patriotic or firefighter/police/medical personnel themes.

Hum 2075: Comfort and Care.

Hum No.	Size	Trademark	Current Value
2075	4-1/4"	TMK-8	$175-$255

Hum 2076: Open Number

Hum 2077/A: First Bloom

Master sculptor Helmut Fischer modeled First Bloom in 1999, and the figurine bears an incised copyright date of that year. It was released in the fall of 1999 at select retailers only with other retailers added in by early 2000. Pieces produced in the first year of production bear the "First Issue 2000" special backstamp along with TMK-8. The original issue price was $85. First Bloom is considered a companion to A Flower For You (Hum 2077/B), which was released the same year.

An ornament variation (Hum 2077/A/0) was released the same year. It was available exclusively in the United States.

Hum 2077/A: First Bloom.

Hum No.	Size	Trademark	Current Value
2077/A	3-1/4"	TMK-8	$70-$75
2077/A/0	3"	TMK-8	$70-$75

Hum 2077/B: A Flower For You

Modeled by master sculptor Helmut Fischer in 1999, A Flower For You carries an incised copyright date with that year. It was a new release for 2000. Pieces produced in the first year of production bear the "First Issue 2000" special backstamp, along with TMK-8. The original issue price was $85. A Flower For You is considered a companion to First Bloom (Hum 2077/A), which was released the same year.

An ornament variation (Hum 2077/B/0) was released the same year. It was available exclusively in the United States.

Hum 2077/B: A Flower for You.

Hum No.	Size	Trademark	Current Value
2077/B	3-1/4"	TMK-8	$70-$75
2077/B/0	3"	TMK-8	$70-$75

Hum 2078: My Toy Train

This figurine of a boy holding his toy locomotive was released in 2003 with a "First Issue 2003" backstamp. It is paired with a Sentiment Occasion base and is part of the "Create-a-Gift" series. It has an incised 1999 copyright date and TMK-8.

Hum 2078: My Toy Train.

Hum No.	Size	Trademark	Current Value
2078	3-1/2"	TMK-8 OE	$69.59 retail

Hum 2079/A: All By Myself

A new release for 2003, All By Myself measures 3-3/4" and is a companion piece to Hum 2079/B, Windy Wishes. It has a

"First Issue 2003" backstamp, incised 2000 copyright date, and TMK-8. It was modeled by master sculptor Helmut Fischer in 1999.

This piece was also available with the Cape Hatteras Lighthouse Hummelscape.

Hum 2079/A: All By Myself.

Hum No.	Size	Trademark	Current Value
2079/A	3-3/4"	TMK-8	$100-$140

Hum 2079/B: Windy Wishes

This figurine is the companion to All By Myself, Hum 2079/A. It is slightly bigger at 4". It was a new release for 2003. It has a "First Issue 2003" backstamp, incised 2000 copyright date, and TMK-8. It was modeled by master sculptor Helmut Fischer in 1999.

Hum 2079/B: Windy Wishes.

Hum No.	Size	Trademark	Current Value
2079/B	4"	TMK-8	$100-$140

Hum 2080/A: Sharing a Story

Sharing a Story depicts a little girl reading to her kitten. The two are snuggled together with the cat's paws on the page of the book. The piece includes a bench that the girl sits on; however, the bench is made in Asia. A Fireside Fun Assortment (made in Asia) of a brick oven with milk jug, two kittens, and a puppy is sold separately. Each of the Fireside Fun Assortment pieces can be purchased separately as well. Hum 2080/B can also be displayed with Hum 2080/A as part of this set, but is sold separately. Issued in the fall of 2010, this figurine is a TMK-9.

Hum 2080/A: Sharing a Story.

Hum	Size	Trademark	Current Value
2080/A	5-1/4"	TMK-9 OE	$299 retail

Hum 2080/B: Here I Come

Here I Come depicts a little boy who has just learned to crawl. He wears a yellow bib that features an outline of a duck.

A Fireside Fun Assortment (made in Asia) of a brick oven with milk jug, two kittens, and a puppy is sold separately. Each of the Fireside Fun Assortment pieces can be purchased separately as well. Hum 2080/A can also be displayed with Hum 2080/B as part of this set, but is sold separately. Issued in the fall of 2010, this figurine is a TMK-9.

Hum	Size	Trademark	Current Value
2080/B	2-1/2"	TMK-9 OE	$160 retail

Hum 2080/B: Here I Come.

Hum 2080/J: Sharing a Song

Sharing a Song depicts a young boy sitting on a chair playing his guitar. The chair on which he sits is made in Asia. A TMK-9 figurine with the TMK-9 backstamp, the figurine is a perfect match to Hum 2080/A and Hum 2080/B.

The Fireside Fun Assortment Set, consisting of brick oven with milk jug, two kittens, and a puppy, all made in Asia, is also available for purchase. Each piece in the set can be purchased separately as well.

Hum No.	Size	Trademark	Current Value
2080/J	4-3/4"	TMK-9	$250

Hum 2080/J: Sharing a Song.

Hum 2081: Open Number

Hum 2082: Oh, No!

Oh, No! was produced in a special edition of only 250, with each piece signed and numbered by Ulrich Tendera.

Hum No.	Size	Trademark	Current Value
2082	5"	TMK-8	$399

Hum 2082: Oh, No!

Hum 2083: Open Number

Hum 2084/A: Jump for Joy

Sculpted by Helmut Fischer, Jump for Joy was issued in 2004 with a "First Issue 2005" backstamp, incised 2001 copyright date, and TMK-8. The first 2,500 were released to the North American market in 2004 with a Goebel artist signature, "First Issue 2005" backstamp, TMK-8, and a teddy bear-decorated base.

A limited edition of 100 Arbeitsmuster Editions were available in October 2004 in North America to members of the M.I. Hummel Club. This edition had an incised 2001 copyright date, "First Issue 2005" backstamp, and TMK-8.

Hum 2084/A: Jump for Joy.

Hum No.	Size	Trademark	Current Value
2084/A	5-1/4"	TMK-8 OE	$195-$305

Hum 2084/B: Count Me In

Sculpted by Helmut Fischer, Count Me In was issued in 2004 with a "First Issue 2005" backstamp, incised 2001 copyright date, and TMK-8. The first 2,500 were released to the North American market in 2004 with a Goebel artist signature, "First Issue 2005" backstamp, TMK-8, and a train-decorated base.

A limited edition of 100 Arbeitsmuster Editions were available in October 2004 in North America to members of the M.I. Hummel Club. This edition had an incised 2001 copyright date, "First Issue 2005" backstamp, and TMK-8.

Hum 2084/B: Count Me In.

Hum No.	Size	Trademark	Current Value
2084/B	5-1/4"	TMK-8	$195-$305

Hum 2085: Little Farm Hand

A 1999 release, Little Farm Hand was a limited and numbered edition of 25,000 pieces worldwide. First designed by master sculptor Helmut Fischer in 1998, it carries a 1998 incised copyright date as well as TMK-8. Because it is a limited edition, it does not carry the "First Issue" backstamp. The figurine came with a free Millennium Harvest Hummelscape. The original issue price was $198.

This piece, which is a companion to Spring Sowing (Hum 2086), is now considered a closed edition.

Hum No.	Size	Trademark	Current Value
2085	4-3/4"	TMK-8	$195-$225

Hum 2085: Little Farm Hand.

Hum 2086: Spring Sowing

Modeled by master sculptor Helmut Fischer in 1999, this figurine was released in 2000 as a limited and numbered edition of 25,000 pieces. It carries an incised 1999 copyright date as well as TMK-8. Because it is a limited edition, it does not have a "First Issue" backstamp. The figurine came as a collector's set with free Seeds of Friendship Hummelscape. The original issue price was $198.

Hum 2086: Spring Sowing.

Hum No.	Size	Trademark	Current Value
2086	3-1/2"	TMK-8	$195-$225

Hum 2087/A: Sharpest Student

Released in the spring of 2000, this figurine was an exclusive edition for members of the M.I. Hummel Club in club year 2000-2001. Master sculptor Helmut Fischer modeled this piece in 1999, so it bears an incised 1999 copyright date along with TMK-8 and club exclusive backstamp. The original issue price was $95.

Sharpest Student is considered a companion to Honor Student (Hum 2087/B).

Hum 2087/A: Sharpest Student.

Hum No.	Size	Trademark	Current Value
2087/A	4"	TMK-8	$50-$95

Hum 2087/B: Honor Student

Modeled by master sculptor Helmut Fischer in 1999, this figurine was the free gift for members of the M.I. Hummel Club renewing in club year 2000-2001. It was released in 2000 and bears a 1999 incised copyright date as well as TMK-8 and exclusive club backstamp.

Hum 2087/B: Honor Student.

Hum No.	Size	Trademark	Current Value
2087/B	3-3/4"	TMK-8	$50-$95

Hum 2088/A: Playing Around

Released in May 2003 for M.I. Hummel Club year 27, this 4" figurine was the third in the "Clowning Around" series. Like the others in the series, Playing Around was released to club members only and was retired after one year. See Hum 2088/B, Hum 2089/A, and Hum 2089/B for the other series pieces.

Hum No.	Size	Trademark	Current Value
2088/A	4"	TMK-8 EE	$140-$200

Hum 2088/A: Playing Around.

Hum 2088/B: Rolling Around

The second installment in the "Clowning Around" series, Rolling Around was introduced in 2002. It is a M.I. Hummel Club exclusive and bears the special club backstamp and "EXCLUSIVE EDITION 2002/2003" inscription in addition to TMK-8. As a club year 26 exclusive, Rolling Around was retired on May 31, 2003.

Hum No.	Size	Trademark	Current Value
2088/B	3-1/4"	TMK-8	$140-$200

Hum 2088/B: Rolling Around.

Hum 2089/A: Looking Around

Looking Around was an M.I. Hummel Club exclusive available for the 2001-2002 club year only. It was the first installment in the "Clowning Around" series, which also includes Hum 2088/A and 2088/B. It carries a special club backstamp, TMK-8, and the inscription: "EXCLUSIVE EDITION 2001/2002 M.I. HUMMEL CLUB." It was retired on May 31, 2002.

Hum No.	Size	Trademark	Current Value
2089/A	4-1/4"	TMK-8	$150-$230

Hum 2089/A: Looking Around.

Hum 2089/B: Waiting Around

Released in 2004 for M.I. Hummel Club year 28, this 4-3/4" figurine was the fourth and final piece in the "Clowning Around" series. Like the others in the series, it was released to club members only and was retired after one year. See Hum 2088/A, Hum 2088/B, and Hum 2089/A for the other series pieces.

Hum No.	Size	Trademark	Current Value
2089/B	4-3/4"	TMK-8 EE	$150-$230

Hum 2089/B: Waiting Around.

Hum 2090: Open Number

Hum 2091: Maid to Order

Modeled in 1999, this figurine was issued in 2001 as part of the "Off to Work" series. Those issued in the first year of production carry a special "First Issue 2001" backstamp, along with TMK-8 and incised 1999 copyright date. The 4" figurine came with the Strudel Haus Hummelscape.

Hum No.	Size	Trademark	Current Value
2091	4"	TMK-8	$175-$250

Hum 2091: Maid to Order.

Hum 2092: Make Me Pretty

Another piece in the "Off to Work" series, Make Me Pretty was modeled in 1999 and released in 2001. Those made in the first year of production bear the special "First Issue 2001" backstamp plus TMK-8 and incised 1999 copyright date. This 4-1/4" figurine came with the Day of Beauty Hummelscape.

Hum No.	Size	Trademark	Current Value
2092	4-1/4"	TMK-8	$175-$250

Hum 2092: Make Me Pretty.

Hum 2093: Pretzel Boy

This figurine, which was modeled by master sculptor Helmut Fischer in 1998, was released in 1999 as a companion to Pretzel Girl (Hum 2004). It has a 1998 incised copyright date, TMK-8, and "First Issue 2000 MILLENNIUM" backstamp in the first year of production.

A special edition of this figurine was issued in 2000 for the M.I. Hummel Club Convention in Germany. It was also part of a collector's set, which included a free Bavarian Bier Garten Hummelscape.

The year 2011 marked the celebration of Sister Hummel's 75th anniversary of the beginning of her legacy. Manufaktur Rödental selected 50 figurines to bear the "75th Anniversary" backstamp. Pretzel Boy was one of those figurines. Only 75 of them were available in North America with this backstamp. Each figurine was hand-numbered, with a golden backstamp and a map of North America backstamp. A special porcelain plaque was included, and the notable emblem on the packaging hinted at the contents. Each figurine included a "75 Years of M.I. Hummel" certificate.

Hum 2093: Pretzel Boy.

Hum No.	Size	Trademark	Current Value
2093	4-1/4"	TMK-8	$150-$190

Hum 2094: Christmas Wish

Modeled by master sculptor Helmut Fischer in 1999, this piece came as both a figurine (Hum 2094) and an ornament (Hum 2094/0). The 4" figurine was released in 1999 as a limited edition of 20,000 pieces sold exclusively on QVC on Nov. 17, 1999. It carries a 1999 incised copyright date, along with TMK-8 and special "Exclusive Edition" backstamp. The figurine came as a collector's set with free Musikfest Hummelscape. It has been temporarily withdrawn from production.

The ornament variation was released later in a smaller, 3-1/4" size with TMK-8.

Hum No.	Size	Trademark	Current Value
2094	4"	TMK-8	$125-$175
2094/0	3-1/4"	TMK-8	$50-$70

Hum 2094: Christmas Wish.

Hum 2095: Proclamation

Proclamation made its debut at the 2005 M.I. Hummel Club convention in Boston. "Boston: M.I. Hummel Club 2005 Convention" was printed on the scroll. This event version had an incised 1999 copyright date and TMK-8. Proclamation was released to the general public in 2006 and could be personalized on the blank scroll at various spring artist events that year. This artist version had an incised 1999 copyright date, "Special Edition" and bell backstamps, and TMK-8.

Hum No.	Size	Trademark	Current Value
2095	5-1/4"	TMK-8 OE	$150-$200

Hum 2095: Proclamation.

Hum 2096: Angel Symphony

"Angel Symphony" is a series of little angels that began in 1999. Modeled by master sculptors Helmut Fischer and Marion Huschka between 1999 and 2000, the pieces vary in size from 3-3/4" to 4-1/2". Depending on the year of release, they may bear either a TMK-7 or TMK-8 and incised copyright dates of either 1999 or 2000.

The year 2011 marked the celebration of Sister Hummel's 75th anniversary of the beginning of her legacy. Manufaktur Rödental selected 50 figurines to bear the "75th Anniversary" backstamp. Hum 2096/Q: Heaven and Nature Sing was one of those figurines. Only 75 of them were available in North America with this backstamp. Each figurine was hand-numbered, with a golden backstamp and a map of North America backstamp. A special porcelain plaque was included, and the notable emblem on the packaging hinted at the contents. Each figurine included a "75 Years of M.I. Hummel" certificate.

Hum No.	Size	Year	Name	Current Value
2096/ A	4-1/4"	1999	Angelic Conductor	$95-$135
2096/ C	4-1/4"	1999	Celestial Drummer	$95-$135
2096/ D	4-1/4"	1999	String Symphony	$95-$135
2096/ E	4"	1999	Heavenly Rhapsody	$95-$135
2096/ F	4"	1999	Celestial Strings	$95-$135
2096/ G	4-1/4"	2000	Celestial Reveille	$95-$135
2096/ H*	4-1/2"	2000	Millennium Bliss	$95-$140
2096/ J	4"	1999	Heavenly Horn Player	$95- $135
2096/ K*	4-1/2"	2001	Joyful Recital	$95-$140
2096/ L	3-3/4"	2001	Heavenly Harmony	$95-$135
2096/ M	4-1/4"	2002	Divine Drummer	$95-$135
2096/ N	3-1/4"	2002	Zealous Xylophonist	$95-$135
2096/ P	4-1/4"	2002	Heavenly Hubbub	$95-$135
2096/ Q	4"	2002	Heaven and Nature Sing	$95-$135 75th Anniversary
2096/ R	4-1/4"	2002	Seraphim Soprano	$95-$135
2096/ S	3-1/4"	2002	Triumphant Trumpeter	$95- $135
2096/ U*	4"	2002	Cymbals of Joy	$95-$140
2096/ V	4"	2002	Bells on High	$95-$135

These pieces are part of the "Annual Angel" series and come with dated wooden bases.

Hum 2096/A-V: Angel Symphony.

Hum 2097: Can I Play?

Fifth in the "Moments in Time" collection, Can I Play? was produced in a limited edition of 3,000 in 2006. It has an incised 2003 copyright date, "Moments in Time" and limited edition backstamps, and TMK-8. Can I Play? is a mixed media piece featuring twine ropes on the swing.

Hum No.	Size	Trademark	Current Value
2097	11" x 10-1/4" x 6-1/4"	TMK-8 LE	$930-$1,250

Hum 2097: Can I Play?

Hum 2098: Annual Ornament Series

This is a series of three annual ornaments that began in 2000 with the release of Millennium Bliss (Hum 2098/A). Joyful Recital (Hum 2098/B) was added in 2001, and Cymbals of Joy (Hum 2098/C) was added in 2002. Each is 3-1/2" and shaped like a six-pointed star. TMK-8 appears on the front of the ornaments.

Hum No.	Size	Year	Design	Trademark	Current Value
2098/A	3-1/2"	2000	Millennium Bliss	TMK-8	$10-$20
2098/B	3-1/2"	2001	Joyful Recital	TMK-8	$10-$20
2098/C	3-1/2"	2002	Cymbals of Joy	TMK-8	$10-$20
2098/D	3-1/2"	2003	Rejoice	TMK-8	$10-$20

Hum 2098/A-D: annual ornament series.

Hum 2099/A: Saint Nicholas Day
Ornament

This boot-shaped bas-relief Christmas ornament, measuring 3-1/4" with an incised "M.I. Hummel" signature on the front, was released in 2000 as part of a series of what are now nine decorative ornaments (see Hum 876/A). Those released in the first year of production carry a "First Issue 2000" indicator.

Hum No.	Size	Trademark	Current Value
2099/A	3-1/4"	TMK-8	$10-$20

Hum 2099/A: Saint Nicholas Day ornament.

Hum 2100: Picture Perfect

Modeled by master sculptor Helmut Fischer in 2000, Picture Perfect was the 25th Anniversary Club Commemorative figurine for M.I. Hummel Club members only. It bears an incised 2000 copyright date as well as the "25th Anniversary" commemorative backstamp. Produced in a sequentially numbered worldwide limited edition of 2,500 pieces, it came with a wooden base and porcelain plaque. A companion piece is Camera Ready (Hum 2132).

Hum 2100: Picture Perfect.

Hum No.	Size	Trademark	Current Value
2100	8-1/4"	TMK-8	$2,800-$3,495

Hum 2101/A: A Girl's Best Friend

Modeled in 1999, A Girl's Best Friend was new for 2001. Those produced in the first year of production carry the special "First Issue 2001" backstamp, along with incised 1999 copyright date and TMK-8. A Girl's Best Friend is considered a companion piece to A Boy's Best Friend (Hum 2101/B), which was released at the same time.

Hum 2101/A: A Girl's Best Friend.

Hum No.	Size	Trademark	Current Value
2101/A	4"	TMK-8	$75-$135

Hum 2101/B: A Boy's Best Friend

A Boy's Best Friend, a companion to A Girl's Best Friend (Hum 2101/A), was modeled in 1999 and released in 2001. Those produced in the first year of production bear the special "First Issue 2001" backstamp, along with incised 1999 copyright date and TMK-8.

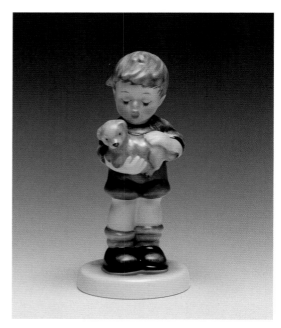

Hum 2101/B: A Boy's Best Friend.

Hum No.	Size	Trademark	Current Value
2101/B	4"	TMK-8	$75-$135

Hum 2102/A: My Heart's Desire

Modeled by master sculptor Helmut Fischer in 2000, My Heart's Desire was introduced in the summer of 2002. It carries a "First Issue 2002" backstamp, as well as incised copyright date of 2000 and TMK-8. It is considered a companion piece to Secret Admirer (Hum 2102/B).

Hum No.	Size	Trademark	Current Value
2102/A	3-3/4"	TMK-8	$105-$140

Hum 2102/A: My Heart's Desire.

Hum 2102/B: Secret Admirer

Another design by master sculptor Helmut Fischer 2000, Secret Admirer was introduced in the summer of 2002. It bears an incised 2000 copyright date and "First Issue 2002" backstamp, as well as TMK-8. It is considered a companion piece to My Heart's Desire (Hum 2102/A).

Hum 2102/B: Secret Admirer.

Hum No.	Size	Trademark	Current Value
2102/B	4"	TMK-8	$105-$140

Hum 2103/A: Puppet Princess

Puppet Princess, which was modeled by master sculptor Marion Huschka in 1999, is a companion piece to Puppet Prince (Hum 2103/B). It was offered as a gift to new 2001-2002 members of the M.I. Hummel Club, who were joining for the first time or renewing membership, and bears the special club backstamp in addition to TMK-8 and an incised 1999 copyright date. It was retired on May 31, 2002.

Hum 2103/A: Puppet Princess.

Hum No.	Size	Trademark	Current Value
2103/A	3-3/4"	TMK-8	$55-$90

Hum 2103/B: Puppet Prince

Modeled by master sculptor Marion Huschka in 1999, Puppet Prince is a companion piece to Puppet Princess (Hum 2103/A). It

was released in 2001 as a M.I. Hummel Club exclusive to new members who joined in that year and bears the special club backstamp and incised 1999 copyright date, along with TMK-8. It was retired on May 31, 2002.

Hum 2103/B: Puppet Prince.

Hum No.	Size	Trademark	Current Value
2103/B	4"	TMK-8	$55-$90

Hum 2104: Sunflower Friends

Modeled in 1999, Sunflower Friends was a M.I. Hummel Club exclusive issued to members as a loyalty piece upon their fifth year of personal membership. Issued in 2001, it carries an incised 1999 copyright date, TMK-8, and special club backstamp.

Hum 2104: Sunflower Friends.

Hum No.	Size	Trademark	Current Value
2104	3-1/2"	TMK-8	$195

Hum 2105: Miss Beehaving

Modeled in 1999, Miss Beehaving was an M.I. Hummel Club exclusive issued to members as a loyalty piece upon their 10th year of personal membership. Issued in 2001, it carries an incised 1999 copyright date, TMK-8, and special club backstamp.

Hum No.	Size	Trademark	Current Value
2105	2-3/4"	TMK-8	$240

Hum 2105: Miss Beehaving.

Hum 2106: Christmas Time

Christmas Time, which was modeled by master sculptor Helmut Fischer in 1999, was released first as a 3-1/4" ornament in 2001 and later as a 4" figurine. The ornament carries mold number 2106/0, whereas the figurine is simply Hum 2106. The figurine bears an incised 1999 copyright date and TMK- 8. It came with a special holiday-themed Hummelscape.

Hum 2106: Christmas Time.

Hum No.	Size	Trademark	Current Value
2106	4"	TMK-8	$150-$200
2106/0	3-1/4"	TMK-8	$40-$50
2106	4"	TMK-9	$89 retail

Christmas Time was re-released in the "Innocent Reflections" series, a series of white ceramic figurines on which a glaze is fired to make it glisten. A coating of 21-karat gold is painted on certain details of each figurine, then fired for 3-1/2 hours. On this figurine, the present and bows in the little girl's hair are painted gold. This figurine is TMK-9.

Hum 2107/A: Bee Hopeful

Modeled in 1999, Bee Hopeful was released in 2000 as a limited and numbered edition of 25,000 pieces. It carries a 1999 incised copyright date, TMK-8, and backstamp to indicate a limited edition. It is considered a companion piece to Little Knitter (Hum 2107/B), which was released the following year.

Hum 2107/A: Bee Hopeful.

Hum No.	Size	Trademark	Current Value
2107/A	4"	TMK-8	$150-$175

Hum 2107/B: Little Knitter

Modeled in 1999, Little Knitter was released in 2001 as the companion piece to Bee Hopeful (Hum 2107/A), which was released the year before. Like its companion, Little Knitter was a limited and numbered edition of 25,000 pieces. It carries 1999 incised copyright date, TMK-8, and special backstamp.

Hum 2107/B: Little Knitter.

Hum No.	Size	Trademark	Current Value
2107/B	4"	TMK-8	$150-$175

Hum 2108/A: Musik Please

Offered in the spring of 2002 as part of the Musik Please collector's set, this piece is the work of master sculptor Helmut Fischer, who designed it in 1999. The set features a 4-1/4" Bavarian girl figurine with an incised 1999 copyright date and a Volkfest display in a limited edition of 15,000 pieces. It is considered a companion piece to Alpine Dancer (Hum 2108/B).

Musik Please was re-released in the "Innocent Reflections" series, a series of white ceramic figurines on which a glaze is fired to make it glisten. A coating of 21-karat gold is painted on certain details of each figurine, then fired for 3-1/2 hours. On this figurine, the girl's hair ribbon and apron are painted gold. This figurine is TMK-9.

Hum 2108/A: Musik Please.

Hum No.	Size	Trademark	Current Value
2108/A	4-1/4"	TMK-8	$150-$175
2108/A	4-1/4"	TMK-9	$99 retail

Hum 2108/B: Alpine Dancer

Offered in the fall of 2001 as part of the Alpine Dancer Collector's Set, this piece is the work of master sculptor Helmut Fischer, who crafted it in 1999. It features a 4-1/4" Bavarian boy figurine with an incised 1999 copyright date and a display. It is considered a companion piece to Musik Please (Hum 2108/A).

Alpine Dancer was re-released in the "Innocent Reflections" series, a series of white ceramic figurines on which a glaze is fired to make it glisten. A coating of 21-karat gold is painted on certain details of each figurine, then fired for 3-1/2 hours. On this figurine, the suspenders and buttons on the boy's pants and jacket are painted gold. This figurine is TMK-9.

Hum 2108/B: Alpine Dancer.

Hum No.	Size	Trademark	Current Value
2108/B	4-1/4"	TMK-8	$150-$175
2108/B	4-1/4"	TMK-9	$99 retail

Hum 2109: Open Number

Hum 2110/A: Christmas Delivery Ornament

This star-shaped bas-relief Christmas ornament, measuring 3-1/2" with an incised "M.I. Hummel" signature on the front, was released in 1999 as part of what is now a series of nine decorative ornaments (see Hum 876/A). Modeled by master sculptor Helmut Fischer in 1999, those issued the first year of production carry a "First Issue 1999" indicator and TMK-7, as well as an incised 1999 copyright date. The newer pieces carry TMK-8.

Hum 2110/A: Christmas Delivery ornament.

Hum No.	Size	Trademark	Current Value
2110/A	3-1/2"	TMK-7	$10-$20
2110/A	3-1/2"	TMK-8	$10-$20

Hum 2111/A: Making New Friends Ornament

Released in 1999, this snowflake-shaped bas-relief Christmas ornament, measuring 3-1/2" with an incised "M.I. Hummel" signature on the front, is part of what is now a series of nine decorative ornaments (see Hum 876/A). Modeled by master sculptor Helmut Fischer in 1999, each carries an incised 1999 copyright date. Those issued the first year of production bear a "First Issue 1999" indicator and TMK-7. The newer pieces bear TMK-8.

Hum 2111/A: Making New Friends ornament.

Hum No.	Size	Trademark	Current Value
2111/A	3-1/2"	TMK-7	$10-$20
2111/A	3-1/2"	TMK-8	$10-$20

Hum 2112: Open Number

Hum 2113: Extra! Extra!

Extra! Extra!—available in several variations including a special exclusive limited edition USO piece as well as an "America: We Stand Proud" piece to commemorate the Sept. 11, 2001 tragedy—

was modeled by master sculptor Helmut Fischer in 1999 and released in 2001. It bears an incised 1999 copyright date and "First Issue" backstamp in the first year of production.

In the wake of the terrorist attacks and the resulting American military effort, Goebel alerted its M.I. Hummel Club chapters that it would donate appropriately

Hum 2113: Extra! Extra!

Hum No.	Size	Trademark	Current Value
2113	5-1/2"	TMK-8	$175-$240
2113	5-1/2"	TMK-9	$199 retail 2011 artists event figurine

themed figurines to local chapters to be used as raffle prizes. Any proceeds from such fund-raising events would then go to benefit the families of the victims. Seven figurines, including this one, were selected as appropriate due to their patriotic or firefighter/police/medical personnel themes.

A limited edition of Extra! Extra! was also available at 2011 artist events.

Hum 2114: Declaration of Freedom

Declaration of Freedom, the fourth in the "Ambassadors of Freedom" series, was produced in a limited edition of 3,000 in 2004. It featured a red, white, and blue eagle backstamp, "Ambassadors of Freedom" inscription, incised 2004 copyright date, limited edition backstamp, and TMK-8. It included a wooden display with brass plaque, booklet by Michael W. Smith, and a CD of patriotic music.

Hum 2114: Declaration of Freedom.

Hum No.	Size	Trademark	Current Value
2114	9"	TMK-8 LE	$250-$350

Hum 2115: Lantern Fun

This mixed media figurine, featuring a wooden stick, ceramic lantern, incised 2003 copyright date, and TMK-8, was issued in 2004. It was part of the "Create-A-Gift" Collection in the North American market when paired with a Sentiment Occasion base. The figurine offered in the European market, as part of the "Through the Years" collection, has a lantern backstamp.

Hum 2115: Lantern Fun.

Hum No.	Size	Trademark	Current Value
115	3-1/4"	TMK-8 OE	$75-$99

Hum 2116/A: One Cup of Sugar

Modeled in 2000, One Cup of Sugar was released new for 2001. It bears a 2000 copyright date and TMK-8. Those made in the first year of production also carry the special "First Issue 2001" backstamp. It is a companion piece to Baking Time (Hum 2116/B), which was released in the same year.

Hum 2116/A: One Cup of Sugar.

Hum No.	Size	Trademark	Current Value
2116/A	3-3/4"	TMK-8	$75-$125

Hum 2116/B: Baking Time

Baking Time was modeled in 2000 and released in 2001. It bears a 2000 copyright date and TMK-8. Those made in the first year of production also carry the special "First Issue 2001" backstamp. It is a companion piece to One Cup of Sugar (Hum 2116/A), which was released in the same year.

Baking Time was re-released in the "Innocent Reflections" series, a series of white ceramic figurines on which a glaze is fired to make it glisten. A coating of 21-karat gold is painted on certain details of each figurine, then fired for 3-1/2 hours. On this figurine, the bowl and spoon are painted gold. This figurine is TMK-9.

Hum 2116/B: Baking Time.

Hum No.	Size	Trademark	Current Value
2116/B	4"	TMK-8	$75-$125
2116/B	4"	TMK-9	$89 retail

Hum 2117-2118: Open Numbers

Hum 2119: Bon Appetite

Bon Appetite is the 12th culinary-themed M.I. Hummel figurine. Released in winter of 2013, this little chef is serving up something special for her guests. She is wearing a little kerchief and an apron to protect her clothing from spatters. Bon Appetite is a TMK-9 figurine and has the TMK-9 backstamp.

Hum No.	Size	Trademark	Current Value
2119	4-3/4"	TMK-9	$279 retail

Hum 2119: Bon Appetit.

Hum 2120: Little Miss Mail Carrier

Hum No.	Size	Trademark	Current Value
2120	4-3/4"	TMK-8 OE	$200-$250

Little Miss Mail Carrier, issued in 2004 with a "First Issue 2005" backstamp, has an incised 2000 copyright date and TMK-8. The first 2,500 pieces released in the North American market have a Goebel artist signature, "First Issue 2005" backstamp, incised 2000 copyright date, TMK-8, and envelope-decorated display base.

The year 2011 marked the celebration of Sister Hummel's 75th anniversary of the beginning of her legacy. Manufaktur Rödental selected 50 figurines to bear the "75th Anniversary" backstamp. Little Miss Mail Carrier was one of those figurines. Only 75 of them were available in North America with this backstamp. Each figurine was hand-numbered, with a golden backstamp and a map of North America backstamp. A special porcelain plaque was included, and the notable emblem on the packaging hinted at the contents. Each figurine included a "75 Years of M.I. Hummel" certificate.

Hum 2120: Little Miss Mail Carrier.

Hum 2121: Soap Box Derby

Soap Box Derby was the first edition in the "Moments in Time" series, which celebrates childhood. Modeled by master sculptor Marion Huschka in 2001 and first available in the fall of 2002, the piece bears the "First Issue 2002" and "Moments in Time" backstamps, along with 2001 incised copyright date. This piece was limited to one year of production only.

Hum No.	Size	Trademark	Current Value
2121	7" x 6-1/2" x 9-1/2"	TMK-8	$900-$1,250

Hum 2121: Soap Box Derby.

Hum 2122: Sweet Nap

This figurine of a sleepy girl features a special backstamp commemorating the 100th anniversary of the birth of Sister M.I. Hummel, TMK-9, and an incised mold number and copyright year. It is the companion to Just Dozing (Hum 451).

Hum No.	Size	Trademark	Current Value
2122	4″	TMK-9	$250-$299

Hum 2122: Sweet Nap.

Hum 2123: Open Number

Hum 2124: Summer Adventure

First available in 2002, Summer Adventure was the third and final edition in the "Wonder of Childhood" collection. The piece came with a wooden base with an attached engraved brass plaque (total height with wooden base is 6-1/2"). It was modeled by master sculptor Helmut Fischer in 2001 and bears an incised 2001 copyright date, special club inscription, bumblebee stamp, and TMK-8. It was an exclusive edition for M.I. Hummel Club members only, offered in club year 26, which ran from June 1, 2002 through May 31, 2003. It was retired on May 31, 2003.

Hum 2124: Summer Adventure.

Hum No.	Size	Trademark	Current Value
2124	5-3/4″	TMK-8	$475-$695

Hum 2125: Teacher's Pet

Modeled by master sculptor Helmut Fischer in 2000 and released in 2002, Teacher's Pet is similar to Little Scholar (Hum 80/2/0), except that it is a girl student rather than a boy student. It carries an incised 2000 copyright date, "First Issue 2002" special backstamp, and TMK-8.

Hum 2125: Teacher's Pet.

Hum No.	Size	Trademark	Current Value
2125	4-1/4″	TMK-8	$110-$175

Hum 2126-2128: Open Numbers

Hum 2129/A: Ring in the Season
Ornament

This pinecone-shaped bas-relief Christmas tree ornament was modeled by master sculptor Helmut Fischer in 2001 and released in 2002 as part of a series of nine decorative ornaments (see Hum 876/A). It measures 3-1/2" and carries an incised "M.I. Hummel" signature on the front and TMK-8 on the back.

Hum 2129/A: Ring in the Season ornament.

Hum No.	Size	Trademark	Current Value
2129/A	3-1/2"	TMK-8	$10-$20

Hum 2130: Nutcracker Sweet

The design of master sculptor Marion Huschka in 2000 and released in 2002 as part of a collector's set, this 6" figurine was a limited edition of 10,000 pieces and bears an incised 2000 copyright date. It was paired with an authentic 5" Fritz von Nutcracker by Steinbach piece made exclusively for Goebel. The set was completed with an heirloom wooden chest.

Manufaktur Rödental re-released Nutcracker Sweet in 2013. The figurine was repainted for this reissue. It is a TMK-9 figurine with the TMK-9 backstamp.

Hum 2130: Nutcracker Sweet.

Hum No.	Size	Trademark	Current Value
2130	6"	TMK-8	$150-$250
2130	6"	TMK-9	N/A

Hum 2131: Open Number

Hum 2132: Camera Ready

Camera Ready, which was modeled by master sculptor Helmut Fischer in 2000, was the 25th Anniversary M.I. Hummel Club commemorative figurine. It carries an incised 2000 copyright date along with a commemorative backstamp. It was available for only one year (2002) and is a companion piece to Picture Perfect (Hum 2100). It features a fabric bow around the teddy bear's neck.

Hum No.	Size	Trademark	Current Value
2132	5-1/2"	TMK-8	$265-$475

Hum 2132: Camera Ready.

Hum 2133: Bashful Serenade

Bashful Serenade was first available in January 2002. Modeled by master sculptor Marion Huschka in 2000, it carries an incised 2000 copyright date, "First Issue 2002" special backstamp in the first year of production, and TMK-8.

Hum No.	Size	Trademark	Current Value
2133	5-1/4"	TMK-8	$400-$475

Hum 2133: Bashful Serenade.

Hum 2134: Wintertime Duet

Hum No.	Size	Trademark	Current Value
2134	4"	TMK-8	$150-$175

Wintertime Duet, a 2002 release, was first introduced on QVC and later made available through regular retailers. Crafted by master sculptor Helmut Fischer in 2000, it is 4" tall, carries an incised 2000 copyright date, and special "First Issue 2002" backstamp. The original suggested retail price was $175.

The year 2011 marked the celebration of Sister Hummel's 75th anniversary of the beginning of her legacy. Manufaktur Rödental selected 50 figurines to bear the "75th Anniversary" backstamp. Wintertime Duet was one of those figurines. Only 75 of them were available in North America with this backstamp. Each figurine was hand-numbered, with a golden backstamp and a map of North America backstamp. A special porcelain plaque was included, and the notable emblem on the packaging hinted at the contents. Each figurine included a "75 Years of M.I. Hummel" certificate.

Hum 2134: Wintertime Duet.

Hum 2135/A: Angelic Drummer

Part of the "Angel Orchestra," Angelic Drummer—sculpted by Helmut Fischer—was issued in 2005 with a "First Issue 2005" backstamp, incised 2000 copyright date, and TMK-8.

Hum No.	Size	Trademark	Current Value
2135/A	4"	TMK-8 OE	$100-$139

Hum 2135/A: Angelic Drummer.

Hum 2135/C: Precious Pianist

Part of the "Angel Orchestra," Precious Pianist—sculpted by Helmut Fischer—is composed of three parts: ceramic angel, ceramic piano, and wooden cloud base. Released in 2005, it has a "First Issue 2005" backstamp, incised 2001 copyright date decal, and TMK-8.

The year 2011 marked the celebration of Sister Hummel's 75th anniversary of the beginning of her legacy. Manufaktur Rödental selected 50 figurines to bear the "75th Anniversary" backstamp. Precious Pianist was one of those figurines. Only 75 of them were available in North America with this backstamp. Each figurine was hand-numbered, with a golden backstamp and a map of North America backstamp. A special porcelain plaque was included, and the notable emblem on the packaging hinted at the contents. Each figurine included a "75 Years of M.I. Hummel" certificate.

Hum 2135/C: Precious Pianist.

Hum No.	Size	Trademark	Current Value
2135/C	3-1/2"	TMK-8 OE	$165-$219

Hum 2135/D: Melodic Mandolin

Part of the "Angel Orchestra," Melodic Mandolin—sculpted by Helmut Fischer—was issued in 2003 with a "First Issue 2003" backstamp. It has incised 2001 copyright date and TMK-8. It is available with the "Christmas Ribbon" base.

Hum 2135/D: Melodic Mandolin.

Hum No.	Size	Trademark	Current Value
2135/D	3-1/4"	TMK-8 OE	$100-$139

Hum 2135/E: Celestial Dreamer

Part of the "Angel Orchestra," Celestial Dreamer—sculpted by Helmut Fischer—was released in 2003 with a "First Issue 2003" backstamp. It has an incised 2001 copyright date and TMK-8. It was released in 2004 as Celestial Dreamer on Cloud candleholder and Celestial Dreamer music box.

Hum No.	Size	Trademark	Current Value
2135/E	3-1/4"	TMK-8 OE	$100-$139

Hum 2135/E: Celestial Dreamer.

Hum 2135/F: Sounds of Joy

Part of the "Angel Orchestra," Sounds of Joy—sculpted by Helmut Fischer—was issued in 2003 with a "First Issue" 2003 backstamp. It has a 2001 copyright decal and TMK-8.

Hum No.	Size	Trademark	Current Value
2135/F	4"	TMK-8 TW	$145-$179

Hum 2135/F: Sounds of Joy.

Hum 2135/G: Rejoice

Part of the "Angel Orchestra," Rejoice—sculpted by Helmut Fischer—was also the fourth piece in the "Annual Angel" series. (The first three pieces in the "Annual Angel" series were Hum 2096/H, 2096/K, and 2096/U.) First issued in 2002, Rejoice has an "Annual Angel 2003" backstamp. The piece features an incised 2002 copyright date, TMK-8, and a yellow wooden star base.

Hum 2135/G: Rejoice.

Hum No.	Size	Trademark	Current Value
2135/G	4"	TMK-8 CE	$100-$145

Hum 2135/H: Angelic Trumpeter

Part of the "Angel Orchestra," Angelic Trumpeter—sculpted by Helmut Fischer—was also the fifth piece in the "Annual Angel" series. First issued in 2003, Angelic Trumpeter has an "Annual Angel 2004" backstamp. It has an incised 2003 copyright date, TMK-8, and a yellow wooden star base.

Hum 2135/H: Angelic Trumpeter.

Hum No.	Size	Trademark	Current Value
2135/H	4"	TMK-8 CE	$100-$45

Hum 2135/J: Spirited Saxophonist

Part of the "Angel Orchestra," Spirited Saxophonist—sculpted by Helmut Fischer—was also the sixth piece in the "Annual Angel" series. First issued in 2004, the piece has an "Annual Angel 2005" backstamp. It also has an incised 2004 copyright date, TMK-8, and a yellow wooden star base. The first 2,500 released in the North American market in 2004 also had a Goebel artist signature.

Hum 2135/J: Spirited Saxophonist.

Hum No.	Size	Trademark	Current Value
2135/J	4"	TMK-8 CE	$100-$165

Hum 2135/K: Angel With Triangle

Part of the "Angel Orchestra," Angel With Triangle—sculpted by Helmut Fischer—was also the seventh piece in the "Annual Angel" series. First issued in 2005, it has an "Annual Angel 2006" backstamp. It also has an incised 2005 copyright date, TMK-8, and a yellow wooden star base.

Hum 2135/K: Angel With Triangle.

Hum No.	Size	Trademark	Current Value
2135/K	4-1/4"	TMK-8 CE	$100-$165

Hum 2135/L: Angel With Carillon

Part of the "Angel Orchestra," Angel With Carillon was sculpted by Helmut Fischer. It was introduced in 2007 and came with a wooden star base.

Hum 2135/L: Angel With Carillon.

Hum No.	Size	Trademark	Current Value
2135/L	4-1/4"	TMK-8 CE	$100-$165

Hum 2135/M: Angel With Accordion

Part of the "Angel Orchestra," Angel With Accordion was sculpted by Helmut Fischer. It was introduced in 2008 and came with a wooden star base.

Hum 2135/M: Angel With Accordion.

Hum No.	Size	Trademark	Current Value
2135/M	4-1/4"	TMK-8 CE	$100-$165

Hum 2135/N Angel With Harp

Another addition to the "Angel Orchestra," Angel With Harp was sculpted by Helmut Fischer. It was introduced in 2009 and is also part of the "Annual Angel" series. A trademark figurine, it has the TMK-9 backstamp.

Hum No.	Size	Trademark	Current Value
22135/N	4"	TMK-9	$100-$165

Hum 2135/N: Angel With Harp.

Hum 2136: The Cat's Meow

A new release for 2003, this 3-1/2" figurine became instantly more collectible within months after the release when Goebel announced that its team of artisans had inadvertently painted the cat on the "First Issue 2003" pieces the wrong color. Factory officials said fewer than 5,000 of these figurines had been painted with a black cat when, in fact, the cat was supposed to be gray. This error in color variation is expected to make those pieces with the black cat rare and, therefore, more valuable in future years.

This figurine is considered a companion piece to Proud Moments (Hum 800), which was released in 2000.

Hum No.	Size	Trademark	Current Value
2136	3-1/2"	TMK-8	$175-$300

Hum 2136: The Cat's Meow.

Hum 2137-2142: Open Numbers

Hum 2143/A: Season's Best

The design of master sculptor Helmut Fischer in 2001, Season's Best was introduced in the summer of 2002. It carries an incised 2001 copyright date, "First Issue 2002" backstamp, and TMK-8. It was sold with a cold cast porcelain ice rink display and is considered a companion to Let's Take to the Ice (Hum 2143/B).

Hum 2143/A: Season's Best.

Hum No.	Size	Trademark	Current Value
2143/A	3-3/4"	TMK-8	$165-$220

Hum 2143/B: Let's Take to the Ice

Introduced in the summer of 2002, Let's Take to the Ice was modeled by master sculptor Helmut Fischer in 2000. It carries a 2000 incised copyright date, "First Issue 2002" backstamp in its first year of production, and TMK-8. Like its companion piece, Season's Best (Hum 2143/A), it was sold with a cold cast porcelain ice rink display.

Hum 2143/B: Let's Take to the Ice.

Hum No.	Size	Trademark	Current Value
2143/B	4"	TMK-8	$165-$220

Hum 2144-2147: Open Numbers

Hum 2148/A: Wait For Me

Modeled by master sculptor Helmut Fischer, Wait For Me was introduced in 2002 as a M.I. Hummel Club exclusive. As such, it carries a special club inscription and bumblebee. It is considered a companion piece to First Mate (Hum 2148/B), the club renewal premium for club year 26. As a club year 26 exclusive, Wait For Me was retired on May 31, 2003.

Hum 2148/A: Wait For Me.

Hum No.	Size	Trademark	Current Value
2148/A	4-1/4"	TMK-8	$50-$100

Hum 2148/B: First Mate

Introduced in 2002 as the M.I. Hummel Club exclusive renewal piece for club year 26, First Mate was modeled by master sculptor Helmut Fischer. It was offered free to club members renewing or new to members from June 1, 2002 to May 31, 2003, when it was retired. It is considered a companion to Wait For Me (Hum 2148/A).

Hum 2148/B: First Mate.

Hum No.	Size	Trademark	Current Value
2148/B	4"	TMK-8	$50-$100

Hum 2149: Open Number

Hum 2150/A: Perfect Pitch

Produced in a limited edition of 5,000, Perfect Pitch became available in fall 2007. It is the companion piece to Hum 2150/B: Cheerful Tune. Perfect Pitch and Hum 2150/B: Cheerful Tune could be purchased as a set.

Hum 2150/A: Perfect Pitch.

Hum No.	Size	Trademark	Current Value
2150/A	5-3/4"	TMK-8	$279

Hum 2150/B: Cheerful Tune

Produced in a limited edition of 5,000, Cheerful Tune became available in fall 2007. It is the companion piece to Hum 2150/A: Perfect Pitch. Cheerful Tune and Hum 2150/A: Perfect Pitch could be purchased as a set.

Hum 2150/B: Cheerful Tune.

Hum No.	Size	Trademark	Current Value
2150/B	6"	TMK-8	$329

2151: Open Number

Hum 2152/A: Dearly Beloved
Trinket Box

Released new for 2003, this heart-shaped trinket box is part of the Bridal Gift Set, which includes three other pieces all featuring the Dearly Beloved (Hum 2003) motif. The other three pieces are: Couple's First Christmas ornament (Hum 2163/A); earthenware framed picture (Hum 2178/A); and earthenware marriage license/storybook (Hum 2179/A).

Hum No.	Basic Size	Trademark	Current Value
2152/A	3-1/4"	TMK-8	$50

Hum 2152/A: Dearly Beloved trinket box.

Hum 2153: Big Announcement

A limited edition 2003 special event piece, this 4-1/2" figurine features a boy carrying a sandwich board that reads "Happy Birthday." It was available at participating retailers nationwide. It carries "SPECIAL EVENT" and "First Issue 2003" backstamps and is referred to as a "tailor-made figurine."

The year 2011 marked the celebration of Sister Hummel's 75th anniversary of the beginning of her legacy. Manufaktur

Hum 2153: Big Announcement.

Hum No.	Basic Size	Trademark	Current Value
2153	4-1/2"	TMK-8	$80-$165

Rödental selected 50 figurines to bear the "75th Anniversary" backstamp. Big Announcement was one of those figurines. Only 75 of them were available in North America with this backstamp. Each figurine was hand-numbered, with a golden backstamp and a map of North America backstamp. A special porcelain plaque was included, and the notable emblem on the packaging hinted at the contents. Each figurine included a "75 Years of M.I. Hummel" certificate.

Hum 2154/A: Patriotic Spirit

Patriotic Spirit, sculpted by Helmut Fischer and Tamara Fuchs, was issued in 2002 with a "First Issue 2002" Exclusive Edition, EE, backstamp. It has an incised 2001 copyright date and TMK-8.

Hum No.	Size	Trademark	Current Value
2154/A	4", 6" with flag	TMK-8 TW	$150-$198

Hum 2154/B: Celebration of Freedom

Celebration of Freedom, sculpted by Helmut Fischer and Tamara Fuchs, was issued in 2002 with a "First Issue 2003" Exclusive Edition, EE, backstamp. It has an incised 2001 copyright date and TMK-8.

Hum No.	Size	Trademark	Current Value
2154/B	4", 6" with flag	TMK-8 TW	$150-$198

Hum 2154/B: Celebration of Freedom.

Hum 2155: Teddy Tales

Teddy Tales was issued as part of a limited edition of 1,000 "Teddy Tales" collectors sets (with the Teddy Bear Picnic Hummelscape) in 2006, featuring "Special Edition" and red bow backstamps, incised 2005 copyright date, and TMK-8.

Hum No.	Size	Trademark	Current Value
2155	3-1/2"	TMK-8 OE	$154-$199

Hum 2155: Teddy Tales.

Hum 2156: Loads of Fun

New in 2007, Loads of Fun depicts a boy playing with a truck. It was sold on QVC.

Hum No.	Size	Trademark	Current Value
2156	4"	TMK-8	$249

Hum 2156: Loads of Fun.

Hum 2157: Full Speed Ahead/ When I Grow Up

Hum No.	Size	Trademark	Current Value
2157	4-3/4"	TMK-8 OE	$150-$300

Full Speed Ahead, a mixed media piece that features a wooden train, was first issued in 2003 with a "First Issue 2003" backstamp. It has an incised 2002 copyright date and TMK-8. A variation called When I Grow Up also is marked

Hum 2157: Full Speed Ahead/ When I Grow Up.

"First Issue 2003" with a "Special Edition" backstamp and a red wooden fire truck. The figurine was also available in Europe in a limited edition (2,000 pieces) Gold Collector Set with a gold wooden train and "First Issue 2003" and "Sonderausgabe Marklin" backstamps.

Hum 2158-2161 Open Numbers

Hum 2162: Baker's Delight

Baker's Delight, the third edition in the "Moments in Time" collection, was produced in a limited edition of 5,000 in 2004. It joins Soap Box Derby (Hum 2121) and Farm Days (Hum 2165). Baker's

Hum No.	Size	Trademark	Current Value
2162	7"	TMK-8 LE	$950-$1,200

Delight features an incised 2002 copyright date, "Moments in Time" and limited edition backstamps, and TMK-8.

Hum 2162: Baker's Delight.

Hum 2163/A: Dearly Beloved
Ornament

Released in 2003, this "Couple's First Christmas" ornament is part of the Bridal Gift Set, which includes three other pieces all featuring the Dearly Beloved (Hum 2003) motif. The other three pieces are: Dearly Beloved trinket box (Hum 2152/A); earthenware framed picture (Hum 2178/A); and earthenware marriage license/storybook (Hum 2179/A).

Hum No.	Basic Size	Trademark	Current Value
2163/A	3-1/2"	TMK-8	$25

Hum 2163/A: Dearly Beloved ornament.

Hum 2164: Me and My Shadow

This special figurine, which was modeled by master sculptor Marion Huschka in 2001, was issued in 2002 along with a limited edition Steiff bear as a commemorative collector's set in honor of the 100th birthday of the teddy bear. The figurine carries an incised 2001 copyright date, commemorative backstamp, and TMK-8. The bear, with white numbered limited edition button-in-ear tag, was made exclusively for Goebel and has a commemorative porcelain medallion attached to its neck bow. The set was limited to 10,000 worldwide.

Hum No.	Size	Trademark	Current Value
2164	6"	TMK-8	$350-$450

Steiff bear and Hum 2164: Me and My Shadow set.

Hum 2165: Farm Days

Released in 2003, this 7-1/2" figurine modeled by master sculptor Helmut Fischer was the second edition in the "Moments in Time" series, which celebrates childhood. It joins Soap Box Derby (Hum 2121) and Baker's Delight (Hum 2162). Farm Days features four children experiencing the joy and wonder of feeding a young calf with a bottle. It bears the "First Issue 2003" and "Moments in Time" backstamps and was limited to one year of production only.

Hum No.	Size	Trademark	Current Value
2165	7-1/2"	TMK-8	$1,000-$1,200

Hum 2165: Farm Days.

Hum 2166: Circus Act

Hum No.	Size	Trademark	Current Value
2166	44-1/4"	TMK-8 OE	$199

Part of the purchase price of Circus Act—introduced in early 2003 in North America as a special preview edition to members of the M.I. Hummel Club—was donated to the Big Apple Circus pediatric hospital clown project. The preview edition has a 2001 copyright date decal, "Commemorative" backstamp, and TMK-8. It also features "Big Apple Circus" on the clown's suitcase.

The regular issue of this figurine, introduced in 2003, has a 2001 copyright date decal, TMK-8, and the Hummel name on the side of the suitcase. Another variation, the European Club Edition, was made available in 2005; it features a "Special Edition 2005" backstamp, TMK-8, 2004 copyright date decal, the Hummel name on the figure's back, and different colored clothes and accessories.

Hum 2167: Mixing the Cake

Mixing the Cake, featuring a girl holding a bag of flour and a mixing spoon, was introduced in 2004 with a "First Issue 2004" backstamp. Collectors in Europe could buy Mixing the Cake as a set with Hum 2168: Today's Recipe and a cookbook. Both versions have an incised 2003 copyright date and TMK-8.

Hum 2167: Mixing the Cake.

Hum No.	Size	Trademark	Current Value
2167	5-3/4"	TMK-8 OE	$200-$300

Hum 2168: Today's Recipe

Today's Recipe, featuring a boy holding a cookbook and a mixing spoon, was introduced in 2004 with a "First Issue 2004" backstamp. Collectors in Europe could buy Today's Recipe as a set with Hum 2167: Mixing the Cake and a cookbook. Both versions have an incised 2003 copyright date and TMK-8.

Hum 2168: Today's Recipe.

Hum No.	Size	Trademark	Current Value
2168	5-1/20"	TMK-8 OE	$200-$300

Hum 2169-2170 Open Numbers

Hum 2171/A: Pretty Performer

Pretty Performer, part of the "Musical Medley" collectors set with Hum 2171/B: Serenade of Songs, was produced in a limited edition of 7,500, of which 5,000 were sold in North America. Released in 2003, the piece has an incised 2001 copyright date, limited edition backstamp, and TMK-8. The set includes a wooden piano base that was brown for the North America market and gold for the European market.

Hum 2171/A: Pretty Performer.

Hum No.	Size	Trademark	Current Value
2171/A	4"	TMK-8	$185

Hum 2171/B: Serenade of Songs

Serenade of Songs, part of the "Musical Medley" collectors set with Hum 2171/A: Pretty Performer, was produced in a limited edition of 7,500, of which 5,000 were sold in North America. Released in 2003, the piece has an incised 2001 copyright date, limited edition backstamp, and TMK-8. The set includes a wooden piano base that was brown for the North America market and gold for the European market.

Hum 2171/B: Serenade of Songs.

Hum No.	Size	Trademark	Current Value
2171/B	4"	TMK-8 LE	$185

Hum 2172: Open Number

Hum 2173: First Flight

First Flight, a boy and his toy airplane, was sculpted by Helmut Fischer and celebrates the 100th anniversary of Orville and Wilbur Wright's first flight on Dec. 17, 1903. It was issued in 2003 in a special edition of 2,000 with a wooden base with brass plaque, TMK-8, and American flag and biplane backstamps. A Kitty Hawk version, with special event markings and an oval commemorative plaque, has TMK-8 and a "Commemorative Issue" backstamp.

Hum No.	Size	Trademark	Current Value
2173	4-1/2"	TMK-8 CE	$150-$200

Hum 2173: First Flight.

Hum 2174/A: Pretty Posey

Pretty Posey is part of the "Pocket of Posies" collector set with Hum 2174/B: Pocket Full of Posies and the Blooming Delights Hummelscape. The figure has an incised 2002 copyright date, TMK-8, and "Special Edition" backstamp. The base is decorated with flowers. Another version on a plain base has a "First Issue 2004" backstamp. The Hummelscape, which features motion and music, was produced in a limited edition of 10,000.

Hum No.	Size	Trademark	Current Value
2174/A	3-1/2"	TMK-8 TW	$80-$110

Hum 2174/B: Pocket Full of Posies

Pocket Full of Posies is part of the "Pocket of Posies" collector set with Hum 2174/A: Pretty Posey and the Blooming Delights Hummelscape. The figure has an incised 2002 copyright date, TMK-8, and "Special Edition" backstamp. The base is decorated with flowers. Another version on a plain base has a "First Issue 2004" backstamp. The Hummelscape, which features motion and music, was produced in a limited edition of 10,000.

Hum No.	Size	Trademark	Current Value
2174/B	3-1/2"	TMK-8 TW	$80-$110

Hum 2175: From the Pumpkin Patch

This figurine of a girl holding a pumpkin was available at artist events and customer appreciation days in 2006. She has TMK-8 and special markings and is a companion to Hum 2011: Little Landscaper With Pumpkin with a ceramic base.

Hum No.	Size	Trademark	Current Value
2175/0	4-1/2"	TMK-8 OE	$120-$150

Hum 2175: From the Pumpkin Patch.

Hum 2176: Open Number

Hum 2177: Shall We Dance

Part of the "Shall We Dance" collector set, which includes the Time to Dance Hummelscape, this little girl with teddy bear was issued in 2003. The figurine has an inscribed 2002 copyright date, TMK-8, and "Premier Edition" backstamp. The Hummelscape was issued in a limited edition of 3,000 and boasts motion and music.

Hum No.	Size	Trademark	Current Value
2177	5-1/2"	TMK-8 OE	$185-$325

Hum 2178/A and Hum 2179/A: Bridal Gifts

New for 2003, this earthenware framed picture (Hum 2178/A) and earthenware marriage license/storybook (Hum 2179/A) are part of the Bridal Gift Set, which includes two other pieces, all featuring the Dearly Beloved (Hum 2003) motif. The other pieces are: Dearly Beloved trinket box (Hum 2152/A) and Dearly Beloved ornament (Hum 2163/A).

Hum 2178/A and Hum 2179/A: Bridal Gifts.

Hum No.	Basic Size	Trademark	Current Value
2178/A	7-1/4"	TMK-8	$75
2179/A	5-1/2"	TMK-8	$50

Hum 2180: The Final Sculpt

Modeled by master sculptor Gerhard Skrobek in 2001 exclusively for his Farewell Tour in 2002, this piece was the last Skrobek completed before retiring from touring at the age of 80. It is a depiction of Skrobek's fond memories at Goebel—specifically his recollection of modeling The Botanist (Hum 351).

Released in 2002, The Final Sculpt was a sequentially numbered limited edition of 8,000 pieces and was available only at selected retailers involved in Skrobek's Farewell Tour. Each piece was signed by Skrobek. The Final Sculpt has a special backstamp, incised 2001 copyright date, and Skrobek silhouette commemorative medallion.

Hum No.	Size	Trademark	Current Value
2180	5-1/4"	TMK-8	$250-$499

Hum 2181: Clear as a Bell

This M.I. Hummel Club exclusive for club year 28 made her debut as part of the "Kinder Choir" series in spring 2004. Hitting the High Note with Lamppost was the companion figurine for that year. Sculpted by master sculptor Helmut Fischer, this Exclusive Edition (EE) figurine has an incised copyright date of 2002, the TMK-8 trademark, and "Club Exclusive" 2004-2005 backstamp.

Hum 2181: Clear as a Bell.

Hum No.	Size	Trademark	Current Value
2181	3-3/4"	TMK-8 EE	$100

Hum 2182: First Solo

This M.I. Hummel Club exclusive for club year 27 made its debut as part of the first year of the "Kinder Choir" series in spring 2003. Too  Shy to Sing (Hum 845) was the companion figurine for that year. A two-tiered wooden display base came with this Hummel, with room for future members of the "Kinder Choir" series. Sculpted by master sculptor Helmut Fischer, this Exclusive Edition (EE) has an incised copyright date of 2002, the TMK-8 trademark, and "Club Exclusive" 2003-2004 backstamp.

Hum 2182: First Solo.

Hum No.	Size	Trademark	Current Value
2182	3-1/2"	TMK-8 EE	$100

Hum 2183: Keeping Time

This M.I. Hummel Club exclusive for club year 30 made its debut as the fourth and final year of the "Kinder Choir" series in spring  2006. Lamplight Caroler (Hum 847) was the companion figurine for that year, and Melody Conductor (Hum 2198) completed the series. Sculpted by master sculptor Helmut Fischer, this Exclusive Edition (EE) has an incised copyright date of 2002, the TMK-8 trademark, and "Club Exclusive" 2006-2007 backstamp.

Hum 2183: Keeping Time.

Hum No.	Size	Trademark	Current Value
2183	3-3/4"	TMK-8 EE	$100

Hum 2184: First Violin

This M.I. Hummel Club exclusive for club year 29 made its debut as the third year of figurine for that year. The second half of the two-tiered wooden base came with this figurine, for future "Kinder Choir" series pieces. Sculpted by master sculptor Helmut Fischer, this Exclusive Edition (EE) has an incised copyright date of 2002, the TMK-8 trademark, and "Club Exclusive" 2005-2006 backstamp.

Hum No.	Size	Trademark	Current Value
2184	3-3/4"	TMK-8 EE	$100

Hum 2184: First Violin.

Hum 2185: Winter's Here

Hum 2185: Winter's Here.

A fine young lad who seems to be ready to sweep the first winter snow of the season was released in 2003. This figurine has a "First Issue 2003" backstamp and an incised 2002 copyright date.

The year 2011 marked the celebration of Sister Hummel's 75th anniversary of the beginning of her legacy. Manufaktur Rödental selected 50 figurines to bear the "75th Anniversary" backstamp. Winter's Here was one of those figurines. Only 75 of them were available in North America with this backstamp. Each figurine was hand-numbered, with a golden backstamp and a map of North America backstamp. A special porcelain plaque was included, and the notable emblem on the packaging hinted at the contents. Each figurine included a "75 Years of M.I. Hummel" certificate.

Hum No.	Size	Trademark	Current Value
2185	5-1/4"	TMK-8 OE	$250

Hum 2186: Open Number

Hum 2188-2189: Open Numbers

Hum 2190: Harvest Time

Harvest Time was inspired by the tradition of the harvest shared by people all over the world. It brings together a pair of boys, one of which is riding in a wheelbarrow, and the beloved M.I. Hummel "Goose Girl," all proud of their accomplishments of the day. It took 43 individual molds to create this figurine. It is sequentially numbered; only 1,000 were made available worldwide. Ten percent of the edition were selected to be artist proofs and were numbered separately. Sculpted by master sculptor Helmut Fischer, this figurine bears TMK-8 and a "Limited Edition" backstamp. A wooden display base and a ceramic plaque stating the limited edition number are included with this figurine, which was released in 2003. It is the companion piece to Hum 2200: Autumn Time.

Hum No.	Size	Trademark	Current Value
2190	13-1/2" L x 6-1/4" W x 8-3/4" H	TMK-8 LE	$3,500

Hum 2190: Harvest Time.

Hum 2187: Benevolent Birdfeeder

This piece was first released in 2003 with a "First Issue 2004" backstamp. 150 Arbeitmeister Editions were made available to M.I. Hummel Club members in North America. The Arbeitmeister Edition also has the "First Issue 2003" backstamp. Both editions of this Hummel have a TMK-8 and an incised 2002 copyright date. This figurine was sculpted by master sculptor Helmut Fischer.

The year 2011 marked the celebration of Sister Hummel's 75th anniversary of the beginning of her legacy. Manufaktur Rödental selected 50 figurines to bear the "75th Anniversary" backstamp. Benevolent Birdfeeder was one of those figurines. Only 75 of them were available in North America with this backstamp. Each figurine was hand-numbered, with a golden backstamp and a map of North America backstamp. A special porcelain plaque was included, and the notable emblem on the packaging hinted at the contents. Each figurine included a "75 Years of M.I. Hummel" certificate.

Hum No.	Size	Trademark	Current Value
2185	5-1/2"	TMK-8 OE	$439

Hum 2187: Benevolent Birdfeeder

Hum 2191-2192: Open Numbers

Hum 2193/4/0: Flowers for Mother

Flowers for Mother was part of the "Create a Gift" collection in North America when paired with the Sentimental Occasion base. This base was not available in Canada. This figurine was first released in 2004. The incised copyright date is 2003, and it has TMK-8. In the European market, this figurine bears a "Bouquet" backstamp.

Hum 2193/4/0: Flowers for Mother.

Hum No.	Size	Trademark	Current Value
2193/4/0	3-1/4"	TMK-8 OE	$100

Hum 2194: Duty Calls

Produced in a limited edition of 3,000 numbered figurines, sculpted by master sculptor Helmut Fischer, Duty Calls is the third of the "Ambassadors of Freedom" series for the AAFES catalog and U.S. Military Exchanges. It has the 2003 incised copyright date, limited edition backstamp, and TMK-8. A brass plaque inscribed "Duty Calls/Ambassador of Freedom" and a wooden base are included, as well as a reproduction of the famous poster by James Montgomery Flagg of Uncle Sam pointing and saying, "I want you."

Hum No.	Size	Trademark	Current Value
2194	7-1/2"	TMK-8 LE	$250-$400
	8-1/4" with	wooden base	

Hum 2195/4/0: Sunflower Girl

Sunflower Girl was part of the "Create a Gift" collection in North America when paired with the Sentimental Occasion base. This base was not available in Canada. This figurine was released in 2004. The incised copyright date is 2003, and it has TMK-8. In the European market, this figurine bears a "Bouquet" backstamp.

Hum	Size	Trademark	Current Value
2194/4/0	3-1/4"	TMK-8 OE	$100

Hum 2195: Sunflower Girl.

Hum 2196: Open Number

Hum 2197: American Spirit

Illustrating the American spirit and the pastime of soapbox derby racing, this piece was first released in 2003 and included a U.S. flag. It was sculpted by Marion Huschka and has TMK-8.

Hum	Size	Trademark	Current Value
2197	4-3/4"	TMK-8 TM	$250

Hum 2197: American Spirit.

Hum 2198: Melody Conductor

The final figurine of the "Kinder Choir" series was released in 2006 for club year 30. Melody Conductor was given free to M.I. Hummel Club members who acquired the eight figurines in the series. It has the TMK-8 and "Club Exclusive" backstamp.

Hum 2198: Melody Conductor.

Hum	Size	Trademark	Current Value
2198	3-1/2"	TMK-8 EE	$100

Hum 2199: First Steps

This figurine was first released as an Arbeitmuster Edition in October 2007. Only 27 of these figurines are "Arbeitmuster," featuring a crimped medal tag signed by Frank Knoch. First Steps was sculpted by master sculptor Helmut Fischer, has TMK-8, and the "First Issue 2008" backstamp.

The year 2011 marked the celebration of Sister Hummel's 75th anniversary of the beginning of her legacy. Manufaktur Rödental selected 50 figurines to bear the "75th Anniversary" backstamp. First Steps was one of those figurines. Only 75 of them were available in North America with this backstamp. Each figurine was hand-numbered, with a golden backstamp and a map of North America backstamp. A special porcelain plaque was included, and the notable emblem on the packaging hinted at the contents. Each figurine included a "75 Years of M.I. Hummel" certificate.

Hum	Size	Trademark	Current Value
2199	5-1/4"	TMK-8 OE	$329

Hum 2200: Autumn Time

A trio of children discovers the world through the changes of the season in Autumn Time. They pass a road sign that shows the way to Convent Siessen and Goebel. This piece symbolized the seven decades of partnership between the Sisters at the Siessen Convent and the artists at Goebel. Helmut Fischer and his team of Annette Barth and Tamara Fuchs worked on this piece of art for a total of 190 hours. The mold was then sliced into 34 different pieces for casting. There were 58 different steps needed during the painting process to complete this limited edition figurine. A total of 1,000 figurines were sold worldwide, with only 400 sold in North America. This figurine came with a wooden base and ceramic certificate of authenticity and bears the edition number. Released in 2005, it has a TMK-8 backstamp. It is a companion piece to Hum 2190: Harvest Time.

Hum 2200: Autumn Time.

Hum	Size	Trademark	Value
2200	12-1/2" L x 6-3/4" W x 9-1/2" H	TMK-8 LE	$2,000-$3,000

Hum 2201: Baby's First Drawing

An exclusive worldwide launch in October 2008 on QVC, Baby's First Drawing presents a baby showing its first creative artistry with paint, paintbrush, and paper. This figurine can also have a Hummelscape added, called Painting Pals. It has a special painting can backstamp to commemorate its release and is a TMK-8.

Hum	Size	Trademark	Current Value
2201	3-1/2"	TMK-8 OE	$299

Hum 2202: Open Number

Hum 2203: Hope

The first figurine in the "Hope" series benefits the National Breast Cancer Foundation. This figurine was introduced in 2004 with a pink ribbon base during the month of October, honoring Breast Cancer Awareness Month. The pink ribbon on the base can be personalized with a name and date. It has the TMK-8 trademark and National Cancer Foundation backstamp.

Hum 2203: Hope.

Hum	Size	Trademark	Current Value
2203	3-1/2"	TMK-8 OE	$99

Hum 2204: Holiday Fun

Part of the "Bavarian Christmas Market Collector Set," Holiday Fun was released in fall 2004 with the Bavarian Christmas Market Hummelscape, which depicts a traditional

Christmas market in Germany. The Hummelscape lights up and plays the "Twelve Days of Christmas." The figurine is a mixed media figurine and has a small ornament hanging from her hand. The set has the "2004 Holiday Edition" and "holly" backstamps and is incised with the 2004 copyright date and TMK-8. The figurine is available separately.

Hum 2204: Holiday Fun.

Hum	Size	Trademark	Current Value
2204	4-1/4"	TMK-8 OE	$230

The year 2011 marked the celebration of Sister Hummel's 75th anniversary of the beginning of her legacy. Manufaktur Rödental selected 50 figurines to bear the "75th Anniversary" backstamp. Holiday Fun was one of those figurines. Only 75 of them were available in North America with this backstamp. Each figurine was hand-numbered, with a golden backstamp and a map of North America backstamp. A special porcelain plaque was included, and the notable emblem on the packaging hinted at the contents. Each figurine included a "75 Years of M.I. Hummel" certificate.

Hum 2205: Troublemaker

The fourth edition of the "Moments in Time" series, Troublemaker is an intricate figurine that was introduced in 2005. It took 40 individual molds. The sections were cast and then put back together again. This figurine was produced in a worldwide limited edition of 5,000, each sequentially numbered, and came with a certificate of authenticity. Troublemaker was modeled by master sculptor Helmut Fischer and features TMK-8.

Hum	Size	Trademark	Current Value
2205	7-1/4"	TMK-8 LE	$1,200

Hum 2205: Troublemaker.

Hum 2206-2208: Open Numbers

Hum 2209/A: Puppet Love

A little girl who loves putting on puppet shows wears a puppet in her left hand. A companion to Hum 2209/B: Puppet Pal, Puppet Love was sculpted by master sculptor Helmut Fischer and released in 2004. The Hummelscape titled Puppet Theater, which plays "Pop Goes the Weasel," has movement with puppets going up and down in the theater. Puppet Love could be purchased separately and features TMK-8

Hum 2209/A: Puppet Love.

Hum	Size	Trademark	Current Value
2209/A	3-1/2"	TMK-8 OE	$139

Hum 2209/B: Puppet Pal

Imagine a boy who loves to put on puppet shows with puppets in both hands. A companion to Hum 2209A: Puppet Love, Puppet

Pal was sculpted by master sculptor Helmut Fischer and released in 2004. The Hummelscape titled Puppet Theater, which plays "Pop Goes the Weasel," has movement with puppets going up and down in the theater. Puppet Pal could be purchased separately and features TMK-8.

Hum 2209/B: Puppet Pal.

Hum	Size	Trademark	Current Value
2209/B	3-1/2"	TMK-8 OE	$139

Hum 2210: Open Number

Hum 2211: Fancy Footwork

Fancy Footwork was introduced in 2005. A young boy dressed in traditional Bavarian lederhosen has his eye on the ball and is ready to score. This TMK-8 figurine is a companion piece to Keeper of the Goal (Hum 2212), Ready to Play (Hum 2274), and She Caught It! (Hum 2265).

Hum	Size	Trademark	Current Value
2211	4-1/4"	TMK-8 OE	$179

Hum 2211: Fancy Footwork.

Hum 2212: Keeper of the Goal

Keeper of the Goal, featuring a boy holding a soccer ball, is a tribute to Germany's love of soccer. This figurine is the companion figurine to Hum 2211: Fancy Footwork, Hum 2274: Ready to Play, and Hum 2265: She Caught It!

The year 2011 marked the celebration of Sister Hummel's 75th anniversary of the beginning of her legacy. Manufaktur Rödental selected 50 figurines to bear

Hum 2212: Keeper of the Goal.

Hum	Size	Trademark	Current Value
2211	4-1/4"	TMK-8 OE	$179

the "75th Anniversary" backstamp. Keeper of the Goal was one of those figurines. Only 75 of them were available in North America with this backstamp. Each figurine was hand-numbered, with a golden backstamp and a map of North America backstamp. A special porcelain plaque was included, and the notable emblem on the packaging hinted at the contents. Each figurine included a "75 Years of M.I. Hummel" certificate.

Hum 2213: Open Number

Hum 2214: What a Smile
Closed Edition

What a Smile was first introduced in January 2005. The figurine depicts a small girl with a flowerpot by her side. This Hummel figurine is the companion to Hum 2215: Gotcha! and Hum 2205: Troublemaker. Master sculptor Helmut Fischer sculpted this figurine in 2004.

Hum 2214: What a Smile.

Hum	Size	Trademark	Current Value
2214	6-1/4"	TMK-8 CE	$279

Hum 2215: Gotcha!

Gotcha! was first introduced in January 2005 and depicts a small boy with a slingshot. This Hummel figurine is the companion to Hum 2214: What a Smile and Hum 2205: Troublemaker. Master sculptor Helmut Fischer sculpted this figurine in 2004.

Hum 2215: Gotcha!

Hum	Size	Trademark	Current Value
2215	6-1/4"	TMK-8 CE	$279

Hum 2216: Homecoming

Homecoming was a new 2005 Hummel figurine and was the fifth piece in the Military Hummel "Ambassadors of Freedom" series. Available for the AAFES catalog and U.S. Military Post Exchanges, it was produced in a limited edition of 3,000 pieces that were sequentially numbered. The base has a red, white, and blue flying eagle backstamp and "Ambassadors of Freedom" inscription.

Hum	Size	Trademark	Current Value
2216	8"	TMK-8 LE	$300-$450

The figurine has an incised 2004 copyright date and a "Limited Edition" and TMK-8 backstamp. The piece comes with a 1-1/4" wooden plaque that is inscribed "Homecoming/Ambassadors of Freedom" and a wooden tree tied with a yellow ribbon.

Hum 2217/A: Do You Love It!

Do You Love It!, first released in 2005, depicts a girl holding a frame with a white background that can be personalized. A partnership between Roger Whittaker and Goebel was later formed to raise funds for Isabella, a charitable organization for children in Kenya, Africa. The figurine depicts a young girl holding a signed picture of Roger Whittaker. Some of the proceeds of the sale of that figurine went to the Isabella charitable foundation. Do You Love It! features a copyright date of 2004 and TMK-8 applied by decal, and has an incised "Hummel" signature on the back of the frame she holds, due to the limited space on the figurine. It is the companion to Hum 2217/B: Look What I Made! In 2013 Manufaktur Rödental made available eight special messages that could be added to this figurine to personalize it.

Hum 2217/A: Do You Love It!

Hum	Size	Trademark	Current Value
2217/A	3-1/4"	TMK-8 OE	$99

Hum 2217/B: Look What I Made!

Look What I Made!, first released in 2005, depicts a boy holding a frame with a white background that can be personalized. A partnership between Roger Whittaker and Goebel was later formed to raise funds for Isabella, a charitable organization for children in Kenya, Africa. The figurine depicts a young boy holding a signed picture of Roger Whittaker. Some of the proceeds of the sale of that figurine went to the Isabella charitable foundation. The piece has a copyright date of 2004 and TMK-8 applied by decal, and has an incised "Hummel" signature on the back of the frame he holds due to the limited space on the figurine. It is the companion to Hum 2217/A: Do You Love It! In 2013 Manufaktur Rödental made available eight special messages that could be added to this figurine to personalize it.

Hum 2217/B: Look What I Made!

Hum	Size	Trademark	Current Value
2217/B	3-1/4"	TMK-8 OE	$99

Hum 2218: Springtime Friends

Springtime Friends, one of the "Spring" figurines in the "Four Seasons" series, has a lamb backstamp. Each figurine in this series bears a special backstamp that matches the animal or season depicted. Springtime Friends has an incised copyright date of 2004 and TMK-8 backstamp. There are no first issue markings.

Hum 2218: Springtime Friends.

Hum	Size	Trademark	Current Value
2218	3-1/4"	TMK-8 OE	$99

Hum 2219: Sunflower Boy

Sunflower Boy is one of the "Summer" figurines in the "Four Seasons" series. Each figurine in this series bears a special backstamp that matches the season it depicts. Sunflower Boy has a watering can and TMK-8 backstamp; it was released in 2005. It is the companion to Hum 2195: Sunflower Girl. There are no first issue markings

Hum 2219: Sunflower Boy.

Hum	Size	Trademark	Current Value
2219	3-1/4"	TMK-8 OE	$99

Hum 2220: School Days

First made available in July 2005, School Days is one of the "Autumn" figurines in the "Four Seasons" series. Each figurine in the "Four Seasons" series bears a special backstamp that matches the season depicted. School Days features pumpkin and TMK-8 backstamps. There are no first issue markings.

Hum 2220: School Days.

Hum	Size	Trademark	Current Value
2220	3-1/4"	TMK-8 OE	$99

Hum 2221: All Bundled Up

All Bundled Up is another of the seasonal figurines. It is part of the "Four Seasons" series and has a chick back stamp. Springtime Friends was also sold as "Springtime Splendor" collectors set. Each figurine in this series bears a special backstamp that matches the animal or season depicted. Springtime Friends has an incised copyright date of 2004 and TMK-8 backstamp; it was released in 2005. There are no first issue markings.

Hum 2221: All Bundled Up.

Hum	Size	Trademark	Current Value
2221	3-1/4"	TMK-8 OE	$99

Hum 2222: A Star for You

The third in the "Swarovski" series, A Star for You is a sequentially numbered limited edition of 7,500. It is a mixed media figurine because it features a Swarovski crystal star. It has an incised 2005 copyright date, and limited edition and TMK-8 backstamps. A matching round tin comes with the figurine.

Hum	Size	Trademark	Edition Value
2222	5"	TMK-8 LE	$359

Hum 2222: A Star for You.

Hum 2223:
Practice Makes Perfect
Girl

First issued in 2005, Practice Makes Perfect Girl has a 2004 copyright date and TMK-8, applied by a decal due to the size of the bottom of the figurine. The Hummel signature is inscribed across the back of the skirt. The piece includes a black base on which the figurine sits with her legs crossed. It is the companion to Hum 771: Practice Makes Perfect Boy.

Hum 2223: Practice Makes Perfect (Girl).

Hum	Size	Trademark	Edition Value
2223	3-1/4"	TMK-8 OE	$139

Hum 2224-2225: Open Numbers

Hum 2226:
Shepherd's Apprentice

Representing summer in the "Four Seasons" collector set, this piece was first released in the European market in 2005 in Summer Landscape: Hummel Pond, followed by the North American release in 2006 as part of the "Animal Friends" collection. It has goat and TMK-8 backstamps. There are no first issue markings.

Hum 2226: Shepherd's Apprentice.

Hum	Size	Trademark	Current Value
2226	3-1/4"	TMK-8 OE	$139

Hum 2227: Morning Call

Representing spring in the "Four Seasons" collector set, Morning Call was first released in the European market in 2005 in Spring Landscape: Hummel Source, followed by the North American release in 2006 as part of the "Animal Friends" collection. It has rooster and TMK-8 backstamps. There are no first issue markings. It resembles Hum 199 and Hum 2085.

Hum 2227: Morning Call.

Hum	Size	Trademark	Edition Value
2227	3-1/4"	TMK-8 OE	$139

Hum 2228: Can't Catch Me

Representing fall in the "Four Seasons" collector set, this piece was first released in the European market in 2005 in Fall Landscape: Hummel Garden, followed by the North American release in 2006 as part of the "Animal Friends" collection. It has goose and TMK-8 backstamps. There are no first issue markings. It resembles Hum 2097.

Hum	Size	Trademark	Edition Value
2228	3-1/4"	TMK-8 OE	$129

Hum 2228: Can't Catch Me.

Hum 2229: Puppy Pal

Representing fall in the "Four Seasons" collector set, this piece was first released in the European market in 2005 in Fall Landscape: Hummel Garden, followed by the North American release in 2006 as part of "Animal Friends" collection. It has puppy and TMK-8 backstamps. It has no first issue markings.

Hum	Size	Trademark	Edition Value
2229	3-1/4"	TMK-8 OE	$9

Hum 2229: Puppy Pal.

Children's Nativity Sets

The following Children's Nativity Set groupings were originally available to purchase as sets of three figurines and may still be found in some local retailers or online stores.

Hum 2230/A, Hum 2230/B, Hum 2230/C: Holy Family Set with Stage

This set includes Mary, Joseph, and Baby Jesus in his crib and the Children's Pageant Center Stage with base and ceramic crèche featuring a stained glass background.

Hum 2230/D, Hum 2230/E, Hum 2230/F: Three Shepherds

This set includes Shepherd with Staff, Shepherd with Milk Jug, Shepherd with Flute, and Children's Christmas Pageant Right Stage with base and background.

Hum 2230/G, Hum 2230/H, Hum 2230/J: Three Kings

This set includes King Melchior, King Balthazar, King Gaspar, and Children's Christmas Pageant Right Stage with base and background.

Hum 2230/M, Hum 2230/N, Hum 2230/O, 2230/P: Angel and Animals

This set includes Angel With Lantern, Angela, Young Calf, Donkey, Sheep Laying, and Sheep Standing. Neither a base nor a background are included in this set. Angela was added in 2006.

Hum 2230/A: Mary

This piece was first released in fall 2005. Mary has an incised 2005 copyright date, TMK-8, and no first issue markings. The M.I. Hummel signature is incised on her cape.

Hum 2230/A: Mary.

Hum	Size	Trademark	Current Value
2230/A	3-1/2"	TMK-8 OE	$149

Hum 2230/B: Joseph

This piece was first released in fall 2005. Joseph has an incised 2005 copyright date, TMK-8, and no first issue markings. The M.I Hummel signature is incised on his cape.

Hum 2230/B: Joseph.

Hum	Size	Trademark	Current Value
2230/B	4-1/4"	TMK-8 OE	$149

Hum 2230/C:
Child Jesus with Manger

This piece was first released in fall 2005. Child Jesus has the 2005 copyright date, M.I. Hummel signature, and TMK-8 on a decal due to the size of the figurine. The Child Jesus is not attached to the manger, which is made of wood and comes with straw. There are no first issue markings.

Hum 2230/C: Baby Jesus With Straw Manger.

Hum	Size	Trademark	Current Value
2230/C	2-1/2"	TMK-8 OE	$45

Hum 2230/D:
Shepherd With Staff

First released in fall 2005, Shepherd with Staff has the Hummel number, 2005 copyright date, M.I. Hummel signature, and TMK-8 applied on a decal due to the size and shape of the figurine. There is no main base for this figurine. Companions are Hum 2230/E: Shepherd with Milk Jug and Hum 2230/F: Shepherd with Flute.

Hum 2230/D: Shepherd With Staff.

Hum	Size	Trademark	Current Value
2230/D	4"	TMK-8 OE	$149

Hum 2230/E:
Shepherd With Milk Jug

First released in fall 2005, Shepherd with Milk Jug has the Hummel number, 2005 copyright date, M.I. Hummel signature, and TMK-8 applied on a decal due to the size and shape of the figurine. There is no main base for this figurine. Companions are Hum 2230/D: Shepherd with Staff and Hum 2230/F: Shepherd with Flute.

Hum 2230/E: Shepherd With Milk Jug.

Hum	Size	Trademark	Current Value
2230/E	4-1/4"	TMK-8 OE	$149

Hum 2230/F:
Shepherd With Flute

First released in fall 2005, Shepherd with Flute has the Hummel number, 2005 copyright date, and TMK-8 applied on a decal due to the size and shape of the figurine. The word "Hummel" is incised on the side of his left leg. There is no main base for this figurine.

Hum 2230/F: Shepherd With Flute.

Hum	Size	Trademark	Current Value
2230/F	3"	TMK-8 OE	$149

Hum 2230/G: King Melchior

First released in fall 2005, King Melchior is standing, wears a crown, and holds an open box. The Hummel number, 2005 copyright date, and TMK-8 are applied on a decal due to the size and shape of the figurine. The word "Hummel" is incised on the back of his cape. There is no main base for this figurine. Companion figurines are Hum 2230/H: King Balthazar and Hum 2230/J: King Gaspar.

Hum 2230/G: King Melchior.

Hum	Size	Trademark	Current Value
2230/G	4-3/4"	TMK-8 OE	$149

Hum 2230/H: King Balthazar

First released in fall 2005, King Balthazar is kneeling and holds a jar. The Hummel number, 2005 copyright date, and TMK-8 are applied on a decal due to the size and shape of the figurine. The word "Hummel" is incised on the back of his cape. There is no main base for this figurine. Companion figurines are Hum 2230/G: King Melchior and Hum 2230/J: King Gaspar.

Hum	Size	Trademark	Current Value
2230/H	3-3/4"	TMK-8 OE	$149

Hum 2230/H: King Balthazar.

Hum 2230/J: King Gaspar

First released in fall 2005, King Gaspar is standing, holds a box, and wears a feather headdress. The Hummel number, 2005 copyright date, and TMK-8 are applied on a decal due to the size and shape of the figurine. The word "Hummel" is incised on the back of his cape. There is no main base for this figurine. Companion figurines are Hum 2230/G: King Melchior and Hum 2230/H: King Balthazar.

Hum	Size	Trademark	Current Value
2230/J	3-3/4"	TMK-8 OE	$149
2230/J	4"	TMK-8	$159

Hum 2230/J: King Gaspar.

Hum 2230/K: Angel With Lantern

First released in fall 2005, Angel with Lantern is standing and holds a lantern. The Hummel number, 2005 copyright date, and TMK-8 are applied on a decal due to the size and shape of the figurine. Angel with Lantern has the word "Hummel" incised on the back of its hem. There is no main base for this figurine. Companion figurines are Hum 2230/L: Angela, Hum 2230/M: Young Calf, Hum 2230/N: Donkey, 2230/O: Sheep, Laying, and Hum 2230/P: Sheep, Standing.

Hum 2230/K: Angel With Lantern.

Hum	Size	Trademark	Current Value
2230/K	4-1/4"	TMK-8 OE	$149

Hum 2230/L: Angela

As an addition to the Children's Nativity Set, Angela was released mid-year in 2006. She is a TMK-8 figurine. Her companions are Hum 2230/K: Angel with Lantern, Hum 2230/M: Young Calf, Hum 2230/N: Donkey, 2230/O: Sheep, Laying, and Hum 2230/P: Sheep, Standing.

Hum 2230/L: Angela.

Hum	Size	Trademark	Current Value
2230/L	3-1/4"	TMK-8 OE	$99

Hum 2230/M: Young Calf

First released in fall 2005, Young Calf is standing looking downward toward the right. The 2005 copyright date and TMK-8 are applied by decal. Young Calf does not have a Hummel number or the M.I. Hummel signature on the figurine. Companion to Hum 2230/K: Angel with Lantern, Hum 2230/L: Angela, Hum 2230/N: Donkey, 2230/O: Sheep, Laying, and Hum 2230/P: Sheep, Standing.

Hum	Size	Trademark	Current Value
2230/M	3-3/4"	TMK-8 OE	$35

Hum 2230/M: Young Calf.

Hum 2230/N: Donkey

First released in fall 2005, Donkey is standing looking to the left. It has a Goebel mark, not a Hummel trademark, and no first issue markings. The donkey does not have a Hummel number or a M.I. Hummel signature on the figurine. Companions are Hum 2230/K: Angel with Lantern, Hum 2230/L: Angela, Hum 2230/M: Young Calf, 2230/O: Sheep, Laying, and Hum 2230/P: Sheep, Standing.

Hum	Size	Trademark	Current Value
2230/N	4"	None OE	$35

Hum 2230/N: Donkey.

Hum 2230/O: Sheep, Laying

First released in fall 2005, Sheep, Laying is looking to the side. It has a Goebel mark, not a Hummel trademark, and no first issue markings. Sheep, Laying does not have a copyright date, Hummel number, or M.I. Hummel signature on the figurine. Companions are Hum 2230/K: Angel with Lantern, 2230/L: Angela, 2230/N: Donkey, and 2230/P: Sheep, Standing

Hum	Size	Trademark	Current Value
2230/O	1-3/4"	None OE	$20

Hum 2230/O: Sheep, Laying.

Hum 2230/P: Sheep, Standing

First released in fall 2005, Sheep, Standing is looking slightly to the right side. It has a Goebel mark, not a Hummel trademark, and no first issue markings. Sheep, Standing does not have a copyright date, Hummel number, or M.I. Hummel signature on the figurine. Companions are Hum 2230/K: Angel with Lantern, 2230/L: Angela, 2230/N: Donkey, and 2230/O: Sheep, Laying.

Hum	Size	Trademark	Current Value
2230/P	2-1/2"	None OE	$25

Hum 2230/P: Sheep, Standing.

Hum 2230/S: Watchful Vigil

This new addition to the Children's Nativity Set was released in summer 2007. The young boy is standing and holding a candle, keeping a peaceful Christmas vigil. The figurine has TMK-8.

Hum 2230/S: Watchful Vigil.

Hum	Size	Trademark	Current Value
2230/S	4"	TMK-8 OE	$149

Hum 2230/T: Little Blessings

This new addition to the M.I. Hummel Children's Nativity Set was released in the summer of 2007. The seated angel is in the tradition of the famous "Hummele" figurine. It is a self-portrait of young Berta Hummel and has TMK-8.

Hum 2230/T: Little Blessings.

Hum	Size	Trademark	Current Value
2230/T	3-1/4"	TMK-8 OE	$99

Hum 2231: Friendly Feeding

Released in 2005 in the European market and then in 2006 in the North American market, Friendly Feeding is part of the "Animal Collection" series. Companions are Hum 2226: Shepherd's Apprentice and Hum 2227: Morning Call. There are a total of eight figurines in the series. Each figurine in the "Animal Collection" series has a special backstamp that matches the animal depicted. Friendly Feeding has the calf backstamp, TMK-8 backstamp, and incised 2005 copyright date. There are no first issue markings.

At presstime, Manufaktur Rödental planned to re-release Friendly Feeding in 2013 as a TMK-9 figurine bearing the TMK-9 backstamp. A new description was not available.

Hum 2231: Friendly Feeding.

Hum	Size	Trademark	Current Value
2231	3-1/4"	TMK-8 OE	$139
2231	3-1/4"	TMK-9	$119 retail

Hum 2232: Let's Be Friends

Released in the European market in 2005 and then in 2006 in the North American market, Let's Be Friends is one of the pieces in the "Animal Collection" series. It is also part of a set representing autumn in the "Four Seasons" series. Each figurine in the "Animal Collection" series bears a special backstamp that matches the animal depicted. Let's Be Friends has a squirrel backstamp, TMK-8 backstamp, and has no first issue markings.

Hum 2232: Let's Be Friends.

Hum	Size	Trademark	Current Value
2232	2-1/2"	TMK-8 OE	$125

Hum 2233: Light of Hope

This is the second figurine in the "Hope" series, which benefits the National Breast Cancer Foundation. Featuring a pink ribbon  around the base of the figurine, it was first released in October 2005 during Breast Cancer Awareness Month. The pink ribbon on the base can be personalized with a name and date. The mixed media figurine, depicting a young girl holding a lantern by a metal chain, is the companion to Hum 2203: Hope and Hum 2240: Heart of Hope. It has TMK-8 and the National Cancer Foundation backstamp.

Hum 2233: Light of Hope.

Hum	Size	Trademark	Current Value
2233	3-1/2"	TMK-8 OE	$99

Hum 2234: Night Before Christmas

The Night Before Christmas set includes a Hummelscape titled Night Before Christmas. The Hummelscape features a Christmas  tree, star, and fireplace that lights up with fiber optics. The new Hummel with the Hummelscape has a motif on the book. The figurine in the set has a "Holiday Special Edition" and red bow backstamps, incised 2005 copyright date, and TMK-8 backstamp. The original figurine doesn't have anything written on the book.

Hum 2234: Night Before Christmas.

Hum	Size	Trademark	Current Value
2234	4"	TMK-8 OE	$230

Hum 2235: Lucky Friend

Released in June 2006 as part of the "Heart of Hummel" collection, Lucky Friend depicts a young girl carrying a young pig in a basket with a heart on it. Lucky Friend is sold individually or as part of a set of the four "Heart of Hummel" figurines. Each "Heart of Hummel" figurine bears a special heart backstamp and was produced in a worldwide limited edition of

Hum 2235: Lucky Friend.

Hum	Size	Trademark	Current Value
2235	4-1/2"	TMK-8 LE	$219

5,000 pieces. A total of 2,500 of the pieces were offered as part of a sequentially numbered, limited edition set with all the same number. The 2,500 limited editions with the same number had to be ordered as a set of four, which includes Lucky Friend, Hum 624: Fresh Blossoms, Hum 908: Gone A-wandering, and Hum 2237: Sunday Stroll. The foursome is packed inside a handsome collector tin.

Hum 2236: Sleigh Ride

Sleigh Ride was made available in fall 2005 in the European market and then in 2006 in the North American market. It is part of the "Four Seasons" collector series Wintertime Wonders set. The base features a special snowflake paying tribute to the winter season, TMK-8, and no first issue markings. Each of the "Four Seasons" figurines has a special backstamp representing the season in which the figurine is part.

Hum	Size	Trademark	Current Value
2236	3-1/4"	TMK-8 OE	$139

Hum 2236: Sleigh Ride.

Hum 2237: Sunday Stroll

Released in June 2006 as part of the "Heart of Hummel" collection, Sunday Stroll depicts a young boy walking his dachshund with a heart on its collar. Sunday Stroll is sold individually or as part of a set of four "Heart of Hummel" figurines. Each "Heart of Hummel" figurine bears a special heart backstamp and was produced in a worldwide limited edition of 5,000 pieces. A total of 2,500 of the pieces were offered as part of a sequentially numbered, limited edition set with all the same number. The 2,500 limited editions with the same number had to be ordered as a set of four, which includes Sunday Stroll, Hum 624: Fresh Blossoms, Hum 908: Gone A-wandering, and Hum 2235: Lucky Friend. The foursome is packed inside a handsome collector tin. QVC sold the first 100 sets.

Hum	Size	Trademark	Current Value
2237	4-1/2"	TMK-8 LE	$199

Hum 2237: Sunday Stroll.

Hum 2238-2239: Open Numbers

Hum 2240: Heart of Hope

This is the third figurine in the "Hope" series, which benefits the National Breast Cancer Foundation. It was first released in October 2006 during Breast Cancer Awareness Month and is a mixed media figurine. It has the known pink ribbon around the base of the figurine. The ribbon can be personalized with a name and date. Heart of Hope is the companion to Hope (Hum 2203) and Light of Hope (Hum 2233). It features TMK-8 and the National Breast Cancer Foundation backstamp.

Hum	Size	Trademark	Current Value
2240	3-1/2"	TMK-8 OE	$100

Hum 2240: Heart of Hope.

Hum 2241: Coming From the Woods

Holiday Dreaming Collector's Set

Part of the Holiday Dreaming Collector's Set, Coming From the Woods was released in 2006. It is part of the Holiday Time Toy Shop Hummelscape, which depicts a holiday-decked toyshop and a young boy carrying a Christmas tree. Both the figurine and the Hummelscape were first sold on QVC, then were available at local retailers. The figurine is a Holiday 2006 Special Edition with an evergreen tree and

Hum 2241: Coming From the Woods.

Hum	Size	Trademark	Current Value
2241	4-1/2"	TMK-8 OE	$219
With HummelScape			$259

TMK-8 backstamp. The figurine is available separately.

The year 2011 marked the celebration of Sister Hummel's 75th anniversary of the beginning of her legacy. Manufaktur Rödental selected 50 figurines to bear the "75th Anniversary" backstamp. Coming From the Woods was one of those figurines. Only 75 of them were available in North America with this backstamp. Each figurine was hand-numbered, with a golden backstamp and a map of North America backstamp. A special porcelain plaque was included, and the notable emblem on the packaging hinted at the contents. Each figurine included a "75 Years of M.I. Hummel" certificate.

Hum 2242: Spring Step

Spring Step, part of the "Sounds of Spring" collection, is an M.I. Hummel Club year 31 exclusive. "Sounds of Spring" is a 12-piece collection that depicts the May Day festival in Germany. Spring Step features a young boy holding a dancing hoop with flowers, stepping to the music. The "Sounds of Spring"

collection has three individual bases on which the 12 figurines can be displayed. "Spring Step" comes with the right side base when all 12 of the figurines in the "Sounds of Spring" collection are purchased. It is a TMK-8. Hum numbers 912/A/B/C/D are based on Hum 348: Ring Around the Rosie and were reconfigured for this collector's set.

Hum 2242: Spring Step.

Hum	Size	Trademark	Current Value
2242	5-1/4"	TMK-8 EE	$125

Hum 2243: Spring Tune

Spring Tune, part of the "Sounds of Spring" collection, is an M.I. Hummel Club year 31 exclusive. Spring Tune features a young boy with a tuba. "Sounds of Spring" is a 12-piece collection that depicts the May Day festival in Germany. The set includes Spring Tune, Hum 912/A: Spring Time, Hum 912/B: Spring Waltz, Hum

912/C: Spring Love, Hum 912/D: Spring Fancy, Hum 2242: Spring Step, Hum 2244: Spring Song, and Hum 2245: Spring Sweetheart. Hum numbers 912/A/B/C/D are based on Hum 348: Ring Around the Rosie and were reconfigured for this collector's set.

Hum 2243: Spring Tune.

Hum	Size	Trademark	Current Value
2243	4"	TMK-8 EE	$125

Hum 2244: Spring Song

Spring Song, part of the "Sounds of Spring" collection, is an M.I. Hummel Club year 31 exclusive. Spring Song features a young boy with a small horn. The "Sounds of Spring" collection has three individual bases on which the 12 figurines can be displayed. "Spring Song" comes with the left side base when all 12 figurines in the "Sounds of Spring" Collection are purchased. It is a TMK-8. "Sounds of Spring" is a 12-piece collection that depicts the May Day festival in Germany. The set includes Spring Song,

Hum 912/A: Spring Time, Hum 912/B: Spring Waltz, Hum 912/C: Spring Love, Hum 912/D: Spring Fancy, Hum 2242: Spring Step, Hum 2243: Spring Tune, and Hum 2245: Spring Sweetheart. Hum numbers 912/A/B/C/D are based on Hum 348: Ring Around the Rosie and were reconfigured for this collector's set.

Hum 2244: Spring Song.

Hum	Size	Trademark	Current Value
2244	4"	TMK-8 EE	$125

Hum 2245: Spring Sweetheart

Spring Sweetheart, part of the "Sounds of Spring" collection, is an M.I. Hummel Club year 31 exclusive. Spring Sweetheart depicts a young boy with a dancing hoop. "Sounds of Spring" is a 12-piece collection that depicts the May Day festival in Germany. The "Sounds of Spring" collection has three individual bases on which the 12 figurines can be displayed. "Spring Sweetheart" comes with the central rotating dance floor and Maypole when all 12 figurines in the "Sounds of Spring" collection are purchased.

It is a TMK-8. The set includes Spring Sweetheart, Hum 912/A: Spring Time, Hum 912/B: Spring Waltz, Hum 912/C: Spring Love, Hum 912/D: Spring Fancy, Hum 2242: Spring Step, Hum 2243: Spring Tune, and Hum 2244: Spring Song. Hum numbers 912/A/B/C/D are based on Hum 348: Ring Around the Rosie and were reconfigured for this collector's set.

Hum 2245: Spring Sweetheart.

Hum	Size	Trademark	Current Value
2245	5-1/4"	TMK-8 EE	$125

Hum 2246: Let Me Help You

Hum	Size	Trademark	Current Value
2246	4"	TMK-8 OE	$299

Let Me Help You, a companion to Time Out (Hum 470), was first released in 2007. The first year of production has the First Issue backstamp. Ninety-three pieces of this figurine were available with  "Arbeitsmuster" status. A crimped metal tag signed by Frank Knoch, head of Product Development, was included. The Arbeitsmuster editions were available only to M.I. Hummel Club members. This piece was first sculpted by master sculptor Helmut Fischer and has a TMK-8 backstamp.

Hum 2246: Let Me Help You.

The year 2011 marked the celebration of Sister Hummel's 75th anniversary of the beginning of her legacy. Manufaktur Rödental selected 50 figurines to bear the "75th Anniversary" backstamp. Let Me Help You was one of those figurines. Only 75 of them were available in North America with this backstamp. Each figurine was hand-numbered, with a golden backstamp and a map of North America backstamp. A special porcelain plaque was included, and the notable emblem on the packaging hinted at the contents. Each figurine included a "75 Years of M.I. Hummel" certificate.

Hum 2247: Gretl

Hum	Size	Trademark	Current Value
2247	3-3/4"	TMK-8 OE	$219

Gretl, part of the 2007 "Premier" collection, was available at the M.I. Hummel Club's 30th Anniversary Oktoberfest celebration  at the Hofbräuhaus, Las Vegas. A commemorative edition was available. It is the companion to Trail Blazer (Hum 2045) and has TMK-8.

The year 2011 marked the celebration of Sister Hummel's 75th anniversary of the beginning of her legacy. Manufaktur Rödental selected 50 figurines to bear the "75th Anniversary" backstamp. Gretl was one of those figurines. Only 75 of them were available in North America with this backstamp. Each figurine was hand-numbered, with a golden backstamp and a map of North America backstamp. A special porcelain plaque was included, and the notable emblem on the packaging hinted at the contents. Each figurine included a "75 Years of M.I. Hummel" certificate.

Hum 2247: Gretl.

Hum 2248: Special Delivery

Special Delivery, depicting two young girls, one holding flowers and the other holding a crystal box wrapped in red ribbon, is the fourth figurine in the "Swarovski" series and was produced in a worldwide limited edition of 7,500 pieces. The piece came with a certificate of authenticity and a commemorative tin box. Considered a mixed media figurine, it features earthenware, crystal, and fabric. It is marked TMK-8 and was released in 2006.

Hum	Size	Trademark	Current Value
2248	5-3/4"	TMK-8 LE	$350

Hum 2248: Special Delivery.

Hum 2249: Marmalade Lover

Hum	Size	Trademark	Current Value
2249	4-1/4"	TMK-8 OE	$289

Marmalade Lover captures a little girl's sweet tooth for homemade marmalade. There are two major differences in this figurine: the M.I. Hummel Club Preview Edition has a green marmalade jar and "Club Exclusive" backstamp. Only 1,500 of the club exclusive were available in North America. Club members and the general public who purchased the figurine now get a blue marmalade jar. This figurine was sculpted by master sculptor Helmut Fischer and was released in spring 2008.

Hum 2250: Learning to Share

Learning to Share was the sixth edition in the "Moments in Time" series. With a book and doll forgotten, a little girl learns to wait her turn on the rocking horse. Produced in a worldwide limited edition of 3,000 pieces, it came with a numbered certificate of authenticity and is hand-numbered on the bottom of the base. It made its debut at artist events, at customer appreciation events, and on QVC in the fall of 2006. This figurine was sculpted by master sculptor Helmut Fischer and has TMK-8 on the base of the figurine.

Hum	Size	Trademark	Current Value
2250	8-1/2" L x 7" H x 6-1/4" W	TMK-8 LE	$1,200

Hum 2250: Learning to Share.

Hum 2251: Swimming Lesson

Swimming Lesson, with a special duck backstamp, was new for 2007. It was an addition to the "Animal Friends" collection and is marked TMK-8.

Hum	Size	Trademark	Current Value
2251	2-3/4"	TMK-8 OE	$99

Hum 2251: Swimming Lesson.

Hum 2252: Joy of Hope

Joy of Hope, the first double figurine in the "Hope" series, is a mixed media figurine featuring two cheerful girls with a pink cloth ribbon on a pink ribbon base. It is the fourth in the series. Its Hummel companions are Hope (Hum 2203), Light of

Hum 2252: Joy of Hope with pink ribbon base.

Hum	Size	Trademark	Current Value
2252	4"	TMK-8 OE	$219

Hope (Hum 2233), and Heart of Hope (Hum 2240). Joy of Hope was first released in October 2007 during Breast Cancer Awareness Month. The proceeds benefited the National Cancer Foundation. A pink ribbon glass ornament was given away as a thank you gift. Joy of Hope has TMK-8.

Hum 2253: Open Number

Hum 2254: Susi

Susi was a 2008 Customer Appreciation Days figurine and came with or without a base. Susi, with the Blue Cloud base for personalization, has a Special Edition Gold Star backstamp and a space for the artist's signature. To obtain the Blue Cloud base, a collector needed to attend an artist event from October through December 2007. Susi was the final addition to the Children's Nativity Series.

Hum 2254: Susi.

Hum	Size	Trademark	Current Value
2254	4-3/4"	TMK-8 OE	$159

Hum 2256: Open Number

Hum 2257: Little Concerto

Little Concerto is a two-piece figurine: piano and young pianist on a piano bench. This is the first Hummel figurine featuring a child sitting at a piano. The sheet music bears the actual notes of "Eine Kleine Nachtmusik" (A Little Night Music), one of Mozart's compositions.

The first 2,500 pieces were made available to M.I. Hummel Club members as a Club Preview Edition worldwide with a bee on the music reflecting this special edition. The open edition does not have the bee on the sheet music. This figurine was sculpted by master sculptor Helmut Fischer and has the TMK-8 backstamp.

Hum	Size	Trademark	Current Value
2257	3-1/4"	TMK-8 OE	$219

Hum 2255: Forever Friends

Forever Friends depicts two girls watching a swan and her cygnet. The piece was produced in a hand-numbered limited edition of 1,000 figurines worldwide with only 500 figurines allotted for North America. It came with the "Limited Edition" backstamp and a certificate of authenticity. Forever Friends was sculpted in 2006 by master sculptor Helmut Fischer and released in 2007. The backstamp also states that it is a TMK-8.

Hum 2255: Forever Friends.

Hum	Size	Trademark	Current Value
2255	10-1/4" x 8" x 8"	TMK-8 LE	$2,750

Hum 2257: Little Concerto.

Hum 2258: For Mommy

A mixed media figurine, For Mommy has a ribbon-made bouquet of flowers, which the young girl is holding. A ceramic bouquet pin is included. It is a TMK-8 figurine.

The year 2011 marked the celebration of Sister Hummel's 75th anniversary of the beginning of her legacy. Manufaktur Rödental selected 50 figurines to bear the "75th Anniversary" backstamp. For

Hum 2258: For Mommy.

Hum	Size	Trademark	Current Value
2258	4-1/2"	TMK-8 OE	$189

Mommy was one of those figurines. Only 75 of them were available in North America with this backstamp. Each figurine was hand-numbered, with a golden backstamp and a map of North America backstamp. A special porcelain plaque was included, and the notable emblem on the packaging hinted at the contents. Each figurine included a "75 Years of M.I. Hummel" certificate.

Hum 2259: A Gift for You

A Gift for You, showing a boy carrying a bouquet of flowers and lebkuchen, was first introduced in Germany in spring 2008 and was first offered in the United States on QVC. It has a "First Issue" backstamp and comes with a lapel pin that says, "Fur dich" (for you). It was first sculpted by Helmut Fischer in 2007. It has TMK-8 and an incised 2007 copyright date.

Hum 2259: A Gift for You with heart pin.

Hum	Size	Trademark	Current Value
2259	4-1/4"	TMK-8 OE	$179

The year 2011 marked the celebration of Sister Hummel's 75th anniversary of the beginning of her legacy. Manufaktur Rödental selected 50 figurines to bear the "75th Anniversary" backstamp. A Gift for You was one of those figurines. Only 75 of them were available in North America with this backstamp. Each figurine was hand-numbered, with a golden backstamp and a map of North America backstamp. A special porcelain plaque was included, and the notable emblem on the packaging hinted at the contents. Each figurine included a "75 Years of M.I. Hummel" certificate.

Hum 2260: Open Number

Hum 2261: Story Time

Story Time was a "Moments in Time Series VII" figurine produced in a worldwide limited edition of 3,000 pieces released in 2008. Each figurine was hand numbered and came with a certificate of authenticity. Story Time was sculpted by master sculptor Helmut Fischer. Fourteen molds were required to complete the complex piece depicting a girl reading to her sleeping brother on a couch with the family cat. It is a TMK-8 figurine.

Hum	Size	Trademark	Current Value
2261	6-1/4"	TMK-8 LE	$1,000

Hum 2261: Story Time.

Hum 2262: How Can I Help You?

How Can I Help You? was a commemorative of the 2007 M.I. Hummel Convention held in St. Paul, Minnesota. It came with a little table labeled for the convention along with a welcome sign. QVC launched it as Christkindlmarkt Collector Set. The figurine, which depicts a little girl holding a traditional unwrapped sweets bag, does not sit on a traditional round base. The figurine name is decaled on the bottom of the base because

Hum	Size	Trademark	Current Value
2262	4"	TMK-8	$169

there is no room for it on the side. The Hummelscape depicts a Christkindlmarkt shop that, when batteries are added, lights up the lantern and window. The Hummelscape plays "First Day of Christmas" when the music box key is wound. The figurine was sculpted by master sculptor Helmut Fischer and has TMK-8.

Hum 2263: Christmas Morning

Christmas Morning depicts a brother and sister opening their gifts on Christmas morning. Produced in a limited edition of 4,000 pieces worldwide, only 1,800 of the piece were available in North America. First sculpted by master sculptor Marin Huschka in 2006, this figurine has a special backstamp and certificate of authenticity. It has TMK-8 and an incised 2006 copyright.

Hum	Size	Trademark	Current Value
2263	7-1/2"	TMK-8 CE	$600

Hum 2263: Christmas Morning.

Hum 2264: Christmas Treat

The M.I. Hummel Holiday Treats Collector's Set was a new 2007 Hummel figurine with a Sweet Shop Hummelscape. It was

introduced on QVC in October 2007 and was the second edition to the "Christmas Wishes" series. The Holiday Treats Collector's Set includes Christmas Treat and a Hummelscape; the figurine features a playful West Highland terrier waiting for a holiday treat. There is a special 2007 backstamp, "Holiday 2007 Special Edition" with a West

Hum 2264: Christmas Treat.

Hum	Size	Trademark	Current Value
2264	4-1/2"	TMK-8 OE	$219

Highland terrier and TMK-8 on the bottom of the figurine base.

The year 2011 marked the celebration of Sister Hummel's 75th anniversary of the beginning of her legacy. Manufaktur Rödental selected 50 figurines to bear the "75th Anniversary" backstamp. Christmas Treat was one of those figurines. Only 75 of them were available in North America with this backstamp. Each figurine was hand-numbered, with a golden backstamp and a map of North America backstamp. A special porcelain plaque was included, and the notable emblem on the packaging hinted at the contents. Each figurine included a "75 Years of M.I. Hummel" certificate.

Hum 2265: She Caught It!

Fifth in the "Swarovski" series, this limited edition of 7,500 pieces was introduced in 2008. It shows a young girl who has caught a crystal soccer ball and a young boy looking impressed. A certificate of authenticity is included as well as a keepsake tin box. It is a TMK-8 figurine.

Hum	Size	Trademark	Current Value
2265	4-3/4"	TMK-8 LE	$349

Hum 2265: She Caught It!

Hum 2266: Mayor

Part of the 10-figurine "Marketplatz" series, Mayor is pretending to be the local mayor. Released in 2008, Mayor has a special backstamp that commemorates his playful dress-up profession. Master sculptor Helmut Fischer sculpted Mayor in 2007. It has TMK-8 and the 2007 copyright incised on the base. The Marketplatz, a five-piece village backdrop with a working clock, lamppost, two-piece fountain, and cobblestone base, was available to display the figurines.

Hum	Size	Trademark	Current Value
2266	3-1/4"	TMK-8 OE	$99

Hum 2266: Mayor.

Hum 2267: Little Cobbler

Part of the 10-figurine "Marketplatz" series, Little Cobbler is pretending to be a local merchant repairing shoes. Little Cobbler has a special backstamp that commemorates his playful dress-up profession. Master sculptor Helmut Fischer sculpted the piece in 2007. It has TMK-8 and the 2007 copyright incised on the base. It was also was available through QVC as a set with a bench. At presstime, Manufaktur Rödental planned to re-release Little Cobbler in 2013 as a TMK-9 figurine with the TMK-9 backstamp. A new description was not available.

The Marketplatz, a five-piece village backdrop with a working clock, lamppost, two-piece fountain, and cobblestone base, was available to display the figurines.

Hum	Size	Trademark	Current Value
2267	3-1/4"	TMK-8	$99
2267	3-1/4"	TMK-9 OE	$119 retail

Hum 2267: Little Cobbler.

Hum 2268: Littlest Teacher

Part of the 10-figurine "Marketplatz" series and Littlest Teacher Collector's Set, Littlest Teacher is pretending to be a teacher in a village school. This figurine was released in 2008. A QVC premier, The Littlest Teacher Collector's Set features a classroom Hummelscape showing Littlest Teacher instructing a teddy bear and a doll. Littlest Teacher has a special backstamp that commemorates her playful dress-up profession. Master sculptor Helmut Fischer sculpted Littlest Teacher in 2007. It has TMK-8 and the 2007 copyright incised on the base. The Marketplatz, a five-piece village backdrop with a working clock, lamppost, two-piece fountain, and cobblestone base, was available to display the figurines.

In 2013 Manufaktur Rödental reintroduced Littlest Teacher as a TMK-9 figurine bearing the TMK-9 backstamp.

Hum	Size	Trademark	Current Value
2268	3-1/4"	TMK-8 OE	$99
2268	3-1/4"	TMK-9 OE	$119

Hum 2268: Littlest Teacher.

Hum 2269: Be My Guest

Part of the 10-figurine "Marketplatz" series, Be My Guest is pretending to be a local merchant selling root beer. This figurine was released in 2008 and has a special backstamp that commemorates his playful dress-up profession. Master sculptor Helmut Fischer sculpted Be My Guest in 2007. It has TMK-8 and the 2007 copyright incised on the base. The Marketplatz, a five-piece village backdrop with a working clock, lamppost, two-piece fountain, and cobblestone base, was available to display the figurines.

Hum 2269: Be My Guest.

Hum	Size	Trademark	Current Value
2269	3-1/4"	TMK-8	$99

Hum 2270: Little Seamstress

Part of the 10-figurine "Marketplatz" series, Little Seamstress is pretending to be a local seamstress making and mending clothes. This figurine was released in 2008 and has a special backstamp that commemorates her playful dress-up profession. Master sculptor Helmut Fischer sculpted Little Seamstress in 2007. It has TMK-8 and the 2007 copyright incised on the base. The Marketplatz, a five-piece village backdrop with a working clock, lamppost, two-piece fountain, and cobblestone base, was available to display the figurines.

Hum 2270: Little Seamstress.

Hum	Size	Trademark	Current Value
2270	3-1/4"	TMK-8	$99

Hum 2271: Proud Baker

Part of the 10-figurine "Marketplatz" series, Proud Baker is pretending to be a local baker selling her baked goods. This figurine was released in 2008 and has a special backstamp that commemorates her playful dress-up profession. Master sculptor Helmut Fischer sculpted Proud Baker in 2007. It has TMK-8 and the 2007 copyright incised on the base. The Marketplatz, a five-piece village backdrop with a working clock, lamppost, two-piece fountain, and cobblestone base, was available to display the figurines.

Hum 2271: Proud Baker.

Hum	Size	Trademark	Current Value
2270	3-1/4"	TMK-8	$99

Hum 2272: Market Girl

Part of the 10-figurine "Marketplatz" series, Market Girl is pretending to go to the market. This figurine was released in 2008 and has a special backstamp that commemorates her playful dress-up profession. Master sculptor Helmut Fischer sculpted Market Girl in 2007. It has TMK-8 and the 2007 copyright incised on the base. It was also was available as a set, Market Girl and an apple tree, through QVC. The Marketplatz, a five-piece village backdrop with a working clock, lamppost, two-piece fountain, and cobblestone base, was available to display the figurines.

Hum 2272: Market Girl.

Hum	Size	Trademark	Current Value
2272	3-1/4"	TMK-8 OE	$99

Hum 2273: Spring Gifts

Spring Gifts, an M.I. Hummel Club exclusive for club year 32, is a mixed media figurine, the first of its kind as a club renewal gift. The fabric bouquet of flowers is wrapped with ribbon and

Hum	Size	Trademark	Current Value
2273	4"	TMK-8	$125

is held high with a wooden stick. It complements the "Sounds of Spring" collection. It is a TMK-8 figurine.

Hum 2274: Ready to Play

Part of the "Premier" collection and released in 2007, this figure features a girl ready to play soccer—a tribute to female athletes all over the world. It was made to honor the lover of soccer in Germany. It is the first young girl figurine to be wearing lederhosen. She is a companion to Keeper of the Goal (Hum 2212), Fancy Footwork (Hum 2211), and She Caught It! (Hum 2265). It is a TMK-8 figurine.

Hum 2274: Ready to Play.

Hum	Size	Trademark	Current Value
2274	4-3/4"	TMK-8 OE	$179

Hum 2275: Summer Castles

Summer Castles depicts what children and summer have in common and is part of a set called Summertime Friends. Its companion is Summer Delight (Hum 2276). A barefooted boy plays in the sand. This worldwide limited edition was released in summer 2008. Only 5,000 figurines were made worldwide, were hand-numbered, and had a certificate of authenticity. A QVC exclusive launch in July 2008 sold this figurine as the Summertime Friends set with limited edition numbers 1-150. This figurine was sculpted by master sculptor Helmut Fischer. It has a TMK-8 trademark.

Hum 2275: Summer Castles.

Hum	Size	Trademark	Current Value
2275	5-3/4"	TMK-8 LE	$269

Hum 2276: Summer Delight

Summer Delight depicts what children and summer have in common and is part of a set called Summertime Friends. Its companion is Summer Castles (Hum 2275). A young girl waters her flower garden. This worldwide limited edition was released in summer 2008. Only 5,000 figurines were made worldwide, were hand-numbered, and had a certificate of authenticity. A QVC exclusive launch in July 2008 sold this figurine as the Summertime Friends set with limited edition numbers 1-150. This figurine was sculpted by master sculptor Helmut Fischer. It has a TMK-8 trademark.

Hum	Size	Trademark	Current Value
2276	5-3/4"	TMK-8 LE	$269

Hum 2276: Summer Delight.

Hum 2277/A: Follow Your Heart
With or without holiday decoration

Follow Your Heart depicts a young girl who holds a heart-shaped plaque that can be personalized. The plaque is either a plain white heart with a red border, or a snowflake background behind the heart with a red border that says "Happy Holidays" or "Tis the Season" with a striped bow and a small evergreen branch.

Hum	Size	Trademark	Current Value
2277/A	3-1/4"	TMK-8 OE	$99-$120

Hum 2277/B: With All My Heart
With or without holiday decoration

With All My Heart depicts a young boy holding a heart-shaped plaque that can be personalized. The plaque is either a plain white heart with a red border, or a snowflake background behind the heart with a red border that says "Happy Holidays" or "Tis the Season" with a striped bow and a small evergreen branch.

Hum	Size	Trademark	Current Value
2277/B	3-1/4"	TMK-8 OE	$99-$120

Hum 2278: Just Ducky

Just Ducky was released exclusively by the Danbury Mint in winter 2008. It was produced as a limited edition of 5,000 figurines and has a special backstamp. At artist events in 2008 throughout North America, many of these figurines were sold with master artist Ulrich Tendera's signature. This is a mixed media figurine. It has a wooden duck tethered by a string to the little girl. Members of local chapters of the M.I. Hummel Club

Hum	Size	Trademark	Current Value
2278	2-3/4"	TMK-8	$50

who attended the 2009 Niagara-Buffalo National Convention received this figurine as a gift for attending the convention. Ulrich Tendera signed the ceramic base commemorating the event, which came with the figurine. It is a TMK-8 figurine.

Hum 2279: Look at Me!
With Bavarian flag

A carefree, barefoot little girl rides her tricycle in Look At Me!, a companion figurine to Oh, No! (Hum 2082). Look at Me! was launched by QVC as a collector's set. A Hummelscape features music and movement when the wind-up base turns, allowing the figurine to go around the park past a bird sanctuary and garden. The music box plays "In the Good Ol' Summertime." This

Hum 2279: Look At Me!

Hum	Size	Trademark	Current Value
2279	4-1/4"	TMK-8 OE	$229

figurine was originally sculpted by master sculptor Helmut Fischer. The figurine has a "First Issue" backstamp and an incised TMK-8.

The year 2011 marked the celebration of Sister Hummel's 75th anniversary of the beginning of her legacy. Manufaktur Rödental selected 50 figurines to bear the "75th Anniversary" backstamp. Look at Me! was one of those figurines. Only 75 of them were available in North America with this backstamp. Each figurine was hand-numbered, with a golden backstamp and a map of North America backstamp. A special porcelain plaque was included, and the notable emblem on the packaging hinted at the contents. Each figurine included a "75 Years of M.I. Hummel" certificate.

Hum 2280: Christmas Duet

A caroling sister and brother stand close together to keep warm and share the sheet music for "Silent Night" in Christmas

Duet. The Hummelscape is a church that lights up and plays 12 different Christmas carols. Both the figurine and Hummelscape were available on QVC in time for the Christmas 2008 holidays. Christmas Duet was sculpted by master sculptor Helmut Fischer. This figurine has two special backstamps: "Holiday 2008 Special Edition" or a music book with TMK-8.

Hum 2280: Christmas Duet.

Hum	Size	Trademark	Current Value
2280	4-1/4"	TMK-8 OE	$229

The year 2011 marked the celebration of Sister Hummel's 75th anniversary of the beginning of her legacy. Manufaktur Rödental selected 50 figurines to bear the "75th Anniversary" backstamp. Christmas Duet was one of those figurines. Only 75 of them were available in North America with this backstamp. Each figurine was hand-numbered, with a golden backstamp and a map of North America backstamp. A special porcelain plaque was included, and the notable emblem on the packaging hinted at the contents. Each figurine included a "75 Years of M.I. Hummel" certificate.

Hum 2281: Puppy's Bath

Debuting first on QVC in the fall of 2009, this figurine depicts a little boy taking his bath while his puppy wants to join him. It bears TMK-9 and the 100th birthday year backstamp. The 100th birthday year backstamp was only available for 2009 production. The figurine was sculpted by master sculptor Helmut Fischer.

Hum	Size	Trademark	Current Value
2281	4"	TMK-9 OE	$379

Hum 2281: Puppy's Bath.

Hum 2282/A: Precious Bouquet

A Precious Bouquet, which debuted on QVC, features a little girl holding a bunch of flowers with a ribbon in her hair and a bee symbol tucked among the flowers. This figurine is a companion to Full of Charm (Hum 2282/B). It bears TMK-9 and 100th birthday year backstamp. The 100th birthday year backstamp was only available for 2009 production. The figurine was sculpted by master sculptors Helmut Fischer and Tamara Fuchs. A wooden heart base was also available for purchase to display this figurine, along with Full of Charm. The wooden base was made in Asia.

Hum 2282/B: Full of Charm

Full of Charm, which debuted on QVC, depicts a little boy holding a bouquet of flowers for someone special with a bee symbol tucked among the flowers. This figurine is a companion to Precious Bouquet (Hum 2282/A). It bears the TMK-9 and 100th birthday year backstamp. The 100th birthday year backstamp was only available for 2009 production. The figurine was sculpted by master sculptors Helmut Fischer and Tamara Fuchs. A wooden heart base was also available for purchase to display this figurine, along with Precious Bouquet. The wooden base was made in Asia.

Hum 2282/A: Precious Bouquet.

Hum 2282/B: Full of Charm.

Hum	Size	Trademark	Current Value
2282/A	5-1/4"	TMK-9 OE	$219

Hum	Size	Trademark	Current Value
2282/B	5-1/4"	TMK 9 OE	$219

Hum 2283/II: Winter Friend

A companion to Making New Friends, Winter Friend was released in 2008 as a mixed media figurine of a child wrapping a scarf around a snowman holding a straw broom. Master sculptor Helmut Fischer first sculpted this figurine in 2007. It is one of the last TMK-8 figurines made by Goebel, has a "First Issue" backstamp, and has an incised 2007 copyright.

Hum 2283/II: Winter Friend.

Hum	Size	Trademark	Current Value
2283/II	6-1/2"	TMK-8	$569 retail

Hum 2284: Butterfly Wishes

Sixth in the "Swarovski" series, this figurine was first released as a limited holiday launch in December 2008. Three crystal butterflies flutter in a garden around a glistening bouquet of flowers held by the older of the two girls in the figurine. The younger girl intently watches the butterflies. It is one of the last M.I. Hummel figurines made with the Goebel TMK-8 trademark.

Hum 2284: Butterfly Wishes.

Hum	Size	Trademark	Current Value
2284	4-1/4"	TMK-8	$350

Hum 2285: Strolling With Friends

Offered exclusively first by Danbury Mint in 2009, this figurine depicts a boy and girl on a walk with a friendly puppy who wants to play. It is one of the first figurines to bear TMK-9 and also commemorates the 100th anniversary of Sister Maria Innocentia Hummel's birth.

Hum 2285: Strolling With Friends.

Hum	Size	Trademark	Current Value
$529	5-1/4"	TMK-9	$529

Hum 2287: Wishing on a Star

Wishing on a Star is a mixed media figurine of a little girl holding a shining Swarovski crystal star and wishing for a bright future for herself and the world. It has a TMK-9 backstamp.

Hum 2287: Wishing on a Star.

Hum No.	Size	Trademark	Current Value
2287	4"	TMK-9 OE	$169 retail

Hum 2288: Sister's Children

Sister's Children celebrated the 100th anniversary of Sister M.I. Hummel's birth. This commemorative limited edition honors her artistry, vision, and loving spirit. Manufaktur Rödental released this figurine on her birthday: May, 21, 2009. It bears TMK-9, "100 Years M.I. Hummel" backstamp, and the number of the figurine on the bottom of the base. A numbered certificate of authenticity is included.

Hum	Size	Trademark	Current Value
2288	12-1/4" H x 17" L x 11" W	TMK-9 LE	$6,750

Hum 2288: Sister's Children.

Hum 2290: Sailing Lesson

Sailing Lesson is one of the first figurines made under Manufaktur Rödental. It is the eighth piece in the "Moments in Time" series. A total of 2,000 pieces were made worldwide. It has the special "100 Years M.I. Hummel" and TMK-9 backstamps, and has a numbered certificate of authenticity.

Hum 2290: Sailing Lesson.

Hum	Size	Trademark	Current Value
2290	9" H x 9-3/4" L x 7" W	TMK-9 LE	$1,700 retail

Hum 2291/A: Up and Down

An M.I. Hummel Club year 35 exclusive, Up and Down is the first of four figurines in the "Carousel" series. It depicts a little girl on a carousel horse at a carnival. This figurine is a TMK-9 and has the TMK-9 backstamp as well as the 2011 M.I. Hummel Club exclusive backstamp. To complete this series, a carousel (made in Asia) with lights, which plays the "Carousel Waltz," is available for $139.

Hum 2291/A: Up and Down.

Hum	Size	Trademark	Current Value
2291/A	5"	TMK-9	$349 retail

Hum 2291/B: Swan Chariot

Swan Chariot is an M.I. Hummel Club year 37 exclusive figurine depicting a little girl sitting in a swan chariot on a carousel. The

third of four figurines in the "Carousel" series, this piece is a TMK-9 with the TMK-9 backstamp and the 2013 M.I. Hummel Club exclusive backstamp. To complete the series, a carousel (made in Asia) with lights, which plays the "Carousel Waltz," is available for purchase for $139 retail.

Hum 2291/B: Swan Chariot.

Hum	Size	Trademark	Current Value
2291/C	3-3/4"	TMK-9 EE	$379 retail

Hum 2291/C: Beep Beep

A M.I. Hummel Club year 36 exclusive, Beep Beep is the second of four figurines in the "Carousel" series. It depicts a little boy in an

old-fashioned racecar. This figurine is a TMK-9 and has the TMK-9 backstamp and the 2012 M.I. Hummel Club exclusive backstamp. To complete this series, a carousel (made in Asia) with lights, which plays the "Carousel Waltz," is available for $139.

Hum 2291/C: Beep Beep.

Hum	Size	Trademark	Current Value
2291/B	3-1/4"	TMK-9	$379 retail

Hum 2291/D: Round We Go

Round We Go is an M.I. Hummel Club year 38 exclusive figurine. It is the fourth and final figurine in the "Carousel" series, released earlier than planned in the summer of 2013. Round We Go, featuring a little boy on a carousel horse, is a TMK-9 figurine with both TMK-9 and 2013 M.I. Hummel Club exclusive backstamps. To complete the series, a carousel (made in Asia) with lights, which plays the "Carousel Waltz," is available for purchase for $139 retail.

Hum	Size	Trademark	Current Value
2291/D	4-3/4"	TMK-9 EE	$379 retail

Hum 2291/D: Round We Go.

Hum 2292: Cuddle Bear

Cuddle Bear is an M.I. Hummel Club Member Exclusive for club year 37 in 2013. A young girl dressed in a red dress, white collar, green apron, grey short socks, and brown shoes, with a blue bow in her brown hair, holds her favorite brown teddy bear. Cuddle Bear is a gift for members who renew their M.I. Hummel Club membership.

Hum 2292: Cuddle Bear.

Hum	Size	Trademark	Current Value
2292	4"	TMK-9 EE	$70

Hum 2293: Parlor Pal

Parlor Pal was the M.I. Hummel Club year 36 free gift for renewing a M.I. Hummel Club membership. It depicts a young boy carrying two ice cream cones. At 4" tall, he is larger than some other recent club gift figurines. Parlor Pal is a TMK-9 figurine.

Hum 2293: Parlor Pal.

Hum No.	Size	Trademark	Current Value
2293	4"	TMK-9	$90

Hum 2294: Hope for Tomorrow

Hope for Tomorrow was the fifth piece in "Hope" series in 2010. This figurine features a little girl standing under an umbrella with her hand stretched out to see if the rainstorm has ended. A pink ribbon base came with the figurine. A portion of the proceeds benefited the National Breast Cancer Foundation. Hope for Tomorrow is a TMK-9 figurine.

Hum 2294: Hope for Tomorrow.

Hum No.	Size	Trademark	Current Value
2294	4"	TMK-9 OE	$169 retail

Hum 2296: Little Luck

Little Luck was the M.I. Hummel Club exclusive year 34 figurine of a young boy holding a golden horseshoe. It was the second of a three-part series of mixed media Lucky Charm figurines, each holding a golden charm. It has the TMK-9 backstamp. It was available to M.I. Hummel Club members beginning in summer 2010.

Hum 2296: Little Luck.

Hum	Size	Trademark	Current Value
2296	3-1/4"	TMK-9 EE	$55

2295: Open Number

Hum 2297: A Lucky Bug

A Lucky Bug was the M.I. Hummel Club exclusive year 33 figurine of a young girl holding a golden ladybug charm–German symbol of good luck. It was the first of a three-part series of mixed media Lucky Charm figurines, each holding a golden charm. A key ring was also available. It has the TMK-9 backstamp.

Hum	Size	Trademark	Current Value
2297	3-3/4"	TMK-9 EE	$55

Hum 2297: A Lucky Bug
Key Ring

One side of A Lucky Bug key ring features a motif in bas relief with a gleaming golden ladybug charm. The back has TMK-9 incised into the chrome.

Hum	Size	Trademark	Current Value
2297	2"	TMK-9 Key Ring	$10

Hum 2297: A Lucky Bug.

Hum 2298: My Lucky Heart

An M.I. Hummel Club year 35 thank you gift, My Lucky Heart is the third and final mixed media Lucky Charm figurine in which a girl holds a golden heart on a pole. It has the TMK-9 backstamp.

Hum 2298: My Lucky Heart.

Hum No.	Size	Trademark	Current Value
2298	3-1/4"	TMK-9 EE	$55

Hum 2299-2300: Open Numbers

Hum 2303: Giddy-Up

Giddy Up was a QVC exclusive until August 2010, and now can be purchased at local Hummel retailers. Giddy Up features a tired little girl lying on her rocking horse. She is holding her favorite doll.

Hum 2303: Giddy-Up.

Hum	Size	Trademark	Current Value
2303	4-3/4"	TMK-9 OE	$299

Hum 2301: Sparkling Shell

Sparkling Shell was the seventh edition in the "Swarovski" series figurine released in April 2010, depicting a boy and girl returning from a walk. It is a mixed media piece: The girl holds a Swarovski Crystal shell and the boy holds a wooden fishing pole with string and hook. A TMK-9 figurine with the TMK-9 backstamp, Sparkling Shell was produced in a limited edition of 3,000 figurines, is numbered, and includes a certificate of authenticity.

Hum 2301: Sparkling Shell.

Hum	Size	Trademark	Current Value
2301	6"	TMK-9 LE	$459 retail

Hum 2304-2308: Open Numbers

Hum 2309/A: Just for You

Released in April 2010, Just for You shows a young girl with her kitten, holding a sunflower in her right hand and a card with flowers on it in the left hand. It is a companion figurine to Only for You (Hum 2309/B). It has a unique base, which fits together so you can keep these two figurines close together. It is the first of its kind in M.I. Hummel history.

Hum 2309/A: Just for You.

Hum	Size	Trademark	Current Value
2309/A	5-1/2"	TMK-9 OE	$359 retail

Hum 2309/B: Only for You

Released in April 2010, Only for You features a young boy with his puppy, holding a cake with a heart on it in his right hand. It is a companion figurine to Just for You (Hum 2309/A). It has a unique base, which fits together so you can keep these two figurines close together. It was the first of its kind in M.I. Hummel history.

Hum 2309/B: Only for You.

Hum	Size	Trademark	Current Value
2309/B	5-1/2"	TMK-9 OE	$359 retail

Hum 2310: Precious Pony

Precious Pony depicts a young girl getting to know her colt. This figurine was released in 2010 and has TMK-9.

Hum 2310: Precious Pony.

Hum	Size	Trademark	Current Value
2310	4"	TMK-9 OE	$229 retail

Hum 2311: Curious Colt

Curious Colt features a young boy being playful with his colt. This Hummel was released in 2010 and has TMK-9.

Hum	Size	Trademark	Current Value
2311	4"	TMK-9 OE	$229 retail

Hum 2311: Curious Colt.

Hum 2312: Teeter-Totter Time

Teeter-Totter Time, the ninth piece in the "Moments in Time" series, was released in the fall of 2010. It depicts a boy and girl on a teeter-totter. The girl holds a teddy bear and the boy's dog is along for the fun. Teeter-Totter Time was produced in a limited edition of 2,000 figurines worldwide. It has the TMK-9 and "Moments in Time" backstamps and is a numbered figurine. It came with a numbered certificate of authenticity.

Hum	Size	Trademark	Current Value
2312	7-1/4"	TMK-9 LE	$1,100

Hum 2312: Teeter-Totter Time.

Hum 2313: No Bed Please

No Bed Please features a little boy with blanket and teddy bear who does not want to go to bed. A TMK-9 figurine, it was introduced in 2010.

Hum	Size	Trademark	Current Value
2313	4-1/4"	TMK-9 OE	$189 retail

Hum 2313: No Bed Please.

"Founders Collection"

The "Founders Collection" of annual figurines depicts family memories from Herr Jörg Köster, owner and managing director of Manufaktur Rödental. The first 10 figurines, which will be auctioned, will be signed by Herr Köster in blue ink as well as have the "Founders Collection" and TMK-9 backstamps. The remaining figurines will receive a signature facsimile in black. The figurines will be numbered sequentially with a certificate of authenticity. All proceeds from the auctioned figurines will go to children's charities. A portion of the proceeds from the figurines sold through normal retail channels will also go to charity.

Hum 2314: First Piano Lesson

First in the annual "Founders Collection" made-to-order figurine, First Piano Lesson is a mixed media piece. The figurine was created by master sculptors and painters at Manufaktur Rödental. The grand piano is crafted of fine hardwood (made in Asia). First Piano Lesson was the first Hummel in which a girl plays a piano. It was available in 2010.

Hum 2314: First Piano Lesson.

Hum	Size	Trademark	Current Value
2314	3-1/4"	TMK-9 LE	$299

Hum 2315: Angel of Peace

Angel of Peace is the 2010 Annual Angel. The cherub holds a white dove, wishing for peace throughout the world. It has a TMK-9 backstamp.

Hum 2315: Angel of Peace.

Hum No.	Size	Trademark	Current Value
2315	4-3/4"	TMK-9 OE	$159 retail

Hum 2316: O' Tannenbaum

O' Tannenbaum depicts a choir boy singing with his trusty friend (a dog) in front of a Christmas tree. This TMK-9 figurine was available in fall of 2010.

Hum No.	Size	Trademark	Current Value
2316	7"	TMK-9 OE	$419 retail

Hum 2316: O'Tannenbaum.

Hum 2317: Open Number

Hum 2318/A: A Prayer for You

Girl

A Prayer for You features a little girl holding a teddy bear and saying a prayer. It is a companion piece to Hum 2318/B: A Prayer for Everyone. Introduced in spring of 2011, it is a TMK-9 figurine with TMK-9 backstamp.

Hum 2318/A: A Prayer for You.

Hum No.	Size	Trademark	Current Value
2318/A	4-1/4"	TMK-9 OE	$179 retail

Hum 2318/B: A Prayer for Everyone

Boy

A Prayer for Everyone depicts a little boy holding a clown doll and saying a prayer. It is a companion to Hum 2318/A: A Prayer for You. Introduced in spring of 2011, it is a TMK-9 figurine with TMK-9 backstamp.

Hum 2318/B: A Prayer for Everyone.

Hum No.	Size	Trademark	Current Value
2318/B	4-1/2"	TMK-9 OE	$179 retail

Hum 2319: First Two Wheeler

First Two Wheeler was the second edition in the "Founder's Collection" series. It was a limited edition figurine limited to the number of pieces ordered by March 31, 2011. It depicts a young boy anxious to learn how to ride his two-wheeler bicycle. It has the "Founder's Collection" series backstamp as well as the TMK-9 backstamp.

Hum No.	Size	Trademark	Current Value
2319	4-3/4"	TMK-9 LE	$349 retail

Hum 2319: First Two Wheeler.

Hum 2320: Follow That Fawn

Follow that Fawn was a Masterpiece Worldwide Limited Edition of 1,000 figurines released in 2011. It depicts two girls and a boy in the forest coming upon a fawn. The little girl kneeling has a basketful of blueberries and is offering some to the fawn, who is lying down below three evergreen trees. The two children standing are making sure they are quiet. The boy is holding a basketful of fruit. Each figurine is numbered, has a special backstamp along with the TMK-9 backstamp, and comes with a certificate of authenticity.

Hum No.	Size	Trademark	Current Value
2320	9-3/4" H x 11" L x 7" W	TMK-9 LE	$3,200 retail

Hum 2320: Follow That Fawn.

Hum 2321: The Little Banker

Introduced in 2013, The Little Banker is saving his change. A young lad, dressed in a blue jacket, white shirt (not all tucked in), and black pants, is holding a coin and standing by a white piggy bank with a painted heart, scrollwork, and silver markings. Little Banker is a TMK-9 figurine with the TMK-9 backstamp.

Hum 2321: The Little Banker

Hum	Size	Trademark	Current Value
2321	4-3/4"	TMK-9 OE	N/A

Hum 2322/A-D: Basket Buddies

Basket Buddies is based on Sister Hummel's relationship with her nephew, Alfred, and her niece, Traudl (Alfred's sister). There are four figurines: Hum 2322/A: Alfred (baby boy), Hum 2322/B: Traudl (baby girl), Hum 2322/C: Teddy Bear, and Hum 2322/D: Basket, in which two of the three figurines can sit. Basket and Teddy Bear are made in Asia. Released in 2011, the girl and boy figurines have the TMK-9 backstamp. These figurines can be purchased as a set or individually.

Hum 2322/A-D: Basket Buddies set.

Hum No.	Size	Trademark	Current Value
2322/A-D	Various	TMK-9 OE	$429 set
2322/A	3"	TMK-9 OE	$179
2322/B	3-1/4"	TMK-9 OE	$179
2322/C	2-1/2"	TMK-9 OE	$40
2322/D	3" H x 2-1/4" L	TMK-9 OE	$40

Hum 2323: Sweetheart

Boy

A mixed media figurine, Sweetheart is the eighth edition in the "Swarovski" series. A young lad holds a heart-shaped Swarovski crystal. He is a companion to Hum 2329: A Simple Wish (Girl). Sweetheart was produced in a limited edition of 3,000 figurines. A TMK-9 figurine, it has the trademark backstamp, is numbered, and has a certificate of authenticity.

Hum 2323: Sweetheart.

Hum No.	Size	Trademark	Current Value
2323	3-3/4"	TMK-9 OE	$179 retail

Hum 2324: Cuddly Calf

Cuddly Calf is part of the "Farm Animal" series. It features a little boy kneeling with a young calf. It is a companion to Hum 2325 and Hum 2326. Released in spring 2011, it has the TMK-9 backstamp. A dog in a doghouse, fence, and wagon, all made in Asia, are accessories to this series.

Hum 2324: Cuddly Calf.

Hum No.	Size	Trademark	Current Value
2324	3-1/2"	TMK-9 OE	$249 retail

Hum 2325: Prized Pig

Prized Pig is part of the "Farm Animal" series. It depicts a boy holding a young pig in his arms. It is a companion to Hum 2324 and Hum 2326. Released in spring 2011, it has the TMK-9 backstamp. A dog in a doghouse, fence, and wagon, all made in Asia, are accessories to this series.

Hum No.	Size	Trademark	Current Value
2325	4-1/4"	TMK-9 OE	$229 retail

Hum 2325: Prized Pig.

Hum 2326: Hee Haw

Hee Haw is part of the "Farm Animal" series. It depicts a young girl feeding a donkey. It is a companion of Hum 2324 and Hum 2325. Released in spring 2011, it has the TMK-9 backstamp. A dog in a doghouse, fence, and wagon, all made in Asia, are accessories to this series.

Hum No.	Size	Trademark	Current Value
2326	4-1/4"	TMK-9 OE	$299 retail

Hum 2326: Hee Haw.

Hum 2327: Angel of Hope

Angel of Hope was the 2011 Annual Angel, modeled by master sculptor Tamara Fuchs. An angel holding a glowing candle, this figurine is part of the "Annual Angel" series. It is a TMK-9 figurine and has the TMK-9 backstamp along with the year 2011.

Hum 2327: Angel of Hope.

Hum No.	Size	Trademark	Current Value
2327	4-3/4"	TMK-9 OE	$179 retail

Hum 2328: Shine So Bright

Shine So Bright was produced in a worldwide limited edition of 2,000 figurines in 2011. It depicts two sisters trimming the tree with a basketful of ornaments. There are eight Swarovski Crystal ornaments, six on the tree, one in the basket, and one in the girl's hand. A kitten sits at the feet of the girl by the tree.

Hum 2328: Shine So Bright.

Hum No.	Size	Trademark	Current Value
2328	7" H x 7" L x 4" W	TMK-9 LE	$619 retail

Hum 2329: A Simple Wish

Girl

A Simple Wish is the eighth edition in the "Swarovski" series. It is a mixed media figurine with a little girl holding a flower in

her right hand and a Swarovski crystal in her left hand. She is a companion to Hum 2323: Sweetheart. Simple Wish was produced in a limited edition of 3,000 figurines. It is a TMK-9 figurine with TMK-9 backstamp, is numbered, and includes a certificate of authenticity.

Hum 2329: A Simple Wish.

Hum No.	Size	Trademark	Current Value
2329	4"	TMK-9 OE	$179 retail

Hum 2330: Song of Hope

Song of Hope is the sixth in the "Hope" series. A young girl holding sheet music is singing a song of hope that represents optimism and the spirit of women fighting breast cancer. A portion of the proceeds goes to the National Breast Cancer

Foundation for research, detection, and education. Song of Hope comes with a pink ribbon base. It is a TMK-9 figurine and has the TMK-9 backstamp.

Hum 2330: Song of Hope.

Hum No.	Size	Trademark	Current Value
2330	4"	TMK-9 OE	$179 retail

Hum 2331: Cuddly Kitty

Introduced in spring 2011, Cuddly Kitty was an M.I. Hummel Club Year 35 Exclusive. It features a little girl cuddling a kitten. A TMK-9 figurine, Cuddly Kitty has the TMK-9 backstamp and the 2011 M.I. Hummel Club backstamp.

Hum No.	Size	Trademark	Current Value
2331	4"	TMK-9 OE	$179 retail

Hum 2331: Cuddly Kitten.

Hum 2332: Fun in the Sun

Fun in the Sun was an exclusive Artist Event Figurine in 2011. It was only available for purchase at artist events that year. It depicts a little girl swimming in a tub with her rubber duck. A TMK-9 figurine, it has the TMK-9 backstamp.

Hum 2332: Fun in the Sun.

Hum No.	Size	Trademark	Current Value
2332	4"	TMK-9 EE	$419 retail

Hum 2333: Tag Along Teddy

Tag Along Teddy is a collector's set in collaboration with Steiff Toys. It depicts a girl giving her Steiff teddy bear a ride. It is a mixed media figurine released in 2011. A worldwide limited edition of 499 pieces was produced and included a Stieff bear. It is a TMK-9 figurine, has the TMK-9 backstamp, is numbered, and has the special backstamp.

Hum 2333: Tag Along Teddy.

Hum No.	Size	Trademark	Current Value
2333	8" H x 10-1/4" L x 5-1/4" W	TMK-9 LE	$1,800 retail

Hum 2334/A: A Little TLC
Girl

A playmate of Hum 2334/B, A Little TLC reminds us of a time when children visited the "doll doctor" (usually Mom or Dad) for a repair of a favorite special friend. A Little TLC was released in the winter of 2012 and is a TMK-9 figurine.

Hum 2334/A: A Little TLC.

Hum No.	Size	Trademark	Current Value
2334/A	5-1/4"	TMK-9 OE	$299 retail

Hum 2334/B: A Little Boo Boo
Boy

A playmate of Hum 2334/A, A Little Boo Boo reminds us of a time when children visited the doll doctor (usually Mom or Dad) for a repair of a favorite special friend. A Little Boo Boo was released in the winter of 2012 and is a TMK-9 figurine.

Hum 2334/B: A Little Boo Boo.

Hum No.	Size	Trademark	Current Value
2334/B	5-1/4"	TMK-9 OE	$299 retail

Hum 2335: Tippy Toes

Tippy Toes is the third piece in the "Founder's Collection," a special limited edition made-to-order figurine. Expected delivery was fall of 2012. The little girl, who dreams of one day being a principal dancer in her favorite children's ballet, gracefully practices her routine. Jörg Köster, managing director of Manufaktur Rödental, stated, "Tippy Toes is not just about ballet. It's about pursuing your dreams." This figurine has the "Founders Collection" backstamp and is a TMK-9.

Hum No.	Size	Trademark	Current Value
2235	4-3/4"	TMK-9 LE	$349 retail

Hum 2335: Tippy Toes.

Hum 2336: Just a Sprinkle

Just A Sprinkle is the ninth edition in the "Swarovski" series. A tribute to spring, this figurine features a young girl watering a flowerpot filled with flowers made of Swarovski crystals. Produced in a limited edition of 1,999, it is a TMK-9 figurine.

Hum No.	Size	Trademark	Current Value
2336	6"	TMK-9 LE	$419 retail

Hum 2336: Just a Sprinkle.

Hum 2337: First Kiss

First Kiss shows the surprise of a stolen kiss. A little girl takes the initiative to steal a kiss from an unsuspecting little boy. It is a TMK-9 figurine and was released in summer of 2012.

Hum No.	Size	Trademark	Current Value
2337	5-1/2"	TMK-9 OE	$499 retail

Hum 2337: First Kiss.

Hum 2338: Hope Blossoms

Hope Blossoms is the seventh in the "Hope" series and is a mixed media figurine. A young girl holds a watering can with a heart and a Swarovski crystal flower in her hair. The pink ribbon base comes with the figurine. A portion of the proceeds go to the National Breast Cancer Foundation. Hope Blossoms has a TMK-9 backstamp and was released in fall of 2012.

Hum 2338: Hope Blossoms.

Hum No.	Size	Trademark	Current Value
2338	3-3/4"	TMK-9 OE	$179 retail

Hum 2339: Angel of Comfort

The 2012 Annual Angel, Angel of Comfort is a winged cherub gently carrying a sweet white lamb. She is dressed in a yellow gown with red dots. It is a TMK-9 figurine with the TMK-9 backstamp as well as the year 2012 on the figurine.

Hum 2339: Angel of Comfort.

Hum No.	Size	Trademark	Current Value
2339	4-3/4"	TMK-9 OE	$179 retail

2340: Pampered Puppy

Pampered Puppy is a Masterpiece Edition anticipated to be released in 2013. When released, it will be in a worldwide limited edition of 999 figurines. The numbered figurine will be a TMK-9 with Masterpiece Edition and TMK-9 backstamps. No further information was available at presstime.

Hum No.	Size	Trademark	Current Value
2340	9-1/2" H x 8-1/4" L	TMK-9 LE	N/A

Hum 2341: Candy Cutie

Candy Cutie invites you to remember the sweets you enjoyed as a child. This figurine depicts a child from Germany holding a scoop of candy placed into a small paper cone or "Zuckertüte" purchased at the market or carnival. Candy Cutie figurine was released in 2012 and is a TMK-9 figurine.

Hum No.	Size	Trademark	Current Value
2341	4-1/4"	TMK-9 OE	$199 retail

Hum 2341: Candy Cutie.

Hum 2342: Ready or Not

Ready or Not is the 11th edition of "Moments in Time." It captures children playing a game of hide and seek, with a young girl counting to 10 and a little boy hiding. A black and white kitten tries to give away his hiding place. A TMK-9, Ready or Not was a limited edition figurine of 1,999 pieces worldwide. Each figurine is numbered with a certificate.

Hum No.	Size	Trademark	Current Value
2342	9-1/4"	TMK-9 LE	$1,100 retail

Hum 2342: Ready or Not.

Hum 2343: Little Lawyer

Little Lawyer is a mixed media figurine of a boy with metal-framed glasses perched on his head. It represents children imitating adult occupations. Little Lawyer has a "First Issue" backstamp along with the TMK-9 backstamp.

Hum 2343: Little Lawyer.

Hum No.	Size	Trademark	Current Value
2343	4-3/4"	TMK-9 OE	$199 retail

Hum 2344: Country Figurine—Germany

Country Figurine—Germany features a young lad dressed in lederhosen, vest, hat, shoes, and socks traditionally found in Bavaria. He also is carrying a plate of sausage with a pretzel in one hand and a drink in the other hand. This figurine has a "First Issue" backstamp, "Country" backstamp, German flag, and TMK-9 backstamp.

Hum 2344: Country Figurine—Germany.

Hum No.	Size	Trademark	Current Value
2344	6"	TMK-9 OE	$599 retail

Hum 2345: Let's Start
Summer Olympian

Let's Start was produced in a limited commemorative edition in honor of the 2012 Summer Olympics. A young boy is proudly carrying the torch in hopes of bringing home a gold medal. Production was limited to the number of orders received by July 31, 2012. It has a special commemorative backstamp and is a TMK-9 figurine.

Hum 2345: Let's Start.

Hum No.	Size	Trademark	Current Value
2345	5-1/2"	TMK-9 LE	$599 retail

Hum 2346: It's My Turn

It's My Turn features a little boy practicing his soccer moves while a little gray puppy tries to take possession of the ball. It's My Turn is a TMK-9 figurine.

Hum 2346: It's My Turn.

Hum No.	Size	Trademark	Current Value
2346	6-1/2" TMK-	TMK-9 LE	$419 retail

Hum 2347: Open Number

Hum 2348: Grandma's Treasures

Grandma's Treasures depicts an old fashioned scene at Grandma's house of a toddler sitting on Grandma's lap to have a story read to him or her. The siblings or cousins come to visit and explore the many treasures found at Grandma's house, especially in the attic. This figurine was produced in a worldwide limited edition of 399 pieces and is a TMK-9.

Hum No.	Size	Trademark	Current Value
2348	16-3/4" L x 9" H x 8-1/4" W	TMK-9 LE	$4,990 retail

Hum 2348: Grandma's Treasures.

Hum 2349: Teaching Time

Teaching Time is a mixed media figurine of a girl with metal-framed glasses on her head. It represents children imitating adult occupations. Teaching Time has a "First Issue" backstamp along with the TMK-9 backstamp. Chalkboard Display was also available for purchase separately to go along with Teaching Time. Chalkboard Display is made in Asia.

Hum 2349: Teaching Time.

Hum No.	Size	Trademark	Current Value
2349	4-3/4"	TMK-9 OE	$199 retail

Hum 2350: Just Fishin'

Just Fishin' was the 12th edition "Moments in Time" figurine released in 2013. Two young boys are fishing where they shouldn't be and catch a boot with a fish in it. One lad is sitting on the dock and the other is behind the railing, helping pull in their catch. Produced in a limited edition of 1,999 figurines worldwide, Just Fishin' is a mixed media piece with a rope for a fishing line. It has the TMK-9 and "Moments in Time" backstamps and a limited edition number. A certificate of authenticity is included.

Hum 2350: Just Fishin'.

Hum No.	Size	Trademark	Current Value
2350	7"	TMK-9 LE	N/A

Hum 2351: Wings of Hope

Wings of Hope, released in 2013, is the eighth edition in the "Hope" series. A young girl in a blue dress and white blouse holds a yellow bird in her hands. A pink ribbon base, which is made in Asia, is included with the figurine. A portion of the proceeds is donated to the National Breast Cancer Foundation. Wings of Hope is a TMK-9 figurine with TMK-9 and National Breast Cancer Foundation backstamps.

Hum 2351: Wings of Hope.

Hum No.	Size	Trademark	Current Value
2351	4"	TMK-9 OE	N/A

Hum 2352: All Yours

All Yours, the 2013 Annual Angel, features a little cherub dressed in light green with three-leaf scrollwork, holding a red heart to share her love of the season. A TMK-9 figurine, it has the TMK-9 backstamp with 2013 Annual Angel written on the base.

Hum 2352: All Yours.

Hum No.	Size	Trademark	Current Value
2352	4-1/2"	TMK-9 OE	N/A

Hum 2353: Bless Your Home

Bless Your Home, new for 2013, depicts a cherub in a white tunic with blue circles kneeling next to a house with a key in her left hand. She is holding her right hand over the house to bless it, and is keeping watch over the family inside. Bless Your Home is a TMK-9 figurine with the TMK-9 backstamp.

Hum No.	Size	Trademark	Current Value
2353	3″	TMK-9 OE	N/A

Hum 2353: Bless Your Home.

Hum 2354: Tell Me a Story

Tell Me a Story, anticipated to be released sometime in 2013, will be a TMK-9 figurine with the TMK-9 backstamp. No further information was available at presstime.

Hum No.	Size	Trademark	Current Value
2354	3″	TMK-9	N/A

Hum 2355: Little Skipper

Little Skipper is the fourth edition in the "Founder's Collection" and features a young boy at his workbench making sailor's knots in his rope so he can launch his boat. It is a mixed media figurine with a wooden table and rope. Little Skipper has a special "Founder's Collection" backstamp and TMK-9 backstamp and is numbered. Production was limited to the number of orders placed by March 2013. A numbered certificate of authenticity is also included.

Hum No.	Size	Trademark	Current Value
2355	4″	TMK-9 LE	$349 retail

Hum 2355: Little Skipper.

Hum 2356: Country Figurine— United States of America
Rodeo Roundup

Rodeo Roundup represents the United States of America and is the second in the "Country" series. Released in 2013, Rodeo Roundup depicts a young boy dressed in western cowboy attire, including a brown cowboy hat, red scarf, white shirt, brown pants with a knee patch, and black shoes. It is a mixed media TMK-9 figurine with TMK-9 and "Country" backstamps and U.S. flag.

Hum No.	Size	Trademark	Current Value
2356	6"	TMK-9	N/A

Hum 2356: Country Figurine—U.S.A./Rodeo Roundup.

2357: Open Number

Hum 2358: Noisemakers

Noisemakers, the 10th edition in the "Moments in Time" series, depicts a trio of musical performers – two brothers and a dog – and their younger sister covering her ears in dismay. Released in May of 2011, it was produced in a worldwide limited

Hum No.	Size	Trademark	Current Value
2358	7"	TMK-9 LE	$1,400 retail

edition of 2,000 figurines. It has the special "Moments in Time" backstamp, TMK-9 backstamp, and is numbered.

Hum 2358: Noisemakers.

Hum 3011: Carousel

Carousel is the display accessory to Hum 2291/A: Up and Down, Hum 2291/B: Swan Chariot, Hum 2291/C: Beep Beep, and Hum 2291/D: Round We Go in the "Carousel" series. It is made of porcelain with a wood platform for the Hummel figurines. When turned on, the carousel moves, lights up, and plays the famous "Carousel Waltz." This accessory is made in Asia.

Hum 3011: Carousel.

Hum 3012, 3015-3021: Ball Ornaments

Although not produced by Goebel and no longer by any other company, these ball ornaments do carry Hummel model numbers. Each measures 3" in diameter and features the design of one of the M.I. Hummel figurines. They can be found only on the secondary market.

Hum No.	Size	Design	Trademark	Current Value
3012	3"	Celestial Musician	TMK-8	$30-$40
3015	3"	Christmas Angel	TMK-8	$30-$40
3016	3"	Angel Duet	TMK-8	$30-$40
3017	3"	Angel Serenade	TMK-8	$30-$40
3018	3"	Christmas Song	TMK-8	$30-$40
3019	3"	Festival Harmony With Flute	TMK-8	$30-$40
3020	3"	Festival Harmony With Mandolin	TMK-8	$30-$40
3021	3"	Heavenly Angel	TMK-8	$30-$40

Plaques

M.I. Hummel Club Plaque

Exclusive for M.I. Hummel Club members, the white and gold lettered plaque depicts the TMK-9 backstamp.

Item Number	Size	Current Value
828900	2-1/2" H x 3-1/4" L	$59 retail

M.I. Hummel Door Plaque

This earthenware door plaque is oval in shape and is available in either the Umbrella Boy or Umbrella Girl motif. The M.I. Hummel signature is incised on the front of the plaque. Personalization is available also.

Hum No.	Size	Current Value
152/A (personalization)	5-1/4"	$59 retail
152/B (personalization)	5-1/4"	$59 retail

Glossary

The following is an alphabetical listing of terms and phrases found in this book as well as other related books, references, and literature during the course of collecting Hummel items. In some cases, they are specific and unique to Hummel collecting while others are generic in nature, applying to other earthenware, ceramic, and porcelain as well. Refer to this glossary whenever you read or hear something you don't understand. Frequent use of it will enable you to become well versed in collecting Hummel figurines and other related items.

Air Holes: Small holes under the arms or other unobtrusive locations to vent the hollow figures during the firing stage of production. This prevents them from exploding as the interior air expands due to intense heat. Many pieces have these tiny little holes, but often they are difficult to locate. Those open at the bottom usually have no need for these holes.

Air Holes: Small holes under the arms or other unobtrusive locations to vent the hollow figures during the firing stage of production. This prevents them from exploding as the interior air expands due to intense heat. Many pieces have these tiny little holes, but often they are difficult to locate. Those open at the bottom usually have no need for these holes.

Anniversary Plate: In 1975 a 10" plate bearing the Stormy Weather motif was released. Subsequent anniversary plates were released at five-year intervals. 1985 saw the third and last in the series released.

Annual Plate: Beginning in 1971, the W. Goebel firm began producing an annual Hummel plate. Each plate contains a bas-relief reproduction of one of the Hummel motifs. The first was originally released to Goebel factory workers in 1971, commemorating the 100th anniversary of the firm. This original release was inscribed, thanking the workers. At the same time, the first in a series of 25 was released to the public. That series is complete and a new series began in 1997.

Anniversary Exclusives: The M.I. Hummel Club designated certain figurines to be offered exclusively to its members for 5, 10, 15, 20, 25, or 30 years of membership.

Anniversary Pins: A member who is celebrating his or her 5th, 10th, 15th, 20th, 25th, or 30th year of membership receives a special pin to mark the occasion.

ARS: Latin word for "art."

ARS AG: ARS AG, Baar, Switzerland, holds the two-dimensional rights for many of the original M.I. Hummel drawings as well as the two-dimensional rights for reproductions of M.I. Hummel products made by Goebel.

Ars Edition: Ars Edition was formerly known as Ars Sacra Josef Mueller Verlag, the German publishing house that first published Hummel art, producing and selling postcards, postcard-calendars, and prints of M.I. Hummel. Today, Ars Edition GmbH is the exclusive licensee for publishing Hummel (books, calendars, cards, stationery, etc.) Owner: Marcel Nauer (grandson of Dr. Herbert Dubler).

Ars Sacra: Trademark on a gold foil label sometimes found on Hummel-like figurines produced by Herbert Dubler. This was a New York firm that produced these figurines during the years of World War II when Goebel was forbidden by the Nazi government to produce Hummel items. Ars Sacra is also the original name of the Ars Edition firm in Munich. Dubler was a son-in-law of Mr. and Mrs. Mueller, the owners of Ars Edition, formerly Ars Sacra, Munich. Although there was some corporate connection for a very short time between Mueller and Dubler, there is no connection between the Mueller Ars Sacra firm and the Hummel-like figurines produced by Dubler under the name "House of Ars Sacra" or the statement "Produced by Ars Sacra." Please see the discussion on the Dubler figures elsewhere in this volume. Here are a few terms every M.I. Hummel collector should know:

Approved Figurine Designation: Once a figurine has been approved, it officially receives its Hummel number and its name in English.

Arbeitsmuster: A "working sample" used as reference during a figurine's production. Some Arbeitsmuster figurines carry a backstamp, some carry a metal tag, and some have both.

Arbeistmuster Backstamp: Sometimes placed on "Arbeitsmuster" (working sample) figurines when the sample was produced. Some Arbeitsmuster figurines carry a backstamp, some carry a metal tag, and some have both.

Archive (Archives): When a figurine has been approved, at least one piece is placed in the archives for posterity. At times working samples and painting samples were also placed in the archives. No one knows why this was done, but it was probably simply because no one knew what to do with the samples when they were not needed.

Artist's Sample: See Master Sample.

Artist's Mark: This is the signature of the artist who painted the face on a particular Hummel. It is usually the artist's initials along with the date. These markings appear in black on the base of the figurine.

Authorized M.I. Hummel Club Retailer: A merchant granted the authority by an official "M.I. Hummel" distributor to redeem M.I. Hummel club exclusive editions and promote the club.

Baby Bee: Describes the trademark of the factory used in 1958—a small bee flying in a V.

Backstamp: Backstamp is usually the trademark and any associated special markings on the underside of the base, the reverse, or backside of an item.

Basic Size: This term is generally synonymous with standard size. However, because the sizes listed in this book are not substantiated initial factory released sizes, it was felt that it would be misleading to label them "standard." "Basic size" was chosen to denote only an approximate standard size.

Bas-relief: A raised or sculpted design, as on the annual bells and the annual plates, as opposed to a two-dimensional painted design or decal.

Bee: A symbol used since about 1940 in various forms, as a part of or along with the factory trademark on Hummel pieces until 1979, when the bee was dropped. It was reincorporated in the special backstamp used on the M.I. Hummel exclusive pieces and a bee variation was again reinstated with new trademark (TMK-8) introduced in 2000.

Bisque: A fired but unglazed condition. Usually white but sometimes colored.

Black Germany: Term used to describe one of the various wordings found along with the Hummel trademarks on the underside of the pieces. It refers to the color used to stamp the word "Germany." Many colors have been used for the trademarks and associated marks, but black generally indicates the figure is an older mode; however, this is not an absolutely reliable indicator.

Bookends: Throughout the collection of Goebel-made Hummel items are bookends. Some are the regular figurines merely attached to wooden bookends with some type of adhesive. Some, however, are different. The latter are made without the customary base and then attached. The regular pieces, when removed from the wood, have the traditional markings. Those without the base may or may not exhibit those markings.

Candleholder: Some Hummel figurines have been produced with provisions to place candles in them.

Candy Bowl/Candy Box/Candy Dish: Small covered cylindrical box with a Hummel figurine on the top. Design changes have been made in the shape of the box/bowl/dish over the years, as well as in the manner in which the cover rests upon the bowl. See individual listings.

Closed Edition (CE): A term used by the Goebel factory to indicate that a particular item is no longer produced and will not be placed in production again.

Closed Number (CN): A term used by the Goebel factory to indicate that a particular number in the Hummel mold number sequence has never been used to identify an item and never will be used. A caution here: Several unquestionably genuine pieces have been found over the years bearing these so-called closed numbers.

Club Exclusive: This refers to the products made for membership premiums and for sale exclusively to members of the M.I. Hummel Club. Each of these bears a special club backstamp to identify it as such.

Collector's Plaque: Same as the dealer plaque except it does not state "authorized dealer," as most later dealer plaques do. Frequently used for display with private collections (see Dealer Plaque).

Copyright Date: The actual year the original mold was made. Often the mold is made, but figures are not produced for several years afterward. The copyright date is sometimes found along with other marks on older pieces but not always. All pieces currently being produced bear a copyright date.

Crazing: A fine web-like cracked appearance in the overglaze of older porcelain and earthenware. It occurs on Hummel figurines from time to time, mostly on older pieces. Crown Mark (TMK-1): One of the early W. Goebel firm trademarks. Has not been used on Hummel figurines and related pieces since sometime between 1949 and 1950.

Current Mark: For many years, this was a term describing the trademark being used at the present time. It has become a somewhat confusing term, for what is current today may not be tomorrow. Most collectors and dealers have come to use a descriptive term such as the "Crown Mark" or the use of trademark number designations such as Trademark No. 1 (TMK-1) for the Crown Mark, for instance. The number designation is usually shortened to "trademark one" when spoken or "TMK-1" when written.

Current Production: Term describing figurines, plates, candy boxes, etc., supposedly being produced at the present time. They are not necessarily readily available because the factory maintains the molds, but doesn't always produce the figure with regularity.

Dealer Plaque: A plaque made and distributed by the Goebel firm to retailers for the purpose of advertising the fact that they are authorized dealers in Hummel figurines and related articles. The plaques always used to have the Merry Wanderer figure incorporated into them. Earlier models have a bumblebee perched on the top edge (see Collector's Plaque). In recent years, the figurine associated has not always been the Merry Wanderer. For more detailed information, see the listing for Hum 187.

Decimal Designator: Many earlier Goebel Hummel figurines exhibit a decimal point after the mold number, i.e.: "154." This is ostensibly to mean the same thing as the "slash" mark (/). The use of the slash mark means that there is another, smaller size of the piece either in existence, planned, or at least in prototype. The decimal is also used to make it easier to clarify the incised mold numbers and to help determine whether a number is, for instance, a 66 rather than a 99. The decimal is not always found alone with the number. Some examples are 49./0., 51./0., and 84./5.

Display Plaque: See Collector's Plaque and Dealer Plaque.

Doll Face: See Faience.

Doughnut Base: Describes a type of base used with some figures. Looking at the bottom of the base, the outer margin of the base forms a circle or oval, and a smaller circle or oval within makes the base appear doughnut-like.

Doughnut Halo: The only figures on which these appear are the Madonnas. They are formed as a solid cap type, or molded so that the figure's hair protrudes through slightly. The latter are called "Donut Halos."

Double Crown: From 1934 to 1938, there were many figures produced with two Crown WG marks. This is known as the Double Crown. One of the crowns may be a stamped crown and the other incised. Pieces have been found with both trademarks incised (see earlier section on trademarks). Thereafter, only a single Crown Mark is found.

Embossed: An erroneous term used to describe incised (see Incised).

Exclusive Edition (EE): Figurines only created for M.I. Hummel Club members. This edition also bears a special club backstamp and is not released to the general public for sale. These editions can be found on the secondary market.

Faience (Doll Face): Faience is defined as brilliantly glazed, bright-colored fine earthenware. More commonly called "doll face" pieces by collectors, this describes the few Hummel figurines that were made by Goebel in the early days of paint and finish experimentation. Several have made it into collectors' hands.

Final Issue: A term used to refer to a figurine that has been permanently retired from production.

First Issue: A term used to refer to a figurine produced during the first year of its production.

Fink, Emil: Publisher of a limited number of postcards and greeting cards bearing the art of M.I. Hummel. All U.S. copyrights of cards published by Fink Verlag are owned by ARS AG, Zug, Switzerland.

Font: A number of pieces have been produced with a provision for holding a small portion of holy water. They can be hung on the wall. Often referred to as holy water fonts.

Full Bee (TMK-2): About 1940, the W. Goebel firm began using a bee as part of its trademark. The Full Bee trademark has been found along with the Crown trademark. The Full Bee is the first bee to be utilized. There were many versions of the Full Bee trademark. The first Full Bee is sometimes found with (R) stamped somewhere on the base.

Germany (W. GERMANY, West Germany, Western Germany): All have appeared with the trademark in several different colors.

Goebelite: This is the name the Goebel firm gave to the patented mixture of materials used to form the slip used in pouring and fashioning the earthenware Hummel figurines and other related Hummel pieces. Not often heard.

High Bee: A variation of the early Bee trademarks wherein the bee is smaller than the original bee used in the mark and flies with its wings slightly higher than the top of the V in the trademark.

Hollow Base: A base variation. Some bases for figures are solid and some are hollowed out and open into a hollow figure.

Hollow Mold: An erroneous term actually meaning hollow base, as above. All Hummel pieces are at least partially hollow in finished form.

Holy Water Font: See Font.

Hummel Mark (TMK-7): This mark was introduced in 1991. It is the first trademark to be used exclusively on Goebel products utilizing M.I. Hummel art for its design.

Hummel Number or Mold Number: A number or numbers incised into the base or bottom of the piece, used to identify the mold motif and sometimes the size of the figure or article. This designation is sometimes inadvertently omitted, but rarely.

Hummelscape: A decorative piece of cold cast ceramic scene to enhance a display of a particular Hummel. Most have very detailed backgrounds. The scapes are made in China.

Incised/Indented: Describes a mark or wording that has actually been pressed into the surface of a piece, rather than printed or stamped on the surface. It is almost always found beneath the base.

Jumbo: Sometimes used to describe the few Hummel figurines that have been produced in a substantially larger size than the normal range—usually around 30". (See Hum 7, 141, and 142.)

Light Stamp: See M.I. Hummel. It is thought that every Hummel figurine has Sister M.I. Hummel's signature stamped somewhere on it, but some apparently have no signature. In some cases, the signature may have been stamped so lightly that in subsequent painting and glazing all but unidentifiable traces are obliterated. In other cases, the signature may have been omitted altogether. The latter case is rare. The same may happen to the mold number.

Limited Edition: An item that is limited in production to a specified number or limited to the number produced in a defined period of time.

Master Sample/Mahlmuster/Master Zimmer: This is a figurine or other item that is the model from which artists paint the newly fashioned piece. The Master Sample figurines usually have a red line painted around the flat vertical portion of the base. It is known variously in German as the Mahlmuster, Master Zimmer, Muster Zimmer, or Originalmuster. There is another notation sometimes found on the base: "Orig Arbt Muster." These are abbreviations for the German words "Original Working Model."

M.I. Hummel® (Maria Innocentia Hummel): This signature, illustrated below, is supposed to be applied to every Hummel article produced. However, as in Light Stamp above, it may not be evident. It is also reasonable to assume that because of the design of a particular piece or its extremely small size, it may not have been practical to place it on the piece. In such cases, a small sticker is used in its place. It is possible that these stickers became loose and were lost over the years. The signature has been found painted on in some instances but rarely. It is also possible to find the signature in decal form, brown in color. From the late-1950s to early 1960s, Goebel experimented with placing the signature on the figurines by the decal method, but abandoned the idea. A few of the pieces the company tried it on somehow found their way into the market. Collectors should also take note of the fact that sometimes the signature appears as "Hummel" without the initials. This is also seldom found.

Mel: There are a few older Hummel figurines made by Goebel that bear this incised three-letter group along with a number. It is supposed that they were prototype pieces that were never placed in production, but at least three were.

Mold Induction Date: See Copyright Date.

Missing Bee Mark (TMK-6): In mid-1980, the Goebel company changed the trademark by removing the familiar "bee" mark collectors had grown accustomed to associating with M.I. Hummel items. It came to be known as the "Missing Bee" mark (TMK-6) for a while.

Mixed Media: Allows for inclusion of detail on a figurine that could not be carried out in earthenware, such as the wooden sled on Hum 2074: Winter Sleigh Ride or Hum 2278: Just Ducky. Also used to describe items incorporating Swarovski crystals.

Model Number: See Mold Number.

Mold Growth: There have been many theories in the past to explain the differences in sizes of figurines marked the same and with no significant differences other than size. The explanation is that in the earlier years of molding, the molds were made of plaster of paris and had a tendency to wash out and erode with use. Therefore, successive use would produce pieces each being slightly larger than the last. Another possible

explanation is that Goebel had been known to use more than one mold simultaneously in the production of the same figure and market them with the same mold number. The company developed a synthetic resin to use instead of plaster of paris in 1954. Although this is a vast improvement, the new material still has the same tendencies but to a significantly smaller degree.

Mold Induction Date (Copyright Date): An incorrectly used term in reference to what is actually the copyright date. See Copyright Date.

Mold Number: The official mold number used by Goebel that is unique to each Hummel item or motif used. See section on the explanation of the mold number system earlier in this chapter for an in-depth discussion.

Mother Mold Sample: When Goebel proposed a new figurine, the piece was modeled, a mother mold made, and usually three to six sample figures were produced and then painted by one of Goebel's master painters. These were for the convent and others to examine and either approve for production, suggest changes, or reject completely, as the case may be. Typically, never more than six to eight of these were produced. Sometimes the final approved models were marked with a red line and placed into service as a master sample for the artists. Although the mother mold samples do not necessarily have the red line, they are identifiable by the black ink within the incised mold number.

Mould: European spelling of Mold.

Muster Zimmer: See Master Sample.

Narrow Crown: Trademark used by the W. Goebel firm from 1937 to the early 1940s. To date, this trademark has never been found on an original Hummel piece.

One-Line Mark: See Stylized Bee.

Open Edition: Designates the Hummel figurines presently in production or in planning. It does not mean all are in production, only that it is "open" for production. Not necessarily available.

Open Number: A number in the numerical sequence of factory-designated Hummel model numbers that has not been used to identify a piece but may be used when a new design is released.

Out of Production: A confusing term sometimes used to indicate that an item is not of current production but may be placed back in production at some later date. The confusion results from the fact that some with this designation have been declared closed editions, and others have been returned to production, thus leaving all the others in the classification in limbo.

Orig Arbt Muster: A marking sometimes found beneath the base of a figurine. It is the abbreviation for the German words roughly translated to mean "Original Working Model."

Overglaze: See White Overglaze.

Oversize: A term sometimes used to describe a Hummel piece larger than that which is currently being produced. These variations could be due to mold growth (see Mold Growth).

Painter's Sample: See Master Sample.

Possible Future Edition (PFE): A term applied to a Hummel mold design that does exist but has not yet been released.

Production Mold Sample: A piece that is cast out of the first production mold.

Prototype: A proposed figurine or other item that must be approved by those with the authority to do so. It is further restricted to mean "the one and only sample," the first out of the mother mold. This is the one presented to the Siessen Convent for its approval/disapproval. See Mother Mold Sample.

Quartered Base: As it sounds, this is descriptive of the underside of the base of a piece being divided into four more or less equal parts.

Rattle: M.I. Hummel figurines are hollow inside. Sometimes when the figurine is fired, a small piece of clay will drop off. This causes a slight rattle inside the figurine. This by no means is a flaw, since it doesn't detract from the appearance.

Red Line: A red line around the outside edge of the base of a figurine means that the piece may have once served as the model for the painters.

Reinstated: A piece that is back in production after having been previously placed in a non-production status for some length of time.

Sample Model: A prototype piece modeled for the approving authorities. May or may not have gained approval. See Mother Mold Sample.

Secondary Market: When an item is bought and sold after the initial purchase, it is said to be traded on the secondary market.

Size Designator: Method of identifying the size of a figure. It is found in conjunction with the Hummel mold number on the bottom of the figure.

Slash-Marked: From time to time, a figure or a piece will be found with a slash or cut through the trademark. There are two theories as to the origin of this mark. Some think it is used to indicate a figure with some flaw or imperfection, although several figures with slash marks are, upon close examination, found to be in excellent, flawless condition. The other theory is that some figures are slash-marked to discourage resale of pieces given to or sold at a bargain price to factory workers.

Small Bee: A variation of the early Full Bee trademark wherein the bee is about half the size of the original bee.

Split Base: When viewing the bottom of the base of a piece, it appears to be split into sections. Generally refers to a base split into two sections, but could readily be used to describe more than two sections.

Stamped: A method of placing marks on the bottom of a figure wherein the data is placed on the surface rather than pressed into it (see Incised).

Standard Size: As pointed out in the section on size designators, this is a general term used to describe the size of the first figure to be produced, when there are more sizes of the same figure to be found. It is not the largest, nor the smallest, only the first. Over the years, as a result of mold design changes and possibly mold growth, all figures marked as standard are not necessarily the same size (see Basic Size).

Stylized Bee (TMK-3): About 1955, the traditional bee design in the trademark was changed to reflect a more modern "stylized" version. Also sometimes called the "One-Line Mark."

Temporarily Withdrawn: Similar to "out of production," but in this case it would be reasonable to assume that the piece so described will be put back into production at some future date.

Terra Cotta: Literally translated from the Latin it means "baked earth"; a naturally brownish-orange earthenware.

Three Line Mark (TMK-4): A trademark variation used in the 1960s and 1970s.

Underglaze: A term describing anything that is found underneath the glaze as opposed to being placed after the glazing.

U.S. Zone or U.S. Zone Germany: During the American occupation of Germany after World War II, the Goebel company was required to apply these words to its products. After the country was divided into East Germany and West Germany in 1948, they began using "West Germany" or "Western Germany." The various configurations in which these words are found are illustrated in the above section on trademarks.

White Overglaze: After a piece has been formed, a clear glaze is applied and fired, resulting in a shiny, all-white finish.

Bibliography

The Official M.I. Hummel Price Guide, Krause Publications, 700 E. State St., Iola, WI 54990. 2010.

Luckey's Hummel Figurines and Plates, 12th edition, Krause Publications, 700 E. State St., Iola, WI 54990. 2003.

M.I. Hummel Guide for Collectors, M.I. Hummel Marketing, 3705 Quakerbridge Rd., Suite 105, Mercerville, NJ 08619. 2000.

M.I. Hummel: I Want to Give Joy! A Fateful Woman's Career, ARS Edition Ltd., Munich, Germany. 2009.

The No. 1 Price Guide to M.I. Hummel Figurines, Plates, Miniatures, & More..., 10th edition, Reverie Publishing Co., 130 South Wineow St., Cumberland, MD 21502. 2003 and 2006.

Warman's Hummel Field Guide, Krause Publications, 700 E. State St., Iola, WI 54990. 2004.

Warman's M.I. Hummel Field Guide, 2nd edition, Krause Publications, 700 E. State St., Iola, WI 54990. 2012.

Index

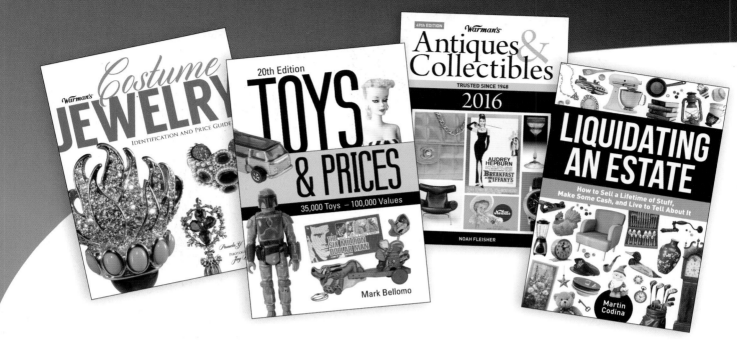
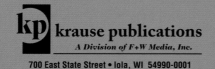